- poor administrator
- too many topics

Harvard Middle Eastern Studies

1. *Desert Enterprise : The Middle East Oil Industry in its Local Environment*. By David H. Finnie. 1958.
2. *Middle Eastern Capitalism: Nine Essays*. By A. J. Meyer. 1959.
3. *The Idea of the Jewish State*. By Ben Halpern. 1961.
4. *The Agricultural Policy of Muḥammad 'Alī in Egypt*. By Helen Anne B. Rivlin. 1961.

Harvard Middle Eastern Studies 4

THE AGRICULTURAL POLICY OF MUḤAMMAD 'ALĪ IN EGYPT

من لا يرضى بحكم موسى رضي بحكم فرعون

"He who is not satisfied with the government of Moses, will be satisfied with the government of Pharaoh."

(A proverb of the Egyptian *fallāḥīn* during the reign of Muḥammad 'Alī)

The AGRICULTURAL POLICY *of* MUḤAMMAD ʻALĪ IN EGYPT

by Helen Anne B. Rivlin

HARVARD UNIVERSITY PRESS
Cambridge, Massachusetts
1961

Distributed in Great Britain by Oxford University Press, London

Library of Congress Catalog Card Number 61-5251

Made and printed in Great Britain by
William Clowes and Sons, Limited, London and Beccles

To my dearest

MOTHER

with love and thanks

PREFACE

The present study was initiated before King Fārūq abdicated the throne of Egypt in 1952, thereby ending the dynasty established by his illustrious great-great-grandfather, Muḥammad 'Alī al-Kabīr. Even before the demise of the late Egyptian ruling house, a new appraisal of its founder's career had become desirable to rectify the distortions foisted upon a credulous public by official historiographers and other persons infatuated with the Muḥammad 'Alī legend. Dr. J. Heyworth-Dunne in his admirable monograph published twenty years ago, *An Introduction to the History of Education in Modern Egypt*, took the first step in setting the record straight and also showed the direction which research must take if a truly unbiased and balanced history of the Muḥammad 'Alī reign is ever to be written.

The most pressing research needs fall within the domain of Muḥammad 'Alī's domestic policies, which have either been neglected by previous writers or simply glossed over. To meet these needs, at least in part, Sir Hamilton Gibb, formerly Laudian Professor of Arabic in the University of Oxford and now University Professor, Jewett Professor of Arabic, and Director of the Center for Middle Eastern Studies at Harvard University, recommended for my thesis subject the problem of Muḥammad 'Alī's agricultural policy. My book is an outgrowth of this doctoral thesis written at Oxford under the direction of Professor Gibb.

The purpose of my research has been to discover if Muḥammad 'Alī had an agricultural policy and then to describe it. Since Egypt's economy in the nineteenth century was dependent almost entirely upon agriculture, the problem of agricultural policy proved far more complex than I had anticipated. It has, in fact, necessitated an analysis of land tenure, administrative practices, taxation, crop production, trade, industry, manpower resources, and irrigation. Furthermore, Muḥammad 'Alī's policy towards agriculture was frequently determined by political considerations rather than economic ones. I have had, therefore, to consider the interplay of political forces and to study the role of politics in the shaping of economic policy.

The material I have collected could, undoubtedly, have been presented in different ways and could have served different purposes. It would have been especially relevant for our time to have departed entirely from the original problem in favor of a thorough review of Egyptian economics during Muḥammad 'Alī's period as an interesting illustration of economic planning in an underdeveloped area. I have resisted the temptation to do this because I possess none of the competence which a trained economist would bring to such a study and because the problem which prompted my research in the first place needed to be resolved. My primary responsibility, as I have interpreted it, has been to settle an historical problem, not to write an economic survey of Egypt during the first half of the nineteenth century.

The organization of this book was partly determined by the necessity either to prove or to deny the existence of a well-defined agricultural policy carried out by Muḥammad 'Alī during the course of his reign. By breaking down the problem under investigation into its component parts, I could deal with it more efficiently and with greater clarity. These component parts are not necessarily related to each other but only to the central problem; their position in the book, therefore, has no special significance. Individually, however, their relevance is not confined to the general problem alone. They are interesting in their own right. The chapter on irrigation, for example, throws light on the general problem but at the same time deals with Egyptian irrigation as such and can be read separately by anyone interested in the history of Egyptian irrigation. Thus, by this form of organization, my material has been made to serve a double purpose. This organizational form has the added advantage of allowing for the inclusion of all available data so that other scholars may be spared the task of going over the same ground again. I think, too, that scholars in other disciplines who may wish to benefit from my research will find the material more accessible because of the plan of organization which I have followed.

The material for this book has been drawn exclusively from published and unpublished Western sources and selected published Middle Eastern sources. All the translations quoted in this book are, of course, my own. I have not used unpublished Egyptian or Turkish archival material and recognize that there are gaps in my data which may possibly be filled after these Egyptian and Turkish archives have been systematically searched. Even so, my work as it now stands presents much new material and offers new interpretations based on the evidence which I have collected. Although further research may indeed fill the remaining lacunae and correct mistakes, I rather doubt that it will contradict very substantially the composite picture which I have created out of isolated facts derived from a large number of sources from various countries and never previously brought together. Nonetheless, I certainly hope that future historians and other social scientists, especially those having access to the largely untapped sources of material in the Middle East, will complete the task which I have begun.

Of the many problems with which I have been confronted in this work, none has been so troublesome as that of seeking out the correct spelling of local terms, proper names, and place-names. The difficulty of the problem has been greatly compounded by the fact that contemporary usages do not always correspond with nineteenth-century usages so that dictionaries can be misleading or even useless. Furthermore, Turkish terms and names were often employed in Egypt during the period under examination. In addition, my European sources were extremely individualistic in the transliterations of terms and names, often making confusing mistakes and thus contributing to my difficulties in tracing the correct spelling of terms and names.

To the best of my knowledge, the terms I have used in this book do conform to nineteenth-century usages. I have given a letter-by-letter transliteration, even of familiar terms, according to the system laid down in Special Publication No. 78, *The Transliteration of Arabic and Persian*, published by the Department of the Interior, United States Board on Geographical Names, Washington, D.C., November 1946. This has been done for the sake of consistency and to enable anyone wishing to consult an Arabic dictionary to do so with comparative ease. With few exceptions, all Turkish names and terms have been Arabicized to avoid the confusion which two systems of transliteration would have caused. Students will find it very easy to find these Arabicized terms in an Ottoman Turkish dictionary because of the letter-by-letter transliteration. To be sure, Egypt had a Turkish administration in this period rather than an Arab one and I should perhaps have Turkified Arabic words rather than the contrary. I feel, however, since I am writing for a twentieth-century audience for whom Egypt is an Arab country, that I am justified in adopting the practice of Arabicizing Turkish words.

In a few cases, although not in all, words that have come into the English language have been spelled according to their English dictionary spelling; also some place names have been retained in their familiar form. Sultan, pasha, bey, Bedouin, Cairo, and Alexandria are examples of this practice. My decisions in specific cases will most certainly be questioned by some people. These were sometimes made rather arbitrarily, I must admit, but once they were made, I have tried to be consistent in the spelling decided upon wherever the word appears in the text.

I have followed the practice of assimilating the "l" of the Arabic article to the *solar letters* and in a few cases the "j" has been changed to "g" according to Egyptian Arabic usage, for example, Gīzah, Girgā. Plurals, with few exceptions (e.g., *fallāḥīn*), have been formed by adding an "s" instead of the Arabic plural. Certain unfamiliar practices not usually followed by European authors have been used upon the recommendations of my good friend Muḥammad Abdulhayy Sha'bān, an Egyptian scholar now associated with the Center for Middle Eastern Studies, who has checked all the transliterations with an eye to their accuracy and to bringing them into conformity with Egyptian usage. Finally, there have been some instances where I have been unable to trace the Arabic or Turkish spelling of a term or name and have been obliged to retain the form given by my source, for example, Divan Roodaway in Appendix III.

I cannot even begin to list the names of the many people who, either directly or indirectly, have encouraged me throughout my academic career and have made it possible for this book to be written. To all these unnamed teachers and friends I wish to extend my thanks. I hope I have not disappointed their high expectations. I am indebted most of all to Sir Hamilton Gibb for the continuing interest which he has shown in my work. As I have already pointed out, the subject of this study was suggested by him and my doctoral thesis was written under his direction. My debt to Professor Gibb does not end there, however. He has spent much time in looking over the revised manuscript, making invaluable suggestions, and is largely responsible for the publication of this work. His great knowledge, his special genius as a teacher, his profound humility and scholarly generosity, and his personal kindness have been a great inspiration to me. My achievements, whatever they are, are the results of his influence; my faults are entirely my own. I shall be forever grateful to Professor Gibb for all he has done for me but, even more, for all he has meant to me.

Three other people have played an enormous role in making this book possible. They are Professor William Langer of Harvard University, Mrs. Bernice Brown Cronkhite of Radcliffe College, and Mr. John Marshall of the Rockefeller Foundation, all of whom gave me encouragement at particularly crucial moments in my career, thereby contributing to the successful completion of this book. The stories which circulate among the students or former students of Harvard University concerning Professor Langer form the folk-lore of a great institution which delights generation after generation of students. The story which remains to be told of Professor Langer can only be touched upon here. From the moment when I first met him in 1949 as a graduate student at Radcliffe College, Professor Langer has never been too busy with his own work at Harvard, never too preoccupied with affairs of state in Washington, never too ill at various times to give me the advice, encouragement, and help which I have needed at different stages of my academic career. It is this story of devotion to his students of which my own experience is but one example that will be the one inscribed in the hearts of those who have known him. Dean Cronkhite, too, has exhibited the same kind of devotion which will be greatly missed when she retires from Radcliffe College. Without her constant support, I am not sure I should have had the courage to overcome all obstacles. Finally, I wish to thank Mr. Marshall who, without knowing anything about me, had the sensitivity and the imagination to respond to my need.

I must also thank Professor J. C. Hurewitz of Columbia University who read my manuscript and made helpful suggestions and Mr. D. W. Lockard, Associate Director of the Center for Middle Eastern Studies at Harvard University, who has been so patient with me personally and has worked so hard to get this book published. My very dear friend Mrs. Justine Phillips deserves much of the praise and none of the criticism for the editorial work done on the last revision of this manuscript. Under the most difficult circumstances, she steadfastly worked with me to improve the presentation of this work in its final form. She could not correct all of my shortcomings as a writer, but she assuredly overcame some of them. Mrs. Martha Smith and Miss Carol Cross of the Center for Middle Eastern Studies who shared in the typing of the manuscript took such personal interest in their work on it that they have almost as much right as I to claim it for their own. Mr. Muḥammad Abdulhayy Sha'bān who advised me on the transliteration of the Arabic terms and names contributed greatly to the accuracy of this work. Finally, I owe thanks to the Harvard University Press and its able editorial staff for the help which I have received in the publication of this book.

I wish also to acknowledge the kind assistance I have received from the staff of Widener Library, the British Museum, the Bodleian, the

Griffith Institute at Oxford, and the library of the School of Oriental and African Studies and to extend special thanks to the Deputy Keeper of the Records at the Public Record Office, Dr. Carl Ludwig Lokke of the National Archives, and M. Amédée Outrey, head of the archives of the Ministère des Affaires Etrangères, for the privilege of using the records in their keeping and for the aid which members of their staffs so generously gave me during the course of my research.

In conclusion, I wish to thank the American Council of Learned Societies for their grant to attend Harvard Summer School in 1950 where I first met Professor Gibb and made the arrangements to pursue my studies which have culminated in this book; Radcliffe College, which granted me the Alice Mary Longfellow Fellowship, and also the kind ladies of the Women's Scholarship Association of Boston, Massachusetts, who supplied additional funds for my first year of study at Oxford (1951–52); the A.A.U.W. Educational Foundation which granted me the Margaret E. Maltby Fellowship (1952–53) and also the Anthony Eden Fund, which covered the cost of my second year of study at Oxford; Oxford University, which granted me the D. Phil. in 1953; Lady Margaret Hall, my college, which made my stay in Oxford so agreeable; the Rockefeller Foundation, which awarded me a post-doctoral traveling fellowship (1954–55) for further research and study in England and France; the Rockefeller Foundation and the Center for Middle Eastern Studies at Harvard University, which provided me with the funds and the opportunity to prepare this book; and the Center for Middle Eastern Studies, which has contributed so magnanimously towards the cost of publication of this book.

West Hyattsville, Maryland H. A. R.
March 1959

CONTENTS

TABLES

Appendix II

Appendix VI

Appendix VII

Notes

MAPS

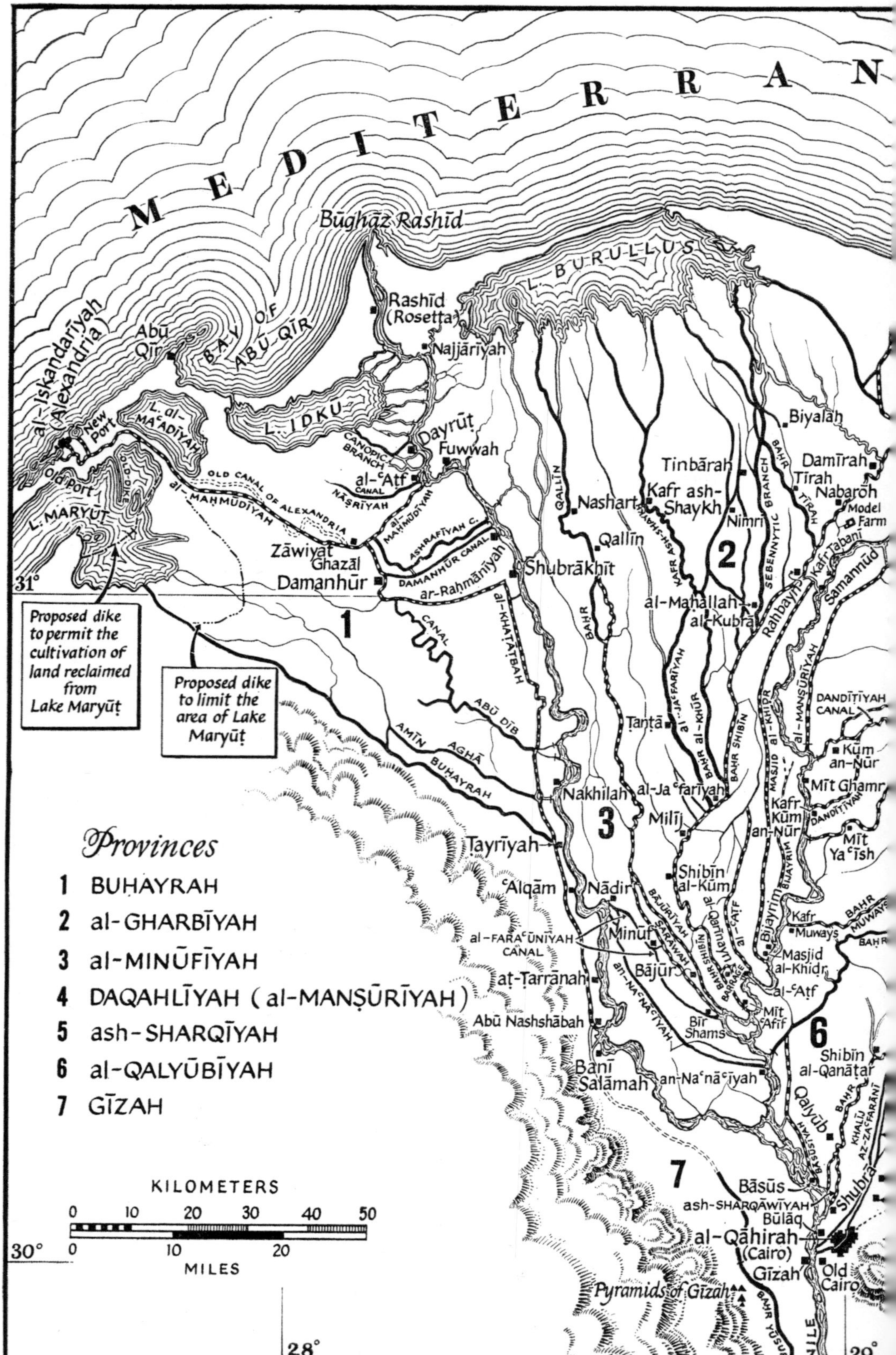
M E D I T E R R A N
Būghāz Rashīd
L. BURULLUS
al-Iskandarīyah (Alexandria)
Abū Qīr
BAY OF ABŪ QĪR
Rashīd (Rosetta)
Najjārīyah
L. al-Maᶜadīyah
L. IDKU
New Port
Old Port
OLD DIKE
L. MARYŪṬ
CANOPIC BRANCH
Dayrūṭ
Fuwwah
al-ᶜAṭf
OLD CANAL OF ALEXANDRIA
al-MAḤMŪDĪYAH
NAṢRĪYAH CANAL
al-MAḤMŪDĪYAH
ASHRAFĪYAH C.
DAMANHŪR CANAL
Zāwiyat Ghazāl
Damanhūr
ar-Raḥmānīyah
Shubrākhīt
31°
Proposed dike to permit the cultivation of land reclaimed from Lake Maryūṭ
Proposed dike to limit the area of Lake Maryūṭ
1
CANAL
al-KHAṬĀṬBAH
ABŪ DĪB
AMĪN AGHĀ
BUḤAYRAH
QALLĪN
Nashart
Qallīn
BAḤR
Kafr ash-Shaykh
KAFR ASH-SHAYKH
Tinbārah
Nimrī
2
Biyalah
Damīrah
Tīrah
Nabarōh
Model Farm
Kafr Ṭabanī
Samannūd
SEBENNYTIC BRANCH
BAḤR TĪRAH
al-Maḥallah al-Kubrā
Rahbayn
Ṭanṭā
al-JAᶜFARĪYAH
BAḤR al-KHŪR
BAḤR SHIBĪN
MASJID al-KHIḌR
al-MANṢŪRĪYAH
DANDĪṬĪYAH CANAL
Kūm an-Nūr
Mīt Ghamr
Kafr Kūm an-Nūr
Mīt Yaᶜīsh
Nakhilah
al-Jaᶜfarīyah
3
Milīj
Tayrīyah
Shibīn al-Kūm
ᶜAlqām
Nādir
BĀJŪRĪYAH
SARAWAH
al-Qarīnayn
al-ᶜAṬF
BIJAYRIM
Bijayrim
Kafr Muways
BAḤR MUWAYS
al-FARAᶜŪNIYAH CANAL
Minūf
Masjid al-Khiḍr
Bājūr
al-ᶜAṭf
aṭ-Ṭarrānah
an-NAᶜNAᶜIYAH
BARRAGE
Mīt ᶜAfīf
Abū Nashshābah
Bīr Shams
6
Shibīn al-Qanāṭar
Banī Salāmah
an-Naᶜnāᶜiyah
Qalyūb
BAḤR
KHALĪJ AZ-ZAᶜFARĀNĪ
BĀSŪSĪYAH
7
Bāsūs
ash-SHARQĀWĪYAH
Shubrā
Būlāq
al-Qāhirah (Cairo)
Gīzah
Old Cairo
Pyramids of Gīzah
BAḤR YŪSUF
NILE
Provinces
1 BUḤAYRAH
2 al-GHARBĪYAH
3 al-MINŪFĪYAH
4 DAQAHLĪYAH (al-MANṢŪRĪYAH)
5 ash-SHARQĪYAH
6 al-QALYŪBĪYAH
7 GĪZAH
KILOMETERS
0 10 20 30 40 50
0 10 20
MILES
30°
28°
29°

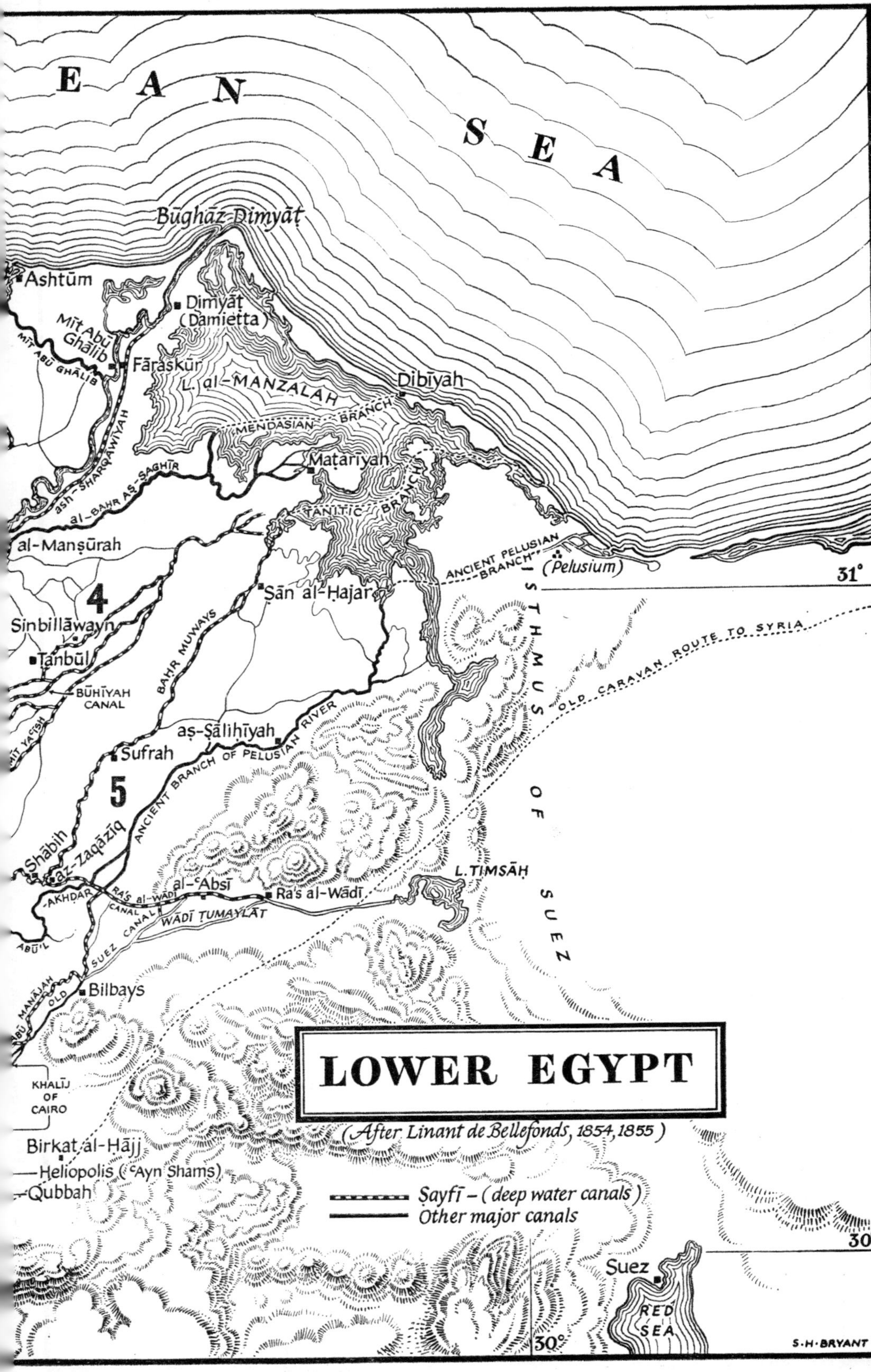
E A N
S E A
Būghāz Dimyāṭ
Ashtūm
Dimyāṭ
(Damietta)
Mīt Abū Ghālib
MĪT ABŪ GHĀLIB
Fāraskūr
L. al-MANZALAH
Dibīyah
MENDASIAN BRANCH
Maṭarīyah
ash-SHARQĀWIYAH
al-BAHR AṢ-ṢAGHĪR
TANITIC BRANCH
al-Manṣūrah
ANCIENT PELUSIAN BRANCH
(Pelusium)
31°
4
Ṣān al-Ḥajar
Sinbillāwayn
Tanbūl
BUḤĪYAH CANAL
BAHR MUWAYS
ISTHMUS OF SUEZ
OLD CARAVAN ROUTE TO SYRIA
aṣ-Ṣāliḥīyah
Sufrah
ANCIENT BRANCH OF PELUSIAN RIVER
5
Shābih
az-Zaqāzīq
L. TIMSĀḤ
al-ᶜAbsī
Ra's al-Wādī
RA'S al-WĀDĪ CANAL
AKHḌAR
WĀDĪ ṬUMAYLĀT
SUEZ CANAL
ABŪ'L MANĀJAH
OLD
Bilbays
LOWER EGYPT
(After Linant de Bellefonds, 1854, 1855)
KHALĪJ OF CAIRO
Birkat al-Ḥājj
Heliopolis (ᶜAyn Shams)
Qubbah
Ṣayfī – (deep water canals)
Other major canals
30°
Suez
RED SEA
30°
S·H·BRYANT

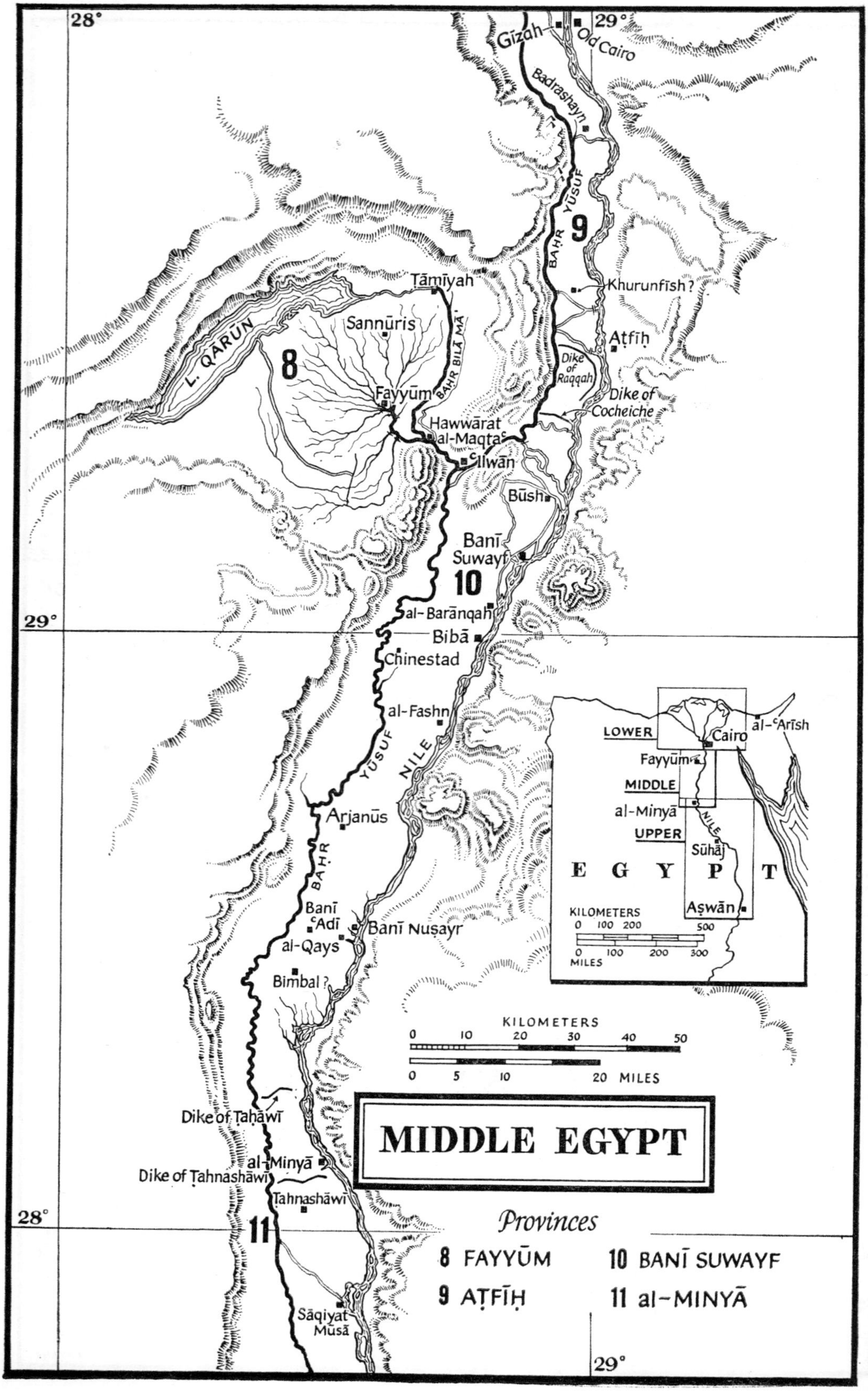
MIDDLE EGYPT
28°
29°
Gīzah
Old Cairo
Badrashayn
BAḤR YŪSUF
9
Khurunfīsh ?
Aṭfīḥ
Dike of Raqqah
Dike of Cocheiche
Ṭāmīyah
Sannūris
L. QARŪN
8
Fayyūm
BAḤR BILĀ MĀ'
Hawwārat al-Maqṭaᶜ
ᶜIlwān
Būsh
Banī Suwayf
10
al-Barānqah
Bibā
Chinestad
al-Fashn
NILE
Arjanūs
Banī ᶜAdī
Banī Nuṣayr
al-Qays
Bimbal ?
Dike of Ṭaḥāwī
al-Minyā
Dike of Ṭahnashāwī
Ṭahnashāwī
11
Sāqiyat Mūsā
KILOMETERS
0 10 20 30 40 50
0 5 10 20 MILES
LOWER
MIDDLE
UPPER
Cairo
al-ᶜArīsh
Fayyūm
al-Minyā
Sūhāj
Aṣwān
E G Y P T
KILOMETERS
0 100 200 500
0 100 200 300
MILES
Provinces
8 FAYYŪM
9 AṬFĪḤ
10 BANĪ SUWAYF
11 al-MINYĀ

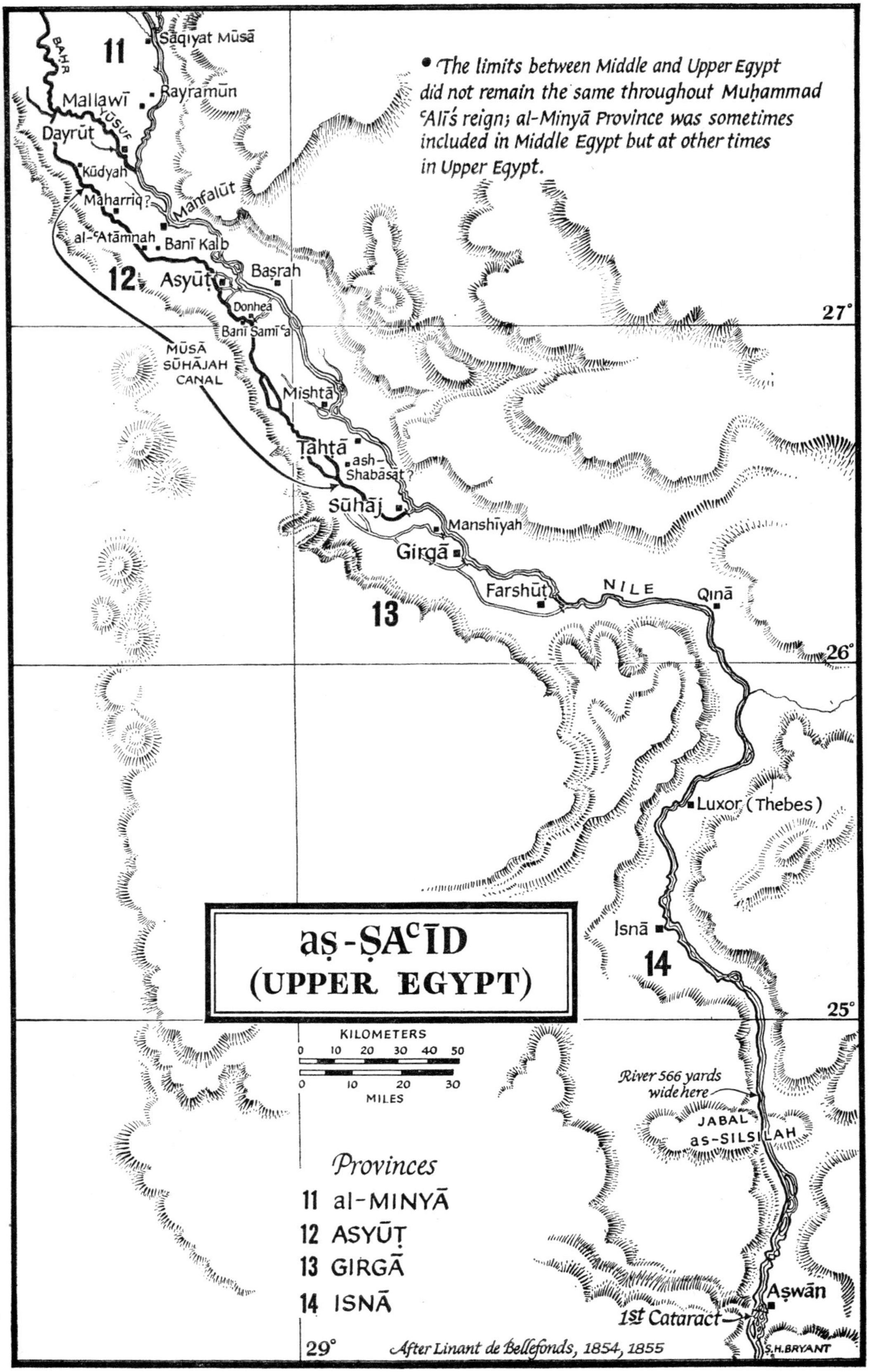

• The limits between Middle and Upper Egypt did not remain the same throughout Muḥammad ʿAlī's reign; al-Minyā Province was sometimes included in Middle Egypt but at other times in Upper Egypt.
11
12
13
14
BAḤR YŪSUF
Sāqiyat Mūsā
Mallawī
Rayramūn
Dayrūt
Kūdyah
Maharriq?
Manfalūt
al-ʿAtāmnah
Banī Kalb
Asyūṭ
Baṣrah
Donhea
Banī Samīʿa
MŪSĀ SŪHĀJAH CANAL
Mishtā
Ṭahṭā
ash-Shabāsat?
Sūhāj
Manshīyah
Girgā
Farshūṭ
NILE
Qinā
Luxor (Thebes)
Isnā
River 566 yards wide here
JABAL as-SILSILAH
Aṣwān
1st Cataract
27°
26°
25°
29°
aṣ-ṢAʿĪD (UPPER EGYPT)
KILOMETERS
0 10 20 30 40 50
0 10 20 30
MILES
Provinces
11 al-MINYĀ
12 ASYŪṬ
13 GIRGĀ
14 ISNĀ
After Linant de Bellefonds, 1854, 1855
S.H. BRYANT

THE AGRICULTURAL POLICY OF MUḤAMMAD ʻALĪ IN EGYPT

CHAPTER I

INTRODUCTION

Egypt has been the stage on which many actors have played—and each has left his mark on the country: the Babylonian, the Hittite, the Persian, the Greek, the Roman, the Byzantine, the Arab, the Ayyūbid Kurd, the Circassian, the Turk, the Frenchman, and the Briton. Each conquest has left a residue of foreign culture which has been absorbed by Egypt and has become an integral part of its history. The remains of these foreign conquests can be recognized not only in the many monuments but in the institutions of the country; in fact, the overlapping of ancient institutions presents numerous historical problems. For the purposes of this study, however, it is enough to be conscious at all times that the Egyptians are an ancient people with roots in many cultures. Furthermore, it should be noted that, despite the great diversity of external influences, there is a peculiar quality of timelessness and changelessness in the Egyptian scene which stems from the fact that no conqueror and no foreign culture can change the physical geography of a country. The Nile River which rises and falls with amazing regularity has given the Nile Valley an individual character that time and governments have scarcely altered. Indeed, it has frequently been said that the Nile *is* Egypt; for without its presence Egypt would disappear under the desert sands which constantly encroach upon the fertile lands on the banks of the river. The Nile not only determines the existence of Egypt itself, but it also in many ways fixes the type of government and institutions the Egyptian people can have. For example, an incontrovertible fact of Egyptian life is that there must always exist a highly centralized administration to direct the distribution of water from one end of the country to the other. It is, then, inconceivable that Egypt could ever be divided for any length of time among warring chieftains and survive as a state; the welfare of all depends upon maintaining the unity of the central government so that the economic structure of the country is not destroyed.

Egypt at the end of the eighteenth century had been part of the Ottoman Empire since 1517. Its independent existence under the Circassian

Mamlūk dynasty had ended when Salīm I, the Ottoman Sultan, conquered the country; it then became an Ottoman province or *pāshāliq* and retained this status until 1914 when the British declared a protectorate over Egypt.[1] Salīm died shortly after his conquest of Egypt and in 1520 Sulaymān the Magnificent or the Lawgiver (al-Qānūnī) became Sultan of the Ottoman Empire. During the reign of Sulaymān Ottoman administration was firmly established in Egypt and a body of administrative ordinances was promulgated.

From the time of Sulaymān's reign the governor of the Egyptian province was the pasha (*wālī* or *beylerbeyi*) who was appointed annually by the sultan and ruled in conjunction with a Great *Dīwān* and a Small *Dīwān*. The Great *Dīwān*, which dealt with the general business of government, was made up of various administrative officers, representatives of the seven Ottoman army corps (*ūjāqs*) stationed in Egypt for purposes of defense, internal security, and enforcement of tax collection, and finally, the principal religious leaders. The Small *Dīwān*, usually referred to as The *Dīwān*, included simply the chief administrative and military officers and dealt with the current business of government, reserving only matters of the greatest importance to the Great *Dīwān*. Egypt itself was divided into *sanjaqs* or provinces, each of which was placed under the control of a governor.[2]

The government of Egypt, as established by Salīm and Sulaymān, was not in itself oppressive; its primary aim was to guarantee the preservation of Ottoman control without effecting radical alterations of indigenous institutions. It was a government of checks and balances which was intended to prevent any one person or group from upsetting the equilibrium and assuming control. The system broke down when the pashas became corrupt and ineffective and when the gradual integration of the *ūjāqlīs* with the Egyptian population, brought about by their intermarrying, becoming artisans, and joining craft guilds, destroyed the corps as an effective fighting force. The *ūjāqlīs*, while maintaining their army pay and other army privileges, eventually lost their discipline and competence as soldiers; consequently the defense of Egypt fell into the hands of the Circassians and other white slaves who had been purchased by the officers of the *ūjāqs* and carefully trained both in the arts of war and government. The new Mamlūks enrolled in the various *ūjāqs* and it became customary for them to receive the provincial governorships and other offices of responsibility. As the power of the pasha and of the regular *ūjāqlīs* declined, then, that of the Mamlūks increased.

By the eighteenth century factionalism in the *ūjāqs*, which were now completely dominated by the Mamlūks, was extremely intense. At the time, the military was divided into two rival groups, each supporting one of the two rival families in Cairo (al-Qāhirah)—al-Qāsimīyah and al-Fiqārīyah. Intrigue and hostility caused frequent pitched battles between these two parties, but as the fighting took place in the open field, little injury was caused to anyone but the contenders. The winning faction would place its leader in the office reserved for the principal bey, the governorship of Cairo, and the man who became governor was known as the *Shaykh al-Balad*. The *Shaykh al-Balad* was *de facto* ruler of Egypt. There was nothing which the pasha could do to restrain his power; in fact, if the pasha displeased the *Shaykh al-Balad* and the other beys, he was informed that he was *persona non grata* and was forced to descend from the Citadel and to leave Egypt. The beys would inform the sultan of this fact and would request that a new appointee be sent. Ottoman control had thus become an empty symbol, for the *Shaykh al-Balad*, supported by the Mamlūks of his party, was in a strong position to resist outside control.

Gradually, even this symbol became too restrictive for the ambitious Mamlūk chiefs who successively sought power by a series of rebellions. ʻAlī Bey al-Kabīr, who became *Shaykh al-Balad* in 1767, first decided to strike for independence after he had strengthened his army by investing in more and more Mamlūks and had consolidated his control over all Egypt from Aṣwān to the Mediterranean. In November 1768 he declared his independence and began to regularize the administration of Egypt, to correct various abuses, and to strike his own money; he ordered that his name instead of the sultan's should be pronounced in the *khuṭbah* (sermon). He negotiated with the Venetians and the Russians to support him in his program of military expansion at the expense of the Ottoman Empire; he conducted a campaign against the Holy Cities and al-Yaman in 1770; and when he captured Makkah, the new *sharīf* sent him a letter of homage and named him sultan, ruler of Egypt and the two seas.

ʻAlī Bey was finally destroyed by his own general and former Mamlūk, Muḥammad Bey Abū 'dh-Dhahab, who joined forces with his enemies and defeated him. He then fled to Syria and Muḥammad Bey Abū 'dh-Dhahab became *Shaykh al-Balad* in 1772. On April 9, 1773, ʻAlī Bey decided to march against Muḥammad Bey Abū 'dh-Dhahab, to re-establish himself as ruler of Egypt, but was defeated and taken to

Cairo where he died and was buried on May 8, 1773. Then, in 1775, Muḥammad Bey Abū 'dh-Dhahab also died, and two Circassian beys of his house, Ibrāhīm Bey and Murād Bey, decided to rule Egypt as a duumvirate. They were eventually challenged and defeated by Ismā'īl Bey, a protégé of 'Alī Bey, and took refuge in Upper Egypt, but soon after Ismā'īl became *Shaykh al-Balad* (July 18, 1777) his two enemies attacked and defeated him. Finally, in February 1778 Ibrāhīm became *Shaykh al-Balad* and Murād became *amīr al-ḥajj* (the leader of the pilgrimage to Makkah and al-Madīnah); but they ruled the country together. Their alliance was not a peaceful one. During the next few years they separated several times and then came back together. After their reconciliation of January 12, 1785, they informed the Sultan that they would no longer pay the annual remittance from Egypt and would only accept the responsibility for sending provisions to Makkah.

The Porte decided that the time had come to strike a blow against the rebellious Mamlūk chiefs and the Ottoman admiral, Qapūdān Ḥasan Pasha, was sent to re-establish Ottoman control in Egypt. He landed at Alexandria (al-Iskandarīyah) on June 23, 1786, and defeated the forces of Murād and Ibrāhīm, both of whom escaped to Upper Egypt. Ḥasan Pasha entered Cairo in August 1786 but on September 27, 1787, before he had time to destroy the power of the beys, to re-establish the old Ottoman militia, or to reaffirm the control of the Ottoman Pasha, he was recalled to Istanbul to fight in the war against Russia. Ismā'īl Bey became *Shaykh al-Balad* once more after Ḥasan's departure and held this office until April 20, 1791, when he died during an epidemic; thereupon, Ibrāhīm and Murād marched upon Cairo and took control of the country. They exploited the population ruthlessly; trade practically ceased; taxes on the land were increased; and they again informed the Sultan that they would not send the annual remittance. Their arbitrary rule and abusive exactions continued until the arrival of the French expeditionary army in July 1798.

In sum, the Ottoman conquerors had provided Egypt with an administrative machine by which the country could be ruled equitably while, at the same time, the prerogatives of the Ottoman sultan were maintained. However, decline in control by the central government at Istanbul and the degeneration of the Turkish militia in Egypt provided the opportunity for an increase in the power of the Mamlūks and the eventual re-emergence of a kind of new Mamlūk state in Egypt. First attempts at throwing off Ottoman domination had begun with 'Alī Bey's declaration of independence; his successors occasionally showed themselves loyal to the Ottoman connection, but they evaded their responsibilities as much as possible. The tribute was paid infrequently and eventually ceased altogether. The Sultan, considering the Mamlūk chiefs rebels against his authority, was unable to reassert control because of his military commitments elsewhere. Consequently, Ottoman power was weakened while that of the Mamlūks increased.

This struggle for power in Egypt in the eighteenth century was confined primarily to the ruling cliques. It affected the population only when greater demands were made for supplies and taxes. To be sure, Bedouin incursions and factional strife among the beys had an unsettling effect upon the life of the country, but society was saved from complete disorganization by the administrative bureaucracy which continued to function regardless of who was in power. Furthermore, the inhabitants of the countryside and the towns had developed techniques for adjusting their lives to existing political conditions. Virtually the only link between the Egyptian people and their rulers was through the system of taxation. Each popular group—merchants or artisans or cultivators—was, in fact, organized independently into a corporate body, each with its own leadership. Allegiance was to the corporate body rather than to the sultan or the ruling class. Under normal circumstances none of the groups interfered with one another, their only points of contact being in the exchange of services, in communal participation in religious ceremonies, and through the *ṣūfī* fraternities. All relations with the governing authorities were conducted through their *shaykhs*, who were responsible for the maintenance of order and the collection of taxes. Western travelers to Egypt in the eighteenth century completely misunderstood this situation. They saw nothing but political anarchy and concluded that government was based only on a system of exploitation and provided no protection for the population. The Turco-Mamlūk regime in Egypt was, in fact, neither anarchic nor arbitrary; it was static and reactionary. Still, when the old equilibrium which had maintained for centuries the elements of Egyptian society was upset by the introduction of external factors, it became essential to replace outmoded forms of social organization and political institutions with more appropriate ones.[3]

Events in Europe during the second half of the eighteenth century were to have a profound effect upon Egyptian history. The Seven Years War, which began in 1756 and was terminated by the Peace of Paris in 1763, brought such territory to England as to change the current of

British history. France, on the other hand, had been evicted from India as a military power, retaining only trading stations at Pondichéry and elsewhere; she ceded her North American territories east of the Mississippi River to Great Britain and those west of the river to Spain; all the neutral islands of the West Indies went to Britain with the exception of the neutral island of St. Lucia which France was allowed to retain along with the islands of Guadeloupe and Martinique; finally, France restored Minorca to the British and also ceded Senegal to them. These victories and territorial acquisitions and the simultaneous development of her commercial prosperity left Great Britain economically more sound than before. Industrial developments at this time in Europe, but particularly in Britain, stimulated a race for the commercial and industrial supremacy of the world, a contest from which Great Britain now emerged the undisputed leader. The Ottoman Empire, which possessed no effective military force at a time when the West was advancing in military science and was moving into a period of dynamic expansion, became the logical object of prey for European powers and was finally shaken from its state of complacency and blind confidence in Ottoman superiority in the 1730's when it was attacked by Russia and Austria. It became even more conscious of its critical position when it was defeated by Catherine II of Russia in the war which ended with the Treaty of Kūchūk Kaynarji of July 21, 1774. Russia's aggressive policy towards the Ottoman Empire continued, until in 1787 the Turks felt impelled to declare war upon Russia. Once again they were defeated and the Treaty of Jassy of January 9, 1792, brought Russian control to the Dniester River.

The Ottoman Sultan, Salīm III, hoped that the end of the war in 1792 and Catherine's death would allow a period of respite from Russian aggression which would enable him to introduce his reforms, the *Niẓām Jadīd*. He expected by these reforms to halt the process of internal decay and to protect the state from external attack. The reactionary Janissaries obstructed his attempts at reform, however, while the Sultan became too deeply involved in the wars of the Napoleonic period to enforce his program. In 1807 the death of the *muftī* of Istanbul, who had supported Salīm in his reform measures, produced an alliance against the throne of the leading Janissaries with the new *muftī*, who, like most of the *ʿulamā*', was inimical to Salīm's reforms. The Janissaries revolted and deposed Salīm, and Muṣṭafā IV became Sultan on May 29, 1807. An attempt to restore Salīm was made by Muṣṭafā Bayrāqdār,[4] Pasha of Ruschuk, in 1808, but Salīm was murdered at the moment of

Bayrāqdār's victory. The infuriated Bayrāqdār dragged Muṣṭafā off his throne and replaced him with Maḥmūd II, who became *Pādishāh* of the Ottoman world on July 28, 1808. Salīm's program of reforms, which in large part caused his death, was pursued by Maḥmūd II during the course of his reign, although he moved slowly and stealthily in his campaign against the conservative and reactionary forces in the empire.

Russian victories in the eighteenth century and the revival of French imperial ambitions after the French Revolution led to a policy of jealous watchfulness on the part of all the European Powers who wished to share in the spoils to be obtained at the expense of the Ottoman Empire. This policy, coupled with the universal anxiety to prevent a general European war after Napoleon's defeat in 1815, was to dominate the diplomatic scene for over a century. The integrity of the Ottoman Empire became the watchword of the nineteenth century, particularly for Great Britain, not because of Europe's reverence for the Empire but because of the need to prevent a general conflict among the Powers madly engaged in a scramble for a larger share of the booty.

The French occupation of Egypt was only a chapter in this great international struggle for empire, power, and commercial and industrial advantages. The idea of converting Egypt into a French colony did not originate with the Directory, but had been first broached in a *mémoire* prepared by the philosopher Leibnitz in which he outlined for Louis XIV the advantages to be derived from a French conquest of Egypt.[5] The matter of launching a campaign against Egypt had also been pressed on Louis XV, but without effect.[6] An opportune moment for the fulfillment of this project finally came during the wars between the new French Republic and Europe. Napoleon's victories over Austria in Italy and the signing of the Treaty of Campoformio in October 1797 had left Great Britain and France directly opposed. The French now considered a plan for the invasion of Great Britain, but decided that the risk was too great and that it would be wiser to attack Great Britain at vulnerable points in her overseas possessions. Both Talleyrand and Napoleon pushed the proposal for invading Egypt. The Directory finally agreed to send an expeditionary force to the Orient, a project which had three principal aims: (1) to strike a direct blow at Great Britain by obtaining mastery of the best route to India; (2) to found a flourishing colony and to exploit the great resources of Egypt; and (3) to provide for the scientific exploration both of ancient and modern Egypt. It has also been said that a fourth aim of the Directory was to rid itself of its ambitious, popular, and far too successful general,[7] but it is unlikely that any government would have deprived itself of the services of an army and fleet merely to rid itself of a potentially dangerous opponent.

The pretext for the invasion was the punishment of the Mamlūk chiefs, Ibrāhīm and Murād, who had failed to comply with French demands with regard to settling the complaints of French merchants in Egypt. General Bonaparte was appointed chief of the Army of the Orient consisting of 40,000 of the best soldiers who had fought under his standard in the Italian campaign. Not only soldiers but also scholars were included in the expeditionary force. One academician, writing many years later, claimed that a wild enthusiasm swept over French scholars who wished to accompany Napoleon. "It was," he said, "like the epidemic of madness which seized our ancestors at the time of the Crusades."[8] All who participated in the expedition were filled with a sense of historic destiny. The extent of their eventual disillusionment was commensurate with the high hopes awakened in their breasts.

On July 2, 1798, the French captured Alexandria, and by July 7 Bonaparte had begun his march on Cairo through hostile countryside. French letters intercepted and published by the British tell the tale of the suffering of the soldiers from heat, hunger, and thirst and of the massacre of stragglers by marauding Bedouin tribesmen.[9] The army finally came within sight of Cairo, and on July 21, 1798, the decisive battle between the French army and the Mamlūks was fought in the shadow of the Pyramids of Gīzah (Jīzah). The Mamlūk cavaliers, dressed in their finest armor and laden with gold and jewels, lacked the speed and military knowledge necessary to combat the most modern and finest fighting force of its time. Islamic chivalry lost the day at the Battle of the Pyramids, just as at Agincourt French chivalry had been destroyed several centuries earlier by English bowmen. The battle demonstrated once and for all time that the Mamlūks were an outmoded fighting force, totally ineffective in modern warfare; it was such proof that was to stimulate the reformers of the Ottoman Empire to reorganize and modernize their armies to withstand external attack from the West.

On July 25, 1798, Napoleon made a triumphal entry into Cairo. All *shaykhs* and members of the former regime who had not taken flight came to make submission. Ibrāhīm Bey fled to Syria, whereas the debris of Murād's army, fleeing to the south, was followed by a military force under General Desaix, who finally conquered aṣ-Ṣaʿīd (Upper Egypt) for the French. Egypt had been successfully occupied, but three factors were to shatter all prospects of converting the country into a French colony. First, the destruction of the French fleet at Abū Qīr by Lord Nelson on August 1, 1798, left the French occupation forces at the mercy of the British who were in complete control of the seas and able to cut off all supplies and reinforcements from France. Next, the hostility of the Egyptian population was never removed. European civilization and attempts at reform were not only disliked by the Egyptians, but were factors largely responsible for two extremely bloody insurrections in Cairo. The Mamlūks had been tyrants, but they were Muslims; their administration might appear chaotic to the outsider, but it had been understood by the Egyptians who knew how to evade the worst aspects of arbitrary rule. When the French were finally forced to evacuate, the population joyously welcomed the return of their Turkish overlords. They may sometimes have regretted the departure of the French, but in the final analysis, a bad Muslim ruler was far more acceptable to them than a good infidel. The final factor was the hostility of the Sublime Porte upon whose support Napoleon had counted, but the Turks persisted in their demands for his evacuation of Egypt.

The inherent danger of his position forced General Bonaparte to seek ways by which to reconcile the Egyptian people to French domination. He announced to their representatives that he wished to change none of the existing institutions or traditional taxes, that he planned only to eliminate arbitrary exactions and to introduce a regular system of tax collection. It was unfortunate for the French that the Egyptian people did not understand the "blessings" of orderly government procedures. They had managed occasionally to escape the abuses of the Mamlūks, but the French tax collectors left no loopholes for such evasion. Instead, recalcitrant villages were burned and demolished by French contingents stationed in the countryside; in fact, economic pressures on the French even forced them to fall into patterns of extortions not too unlike those of the Mamlūks. The first insurrection of Cairo of October 21, 1798, had been forcefully repressed, but Napoleon had no choice now but to show moderation towards the population, since his army, trapped in Egypt, remained in constant peril of annihilation by a hostile populace. Furthermore, he was obliged to be particularly circumspect at this time, for the Porte, urged on by the British with whom a Treaty of Alliance had been signed on January 5, 1799, declared war upon France and a Turkish attack upon the French in Egypt became imminent. Napoleon decided to act quickly to forestall attack. He left an army of 2,500 men under General Desaix in Upper Egypt, two battalions at Cairo, and a contingent under General Dugua in the Delta. He then set out with the rest of his army for Syria in February 1799.

This Syrian campaign, in which Napoleon lost more than one third of the French army in combat and from disease, was a failure because of the assistance rendered to the Turkish land forces by the British fleet under Commodore Sidney Smith. Bonaparte's defeat at 'Akkah delivered the death blow to his plans for establishing an empire in the Orient, his real intention, he later claimed: "If I had taken Acre ['Akkah]," he said, "I would have gone to Constantinople and would have established my dynasty there." He blamed Sidney Smith for causing him to miss his great destiny.[10] Napoleon's intention at the time of the Syrian campaign was probably not so grandiose as he chose to believe during his exile at St. Helena when he indulged in this recollection of the past.

When Napoleon returned to Egypt, he made his entry into Cairo on June 14, 1799, as a triumphant general returning from a successful war. Strict censorship had prevented the truth of his failure in Syria from leaking out. He declared to the Egyptians that at last the Turkish yoke, far more fearful than that of the Mamlūks, had been destroyed and that Egypt was no longer part of the Ottoman Empire. Then, on July 11, 1799, a Turkish force of 18,000 men was landed at Abū Qīr by the British fleet, but on July 25, 1799, Napoleon attacked the Turks and won a brilliant victory. By August 2, 1799, the last Turkish resistance disappeared and Egypt was saved for France, at least for the time being. In the meantime, Napoleon had obtained newspapers from Sidney Smith which contained news of the latest developments in Europe. He decided to return to France and on August 23, 1799, he and several of his principal generals embarked secretly on the *Muiron* and left Egypt and the remnants of his once great army under the control of General Kléber.

The French army and French *savants* remained in Egypt for two more years, abandoned by their leader and resigned to their fate. They criticized Napoleon for deserting them; General Kléber himself described in strong language in a report to the Directory dated October 7, 1799, the untenable position in which Napoleon had left the French in Egypt. He stated that the only course remaining to them was to make peace with the Porte.[11] There were valid reasons for his pessimism. In a dispatch dated September 22, 1799, Poussielgue, controller of expenses of the army and administrator-general of Egyptian finances, reviewed for the Directory's benefit the financial difficulties confronting the army in Egypt and the impossibility of holding on under the circumstances. "We have here, on every side of us," he wrote, "ten thousand secret enemies to one open friend. . . . Egypt is a very fine country; our dreadful situation in it is merely the effect of circumstances. It proves only that we are arrived too soon, and that the time is not yet come for us to establish ourselves."[12] Duplicate copies of both dispatches were intercepted by the British who were consequently well informed of the true conditions of the French in Egypt and could negotiate from strength.

The French in Egypt were divided into two parties: the first, headed by Kléber and supported by the majority of the army, favored the abandonment of Egypt; the second, headed by General Menou, favored remaining in Egypt and fulfilling the program of converting Egypt into a French colony. Menou's party was unable to make headway against the pressures of the other group and Kléber began to negotiate with the Turks. Accordingly, under the terms of the Convention of al-ʻArīsh signed January 24, 1800, by the French and Turkish plenipotentiaries in the presence of Sidney Smith, an armistice of three months was declared and preliminary steps for French evacuation were initiated. The Egyptians were delighted by the news that the French were about to leave. "Blessed be the year," they declared, "when these infidel dogs leave us; the day of their departure will be a happy one."[13]

Meanwhile, the British government, reluctant to allow the return of such a large military force to France while the continental war was in progress, sent instructions that Sidney Smith was to agree only to a convention whereby the French would surrender as prisoners of war, but the Convention of al-ʻArīsh had already been signed before Smith received his new instructions. When Kléber learned of British opposition to the evacuation, he was angered by the humiliation which the British wished to impose upon him and his troops. He issued an order of the day to his troops stating that such insolence could only be answered by fresh victories.[14] It is possible that the stiffening of Kléber's stand at this moment was due less to his resentment of the dishonorable terms imposed by the British than to the fact that he had by this time learned that his critical dispatch of October 7 in which he had denounced Napoleon was never destined to reach the five members of the Directory to whom it was addressed. It came, instead, into the hands of Napoleon who, upon his return to France, became First Consul of the French Republic. This very embarrassing situation made it imperative for Kléber to re-establish his position by making a good showing in Egypt. This he did at the Battle of Heliopolis (ʻAyn Shams) on March 20, 1800, when the French defeated a large Turkish army under Yūsuf Pasha. During the course of the battle, the second insurrection of Cairo occurred and lasted until April 25, 1800, when the French army made a victorious entry into the rebellious city. But Kléber accomplished little during the brief period in which he ruled Egypt. He was assassinated on June 14, 1800, and the French troops, wholeheartedly devoted to him, grieved over his death and never became reconciled to his successor, General Menou, who was well-known for his colonial views and was the laughing stock of the army because of his obesity, his conversion to Islām, and his marriage to a very young Egyptian girl.

General Jacques ʻAbd-allāh Menou, formerly a Baron of the *ancien régime* in France, deputy of the Nobility of Touraine to the Estates-General at the time of the French Revolution, had thrown in his lot with the revolutionaries and later with Napoleon. He was senior officer in Egypt at the time of Kléber's assassination. Disliked by the other officers who had no respect for his capacities as a soldier, ridiculed by the French soldiers, he nevertheless received firm support from the chief of state, Napoleon Bonaparte, and set himself the task of reforming the Egyptian administration and the tax structure of the country. For approximately nine months he enjoyed a period of peace during which he began to put down sturdy roots for a permanent occupation of Egypt by France. The Egyptians resigned themselves to the inevitability of French rule and began to fraternize with the French, while the French soldiers, although bored by the long occupation and homesick for France, settled down to a long exile and began to take an interest in the local people and the country.

Menou's program of reform was terminated, however, by a new invasion by the British and Turks. After a French defeat at the Battle of Nicopolis on March 13, 1801, and the indecisive outcome of the Battle of Canopus on March 21, 1801, Menou, undecided what to do, did the minimum possible while awaiting reinforcements from France promised to him by Napoleon. The British, under the command of General Hutchinson after General Abercromby's death from fatal wounds received during the Battle of Canopus, prepared a three-pronged attack upon Cairo in conjunction with the Turkish army which came to Egypt by way of Syria. Instead of taking proper precautions, Menou quarreled with his generals and did nothing, but the success of the British plan persuaded General Belliard in Cairo to capitulate on June 27, 1801, and to enter into negotiations. On July 10, 1801, General Belliard, at the head of 13,754 officers and soldiers, started for Rosetta (Rashīd) where they embarked for France on August 7. Ten thousand French still remained in Egypt under Menou at Alexandria. Napoleon urged Menou to resist as long as possible, maintaining that if he continued to occupy Alexandria, the French could hope to wring favorable concessions from the British at the conference for discussions preliminary to the Treaty of Amiens which was scheduled to begin in London in November 1801. Events in Egypt moved too quickly, however. Hutchinson besieged Alexandria and Menou, fearful of the threat of famine and plague, decided to capitulate. A treaty of evacuation was signed on September 2, 1801, and within a month the last French troops were evacuated. Out of 40,000 soldiers who had taken part in the French expedition, only 24,000 men returned to France. At the London conference of November 1801 both France and Britain agreed to recognize the re-establishment of Turkish sovereignty in Egypt; this recognition was incorporated in the Treaty of Amiens signed on March 27, 1802, and was reinforced by the Franco-Turkish Treaty signed June 25, 1802.

It is impossible to gauge with any degree of accuracy the influence of any person, institution, or event upon the course of a nation's history. Nevertheless, it has frequently been claimed in exaggerated terms that modern civilization was introduced into Egypt during the period of the French occupation, largely through the efforts of the French scholars who accompanied Napoleon. The work of the French *savants* remains as a permanent tribute to French scholarship, but it must be recognized that the scholars' greatest achievement was enlightening the West about Egypt rather than influencing the Egyptians. Three years, in any case, is a very brief period for the representatives of one civilization to leave a lasting impression upon those of another. Besides, the immediate needs of the occupation army took precedence over idealistic long-range reforms which might have revolutionized Egypt. The critical financial situation in which Napoleon and his successors found themselves led instead to oppressive measures reminiscent of Mamlūk tyranny. There was indeed only a very brief period of peace in the country. For the most part, it was the scene of continuous struggle: Bedouin raids, Mamlūk battles, city insurrections, and village revolts. Along with native discontent, there was also the discontent of the army, unpaid, badly clothed, homesick, disillusioned, unhappy to be in the backwoods of events while new glory was to be gained on European battlefields, hated by the Egyptians, and bearing them no love in return. Perhaps Menou and his party of colonizers might have influenced Egypt profoundly had the occupation continued, but under the circumstances French influence could not have survived the French occupation for long without being renewed through other channels.

Many French ideas were reintroduced in Egypt during Muḥammad 'Alī's[15] reign by men like Drovetti and Mengin and by the numerous French officers who either remained in Egypt after the French withdrawal or returned at a later date when Napoleon lost his power and officers, like Colonel Sève (Sulaymān Pasha), and other supporters of Napoleon were obliged to leave France to seek their fortunes elsewhere. French influence also came into Egypt during Muḥammad 'Alī's reign by way of the educational missions to France under the supervision of Jomard, one of the French *savants* of the French expedition. Another source of French influence was the Saint-Simonians who flocked to Egypt in the 1830's to assist in the construction of the Barrages. These Saint-Simonians, who dreamed of wedding the East and West by building a canal through the Isthmus of Suez, were the heirs of the French engineers of the expeditionary army who had made careful surveys of Egypt and had published their findings in a series of remarkable articles. The French expedition had also loomed large in the minds of the French romantics of the post-Napoleonic era and innumerable travelers were making pilgrimages to Egypt. Artisans, engineers, experts of all sorts came, too. Thus, French influence in Egypt was not simply the outcome of the three-year occupation of the country by Napoleon's Army of the Orient but was, rather, the result of a continuing stream of French influences of many kinds which combined to make French civilization the predominant European influence in Egypt during, as well as after, Muḥammad 'Alī's reign.

Subsequent to the evacuation of the French expeditionary army, there developed an intense struggle among competing groups for control of Egypt. Ottoman policy was directed towards the exile of the Mamlūks from Egypt and the re-establishment of Turkish control over the country, but the Mamlūks sought to return to their former position of control and looked for complete emancipation from Ottoman domination. Headed by four chiefs, Ibrāhīm Bey, 'Uthmān Bey al-Bardīsī, Muḥammad Bey al-Alfī, and 'Uthmān Bey Ḥasan, they dissipated much of their energy and strength in inner factional disputes, especially in those between 'Uthmān Bey al-Bardīsī and Muḥammad Bey al-Alfī, who were competing for leadership of the entire body of Mamlūks. Both the Turks and the Mamlūks attempted to obtain diplomatic and military support from France and Great Britain, whereas the French and British governments backed one or the other group or faction as it furthered their own interests in the great international struggles of the period. Negotiations between the Turks and Mamlūks, with the British acting as intermediaries, failed to produce a compromise solution; the Mamlūks, in open rebellion against their sovereign, withdrew to Upper Egypt from where they carried on their struggle against the Turks, while Muḥammad Bey al-Alfī went to plead their cause in Great Britain.

When the British withdrew from Egypt on March 14, 1803, in accordance with the terms of the Treaty of Amiens, the Turkish-Mamlūk struggle entered a new phase. The struggle for control of the country which had to this point been confined to the two main parties—Turk and Mamlūk—was complicated by a split in the Turkish party between, on one side, Khusraw Pasha, the Ottoman *wālī* in Egypt, supported by the 'Uthmānlī troops (the Janissaries), and, on the other side, the Albanian mercenaries headed by Ṭāhir Pasha. When the Albanian troops mutinied in Cairo for their pay on April 12, 1803, Khusraw Pasha fled from the Citadel and took refuge in Damietta (Dimyāṭ), while Ṭāhir Pasha assumed the position of *qā'immaqām* (governor of Cairo) and asked the Sultan to appoint a new *wālī*. Ṭāhir realized that he could not control Egypt without additional support and invited the Mamlūks to return to Cairo to assist him in holding the country, but before their arrival he was murdered by the Janissaries on May 25, 1803. Muḥammad 'Alī, second in command of the Albanian troops, replaced Ṭāhir, but was threatened by the attempt of Aḥmad Pasha of al-Madīnah, then in Cairo, to assume leadership at this critical moment. Muḥammad 'Alī feared that if Aḥmad succeeded the Albanians would lose their stranglehold on the country. He, therefore, decided to follow the course chosen by Ṭāhir and entered into an alliance with the Mamlūks. He defeated Aḥmad's forces and with the Mamlūks restored order in Cairo. An expedition of Albanian and Mamlūk troops then hurried to Damietta where Khusraw was gathering forces for an attack upon Cairo and on July 1, 1803, engaged in battle with Khusraw who was defeated, brought back to Cairo, and imprisoned in the Citadel.

On July 8, 1803, ʿAlī Pasha Burghul, appointed by the Sultan as *wālī* of Egypt, arrived in Egypt to replace Khusraw. He only then learned of Ṭāhir's murder and the re-entry of the Mamlūks into Cairo. He promptly sent a conciliatory letter to the Mamlūks, informing them that the Sublime Porte would extend full pardon on certain conditions that he listed (see Chapter III). These conditions were acceptable to the Mamlūks who allowed ʿAlī Pasha to come to Cairo and assume office. Soon after his arrival, though, he began to intrigue with Muḥammad ʿAlī against the Mamlūks, but Muḥammad ʿAlī was not prepared to be drawn into his intrigue. He informed al-Bardīsī Bey of ʿAlī's treachery and urged him to depose him from office. ʿAlī was ordered to leave Egypt, but before he could embark at Alexandria, he was assassinated on January 31, 1804, by order of al-Bardīsī Bey.

Upon Muḥammad Bey al-Alfī's return to Egypt from England on February 14, 1804, he was attacked at Gīzah by Albanian troops under Muḥammad ʿAlī's command in accordance with al-Bardīsī's decision to rid himself of his opponent, who had already announced that he had obtained British backing for himself. Al-Alfī Bey managed to escape to Upper Egypt, and Muḥammad ʿAlī now recognized that the split in Mamlūk ranks offered him a splendid opportunity to make a bid for power. He demanded, on behalf of his troops, the arrears of pay which al-Bardīsī owed. To meet this demand, al-Bardīsī was obliged to levy a special tax upon the population of Cairo. Full opprobrium for this act fell upon al-Bardīsī, although Muḥammad ʿAlī had been essentially responsible. When the people revolted against this new exaction, Muḥammad ʿAlī entered the Great Mosque and declared to the insurgents that the new tax was abolished and that no reprisals would be made against the rebellious populace. His popularity with the Cairenes dated from this occasion. Muḥammad ʿAlī then decided to take the offensive against the Mamlūks. He first besieged al-Bardīsī's residence on March 11, 1804, and bribed his Turkish troops to desert him. The homes of the other beys were also attacked, and, by March 12, Muḥammad ʿAlī was in full command of Cairo. Al-Bardīsī and the other Mamlūks managed to escape to the desert and from there fled to Upper Egypt.

Muḥammad ʿAlī, placing little reliance upon the loyalty of his Albanian troops and also wishing to legalize his position, decided to release Khusraw Pasha from imprisonment and to re-establish him as Pasha of Egypt, but his Albanian troops, who held Khusraw responsible for the murder of Ṭāhir, refused to accept him and demanded his return to Istanbul. The Albanians found Khūrshīd, Governor of Alexandria, acceptable, however, and he was summoned by Muḥammad ʿAlī to serve as Pasha of Egypt and was confirmed in this office by the Sultan. Later, during the summer of 1804, while Muḥammad ʿAlī was campaigning against the Mamlūks, Khūrshīd Pasha, anxious to strengthen his position against the Albanians, invited a troop of five hundred Dalāt[16] from Syria to come to Egypt. When Muḥammad ʿAlī learned of their arrival, he hastened back to Cairo on the pretext that his troops were demanding their pay. As Khūrshīd was unable to settle his accounts with Muḥammad ʿAlī, the Albanians formed an alliance with the Dalāt, also in arrears of pay, and together they pillaged Cairo to raise funds. At the same time, Muḥammad ʿAlī began his intrigue with the *shaykhs* and notables of the city. He encouraged them to present a list of demands to Khūrshīd calling for the removal of troops from the city and a promise that no unlawful taxes should henceforth be levied upon the country and that communications with Upper Egypt should be restored. When Khūrshīd refused to consider any demands made upon him by the Egyptians, Muḥammad ʿAlī stated that he was prepared to carry them out, provided he became Pasha of Egypt. The *ʿulamā'*, led by as-Sayyid ʿUmar Makram, then declared that, since Khūrshīd was a tyrant, they were entitled to remove him from office in accordance with an ancient Muslim prerogative, the right of the people to depose an unjust ruler.[17] Accordingly, on May 14, 1805, they proclaimed Muḥammad ʿAlī *wālī* of Egypt and proceeded to the Citadel to demand Khūrshīd's withdrawal. Khūrshīd refused to leave the Citadel and contemptuously declared that his authority came from the Sultan and that he would certainly not accept decisions made by a group of *fallāḥīn*.[18] He called upon the Dalāt to come to his aid for the sake of religion and in defense of the honor and laws of the Empire, but the Dalāt refused to give him their support and allied themselves instead with Muḥammad ʿAlī and as-Sayyid ʿUmar Makram. Between May 18 and June 17, 1805, Muḥammad ʿAlī tried to prevail upon Khūrshīd Pasha to abandon the Citadel, but he refused. Hostilities were postponed by agreement between the two sides, pending instructions from the Sultan, but on June 17, before the Sultan's decision was received, the Pasha began to bombard the city. Muḥammad ʿAlī then ordered that cannons and mortars should be transported to the Muqattam Hills overlooking the Citadel and began to bombard the Pasha's position. At the end of July 1805, Ṣalāḥ Aghā, an emissary from the Sultan, arrived in Egypt. As soon as he had ascertained the strength of both parties and recognized the superior position of Muḥammad ʻAlī in the conflict, he instructed Khūrshīd to surrender and on behalf of the Sultan confirmed Muḥammad ʻAlī as the new *wālī* of Egypt. After lengthy negotiations, Khūrshīd agreed to leave the Citadel and to withdraw from Egypt. Muḥammad ʻAlī thus came to power with the support of the people of Cairo and with the agreement of the Sublime Porte.

Muḥammad ʻAlī was Pasha of Egypt *de jure*, but *de facto* he controlled only Cairo. The rest of the country remained in the hands of the competing Mamlūk factions and of the Bedouin tribes who had taken advantage of the unstable political situation to pillage the countryside for their own profit. Muḥammad ʻAlī's position was thus extremely precarious. He centered his attention on retaining the Sultan's support and on overcoming the intrigues in Istanbul initiated by Muḥammad Bey al-Alfī. By judicious bribery he gained his aims and frustrated an attempt in 1806 to remove him from office in Egypt and to appoint him Pasha of Salonika. The renewal of hostilities between Turkey and Russia on December 27, 1806, and the alignment of Russia and Great Britain against Turkey and France led the Sultan to reconfirm Muḥammad ʻAlī in office, but he was urged to arrange a reconciliation with the Mamlūks and to cooperate with them in combating any attempt by the enemy to occupy the country. Muḥammad ʻAlī then consented to work for a compromise with all the Mamlūk parties and entered into negotiations with them. By January 28, 1807, before these negotiations could be brought to a close, Muḥammad ʻAlī's two principal enemies in Egypt, ʻUthmān Bey al-Bardīsī and Muḥammad Bey al-Alfī, were dead. His position was again briefly threatened at the time of the occupation of Alexandria by the British (March 17–September 19, 1807), but this danger soon passed with the defeat and evacuation of the British troops. Negotiations with the Mamlūks were resumed, but Ibrāhīm Bey, ʻUthmān Bey Ḥasan, and the remnant of Murād Bey's party still refused to come to terms with Muḥammad ʻAlī. By 1808 peace was arranged with the Muḥammad Bey al-Alfī faction, now headed by Shāhīn Bey, but this peace proved to be only an uneasy truce which was disturbed several times by the Mamlūks. Finally, when the Sultan urged Muḥammad ʻAlī to take up arms on his behalf against the Wahhābīs in Arabia, the Pasha decided to destroy the Mamlūks completely. On March 1, 1811, he treacherously massacred the majority of the Mamlūks and by 1812 those who had not escaped to Nubia were annihilated by Muḥammad ʿAlī's command.

The drama was at an end. The ruling class of Egypt which had held power for so long was finally wiped out and Muḥammad ʿAlī was firmly in power. He had survived the struggle for power, no mean achievement, but continued survival was contingent upon his ability to resist any attempt by the Sultan to remove him from office. The Ottoman government's policy toward the Mamlūks had envisaged the re-establishment of absolute Turkish control over Egypt and Muḥammad ʿAlī had served as a tool in that design, but it was certainly never the Sultan's intention to destroy one adversary merely to create another more dangerous. Unfortunately for Ottoman rule, the Sultan failed to take the proper measure of the man whom he appointed as his viceregent in Egypt and when he finally did, it was too late.

CHAPTER II

LANDHOLDING IN EGYPT BEFORE THE FRENCH OCCUPATION

The system of landholding in Egypt at the end of the eighteenth century dated from the Ottoman conquest, although vestigial remnants from previous dynasties existed also. Neither the Ottomans nor their predecessors began their rule with a *tabula rasa*; each ruling dynasty made some concession to or compromise with conditions prevailing at the time of conquest.[1] Innumerable variations in landholding evolved from this process, all, however, falling within the framework of Islamic land categories[2] modified by customs and usages which gradually acquired the force of law.

Early in the Ottoman period an examination into the ways of landholding in Egypt was made and land titles were subjected to close scrutiny. If landholders possessed land without valid titles or failed to conform to the terms stipulated in their deeds of concession, their land was joined to the body of state lands and subjected to the *mīrī* on land levied by the Ottoman conquerors.[3] Much of the agricultural land of Egypt was integrated into the national domain at this time. All titles to endowments (i.e., *waqfs*) and pensions held by soldiers and religious beneficiaries in land, money, or payment in kind (*ar-rizaq al-jayshīyah* and *ar-rizaq al-aḥbāsīyah*) were also inspected. Such verification of titles at times of dynastic change was no innovation and was, in fact, a device by means of which the abuses in landholding which periodically developed could be corrected.[4] Thus, Muḥammad ʻAlī's claim to the right of employing this same procedure soon after Maḥmūd II came to the Ottoman throne was clearly based upon historical precedents. In 1809 he upheld this right by arguing that whenever a sultan or his representative died or was deposed, the change of rulers necessitated the re-examination of all titles and the renewal of all privileges.[5]

In the *Qānūn-nāmah* of Sulaymān the task of administering the state domains and collecting taxes with which state lands were burdened was assigned to (1) government officials, specifically the *kāshifs*, or (2) Arab *shaykhs* who controlled large areas of Egypt or (3) agents (*'āmils*) selected from among rich individuals who could pay the government for the privilege of acting as its agents. The system of *iltizāms* or tax farms which finally emerged was undoubtedly an outgrowth of the work of the latter.[6] By the end of the eighteenth century, state lands were almost universally distributed throughout Egypt in the form of *iltizāms* and fell into the hands of the wealthiest and most powerful men, most of whom were Mamlūks. Of the six thousand *multazims*, tax farmers (that is, holders of *iltizāms*), it was estimated that three hundred were Mamlūks who held more than two thirds of the cultivable land in Egypt. The balance was held by non-Mamlūk *multazims*, whose holdings were sometimes so small as to provide them with only the barest subsistence.[7]

An *iltizām* was an estate which was granted through the government bureau in charge of land registration (*Rūznāmah*) for a year or a term of years. The grant was awarded to the highest bidder at an auction or by means of a private arrangement with this bureau. Upon payment in advance of an amount equal to one year's portion of that part of the land tax payable from the estate's income to the government (i.e., the *mīrī*), the *multazim* was issued a title deed to the lease (*taqsīṭ*) by the *Rūznāmah*, which also addressed a letter to the notables and inhabitants of the estate (*namīqah*) instructing the villagers to obey the *multazim* and to pay him the amount of taxes authorized by the terms of the title deed. The substance (*raqabah*) of the land was retained by the state; the *multazim* acquired only the right to its use (*taṣarruf*), a right which he shared with the peasants (*fallāḥīn*) who worked that portion of the *iltizām* reserved for them (*arḍ al-fallāḥ*) and on which they paid taxes to the *multazim*. The *multazim's* profit was derived partially from the taxes which he collected on the *arḍ al-fallāḥ*—the *fā'iẓ*[8] and, in the eighteenth century, the *muḍāf* and *barrānī*—but mostly from the income he obtained from working the portion of the *iltizām* assigned for his exclusive enjoyment (*arḍ al-waṣīyah*). The *waṣīyah*, however, did not become his private property and could be exploited for his account only so long as he retained the leasehold on the *iltizām*. He was, moreover, obliged to deduct from his total profit the administrative costs of tax collecting, the expenses for providing hospitality to travelers, the upkeep of certain public buildings, and the maintenance of the irrigation system.[9]

Although an *iltizām* was legally only a temporary concession of the right to farm the taxes of a parcel of *mīrī* land and the leasehold could, theoretically, be revoked by the state or given to a wealthier or more influential person, in practice certain customary procedures gradually were evolved that conferred upon the tax farmers rights and privileges that closely resembled those attached to private property and, in fact, encroached upon the rights of the state. The decline in Ottoman domination over Egypt in the eighteenth century accelerated this process by enabling the beys, and the Mamlūks in general, to usurp prerogatives which fell within the sovereign's domain. Hereditary rights developed which were recognized by custom. The children and white Mamlūks of a *multazim* (or whoever was mentioned in the will, if one existed, of the deceased) could inherit the leasehold upon payment to the pasha, as representative of the sultan, of a tax called *ḥulwān*, which amounted to a sum not exceeding the total *fā'iẓ* for three years. The payment of the *ḥulwān*, in effect, constituted a kind of repurchase of the land. Upon its payment, the *Rūznāmah* registered the changes in landholding and issued a new *taqsīṭ* to the heirs. If a *multazim* died without children and intestate, or if the heirs failed to pay the *ḥulwān*, the land reverted to the state.[10]

The *multazim* also acquired the privilege, by the eighteenth century, of selling or donating his rights to any portion of the *iltizām* to another *multazim*. Selling, in this context, actually meant renting or leasing, for a price, the right to enjoy the usufruct of the land. The *multazim* could reclaim his land upon repayment of the purchase price, as the sale was usually only a temporary arrangement to enable him to raise a loan. It was incumbent upon the *multazim* to sell or donate an equal proportion of *waṣīyah* land and *fallāḥ* land. To protect the rights of the *fallāḥīn*, it was always the practice to divide both the *arḍ al-fallāḥ* and the *arḍ al-waṣīyah* of the *iltizām* into twenty-four parts (*qīrāṭs*) so that the sale or donation of part of the *arḍ al-fallāḥ* necessitated the loss to the *multazim* of a proportionate part of his *arḍ al-waṣīyah*. After the transfer was registered by a Muslim official (*efendī*) in the *Rūznāmah*, the judge (*qāḍī*) issued a title deed (*ḥujjah*) to the purchaser. The pasha received no benefits from this kind of transaction, but it was customary to pay his scribes, as a kind of confirmation tax, twenty-eight *medins* (40 *medins* [paras] = 1 piaster) per *qīrāṭ* of land transferred. A fee of 1 per cent of the selling price and 1 per cent of the *mīrī* on the land went to the *efendī* who registered the change. The *qāḍī* received 2 per cent.[11]

It was the custom in Lower Egypt, in the Fayyūm, and in Middle Egypt below Aṭfīḥ for a fixed area of the *arḍ al-fallāḥ* to be cultivated by individual families, although no rights of private property were thereby conferred. These definite portions were known as *athar* (plu. *âthār*) land (also called *atharīyah* land), *athar* meaning vestige, trace, tradition, usage, and were handed down from father to son. The *multazim* could remove the peasant (*fallāḥ*) from this land only if he failed to pay his taxes or cultivate his land. The procedure for dispossessing the defaulting *fallāḥ* consisted of the *multazim's* bringing him before the legal authorities and declaring before witnesses that the *fallāḥ* had defaulted in the payment of taxes. With this act the *fallāḥ* was dispossessed. The *multazim* could then turn the land over to another *fallāḥ* who was usually chosen by the *shaykh al-balad.* Generally the dispossessed *fallāḥ* was not alienated from his land permanently. If he was able to pay his arrears, he could reclaim possession of his land. In cases where the *fallāḥ* was too heavily burdened and unable to meet the *multazim's* demands, he might choose to abandon his land. He was then replaced by another *fallāḥ* selected by the *shaykh al-balad* and confirmed by the *multazim.* So long as a *fallāḥ* cultivated his land and paid his taxes, he was free to cultivate the land as he chose.

On the other hand, in Upper Egypt, from Girgā (Jirjā) to the Cataracts, families did not work a fixed portion of land, because variations in cultivable land caused by the floods made it difficult to establish separate boundaries. No *waṣīyah* land existed farther south than al-Minyā and no *athar* land was found south of Girgā. Families were, however, entitled to a certain proportion of the land, although in view of its superfluity this right was of little significance. Cultivable land was distributed to individuals each year after the inundation of the Nile in accordance with their ability to cultivate it; this land was designated *bi'l-masāḥah* or land by the measure. This practice could sometimes be found below Girgā also, but there it was usual for the *fallāḥ's* land to be *athar.*[12]

A *fallāḥ* could sell or donate his *athar* land to another *fallāḥ* except in Middle Egypt where there was always more land than cultivators. In addition, if a *fallāḥ*, for some reason, could not work all his land or required a loan, he had recourse to two kinds of transactions. In the first, known as *gharūqah* (a form of mortgage),[13] the *fallāḥ* leased his land to another *fallāḥ* until he was able to repay the amount he had received. He could then reclaim his land. In such cases of sale, donation, and *gharūqah*, the *qāḍī* had to confirm the transfer of land from one person to the other. The second transaction required no legal confirmation by the *qāḍī* as it was usually arranged privately between two *fallāḥīn*; one *fallāḥ* would rent to the other the use of his *athar* land for a single year after which it had to be returned to the original holder.

Inheritance of *athar* land, based on custom rather than right, was of a restricted nature, however, and depended upon the good will of the *multazim* in whose *iltizām* the *athar* land was situated. The heir of a deceased *fallāḥ* was expected to pay to the *multazim* a kind of tax of investiture which, depending upon the *multazim's* generosity, might amount to as much as three times the annual revenue of the land. Frequently the heir did not pay this tax unless forced to do so by the *multazim* who could, if he desired, refuse to allow the *fallāḥ* to enter upon his patrimony until he had done so. When a *fallāḥ* died without heirs, his land remained within the *multazim's* jurisdiction, whereas his personal property, such as the house, furniture, and flocks, were claimed by the public treasury. The *qāḍī* dealt with all questions of *fallāḥ* successions and the sale of houses and furniture and charged a fee in accordance with the means of his clients.[14]

There was also a class of landless peasants who worked for other *fallāḥīn*. The phenomenon of such a class existing in a country with an excess of land was due to the power of *multazims* to dispossess *fallāḥīn* who failed to pay their taxes. Unless a dispossessed *fallāḥ* migrated to another part of the country, he had no alternative but to work for someone else. Not all peasants who worked for others were necessarily without land, however, as it was also customary for peasants who held land to hire themselves out as laborers when the flood failed to water their own lands. They usually went to other villages where work was available.[15]

Shaykhs al-balad were granted portions of village land exempted by *multazims* from one of the extraordinary taxes (*barrānī*) partly to pay for various administrative duties which they performed and partly to cover the expense of providing hospitality to travelers. This type of concession was known as *masmūḥ ash-shaykh*. As the office of *shaykh al-balad* usually passed from father to son, these lands were also inherited by the heirs of the *shaykhs al-balad*.[16]

Another important group of landholders in Egypt was of Bedouin origin. The settlement of these nomads began as early as the Arab conquest and continued thereafter until large tracts of land, especially in Middle and Upper Egypt but also in the Fayyūm and in Lower Egypt, were cultivated by them. The *Qānūn-nāmah* of Sulaymān recognized the importance of the Bedouin element and assigned to the Arab *shaykhs* (*mashāyikh al-ʻarab*) the task of supervising land cultivation and tax collection on behalf of the government in the extensive areas under their control. As more and more tribes gravitated to Egypt, the Arab *shaykhs* gradually assumed the role of hereditary *multazims* and the most important of them possessed almost unlimited powers in the regions under their domination. This was particularly the case in Upper Egypt which had been settled by the Hawwārah tribe. Far from the center of control at Cairo, Upper Egypt existed almost as an autonomous area and developed indigenous practices varying from those to be found elsewhere in Egypt. In the middle of the eighteenth century the last *shaykh* of the Hawwārah tribe to exercise absolute control over Upper Egypt from Asyūṭ to Aṣwān was the Amīr Hammām. He provided the government at Cairo with approximately 150,000 *ardabbs* of wheat and received in return a free hand to collect taxes and to govern the area. His administration was notably stable and Upper Egypt prospered under his rule.

In 1769, however, ʿAlī Bey al-Kabīr decided to break the power of the great Arab *shaykhs*. He launched a campaign against ash-Shaykh Hammām in Upper Egypt and also against ash-Shaykh Suwaylim ibn Habīb of the Saʿd confederacy, who controlled al-Qalyūbīyah Province. Both were defeated; ibn Habīb died in battle and Hammām died shortly after his defeat. ʿAlī Bey did not remain in control of the government at Cairo long enough to establish a stable administration to replace the one that he had destroyed in Upper Egypt, which soon became a place of refuge for Mamlūks chased out of Cairo by their enemies. In fact, from the death of Hammām in 1769 until 1811 when the Mamlūks were massacred by Muḥammad ʿAlī, Upper Egypt was in a state bordering upon political anarchy. The Mamlūks who fled there extorted as much as they could from the local population and did little to maintain the irrigation system or to provide security. Later, during the French occupation, the land which had been held by Mamlūks in Upper Egypt was joined to the national domain for the profit of the French Republic; it was administered by French officials until 1800 when General Kléber and Murād Bey signed an agreement by which Murād was recognized as governor of Upper Egypt on condition that he acknowledge the sovereignty of France. Murād ignored the rights of the former landholders and granted *iltizāms* to his most important adherents. After the withdrawal of French troops from Egypt in 1801 and during the years of struggle which followed, Upper Egypt was controlled by various Mamlūk factions who sought refuge there in defiance of the Sultan and his representatives at Cairo. The control of Upper Egypt and the payment of taxes to Cairo became a bargaining point in the negotiations between the Mamlūks and Muḥammad ʿAlī until their final annihilation when Upper Egypt was subjected to direct control by the government at Cairo.

A survey of all land in Upper Egypt was made annually. The village land was then divided by the *shaykhs al-balad* among the cultivators, either *fallāḥīn* or Bedouins. Villages that paid their taxes in kind deducted them from the total harvest and divided the balance between the cultivators and the *multazims*, whether Arab *shaykhs* or fugitive Mamlūks; when taxes were paid both in kind and in money, the proportion paid was usually determined by the quality of the land and the rapacity of the *multazims*. The Bedouin cultivators in Upper Egypt and elsewhere, many of whom still maintained a semi-nomadic existence, commonly resorted to violence to obtain better land, often refusing to pay their taxes or forcing the *fallāḥīn* to bear a larger share of the taxes so they could pay less. Furthermore, they frequently tampered with the irrigation system for their own advantage. They also confiscated supplies from the peasants, if their own lands failed to provide them with an adequate yield. The *fallāḥīn* tolerated these depredations, because the Bedouins, even those who were fully settled or semi-nomadic, carried arms and retained the traditions of fighting men and frequently protected the *fallāḥīn* against the marauding of other Bedouins who still lived a purely nomadic existence.[17]

The *iltizāms* were maintained as long as they constituted a stable economic unit which continued to function irrespective of political revolutions within the ruling institution and produced the revenue which the government required. A well-developed system of administration at the local level thus emerged which was able to absorb the shock of numerous political revolutions and, in fact, to serve as a basis for administration even after the disappearance of the *iltizām* as a system of landholding. Since most of the *multazims* were absentee landlords residing in Cairo, the management of the *iltizāms* rested with local officials, each of whom had duties and responsibilities that cannot always be precisely defined because of disagreement and discrepancies which appear in the sources and also because of diversity in local customs.[18] For example, a *multazim* may have been represented by a *qāʾimmaqām* whose function was to protect his interests in the *iltizām*. On the other hand, it is argued that the *qāʾimmaqām* was a Mamlūk assigned by the provincial bey to most villages to carry out on the lowest administrative level the duties and responsibilities which the government undertook on behalf of the *multazims*, namely, maintaining security in the village, protecting cultivators against the Bedouins, settling disputes in the village, and, whenever necessary, assisting the *multazim* in collecting taxes. Regardless of whether the *qā'immaqām* was appointed by the *multazim* or the bey, however, his functions were in effect identical in either case—he safeguarded the interests of the *multazim*.[19]

Where an *iltizām* was very large, the *multazim* would usually appoint a Copt steward (*mubāshir*) who had several Copt scribes to assist him. This *mubāshir* appointed all the money-changers (*ṣarrāfs*) in the *iltizām*, corresponded with them, and kept separate registers of the land taxes (*mīrī*, *al-māl al-ḥurr*, and *barrānī*) for each village. There were three sets of registers of *al-māl al-ḥurr* and the *barrānī*. One set was kept by the *mubāshir*, a second by the village *ṣarrāf*, and a third was deposited with the representative of the village (*shāhid*) for the use of the villagers. No general register of *al-māl al-ḥurr* existed in Egypt.[20]

The *multazim* divided the *iltizām* into portions over which he appointed a *shaykh al-balad* who received his orders and transmitted them to the *fallāḥīn* placed under his jurisdiction. Each *shaykh al-balad* was responsible for supervising the cultivation in his portion and for preventing any misconduct or negligence which could affect the interests of the *multazim*. For example, if peasants abandoned their land or committed some serious error of which the *shaykh* failed to inform the *multazim*, he was held responsible for the payment of their taxes. Most villages, whether held by one or several *multazims*, had an average of eight to ten *shaykhs al-balad*, and in some cases there were as many as twenty or more. The most eminent of their number was known as the *shaykh* of the *shaykhs* (*shaykh al-mashāyikh*), and he fulfilled the same function with regard to his colleagues as they towards the *fallāḥīn* under their supervision; he served, in fact, as the focal point in the village and held it together. He was also justice of the peace and acted as arbitrator in disputes among members of the village. His authority was not confined to the peasants, however, but extended over all inhabitants, including the village artisans and merchants. The chief *shaykh*, if no *qā'immaqām* was stationed in the village, represented the *multazim* when he was absent. Sometimes the *shaykh al-balad* was obliged periodically to present the *multazim* with a certain amount of money to retain his office, but this practice was by no means universal. His post was usually a hereditary one, subject to confirmation by the *multazim* who might appoint a richer or more esteemed member of the community. Generally, however, the *multazim* selected one of the *shaykh's* children to succeed and an exchange of gifts occurred.[21]

Each village had one Copt *ṣarrāf* appointed by the *mubāshir* or, if there was no *mubāshir*, by the *multazim*. His task was to gather the revenue collected by the *shaykhs al-balad* from the *fallāḥīn*, to verify the value of the specie transmitted to him, and to pay administrative expenses incurred locally. The village also had a *shāhid*, or witness, selected from the *fallāḥīn* of the village by them with the concurrence of the *multazim*. Where there were several *multazims* in a village, the principal one confirmed the selection of the village *shāhid*. The *shāhid's* major qualification was his ability to read and to count. He watched over the interests of the *fallāḥīn* and retained the register which included information concerning the nature and extent of all the land in the village, the name of each inhabitant and the property he held, and the changes in holdings which occurred.

As taxes could be levied only on watered land that had been cultivated, a survey was made annually. It was sometimes carried out by a Copt official, the *massāḥ*, surveyor, but it was usually performed by the *khawlī*, an official who supervised the cultivation of the *multazim's arḍ al-waṣīyah*. The village *ṣarrāf* witnessed the survey, wrote down the measurements, and made the necessary calculations. The *shaykh* also witnessed the survey in his portion. In years when a large part of the land remained dry (*sharāqī*), the *qāʾimmaqām* witnessed the survey, too. Since the *khawlī* frequently was unable to read or write, he relied upon his memory in cases of boundary controversies between *fallāḥīn*. Should he be tempted to make a false survey, the *shaykh* was obliged to denounce him and to recommend someone else for the post.[22]

Two other officials, the *mishadd*[23] and the *ghafīr*, also performed duties in the local government. Those delegated to the *mishadd* are not entirely certain in view of discrepancies in the sources and a difference of opinion regarding the role of the *shaykh al-balad* in tax collecting. According to Lancret, the *mishadd* had no role to play in the business of collecting taxes. He was merely a subordinate of the *shaykh al-balad* and his sole function was to serve as a sort of concierge for the village who knew where everyone lived and directed strangers to whomever they wished to visit; it was also his duty to provide strangers with all their needs, such as food and pack animals. The *shaykh al-balad*, on the other hand, was not only responsible to the *multazim* for the collection of taxes in the part of the village under his jurisdiction, but was authorized by the *multazim* to employ force or even to imprison a defaulting *fallāḥ* at the time. Estève, however, makes no reference to the *mishadd* as concierge of the village. He, furthermore, denies that the *shaykh al-balad* had any right to employ force against delinquent tax payers and claims that this privilege was instead conferred on the *mishadd* by the *multazim*. According to Estève, the *mishadd* informed the village of the *multazim's* orders, carried out his commands whenever the *multazim* wished to deal severely with peasants who misbehaved or were in arrears, and acted upon the request of the *shaykh al-balad* or other village officials in cases where force was necessary in obtaining obedience from the *fallāḥīn*. Estève's view is reinforced in most particulars by the contemporary report of Ḥusayn Efendī, who described the *mishadd* as an official subordinate to the *qā'immaqām* whose primary responsibility was to bring the *fallāḥīn* to the *dīwān* at the time of tax collection.[24] The other officials, the *ghafīrs*, were village policemen whose number varied in each village. They prevented thefts and other crimes and gave warnings of Bedouin attacks. They guarded the *multazim's* house and the harvest and they watched the dikes to prevent their being tampered with out of season.[25]

The *arḍ al-waṣīyah* of the *multazim* was administered in ways which varied from village to village in accordance with the *multazim's* wish. In general the *multazim* might sublet his land to members of the village or farm it directly for his own account. In the first case, he usually rented it to the *shaykhs* who directed the cultivation of the *arḍ al-fallāḥ*. In the second, the *multazim* might hire *fallāḥīn* in the village to work his land at a wage or use the *corvée*, since, in some places, he had the right to use forced labor. In either case, the *multazim* appointed two local officials: the inspector, *khawlī* (the same official who carried out the village land surveys), and the steward (*wakīl*). When wages were paid, the *khawlī* conferred with the *shaykh* regarding the distribution of land to each *fallāḥ*. The *khawlī* and *shaykh* then took into account the needs or demands of each *fallāḥ* when making this distribution. When the *corvée* was used, the *khawlī* distributed land and supervised cultivation. In addition, he was also responsible for maintaining the irrigation system of the *iltizām*. Then, at the time of the harvest, the *wakīl's* responsibilities began. He registered the amount of grain deposited with him, a procedure witnessed by the *shaykh*. When *fallāḥīn* were hired to work the land, the *wakīl* paid their wages; when the *corvée* was used, he paid wages only to *fallāḥīn* who worked the plow. Sometimes, however, the *multazim* allowed him to allot some grain to the poorest cultivators as a token payment for services rendered. (The *multazim* who worked the land for his own account always furnished the necessary animals and seed.) The official in charge of the animals was known as the *kallāf*. He also supervised the flocks, collected wool, butter, and cheese, and served as veterinarian for the village as a whole. All of these officials in the *iltizām* received compensation in the form of exemptions from certain taxes, of specie, and of payment in kind, depending upon the customary usages of the *iltizām* and the degree of corruption which they condoned.[26]

In Upper Egypt the *shaykhs* distributed land which was held communally in the village. Of these the *shaykhs* in Copt villages were Copts, but in mixed villages they were Muslims. The *massāḥ*, surveyor, and his *qaṣṣāb*, an official who carried his surveying instrument, measured the land and noted the amount distributed to each *fallāḥ*. The cultivator was then told in advance the tax for which he was liable; the tax in specie was paid in advance of the harvest and the tax in kind at the time of the harvest. The *shāhid's* register, such as existed in Lower Egypt, was dispensed with, as the annual survey by the *massāḥ* served as the basis for distributing the tax. The *massāḥ* was usually a Copt, though Muslims sometimes served in this capacity. The *shāhid* and *khawlī* aided him in his work and guarded against any propensity which he displayed for partiality or irregularities. The *multazim* also employed a *ṣarrāf* to collect taxes.[27]

Specific duties and responsibilities were reserved for the provincial governors, including the supervision of the irrigation works, the enforcement of tax collection, and the maintenance of public security. A provincial governor was usually a bey, although in some cases a lesser officer, a *kāshif*, was appointed. Each governor was assisted by the provincial troops under his command as well as by subordinate *kāshifs* whom he appointed to act as his lieutenants in the *nāḥiyahs*, subdistricts of the province, by a treasurer (*khazīnah-dār*) to whom the taxes collected in the province were paid, and who, in turn, transmitted the portion of the tax due to the central administration to the *Rūznāmah*, the government bureau to which taxes were paid, and, finally, by a chief scribe who kept the provincial records. The expenses incurred by this provincial administration were defrayed by a special tax collected in each province, the *māl al-kushūfīyah.*[28]

Landholding in Egypt was affected to a significant degree by the widespread practice of creating *waqfs* (pious foundations) in favor of religious and charitable institutions. Full property rights theoretically had to be assigned to the beneficiary upon the establishment of a *waqf*, so that only property held in *mulk* tenure (in full ownership) was eligible for conversion into *waqf*. Generally, urban property alone filled this requirement, most of the agricultural land in Egypt being excluded, since the state retained the right to the substance (*raqabah*) of agricultural land and only granted its use (*taṣarruf*) to landholders. The usual procedure followed in Egypt was to create *waqfs* from the revenue on land rather than on land itself. Such *waqfs* were not true *waqfs* as defined by Muslim law (*Sharī'ah*) and were occasionally annulled, particularly at times of dynastic change. At the time of the Ottoman conquest the deeds of all religious endowments were carefully scrutinized to insure that the revenues assigned to religious and charitable institutions were employed in conformity with the wishes of their donors. Long-standing abuses were corrected and requisite adjustments were made in the two main kinds of religious endowments in existence at the time of the conquest: (1) *waqf* (plu. *awqāf*) and (2) *ḥubus* (plu. *aḥbās*).

The first type of endowment, the *waqf*, consisted of *al-awqāf as-sulṭānīyah* (royal *waqfs*), the revenue of which was allotted to Makkah and al-Madīnah and to charitable works, and the private *waqfs* established by individuals for various religious and charitable works. Estève lists five *al-awqāf as-sulṭānīyah* confirmed by the Ottomans and still in existence in Egypt at the close of the eighteenth century:

1. *Waqf ad-Dashīshah al-Kubārah*—established by a Circassian Sultan.
2. *Waqf al-Murādīyah*
3. *Waqf al-Muḥammadīyah*
4. *Waqf al-Aḥmadīyah*
5. *Waqf al-Ḥaramayn*

(2–5:) established by Sultans Murād, Muḥammad, and Aḥmad, three Sultans who occupied the throne in Istanbul, before Salīm I.

It is unlikely that the fifth was a single *waqf*. It was, rather, a group of *waqfs* (*awqāf al-Ḥaramayn*) from whose revenues the holy cities of Makkah and al-Madīnah were provided with annual payments in money and kind. As revenues from the other four *waqfs* were also assigned to the holy cities, the distinction between them and the *awqāf al-Ḥaramayn* is unclear. Both the lands of *al-awqāf as-sulṭānīyah* and *awqāf al-Ḥaramayn* were farmed out to *multazims*. Each year their *mubāshirs* paid to the supervisors (*nāẓirs*) of the *waqfs* the amount due in money and kind. The *nāẓirs*, in turn, transferred the required amount to the *rūznāmjī*, head of the *Rūznāmah*; the latter transmitted it to the *amīr al-ḥajj*. Revenues from the *awqāf al-Ḥaramayn* were paid directly to the *rūznāmjī* instead of to *nāẓirs* as in the case of the other *waqfs*. Estève also listed as extant eight private *waqfs* which were confirmed by Sultan Salīm I at the time of the Ottoman conquest. The Sultan imposed the *mīrī* upon them which their *nāẓirs* paid thereafter to the *rūznāmjī*:

1. *Sulaymān Pasha*,
2. *as-Sulṭān al-Ghūrī*,
3. *as-Sulṭān al-Ashraf*,
4. *as-Sulṭān Baybars*,
5. *al-Wazīr Khayr Bey*,
6. *as-Sulṭān Qā'it-Bāy*,
7. *ʻUbayd-allāh*,[29]
8. *al-Wazīr Yash Bey*.[30]

In addition to *waqfs*, the Ottoman conquerors also found a second kind of religious endowment in Egypt known as *ḥubus* (plu. *aḥbās*), a type which did not require the donor to confer absolute ownership to property upon the religious or charitable institution in whose favor the endowment was made. At various periods in the past, rulers of Egypt had converted state land into *aḥbās* to provide a livelihood for pious persons connected with the religious cult and to support specific religious and charitable institutions. The revenues from lands so constituted were assigned as pensions or *rizaq* (sing. *rizqah*) to individuals or religious and charitable institutions and were paid by the state treasury (*bayt al-māl*) to these beneficiaries in money or in kind. The Ottoman conquerors confirmed the *rizaq* which continued to be paid after the conquest. These pensions were known as *ar-rizaq al-aḥbāsīyah*, that is, pensions derived from lands belonging to the class of *ḥubus*.[31]

As political conditions in Egypt during the course of Ottoman domination became more unstable, landholders, anxious to protect their sources of revenue for themselves and their heirs, obtained permission from the sovereign or his representative to convert their usufructuary rights, usually to their *waṣīyahs*, into pious foundations. Sovereigns rarely refused to grant permission in view of the religious character of the donations. In these circumstances the status of the land did not change; the *raqabah* was retained by the state and the land continued to be burdened with the *mīrī*. By the end of the eighteenth century, much Egyptian agricultural land had been thus converted into *aḥbās* and the shift had been made in the meaning of the term *ar-rizaq al-aḥbāsīyah* to signify lands converted into *aḥbās* rather than the pensions from such lands. Many *ar-rizaq al-aḥbāsīyah* formed after the Ottoman conquest were established by landholders for the benefit of their heirs until the extinction of their line, when the revenues reverted to the religious or charitable foundations for whom the endowments were made. Such donations were designated family or *ahlī* endowments, as distinct from *khayrī*, wherein the religious institutions began to enjoy the revenues from the land immediately. By the establishment of *ahlī* endowments, the donors safeguarded their sources of revenue for themselves and their heirs from the rapacity of the ruling class. Furthermore, they also prevented the dissipation of the family's wealth by extravagant heirs.[32]

Whether these endowments were free of tax, as has been claimed, is a debatable point.[33] The sultan had the privilege of waiving all claims to the *mīrī*, but it was a right which most sultans preferred to avoid. However, donations often did appear to be tax free, since donors who converted their *waṣīyah* lands into *rizaq* frequently agreed to pay the amount of the *mīrī* with which these lands were burdened out of revenues derived from other sources. It is conceivable that after a period of years the necessity of paying the tribute from other revenues was overlooked or conveniently forgotten. The matter becomes clearer in an example of a *multazim* who endowed all the land of his *iltizām* and not merely his *waṣīyah*. In this case, the beneficiary was obliged to pay the *mīrī* levied on the *iltizām*.[34] Endowments of entire *iltizāms* occurred only rarely; nevertheless, those that were created emphasize the fact that *rizaq* were not relieved of *mīrī* unless some special arrangements had been made by their donors to relieve them of tax. Even with the payment of the *mīrī*, though, the beneficiaries of *ar-rizaq al-aḥbāsīyah* were better off than holders of *iltizām* land. They were not burdened with all the supplementary taxes, such as the *barrānī*, levied by *multazims*. *Rizaq* in Upper Egypt were considered more desirable than those in Lower Egypt because they were frequently augmented in size by Nile deposits; since land surveys were rarely accurate, the taxes on these *rizaq* were even less than those collected on *ar-rizaq al-aḥbāsīyah* located in Lower Egypt. Holders of *ar-rizaq al-aḥbāsīyah* often paid the pasha a light tax known as *māl al-ḥimāyah*, tax of protection, the payment of which insured the beneficiaries of the pasha's protection in the collection of their revenues.[35]

All *ar-rizaq al-aḥbāsīyah* were inscribed in the registers of *rizaq* of *ad-Dīwān as-Sulṭānī* by the *efendī* called *kātib ar-rizaq* attached to the *Dīwān ar-Rizaq al-Aḥbāsīyah*. A separate register for every province in Egypt was maintained, on the cover of which appeared a monogram (*ṭurrah*) and the name of the province. These separate registers were kept to facilitate research and verification of the rights of beneficiaries in cases of doubt. Great care and accuracy throughout the centuries were exercised in the registration of the *rizaq* and in recording their transfers to new beneficiaries. A *sanad* or deed called *al-ifrāj*, written in beautiful Arabic calligraphy, was prepared and initialed by the *efendī*. The deed bore a *ṭurrah* containing the name of the *wālī* and was sealed with his great seal. The *daftardār's* or chancellor's seal was also placed on the document. A second document, *at-tadhkirah*, was prepared, initialed, and sealed at the same time and contained a résumé of the main points appearing in *al-ifrāj*. The *efendī* was paid for his services by the pasha and enjoyed an additional income from the sums he charged when registering a *rizqah* or entering a note of transfer.[36]

Each *rizqah* had its administrator (*mutawallī*) and supervisor (*nāẓir*).[37] The land was worked in the same way as *waṣīyah* land; it was either hired out to *fallāḥīn* or cultivated directly by the *mutawallī*. The *mutawallī* rendered his accounts to the *nāẓir* and, where no *nāẓir* existed, to the *qāḍī* of the place. The *nāẓir* collected the revenues and distributed them in accordance with the wishes of the founder of the *rizqah* as specified in the deed. The beneficiary of a *rizqah* (*mutaṣarrif*) enjoyed his revenue for life. Upon his death, the *nāẓir* or *qāḍī*, if there was no *nāẓir*, was obliged to pay his heirs the revenue to which they were entitled. These benefits were inherited by his heirs of either sex in equal shares, unlike those of *mulk* property of which the female, in accordance with inheritance laws in the *Sharīʿah*, received one share and the male two shares. The names of the new beneficiaries were entered in the judicial roll of the *qāḍī*; the transfer was entered in the register of the *kātib ar-rizaq* and deeds were issued as proof of title. No collateral branch of the family could inherit these rights. If no direct heirs existed, the line was considered extinct and the revenues from the *rizqah* went to the religious institutions to which the bequest had been made.[38]

Lands bequeathed to religious or charitable institutions could never be sold. However, if the beneficiary required money, he was allowed the right of temporary cession (*al-muddah aṭ-ṭawīlah*). The cession could be made for a period of ninety years; the beneficiary received a lump sum at the time of cession and a small annual rent (*ajr*) by which the memory of the cession was retained. The amount of the *ajr* could never be increased. At the end of ninety years the property might be reclaimed by the original beneficiary or his heirs if no improvements had been made; otherwise the person to whom the property had been ceded or his heirs might remain in possession, provided the *ajr* continued to be paid. The *qāḍī* decided in cases of disagreement.[39]

By the end of the eighteenth century, it was clear that numerous abuses had developed in all categories of *waqf* holdings. Many people held *ar-rizaq al-aḥbāsīyah* and *awqāf* land to which they had no legal title. Moreover, they frequently diverted revenues from their proper object, allowed religious institutions to fall into a state of decay, and starved charitable works for lack of revenue. Even rights of legal beneficiaries were often ignored or forgotten. The most powerful people in the villages, who had obtained the use of *waqf* lands at small rents, often failed to meet their obligations and pocketed all the revenues for their own use. Eventually privileges they assumed illegally became firmly entrenched in the customary practices of the country and were sanctified by the support of religious leaders who were not always disinterested parties and often usurped the revenues of *waqf* land for their own benefit to the detriment of religious and charitable institutions. *Ar-rizaq al-aḥbāsīyah*, whose beneficiaries always insisted upon their religious character and their inviolability, were particularly vulnerable to confiscation by the state, because the donation of their revenues to religious institutions, while in theory not affecting the status of the land, did in fact immobilize a large part of Egyptian soil. The rulers of Egypt at various periods attempted unsuccessfully to free these lands in order that they might be placed upon the same footing as other state lands. It was, however, Muḥammad ʻAlī in the nineteenth century, who, by largely directing his policy regarding land tenure against *ar-rizaq al-aḥbāsīyah*, finally brought about reforms which proved to be the forerunners of those introduced by the government at Istanbul through the promulgation of the Ottoman Land Laws of 1858.[40]

The system of landholding which had developed in Egypt in the three centuries of Ottoman rule had grown out of the privileges obtained by the landholding classes after the Ottoman conquest. These privileges had congealed into a static pattern which the growth of customary practices had helped to perpetuate. To be sure, by the eighteenth century an equilibrium had been struck between the interests of the landholders and the peasants, but the entire landholding system of Egypt had become thoroughly unprogressive. Soon the Ottoman Empire's need for revenue, brought about by the impact of external events, would reveal the inadequacies of this fossilized system of landholding and would contribute to its complete transformation during the course of the nineteenth century.

CHAPTER III

CHANGES IN EGYPTIAN LAND TENURE: 1798–1815

If the Ottoman Empire was to meet the challenge of a changing world in the nineteenth century, it was vital that the Empire should be reformed. A prerequisite to any such reform, however, was a greatly increased revenue. It was inevitable, therefore, that the resulting search for untapped sources of revenue would be accompanied by a re-evaluation of the system of landholding in the Empire and that changes would be introduced to give the government a greater share of the revenue derived from land.

The earliest example of this close connection between general reform and changes in land tenure came in the last decade of the eighteenth century when Sultan Salīm III made an impressive attempt to meet the demands of a new age by introducing the *Niẓām Jadīd* (new system).[1] Accordingly, two measures of 1792, each of great significance for landholding in the Ottoman Empire, were designed to create new sources of revenue to pay the cost of the institutions that Salīm sought to introduce. The first called for the immediate cancellation of the *zi'āmats* and *tīmārs*[2] held by persons who had failed to fulfill the duties attached to the grants and for the eventual resumption of all such estates by the Sultan upon the death of their holders. The second abolished the farming of taxes; officers of the royal treasury were henceforth to collect all taxes. Salīm, however, was prevented from enforcing general reform by his preoccupation with his conflict with Russia, his involvement in the Napoleonic Wars, and the resistance of the conservative elements in the Empire to innovations.[3]

The Sultan could not implement the *Niẓām Jadīd* at home, but he, nevertheless, hoped to re-establish his authority over Egypt and to obtain control of the sources of revenue after the French withdrawal in 1801. To forestall opposition to his policies he based his right to make radical reforms on the Islamic law of conquest, rather than insisting upon his right to introduce the *Niẓām Jadīd*. The Sultan took the position that the conquest of Egypt by the French canceled the conditions laid down by Salīm I at the time of the original conquest of Egypt by the Ottoman Turks (see Chapter I, note 1) and that, consequently, all arrangements which had evolved during the course of Ottoman rule had become null and void; he held also that the Turkish reconquest of Egypt from the infidel by force of arms gave the sultan full right to lay down the conditions by which the conquered territory was to be ruled and that it gave him, both as Sultan and *Imām*, the legal right to the ownership of the land of Egypt and the privilege to reconstitute that land in any manner he saw fit.[4]

The French troops under General Belliard had no sooner evacuated Cairo (July 10, 1801) when the Turks took their first step to carry out the Sultan's policy. Yūsuf Pasha, *wazīr* in command of the Turkish forces in Egypt, issued instructions to all villages not to pay taxes to their *multazims* without his consent. He then informed the *multazims* that payment of taxes to the new administration would be made retroactive from 1798 to 1801 (A.H. 1213, 1214, and 1215), that is, for the entire period of the French occupation. The *multazims* protested, stating they could not possibly pay any taxes until the *wazīr's* order to the inhabitants to refuse tax demands was rescinded. This refusal by the *multazims* to pay the taxes for the three years of the French occupation prompted the *wazīr* to revoke their right to collect taxes and to instruct the Copts to proceed immediately to the villages for the purpose of collecting taxes directly for the account of the government. Shortly afterwards, the *multazims* demonstrated in front of Yūsuf Pasha's residence. In response to this demonstration, Yūsuf agreed to withdraw his order and to allow the *multazims* to collect taxes as usual, but the imperial *daftardār*, Sharīf Efendī, refused to acquiesce in this concession. The matter of the collection of taxes on the *iltizāms*, therefore, was left in a state of confusion.

While this struggle with the *multazims* was taking place, the Turkish administrators were also examining the titles of *ar-rizaq al-aḥbāsīyah* and *al-awqāf as-sulṭānīyah* to ascertain whether these titles had been recorded in the *daftars* (registers) of *rizaq* as required and also to check whether the revenues from these lands were being employed in accordance with the terms of their original bequests. After completing their investigations, the Turks then imposed the *māl al-ḥimāyah* (tax of protection) at the rate of approximately ten paras per *faddān* upon everyone holding a valid deed; a new deed was issued in the meantime. Those who could not or would not produce valid deeds lost their rights to the use of their lands, which were then given to anyone who paid the treasury the *ḥulwān* amounting to three years of the *fā'iẓ* on the land.[5]

The Sultan then decided that his new policy would never succeed so long as his authority could be challenged by the Mamlūks. He, therefore, decided to get rid of them. An attempt to destroy the Mamlūks both in Cairo and Alexandria was made by the Turks in October 1801, but it failed because of British interference on their behalf. Salīm was so annoyed that he addressed a letter to King George III and requested the King to instruct the commanding officer of British troops in Egypt, General Hutchinson, to meddle no more in a matter of no concern to the British. He also informed the British Embassy at Istanbul of the terms he was willing to concede to the Mamlūks:

(1) the beys and their Mamlūks would be allowed to go to other Ottoman provinces;

(2) the Sultan guaranteed their lives if they left peacefully;

(3) they would be permitted to take their personal property;

(4) their houses in Egypt would be sold to the natives of the country and the proceeds of sale would be given to their owners;

(5) the Sultan would grant annual pensions to the beys and their *kāshifs* to compensate them for loss in revenues from their land;

(6) this land would revert to the Porte in accordance with the laws of the Ottoman Empire.[6]

The Mamlūks, however, rejected the Sultan's terms and fled to Upper Egypt where the struggle between the Turkish and Mamlūk forces continued. The British then tried to mediate between the Sultan and the Mamlūks. On several occasions it appeared that the British would obtain an agreement, but before the matter could be settled they were obliged to leave Egypt, in compliance with the terms of the Treaty of Amiens. Several months later, however, in July 1803, 'Alī Pasha Burghul, the new governor (*wālī*) of Egypt, did bring a pardon from the Sultan in which these terms were agreed upon:

(1) the Mamlūks would be allowed to remain in Egypt;

(2) only fifteen purses of revenue (*fā'iẓ*) and the *ḥulwān* due on land which had been vacant for eight years would be allowed to each one;

(3) the *waṣīyahs*, *muḍāfs*, and *barrānīs* would be joined to the *mīrī*;

(4) decisions in regard to the administration of the country, the collection of the *mīrī*, and the control of frontiers (ports) would rest with the Pasha and the *rūznāmjī* who accompanied him. Customs and the

tax farms, granted in accordance with the *Niẓām Jadīd*, would be controlled by the *daftardār* who was due to arrive in Egypt.

The Mamlūks accepted these conditions, although it meant that only a shadow of their former power and sources of revenue remained to them. Peace seemed at last in sight. Unfortunately, however, 'Alī Pasha soon began to intrigue against the Mamlūks; he was removed from office and finally assassinated by their order. The struggle for power was intensified and the final outcome hung in the balance when Muḥammad 'Alī became Pasha of Egypt in May 1805.[7]

Sultan Salīm's attempts to restore undisputed Turkish control over Egypt, to place the sources of revenue under the direct control of the state, and to exile the old privileged class had all failed. The measures which he had authorized, however, were to serve as precedents for Muḥammad 'Alī who, it became apparent later on, supported this movement for reform in the Ottoman Empire generally and in Egypt in particular. Whether he did so out of a sense of personal conviction, or with the intention of ingratiating himself with the reforming sultans, Salīm III, Maḥmud II, and also the reform party as a whole, or merely out of necessity can only be conjectured. Nor is it possible to know precisely the time and circumstances of his adherence to the reform movement. It would be helpful in tracing the evolution of Muḥammad 'Alī's thinking if exact information were available concerning the intellectual milieu in Cavalla where he grew up. Such information is not available, but it does seem extremely unlikely that he remained ignorant of the early attempts at reform made by Salīm III in 1792. In any event, when Muḥammad 'Alī came to Egypt, he was soon exposed to the reforming ideas of the Sultan and later was certainly familiar with the details of the revolutions in Istanbul and the issues in dispute. Accordingly, there can be no doubt whatsoever that many of his policies were inspired, at least in part, by Salīm's program of reform; in fact, conditions in Egypt were favorable early in Muḥammad 'Alī's reign for the introduction of reforms which Salīm had attempted prematurely in the Empire as a whole. It would appear, also, that Sultan Maḥmūd II, when he came to the Ottoman throne, not only did not object to the measures introduced in Egypt by Muḥammad 'Alī but may even have encouraged them. In fact, it seems that Maḥmūd actually learned from the experiences of his Egyptian viceroy, for when the time was ripe he adapted a number of Muḥammad 'Alī's more successful measures to the requirements of the rest of the Empire.

Muḥammad 'Alī's specific policies concerning landholding were influenced not only by the Turkish reform movement but also by the land reforms undertaken by the French during their occupation of Egypt. His source of information regarding French reforms, the most important of which never passed the planning stage, can only be surmised. There were numerous Egyptians, like al-Jabartī, *shaykhs* of al-Azhar, and Copts, in close touch with affairs during the French occupation, who could have instructed Muḥammad 'Alī. Furthermore, there were Frenchmen, both those who stayed behind after the French withdrawal and those who came to Egypt during Muḥammad 'Alī's reign, who were undoubtedly acquainted with French policies during the occupation and could therefore have recommended reforms akin to those originally projected by Napoleon and Menou. Although the precise source of his information is not ascertainable, it can certainly be assumed that the details of the French land reforms were brought to Muḥammad 'Alī's attention early in his reign. These French land reforms, like those of the Turks, were intimately connected with the problem of increasing the sources of revenue to pay the cost of government, both civil and military. The need for land reform became crucial for the French when Napoleon found himself totally dependent upon local sources of revenue after Lord Nelson destroyed the French fleet at Abū Qīr on August 1, 1798. His difficulties were further intensified by his failure to win a decisive victory over the Mamlūks and his only partial conquest of Egypt; the rest of the country had still to be subjugated province by province and peace was never fully attained. The Mamlūks continued to harass the French in Upper Egypt until shortly after Bonaparte's departure for France when General Kléber concluded a treaty of peace with Murād Bey; also the lawlessness of the natives in the countryside and the predatory raids of the Bedouins combined to keep the country in a perpetual state of unrest. Large military contingents in the provinces alone enabled the French to bring some order to the countryside, but even so, the provincial administrators were only partially successful in governing their provinces.

Isolated from France and in the midst of a hostile population, Napoleon had to move cautiously. Early in August 1798 he confirmed the *multazims* in their *iltizāms* after registration of their title deeds (*taqsīṭs*) in order to enlist their support for the new regime and to insure the payment of taxes in their villages. Two thirds of the land of Egypt formerly held by Mamlūk *multazims* was joined, however, to the state domain for the profit of the French Republic and was administered directly by French officials. Taxes were collected by Copts who were supervised by French inspectors, but in spite of the use of military force the peasants frequently evaded demands for taxes in money or produce.[8]

Soon after these preliminary measures were taken, the French did make a serious attempt to introduce reforms in the system of Egyptian landholding. Napoleon and the Arab historian, al-Jabartī, provide somewhat different but complementary versions of the discussions which were held in connection with the introduction of these reforms; from the two reports there emerges a fairly clear picture of the character of the reforms which Napoleon envisaged. In his memoirs dictated to General Bertrand at St. Helena, Napoleon reported that the question of a thorough land reform had been discussed by representatives from all parts of Egypt in the General *Dīwān* that met between October 4 and October 20, 1798, that the pros and cons of ending the tax-farming system of *iltizāms* had been debated, and that it was finally decided that the *multazims*, who were greatly reduced in number in any case, should receive as compensation for the loss of their concessions both the right to the possession of their *waṣīyah* land and also an indemnity for the loss in revenue from taxes imposed upon *athar* land in the *iltizāms*. *Athar* land was to remain in the possession of the peasants, whereas lands donated to religious institutions would be rented for a ninety-nine year period in emphyteusis. The rate of tax to be levied on all land was also discussed.

In al-Jabartī's version a series of discussions was held in the Small *Dīwān* that was formed from the General *Dīwān*. These discussions, as described by al-Jabartī, centered, first of all, around the decree of September 16, 1798, which called for the establishment of a registration office to which all owners of *mulk* property (*aṣḥāb al-amlāk*) had to present their titles for registration within a limited time or suffer confiscation of their property for the profit of the French Republic; it stipulated, furthermore, that a tax of 2 per cent was to be levied at the time of registration upon the assessed value of the property after which a new deed would be issued, that heirs of property held in valid title must enter claims for their share of the inheritance within twenty-four hours from the time of decease of the owner or the property would escheat to the state, and that an inheritance tax was to be charged in accordance with the value of the property. This decree also listed other taxes: death taxes; a tax on creditors making claims upon the property of deceased persons; taxes on pensions, donations, sale of land, civil and criminal cases, witnesses, travel, births, contracts, rent collections. After a lengthy discussion of the decree of September 16, 1798, the Small *Dīwān* decided that a special commission should be established to find some way of reconciling French interests with those of the Egyptian people. The commission was established and its members presented their recommendations at the next meeting of the *Dīwān*. The Small *Dīwān* then turned its attention to two other problems: the establishment of a tariff of taxes and the question of successions as practiced in Egypt. The latter problem was considered too complicated to be dealt with by the *Dīwān*, so a group of *shaykhs* was instructed to draw up a report on the law of successions. Several days later the *shaykhs* presented their report to the *Dīwān* and after some discussion the law of succession according to the *Sharī'ah* was accepted unanimously as the law of the land. The following week the *Dīwān* met again and decided upon the rate of tax to be paid on property: property was divided into three categories—eight French dollars to be paid on the first, six on the second, and three on the third.[9] Property renting for less than one dollar (*riyāl*) per month was exempted from tax. Shops, inns, baths, and oil-pressing establishments were to be taxed thirty to forty dollars according to their importance. Al-Jabartī then reports that copies of the ordinance as modified by the *Dīwān* were posted in all streets and sent to all the notables in the country, that engineers were assigned to survey the property to determine the category of taxes into which each one fell, and that they prepared lists indicating where the properties were located, their category, and the names of their owners.

Both Napoleon's memoirs and al-Jabartī's journal confirm that all categories of property and land were to be registered and taxed in accordance with a fixed tariff and that a scale of taxes on all legal transactions entailing property was to be established. These proposed reforms never materialized, however, as the Cairo insurrection of October 21 and 22, 1798, which underscored the resentment felt by the people towards these changes, put an end to Napoleon's plans. The prescribed taxes were levied after the suppression of the insurrection, but they were levied as forced contributions rather than part of a general scheme of land reform.[10]

After General Kléber's assassination on June 14, 1800, the governorship of Egypt passed into the hands of General Jacques 'Abd-allāh Menou. Menou may have lacked capacities as a soldier, but as an administrator he showed real talent. Had he remained longer as head of the Egyptian government, basic reforms in the system of taxation of the land would have been introduced by him and would have affected Egyptian landholding radically. Menou's double aim was to establish a French colony firmly in Egypt and to provide for the welfare of the Egyptian people. Accordingly, he introduced reforms in the central and provincial governments to check the growth of inefficiency, negligence, and malversation of public revenue by the French administrators themselves; the financial administration was reorganized and tightened to prevent dilapidation by the Copt tax collectors; a long list of taxes, only few of which were actually new to Egypt, was levied at fixed rates, but these taxes, although heavy, had the virtue of being definite. Menou also established representative bodies in the cities and in the provinces to develop a sense of responsibility among Egyptians; judiciary reforms were introduced; peace treaties with a number of Arab tribes were signed; new concessions were made to Murād Bey in Upper Egypt to gain his support and to maintain peace in the south; studies were made of the Egyptian irrigation system and some of the more urgent work was carried out by irrigation engineers; an industrial program was projected for the future; experiments for developing new agricultural crops and stimulating existing ones were carried out.

The most important reform which Menou planned to introduce to Egypt was a thorough-going tax reform on land. The project, which remained on paper, is extremely interesting because of its basic similarity to the developments which later occurred during Muḥammad 'Alī's reign. This similarity may be explained in several ways: the likeness may be simply coincidental; or it may indicate that conditions of land tenure and the state of public opinion in Egypt could produce only one kind of reform, whether proposed by Menou or by Muḥammad 'Alī; or, finally, Muḥammad 'Alī, if he had access to the plan, may have borrowed from it when he formulated his own program of reform. Menou's plan included the following points:

(1) All existing taxes (the *mīrī*, *fā'iẓ*, *muḍāf*, *barrānī*, and so on) levied on land were to be abolished.

(2) A single tax was to be collected, the rate of which was to be based upon the number of *faddāns* in the village and the quality of the land taxed.

(3) Land was to be divided into three classes. After every annual inundation the General-in-Chief would fix the amount to be collected for each class.

(4) Supplementary dues paid by the *fallāḥīn* to the *multazims*, *shaykhs*, scribes, and the remaining minor officials for canal repairs and other services were to be included in the tax rate.

(5) The provincial controllers would determine the number and quality of *faddāns* in each village and, after assembling the *fallāḥīn*, would inform them of the total amount due from the village. Each landholder could then calculate the exact amount to be paid by him in accordance with the amount and quality of land which he worked. Once this was paid, there would be nothing further for him to pay to anyone.

(6) The General-in-Chief undertook never to increase the amount of the tax and to decrease it in years of bad flood when the land was *sharāqī* (not watered by the Nile) on condition that the *fallāḥīn* should pay the correct tax promptly. If not, the tax would be collected with the assistance of the military and the additional expense of sending troops would be charged to the village.

(7) The total tax would be divided into twenty-four parts: $\frac{12}{24}$ to be reserved for the treasury of the French Republic; $\frac{3}{24}$ to be paid to the *shaykhs*; $\frac{1}{24}$ to cover the cost of irrigation works including the cost of wages to the *fallāḥīn* from whom forced and unpaid labor would no longer be demanded for this purpose; $\frac{1}{24}$ to cover the salaries of the tax collectors; $\frac{7}{24}$ to go as an indemnity to the *multazims* in accordance with the number of parts (*qīrāṭs*) each *multazim* held in a village. This latter sum was either to go to the treasury of the Republic in the case of villages which belonged to the Republic or was to be paid annually to the *multazims* in the form of a pension. Under the scheme, the *multazims* were deprived of their right to collect taxes in villages or to interfere in the administrative or judicial affairs of the village. The *multazims* could, however, opt for an alternative plan which would give them full property rights to their *waṣīyah* land in lieu of the $\frac{7}{24}$ pension.

(8) The land held by the *fallāḥ* was to be his property and to be disposed of as he wished.

(9) All land was subjected to tax whether it was *waṣīyah* land held by *multazims* or *athar* land held by *fallāḥīn*.

(10) The special taxes in kind levied in Upper Egypt were to be abolished with the exception of those on certain designated villages.

(11) No tax was to be levied on *rizqahs* or *waqfs* belonging to the mosques or pious foundations provided that this property was properly registered, registration to be gratuitous. All *waqf* and *rizqah* lands which

were not registered by a certain date were to be confiscated by the Republic.

(12) Village *shaykhs* and Copts were to be appointed, the former to serve as superintendents of tax collection from the peasants and the latter to serve as their subordinates. The *shaykh* superintendents had the additional responsibility of paying the amounts stipulated by the plan to the *multazims* and the other *shaykhs*.

This entire project of tax reform was to have been introduced after a new cadastre had been executed to determine the exact amount and quality of land which was cultivated in Egypt. A survey commission was accordingly established and it was publicly announced that the survey was about to be undertaken. Unfortunately, the survey was destined never to be carried out, for the announcement was published on the eve of the Battle of Canopus of March 21, 1801. The military reverses suffered by the French forces in that battle put an end to the entire project.[11]

When Muḥammad 'Alī became Pasha of Egypt he did not launch a reform program immediately. Instead he devoted the early years of his reign to consolidating his position as the undisputed master of the country and to replacing the privileged classes with his own adherents. The struggle for political domination of Egypt was settled on the field of battle, by intrigue, by bribery, by treachery, and by the expropriation of ancient prerogatives, but the preservation of political authority hinged upon the extent of financial control which Muḥammad 'Alī commanded. In Egypt, as elsewhere in the Ottoman Empire, the road to power had to be paved with gold and its retention depended upon the steady flow of revenue to meet the demands from every side. Muḥammad 'Alī required money to keep his troops faithful,[12] to keep his friends in Istanbul loyal, and to offer bribes whenever necessary.[13]

Such financial pressures forced upon Muḥammad 'Alī the realization that the existing system of landholding was inadequate as a mechanism for producing revenues and must either be improved or changed. French and Turkish precedents emphasized the necessity for caution in tampering with a system so deeply entrenched in and so intimately linked with the religious prejudices of the people, the administration of the country, and taxation. Muḥammad 'Alī therefore proceeded gradually and pragmatically. If a measure worked, he advanced to the next stage, but if resistance to change appeared to threaten his position, he temporized. He moved against one group after the other until by the end of 1815 most of the landholders were either expropriated or annihilated and the greater part of the cultivated land in Egypt was taxed.

The earliest land tax reforms undertaken by Muḥammad ʻAlī were confined to Lower Egypt, Upper Egypt remaining as yet under Mamlūk domination. At first, the Pasha collected only those taxes formerly imposed by the Mamlūks, but in 1806 and 1807, when they proved inadequate, the *shaykhs* of al-Azhar agreed to his also collecting half of the *fā'iẓ*, a tax customarily retained by the *multazims*. In 1807 he not only collected half of the *fā'iẓ*, but he also taxed the *masmūḥ* lands of the *shaykhs al-balad*. Then, in 1808, he went even further. When the 1808 flood proved unsatisfactory, he replaced some of the less powerful *multazims* with members of his family and entourage, relying upon them to maintain the level of cultivation despite the bad flood and to provide him with the revenues he needed. Furthermore, he had an opportunity in 1808 to warn the *shaykhs* of al-Azhar to stop abusing their privileges lest he confiscate their illegally acquired wealth. This opportunity arose when the *shaykhs* demanded that he abolish his tax on food and curb the activities of speculators who, as soon as the news of the low Nile had been announced, had seized all the available foodstuff and had driven up the cost of food. Angered by their demands, Muḥammad ʻAlī retorted that the depressed conditions in the country were attributable to their own selfishness rather than to any other cause. Completely intimidated, the *shaykhs* withdrew, while Muḥammad ʻAlī, on the other hand, already appeared to have decided against making further concessions to the *shaykhs* or allowing them immunity from taxation.[14]

The first step toward a more equitable distribution of the tax burden was taken soon after Maḥmūd II came to the Ottoman throne. Early in 1809[15] Muḥammad ʻAlī decided to try this far more radical tax reform. Not only would he collect half of the *fā'iẓ* from the *multazims* as he had done in the past few years, but he would also impose a tax on *waṣīyah* lands and on *ar-rizaq al-aḥbāsīyah*. Acting on the theory that all decrees emanating from the former Sultan were null and void and must be renewed by the new Sultan or his representative, Muḥammad ʻAlī required each *rizqah* beneficiary (*mutaṣarrif*) to present his deed at the *dīwān* within forty days for renewal or face the consequence of its being canceled and his rights to its benefits transferred to someone else. Muḥammad ʻAlī's new policy was first introduced in Buḥayrah Province where a register was drawn up listing all land, including *waṣīyah* and *rizqah* lands. Letters demanding additional taxes were then sent by the government to the landholders. When the landholders received these letters, they hurried to the *shaykhs* of al-Azhar to complain and to enlist their aid in the struggle against these new taxes. The *shaykhs* agreed to take up the matter with the Pasha who, in their opinion, had now gone entirely too far. The outcome of the conflict which followed between the *shaykhs* of al-Azhar and Muḥammad ʻAlī was to have lasting significance for the history of Egypt.[16]

Muḥammad ʻAlī, who had come to power with the support of the *shaykhs* of al-Azhar, had obtained this support by promising to adopt no new policy without their consent. Therefore, the arbitrary imposition of new taxes was viewed by the *shaykhs* as a violation of Muḥammad ʻAlī's oath, a violation which they could not countenance. When the *multazims* from Buḥayrah Province complained to them, the *shaykhs* after two days' deliberation prepared a petition enumerating their grievances and presented it to the Pasha. Muḥammad ʻAlī chose to ignore it and initiated instead an intrigue by which he hoped to vitiate the power of the *shaykhs*, particularly that of as-Sayyid ʻUmar Makram, chief of the *sharīfs* (*Naqīb al-Ashrāf*),[17] whose personal influence over the people he feared most. At first he attempted to conciliate ʻUmar Makram by promising to follow his advice and by offering him three hundred purses as a gift and an allowance of one purse per day.[18] These bribes had no effect upon as-Sayyid ʻUmar, whose intransigence was due not only to his opposition to the new taxes but also to his desire to uphold the principle of the limitation of power of the ruler. Muḥammad ʻAlī then played upon the vanity of some of the *shaykhs* by inviting them to the Citadel and flattering them with his attentions. He also created a wedge between as-Sayyid ʻUmar and two of the leading *shaykhs*, al-Mahdī and ad-Dawākhlī, who secretly hated ʻUmar and agreed to side with Muḥammad ʻAlī. Finally, the Pasha succeeded in persuading the *shaykhs* to send a delegation to the Citadel to confer with him. He promised them that he would abolish taxes on the *waṣīyahs* and would demand only a quarter of the *fā'iẓ* instead of half, but as-Sayyid ʻUmar, opposing any compromise with Muḥammad ʻAlī on the grounds that it would constitute a betrayal of the people's confidence, accused the *shaykhs* of pusillanimity because of their failure to join him in defense of the rights of the people against arbitrary taxation.

The crisis came when as-Sayyid ʻUmar refused to approve a letter which Muḥammad ʻAlī wished to send to the Sublime Porte concerning the expenditure of four thousand purses. ʻUmar returned the letter with the comment that he could not agree to sign it because the statement of accounts was entirely false. He also remarked that no exact reckoning of the sums extorted by Muḥammad ʿAlī from the people of Egypt would ever be possible. Muḥammad ʿAlī was infuriated. He insisted upon a meeting with ʿUmar, to which the latter agreed on condition that the meeting should take place in the home of the *Shaykh as-Sādāt*[19] rather than in the Citadel. His reply angered Muḥammad ʿAlī still more and he resolved upon ʿUmar Makram's removal from his high office. He called a meeting of the *qāḍī* and *shaykhs* at the home of his son, Ibrāhīm Bey (later Pasha), to which he also invited as-Sayyid ʿUmar, but ʿUmar replied that he was indisposed and was unable to attend. Muḥammad ʿAlī then dismissed ʿUmar and appointed the *Shaykh as-Sādāt* to succeed him as *Naqīb al-Ashrāf*. He commanded ʿUmar to leave Cairo within three days, either for Alexandria or Damietta. When ʿUmar Makram learned of his dismissal and his exile, he calmly stated that he felt no regrets at the loss of his office but that if he could not go to Asyūṭ, his birthplace, he wished to be exiled from the Pasha's domain. The Pasha refused his request and insisted that he go to Damietta, where ʿUmar lived until 1812 when he was allowed to move to Ṭanṭā. In 1819 Muḥammad ʿAlī permitted him to return to Cairo, as he was by this time firmly in power and unafraid of ʿUmar's influence over the people.

With as-Sayyid ʿUmar's disappearance from the political scene, Muḥammad ʿAlī was no longer threatened by the *shaykhs* of al-Azhar. Their ranks split even more over the question of the report which they had to submit to the Sultan concerning ʿUmar Makram's dismissal, and the Ḥanafī *muftī*,[20] as-Sayyid Aḥmad aṭ-Ṭaḥṭāwī, was removed from office because he refused to sign the statement finally agreed upon. By their failure to unite against Muḥammad ʿAlī and by their capitulation to him, the *shaykhs* had forfeited their power to control him. Reduced to a state of complete impotency, the religious leaders could no longer exercise any moral restraint upon the Pasha, who was now free to govern Egypt with unlimited authority.[21]

Economic stagnation and the persistent deterioration of conditions in the country increased Muḥammad ʿAlī's financial difficulties. Extensive tracts of land remained uncultivated because entire villages were deserted by the peasants. Some of the most fertile regions in Egypt presented a picture of desolation. Steadily rising food prices also increased the misery of the population. In the spring of 1809 wheat sold at six times its price during the French occupation; none was to be found in the warehouses and scarcely any in the Nile ports. Only the supply of maize saved the country from starvation. Abnormally high floods in 1809 inundated land that had remained dry for several years, but caused considerable damage in Upper Egypt to the maize and sugar-cane crops and in Lower Egypt to rice, sesame, and cotton crops. High taxes and daily avanias reduced landholders and peasants alike to beggary and despair. In Cairo nothing was bought or sold because of the shortage of goods in the market and the tightness of specie. The intermittent civil war which prevented political and economic stabilization and the burden of taxes imposed by the Pasha both contributed further to the collapse of agriculture and commerce. The troops, in arrears of pay, became restless and began to make urgent demands upon the Pasha. One observer, Drovetti, claimed that Muḥammad 'Alī's position in June 1810 was its most critical since the beginning of his reign.[22] Since all sources of income for meeting even the ordinary needs of government were quickly disappearing, Muḥammad 'Alī was forced to seek drastic remedies.[23]

The first of a series of measures taken by Muḥammad 'Alī in 1810 demonstrated his determination to eradicate corruption from the financial administration and to end the monopoly of the finances of the country by a group of officials who seized every opportunity to enrich themselves. He appointed a supervisor, the *kātib adh-dhimmah*, at the precise moment when tax collections for the current year began, to control the activities of employees in the *Rūznāmah*, some of whom were suspected of misappropriating state funds. He also made an example of three Copt scribes who were found guilty of accepting bribes to falsify the land survey in al-Minūfīyah Province. They were severely bastinadoed and imprisoned.[24] Muḥammad 'Alī also called a conference of *kāshifs* from the provinces to review the general situation in the country, discuss improvements to be undertaken, and fix the amount of taxes which, in their judgment, could be collected. On the basis of the *kāshifs*' recommendations, he established the rate at which taxes were to be levied. Most *multazims* met the government's demands promptly to avoid the additional cost involved when special messengers were sent to force collection; some even advanced sums to *fallāḥīn* unable to pay their taxes. *Fallāḥīn*, however, frequently either sold their livestock and food reserves to meet the excessive demands or abandoned their villages to escape them. A few *fallāḥīn* fled to Syria and Turkey, but most of the fugitives were compelled to return to their villages. Some *multazims* still found they were unable to meet the government's demands and petitioned the Pasha to grant them relief. They were told to relinquish the *taqsīṭs* to their *iltizāms* and to accept as compensation either the prices they had paid for their concessions or pensions equal to the *fā'iẓ*. A few *multazims* were obliged to abandon their *iltizāms* to pay their debts to the treasury.[25]

Since none of these measures produced the desired results, Muḥammad 'Alī decided to eliminate existing tax distinctions on agricultural lands. The matter was discussed at a special council of *shaykhs*, *ūjāqlīs*, and other notables convoked by Muḥammad 'Alī in the autumn of 1810. The Pasha first proposed to increase the rate of the *mīrī* and *fā'iẓ* and to end the anomalous system by which these two taxes remained pegged at a constant figure regardless of changes in the value of currency or the needs of the government. Muḥammad 'Alī considered such a reform to be fair both to *multazims* and *fallāḥīn*, for it would end the necessity of imposing supplementary taxes, the victimization of the population by rapacious tax collectors, the abandonment of the land by *fallāḥīn*, and the ruin of the countryside. The chief of the elders, perhaps at Muḥammad 'Alī's instigation, then called for equalization of the tax burden upon all landholders and criticized the *shaykhs* who held village land for transferring their share of the tax burden to the villagers. An outburst of protest from the *shaykhs* led to arguments which became so exacerbated that the meeting was dissolved. The Pasha then took action without the council's approval. He ordered the preparation of registers of all lands, including inundated, *sharāqī*, *waṣīyah*, *rizqah*, and *masmūḥ* lands, which were henceforth to share obligations equally. He even obtained a legal decision (*fatwā*) from the *muftī* to legalize his action, especially as it pertained to *ar-rizaq al-aḥbāsīyah*. The *fatwā* upheld the argument that since Egypt had been conquered without capitulation, all land in Egypt was tribute-bearing land and could be taxed by the Pasha.[26]

The goal at which Muḥammad 'Alī aimed between 1808 and 1810 was the rectification of the existing landholding system without an introduction of drastic changes in its form. Actually, though, equalization of the tax burden as projected by Muḥammad 'Alī in 1810 was never consummated, as two new factors intervened which altered the course of tax and land reform. First, a marked improvement in Muḥammad 'Alī's financial situation at the end of 1810 relieved him of the necessity of taking precipitate action. The principal cause of this condition was the trading opportunities which developed at the time (see Chapter IX). Secondly, the Pasha, with the concurrence of the Sultan, decided to rid himself of the Mamlūks who not only remained as a permanent threat to his power but also obstructed the achievement of economic unity in Egypt. On March 1, 1811, therefore, he ordered the massacre of a large number of Mamlūks whom he invited to Cairo to attend a special ceremony at the Citadel; the rest were either annihilated in the provinces or driven into exile. By the spring of 1812 there were no Mamlūks in Egypt to challenge Muḥammad 'Alī's authority or to agitate the countryside.[27] The expansion of commerce coupled with the cessation of Mamlūk control in Upper Egypt provided Muḥammad 'Alī with new incentives to break with the past completely. He proceeded vigorously to revise the method of tax collection which, in effect, meant a revision of the entire system of landholding, to organize the administration of the country, and to control the cultivation of crops so that most of the country's agricultural products would flow into government warehouses.

The new policies were first introduced in Upper Egypt after the destruction of the Mamlūks left a political void in that part of the country. In 1811 Muḥammad 'Alī appointed his son, Ibrāhīm Pasha, the *daftardār*, to serve as governor of Upper Egypt. (This appointment was confirmed by imperial rescript [*faramān* or firman] in July 1813.) Ibrāhīm Pasha's first task was to extend the authority of the central government to an area which had been outside its control for years. His second task was to insure the regular flow of revenue into the treasury. Accordingly, he ordered that all land in Upper Egypt should be surveyed: Mamlūk lands; lands held by Hawwārah tribesmen; lands of the non-Mamlūk *multazims* who had retained their concessions during the period of Mamlūk domination in Upper Egypt; all *ar-rizaq al-aḥbāsīyah* lands; and, finally, the *waqfs* which had been established by former sultans of Egypt. After the survey, the land was taxed, the *rizqah* and *waqf* lands being, at first, taxed at half the rate of tax imposed upon *iltizām* lands. Most of the land was then placed under the direct supervision of the government hierarchy; a few of the more influential *multazims* who could produce valid titles to their concessions were allowed to retain at least part of their lands; others received promises of land in Lower Egypt which, however, never materialized; still others obtained a small compensation for the loss of their *iltizāms*; and, finally, even the beneficiaries of *rizqah* and *waqf* lands were deprived of their revenues. The latter protested to the *shaykhs* of al-Azhar who, acting on their behalf, argued that the religious institutions and charitable foundations would be ruined by the confiscation of these revenues by the state. Their arguments had no effect either upon Muḥammad ʻAlī or Ibrāhīm Pasha and Ibrāhīm even insisted that since the revenues of these estates were being employed to wage war in al-Ḥijāz against the Wahhābīs, the enemies of Islām, their use by the state took precedence over their employment for other religious purposes. Ibrāhīm also pointed out that the vast revenues which had been assigned to religious institutions had, in fact, been diverted into the pockets of the administrators of these estates, that most of the religious institutions had fallen into a state of decay, and that these abuses could no longer be countenanced. To the religious institutions which still remained in good condition the state had assigned revenues sufficient to cover maintenance costs and to pay the salaries of such personnel as the prayer leader (*imām*) and the caller to prayer (*mu'adhdhin*). This policy left the *multazims* and those who had profited from the revenues of *ar-rizaq al-aḥbāsīyah* and *waqf* lands little choice but to leave Upper Egypt or to remain simply as cultivators. Ibrāhīm's methods had been extremely ruthless, even brutal, but he achieved the goal coveted by Muḥammad ʻAlī—complete control over the revenues of Upper Egypt.[28]

The relaxation of financial pressure after 1810 postponed similar reforms in Lower Egypt until the middle of 1813. Two interrelated problems confronted Muḥammad ʻAlī in 1813 and evoked the formulation of an accelerated program of reform. First, the cost of waging war in Arabia imposed an enormous strain upon the treasury which could not be met from the ordinary resources of the country. According to Hamont, the war in al-Ḥijāz cost Egypt 100,000 men, 50,000 animals, including horses, dromedaries, and camels, large quantities of wheat which were transported from Egypt, and millions of dollars. Secondly, the profits derived from the grain trade which had supplemented Muḥammad ʻAlī's income for several years were jeopardized by the opening of the Black Sea and the resumption of British trade with Russia.[29] The loss of revenue resulting from the serious decline in grain exports could only be compensated for by finding expedients by which to augment Egyptian resources. In September 1813 Muḥammad ʻAlī resolved upon the following program:

(1) an increase in the area of cultivation for the profit of the Pasha, particularly of land which the landholders were unable to cultivate for lack of funds;

(2) the suppression of supplementary taxes imposed by the *multazims* upon the *fallāḥīn* and their integration into the regular land tax;

(3) the abolition of all immunities on lands belonging to mosques and pious foundations;

(4) the cancellation of special privileges involving tax relief to those of Muḥammad ʻAlī's adherents who had received concessions of land;

(5) the classification of all land according to type and nature of crop grown and the establishment of a uniform land tax for each class;

(6) a simplification of the system of tax collection to insure the flow of a larger proportion of revenue into the treasury instead of into the pockets of Copt scribes and village *shaykhs* who benefited from the irregular and complicated system which existed.[30]

An essential requirement for the implementation of the new policy was the completion of a thorough survey of all land in Egypt. A cadastral survey had been begun in Upper Egypt in 1813 and early in 1814 in Lower Egypt, but by the time of the survey in Lower Egypt Muḥammad ʻAlī had decided upon more drastic measures than originally planned. He accordingly instructed his lieutenant in Egypt, the *kikhyah bey*, to proclaim that all *iltizāms* in Lower Egypt were to be confiscated but that their *multazims* would continue to receive the *fā'iẓ* which would be paid to them by the treasury.[31] A delegation of *shaykhs* thereupon visited the *kikhyah bey* and asked for a delay in the execution of the Pasha's firman to enable them to petition Muḥammad ʻAlī, who was then in al-Ḥijāz. A few days later a demonstration of women occurred at al-Azhar Mosque at which they demanded the withdrawal of the order of confiscation. Although the *kikhyah bey* summoned the *shaykhs* and accused them of inciting these riots to serve their own ends, he did grant the *multazims* the right to harvest their crops which were in the ground. However, many *multazims* found that the *fallāḥīn* were unwilling to work for them.[32] In one case, a *fallāḥ* to whom a *multazim* offered a salary to do the necessary work on his land reportedly replied curtly, "Go find someone else. I am busy with my own affairs. You have no more authority in this country for your day has passed. We have become the *fallāḥīn* of the Pasha."[33]

The cadastre of all cultivated (*maʻmūr*) land in Lower Egypt, including *athar*, *waṣīyah*, and *rizqah* lands, was completed in the spring of 1814. The land was classified and taxed in accordance with the category into which it fell. Since the uniform *faddān* used for the first time during this cadastre was a smaller unit of measurement than was usually employed, between one quarter and one third of the total land was declared in excess of the amount to which their landholders were entitled and was taken over by the government. When the cadastral registers were eventually completed, the *waṣīyah* lands and the lands which were either uncultivated or uncultivable (the so-called *ab'ādīyah* lands) were excluded from them. The rest were registered and taxed with the *mīrī* (or *kharāj*). The *ma'mūr* land, with the exception of *waṣīyah* land, was distributed among the village inhabitants and the amount of each parcel and its tax entered in the cadastral registers.[34] The government, in conformity with customary practice, granted the *shaykhs al-balad* lands known as *masmūḥ al-mashāyikh* to pay for services rendered to the government and to cover the cost of entertaining government officials who passed through or stopped in the villages. Village notables who undertook the responsibility of feeding the poor and travelers also received grants of land referred to as *masmūḥ al-maṣāṭib*. Both types of *masmūḥ* lands were relieved of taxes.[35] The *waṣīyah* lands, excluded from the cadastral registers at this time, were exempted from the full *kharāj* imposed on other village lands and taxed only with *al-māl al-ḥurr*, a far less onerous tax than the new *kharāj*. A special *dīwān*, composed of Ibrāhīm Aghā 'r-Razzāz and ash-Shaykh Aḥmad Yūsuf, was created in the spring of 1814 in Cairo to receive payment of this tax on the *waṣīyahs*; as soon as the tax was paid, a deed (*taqsīṭ*) entitling the *multazim* to the use of his *waṣīyah* land was delivered to him. If the tax remained unpaid, the *multazim* lost the right to his land.[36]

As for *ar-rizaq al-aḥbāsīyah*, the lands declared in excess of the amounts stated in their titles were integrated into village lands and were not differentiated from them. The balance was registered in the names of their beneficiaries or, if their names were not known, in the names of those who actually held and cultivated the *rizqah* land at the time of the survey. The tax imposed upon *ar-rizaq al-aḥbāsīyah* was equal to the tax on other village lands except in cases where the beneficiary of a *rizqah* possessed one of the deeds which had been issued at or since the time of al-Wazīr Yūsuf and Sharīf Efendī. A beneficiary with such a deed could then present it for verification to the special *dīwān* created for the purpose. If its validity was established, he was allowed to pay half the regular rate of tax imposed by the government. Obstacles were created to obstruct verification and heavy fees were collected by the officials at every possible point in the process of verification. Nevertheless, most of the beneficiaries pursued the matter to the end in order to confirm their titles and to obtain tax relief. In a few instances, beneficiaries neglected to do so in the hope that a change in government would cancel Muḥammad ʿAlī's innovations and would restore former rights and customs.

The *shaykhs* protested half-heartedly against the policy of taxing *ar-rizaq al-aḥbāsīyah.* They warned the *kikhyah bey* that the tax would induce the ruin of the mosques and the collapse of religion. The *kikhyah bey* replied that he was unable to interfere, as the responsibility rested with the Pasha and his tax agents, Maḥmūd Bey and al-Muʿallim Ghālī. The *shaykhs* then called upon these officials and were informed that the order to collect these taxes had actually been given the previous year and could not be altered or postponed. They criticized the *shaykhs* for attempting to obstruct the use of these revenues by the Pasha who, at that moment, was fighting a holy war in Arabia. There was nothing for the *shaykhs* to do but to retire and to accept without further protests that which they were powerless to change.[37]

The return of Muḥammad ʿAlī from al-Ḥijāz in June 1815 evoked much enthusiasm from the landholders, for it was rumored that the Pasha planned to reverse the land policy and had already restored land in Upper Egypt to their owners. A few days after arriving in Cairo Muḥammad ʿAlī apologized for the injustices suffered by landholders at the hands of the Copts and promised to remedy the situation. Everyone was elated; it was even rumored in Cairo that Muḥammad ʿAlī intended to impale al-Muʿallim Ghālī and the other Copt chiefs in front of Shubrā Palace. Actually, there was little cause for rejoicing, for it soon became clear that the Pasha had no intentions whatsoever of reversing his land policy. Instead of punishing al-Muʿallim Ghālī, he heaped new honors upon him. Then, when the disgruntled beneficiaries of *rizqahs* descended upon Cairo from all parts of Egypt and marched with flying banners to Qubbah where he was located, Muḥammad ʿAlī ordered his troops to disperse the demonstrators, many of whom were severely beaten by the soldiers. Finally, he refused to change his position concerning the payment of *al-māl al-ḥurr* on *waṣīyah* lands and even withheld the compensation which had been promised to the *multazims* upon confiscation of their *iltizāms* (i.e., the *fāʾiẓ*), pretending that new land registers had to be prepared before payments could be made. In fact, the government seemed to be procrastinating in order to derive full profit from the land for as long as possible. Dissatisfaction among the *multazims* reached such a pitch that the government finally ordered payments to commence at the beginning of August. Even then, only half the *fā'iẓ* was paid.[38]

The political climate in Egypt became truly explosive early in August 1815 owing to the soldiers' revolt against Muḥammad 'Alī's efforts to introduce the *Niẓām Jadīd* (that is, the military organization on French models) in the army. An alliance between the disaffected soldiery and the discontented landholders might have been achieved had Muḥammad 'Alī not handled the revolt forcefully and used all his powers of reconciliation to appease those who had been plundered by the mutineers. The land question was also settled shortly after the August revolt as part of Muḥammad 'Alī's attempt to relieve tension and to prevent further disturbances. In order to propitiate the army chiefs and other distinguished persons in the country injured by his land measures, he now declared that all *multazims* would be allowed to enjoy the revenue from their *waṣīyah* lands without the necessity of paying the government anything for this privilege. He then instructed the officials of the *Rūznāmah* to prepare within twelve days registers containing the additional amounts to be paid to the *multazims* to compensate for the loss of their *iltizāms*. Two *dīwāns* were established for this purpose, one in the Citadel and the other in the city. The first prepared accounts for the *multazims* who were members of Muḥammad 'Alī's entourage and the army chiefs, whereas the second prepared those for the remaining *multazims*. Special favor was shown to the first group, since it was credited not only with the *fā'iẓ* but also with the *muḍāf*, *barrānī*, and gifts which it had enjoyed. The second group of *multazims* was not so fortunate and was credited only with the amount of the *fā'iẓ*. The pensions of both groups were paid during their lifetimes. Neither their pensions nor their *waṣīyah* lands could be inherited by their children; no right of cession during their lifetimes was granted and upon their deaths the pensions and *waṣīyah* land reverted to the state.

Ash-Shaykh ad-Dawākhlī attempted to procure a reversal of Muḥammad 'Alī's policy concerning *ar-rizaq al-aḥbāsīyah* and at one point even obtained the Pasha's promise to return to traditional practices vis-à-vis these lands. Muḥammad 'Alī, however, at a meeting with the *shaykhs* offered to allow the lands to remain with the beneficiaries, provided only that they paid taxes on the land; otherwise, he agreed to take over the land and pay the landholders a pension equivalent to the amount of the *fā'iẓ*. The *shaykhs* raised no objection to these proposals. The final settlement regarding *ar-rizaq al-aḥbāsīyah* included the following terms: (1) they, like the village lands, were taxed with the *mīrī* (*kharāj*) which was collected by the government; (2) their beneficiaries received a life pension that could not be inherited; and (3) the state assumed the cost of maintaining the mosques and charitable institutions. In the latter case, as events were to show, the penurious policy pursued by the state towards religious institutions resulted in the decay of many mosques.[39]

Muḥammad 'Alī had acquired most of the agricultural land in Egypt by the payment of pensions whose real value declined continually because of the steady devaluation in the value of the piaster. Furthermore, the death of the pensioners during the course of his reign reduced the state's liability. Although exact budget information in Egypt during this period is nonexistent, the accompanying excerpts from budget estimates contained in European reports give some idea of the cost to the state of Muḥammad 'Alī's policy of confiscation.[40]

	Piasters	*Purses*
Boislecomte's budget for 1829 lists pensions paid to former *multazims* at 612,000 francs. The piaster was valued at 35 centimes.	2,142,000	4,284
Boislecomte stated that in 1833 the amount of the pensions paid to *multazims* was 525,000 francs.	1,750,000	3,500
Budgets for 1250/1834–35 (Campbell and Colin) list pensions to the *multazims* at	1,250,000	2,500
Duhamel's list of expenses dated 1837 put the amount paid to former *multazims* at	2,000,000	4,000
Murray's budget for 1262/1845–46 included an item covering pensions for *multazims* and Arab chiefs at 1,200,000 francs. (The amount paid to the *multazims* alone is not stipulated.)	4,800,000	9,600
Boislecomte's budget for 1829 included an item to cover salaries to *shaykhs* and the maintenance of mosques at 437,500 francs.	1,531,250	3,062½
Colin's budget for 1250/1834–35 included an item for the same purpose.	1,100,000	2,200

Campbell did not mention salaries to *shaykhs* but listed expenses for mosques.	1,000,000	2,000
Duhamel's report listed two items:		
(1) subvention to compensate persons for revenues derived from the villages which have been withdrawn. (This item might cover pensions to expropriated *rizqah* beneficiaries, although this is uncertain.)	1,500,000	3,000
(2) subvention to maintain mosques and other charitable works to replace revenues derived from *rizqahs* confiscated by the government.	1,029,000	2,058

The revolution in Egyptian land tenure envisaged in part by Salīm III, Napoleon, and Menou had been executed by Muḥammad 'Alī over a period of seven years. Baron de Boislecomte commented years later that these changes actually offended Europeans more than they did native Egyptians. "Property with us," he wrote, "is the foundation of society; but here, actually, it has never been well established nor even clearly defined."[41] The validity of this statement is more apparent than real. It was not the absence of a well-defined concept of property which made the revolution acceptable to the Egyptians; it was, rather, that Muḥammad 'Alī did not do violence to what was a radically different concept of property. The traditional Islamic concepts pertaining to land tenure were, in fact, left intact, since even the confiscation of *ar-rizaq al-aḥbāsīyah* could be justified on theoretical grounds. This point, however, must not obscure the fact that the transformation at the practical level was complete. The old class of landholders was either annihilated or expropriated and the path was cleared for the emergence of a new landholding class. A radical departure from old practices might conceivably have been achieved and a nation of small independent farmers created, but it would have been too much to expect this at the beginning of the nineteenth century in a society such as existed in Egypt and in a land governed by a man raised in the traditions of the Turkish ruling class.

The expropriation of landholders was nothing more than a device for ridding the country of an unsatisfactory tax-collecting agency and for increasing the revenue from the land. No sooner was this end accomplished when Muḥammad 'Alī sought substitutes; for the balance of his reign, he experimented with various forms of landholding with a view to increasing his sources of revenue. Just as the policy of expropriating the old landholding classes evolved slowly and was influenced by internal and external requirements, in like manner the new landholders were created as a result of internal and external pressures. The development of large private estates, characteristic of modern Egypt, originated in the period of Muḥammad ʿAlī. The basis for their foundation, however, was not the desire to create a new landowning class but to facilitate administration and tax collection for the benefit of the government and the new ruling class.

CHAPTER IV

MUḤAMMAD 'ALĪ AND LANDHOLDING REFORM AFTER 1815

As soon as the process of expropriating the land was consummated at the end of 1815, Muḥammad 'Alī converted most of Egypt into a huge government farm under the direct administration of the government hierarchy (see Chapter V) and drew upon the revenue which flowed directly into the state treasury both for governmental and private expenses. At first, though, he did not encourage the formation of private estates, because he wished to reserve the profits derived from agriculture for himself. Furthermore, he had no desire to give his Turkish officers the opportunity to gain personal control or influence over the Egyptian population. "All my ingenuity," he once told Baron de Boislecomte, "has been directed towards attracting Turkish officers to my service. For this, I have had to draw upon the same sources as the Sultan. Fortunately, he pays small salaries. I have paid far more and the officers have come to serve me. It has since been necessary to keep them faithful to me. I have found the way to do so by lavishing upon them money and presents but preventing their becoming proprietors and creating for themselves a personal influence over the population."[1] Towards the end of the 1820's, however, he began to modify his policy. In order to encourage the cultivation of trees along the banks of al-Maḥmūdīyah Canal, he issued an order dated Ṣafar 8, A.H. 1243 (August 31, 1827), which promised tax exemption on all lands, either *ab'ādīyah* or *ma'mūr*, to cultivators who planted acacia trees; this order was soon interpreted to include land on which other types of trees were planted and also lands with walled gardens. Such land, according to the *Sharī'ah*, became *mulk*. The *Rūznāmah* thereupon issued a deed (*taqsīṭ*) which stipulated that the land was granted as *rizqah bilā māl* or estate free from tax. It was then recorded in the *Maḥkamah* court and a *ḥujjah* was issued by the *qāḍī*. The grantee was insured by Muḥammad 'Alī's order to the *Rūznāmah* of al-Muḥarram 5, A.H. 1258 (Feburary 16, 1842), of the right to dispose of his *rizqah bilā māl* by all legal methods of conveyance.

Not only did Muḥammad ʻAlī seek the cultivation of trees and gardens, but he also tried to extend the area of cultivation by encouraging the reclamation of *abʻādīyah* lands. In the *Lā'iḥat zirāʻat al-fallāḥ watadbīr aḥkām as-siyāsah biqaṣd an-najāḥ* of Rajab, A.H. 1245 (January 1830), he authorized the *nāẓirs al-qism* to lease *abʻādīyah* lands to industrious cultivators who promised to reclaim them; *abʻādīyah* lands were also granted to provincial officials. The first such grant on record was dated Jumādā 'l-Âkhirah 4, A.H. 1245 (December 1, 1829). According to Ḥanafī law, anyone, whether Muslim or non-Muslim, who reclaimed *mawāt* or dead land with the permission of the *Imām* was entitled to its enjoyment free from any tax except the tithe or *ʻushr*. Muḥammad ʻAlī did not comply strictly with this legal opinion nor was his policy with regard to *abʻādīyah* land uniform. Sometimes he granted estates from *abʻādīyah* land as *rizaq bilā māl*; sometimes he gave concessions to individuals exempt from tax for a period ranging from three to seven years to compensate them for the expense of their initial investment. He granted to Bedouins *abʻādīyah* lands tax exempt in order to encourage their settlement on the land. No legal title deed was given to them; they received only the formal promise of the viceroy that if they cultivated the land they would be exempted from the *corvée* and from military conscription.[2]

Concessions of *abʻādīyah*, as well as *maʻmūr* land, were made to foreigners, particularly to Greeks who came to Egypt and settled in the country. Many Greeks, successful in trade, accumulated large amounts of capital which they invested in land reclamation. Others who had no capital but were experienced farmers were assisted by Muḥammad ʻAlī who advanced them funds to invest in animals, agricultural implements, and seed. Athanasios Polites claimed for these Greek settlers full credit for giving the first impetus to cultivation in the Delta, especially since they adapted themselves easily to the new methods and crops which Muḥammad ʻAlī introduced. These claims are exaggerated; nevertheless, the Greek contribution to Egyptian agriculture must not be overlooked. Several British merchants also obtained land grants and by 1840 they had made large capital investments on approximately 25,000 acres, some of which were *abʻādīyah* lands which they reclaimed and cultivated.[3]

Islamic law allowed foreigners to hold land provided they paid the *kharāj* with which the land was burdened and submitted to the *jizyah* or capitation tax. The Capitulations, however, acted as a brake upon landholding by foreigners, since one of the privileges which the Sublime Porte had granted them was immunity from all taxation. Before the nineteenth century European governments had issued instructions prohibiting their nationals from holding land, but afterwards, when the European powers no longer considered the Capitulations a privilege but rather a right which they could enforce by exerting pressure upon the Sublime Porte, they allowed the old prohibitions to lapse. It then became British policy to require payment by British nationals of the tax with which the land was burdened, regardless of tax immunity under the Capitulations. Some of the other countries were less scrupulous, however, and insisted upon their Capitulatory privileges while, at the same time, allowing their citizens to accept lands on which the government was entitled to collect taxes. The problem was to become serious and new arrangements to protect the Egyptian government a necessity, but it reached the crucial stage after the reign of Muḥammad 'Alī and falls outside the scope of this work.[4]

Muḥammad 'Alī had only limited success in his grants of estates from *ab'ādīyah* land. In the case of the *rizaq bilā māl* which were granted to cultivators to raise trees and gardens, it was soon discovered that many cultivators accepted the tax exemption but failed to carry out their part of the bargain. To end this situation, Muḥammad 'Alī ordered in a decree dated Rajab 17, A.H. 1256 (September 14, 1840), that no *taqsīṭs* should be issued by the *Rūznāmah* until it was definitely established that the cultivators had fulfilled their undertakings. The government's efforts to reclaim village *ab'ādīyah* land also met with only limited success. One such attempt occurred in Daqahlīyah Province where inefficiency was so great that after six years the reclaimed estate was still operating at a loss.[5] The estates which Muḥammad 'Alī granted to private individuals, especially those granted to high provincial officials, were more successful, but their success was usually gained at the expense of neighboring villages. These high dignitaries obtained the first waters, the best workers from neighboring villages, and the village *shaykhs* rendered all possible assistance to curry favor with them. In this way a few of the governors and high officials reaped benefits with little or no investment on their part. The concessions to the Bedouins also failed to accomplish the goal intended by Muḥammad 'Alī, since the Bedouins had little experience in agriculture and also lacked the necessary animals and agricultural implements. They often turned over their grants to the peasants in the area, either by leasing the land to them or by granting them half-shares. In 1837 Muḥammad 'Alī issued an order which forbade the Bedouins from cultivating land by these means. On Dhū'l-Qa'dah 29, A.H. 1262 (November 18, 1846), an order was issued that grants would be withdrawn if the Bedouins failed to cultivate the lands themselves.[6]

After 1837 there was an increasing number of grants made to members of the viceroy's family, to high Turkish officers, and to other favored individuals, including foreigners. This practice constituted a fundamental change in policy that arose from several causes. First, much land had been abandoned by the peasants because of Muḥammad 'Alī's policies of conscription and excessive taxation. The best agricultural workers were being drawn from the land to fill the ranks of the army and navy. Those who escaped conscription did so by mutilating themselves, thus reducing their ability to work the land, or by fleeing from their villages either to Syria or to the towns. Excessive taxation led to the insolvency of many villages which could not keep abreast of current taxes and accumulated arrears. Second, the system of direct supervision of cultivation, monopoly of crops, and collection of taxes by government agents proved inefficient (see Chapter VI). Third, Muḥammad 'Alī suffered greatly from the world economic crisis of 1836 and wished to reduce the cost of government. By the new policy the new landholders would assume the responsibilities and pay the costs for administering the villages granted to them. Furthermore, since many of them were military officers and high government officials, Muḥammad 'Alī was also able to save the cost of their salaries and pensions by providing them with estates.[7] Fourth, the pressures of the foreign powers upon the Sublime Porte to allow free trade led to the Commercial Treaty of 1838 which was intended to end monopoly in all the provinces of the Ottoman Empire. Muḥammad 'Alī was not able to resist the demands of the foreign consuls to end the system of monopoly which he had introduced as early as 1812, but he circumvented them by assigning the land to his followers who, to maintain his favor, could not deny him the produce from their estates at the prices he was prepared to pay. The system of monopolization by government ended, but monopoly, in a new form, remained. Finally, when Muḥammad 'Alī became hereditary governor of Egypt in 1841 he turned his attention to accumulating wealth, the permanent possession of which was now guaranteed by the Sultan and by the foreign powers. After 1841, the members of the viceroy's family, particularly Ibrāhīm Pasha, and the favorites of Muḥammad 'Alī had one all-consuming interest—the acquisition of enormous personal fortunes.[8]

The great estates formed during these years were of two kinds: the *chafālik* (sing. *chiflik*) and the *'uhad* (sing. *'uhdah*), which were not really estates but rather tax farms bearing a close resemblance to the former *iltizāms*. An *'uhdah* was a concession made to an individual who undertook (1) to assume all responsibility towards the state with regard to the payment of the arrears and the current taxes of insolvent villages and (2) to deliver to the government at fixed prices the produce from the land.[9] Dr. al-Ḥitta claims that as early as 1831 Maḥmūd Efendī was granted an *'uhdah* in al-Qalyūbīyah Province and that other grants were made in Aṭfīḥ Province in 1833.[10] These grants were isolated examples, however, since the policy of assigning land to private landholders really went into effect after 1837. Considerable reluctance was shown at first by wealthy individuals to accept *'uhdahs*, so that when conditions in the country continued to deteriorate Muḥammad 'Alī simply decreed on al-Muḥarram 19, A.H. 1256 (March 23, 1840), that insolvent villages should be granted to the high dignitaries and officers who had grown wealthy in his service. They had no choice in the matter and had to comply with his orders.[11] Muḥammad 'Alī, himself, as well as Ibrāhīm Pasha and other members of his family, also accepted *'uhdahs*. By 1844 a total of 1,205,559 *faddāns* had been converted into *'uhdahs* of which 120,000 *faddāns* belonged to Muḥammad 'Alī, 98,000 *faddāns* to Ibrāhīm Pasha, 75,000 to other members of the viceroy's family, and 912,559 to Turkish officers, high officials, and favorites.[12]

The concessionaire, the *muta'ahhid*, received no proprietary rights. The land remained *athar* land in possession of the *fallāḥīn* in whose name it was inscribed in the cadastral registers. The peasants, indebted to the government, were forced to remain in their villages, to pay the *muta'ahhid* the amount of tax listed in the cadastral registers (which amount, however, could be increased only if the government reassessed all taxes), and to work for the concessionaire as day laborers or sharecroppers. The *muta'ahhid's* profit was derived either from working part of the village land with day labor for his own profit or from a system of sharecropping whereby he supplied seed and capital, while the *fallāḥīn* worked the land in return for half the produce. The royal *'uhdahs* were under the direction of the *Dīwān 'Umūm al-Chafālik wa'l-'Uhad as-Sanīyah*. So far as the others were concerned, the government did not interfere and was only interested in receiving taxes and crops.[13]

Colonel Barnett, British Consul-General in Egypt (1841–1846), who opposed the seizure of lands from the peasantry because it obstructed free trade, recommended that the Sultan should be asked to intervene on behalf of the *fallāḥīn* and to obtain the restoration of property "illegally taken from them." The *fallāḥīn*, however, welcomed the *'uhdahs*, because they were glad to escape exactions by the government authorities and preferred to be under the control of one individual. They also profited from the fact that some of the landholders were sufficiently influential to obtain exemption for them from the *corvée*.[14] The *muta'ahhids*, on the other hand, found the estates a burden in the majority of cases, rather than a source of profit. Hamont explains why this was true for foreign holders of *'uhdahs*. First, they were unable to sell their produce at high prices as the Pasha imposed his own prices upon them. Second, no matter what methods of cultivation they used, they were unable to keep their production costs at the low level maintained by the *fallāḥīn* whose living standards were lower than theirs. Third, they were robbed without compunction by the *fallāḥīn* who felt justified in so doing since, in their opinion, they had been saddled with debts because of Muḥammad 'Alī's extortions and felt, therefore, entitled to the profits derived from the land. In some instances, Hamont admitted, the estates were successful when concessionaires were under the special protection of the viceroy or because their directors had extraordinary managerial capacities. British landholders were probably better off than the Greeks and Armenians because they could dispose of the produce from their estates more freely. The Reverend Stephen Olin who described his visit to the farms of Mr. Larking, at one time the British consul at Alexandria, was informed that they were flourishing. In 1849 'Abbās Pasha, the new viceroy, found that two thirds to three fourths of the *'uhdahs* were in default of taxes. Since many of the *muta'ahhids* were unable to collect the arrears owed to the government, he withdrew their concessions without compensation. The rest were allowed to retain them. No great outcry resulted from his measures, as this form of land grant had proved unsatisfactory.[15]

Chifliks can more properly be designated as private estates than *'uhdahs*, which were merely tax farms. A *chiflik* in its legal connotation was a field varying in size which was cultivated annually by a plow drawn by two oxen and produced a yearly harvest. In its more common usage, however, the *chiflik* included buildings, animals, seed, and agricultural implements, as well as the land which was cultivated. In other words, it was a farm in our sense.[16] In Egypt the term *chiflik* was applied to estates granted to members of the viceroy's family. They were constituted either from reclaimed *ab'ādīyah* land or from *ma'mūr* land which the Pasha withdrew from villages unable to pay taxes. Muḥammad 'Alī's estate at Shubrā was possibly the earliest *chiflik*. In 1809 he ordered the construction of *sāqiyahs* on the banks of the Nile from Cairo to Shubrā to develop gardens en route to his palace there. He also confiscated the lands of the neighboring villages up to Birkat al-Ḥājj and placed them under the supervision of Dhū'l-Fiqār, his *kikhyah*. Every kind of vegetable was raised and became known to the public as the cabbages of the Pasha, the carrots of the Pasha, or the radishes of the Pasha. Flowers of every variety were also cultivated in his newly laid out gardens.[17]

Since it was not the government's policy to dispossess cultivators so long as taxes were paid, *chifliks* began to expand in number and size only towards the end of the 1830's when many villages became insolvent and especially after 1841, when the viceroy's family acquired a durable personal stake in Egypt. In his report of 1844 Barnett listed the amount of *ma'mūr* land converted into *chifliks* at 371,000 *faddāns*, but he failed to specify whether this represented the total area for *chifliks* or if, in addition, some of the estates formed from reclaimed *ab'ādīyah* land were *chifliks*. Since *chifliks* became the property of members of the royal family, they were undoubtedly exempt from paying taxes even though Barnett claimed that all the *ma'mūr* land was liable to tax at a rate of between 27 to 90 piasters per *faddān*.[18] The Citadel archives, according to Dr. al-Ḥitta, contain records concerning *chifliks* at Nabarōh, Najjārīyah, Bashbīsh, Tinbārah, and Sandīlah. Jean Deny in his inventory of the files of the *Dīwān 'Umūm al-Chafālik wa'l-'Uhad as-Sanīyah* also listed *chifliks* at Shubrā, Sanjahā, Baḥr ash-Sharq,[19] Kafr ash-Shaykh, Ma'niyā, and Sharnūb. In addition, there are files for unspecified *chifliks* located in the provinces of al-Qalyūbīyah, al-Minūfīyah, ash-Sharqīyah, and Buḥayrah and in the rice field regions, *Bilād ar-Ruz ash-Sharqān*.[20]

After the Egyptian crisis was settled in 1841, Muḥammad 'Alī invested heavily in *chifliks* that he placed under the direction of government officials whose duties were incorporated in the *Qānūn al-Chafālik*. Each *chiflik* was supervised by a *nāẓir*[21] who coordinated the work of the staff of officials placed under his jurisdiction and made certain that each one performed his assigned task. It was also his duty to punish negligent officials or *fallāḥīn* in accordance with penalties listed in the *Qānūn*. The *chiflik* officials included a *khawlī* and his assistants who directed the cultivation, the *shaykhs al-balad* who supervised the *fallāḥīn*, a veterinarian, trained at the school of Abū Zaʿbal, who took charge of the livestock, an attendant for poultry, warehouse employees, and a weigher. Several officials in the *chiflik* were not responsible to the *nāẓir* but to other officials in the government: the surveyor (*massāḥ*), the tax collectors (*ṣarrāfs*), the chief scribe in the *chiflik* (*kātib ʿarabī*), and the police officer (*mulāhiz*). The surveyor, with the knowledge of the administrator (*mudīr*) and the chief inspector (*mufattish*), was sent by the *Dīwān al-Madāris* to survey the land. He performed the survey in cooperation with the *khawlī* and the *nāẓir* of the *chiflik*. The tax collectors were responsible to the *mudīr*. The chief scribe controlled the work of the scribes under him who recorded all data connected with the work in the *chiflik*. The police officer, also responsible to the *mudīr*, carried out police duties in the *chiflik* and reported to the chief inspector in cases where the *mudīr* was unable to give ample support. The *mudīr* was in turn ultimately responsible for everything connected with the *chifliks* in his *mudīrīyah*. He was to be informed by the *nāẓir* of all the work and problems of each farm; he must coordinate the work of all the *chifliks* under his control; and it was his responsibility to prepare reports which were sent to the chief inspector. In addition, there was a *jurnāljī* who prepared independent reports, *jurnālāt*, which he sent to the chief inspector. The latter had access to Muḥammad ʿAlī's privy council without recourse to any intermediary and it was his duty to keep the privy council informed of the true state of the *chifliks*.[22]

Hamont gives a detailed and probably fairly accurate account of the manner in which *chifliks* were actually managed. After villages were taken over, he writes, an inventory was made of all their men, women, children, animals, and agricultural implements. The *dīwān* named a director (*nāẓir*), usually an officer of the army, navy, or cavalry who was detached from military service. This director and the *shaykhs al-balad* were authorized to search villages and towns for *fallāḥīn* who had abandoned their lands and to force them to return. Inadequate provisions were usually prepared for the *fallāḥīn* and the livestock on new *chifliks* so that both suffered considerable hardship until the first harvest. Although by an order issued in 1837 (A.H. 1253) the *fallāḥīn* were to receive one sixth of the crops in return for their labor, it was never executed, as the officials took the cereals for themselves and left the *fallāḥīn* less than their share. In 1838 (A.H. 1254) the *fallāḥīn* were allowed to work one fifth of the land for their own account. As they did not have the necessary animals to do the work, the government granted them the right to use its animals, a privilege which proved a dead-letter since the government lacked sufficient animals for its own needs. In 1840 (A.H. 1256) it was agreed that the *fallāḥīn* on the viceroy's estates should be paid half in cash and half in kind every Tuesday at the rate of thirty paras for an adult man, fifteen paras for a young man, and ten paras for a boy. Those on Ibrāhīm Pasha's estates received forty paras a day, thirty of which were paid as a bread ration and the rest in cash at regular intervals. They also received part of the crops and were permitted to keep some animals and poultry.[23] Conditions for the *fallāḥīn*, particularly on Muḥammad 'Alī's *chifliks*, were so bad that Hamont once proposed to him that communal kitchens be introduced in each *chiflik* where the *fallāḥīn* could eat in a common dining hall or receive food to take to their homes. He also suggested that weavers should be employed to supply cloth to dress the *fallāḥīn* in the *chifliks* and that workshops should be constructed to extract oil and bleach rice for *fallāḥ* consumption. All his proposals were rejected, however.

One of the chief reasons, Hamont continues, for the failure of *chifliks* was that all of them, regardless of their potential differences, were placed under the same regulations. Orders were accordingly sent from Cairo directing the sowing of cotton in one place and sesame in another when sometimes the reverse should have occurred. Orders also had to pass through a bureaucratic hierarchy which occasioned calamitous delays; it was not infrequent that the end of the sowing season would come before the necessary instructions were received. Workers and animals labored under tremendous pressure resulting often in death in order to compensate for delays caused by bureaucratic red tape. In fact, animal mortality became so serious that directors were held personally responsible for each animal that perished. At least one director was sent to the galleys for permitting too many animals in his *chiflik* to die, but a proposal to allow each director only four deaths after which he would have to bear the additional losses met with so much opposition that it was scrapped. The *nāẓirs*, subservient to the wishes of the central authority, were deprived of all powers of initiative and adopted a nonchalant attitude. They were often placed in charge of as many as ten to fourteen thousand *faddāns*, and, since they could not provide adequate personal supervision, abuses developed. They were expected to perform miracles without sufficient workers, animals, or tools. Although they were granted the right of life and death to prevent thefts, the *fallāḥīn* robbed whenever they could. Accounts too were so badly maintained that they could not be checked, although it was known that many of the *chifliks* operated at a loss. Sometimes an official investigation would be made when *chifliks* failed to provide the quotas for which they were responsible; *nāẓirs* would try then to disguise the real reasons for the failures by blaming the *fallāḥīn* who would be seized and bastinadoed. The *fallāḥīn*, tormented on every side, fled from the land only to be dragged back again, a procedure to which Colonel Barnett refers in a diplomatic dispatch:

Troops were sent from Cairo into the Provinces in aid of the Civil Authorities, and the Mudir of each village was commanded under the severest penalties to give up every peasant who was not proved to belong to his village. The peasants being collected in bodies were then marched with their wives and children under military escort to the villages from whence they had emigrated. From the Province of Bahira alone twelve thousand families have been taken away. The scenes of misery and desolation which ensued upon the removal of these unfortunate creatures from their homes has been described to me as most distressing. It is reported that several peasants have been executed for attempting to make their escape, but I have not sufficient authority for this fact to warrant stating it to Your Excellency otherwise than a report which has reached me. The measure of extreme severity to which the Pasha has had recourse, has no doubt for its principal object to force back to his own Chifflicks the Fellahs whom want and ill-treatment had induced to abandon them.[24]

This situation, however, remained hidden from Muḥammad 'Alī, for everyone recognized that if they wished to be considered efficient by the Pasha they would have to learn the technique of keeping the truth hidden from him. Anyone who attempted to inform him of the truth fell into disgrace; those who painted a favorable, even if untrue, picture received praise. After a tour of the estates, the Pasha would return to Cairo and speak about the fine conditions which existed in the countryside and would praise the officials most notorious for their venality. The members of the *dīwān* were no more anxious than the provincial officials to reveal the truth to Muḥammad 'Alī, so that he was consequently completely ignorant of the true state of affairs in the *chifliks*.[25]

The deplorable conditions in the *chifliks* could not be concealed indefinitely from Muḥammad 'Alī and complaints did finally reach him that led to his instructing the Ministry of Finance to study the problem.

The Ministry referred the matter to al-Ḥaqqānīyah Court.[26] The latter drew up an official report on the basis of information received from the directors of the *chifliks*, but failed to present it to Muḥammad 'Alī, partially because of bureaucratic delay, but mostly from fear of his anger, which the revelations in the report would certainly occasion. The report spoke of the increasing losses suffered by the *chifliks* and of the flight of the peasantry to Syria. Then, in July 1844, an annual meeting of the directors of Muḥammad 'Alī's *chifliks* was called at which the Pasha made unreasonable demands. A number of his close advisers thereupon decided to confront him with the truth. Samī Pasha informed him of the report prepared by al-Ḥaqqānīyah Court and Muḥammad 'Alī insisted upon seeing it, insulting his officers for their cowardice in not giving it to him. There are conflicting statements concerning his reaction to the report. One account stated that as soon as he received the information about the *chifliks* he became violent but was calmed by the suggestion that matters might not be so serious, that he ordered the official report to be sent for and then retired for the night.[27] Another account said that he flew into a violent rage and in the course of his outburst referred to a *Traitor* and a *Miser*, that he named neither one nor the other but that it was believed he considered Ibrāhīm Pasha, whom he suspected of attempting to take over the government, to be the traitor and Sharīf Pasha, president of the privy council, to be the miser.[28] Both versions differ also concerning the moment at which he became hysterical and began to declare that he was tired of the world and would retire from office and make a pilgrimage to Makkah. One stated that it was during the meeting, the other that it was only during the course of the night.[29] In any event, the next day he ordered a large sum of money to be brought to him and began to make preparations for a trip. On July 27, 1844, he left Alexandria for Cairo, accompanied only by his physician and apothecary.

His officers, Ibrāhīm Pasha, Sa'īd Pasha, Attin Bey, Samī Pasha, Basilyūs Bey, Bakrī Bey, and Kāmil Pasha, made several attempts to reconcile him by making submission to him in writing in which they declared that none of their number could have been meant by the terms *traitor* or *miser*, that they were willing to hold a Court of Inquiry and to produce the guilty parties. The Pasha would not be reconciled. Everyone was afraid to approach him to discover his real intentions. The foreign consuls then decided to lend their aid by submitting a joint statement which Muḥammad 'Alī would be obliged to receive. In it they said that they had learned of his intention to go to Makkah and expressed their regrets that they had not had the opportunity to bid him personal farewells. They also expressed their hope that he had made necessary arrangements for the conduct of affairs in Egypt during his absence.

By the time of Muḥammad 'Alī's arrival in Cairo, he had obviously reconsidered the whole matter. He promptly assembled his officers at Shubrā Palace on August 5, 1844, and fined them an amount which was said to equal 10,000 purses, of which Ibrāhīm Pasha paid 3,000. Muḥammad 'Alī then spent the first part of August examining the official report of al-Ḥaqqānīyah Court. Thereafter, everything continued as though nothing had happened; the whole project of a pilgrimage to Makkah was dropped; and the Pasha did not delegate any of his powers to Ibrāhīm but carried the full burden of authority by himself. It was generally felt that the whole outburst had been merely a ruse for arousing terror and breaking up intrigues, but the British consul at Alexandria held another opinion: "The indisposition of His Highness has, no doubt, been singular in its circumstances, and its true character is properly a question of medical science. The temporary disorder in the Pasha's mental faculties seems to have depended closely on the shock suffered by the nervous system; and, by degrees as this recovered quiet and a more healthy tone, the projected pilgrimage to Mecca, the morose speculation, and the imputations of treason and the other errors of sickness dispersed from the imagination."[30] At any rate, the "Crisis of 1844" brought no improvements according to Colonel Barnett, who in 1845 found conditions in Egypt still deplorable: "A peasantry groaning under the most cruel oppression and exactions that any people ever submitted to, a starving population forced to work in manufactories, the products of which little more than repay the cost of the raw material, a large army and navy neither paid nor fed, and a higher class converted by the will of the Pasha into landed proprietors, burthened with arrears of taxes due from the Villages made over to them, and often left without labourers to till the soil. . . ."[31] Not until the reign of 'Abbās Pasha (1848–1854) was any real attempt made to relieve the pressures imposed by Muḥammad 'Alī upon the peasantry and the landholders.

At the end of Muḥammad 'Alī's reign there were, then, several categories of landholders: members of the ruling family, the Turkish officers and high government officials, a certain number of foreigners, and peasants. The bulk of the land remained state land subject to the *mīrī* (or *kharāj*) and most of the large landholders were merely tax farmers (*muta'ahhids*) similar to the *multazims* who had been expropriated during the early years of Muḥammad 'Alī's rule. The *muta'ahhids*, like their predecessors, held their land by consent of the ruler and could be deprived of their estates whenever he wished. Part of the land had been granted as *rizaq bilā māl* and as *chifliks*, both of which enjoyed a privileged position. The peasants who remained solvent were allowed to retain their *athar* land but were under government control. A significant redistribution of the land had also occurred between 1820–21 and 1844, as shown in Table 1. In a twenty-three year period the best Delta land most suited to cotton cultivation, had passed into the hands of large landholders. The peasants, on the other hand, held land which did not benefit from the program of irrigation works carried out during Muḥammad 'Alī's reign and on which they were unable to cultivate the more profitable summer crops. Furthermore, the status of peasant-held land remained unchanged; it was state land burdened with the *kharāj* to which the peasants had rights of usufruct only.[32]

TABLE 1. Redistribution of land (in *faddāns*) between 1820–21 and 1844

Area	Peasant land		Land held by large landholders
	1820–21 (A.H.1236)	1844 (A.H.1260)	1844 (A.H.1260)
Lower Egypt	1,003,866	674,914	1,464,559
Middle and Upper Egypt	952,774	1,339,000	112,000
Total	1,956,640	2,013,914	1,576,559

The land law of 1846 did not grant the peasants any rights to private property, as asserted by some; it merely guaranteed by statute privileges formerly regulated by custom which safeguarded peasants from permanent alienation from the land, in many cases in the possession of their families for generations. It provided, first, that only land that had been surveyed at the time of the Cadastre of 1813–14 and had then been mortgaged by a peasant could be reclaimed entirely or in part by him, if he could repay all or part of the mortgage and was able to work all or part of the land. If, however, the person who had mortgaged the land could prove by means of a legal title or by witnesses that the emigrant peasant had ceded to him his rights, the emigrant could not reclaim it. Second, peasants who had possessed land which they had abandoned could reclaim it even if it was in possession of *shaykhs* or had been mortgaged.

Where the land had been granted by the state to another tenant on condition that he pay the arrears with which it was burdened, the emigrant received half of the land he had previously possessed, provided he undertook to pay the back taxes on the portion of land which he received. Finally, a peasant whose land had been confiscated because of his inability to construct *sāqiyahs* in compliance with an order issued in 1826 (A.H. 1242) and in effect until 1835 (A.H. 1251) could obtain part of his land, if he satisfied the authorities that he could cultivate it and if he paid the arrears on the land.[33]

A final question must be posed with regard to Muḥammad ʻAlī's policies toward landholding in Egypt. Did he arrogate to himself powers to which he had no legal claim, powers which belonged of right to the Sultan? Theoretically, the right both to expropriate and reassign land remained the prerogative of the Sultan, though it was undoubtedly the practice for governors in the Ottoman Empire to assume full responsibility in their provinces on behalf of the sovereign. At any rate, the Sultan accepted revenue from Egypt, allowing his subordinate to carry out his policies without interference. So long as the Sultan was too weak to impose his will upon Muḥammad ʻAlī, the matter of right was an academic question and both the Sultan and Muḥammad ʻAlī recognized the true situation without concerning themselves with its legality. After the second Syrian War, Muḥammad ʻAlī received the hereditary governorship of Egypt, and was limited in the conduct of Egyptian internal affairs only by the clause in the imperial firman which stipulated that he was to rule in accordance with the laws of the empire, always taking into account, however, *local requirements and the principles of justice*.[34] This qualifying clause, upon whose insertion Muḥammad ʻAlī had insisted, could be and, in fact, was the clause by which the legality of Muḥammad ʻAlī's measures after 1841 was asserted.

In sum, it might be said that in the first stage of his reign (until the Greek War of Independence) Muḥammad ʻAlī acted in accordance with Sultan Maḥmūd's views of land reform and could not be accused of arrogating powers denied by the Sultan; in the second stage (from the end of the Greek War of Independence to the termination of the second Syrian War) no basic changes in landholding occurred and, furthermore, the Sultan was too weak to control his powerful vassal; in the final stage, Muḥammad ʻAlī construed the Firman of 1841 to mean that he was entitled to act freely with regard to land distribution, limited only by restrictions placed upon him by the *Sharīʻah*.

CHAPTER V

ADMINISTRATION OF EGYPT UNDER MUḤAMMAD 'ALĪ

The *Qānūn-nāmah* promulgated by Sulaymān the Magnificent after the Ottoman conquest of Egypt in the sixteenth century established the basis by which Egypt was to be ruled for the three centuries which preceded Muḥammad 'Alī's reign. The general outlines of the administrative and financial machinery established by Sulaymān remained clearly recognizable throughout this period, although, in the course of time, the *Qānūn-nāmah* was modified, arbitrary interpretations were given to its decrees, new practices were evolved, and control of the Egyptian administration by the central government at Istanbul practically disappeared.[1]

By the eighteenth century, the Mamlūks had emerged as the new ruling class, usurping effective control of the country, while the Turkish pasha appointed by the sultan had become only a phantom administrator subjected to their whims, their caprices, and their tolerance. The Arab historian, al-Jabartī, describes with what regularity these pashas were compelled to descend the Citadel at the insistence of the Mamlūks to make way for new appointees from Istanbul. The Mamlūks also neglected the duties and responsibilities owed to the Turkish sovereign and even ceased to pay the annual contribution to the Sultan's Private Treasury.[2] Finally, in the last decades of the eighteenth century, the Turkish government decided to reassert its power over its Egyptian province. First, the Turks accused the Mamlūks of rebellion against the Sultan and then took advantage of the internecine struggle between the Mamlūk factions to play one group off against the other. They were unable, however, to win any decisive victory over the Mamlūks before the French invasion of Egypt called a halt to the struggle. No sooner had their troops landed in Egypt when the French, professing great friendship for the Sultan, sent assurances to him that the object of the invasion was to aid him in his struggle against the rebellious Mamlūks. The Sultan, however, was not to be so easily duped and cooperated instead with the British in expelling the French from Egypt. As soon as the French troops were withdrawn, the struggle between the Turks and the Mamlūks for the control of Egypt was resumed with new vigor. It was this renewed struggle between the Turks and the Mamlūks which gave Muḥammad ʿAlī his opportunity to capture control of Egypt for himself. During the course of this conflict, Muḥammad ʿAlī shifted from one side to the other as it suited his own interests, at the same time cultivating the good will of the Egyptian notables. He finally succeeded in obtaining the support both of the Egyptian notables and of the Sultan for his candidacy for the office of *wālī* (governor) of Egypt by promising the former that he would adopt no new policy without their consent and by promising the latter that he would accept the duties and responsibilities owed to him, including the payment of the annual remittance to Istanbul. In 1805 he was appointed *wālī* and his appointment was renewed each year thereafter. Muḥammad ʿAlī thus emerged as the governor of Egypt, a country which had passed through civil wars and foreign occupation, had served as the battlefield for the French, British, and Turkish armies, would continue to be the scene of struggle between the Mamlūks and Muḥammad ʿAlī's troops for several years, and finally in 1807 would suffer a British invasion.

Despite political upheavals in Egypt during this entire period some measure of continuity in the administrative and financial machinery of the government persisted. Even during the French occupation, when the Mamlūks and the higher officials in the old bureaucracy were dispersed, those who were willing to collaborate with the French were permitted to remain in government service. The Copts, in particular, were at first given posts of greater responsibility than they had formerly enjoyed. The key positions, however, were held by Frenchmen. After the French withdrawal from Egypt the Turkish government appointed its officers to serve in the administration, but the Copts, who had already lost their position of favor, continued to function at the lower levels. The administration now appeared, however, to be on the verge of collapse, not only because of the ineptness of the Turkish officials who were appointed to govern the country but also because of the struggle for power involving the Turks and the Mamlūks as well as the various groups of soldiers imported into Egypt by the Turks. This struggle was reflected most strongly in the chaotic system of tax collection. The country was devastated by arbitrary and frequent tax levies by competing groups of soldiers; the suffering of the people was so great that Colonel Missett, the British agent in Egypt, reported to his government that he felt the breakdown in the system would cause the people to welcome the occupation of any European power to protect them against the Mamlūks, Albanians, and 'Uthmānlīs.[3] This apparently anarchic situation prevailing at the moment when Muḥammad 'Alī became governor of Egypt, however, disguised the essential fact that there still existed an administration, a minor officialdom, and a body of regulations and customary usages upon which the new Pasha could base his future government. His immediate problem, therefore, was not to reorganize the government but to make it an effective instrument by which he could control the country, collect the taxes he urgently needed, and consolidate his own position so that he could remain in power.

The system of government which was gradually evolved was highly centralized compared to the former regime under Mamlūk domination; once again a Turkish-appointed *wālī* was in complete control, although under circumstances vastly different from those envisaged by the *Qānūn-nāmah* of Sulaymān. The business of the central government was now conducted on two levels, by means of one or more deliberative councils (sing. *majlis*) presided over by *nāẓirs* and by bureaucratic departments (*dīwāns*) also headed by *nāẓirs*. The *majlises* and *dīwāns* were reorganized periodically and varied in number to meet administrative requirements. Although public business was discussed in deliberative councils (similar in character to those established by the *Qānūn-nāmah* and maintained during the period of Mamlūk and French domination) and decisions were made by majority rule as stipulated in an official regulation dated Rabī' ath-Thānī, A.H. 1233 (February–March 1818), these councils had no authority to act without the concurrence of the Pasha; their recommendations had first to be presented to Muḥammad 'Alī for his approval and final authority always rested with him. In 1240/1824–25 two principal councils were organized: (1) *al-Majlis al-'Alī al-Malakī* (or *al-Majlis al-'Alī*) for civil affairs and (2) *Majlis al-Jihādīyah* for military affairs. The former, referred to as the Council of State, was dissolved in 1837 and reformed as *al-Majlis al-Kabīr*, the Great Council or the Great Council of Ministers. *Al-Majlis al-Kabīr* was in turn disbanded in 1254/1838–39; at least, it no longer existed in 1258/1842–43. *Dīwāns* were also established as their need arose, but six principal *dīwāns* carried the burden of administrative functions: (1) interior, (2) treasury, (3) war, (4) marine, (5) public instruction and public works, and (6) foreign affairs and commerce. In addition to numerous departments of secondary importance there were two important *dīwāns* which performed functions belonging rightfully to that of the interior (*Dīwān al-Khidīwī*): (1) *Dīwān al-Katkhudā* (*Kikhyah*), *dīwān* of the lieutenant of the Pasha and (2) *Dīwān ʿUmūm at-Taftīsh, dīwān* of general inspection.[4]

Exact detailed information concerning the development of this *Dīwān ʿUmūm at-Taftīsh* is not available. It appears that in the middle of the 1820's, when the Egyptian provincial administration underwent a drastic reorganization, three *warshahs* (workshops) were established, each of which was headed by a chief (*ra'īs*), a bailiff (*mubāshir*), secretaries (*kātibs*), clerks (*mulāzims*), and a number of *shaykhs*. All three were located at Cairo and placed under the orders of a general director (*nāẓir ʿumūm*). They received inspection reports (*jurnālāt*) prepared in the provinces under their jurisdiction by special officials (*jurnāljīs*). For purposes of inspection, the country was divided into three major divisions: Lower Egypt, Upper Egypt, and Cairo.

Shortly after the establishment of these *warshahs*, the one dealing with Lower Egypt was placed under the control of Muḥammad Sharīf Bey, the Pasha's lieutenant (*kikhyah*), and was transferred to al-Manṣūrah. It now became known as the *Dīwān al-Jurnāl* of Lower Egypt and was placed under the direction of a *nāẓir* who was responsible to the *kikhyah bey*. Still later (in the middle of 1827), Muḥammad ʿAlī came to Lower Egypt on an inspection tour and transferred the *Dīwān al-Jurnāl* of Cairo to his headquarters at al-Jaʿfarīyah. This latter *dīwān* was eventually transferred back to Cairo, but the *Dīwān al-Jurnāl* of Lower Egypt remained in Lower Egypt (at al-Jaʿfarīyah). A further change occurred in 1828 when a new ordinance was issued by which the *warshah* of Middle Egypt was detached from that of Upper Egypt while the *warshah* of Lower Egypt was divided into three separate bureaus. There was now a total of six *warshahs*: three for Lower Egypt, one for Cairo, one for Middle Egypt and the royal estates, and one for Upper Egypt.

Still another reorganization took place when the name *jurnāl* was replaced by that of *taftīsh* and four *warshahs* rather than six became responsible for the task of inspection. The most important of these was the *Dīwān ʿUmūm at-Taftīsh* whose director (*mudīr*) was the *kikhyah bey*. This officer thus served in the capacity of inspector general, but he usually delegated his functions to an assistant (*wakīl*). The decisions of the government and important circulars were issued to all departments through the *Dīwān ʿUmūm at-Taftīsh*. Periodically, also, its director called a meeting of the first secretaries of the principal *dīwāns* to discuss with them administrative problems and to enact, with their agreement, the most essential government regulations. In addition to this *dīwān* there were three other *dīwāns* of inspection, one each for Lower, Middle, and Upper Egypt. Whether there were three or possibly only two other *dīwāns* is not clear. One source insists upon three but a report of 1837 claims that only two inspectors had been appointed, one for Lower Egypt and the other for Middle and Upper Egypt, and this is substantiated by a report of 1838 which states that the inspector (*mufattish*) for Lower Egypt was Ḥusayn Pasha while the inspector of Upper Egypt was Salīm Pasha, no mention being made of an inspector for Middle Egypt. In either case, the provincial *mudīrs* sent their accounts to the inspectors and they, in turn, presented theirs to the inspector general.[5]

The crisis in Muḥammad ʻAlī's financial situation in 1837 led to a major reorganization of the government and the consolidation of various departments. The administrative changes were incorporated in the *Qānūn as-Siyāsat-nāmah* of Rabīʻ al-Awwal, A.H. 1253 (June–July 1837),[6] and new directors (*mudīrs ad-dīwān*) were appointed. After reorganization the *dīwāns* and *mudīrs* and their functions were as follows:

Dīwān	*Mudīr*
1. *Dīwān al-Khidīwī* (Ministry of Interior)	Ḥabīb Efendī
2. *Dīwān al-Īrādāt* (Ministry of Finance)	Bakrī Bey Muḥammad Bey
3. *Dīwān al-Jihādīyah* (Ministry of War)	Aḥmad Pasha Miniklī
4. *Dīwān al-Baḥr* (Ministry of Marine)	Ḥasan Bey
5. *Dīwān al-Madāris* (Ministry of Education and Public Works)	Mukhtār Bey
6. *Dīwān at-Tijārah al-Miṣrīyah wa'l-Umūr al-Ifrankīyah* (Ministry of Commerce and Foreign Affairs)	Bāghūṣ Bey
7. *Dīwān al-Fāwrīqāt* (Ministry of Industry)	——————[7]

Dīwān al-Khidīwī (*Ministry of Interior*). This important *dīwān* dealt with police and judicial matters which did not fall within the competence of the religious or commercial tribunals. It also controlled a total of nineteen separate administrations responsible for matters such as markets, provisions for the Pasha, personal or public, with the exception of military supplies, the pious foundations, al-Maḥmūdīyah Canal, the post, and the mint.[8]

Dīwān al-Īrādāt (*Ministry of Finance*). From the outset of his reign, Muḥammad ʿAlī was concerned with the necessity for strengthening his financial position. Consequently, the financial department of the government took precedence over all others. The central financial administration, located at Cairo, was under the close personal supervision of Muḥammad ʿAlī. Its chief officer was the *daftardār*, who in accordance with the practice established by the *Qānūn-nāmah* was appointed by the Sultan.[9] Aḥmad Efendī became *daftardār* of Egypt in Dhū'l-Qaʿdah, A.H. 1220 (early in February 1806). Eighteen months later his duties were assumed for a brief time by Ḥusayn Efendī ar-Rūznāmjī and then, shortly afterwards (Shawwāl, A.H. 1222 [December 1807]), by Ibrāhīm, the Pasha's eldest son, whom the Sultan appointed *daftardār* and who held this post until July 1813 when he was succeeded by Muḥammad Efendī.[10] The *Rūznāmah*, one of the bureaus of the central financial administration, was responsible for land registration and the collection of the *mīrī*. It was headed by the *rūznāmjī*, chief of the *efendīs*, a corps of Muslim officials employed in the financial department. Ḥusayn Efendī served as the *rūznāmjī* until February 1813, when he was replaced by Muṣṭafā Efendī. The *efendīs*, assisted by various minor officials, kept the land registers, recorded all changes in landholding, prepared the annual tax registers, and kept the accounts of the government's receipts and expenditures. In addition to the permanent bureaus of the financial administration, special *dīwāns* were established periodically to deal with specific problems pertaining to land distribution or the assessment and collection of taxes.[11]

As early as 1810 Muḥammad ʿAlī began to suspect the officials of the *Rūznāmah* of malversation and of appropriating large sums belonging to the state. In March of that year, therefore, he appointed Khalīl Efendī to act as controller of the *Rūznāmah* (*kātib adh-dhimmah*) and instructed that all orders emanating from the *Rūznāmah* should first pass through the hands of this special official and be countersigned by him.[12] These measures did not have the desired effect, for officials of the *Rūznāmah* continued to defraud the government. The principal Copts, including al-Muʿallim Ghālī, chief of the Copt corporation whose members collected the taxes in the country, were arrested several times in 1810 on charges of malversation. These charges were, undoubtedly, well founded, but the arrest of these leading Copt officials also provided

Muḥammad 'Alī with a convenient device for extorting large fines from them. As soon as these fines were paid—and the Copts could usually call upon their coreligionists to assist them in meeting the Pasha's demands—the Pasha would reinstate them in their former positions. Even high Muslim officials were subjected to such treatment by the Pasha. In 1813 Ḥusayn Efendī ar-Rūznāmjī was denounced by several of his subordinates for misappropriating large sums. When he could not make restitution, he was removed permanently from his office. Although Ḥusayn Efendī was probably the victim of the jealousy and intrigue of his subordinates as well as of the Pasha's cupidity, in many cases officials were certainly guilty of cheating the government and these early attempts by Muḥammad 'Alī were, therefore, justified. It was unfortunate, however, that control by the Pasha was not always exercised with justice and was sometimes merely a device used by Muḥammad 'Alī for extortion. Furthermore, his measures proved to be only temporary palliatives. When he became preoccupied with other matters and relaxed his personal control, corruption flourished again and became an integral part of the entire financial administration.[13]

The competence of the *Rūznāmah* was greatly reduced during the course of Muḥammad 'Alī's reign so that by 1837 it formed only one of the nineteen administrations of the *Dīwān al-Khidīwī* and was annexed by the Ministry of Finance around 1265/1848–49.[14] Many of its functions were absorbed even before 1837 by one of the bureaus which formed part of the *Dīwān al-Khidīwī* (*Qalam al-Khazīnah al-Khidīwīyah*). This bureau of the viceregal treasury, generally referred to simply as the *Khazīnah*, controlled the accounts of all the provinces, including al-Ḥijāz and as-Sūdān and prepared monthly and annual statements which were submitted to the viceroy and the Council for Civil Affairs (*al-Majlis al-'Alī*). This arrangement still did not satisfy the Pasha and a new reorganization of the financial administration led to a division of functions among various departments, those which received the government's revenues and those which paid the government's bills. A separate department of receipts (*Dīwān al-Īrādāt*) which at first merely took over certain functions from the *Khazīnah* was created in 1250/1834–35. Then, when it was reorganized in 1837 into two bureaus, one under the direction of Bakrī Bey and the other under Muḥammad Bey, the *Dīwān al-Īrādāt* was assigned the task of keeping the accounts for all the Egyptian provinces, Crete, as-Sūdān, and al-Ḥijāz. It received all revenues with two exceptions. First, the Syrian finances were kept separately by a *mubāshir*, Wāsif Ṭiyāb, and his family, who acted as financial agents for the Egyptian government in Syria, received all taxes, paid all expenses, and rendered an account at the end of the year to the *Khazīnah* at Cairo. Second, the earnings from agriculture remained in the treasury of the Ministry of Commerce and Foreign Affairs, since these earnings were derived from the sale of agricultural produce handled by this ministry. The revenues received from the Egyptian provinces were collected by the provincial *mudīrs* and their assistants. Each *mudīr* came under the jurisdiction of one of the bureaus of the *Dīwān al-Īrādāt* and could appeal to his superior for aid in solving financial problems arising in his province. He was also responsible for presenting to his bureau an annual report dealing with the financial affairs of his province. The *Dīwān al-Īrādāt* did not pay the government's bills. These were dealt with separately by the *Dīwān al-Khidīwī* and, to a limited extent, by the Ministries of War and Marine. For disbursements handled by the *Dīwān al-Khidīwī*, it was required that all bills covering expenses incurred by the government in Egypt and the other countries under Muḥammad 'Alī's control should be submitted for approval to Ḥabīb Efendī, its *mudīr*, and he then authorized the *Khazīnah* to make the necessary payments. To provide some type of supervision over the activities of Ḥabīb Efendī, Bakrī Bey, and Muḥammad Bey, the Pasha also appointed his grandson, 'Abbās Pasha, to serve as inspector general. 'Abbās Pasha not only controlled the various officials of the financial administration but also received and passed judgment on complaints arising from financial matters. If 'Abbās failed to give satisfaction to a complainant, a final appeal could then be made directly to Basilyūs Bey and other members of Muḥammad 'Alī's *dīwān*.[15]

The separation of the accounts of receipts and expenses placed under the control of different officials proved an even slower and more confusing form of administration than had previously existed. By January 1838 it was reported that the finance administration "is a complete and incomprehensible chaos—and what is worse—not any efforts are made, nor any means sought, for remedying this disorder in the finance administration. It may be perhaps said that the machine marches—but you already know in what manner it does march." So long as no regular budget was formed and no bureau of control instituted to regulate all the financial departments, there seemed to be no hope of altering the situation. Since the amounts of receipts and expenses were unknown, there was rich opportunity for corruption. The accounts were kept by the Copts, who were the only ones capable of doing so, which made the situation worse, for the Copts, Campbell maintained, "were universally rogues and thieves—and their accounts are kept in such a way, that although Mehemet Ali has a positive conviction that he is cheated by them, still he cannot discover in what manner."[16]

In February 1838 it was decided that a Budget of Receipts and Expenditures should be established for the ensuing year in which estimates of expenses would be made before expenses were incurred and that general discussions regarding taxes should take place before they were levied. Abuses, however, persisted, as reports to the British Foreign Office indicate:

> But it does not appear that at present any good system of accountancy has been adopted, as different Districts have been apportioned to different ministries to provide their expenses instead of sending their Revenues to the Common Treasury. The present state of things leads to great abuses, as every Minister has a treasury of his own, and seven doors are opened . . . to fraud and abuse, where one in a country like this is already but too many. The Pacha has, however, requested Dr. Bowring to look into the state of his accounts and all the books have been laid open to him in the presence of Abbas Pacha, Bozileus Bey, the Accountant General, Hussein Pacha and several of the Ministers. Dr. Bowring has drawn up a series of suggestions for the improvement of the Public Bookkeeping, which, as they have been received in very friendly spirit by the Pacha may lead to some reform. These suggestions are clear, and admirably adapted for the country.
>
> It is estimated that nearly 40 per cent of the amount taken from the taxpayer never reaches the treasury of the viceroy.[17]

Since the situation in the financial administration did not improve, a further reorganization occurred in Jumādā 'l-Ūlā, A.H. 1260 (May–June 1844), when the *Dīwān al-Īrādāt* was abolished. An attempt was made then to consolidate most of the government's financial business into one department, the *Dīwān al-Mālīyah al-Miṣrīyah* (*dīwān* of Egyptian finances). The *dīwān* was placed under a *nāẓir* who received the rank of pasha (in 1262/1845–46). Sharīf Pasha was appointed to this post.[18] The disorder in the financial administration is of special importance in considering the agricultural policy of Muḥammad 'Alī, for it placed a special burden on agriculture, Egypt's principal source of revenue, which might have been avoided if financial affairs had been more efficiently conducted.

Dīwān al-Jihādīyah (*Ministry of War*). The reorganization of the Ministry of War led to the retirement of about forty Turkish officers who were replaced by promotions from the junior ranks and the military colleges in Cairo. The reorganized ministry was charged with the duties of recruiting, which were to be carried on in accordance with regulations established on the French model, with the training and discipline of troops, with assigning and maintaining them, with the operation of the army medical service and the military hospitals, with the upkeep of army buildings and fortifications, and with the supervision and maintenance of military workshops and stores, powder factory, forage-stores, and bakeries. The *mudīr* was responsible for the purchase of all military stores but was required to consult with General Attin Bey regarding war matériel and with Destouches regarding military stores. A department of finance was to be established within the ministry which was to be located at Cairo and directed by a chief under the Minister of War. He was ordered to pay all arrears owed to the troops and to pay current salaries regularly at the end of every month.[19]

Dīwān al-Baḥr (*Ministry of Marine*). All naval affairs were under the jurisdiction of the Minister of the Marine, including the supervision of naval forces and personnel, the shipyard, stores, naval hospitals and medical services, and the naval treasury. It was placed in charge, also, of all departments in Alexandria which paid expenses not falling within the competency of the *Dīwān al-Khidīwī*.[20]

Dīwān al-Madāris (*Ministry of Education and Public Works*). The ministry was charged with the primary, secondary, and technical schools, the libraries, instrument-stores, and museums, the Barrages of the Delta, the printing press at Būlāq, the Official Gazette (*al-Waqā'i' al-Miṣrīyah*), engineering, stud farms at Shubrā, the sheepfolds of the merino breed of sheep, and telegraph.[21]

Dīwān at-Tijārah al-Miṣrīyah wa'l-Umūr al-Ifrankīyah (*Ministry o, Commerce and Foreign Affairs*). It handled diplomatic relations, the direction and charge of the government warehouses (*shūnahs*), tax farming (*appaltos*), customs, sales and auctions of government produce.[22]

Dīwān al-Fāwrīqāt (*Ministry of Industry*). Various factories in Cairo, such as the *ṭarbūsh* factory, and the industries in the provinces came under the jurisdiction of this ministry.[23]

Duhamel pointed out in 1837 that although the Egyptian government had been reorganized into ministries on the European model by a French advisor, Egypt lacked the necessary personnel to operate a government according to European standards. He felt that since its leadership never changed, no matter what form the government took, the confusion which had existed under the previous organization would remain and would probably increase, as reorganization always involved confusion. He, at that time, asked Muḥammad ʿAlī for some clarification about the changes but noted that the viceroy was in no position to reply, for he was equally confused about the reforms he had sanctioned.[24]

To assist the *wālī* in his task of coordinating the administration and to free him from the burden of details, *Qānūn as-Siyāsat-nāmah* also provided for the establishment of a privy council (*shūrā khāṣṣah*) composed of a *nāẓir* and seven officials, corresponding to the number of ministries created by the *qānūn*, together with their assistants and scribes. A privy council had, in fact, existed prior to the 1837 reorganization of the administration, although it is not known precisely when it was first established. It was originally called the *Dīwān al-Maʿūnah* or *Muʿāwanah* (assistance) or *al-Maʿīyah as-Sanīyah* (the royal suite) until 1248/1832–33, when it became known as *Shūrā 'l-Maʿūnah* (*Muʿāwanah*). In 1260/1844–45 it was designated by its former name, *al-Maʿīyah as-Sanīyah*. The privy council's duties consisted of advising the Pasha on various projects, suggesting measures to improve the country, promulgating the Pasha's orders, verifying the execution of all official business, resolving administrative and financial difficulties referred to it, and bringing together financial statements to be presented to the Pasha. Furthermore, it possessed specific judicial powers in connection with violations of administrative regulations by governmental officials, but these powers were later transferred to a special administrative court (al-Ḥaqqānīyah) established on al-Muḥarram 3, A.H. 1258 (February 14, 1842), to deal with disciplinary and administrative matters previously falling within the jurisdiction of *al-Majlis al-ʿAlī*, *al-Majlis al-Kabīr*, and the privy council.[25] So that the Pasha might be kept well informed of the state of the country, the members of the privy council had the additional responsibility of studying the reports (*jurnāls*) received from the various departments and the resolutions passed at the annual meeting of the general advisory council composed of directors (*mudīrs*) of the *dīwāns* and notables nominated by the Pasha and then of communicating to him the most essential information contained in these documents. Despite the provisions carefully laid down by *Qānūn as-Siyāsat-nāmah*, the privy council never functioned very efficiently; its membership was changed frequently, largely because of disclosures of corrupt practices within the council. In 1841, for example, its president (*nāẓir*), Ḥusayn Pasha, who reportedly used his office for increasing his own personal fortune, was finally denounced to Muḥammad ʿAlī, and the other members of the privy council, all of whom were notorious for their venality, were also punished by the Pasha.[26]

Government at the provincial level evolved gradually under Muḥammad ʿAlī's guidance. The form of decentralized provincial government which had existed in Mamlūk times was not restored by Muḥammad ʿAlī when he first came to power and would have been impracticable, in any event, so long as the country remained disunited and in a state of flux. In the early years of his reign, therefore, Muḥammad ʿAlī simply appointed *kāshifs* to govern those parts of the country under his control, meeting with them periodically and informing them of his wishes with regard to taxation, collection of crops, irrigation works, and other administrative duties. Those parts still under Mamlūk domination were ruled by the beys through *kāshifs* whom the beys themselves appointed independently of the government at Cairo. Then, when Muḥammad ʿAlī achieved sovereignty of the entire country after his destruction of the Mamlūks, he merely divided Egypt into administrative units, whose boundaries fluctuated, to meet administrative necessities and appointed officials to govern them.[27] No officer of rank equal to the bey of Mamlūk times was given complete control of provinces (al-Jabartī did, however, refer in 1817 to governors of provinces, *ḥukkām al-aqālīm*). *Kāshifs* were appointed to supervise the larger administrative units and *qāʾimmaqāms* administered the cantons (*nāḥiyahs*), the smallest administrative units.[28]

The introduction of long-fiber cotton in 1821 promised to provide Muḥammad ʿAlī with a new source of income to carry out his ambitious schemes. Thereafter, the government was frequently reorganized to maximize financial returns and increased in complexity as the business of government became more complex. In fact, military expansion, which had begun before 1821, was accelerated after 1821 when it became financially feasible. Armies were sent against the Greek insurgents and against the Wahhābīs in Arabia, where new disturbances in 1824 required the dispatch of an expeditionary force to maintain order. An army was stationed in as-Sūdān to retain control and a large military establishment was kept in Egypt to check insurrectionary tendencies within the country. The reorganization of the army, the building of a navy, the extension of factories, the construction of palaces, and the development of public works were carried out simultaneously and saw their greatest activity in the optimistic decade of the 1820's when cotton was king and all things seemed possible. The existing governmental organization no longer sufficed for satisfying the increased demands for soldiers, for close supervision of the cultivation of cotton and other crops, and for efficient tax collecting. Muḥammad 'Alī, therefore, decided in 1824 to create provincial governments and to assign to them many of the powers concentrated in the hands of officials in Cairo.[29]

TABLE 2. Egyptian administrative divisions in 1826[a]

Ma'mūrīyah (province)	*Qism* (department)	*Khuṭṭ* (district)	*Nāḥiyah* (canton)
	Lower Egypt		
	1. Qalyūb	3	9
I	2. Bilbays 3. Shābih	6	20
II	4. Mīt Ghamr 5. al-Manṣūrah	4	17
	6. Dimyāṭ	3	9
III	7. Ṭanṭā 8. Fuwwah 9. al-Maḥallah	7	28
IV	10. Milīj 11. Minūf	4	16
V	12. Nakhilah 13. Damanhūr	4	16
	14. Gīzah	2	7
	Upper Egypt		
	15. Aṭfīḥ	—	—
VI	16. Būsh 17. Banī Suwayf	— —	— —
	18. Fayyūm	—	—
VII	19. al-Minyā 20. Manfalūṭ	4	—
	21. Asyūṭ	—	—
	22. Girgā	—	—
	23. Qinā	—	—
	24. Isnā	—	—

[a] John Bowring, "Report on Egypt and Candia," A Report addressed to the Right Hon. Lord Viscount Palmerston and presented to both Houses of Parliament, House of Commons, Sessional Papers 1840, vol. XXI: *Reports from Commissioners*, vol. 6, 120; Jean Deny, *Sommaire des archives turques du Caire*, Société royale de géographie d'Egypte, publications spéciales (Cairo, 1930), 130.

Accordingly, in Rajab, A.H. 1241 (February–March 1826), Egypt was divided into twenty-four *qisms* (departments), some of which were grouped into provinces (*iqlīms*, also referred to as *ma'mūrīyahs*). Fourteen *qisms* were located in Lower Egypt and ten in Upper Egypt (see Table 2, p. 87).

In 1245/1829–30 a new administrative unit, the *mudīrīyah*, was added to those of 1826 and was formed by grouping a number of provinces together under a *mudīr*. The first *mudīrīyah*, the *Mudīrīyah* of the Central Provinces, joined two provinces in Middle Egypt, Banī Suwayf and al-Minyā. It was governed first by Aḥmad Ṭāhir Pasha and then by Maḥmūd Efendī who replaced him in 1250/1834–35. Other *mudīrīyahs* were organized subsequently.

	Mudīrīyah	*Date established*
I	Banī Suwayf and al-Minyā	1245/1829–30
II	al-Gharbīyah	1248/1832–33
III	ash-Sharqīyah	
IV	al-Minūfīyah	1249/1833–34
V	Buḥayrah	
VI	Gīzah	
VII	Asyūṭ and Girgā	
VIII	Qinā and Isnā[30]	

The chief provincial officials and the administrative units under their jurisdiction were as follows:

Official	*Unit*
Mudīr	*Mudīrīyah*
Ma'mūr	*Ma'mūrīyah* (province)
Nāẓir (or *kāshif*)	*Qism* (department)
Ḥākim al-khuṭṭ, assisted by the leading *shaykhs*	*Khuṭṭ* (district)
Qā'immaqām	*Nāḥiyah* (canton)
Shaykh al-balad	Village
Shaykh al-ḥiṣṣah	*Ḥiṣṣah* (portion of village).

These officials were charged with administrative, financial, and police duties and were responsible for the area under their control. Their duties were clearly defined in the various ordinances which were promulgated from time to time. The most important of these was the

Lāʾiḥat zirāʿat al-fallāḥ watadbīr aḥkām as-siyāsah biqaṣd an-najāḥ which was published in December 1829–January 1830 (Rajab, A.H. 1245).

This *lāʾiḥah* (ordinance) was a formal code to guide the provincial administrators and to insure that the administration was carried out efficiently but not unjustly. Checks and balances of every kind were provided to prevent negligence either by officials or *fallāḥīn*. Protective measures for the peasants, who received the right of petition and redress, were included. Unlimited or unrestrained punishments were prohibited by regulation and every infraction of the ordinance had its specific punishment. The ordinance included about seventy violations punishable by bastinado,[31] remittance, prison, or a combination of the three. The violations covered negligence by administrative officials or *fallāḥīn*, thefts, the cutting of dikes, flight from the land, evasion of conscription, conflicts between *fallāḥīn*, murders or injuries by violence, and malversation of any kind. Certain matters included in the regulation were relegated to the *Sharīʿah* courts for judgment, but most violations were judged by members of the civil administration. Although the *Lāʾiḥat zirāʿat al-fallāḥ* was never fully complied with, it does give some idea of the inner workings of the provincial governments by listing the titles of the provincial officials, describing their duties, indicating the type of problems with which the administration was confronted and the methods used to deal with them, and, finally, by enumerating the punishments for violations.[32] The following is a detailed study of the administrative officials and their functions in the provinces as represented in this government ordinance and other sources.

Mudīr. This official was responsible for the execution of the Pasha's orders in his *mudīrīyah* and especially for the collection of taxes and arrears. His duties included the maintenance of the dikes and canals, the supervision of the manufactories in the *mudīrīyah*,[33] and the issuing of directions regarding the sowing of crops and their irrigation. If additional workers were required anywhere in the *mudīrīyah* for the cultivation of land, it was the *mudīr's* responsibility to provide them and to supply whatever other assistance was needed. He was also to render justice impartially within the area of his jurisdiction and to supervise the warehouses (*shūnahs*) and stores and the actions of their employees. Finally, he was required to present to the Ministry of Interior a detailed weekly report (*jurnāl*) concerning his *mudīrīyah*.[34]

Ma'mūr. Prior to the establishment of *mudīrīyahs*, the provincial officials had received directives periodically from the central *dīwāns* located at Cairo. Instructions dealing specifically with agricultural matters had been issued by the *Majlis al-ʻĀmir*.[35] Later, however, instructions were sent to the *ma'mūr* by his *mudīr* with whom he consulted on all matters concerning his *ma'mūrīyah*. Upon receiving his instructions from Cairo,[36] the *ma'mūr* held a meeting of the leading officials under his jurisdiction (*nāẓirs al-qism*, *ḥākims al-khuṭṭ*, and the great *shaykhs*) at which they discussed the problems of distributing the crops which were to be cultivated, taking into consideration the available cultivators and the amount of cultivable land within the confines of each *nāḥiyah*. They also discussed the distribution in every village (*balad*) of water-raising devices (*sāqiyahs*, *tābūts*, and *shādūfs*).

The *ma'mūr* bore ultimate responsibility for all the work in the villages under his supervision. He therefore sent out inspectors to see that none of the *fallāḥīn* were neglectful of their tasks and demanded detailed registers from each village of the crops actually sown. He also advised on the planting of trees near suitable waterways. He made personal tours of inspection in all of the *nāḥiyahs* and heard cases against officials, ordering, where necessary, the restitution of wrongful demands and punishing the offenders by committing them to prison in accordance with regulations. Periodically, he would summon the *nāẓir al-qism* and the *khuṭṭ* officials to discuss with them measures to improve the administration of the districts and the discharge of taxes. He would also inquire of them concerning the manner in which the various officials in the *ma'mūrīyah* performed their duties. He required that they should not only investigate carefully the manner in which officials carried out their duties but also the way in which they acquired their food, whether by purchasing it at the current price or for less or acquiring it at no cost.

The *ma'mūr* had also to see that taxes were collected and crops brought to the government *shūnahs*. In instances where taxes remained in arrears, the *ma'mūr* summoned the *shaykhs* from the *khuṭṭs* and instructed them to make up these arrears within a fixed time. If, however, villages remained in arrears, the *ma'mūr* tried to find some satisfactory way of enabling the cultivators to pay their taxes; if he failed in this, he then made adjustments at the beginning of the financial year to enable the cultivators to pay at least part of their taxes in kind after the harvest.

The *ma'mūr* was required, also, to search for *fallāḥīn* who had abandoned their land—usually to escape conscription or the burden of taxation—and to bring them back. When fugitives from other *ma'mū-rīyahs* were found in his area, he was obliged to deliver them up. In conjunction with this duty the *ma'mūr* had the additional responsibility of ascertaining whether the passes issued to peasants having legitimate reasons for leaving their villages were being bestowed in accordance with regulations. Finally, the *ma'mūr* was responsible for the industrial works carried on in the province.[37]

Nāẓir al-qism. The *nāẓir* was responsible for all the work performed in his department. He appointed a *qā'immaqām* and a *khawlī* to serve in each village and supervised their activities as well as those of the *khuṭṭ* officials; but to see that work was being carried out correctly, he traveled continually from one village to the other. In the villages, he inspected the registers to determine whether the monthly deliveries required from them were being made. He insisted at all times that these deliveries and all other demands of the government should be made punctually and checked the accounts of the tax collectors (*ṣarrāfs*) in the villages to determine whether payments had been made. If payments had not been made, he would demand an explanation from the *shaykhs al-ḥiṣṣah* whom, if they could present no legitimate excuse, he would punish for failing in their duties.

It was the *nāẓir's* responsibility, also, to inspect all dams and irrigation works before the annual inundation of the Nile and to determine whether they were in working order. If they were not and he needed help to correct the situation, he could request the *ma'mūr* to supply men from outside his department to assist him. He had the additional responsibility of ascertaining whether any of the land which was uncultivated at the time of the Cadastre of 1813–14 and classified as *abʻādīyah* land had become cultivable because of adequate watering. If so, he was authorized to lease this land to any diligent cultivator desiring the benefits which could be derived from it, provided the peasant agreed to reclaim it.

Furthermore, he conferred with the great *shaykhs* concerning the even distribution of land and labor among the villages, arranging for a more equitable redistribution whenever necessary. He also demanded of the great *shaykhs* that they supply him each month with a list of fugitives from the land. He then sought them and if they had escaped to a village in another province he applied to the *ma'mūr* about them.

When they were returned, the *nāẓir al-qism* listened to their complaints; if he found they were justified, he punished the *qā'immaqām*, *shaykh*, or *ṣarrāf* concerned and insisted upon an end to the abuses which gave rise to the peasants' complaints.

The *nāẓir al-qism* also supervised the activities at the *shūnahs* and exercised control over their employees, punishing them, as well as any other officials in his department, for even the slightest misconduct. At harvest time, the *nāẓir* sent to the *qā'immaqāms* sealed weights and measures and then sent out spies (*baṣāṣīn*) to see that these weights and measures were actually used by the employees at the *shūnahs* who might otherwise try to cheat the *fallāḥīn*.[38] The *nāẓir* was particularly careful that the *ṣarrāfs* in the *nāḥiyahs* should perform their tasks with scrupulous accuracy and honesty. He exercised judicial functions, as well, by hearing cases which fell within the scope of administrative law, referring the cases under religious law to the proper authorities. Finally, the *nāẓir al-qism* was responsible for the industrial work carried out in his department. Then, each month, he sent a report to the *ma'mūr* of his province, giving full details on all pertinent matters, such as the state of public works and agriculture in his department.[39]

Muḥāsib of the qism. The departmental accountant (*muḥāsib*) controlled the financial administration of the *qism*. He was responsible for the activities of the *ṣarrāfs* in the *nāḥiyahs* and therefore would not allow any tax collector who had failed to clear his accounts for the previous year to collect taxes in the villages. Furthermore, deficits appearing in the accounts of a *ṣarrāf* had to be paid by his guarantor, the supervisor of the *ṣarrāfs* (the *mubāshir*). Once the *ṣarrāfs* had cleared their accounts with the *muḥāsib*, they were allowed to return to their *nāḥiyahs*. The *muḥāsib* continued to supervise their activities, however, demanding promptness in the exercise of their duties and requiring monthly statements of their collections. In addition to supervising the *ṣarrāfs*, the *muḥāsib* also supervised the clerks (*kātibs*) of the warehouses of the bleaching establishments (*mabyaḍah*) as well as the warehouses to which crops were brought.[40]

Ḥākim al-khuṭṭ and mashāyikh al-khuṭṭ. After the meeting of the officials of the *ma'mūrīyah* where the *khuṭṭ* officials were told the quota of crops required by the government from each district, they, in turn, assembled the officials in each of the cantons of their *khuṭṭ* (the *qā'immaqāms* and *shaykhs al-ḥiṣṣah*), informed them of the amounts which would be required from each *nāḥiyah*, and arranged for the distribution of irrigation machines. Then, when the inundation occurred, they supervised the irrigation of the villages, gave instructions for the distribution of land to be used for each crop, and made certain that the *shaykhs* and *fallāḥīn* prepared the land and sowed the crop in accordance with the instructions laid down by government regulations. If they discovered any shortages of animals or seed in a village, they were required to make up the deficiencies from other villages in the district.

Once sowing had been completed, the land was surveyed and a register listing the amounts due from each peasant prepared, sealed by the *qā'immaqām*, and sent to the council (*dīwān*) of the *ma'mūrīyah*. The *fallāḥīn* were not required, however, to pay the amounts listed in the register if the yield had failed to meet expectations, but it was essential for the *ḥākim al-khuṭṭ* to inform his superior, the *nāẓir*, of this fact so that he in turn could pass on the information to the *ma'mūr*. Before doing so, the *ḥākim al-khuṭṭ* had first to make certain that the actual yields had been turned over at the time of the harvest. For this purpose he supplied at harvest time guards (*ghafīrs*) and measurers of grain for the threshing floors of each village and instructed the village scribe to be present each day at the threshing floor to record the amount being threshed. The scribe's daily record was then turned over to the *qā'immaqām* who, in turn, supplied a copy to the *ḥākim al-khuṭṭ* and the *shaykhs al-khuṭṭ* to serve as a check-list for them against the amounts actually received in the *shūnahs*. If the anticipated yields had actually been produced, the *fallāḥīn* were, of course, required to pay their taxes in full. Furthermore, any *fallāḥ* who was in arrears had both the amount of his arrears and his current taxes deducted from the crops which he brought to the warehouse.

The *ḥākim al-khuṭṭ* and *shaykhs al-khuṭṭ* were required to secure the collection of all taxes. For this purpose they toured the villages under their supervision continually, calling monthly meetings of the *nāḥiyah* officials (*qā'immaqām*, *shaykhs al-ḥiṣṣah*, and *ṣarrāf*) and examining the registers of the canton, *ḥiṣṣah* by *ḥiṣṣah* and name by name. If they discovered that landholders had delayed payment, they then inquired of the delinquent taxpayers the reason for their delay, bringing pressure to bear, if necessary. They also made certain that the *ṣarrāfs* were collecting the correct amounts from the *fallāḥīn*, demanding of these tax collectors that they produce receipts or money when rendering their accounts.

In the event *corvée* labor was required for working the land or for cleaning canals and strengthening dikes, the *khuṭṭ* officials, in conjunction with the *ma'mūr*, had to arrange for such labor from within their districts or from neighboring districts. They had the additional responsibility of apportioning the government's demands for *corvée* labor for public works projects among all the *nāḥiyahs* in their district. The district officials also had specified duties with regard to the village industries; they had to supervise closely the distribution of flax by the *qā'immaqāms* and *shaykhs al-ḥiṣṣah* to the women of the village *ḥarīms* in which the flax was spun, to ascertain whether the quantity of twist returned to the warehouses was correct, and in addition to assist the *shaykhs* of the weavers in making their monthly shipments of cloth for bleaching.

The *ḥākim al-khuṭṭ* had to make certain that all peasants of the district were in their own villages and to search for fugitives. A peasant was considered a fugitive whenever he left his village without an identity card (*tadhkirah*), though he could always receive one from the *ḥākim al-khuṭṭ* and go to another *nāḥiyah*, provided the *shaykh* of his village would act as his guarantor.[41] Should the *ḥākim al-khuṭṭ* discover in his district a peasant from some other region, he was required to question him as to his name, village, and *ma'mūrīyah*. If the *fallāḥ* possessed an identity card he could remain, but otherwise the *ḥākim* was required to return the fugitive to the latter's *ma'mūr*. If the secret police or spies (*baṣāṣīn*) of the *ma'mūr* found a fugitive in a village where one of the *shaykhs* of the district resided, the *shaykh al-khuṭṭ* was punished by being required to pay the sums due from the fugitive. Should the same thing occur a second time, however, the *shaykh* was not only required to pay the sum due from the fugitive but was also dismissed from office. If a fugitive was found in a village other than in one where a *shaykh al-khuṭṭ* resided, then the *shaykh* of that village was beaten with a cudgel (*nabbūt*) and in addition was required to pay one hundred piasters to the spy who discovered the fugitive.

Finally, if the *ma'mūr* found that the *khuṭṭ* officials were neglectful of their duties, he chastised them the first time, but the second time they received corporal punishment—the *ḥākim al-khuṭṭ* receiving fifty strokes with a cane (*ʿaṣāyah*) carried out by the *nāẓir al-qism* and the *shaykhs* receiving one hundred lashes with a *kurbāj* (a whip made from the hide of a hippopotamus) executed, in this case, by the *ma'mūr* himself. If they were found guilty a third time, they were simply dismissed and replaced by other appointees.[42]

Qā'immaqām and mashāyikh al-ḥiṣṣah (*mashāyikh al-balad*). A canton (*nāḥiyah*) was a subdivision of the district (*khuṭṭ*) and was, in turn, divided into separate portions or *ḥiṣṣahs*. The chief officer in the canton was the *qā'immaqām an-nāḥiyah* (canton lieutenant) who bore ultimate responsibility for affairs in his canton, but it was the *mashāyikh al-ḥiṣṣah* who carried out most of the administrative tasks in the portions under their jurisdiction. These *shaykhs al-ḥiṣṣah* usually inherited their posts from their fathers, but they also were frequently chosen by the government for their ability, the government, in such cases, disregarding hereditary claims. In return for the duties which they undertook on behalf of the government the *shaykhs* received special grants of land and the right to employ *fallāḥīn* to cultivate it.

Among their many duties and responsibilities the protection of the peasants in their portions was one of the most important; if a *shaykh* was incapable of giving protection, then he would request assistance from the district officials, the *ḥākim al-khuṭṭ* and the great *shaykhs*. If the district officers were also unable to provide for the adequate defense of the peasants, they informed the *qā'immaqām* of this fact and then appealed to the *nāẓir al-qism* for help. Another important duty for the *shaykh* was to report to the *qā'immaqām* whenever a *fallāḥ* was missing from his *ḥiṣṣah* so that a search could be undertaken and the missing *fallāḥ* brought back. A peasant could leave his land only after receiving the consent of his *shaykh* and the *qā'immaqām* and after having obtained an identity card (*tadhkirah*) from the *ḥākim al-khuṭṭ*. Should a *shaykh* discover a stranger from another canton in his *khuṭṭ* without an identity card, he had to arrest him and send him to the *nāẓir* or *ma'mūr* or risk punishment, as set forth in the regulations, if the fugitive was found in his area at the time a search was being conducted by the authorities.

The *qā'immaqām* and the *shaykhs al-ḥiṣṣah* shared the responsibility for keeping the irrigation system in their locality in good working order. They had to arrange for the cleaning of canals and the reinforcement of dikes. Should they need help to perform these tasks, particularly if a breach occurred in the dikes which had to be repaired without delay, they could call upon the *ḥākim al-khuṭṭ* and the *shaykhs al-khuṭṭ* to bring men from other *nāḥiyahs* to assist them. At the time of the flood, the *qā'immaqām* assembled the *shaykhs al-ḥiṣṣah* to assign the tasks each had to perform, together with their *fallāḥīn*, in regulating the irrigation of the fields within the canton according to the rules of basin irrigation.

Then, when the land had been inundated and the water finally drained off, the canton officials had first to select the land for the sowing of specific crops as required by the council of the *ma'mūrīyah* and then to supervise the preparation of the land and the sowing of crops, both of which had to be done precisely in the manner set forth in the government ordinance. This done, a survey was made and then the *qā'immaqām* and *shaykhs* met to prepare detailed reports indicating the amount and location of each crop. After these reports were completed, they were sealed by the *qā'immaqām* and sent to the *nāẓir al-qism* or to the council of the *ma'mūrīyah* each *shaykh al-ḥiṣṣah* retaining a duplicate of the report dealing with his own portion.

While the crops remained in the ground, it was the constant responsibility of the *shaykhs al-ḥiṣṣah* to supervise their cultivation and irrigation and to punish any *fallāḥīn* who were negligent. If a *shaykh* discovered that a *fallāḥ* had failed to cultivate his fields as required, he punished him by whipping him twenty-five times with the *kurbāj*. Three days later the *shaykh* inspected the *fallāḥ's* fields once again and if the peasant had not yet completed the necessary cultivation the *shaykh* was authorized to whip him fifty times. An inspection took place after another three days and this time the negligent *fallāḥ* received one hundred lashes. If a peasant proved incapable of working his land, the *shaykh* was obliged to transfer it to those who were able. He could, if he found a peasant in the *khuṭṭ* who was there legally and who had no land of his own, assign it (and excess land, in general) to him as *athar* land. Frequently, however, there were no peasants in his portion who could work more land and so he had either to cultivate it himself or, if he was unable to do so, to turn it over to a neighboring *shaykh*. In instances where a *fallāḥ* needed an animal to plow his fields (his *athar* land), the *qā'immaqām* and *shaykh* either arranged for him to receive the loan of an animal from another peasant, who had completed his work, at the rate of four piasters per *faddān* for winter (*shitwī*) cultivation and three piasters for spring or autumn (*nīlī*) cultivation or else the *shaykh* would assist the peasant by supplying without charge one of his own animals for plowing. Then, at the time of summer (*ṣayfī*) cultivation the *qā'immaqām* and *shaykhs al-ḥiṣṣah* saw to the maintenance of the *sāqiyahs* and *shādūfs* and supervised their use, making certain that land in the proximity of these irrigation implements was being cultivated and redistributing it, if necessary, so that the quota for summer crops would be met.

The *shaykhs al-ḥiṣṣah*, together with the *qā'immaqām*, supervised the payment of taxes to the *ṣarrāfs* by the *fallāḥīn* to prevent any delay in the task of the former. At the same time they kept strict watch over the conduct of the *ṣarrāfs*, checking the receipts of the peasants issued by the *ṣarrāfs* against the registers in the government warehouses. If they found that a *ṣarrāf* did not exercise proper diligence in his work or if he had collected more taxes from the canton than were required, they informed the *nāẓir al-qism* and the latter investigated the charges and took proper measures to remedy the situation.

The canton officials had numerous other duties, such as providing people for the *corvée*, accompanying their men, supervising their work, and preventing their flight from the *corvée*. They also provided conscripts for the army and navy as well as workers for the industries, making for the remaining peasants an equitable redistribution of the land of those who were taken from the village. They assisted the officials in charge of the local industries (spinning and weaving) with the delivery of the flax to the village *ḥarīms* as well as with the collection of the twist, and also with the collection from the weavers of the cloth that was to be bleached. They distributed among the peasants the demands for butter as well as those for dung-cakes for the kitchens of the troops.

The officials of the *nāḥiyah*, who had almost absolute control over the peasants, were themselves controlled by their superiors lest they abuse their power by failing, for instance, to distribute all government demands fairly among the peasants in rotation or by beating the peasants on false charges or, finally, by forcing the peasants to work their lands out of turn, either without pay or to the detriment of the cultivation of the peasants' own lands. Those officials who had failed to carry out their duties as required were punished by the *ḥākim al-khuṭṭ* as stipulated in the regulations. These punishments varied. In the case of negligence in the supervision of cultivation, for example, the erring official was chastised the first time he was found guilty. The second time he received one hundred lashes with the *kurbāj*; the third time, two hundred under the supervision of the *nāẓir al-qism*; the fourth time he was dismissed and a new appointment was made.[43]

Ṣarrāf. Taxes were collected by the *ṣarrāf* of the *nāḥiyah*. Each year he received the reports of the land survey which were drawn up after the annual flood and then calculated the amount of tax in money and kind for each peasant, basing his calculations on the quantity and type of crops which the peasant had sown. His calculations also took into account the different categories of land, especially the land which was irrigated by means of a *sāqiyah*, which was more valuable and, therefore, more heavily taxed. The *ṣarrāf* then prepared a tax register containing the names of all the peasants in the *nāḥiyah*, the amount of tax which each one owed, and other pertinent information. Once the tax register was drawn up, the *ṣarrāf* was prohibited from demanding more than appeared in the register. Occasionally, however, a *ṣarrāf* attempted to circumvent this prohibition in order to make up his own losses. In such cases it was the responsibility of the *shaykhs* to safeguard the interest of the peasants by protesting against these illegal extortions. At the same time the *shaykhs* were required to assist the *ṣarrāf* in the collection of all taxes listed in the register. If a peasant failed to pay his taxes, then his *shaykh*, accompanied by the *qā'immaqām* and a *ghafīr*, demanded prompt payment from him, these officials being authorized to employ force whenever the peasant proved unwilling to meet his obligations.

Normally, a peasant met his tax commitment by bringing his crops to the government warehouse where the *shūnah* officials deducted from the total delivery the amount demanded as taxes, giving the peasant a voucher for the balance as well as for the amount deducted for taxes. This transaction was witnessed by the *shaykh al-ḥiṣṣah* and the *khawlī*[44] and sometimes by the *qā'immaqām* and the *ṣarrāf*. The canton officials were interested not only in protecting the interests of the peasant but also in ascertaining whether the quotas required of the *ḥiṣṣah* and *nāḥiyah* were being met. The peasant then brought his vouchers to the *ṣarrāf* who credited his account with their amount. The *ṣarrāf's* records had to be maintained with strictest accuracy, for they were checked against the warehouse records and the records of the *dīwān* of the *ma'mūrīyah* for discrepancies.

Not only were these tax collectors closely watched but severely punished if they failed in their duties in any way. If, for example, a *ṣarrāf* was found to be negligent, he received one hundred lashes with the *kurbāj* for a first offense. He was dismissed and replaced upon a second offense. In cases of embezzlement, he was forced to refund the money. If he could not, then his guarantor had to supply the money while the *ṣarrāf* received a jail sentence of one year in the prison at Alexandria and was denied employment by the state thereafter.[45]

Khawlī. This official was charged with the supervision of the work both on *maʿmūr* and *abʿādīyah* lands where crops such as cotton required special attention. He was to keep the *qā'immaqām* of the *nāḥiyah* and each *shaykh al-ḥiṣṣah* informed of the work. In case of neglect by the *qā'immaqām* or the *shaykhs*, the *khawlī* was to inform the *khuṭṭ* officials, the *nāẓir al-qism*, or the *ma'mūr*. He was charged also with the task of supervising artificial irrigation and making the land survey. He had to make sure that the land sown with *ṣayfī* crops was weeded and inform the *qā'immaqām* and *shaykhs* of the growth of weeds. At the time of the cotton harvest, he would check the crop. If he found that cotton had fallen to the ground because the owner had not gathered it on time, he would inform the *qā'immaqām* and *shaykhs*. He informed them also if he found that the owner had not extracted the seeds from the flax on time. If he found a *fallāḥ* wronging another *fallāḥ* at the time of sowing or harvesting, he investigated the cause of the argument and reported the names of the contenders to the *qā'immaqām* and *shaykhs*.[46]

Mishadd and Ghafīr. These officers checked the *fallāḥīn* daily and watched them night and day to prevent them from abandoning the village. If one of the *fallāḥīn* or *shaykhs* should run away, they were to seek him out. If a stranger came to the *nāḥiyah* secretly, they would examine him, place him under arrest, and bring him to the *qā'immaqām* and the *shaykh al-balad*. They also carried out the orders of the *dīwān* with regard to the gathering of butter, hay, and dung-cakes from the *fallāḥīn*, recruited men for the *corvée* and supervised them; they protected the spinners and *shaykhs* of the weavers; they brought the *fallāḥīn* to the *dīwān* to settle their accounts either in specie or in kind, and in general, carried out all instructions from the *dīwān*.[47]

Nāẓir and other officials of the government shūnahs. There were three types of *shūnahs* (warehouses), one for goods coming from Europe, another for goods originating in Africa and the Orient, for example, gum and ivory from Sinnār and Kurdufān and coffee from al-Yaman, and a third for Egyptian commodities. Goods in the last category entered two sorts of warehouses, one for such agricultural products as cotton, cereals, rice, safflower, indigo, opium, tobacco, silk, dried vegetables, linseed, dates, flax, and sugar, or another for manufactured goods like linen and cotton cloth, hides, saltpeter, ammonia, and mats. *Shūnahs* were further divided into wholesale and retail warehouses. The wholesale *shūnahs* for goods coming from Europe were in the hands of European businessmen and a few Levantine traders who bought these goods to sell to merchants in the bazaars and to the agents who traded in as-Sūdān. The retail *shūnahs* of this category belonged to Muslim, Copt, and Jewish merchants who possessed shops in the bazaars. The *shūnahs* for merchandise from Africa and the Orient, with the exception of mocha coffee from al-Yaman, which was a government monopoly, belonged to local merchants. The *shūnahs* for Egyptian products which were exported belonged to the government, whereas the *shūnahs* which contained produce for internal consumption, with the exception of certain foodstuffs traditionally disposed of by the government, were in the hands of merchants who had booths in the covered markets.[48]

Only the *shūnahs* that received Egyptian commodities handled by the government are pertinent for discussion here. This *shūnah* was headed by a *nāẓir* who supervised the issuing of receipts or vouchers given to persons who brought crops or manufactured items to the warehouse. He was responsible for seeing that every item as it came from the village was checked against the statement prepared in the village. The amounts received had to conform exactly to the information given by the *ṣarrāf* of the *nāḥiyah*; only then did the *nāẓir* place his seal upon the vouchers. The warehouse scribe (*kātib*), the grain measurer (*kayyāl*), and the weigher (*qabbānī*) carried out the various tasks connected with the preparation of these vouchers and every precaution was taken to prevent their dishonesty or their defrauding the people. For example, all weighing and measurements had to be checked by a second grain measurer and weigher. The scribe had to prepare a statement of accounts every day and explain any deficiencies appearing in his records. Also, the *nāẓir* controlled the brokers (sing. *simsār*) who priced the crops such as flax, cotton, and indigo to see that they placed neither a higher value on the crops of those who had bribed them or a lower value on the crops of those who had failed to bribe them. If the *nāẓir* suspected the brokers, he informed the *ma'mūr* who ordered a re-evaluation of the crops by another broker and corrected any inaccurate evaluations which were revealed. Generally speaking, it was the *nāẓir's* responsibility to control all the employees of the warehouse to see that they took nothing from the peasants which was not stipulated in the regulations.

The *nāẓir* was assisted by an accountant (*muḥāsib*) who checked the warehouse accounts and turned them over to the *dīwān* of the *qism* at the prescribed times. The accountant also informed the warehouse overseer whenever the villages failed to produce their quotas and the *nāẓir* then passed on this information to the *ma'mūr*. The accountant also saw to it that the seeds which had been issued to the peasants were deducted from the amounts delivered by them after the harvest.

The warehouse *nāẓir* also supervised the loading of the boats, allowing crops to be loaded only on those boats accompanied by a skipper (*qapūdān*) who came from the region, and thus, presumably, he protected the interests of the region against dishonest boatmen. The *nāẓir* made certain that the boats were not loaded beyond their capacity. Furthermore, he took a sample of each crop as it was being loaded and put it in a sealed jar, which he then entrusted to the custody of the skipper of each boat and for which he received a receipt in return. Each boat then proceeded to one of the central warehouses established by the government where the skipper was required upon his arrival to relinquish the samples in the sealed jar to the *nāẓir* of the central *shūnah*. The latter determined whether the quality of the shipment was the same at the end of the voyage as it had been at the outset, basing his judgment on a comparison between the sample and the rest of the consignment. These precautions were necessary because some of the boatmen sprinkled water on their shipments and added sand as well, in an attempt thereby to defraud the *nāẓir* of the central warehouse; if they were found guilty of this offense they faced confiscation of their boats and life imprisonment in the prison at Alexandria.[49]

Nāẓir of the shipyards. This official had to furnish the skipper of each boat with a sealed certificate (*tadhkirah*) stating its capacity and to issue instructions to all *qapūdāns* to guard against overloading. The object of this regulation was to prevent boatmen from overloading their vessels, thereby risking water damage or even total loss of cargoes belonging to the government.[50]

Despite this tight administrative organization established by Muḥammad ʻAlī, the provincial officials were unable to satisfy the constant demands made upon them for crops, taxes, and men to serve in the army. Changes occurred daily in every branch of public affairs, owing, Colonel Patrick Campbell maintained, "to the government's feeling the evils of many parts of its system, and wishing to correct them, without knowing how to do so, and which causes a constant vacillation and change in its measures."[51] Muḥammad ʻAlī changed his officers in the central administration constantly; he sent out the highest government officials to the country on tours of inspection; councils of provincial administrators and top government officials conferred frequently; the

Pasha made personal inspection tours and met with provincial officers to discuss agricultural matters. Nevertheless, crops failed to meet expectations, taxes were greatly in arrears, and the *fallāḥīn* were crushed under the burdens imposed upon them.

In 1826 Muḥammad 'Alī ordered his principal officers to make a tour of the provinces to ascertain the reasons for the general decline which had set in. They were ordered to report to him all cases of dilapidations and avanias committed by the provincial administrators and to enter into every detail of administration in the provinces, rendering justice in every case and punishing those who had expropriated or misappropriated funds. They were to make every effort to obtain tax arrears amounting to 133,000,000 francs and, finally, they were to suggest means for remedying the situation. Among the officers sent were the former *kikhyah bey*, Maḥmūd, who had been dismissed from office in 1826 and replaced by Sharīf Bey;[52] the new *kikhyah bey*, Sharīf; the *daftardār* Ḥamīd Pasha; Ibrāhīm Aghā; and others. It was Henry Salt's opinion that the persons whom Muḥammad 'Alī had sent to the provinces were not likely to find the trouble or, if they did, to tell him the basis for it. At any rate, the investigators were displeased with the arrangements which kept them in the provinces. So that nothing would be neglected while these officers were traveling, Muḥammad 'Alī dealt with all government business in the capital. He sat in judgment in his *dīwān* every day from eight to ten hours. His activity was so great that he accomplished all current business and hoped by his example to stimulate his officers. Finally, in May 1826 he held a meeting at Ṭanṭā for three days at which his officers submitted their reports.[53]

Conditions in Egypt continued to deteriorate so that many *fallāḥīn* fled from the countryside. The causes for general misery in the country were attributed by Henry Salt to the monopoly system and to oppressive taxation. "Pharaoh," he once said, "by the advice of Joseph contented himself with a fifth but the Pasha is scarcely content with two-thirds."[54] Ibrāhīm Pasha (after his return from his campaign against the Greeks in their War of Independence) served as *kikhyah* of Muḥammad 'Alī and in this capacity called a meeting in 1829 of the principal officers of the civil and military departments of the government as well as of the important provincial officers. The assembly then discussed means by which to correct abuses and ameliorate the wretched state of the peasants without reducing taxes. This assembly, called his "Parliamento" by Ibrāhīm, sat for some time; it was presided over by Ibrāhīm and attended by four hundred persons, including Copt scribes. All members of the assembly were sworn to secrecy, the Christians on the Gospels and the Muslims on the Qur'ān. Sessions began an hour before sunset and continued through most of the night, with no one even being allowed any refreshments while the meetings were in progress. The *Lā'iḥat zirāʻat al-fallāḥ* of Rajab, A.H. 1245, was undoubtedly published in consequence of the discussions of Ibrāhīm's "Parliamento."[55]

Ibrāhīm's "Parliamento" set a precedent for assemblies of a similar sort. Each year thereafter officials selected from the leading families in the provinces were ordered by Muḥammad ʻAlī to participate in a meeting dealing with problems of rural administration. These annual assemblies were usually presided over by ʻAbbās Pasha and the results of their deliberations were submitted to Muḥammad ʻAlī for his approval. At the meetings, the provincial administrators reported upon the districts under their jurisdiction: the extent of the work carried out on the dikes, the excavation of canals, the means which they employed to extend cultivation, and their success in the collection of taxes.[56]

Muḥammad ʻAlī was not prepared, however, to relinquish the direction of the administration to anyone. Instead, he continued to exercise personal control over every phase of government. He became particularly engrossed in the conduct of the internal affairs of Egypt after the successful conclusion of the first Syrian War. In October 1833 he explained to Colonel Patrick Campbell, the British Consul-General, that he had had enough of wars during his life and that he was now desirous of peace and "of attending to the administration of his dominions." This, in fact, seems to have been his main objective for several years. He accordingly made periodic tours in the countryside to inspect the manner in which the work and tax collection were handled by his administrators; he examined cultivation, canals, and *shūnahs*; and he received reports regarding the conduct of government officials. He visited the Delta provinces in October 1834 and in February 1835, while Ibrāhīm Pasha replaced him in Cairo; he traveled to Upper Egypt as far south as Isnā, accompanied by the consuls of France, Austria, and Russia. Muḥammad ʻAlī remained several days at various points en route where he examined the accounts of the governors and the *shaykhs* of the towns and villages; he studied every small detail of rural economy and gave the impression of being a farmer inspecting his property rather than a prince visiting his state. In 1837 Colonel Duhamel mentioned that for the preceding two years Muḥammad 'Alī had moved about constantly, assuming that if he inspected everything personally the land would be cultivated with greater care and his employees would find it difficult to cheat him.[57] It was, however, unfortunate that these efforts of the Pasha were to lead to no vital or lasting administrative reforms.

CHAPTER VI

THE FAILURE OF THE EGYPTIAN ADMINISTRATIVE SYSTEM: CIVIL SERVICE AND GOVERNMENT REGULATION OF THE AGRICULTURAL POPULATION

> If the Lord had provided him with a sense of justice equal to his qualities of determination, leadership, energy, organizing ability, and capability, he would have been the miracle of his age.
>
> al-Jabartī, IX, 199 (IV, 258)

The prime objective of Muḥammad 'Alī's administrative policy had been the creation of an efficient instrument for carrying out his ambitious schemes; yet none of the administrative changes which he had introduced in pursuit of this objective had produced the desired effect. In fact, disorder reigned in every part of the government with the situation becoming progressively worse. The principal causes for the failure of this administrative policy lay in the character of the government bureaucracy, in the policy of government control and supervision of the economic activities of the agricultural population, and, finally, in the unrealistic financial demands upon the Egyptian people made by the Pasha.

Muḥammad 'Alī frequently complained that he could rely upon no one to implement the policies he had laid down and a number of Europeans felt that he was justified in his complaints, observing that once a project left the Pasha's personal supervision it atrophied, remaining unfinished or badly directed. They placed the entire blame for this situation upon Muḥammad 'Alī's officers, accusing them of indolence and incompetence. These foreign observers failed to perceive, however, that the Pasha was himself largely responsible for the deficiencies of the government bureaucracy. As early as November 1816 (al-Muḥarram, A.H. 1232) al-Jabartī noted that Muḥammad 'Alī tended to surround himself primarily with persons who never disagreed with him and who showed a general disposition to approve and assist him in his various projects for increasing his revenues.[1] Those who continued to remain close to the Pasha were usually servile apologists and frequently adventurers seeking to further their own interests and personal gain by flattering him, stimulating in him illusions of power, and encouraging new works which were neither within his means nor of profit to the country. Furthermore, the entourage which surrounded Muḥammad ʻAlī became a theater of intrigue and rival pretensions. By 1837 there were two parties who contended for his favors and exclusive confidence. The first party called itself the "Moreate" party and consisted of several Turks who had followed Ibrāhīm Pasha in the war in the Morea. They had been placed in their position through Ibrāhīm's influence. The second was the Armenian party which was headed by Yūsuf Bāghūṣ Bey and included all the young men who had been educated in France and England. The nucleus of a third party formed around Ibrāhīm Pasha and was composed of his generals, who were devoted to him. This group sympathized more with the "Moreate" party.

The men closest to the Pasha in 1837 were Samī Bey, Aḥmad Pasha Miniklī, Sharīf Pasha, Muṣṭafā Pasha, Mukhtār Bey, Yūsuf Bāghūṣ Bey.[2] With the exception of the latter, none of the group who surrounded Muḥammad ʻAlī was sincerely devoted to him, despite the honors and riches he heaped upon them. They were attached to him by self-interest alone. None of his subordinates dared to contradict the Pasha or show disapproval of any of his projects, for if one did he would be certain to be considered an enemy and sent away to some distant place or exiled from the country. Consequently, no one would tell him the truth, neither his Turkish officers nor the foreigners in his employ. The Egyptians whom he had sent to Europe on educational missions and who occupied government posts were equally reluctant to reveal their true opinions. His circle of advisers chose, rather, to treat him as though he were an oracle, echoing his every statement and pretending his judgments were infallible. At the same time no one would act quickly, being certain that a change in plans would unquestionably be announced. The result was that although Muḥammad ʻAlī was despotic, he was badly obeyed.[3]

Convinced as he was that "the Government best calculated to increase the power, the happiness and the prosperity of a country was that which combined justice and humanity and talent for government with absolute power,"[4] Muḥammad ʻAlī refused to delegate power to anyone and thereby failed completely to develop among his officials an *esprit* which could stimulate in them a sense of responsibility or a concept of public service. Colonel Duhamel, the Russian Consul-General, once expressed the opinion that the worst calamity which had befallen Muḥammad 'Alī's government was the necessity of employing Turkish officials for public offices. There were Turks, he said, who were honest men of good faith, but those who had come to Egypt had come to seek positions and to make a fortune. All that could be said of them was that they had all the vices and none of the virtues of their race. Individuals with any principles of morality, honor, probity, or patriotism were rare exceptions. It was not to be wondered at, then, that all the best intentions of the viceroy were misunderstood, that the vicious and vexatious orders which were issued were carried out too rigorously. Each public functionary in his own sphere was guilty of the most shameful dilapidations and the most crying exactions.[5] The administration was, consequently, corrupt from top to bottom. Everyone, as Hamont reported, cheated the government or the *fallāḥīn*:

> The inspectors sell themselves to the governors, then the latter fleece the *fallāḥ*. Everyone, to the lowliest servant of a miserable Turk demands money from the inhabitants. Taxes, judgments, favors, everything is arbitrary, and this arbitrariness spreads each day.[6]

There was no government order which could not be circumvented for a price. The influential people in the country were allowed every privilege and took advantage of every situation. Collusion and venality appeared in the survey of the land, in the collection of taxes, in the transport of goods to government *shūnahs*, in the weighing and in the measuring, and the spoils were shared by all concerned. If anyone was caught by a government inspector in an act of corruption, he could usually bribe the official and evade the penalty subscribed. Posts were bought and sold and each official oppressed those he governed in order to redeem the cost of his office. Not the smallest government service could be obtained without some gratuity.[7]

This corruption in the administration was intensified by Muḥammad 'Alī's policy of withholding salaries and of making unreasonable demands upon those who accumulated large fortunes in his service. Nominally, government officials were well provided for to insure the maximum service and loyalty from them.[8] In reality, money was found for every purpose except the payment of salaries, which were left in arrears for months and sometimes for years.[9] When they were eventually paid, officials received government assignations which could only be redeemed at a discount. Under the circumstances they became neglectful in the performance of their duties. Although appointed to supervise the peasants, the discontented Turkish officials usually slept or sat smoking at a distance while the peasants, who were also dissatisfied, performed their work with lassitude. Most serious was their neglect of the irrigation works for which they were responsible, the fearful destruction caused by floods being frequently attributable to their negligence.[10]

The highest Turkish officials in the government suffered likewise from Muḥammad 'Alī's policy. Many of them had been drawn into the Pasha's service by promises of large salaries; in fact, some of the governors received the equivalent of 20,000 to 40,000 francs per annum, at least on paper.[11] Muḥammad 'Alī was jealous of their wealth, however, and periodically demanded financial assistance from them. In 1826 he levied "voluntary" contributions on his high officials. Each was obliged to contribute large sums and, in addition, a small sum of money was substituted for the rations allotted to them; even this sum was put in arrears.[12] When he became extremely pressed for money in 1837, he forced the high dignitaries and officers who had grown wealthy in his service to accept the responsibility for paying the taxes of insolvent villages and allowed them no opportunity to refuse.[13] Furthermore, he levied huge fines upon them, if they failed in the performance of their duties. Finally, he insulted them, often humiliated them, and resorted to extraordinary devices to obtain their complete obedience, as Colonel Charles John Barnett, British Consul-General, reported in 1843:

> A few days ago the Pasha assembled all his principal officers and called upon them to take an oath that they would serve him faithfully, and that each would report to him without reserve any case of abuse of authority or neglect of duty which might come to his knowledge.
>
> The Pasha allowed them twenty-four hours to consider the matter and to offer any observations they might think proper. The next morning the oath was taken by all upon the Koran before Ibrahim Pasha without a remark being made.
>
> This rather extraordinary and novel proceeding, as it was totally unlooked for, caused a good deal of surprise; but I fear that the expedient the Pasha has had recourse to with a view of correcting the numerous abuses which exist in all the Branches of Administration will fail of producing greater honesty and fidelity among those he employs until they are more regularly paid for the services he requires from them.[14]

Corruption, then, flourished at all levels of the administration owing to the Pasha's shortsighted policy of withholding payments of salaries to his officials and of extorting huge sums from his chief officers; since he persisted in this mistaken policy, corruption was never eradicated from his administration.

The Turkish officials were obstructive as well as corrupt. Their obstructiveness was an offshoot of the Pasha's policy of favoring European and European-trained employees. The Turkish officials, who were jealous of this special preference shown by the Pasha, placed thousands of obstacles in the path of his manifold plans under the mask of absolute obedience.[15] Their resentment mounted when Muḥammad 'Alī introduced his policy of eliminating Turks from the civil administration and of replacing them with Egyptians for whom the Turks felt nothing but contempt. The replacement of Turks by Egyptians did not occur suddenly. The idea was probably implanted in Muḥammad 'Alī's mind by Drovetti in 1826 when the latter suggested to the Pasha that he should dismiss all Turkish *kāshifs* and *qā'immaqāms* in the civil administration and that he should replace them with Egyptians. The Pasha rejected the proposal and was applauded at the time by those who disapproved of Drovetti's recommendation.[16] In 1833, however, shortly after the first Syrian War, he began to replace the Turks in the lower echelons of the civil administration when he discovered that serious abuses had crept into the administration while he had been preoccupied with the war and that many Turkish officials had been guilty of misappropriating government funds. He eliminated the Turkish intermediaries between the Egyptian *shaykhs* and himself, therefore, informing the *shaykhs* that they were to communicate directly with him.[17] "No one," he declared at the time, "will be able to complain anymore. The *fallāḥīn* are now equal to the Turks."[18] Baron de Boislecomte saw in this policy the beginnings of municipal government. "Does not this measure," he once wrote, "seem to Your Excellency to be the creation of municipal government which was the beginning of the emancipation of the communes and of European civilization?"[19] Boislecomte was, unfortunately, unduly optimistic. Conditions in Egypt were, in fact, very unlike those out of which European municipal government had evolved; the end results were equally dissimilar.

The policy of substituting Egyptians for Turks not only antagonized the latter but also failed to produce the anticipated improvement in the Pasha's financial position. Furthermore, it was extremely unpopular among the Egyptians themselves who summed up their feelings in a proverb which became current at the time: "The oppression of the Turks, rather than the justice of the Arabs."[20] There were several reasons for this attitude. First, the peasants found it difficult to conceive that one of their own people could be anything other than a *fallāḥ*, for the notion that they must be ruled by a foreign ruling class was deeply engrained in the people. Second, although they hated the Turks, they had usually found them accessible and willing to hear their complaints. Finally, they considered the policy a trick by the Pasha to extract their last para. The Turk was rapacious, but the Arab *shaykhs* were *fallāḥīn* and knew the peasants' every device to evade government extortions. "The Pasha is cunning," Hamont was told. "We are lost. They appoint *fallāḥ* governors, and they will deprive us of our last shirt!"[21] The peasants' fears were entirely justified, for the new Egyptian *ma'mūrs* and lesser officials did, in fact, prove to be less compassionate towards them than the Turks had been.[22] "Most of the Turkish governors of districts used to exercise great oppression over the fellaheen," wrote Lane, "but since persons of the latter class have been put in the places of the former, they have exceeded their predecessors in tyranny; and it is a common remark, that they are 'more execrable than the Turks.'"[23]

The Egyptian officials, more fearful of Muḥammad 'Alī than the Turkish officials had been and anxious to demonstrate their competence, performed their tasks conscientiously and rigorously, but, in so doing, produced the deplorable conditions described by Hamont:

> Vain, arrogant, servile, jealous, they exceed the limits established by their predecessors. And if Muḥammad 'Alī intended by elevating them to their positions to snatch the last sou from the *fallāḥ*, he has found in the *fallāḥ* administrators men capable of fulfilling this frightful end. Beatings never cease. The *fallāḥīn* are forced to sell everything to obtain cash: cows, calves, sheep, goats, and even the silver foot and nose rings of the Egyptian woman! They torture the men; they beat and imprison the women. The *fallāḥīn* dressed in rags occasionally excited the Turk to pity, but he can never obtain the slightest delay from his compatriots.
>
> And when they are denuded of everything, the *fallāḥ* governors, as an example to others, send them to the galleys like vagabonds, idlers, or thieves. Nobody escapes the attention of the parvenu. He knows the names of the inhabitants, their possessions; he knows their tricks, their dodges; nothing can be hidden from him; he oppresses the people, ruins villages, and everywhere he goes, misery and desolation follow him.[24]

The Egyptian *ma'mūrs* received three hundred francs per month plus a diamond decoration, a far lower salary than their Turkish predecessors had received.[25] Muḥammad 'Alī thereby reduced his own administrative costs, but increased the burden of the *fallāḥīn*, for the new officials quickly implemented their incomes at the expense of the peasants. It was, in fact, held that "an Arab who did not possess a single sou at the time of being made a shaykh or a governor, in two or three years is master of three or four horses, and twenty or thirty head of cattle, and this is screwed out of the poor fellah."[26]

In order to prevent further deterioration of conditions in the country, Muḥammad 'Alī in 1837 reconsidered the possibility of using only Turks, but because he became preoccupied with the political events leading up to the second Syrian War and with the war itself, he took no action in this direction. In fact, he paid little attention to Egyptian administrative problems during this entire period and his close advisers were careful to withhold from him the true facts concerning conditions in the country and the persistence of abuses in the provinces. After the war the consequences of his neglect became apparent, but instead of removing his Egyptian officials he employed even more Egyptians in subordinate positions to replace the large number of foreign employees, particularly French and Italian, whom he had dismissed in 1841 after deciding upon a policy of retrenchment. The administration probably suffered little from this policy, since many of these foreigners were mere adventurers who had come to Egypt to make their fortune. They had been hired by Muḥammad 'Alī originally, because he had maintained that out of fifty men who had offered their services to him, forty-nine had been false stones, but that he had given them all a chance to find the one real diamond, believing that in the end he would repay himself a hundredfold by obtaining the services of one such person.[27] He simply decided in 1841 to dispense with the dross and retain only his most trustworthy foreign advisers.

Muḥammad 'Alī's policy of using Egyptians in his administration was, undoubtedly, unpopular among the Turks, the foreign powers whose nationals had been dismissed, and the Egyptians themselves; nor did it improve the caliber of the government bureaucracy at the time. Nevertheless, it proved of great significance for Egypt in the long run, for it led to the formation of an Egyptian bureaucratic class. An important by-product of the policy was the gradual substitution of Arabic as the administrative language of the government. The administrative hierarchy, however, by no means consisted of Egyptians alone. Foreigners still retained important posts and, what is even more significant, the highest officials in the government continued to be recruited from the Turkish ruling class.[28]

The government bureaucracy, then, apathetic, corrupt, obstructive, resentful, and unpopular, impeded rather than promoted the Pasha's efforts to reform his administration, but it was not alone responsible for the failure of the Egyptian administration. The government's failure resulted, also, from its practice of controlling and supervising the economic activities of the agricultural population, a policy which began in 1812 when the commercial opportunities provided by the Napoleonic Wars and the massacre of the Mamlūks made it economically advantageous and politically feasible to seize control of the entire economic life of the country. The introduction of a government monopoly of crops began in 1812 in Upper Egypt where the entire grain crop was seized for the account of the government by the *kāshifs* who were instructed to prohibit the direct sale of grain by the cultivators to the merchants and to collect all cereal, including the amount reserved by the peasants for their own consumption. In order to insure that the peasants did not conceal any of the grain, government agents made unexpected searches in *fallāḥ* homes, confiscating whatever grain they found. The grain was then assembled at a point of debarkation, loaded on boats provided by the Pasha, shipped to Lower Egypt, and sold to Europeans at one hundred piasters per *ardabb*.

The rice crop was the first to be monopolized in Lower Egypt. Instead of the former practice whereby peasants had received advances from the merchants and had then sold them their rice crop, the government scribes now advanced seeds and animals to the peasants while the local *mubāshirs* supervised the cultivation. The harvest was taken to a designated place in the *nāḥiyah*, a fixed price was assigned to the crop, and after expenses of cultivation and the employees' salaries had been deducted, the *fallāḥīn* received a voucher for the balance. The rice was then bleached by owners of bleaching machines who were taxed at the rate of from three to five sacks of rice per year for each machine. Arrangements for the sale of the bleached rice was made by the government *dīwān*; the local merchants were charged 100 piasters or more per *ardabb* while the European merchants who bought rice for export to Europe and Turkey paid even higher prices.

The government's new policy of monopolizing agricultural produce prejudiced the interests of the Egyptian cultivators. For one thing, the peasants were obliged to turn their crops over to the Pasha at a low price and, therefore, derived no benefit from the high prices which Muḥammad ʿAlī received from the foreign merchants. Furthermore, they merely received tax credits instead of payment for their crops, suffering in this transaction also, as the tax credits were calculated in paper currency at a fixed value, rather than in its equivalent in hard currency, whose true value was far higher.[29] In addition, the peasants were the victims of the fraudulent practices of the government officials who cheated them in the evaluation and measurement of crops. Finally, they were obliged to pay the costs of transporting their crops to the central depot. Yet another hardship for the cultivators resulted in 1812 from the seizure of crops by the government, this seizure producing a serious shortage of cereal for local consumption. The only grain available was to be found in limited supplies in some of the villages of Middle Egypt, but this was shipped to the markets of Lower Egypt where it was sold at inflated prices to consumers (36 piasters per *ardabb* as compared to 7 piasters during the French occupation). As a result of all these factors, serious discontent developed among the peasantry and several uprisings against tax collectors and the troops who accompanied them occurred in 1812 in Upper Egypt; the insurgents were brutally suppressed, several villages burned, and their inhabitants massacred. Such outbursts did not deter Muḥammad ʻAlī, however. He extended his monopolies in 1816 to include flax, sesame, safflower, safflower seed, indigo, cotton, beans, and barley and, eventually, most of the crops grown in Egypt were monopolized by him.[30]

The *fallāḥīn* continued to resist the restrictions placed upon their liberty to cultivate and market their crops as they chose. In 1816 they objected to an order to provincial administrators to force them to cultivate double the quantity of flax, chick peas, sesame, and cotton over that of the previous year, since they could not sell these products for their own benefit; they opposed, too, an increase in the area given over to the cultivation of those crops subjected to the system of monopoly. They sought the intervention of influential persons on their behalf. Some were successful in receiving a waiver to the order, but the majority were unable to obtain satisfaction and were constrained to carry it out. To prevent sabotage the Pasha commanded that *fallāḥīn* who diverted even a small part of their harvest for sale on the open market were to be severely punished. The *mubāshirs* and *kāshifs* in the *nāḥiyahs* were instructed to keep strict account of all crops in the ground and to maintain a careful check until they were ready for delivery. When the harvest failed to produce the anticipated amount of wheat, beans, and maize, orders were issued to provincial administrators to force villages to make up the deficit; the *shaykhs al-balad* then apportioned their quotas among the *fallāḥīn* under their jurisdiction and collected them at 8 dollars per *ardabb*, only half of which was paid and the other half credited to the coming year's tax payment. The entire rice harvest also went to the Pasha at his price; he arranged for it to be beaten, cleaned, and bleached at his expense and established a new type of machinery for this purpose. Rice and the other monopolized cereals were destined for export at high prices. Wheat sold in the export market for as much as 150 piasters per *ardabb* in 1816 and other crops sold at prices fixed at equally high rates.[31]

Monopoly of crops was not confined to exports only, but extended also to crops intended for local consumption. *Fallāḥīn* were forced to hand over their entire crop to the government. The rice monopoly, for example, was so stringently upheld that peasants were prohibited from retaining part of their crop for private use; in 1816 Muḥammad ʿAlī went so far as to instruct the provincial administrators to forbid the population to eat beans, chick peas, fenugreek, and vegetables. Muḥammad ʿAlī bought the entire crop of beans, one of the principal foods of Egyptians, and then resold it to the native population for more than he had paid at a price which increased from 50 to 80 paras. This policy and the export of a large proportion of the harvest resulted in shortages of basic foodstuffs in Egypt. Al-Jabartī reported in the spring of 1816 that no cereals could be found on the market, that the Pasha sold 1,000 *ardabbs* of his wheat to merchants at 1,250 paras (31 piasters and 10 paras) per *ardabb*, and that it was snapped up within two days despite his order to merchants to limit the sale to two kilograms at a time. The lack of bread in Cairo caused so much protest that Muḥammad ʿAlī ordered another 1,000 *ardabbs* of wheat to be distributed to merchants at 24 piasters per *ardabb* and commanded that only one kilogram be sold per person. The monopolization of crops for sale in Egypt thus caused much hardship and bitter resentment.[32]

The monopoly system was modified in time, as it proved such a great irritant, particularly since the government's export policy frequently left an insufficient supply of food in the country. Food shortages around 1831 forced the Pasha to allow the peasants to cultivate wheat, *dhurah* (maize), beans, and barley freely. He still prohibited their direct sale to merchants for export, but he permitted the cultivators to sell them locally after tax deductions had been made, retaining the right, however, to purchase four hectoliters per hectare of each of these crops at fixed prices. Then, in 1834, he suppressed the octroi tax and permitted free trade between towns and villages of all agricultural and industrial goods. When he was asked the effect he thought his policy of relaxation would have, Muḥammad 'Alī replied "that he believed he would be a gainer in revenue and he *knew* he would gain in the affections of the people."[33] Further modifications in the monopoly system occurred, but they did not alter the system very significantly. Generally speaking, the government continued to designate the crops to be raised; the peasants were obliged to deliver their crops at government prices; crops such as wheat, *dhurah*, beans, and barley, which the *fallāḥīn* were permitted to sell locally for their own account, were heavily taxed and their prices controlled; and finally, Muḥammad 'Alī continued to reserve for himself the entire export trade.[34]

Each *fallāḥ* had an open account with the government warehouse (*shūnah*) which was located at one of the chief towns in the province. He delivered his produce to the *shūnah* at his own risk and was obliged to sell his crops to the government at fixed prices.[35] He received receipts for his crops which he had to present at the end of the year when his account was closed. After his taxes and the advances for seed, animals, and irrigation machinery (for which he paid not only the capital cost but also interest) were deducted, he found that instead of being free with a surplus for his year's labor, he was more usually in debt. The exactions of the government officials further added to the burdens of the peasant. The *fallāḥ*, who was obliged to furnish the government with one *qinṭār* of butter for every *faddān*, found that the officials invariably increased this to one and one half to two *qinṭārs* and divided the surplus among themselves. They also reduced the amount of seed which the government furnished the *fallāḥ* from one *ardabb* to three quarters of an *ardabb*. The *fallāḥ* was obliged to accept this reduced amount and turn over to the government the full measure when repaying the advance. Officials also cheated the *fallāḥ* in the weighing of and payment for the crops he produced. And, as if this were not enough, the *fallāḥ* might also find that suddenly the rate of taxes had increased. Finally, if he was by chance the creditor of the government, he would be paid in assignations which he could only redeem at a considerable discount and with much trouble. In 1836 Muḥammad 'Alī decided to pay the peasants in cash to get them to deliver the goods. Usually, however, the peasants were paid at the convenience of the district administrator rather than at the time of delivery and even more frequently the surplus was simply credited to the next year's tax bill. Therefore, the *fallāḥīn* often preferred to sell their crops underhandedly to obtain some cash to supply their basic needs, occasionally selling them at prices lower than those obtained from the government.[36]

At the end of the year, the accounts for the entire village were prepared and all the receipts had to be presented to be checked against the total amount of taxes for which the village was responsible. Frequently, when the village failed to cultivate all its land and the discrepancy was exposed, the village chief would describe the difficulties encountered during the year, but the *dīwān* accepted no excuses and told the village officials that full taxes had to be paid. Sometimes the peasants begged for delays, but the government administrators would usually bastinado the unwilling *fallāḥīn* to force payment. It was a time-honored tradition among Egyptian peasants to resist the payment of taxes, but under Muḥammad ʿAlī's government they were often unable to pay, even if they had wanted to do so. If the peasants simply could not pay, the government officials then seized the animals or other assets which could be found in the village. Often, too, taxes were collected, but were not entered in the government registers so that the peasants were forced to pay taxes twice. Sometimes the government, pressed for money, demanded taxes in anticipation for an entire year. If the Pasha decided to make some allowances to the *fallāḥīn*, his orders were frequently evaded by the *kāshifs*, *qāʾimmaqāms*, *shaykhs*, and Copt scribes who sought to benefit from such evasion.

The only escape from exorbitant demands and extortions was to abandon the land; the *fallāḥīn* and even the *shaykhs* in charge, therefore, unable to meet the demands of the government, took flight. So many peasants took this course that the governor of Buḥayrah, Aḥmad Pasha, came to Alexandria on August 31, 1827, to force all those who had fled to Alexandria to return to their villages. Muḥammad ʿAlī himself became so concerned with the problem in 1827 that he undertook a tour of parts of the country to seek some remedy for the continual emigration of peasants who could not meet their taxes. Thereafter, orders were issued periodically to seize *fallāḥīn* who left their own villages to seek employment elsewhere and the heads of villages were commanded under the most severe penalties to give up *fallāḥīn* not belonging to their villages. A *shaykh* of a village near Cairo was condemned to death in 1844 for helping peasants evade the authorities and a public notice was posted throughout Alexandria giving details of the execution and ordering all *fallāḥīn* in Alexandria to go home (see Appendix III). Troops assisted the civil authorities in collecting the peasants with their wives and children and they were marched under military escort to their villages. The abandonment of the land by the *fallāḥīn* remained a problem for most of Muḥammad 'Alī's reign; before the first Syrian War, many left Egypt, but after 1832 they sought refuge in Egyptian cities.[37]

The government administrators were obliged to use the most brutal methods to collect taxes, for if they did not, they often found themselves accused of corruption or indolence by the *dīwān* and were severely punished (see Appendix IV for a secret order obtained surreptitiously in 1833). Hamont reported a visit to a village where he met an old man who told him that on the previous day the tax collectors had come and that, although he had attempted to hide, he was found and beaten by them. He defended them by saying that they could not do otherwise, as they were under stringent instructions to collect the taxes. He went on to explain that this village had once been prosperous, but was now practically deserted as most of the *fallāḥīn* had been conscripted into the army, factories, and the *corvée*; and yet, he pointed out, the government still expected the same harvests and taxes, although most of the men had been taken away.[38] Indeed, the government accepted no losses to itself and insisted that the population which remained in Egyptian villages should bear all the taxes. If a *fallāḥ*, a village, or a canton could not pay taxes, the indebtedness had to be assumed by other *fallāḥīn*, villages, and cantons. The system of solidarity, as it was known, extended throughout the country. Bowring justified it on the grounds that the *shaykhs* or powerful landholders often attempted to shift the distribution of taxes onto the *fallāḥīn* and that with all the taxpayers responsible the peasants' interests were safeguarded. Boislecomte pointed out that the only redeeming feature of this practice was that it became the interest of the entire village to discourage indolence. Other writers noted that it had the opposite effect and made everyone indolent. Eventually the system of solidarity was revoked, in theory at least, if perhaps not in practice.[39]

The monopoly system, then, affected the agricultural population adversely. First, it deprived the cultivators of any incentive to improve themselves. Unlike the Mamlūk government, which had always left matters of cultivation entirely to the *fallāḥīn* and had allowed them, after paying their taxes, to enjoy the fruits of their labors, Muḥammad

ʻAlī left nothing to the initiative of the peasants. He excluded them entirely from the benefits which they might have derived from the commercial opportunities that had developed during his reign and then ruined them, finally, by excessive taxation. Furthermore, by introducing the monopoly system, he had brought the peasants face to face with the government bureaucracy for the first time. In the period of the Mamlūks only the village *shaykhs* had dealings with the ruling class, whereas the cultivators had enjoyed almost complete autonomy within their villages and had been safeguarded by the customary practices which had grown up and through which their interests had been protected. During Muḥammad ʻAlī's reign, on the other hand, the bureaucracy, under ruthless pressure from the Pasha, disregarded customary practices and tyrannized the Egyptian *fallāḥīn*. The result was misery and deprivation for the Egyptian agricultural population. Thus, the combination of an inefficient, corrupt, and disgruntled bureaucracy and an oppressed agricultural population contributed greatly to the failure of Muḥammad ʻAlī's administration. It is obvious, therefore, that no amount of reorganization of the administration, no mere publication of government ordinances like the *Lā'iḥat zirāʻat al-fallāḥ* could possibly have corrected the situation until these fundamental causes for failure had been eliminated.

CHAPTER VII

THE FAILURE OF THE EGYPTIAN ADMINISTRATIVE SYSTEM: FINANCES

يبني قصراً ويهدم مصراً

"He builds a palace and ruins a city [Egypt]."
(A *fallāḥ* proverb during Muḥammad 'Alī's reign)[1]

The financial pressures imposed upon the limited population of Egypt[2] constituted the third and probably the most important of the principal reasons for the failure of Muḥammad 'Alī's administration. The Pasha's resources were constantly taxed beyond their capacity by the drain placed upon them by his wars, by the remittances to the Sultan,[3] by the expenses connected with the lands he had been granted or had conquered, by the construction of palaces and factories, and by the huge public works program which he had undertaken. "We cannot be surprised at the Viceroy's pecuniary embarrassments," remarked British Consul-General Barker on one occasion, "but rather that with such means, the machinery of this extraordinary government is kept still going."[4] Muḥammad 'Alī had, undoubtedly, accomplished many projects which only a few years before would have been considered the dreams of a madman, but even these successes had only been achieved by straining the Egyptian economy to a point verging on disaster.[5]

A chronic shortage of revenue plagued Muḥammad 'Alī throughout his reign; yet he remained completely unrealistic in his demands, having exaggerated notions concerning the amount of revenue that was obtainable.[6] Exact figures concerning his revenue cannot be known in view of the absence of an accurate bookkeeping system, the secrecy which was generally maintained by the Pasha concerning the true state of his finances (or his own ignorance of the true facts), and the instability and inflationary character of his monetary system. One can, however, derive some impression from the accompanying set of figures prepared by Baron de Boislecomte.[7]

Year	*Piasters*	*Francs*
1805	5,000,000	8,000,000
1812	23,000,000	23,000,000 [*sic*]
1821	70,000,000	50,000,000
1825 and 1826	200,000,000	100,000,000
1829	230,000,000	90,000,000
1833	253,000,000	76,000,000
1846–47	300,201,729[8]	75,050,432

These figures demonstrate that the increase in Muḥammad ʻAlī's revenues in the currency of the country was over sixty times greater in 1846–47 than it had been in 1805, a colossal achievement were it not for the fact that this increase merely reflects the degree of inflation from which the Egyptian economy had suffered. The Pasha's real income is more accurately gauged by a comparison of the figures in a foreign currency, such as the franc, which remained relatively stable. Such a comparison reveals that Muḥammad ʻAlī's real income had increased at a much more moderate rate during the course of his reign, apparently reaching its peak in the 1820's[9] and falling off noticeably towards the end of his reign. Even so, this real income was nine and one half times greater in 1846–47 than it had been in 1805, certainly an impressive increase, but still one insufficient to satisfy the inordinate ambitions of the Pasha and one achieved only at great cost to the Egyptian people.

The fact is that Muḥammad ʻAlī's revenues never kept pace with his needs and the inflationary character of the Egyptian currency posed an especially vexing problem. The Egyptian monetary system requires a separate study,[10] but the table showing the decline in the value of the piaster which Baron de Boislecomte sent to his government in 1833 is pertinent here (see Table 3).[11] Muḥammad ʻAlī made several unsuccessful attempts to combat the decline of the piaster,[12] but the monetary improvisations to which he resorted weighed heavily upon the people. Foreign commerce was severely affected by the instability of the currency, as sound money disappeared from the market and insufficient specie circulated to serve the commercial needs of the country. Money transactions were rarely made without much dispute and difficulty, a serious hindrance to selling in a country of limited credit; consequently, commerce languished.[13] In Boislecomte's opinion the diminution in the value of the piaster did not affect the local population, as internal wages, prices, and taxes fluctuated in proportion to currency fluctuations.

TABLE 3. Decline in the piaster, 1773 to 1833, based on a comparison of the value of the piaster with the Spanish pillared dollar and French franc[a]

Date	Value of Spanish pillared dollar in piasters		Value of piaster in French francs	
1773	2 piasters,	10 paras	2 francs,	20 centimes
July 5, 1798	3	30	1	40
1822	12	20	—	40
1830	15	20	—	35
July 1833	19	20	—	30

[a] Georges Douin, *La mission du Baron de Boislecomte. L'Egypte et la Syrie en 1833*, Société royale de géographie d'Egypte, publications spéciales (Cairo, 1927), 130.

It was only of importance, he said, when piasters were converted into foreign specie in connection with foreign trade.[14] In actual fact, currency instability had disastrous effects internally even more than externally, since the wages and prices which the *fallāḥīn* received for their crops never matched the currency fluctuations, whereas the price of goods for internal consumption and taxes did. Thus, the cost of living rose constantly.

In an effort to combat the monetary problem, Muḥammad 'Alī resorted to devices which were economically unsound and burdensome to all classes. One such device was the issue of paper currency known as assignations, which were promissory notes on the Egyptian treasury or *khazīnah*. He used this currency locally to pay government expenses, including the payments to the *fallāḥīn* for crops he had purchased from them. At the same time he insisted upon the payment of taxes to the government in cash as well as in kind.[15] When Muḥammad 'Alī refused to accept his own assignations from the *fallāḥīn* in payment of taxes, six villages in ash-Sharqīyah rebelled in August 1826 but were repressed by a regiment of the *Niẓām Jadīd*.[16] For the most part, however, the peasants conformed to the Pasha's requirements without protest, resorting to merchants or brokers who converted the assignations at a considerable discount. Then, in 1827 the Pasha decided to save a large amount of money at the expense of the merchants and brokers who had accepted these assignations from the population. He issued an order that the circulation of Treasury assignations was to cease and that they were to be presented to the Bureau of Accounts for verification. When the merchants complied with this order, the amounts which they owed to the government were deducted from the total number of assignations in their possession while the balance was redeemed by payments in merchandise or manufactured goods, the entire transaction being conducted in such a way that the assignations redeemed by the merchants dropped in value by 18 to 20 per cent. Thereafter, the merchants refused to accept assignations from anyone except at a discount of from 20 to 30 per cent.[17]

The inflationary character of money is significant in considering the increase in taxation during Muḥammad ʻAlī's reign, particularly with regard to the increase in land taxes from which the Pasha continued to derive the major portion of his income.[18] During the last years of the reign of the Mamlūks, land taxes had fallen into three groups: (1) *al-māl al-ḥurr*, consisting of the *mīrī*, which was earmarked for the Sultan's Private Treasury, and the *fā'iẓ*, the portion of the tax assigned to the *multazim* as his profit; (2) *māl* (or *khidmat*) *al-kushūfīyah*, used to pay for the maintenance of the provincial troops and for the administrative expenses of the district governed by the *kāshif*; and (3) *muḍāf* and *barrānī* and other supplementary taxes which had originated as extraordinary taxes but continued to be collected over and above legal taxes. These taxes had been collected in specie and in kind. With the exception of the *mīrī*, taxes had not been fixed but had been limited only by the capacity of the land to produce and the *fallāḥīn* to pay.[19]

In addition to taxes paid to the *multazims* and to the government the peasants had been obliged to compensate the Copts with a service tax (*khidmah*), for during Mamlūk times only the chief scribe in the service of the bey had received an allowance from the latter of 6 paras per day to cover overhead expenses. The other Copts had received a commission on the proceeds of the taxes collected. The *kāshif's* scribe had received 5 paras per *pataque* (90 paras) of the amount collected.[20] Village scribes had received 2 paras plus the food furnished to them by the villagers. This commission, totaling 7 paras, had been in addition to the amount of the tax for which the *fallāḥīn* were responsible. When the commission had been paid in kind, it had amounted to 5 or 6 *ardabbs*[21] for each 100 *ardabbs* collected. The *massāḥ* had received 18 to 30 paras for his work, depending upon the locality. In addition to this commission, which had been legally allowed by the government, the Copts had found additional sources of income: first, they often had acted in collusion with the *shaykhs al-balad* to obtain a larger portion of the proceeds than that to which they were entitled; second, they had benefited from frauds in the surveys by coming to private agreement with individual *fallāḥīn* to make certain that the latter not be registered to pay tax for more land than they cultivated or, on the other hand, to arrange that a lesser amount be entered in the register than the actual amount of land held; and finally, the Copts often had used two different measures when calculating the payment of taxes in kind, that is, a larger measure when collecting the grain from the *fallāḥīn* and a smaller measure when making their remittances to their superiors. The total profit that the Copts had received through these extra-legal means had been divided among all the members of the Copt corporation, including the *kāshif's* scribe. The bey's scribe had maintained some measure of aloofness by not becoming involved in the details of the fraud, but he had demanded a payment in addition to his annual allowance from the bey from each *kāshif's* scribe in the province under his administration, amounting to from 2,000 to 3,000 *pataques* each (180,000 to 270,000 paras). The *kāshif's* scribe also had received additional revenue from selling the posts of *massāḥ* and village scribes to his compatriots.[22]

This financial administration had been dislocated by the French occupation and the period of disorganization which followed. Consequently, Muḥammad 'Alī's first task was to re-establish the former system of tax collection on a regular basis. Annual tax registers were prepared in which were recorded the area of inundated land and the taxes due to the government from each landholder. Ibrāhīm, accompanied by Muslim *efendīs* from the *Rūznāmah* and a number of Copt *mubāshirs*, went to al-Qalyūbīyah shortly after he was appointed *daftardār* in December 1807 in order to survey the area of irrigated land and to regulate taxes. Tax rates were fixed in accordance with the financial exigencies of the moment. In 1806 the Pasha ordered a forced collection from *multazims* and *fallāḥīn* and promised to deduct these sums from taxes and rents the following year. The *multazims* complained to the *shaykhs* of al-Azhar who spoke on their behalf to Muḥammad 'Alī. He convinced them of his pressing need for revenue and a compromise solution was reached: three quarters of the amount demanded would be paid, half by the *multazims* and a quarter by the peasants. In addition, the *multazims* were also to pay half of their *fā'iẓ* (profit). In 1807 taxes were again demanded in anticipation and included half the *fā'iẓ*, all the customary taxes, the tax paid to officials who came to villages on government business (*ḥaqq aṭ-ṭarīq*), and the new announcement tax, the *bushārat al-furdah*. The latter tax, similar to the Mamlūk tax (*'ādat awrāq shitwī waṣayfī*) that covered the cost of letters sent to villages to inform them that someone would soon be coming to collect taxes, was paid to the agent who was sent by the tax collector to announce his imminent arrival. Villages were forced to pay not only the man who made the collection, therefore, but also the person who brought the announcement of his coming. In one year a sum of 70,000 purses (35,000,000 piasters) was extorted from the peasants for the announcement tax alone. The rate of taxes rose in 1807 to 15 and 16 *pataques* (1,350 and 1,440 paras) per *faddān* as compared to 3 *pataques* (270 paras) which were paid during the French occupation.

Muḥammad 'Alī was forced to make these excessive demands at this time because his troops were owed their wages and were clamoring for payment. They indulged in all kinds of outrages against the native population; according to al-Jabartī, such atrocities were committed that the population wished that Egypt were occupied by a European power, any European power, just to rid the country of the "hordes who have no faith, no law, no rules of conduct." The soldiers replied to the people who expressed their feelings openly: "The Egyptians are not Muslims for they detest us and would prefer Christians."[23] Muḥammad 'Alī's attempts to restrain the soldiers only caused new outbursts of indignation and further demands for pay. When the troops revolted in October 1807, one report put the sum owed to the soldiers at 60,000 purses. Muḥammad 'Alī quashed the revolt, but he had to agree to pay the soldiers three months' pay, the balance of their claims being canceled. To meet this commitment Ibrāhīm levied a tax in December 1807 of 450 paras per *faddān* of irrigated land, in addition to the *ḥaqq aṭ-ṭarīq*, the *muḍāf*, the *barrānī*, and the regular taxes due to the *multazims*. One foreign representative reported that the excessive taxation weighed so heavily upon the people that the danger of another revolution appeared imminent.

Muḥammad 'Alī demanded in 1808 that each *qīrāṭ* of land be taxed 7,700 paras, but the *rūznāmjī* warned him that it would be impossible to collect taxes at this rate. When registers were finally established in the spring of 1809, taxes were divided into four categories with a difference of 100 paras between each. The first group was fixed at 800 paras and went up to 1,100 paras per *faddān*. Registers were established by the *efendīs* in Būlāq and the Copts in Old Cairo. After the annual flood of

1809 registers were again drawn up and all land was taxed at the rate of 5 *riyāls* per *faddān*, exclusive of the *barrānī* and the *khidmah.*[24] When the registers were completed, they were brought to the Pasha, then in Asyūṭ, by al-Mu'allim Ghālī, Aḥmad Efendī al-Yatīm from the *Rūznāmah*, and 'Abd-allāh Baktāsh at-Turjumān. After he had examined the registers, Muḥammad 'Alī approved and signed them. The tax rates thereafter were continually raised to meet Muḥammad 'Alī's needs and at the same time the area of land subjected to taxation was extended. The peasants continued to pay *al-māl al-ḥurr*, *muḍāf*, and *barrānī* taxes at increased rates, the *khidmah* to the *mubāshirs* and their assistants, the *māl al-kushūfīyah*, and the *ḥaqq aṭ-ṭarīq.*[25]

By 1813 Muḥammad 'Alī's landholding and administrative policies had advanced to the stage where an accurate survey of the land was urgently required to record changes in landholding, to regularize the entire tax structure of the country, and to correct the abuses of preceding years. It had always been the practice in Egypt, even in pre-Islamic times, to have periodic surveys of the land to determine how much was cultivable, as the area of cultivable land was not constant and varied from year to year depending upon the Nile flood. When Egypt had been conquered by the Ottoman Turks, a new cadastre had been carried out and a schedule of taxes established at rates to be paid when the river had reached the height of seventeen cubits, a sliding scale having been established in order to take into account the variations in the level of the river. This tax schedule had been augmented in the sixteenth century but had remained fixed thereafter, at least in theory; in fact, the fluctuation in the value of currency and the rapacity of succeeding administrators had led to the establishment of a body of taxes considered illegal, but gradually sanctified by custom. The basis for determining the tax rested upon the revenue different areas of land could produce; a fixed revenue was obtained by varying the size of the *faddān*, which fluctuated therefore between 200 and 450 square *qaṣabahs*, the length of the *qaṣabah* varying also between 3.75 meters and 3.99 meters in length.[26]

Muḥammad 'Alī's cadastral survey began in the autumn of 1813 and was completed in the spring of 1814. It was carried out by surveyors accompanied by Muslim and Christian scribes and supervised by Maḥmūd Bey, an important government official, and al-Mu'allim Ghālī, the chief of the Copts.[27] A standard *faddān* was introduced and it was decided that henceforth a uniform measurement should be used in land surveys. Uniformity was not always achieved, but on the whole it was.

The length of the *qaṣabah* was reduced to 3 meters 64 centimeters (3 m 64 c), and the total area of the *faddān* was established at 333⅓ square *qaṣabahs*.[28] Cultivators were allowed to retain possession of land classified as excess, provided they paid the additional taxes; some sold their animals and the crops that were still in the ground to raise the necessary funds. Others preferred to emigrate, but, al-Jabartī said, they often returned "like dogs because they were accustomed to such vexations."[29]

Cultivable land was taxed at specific rates for each category of land. Al-Jabartī gave rates of 10, 11, 12, 14, and 15 *riyāls* per *faddān*; Boutros Pasha Ghali said that rates varied from a minimum of 2 *michts* (2¼ piasters per *micht*, i.e., another term for *pataque*), that is, 180 paras, to a maximum of 20 *michts* (1,800 paras) in Lower Egypt and 22 *michts* (1,980 paras) in Upper Egypt.[30] Classification took into account several factors upon which the schedule of the tax was based: the quality of the land cultivated; its proximity to the Nile; local circumstances which varied from year to year, depending upon the flood; and the nature of the crop grown. The cadastral registers contained a description of each parcel of land, its dimensions, the name of the usufructuary holder, and the rate of tax so that each taxpayer knew the amount for which he was responsible. *Waṣīyah* and *ab'ādīyah* lands were excluded from the registers.[31]

All former taxes were now unified into one tax, the *mīrī* (*kharāj*), but the tax rates were fixed at a higher level than had been paid previously. Consequently, villages which were already in debt for as much as 1,000 *riyāls* found their indebtedness increased by from 10,000 to 100,000 *riyāls*. Furthermore, the increase in taxes and tax indebtedness came at approximately the same time that Muḥammad 'Alī introduced his policy of direct interference in agricultural matters, a policy which prevented the peasants from selling their produce in a free market at the current high prices.[32] The unification of taxes into one tax, however, gave a modicum of order to the tax structure of the country. It facilitated the method of tax collecting, thereby enabling Muḥammad 'Alī to introduce reforms into the financial administration, reforms designed to reduce the opportunities for malversation which the former complicated system had encouraged. It thus guaranteed that a greater proportion of the taxes flowed into the government treasury than into the pockets of the Copt scribes and the *shaykhs al-balad*.[33]

The Copts continued to collect taxes, the chief of the Copt corporation being under the supervision of the *daftardār*. Each district governed by a *kāshif* had its Copt official who kept the tax registers. His subordinates collected taxes in the villages with the assistance of the *qā'immaqām* and turned over the specie to the district *ṣarrāf* who verified it and transmitted it to the viceregal treasury.[34] Any official, either Copt or Muslim, who committed an act of embezzlement was removed from office, forced to reimburse the government, and possibly bastinadoed as punishment for himself and as an example to others. The customary service charges (*khidmahs*) collected by the Copts were abolished and replaced by a monthly salary corresponding in scale to the importance of the position of each Copt official. These were punished if they made demands beyond the compensation granted by the government. An order in 1816 prohibited *kāshifs* of *nāḥiyahs* and *mubāshirs* from taking anything for their services, other than a little bread and straw, except at official prices. They were warned that contravention of this order would be severely punished. In 1817 during the month of Rabī' al-Awwal (January–February), A.H. 1232, the Pasha called a meeting at Cairo of all provincial officials and ordered them to render an account of sums received from the *fallāḥīn* over and above the amount they had been instructed to collect. Agents were also sent to different provinces to inquire into the exactions of these functionaries. They interrogated the village *shaykhs* and noted whatever details they were able to obtain, including the number of animals, chickens, and forage that the *fallāḥīn* had given to the government officials. The people readily denounced many of the officials who were then obliged to liquidate their possessions in order to return the additional sums which they had extorted.[35]

The tax schedule established at the time of the 1813–14 cadastre did not remain static, despite the contrary claim made by Muḥammad 'Alī some twenty years later to Dr. John Bowring.[36] In point of fact, reclassifications of the land and changes in the tax schedule took place periodically after 1813–14 and were intimately connected with the economic needs of the Pasha at various stages in his reign. An early example of this fact may be seen in the augmentation of the tax schedule even before the flood of 1817. The increase was ostensibly for the purpose of providing revenues to pursue the war in al-Ḥijāz, but the Pasha did not cancel the tax increase when news of the victories of his troops in Arabia reached him. Nor did he take into account the effect which the insufficient flood of 1817 had had upon agriculture, with the result that many *fallāḥīn* abandoned their land because of their inability to pay the increased taxes.[37] Further reclassifications occurred in 1818 and 1819, although by 1819 the taxes had become so burdensome that many villages were unable to meet the government's demands. The Pasha agreed to forgo payment of tax arrears but insisted upon the payment of current taxes. Ibrāhīm, however, when he returned from his victories in al-Ḥijāz, declared that he would collect not only current taxes but also the arrears which had accumulated over a two-year period. He went with the tax collectors to al-Qalyūbīyah, al-Gharbīyah, and al-Minūfīyah to see that all taxes were paid, but many *fallāḥīn* and *shaykhs al-balad* had abandoned their villages to escape his demands. Those who had remained went into debt to pay the taxes and were forced to sell their animals, furniture, and the jewelry of their wives; there were *shaykhs* who were obliged to pay as much as one thousand *riyāls*. Ibrāhīm successfully collected 100,000 purses on this occasion alone.[38] A further tax increase was levied after the land survey of 1236/1820–21 when land was divided into classes according to its fertility; class I was fixed at 17 *pataques* (1,530 paras) per *faddān* and other lands were taxed at lesser amounts according to their quality. In 1822 taxes ranged from 200 to 2,200 paras (2 to 22 francs) per *faddān* and the land was divided into eleven classes, depending upon the quality of the land, its distance from the Nile, and the type of cultivation; in 1824, first-class land was taxed at 67½ piasters (2,700 paras) per *faddān*.[39]

Bad floods in 1824 and 1825 produced a decrease in revenue. The ill effect of the 1825 flood may be seen from the fact that the Pasha's optimistic hope of harvesting a cotton crop in 1826 of 500,000 *qinṭārs*[40] failed to materialize. The steady decline in exports from 228,078 *qinṭārs* in 1824 to 59,225 *qinṭārs* in 1828 resulted, in part, from these floods.[41] They also increased the sufferings of the people. The peasants were required to pay all their taxes, including even taxes on *sharāqī* lands (lands not inundated at the time of the Nile flood). At the same time, they were impelled to sell their animals which they needed for agricultural work and for operating irrigation machines in order to combat widespread food shortages. An accumulation of tax arrears consequently resulted which, together with the decrease in export revenues, increased the government's financial difficulties.[42] Nevertheless, the government was finally compelled to remit taxes, for the officials who were sent to the provinces in 1826 to investigate the causes for the arrears in taxes reported to Muḥammad 'Alī that the tax burden was too great and had to be alleviated. A decree, therefore, dated al-Muḥarram 4, A.H. 1242 (August 8, 1826), was issued remitting taxes on *sharāqī* lands, and a decree of the same date authorized the remission of taxes where crops had deteriorated because of dryness.[43] The schedule of taxes in 1826 on inundated lands was not reduced, however.[44]

Notwithstanding the flood of 1826, which was more favorable than those of the two preceding years, the government's financial position remained critical. In March 1827 it was estimated that taxes were in arrears for the amount of 210,000 purses[45] and government officials, factory workers, and troops unpaid for months were demanding their salaries. Muḥammad 'Alī convoked an assembly of one hundred and twenty *shaykhs* from the provinces to devise means for forcing the *fallāḥīn* to pay their taxes. After several sessions the *shaykhs* proposed the payment of arrears in instalments, the first payment of 85,000 purses to be made within a few months and the balance within two years. Although Muḥammad 'Alī agreed to this plan, he nevertheless ordered a forced levy of 80,000 purses a few months later to be paid within twenty days and also collected a "voluntary" contribution from his chief officers. A special tax was also placed upon more fertile land to compensate for losses to the public exchequer from land remaining dry and uncultivated.[46] Finally, after the Battle of Navarino (October 20, 1827) Muḥammad 'Alī devoted all his attention to the problems vexing the country with regard to agriculture, conscription, and tax collections.[47] He attempted to correct numerous administrative abuses which made the collection of taxes oppressive; he remitted the taxes of some of the poorer villages; he made some capital advances to the peasants to encourage them to extend the area of cultivation; he ordered that irrigation works be carried out; and he caused some money to be put into circulation in the provinces to ease the monetary shortage. Much of his time was spent in hearing petitions and rendering judgments.[48]

The war in 1828 between Turkey and Russia and favorable floods for several consecutive years combined to rescue Muḥammad 'Alī from his immediate financial straits, but they could not alleviate completely the economic position of the Pasha whose needs increased steadily. The crushing burden of taxation made it impossible for the *fallāḥīn* to keep abreast of the government's demands. By 1832 the figure for arrears owed by the peasants in all Egypt amounted to 3,500,000 dollars.[49] Nevertheless, the Pasha increased taxes in 1833, dividing the land into nine classes taxed at rates ranging from 11 piasters to 72 piasters (from

5 to 30 francs) as shown in Table 4.[50] All these increases in the rates of the land tax during Muḥammad 'Alī's reign were established on no other basis than the government's estimate of the people's capacity to

TABLE 4. Classification of land for tax purposes, 1833, in piasters and in paras[a]

Classification	Piasters	Paras
First-quality land		
Good soil, well cultivated	72	2,880
Mediocre	67½	2,700
Less good	63	2,520
Second-quality land		
Good	55	2,200
Mediocre	50	2,000
Less good	36	1,440
Bad land		
Grade 1	27	1,080
Grade 2	18	720
Grade 3	11	440

[a] Georges Douin, *La mission du Baron de Boislecomte. L'Egypte et la Syrie en 1833*, Société royale de géographie d'Egypte, publications spéciales (Cairo, 1927), 128; Adam Georges Benis, *Une mission militaire polonaise en Egypte*, Société royale de géographie d'Egypte, publications spéciales (Cairo, 1928), II, 47.

pay and such estimates were generally more optimistic than the situation warranted.

Despite these increases in land taxes Muḥammad 'Alī was unable to liquidate his debts. At the beginning of 1834 he owed at least 31,000,000 piasters (62,000 purses) to his troops and to government employees. He tried to raise the money in the country, but conditions were so bad that he had, instead, to cancel an amount of 110,000 purses (3,000,000 dollars) which was due from various individuals, villages, and towns. The merchants came to his rescue by advancing the money he needed to meet his obligations.[51] The following year, the high loss of life during the severe epidemic of bubonic plague aggravated the situation, for Muḥammad 'Alī found that he could not possibly demand full payment of taxes and arrears from the survivors. He was forced, therefore, to cancel approximately 300,000 purses (7,500,000 dollars) as follows: 70,000 purses of arrears, 150,000 purses of the regular land tax, and a special tax exemption of 80,000 purses on lands which had not been adequately inundated in the flood of 1249/1833–34, on lands where public works were being carried on, and on lands where the water had remained too long and planting had not taken place early enough.[52] An increase in trade in 1835–36 relieved the situation somewhat, for the Pasha, wishing to encourage production, paid higher prices to the peasants. Most villages in Lower Egypt could, therefore, meet their current taxes in 1836 and several provinces were even able to pay off their arrears. In Upper Egypt all towns and villages also had managed to pay their current taxes by the spring of 1837, and some even paid their arrears while others arranged to pay them by installments. The total tax arrears still outstanding by the end of spring, 1837, amounted to 190,000 purses.[53] Then, in September 1837, conditions deteriorated once again when the bad flood and a drop in export prices created economic difficulties for the Pasha; it was reported that he had not been in such a serious financial situation for a long time. Famine and the high living costs prevailing in the country affected all classes.[54]

To meet this situation Muḥammad ʿAlī convoked a council of state composed of the *mufattishes* of Upper and Lower Egypt, Salīm Pasha and Ḥusayn Pasha respectively, and all the *mudīrs* of Upper and Lower Egypt. The meetings, presided over by ʿAbbās Pasha, were held at Shubrā for several weeks beginning January 25, 1838. The council's agenda included the following points:

(1) amelioration of agriculture;

(2) examination of accounts of debts due to the government;

(3) examination of duties to be taken off grain and other necessities of life;

(4) discussion regarding the formation of an administrative council to which all matters of finance and administration could in future be referred to in the first instance instead of directly to the Pasha.[55]

The council confined its discussion of item 2 on the agenda to Lower Egypt[56] where taxes were in arrears, in some cases for more than four years. The consensus among the participants at these meetings was that the people could no longer meet the government's demands. Even ʿAbd ar-Raḥmān asked that 60,000 to 70,000 *faddāns* in ash-Sharqīyah province be relieved of taxation.[57] Duhamel's prophecy that there would remain nothing further to take from the cultivators had been fulfilled;[58] excessive taxation, both direct and indirect, had raised the cost of living, increased the misery of the peasants, and had finally culminated in the bankruptcy of many villages.[59] Although the council agreed that the only way the iniquities in the tax system could be overcome was by conducting a complete land survey and by redistributing the land, Muḥammad 'Alī was too impatient to order a new survey involving several years' work. He needed revenues badly and wished to see immediate results. The council finally decided to make another effort to collect arrears insofar as possible. Orders were issued to the governors of the provinces of Lower Egypt to collect a total of 104,000 purses to be paid in monthly installments of 3,250 purses and in addition to collect 450,000 *ardabbs* of *dhurah* for the army. The council then dealt with the other points on the agenda. They also discussed two additional problems: the question of population, especially with regard to a better distribution of land and the elimination of corrupt practices in conscription, and the increase in self-mutilation by *fallāḥīn* seeking to evade conscription (see Chapter XI), a problem which had given rise to real alarm.[60] Although the council of state was alive to the seriousness of the situation in Egypt, it was unable to introduce any real reforms. Consequently, conditions did not improve.

Even the favorable flood of 1838 did not rescue Egypt from its state of financial exhaustion. On several occasions the Pasha claimed that his financial position was good, but such claims were probably acts of bravado, as all available evidence exposes his situation as being far from brilliant. The second war in Syria completed the picture of approaching bankruptcy. The French Consul-General stated in 1839 that measures should be taken speedily to save Egypt from complete ruin and to prevent its falling as a colony into the hands of a foreign nation. Trade diminished to a new low because the merchants feared a blockade of Egyptian ports and because ships kept away during the 1840 crisis. Only by a loan was it considered possible for Egypt to continue the struggle, and the French government was, in fact, approached for a loan of 2,000,000 dollars.[61] It should be pointed out, however, that the foreign consuls were hardly objective observers and are therefore not entirely to be relied upon for a true estimate of the Pasha's financial situation during the years of crisis. It seems safe, though, to say that although there were periods during these years when the situation was not desperate, the total period may be viewed as one when financial collapse seemed almost inevitable unless a speedy decision in the conflict was reached. The state of Muḥammad 'Alī's finances was probably an important factor contributing to his acceptance of the ultimatum by the European powers at the time of the Egyptian crisis.[62]

In 1841 Sa'īd Pasha was sent to the provinces to correct some of the more flagrant abuses and to prepare a report for his father concerning the true conditions in the countryside. It was noted at the time that, not only would the country's internal administration have to undergo complete alteration, but Muḥammad 'Alī would have to be prepared to remit taxes to relieve the *fallāḥīn's* burdens, which were paralyzing their energies.[63]

Land taxes were by no means the only taxes collected in Egypt. In addition, tax farmers (*appaltatores*), who contracted with the government for a period of one or more years, collected customs and taxes levied on various commodities. Muḥammad 'Alī also decided to levy a new capitation tax, the *furdat ar-ru'ūs* (referred to as the *furdah* [*firdah*]), on everyone in Egypt regardless of religion.[64] Only the European residents, excluding European employees of the Egyptian government who had to pay the tax, and the native Egyptians in the employ of foreign consulates were exempted from this tax. The rate was based on the capacity to pay, the amount ranging from 5 piasters to 500.[65] The peasants paid from 30 to 100 piasters, while artisans and merchants paid in accordance with the volume of their trade, but never more than the maximum amount of 500 piasters.[66] The tax was automatically deducted from the salaries of all government employees.[67] This personal tax on Muslims as well as on Christians, being considered an innovation by the Muslim population, caused considerable irritation and hardship.[68] Another personal tax introduced in 1822 was the house tax fixed at 20 to 80 piasters for each house, but resentment was so great that collections had to be suspended temporarily. Eventually, however, the tax, known as *sālyān*,[69] was enforced and each houseowner was obliged to pay one month's rent annually even if the house was unoccupied.[70]

Date trees were also taxed by Muḥammad 'Alī. They had occasionally been taxed in the past by the *multazims*, but it is unknown precisely when this tax was first introduced by Muḥammad 'Alī. A tradition in Egypt, concerning which there is some uncertainty, holds that about 1813 the male date tree was exempted from all taxes, but that in the case of female trees a tax was levied on the gross yield, an area of one square *qaṣabah* around each female tree being tax free at first but taxed later on. In any event, by 1819 a tax had not only been established on dates of all kinds, but also on the branches, leaves, and fiber of the date tree. The dates, according to al-Jabartī, as well as the branches, leaves, and fiber, were collected by treasury officials at a low price, sold to the merchants at a higher price, and the latter, in turn, sold them to the public at a still higher price—ten times higher. The tax on the trees in 1822 was reported as from one to two piasters per annum for every date tree, no mention being made of distinctions between male and female trees. By 1833 the policy of taxation had produced a noticeable decline in the number of trees, Boislecomte estimating their number in the neighborhood of between five and six million. He claimed in July 1833 that Muḥammad 'Alī had just lifted the tax in several provinces to encourage cultivation of date trees. A few years later, however, Bowring reported that a tax of 40 paras was being levied on about two million trees, though Duhamel claimed that date trees were being assessed with direct and indirect taxes at rates amounting to 20, 40, and 50 paras in Upper Egypt per tree and 40, 60, and 100 paras in Lower Egypt.[71]

Taxes did not end here. There was a tax on animals. Camels and sheep were taxed 4 piasters. Bulls and cows were taxed 20 piasters. When they were sold to butchers, they were taxed 70 piasters, and the hides belonged to the government.[72] A trades or professional tax was also levied. Bowring estimated that the tax burden for each individual amounted to approximately £2.0.0. This sum was equal to that paid by the population of Great Britain, twice that paid by the French, and four times that paid by the Spanish population.[73]

The excessive taxation which Muḥammad 'Alī exacted, as well as the policy of direct interference by the government in agricultural matters, had brought unprecedented misery to the Egyptian people. It was almost universally agreed upon by contemporary witnesses that conditions for the Egyptian people were worse than they ever had been.[74] Count Medem once said that, despite the philanthropic sentiments expressed by Muḥammad 'Alī, conditions in Egypt were in a state of steady decline because of three plagues—conscription, monopoly, and vexatious taxes—to which list must be added the bubonic plague of 1835 and the famine of 1837. Colonel Gallice reported that the *fallāḥīn* considered themselves fortunate when they were left sufficiently independent to marry and divorce freely and Colonel Duhamel claimed that although many external changes had been introduced, fundamentally, nothing had changed. Hamont went even further, saying that never in the history of mankind had there been an economic system, whether feudal or slave, which had gone so far as to deprive its workers of food to eat, if for no other purpose than to allow them to continue working. Men, women, and children were all victims of the system. "Hear what one *fallāḥ* said," he wrote. "One day in the *dīwān* of a governor in Upper Egypt, a *fallāḥ*, indignant at the incessant extortions made by government officials, got up suddenly, and throwing the brown linen cloak which covered him over his left shoulder, cried: 'Muḥammad 'Alī is jealous of the lice which devour the *fallāḥ*.'"[75] There were certainly members of the government who were not unaware of the misery which prevailed in the country nor of the different conditions in other countries. As early as 1829 two Egyptian officers, who had been taken as prisoners during the war in Greece, spoke frequently of their constant astonishment at the conditions of the peasants in the European countries through which they had traveled, peasants "whom they were forced to put in comparison with the corresponding class of the people of Egypt—the wretched naked Fellah, starving in his mud-built hovel,[76] five feet high, destitute of even the most indispensable necessaries of life."[77]

The government, in the long run, suffered from its own policies. It was constantly obliged to coerce the *fallāḥīn* who, reduced to absolute pauperism, were reluctant to work. Coercion was justified on the grounds that the *fallāḥīn* were naturally lazy, conservative, and easily satisfied with the barest subsistence. Muḥammad 'Alī himself expressed this opinion more than once, but though some European observers shared it, others asserted, on the basis of their observations, that the *fallāḥīn*, like people everywhere, were interested in accumulating wealth and improving their conditions. If they were given guarantees for the sanctity of property and the end of arbitrary exactions, they would quickly cease to be lazy. In the period of flood they worked day and night to protect their own houses and fields sown with *dhurah*, whereas they showed the greatest lethargy in safeguarding lands and crops from which they received no benefit.[78]

Not only did the *fallāḥīn* refuse to exert themselves, but they used every opportunity to steal. This characteristic was considered almost inherent in their natures; Michaud, who found a confirmation of the fact even in the historian Ammianus Marcellinus, commented: "In this country, theft is like the corruption of manners (*corruption des moeurs*); time has changed nothing; Egypt has lost its glory, but it has conserved its thieves and its prostitutes."[79] Muḥammad 'Alī attempted to root out this evil and went so far as to destroy entire villages suspected of committing acts of piracy or theft. Despite severe penalties and speedy acts of justice, however, the *fallāḥīn* continued to steal not only from the barges which sailed on the Nile, but from government stores. Cheated by the government, they sought to cheat it. They stole the wheat which had not yet been stored; they stole beans and rice; and their Turk overseers, in arrears of pay for months on end, joined the *fallāḥīn* and stole with them.[80]

Muḥammad ʻAlī had not been indolent in any way nor was he given to the pleasures of an oriental potentate. He also believed with the best faith in the world that his people were happy and contented, being convinced, it was said, of that which his blindest panegyrist could have no illusions about. He spoke often of his desire to improve the conditions of the Egyptians in the same breath that he ordered some new exaction and as late as 1847[81] expressed his desire for nothing more than the advancement of his country, exhorting his officers to greater diligence:

> Be it known to you, moreover, that if you do not abandon your old habits, if you do not put away from you all private considerations, if you do not declare the truth in everything, if you do not with diligence and zeal apply yourself to following the right course, and if you do not conduct yourself in such manner as to preserve the rights of the Government, without doubt, I shall be greatly displeased with you all. Since my whole desire is the advancement of this well beloved country, an object to which I in every way consider myself bound, I find myself, also, compelled to punish with severity, and with great heart-burnings and tears in my eyes, all those who do not walk with me in the same straightforward course.[82]

But there was in fact no link between Muḥammad ʻAlī and his people. Oppressed by the highly organized and systematic method of exaction which touched every phase of life and left no opportunities for personal gain, finding that no advantages were to be derived from personal initiative, hard work, and ambition, the Egyptians often regretted the end of the rule of the Mamlūks whose tyranny was proverbial but had, at least, permitted some years of peace and a normal life.[83] "How little the government of Mehmed Aly," commented Barker in 1832, "merits the praise that it receives from individuals interested in its duration; and from travellers who are surprised to find themselves unmolested in a Turkish province." At the same time the French Foreign Minister wrote that although Muḥammad ʻAlī's government appeared superior to that of the Sultan's, it lost some of its brilliance upon closer observation.[84]

CHAPTER VIII

AGRICULTURAL PRACTICES UNDER MUḤAMMAD 'ALĪ

At the end of the eighteenth century Egyptian agriculture was in a depressed state. The cultivation of cash crops requiring a substantial capital investment, such as sugar, rice, and indigo, was difficult because of the lack of capital, whereas the cultivation of cereals requiring a minimum of capital investment was uneconomic because of the shortage of labor.[1] Nevertheless, the impoverished Egyptian peasants were forced to cultivate cereals and were thereupon caught in a vicious circle; for so long as they raised cereals which provided only a small margin of profit, they could never accumulate sufficient capital to plant those crops which provided a large profit.[2] Muḥammad 'Alī broke this stalemate by supplying capital for the cultivation of crops capable of producing the highest margin of profit. Undoubtedly, Egyptian agriculture was greatly stimulated by the Pasha's use of capital in the cultivation of cash crops, but the state of agriculture was by no means ideal during his reign, as the following analysis of Muḥammad 'Alī's agricultural practices shows.

Ṣayfī Cultivation[3]

COTTON. Cotton of a short-staple variety was grown in Egypt prior to the reign of Muḥammad 'Alī to provide the cotton cloth used mostly for cushions and mattresses. Woven by native women, this cotton was raised both in the Delta and in the most southern part of Upper Egypt. In Thebes it was common to plant cotton twice a year, in April and in July. The cotton plant raised in this area was known as *gossypium arborescens*. A *faddān* produced 300 *raṭls* of this cotton, which was sold at 10 to 12 paras a *raṭl* (equal to 0.981 pound). Cotton grown in the Delta was of the variety known as *gossypium herbaceum*, an annual plant, and was planted in April after the wheat crop was harvested. A *faddān* of land planted with this variety produced 1½ to 2 *qinṭārs* of 120 *raṭls* each and was sold at 16 *pataques* per *qinṭār* in peacetime and 9 in wartime when commerce was stagnant. The cotton plant was not uprooted periodically to maintain the maximum yield, but was allowed to remain in the ground until it died.[4]

The cultivation of long-fiber cotton (*al-quṭn al-hindī*) began in 1821[5] and the first large harvest was made in 1822. Since the *fallāḥīn* were acquainted with cotton cultivation which they had practiced for generations on quite a large scale, they could readily adapt themselves to the cultivation of new varieties of the plant. In order that this new variety of cotton might meet the demands of the foreign market, however, it was essential to develop methods which would insure the maximum yield and the best quality of cotton. Experts in cotton cultivation were therefore brought to Egypt from Syria and Asia Minor to supervise cultivation and inquiries were made in America concerning methods of cultivation and the sorting of cotton. The imported experts were assigned to manage the work in a number of villages where the *fallāḥīn* were placed under their direction; they were even given the right to authorize corporal punishment when necessary. These experts selected the most suitable land for cotton cultivation and directed the *fallāḥīn* at every stage of cultivation and preparation of the cotton for export. The results of their efforts were seen after the first consignment was sent to Europe where the weavers classified Egyptian cotton as second only to the Georgian long-fiber variety known as Sea Island cotton. This first consignment, accordingly, fetched high prices.[6]

This favorable reception of Egyptian cotton by the European textile industry induced Muḥammad ʿAlī to extend the area of cotton cultivation and this move, in turn, stimulated his program of irrigation works (see Chapter XII). Old canals were dredged, new ones dug, and a number of canals converted into summer or *ṣayfī* canals. A large number of *sāqiyahs* and *shādūfs* were also installed to lift the water from the canals during the summer, the period of cotton cultivation, when the level of the Nile was at its lowest point.[7] The Pasha ordered that minute attention should be given to every facet of the cultivation, picking, ginning, and packing of cotton. Nothing was to be left to chance. Precise instructions were incorporated in the *Lāʾiḥat zirāʿat al-fallāḥ* concerning the preparation of land before planting, the exact number of times the land was to be plowed and leveled, the preparation of the seed, the method of planting and the distances involved, the care of the soil and the plants after the seed had been planted through hoeing, weeding, and pruning, the irrigation of the plants, the picking of cotton, ginning, packing, the use of the cotton seed after ginning, the delivery of cotton to the *shūnahs*, the uprooting of the cotton plant after three years when it reached its maximum yield, and the use of the soil thereafter for the planting of winter crops. It even went so far as to prohibit the practice of planting vegetables between the rows of cotton plants, a practice which the peasants, particularly those in areas near large cities, had followed in order to increase their own revenue, but one which prevented the proper care of the soil around the cotton plants and was therefore harmful to them.[8] So that there would be no mixture of seed of the indigenous or *baladī* cotton[9] with that of the new varieties such as *al-quṭn al-hindī*, Sea Island, Ceylon, Nankin, and Sinnār,[10] Muḥammad 'Alī instructed the government inspectors to maintain careful supervision over the distribution of seed to the peasants. During the first few years these procedures were strictly adhered to. Then, when Muḥammad 'Alī discovered that the quality of long-fiber cotton had begun to deteriorate, he resumed the cultivation of the *baladī* short-staple variety which required less attention and produced more profit for the treasury. Some of the finer grades of cotton continued to be cultivated but only in limited quantities.[11]

Various factors contributed to the decline in the quality of long-staple cotton. In the first place, the exhaustive nature of the cotton crop caused a decrease in the fertility of the soil. Although on large estates crops were rotated so that an interval of four to five years occurred between the planting of cotton on a particular area of land, in the smaller holdings cotton was planted every three years and sometimes as often as every other year on land which had already grown a cotton crop. The land was further exhausted by the cultivation of intercalary crops (crops, usually vegetables, planted between the cotton plants). There resulted a distinct difference between the amount of cotton grown on the large estates and that grown on the small holdings. The staple of Egyptian cotton began to get shorter and less firm and the plant also degenerated. The failure of the *fallāḥīn* to maintain the high standard of care practiced in the early years also contributed greatly to the decline in quality.[12]

Not only did the quality of cotton cultivation decline, but also the harvesting and the preparation of the fiber for export. The cotton was frequently allowed to remain in the fields until the cotton balls fell to the ground and became dirty, although the *Lā'iḥat zirā'at al-fallāḥ* had ordered that the cotton was to be picked before it fell to the ground; if the *fallāḥīn* failed to do so, the authorities were to be informed and action taken against those who were negligent. Actually, when cotton was removed from the capsules, a task usually performed by children, sufficient care was not taken and the capsules were often smashed. The particles of the capsules were mixed with the fiber from which process originated the complaint that Egyptian cotton was dirty and peppery. As a result, in 1826 it was reported that manufacturers in Alsace preferred Louisiana cotton which was inferior in quality, but cleaner and therefore more suited to manufacturing. After the cotton was removed from the capsules, it was ginned. According to the *lā'iḥah*, one man should gin a *qinṭār* of 125 *raṭls* in about six to eight days, for which he was to receive 5 to 6 piasters plus three meals a day. In 1837, George Gliddon, the consul for the United States government, imported a cotton ginning machine for the Pasha from the United States; it does not appear, however, that the widespread use of American ginning machinery was introduced into Egypt at this time.[13] Although primitive techniques persisted in ginning, the pressing of cotton was successfully mechanized. Instead of having the *fallāḥīn* tread on the cotton to press it, as at first, mechanical presses imported from Great Britain and later manufactured in Egypt by order of the Pasha were employed. These mechanical presses made it possible to press the same quantity of cotton into smaller bales, thereby saving valuable shipping space.[14]

The principal reason for the decline in quality undoubtedly resulted from the fact that cotton was a government monopoly from which the peasants failed to obtain adequate compensation. None of the cotton could be withheld for private sale, whether grown on *athar* land or on private estates. All of it had to be delivered to government *shūnahs* at prices fixed by the Pasha. These prices varied. In the early years they were high to serve as an inducement to the *fallāḥīn* to undertake cotton cultivation. The peasants responded willingly, at first, especially when they recognized that only their *nīlī* crops (mostly *dhurah*) were affected and supposed that since cotton cultivation did not interfere with wheat cultivation, which was planted in a different season, the *dhurah* crop would not be missed.[15] The Pasha made generous advances to the *fallāḥīn* of seed, oxen, and water-raising devices and the *fallāḥīn*, anticipating great profit from the new crop, turned over their best land to cotton cultivation. They carried out the careful instructions for its cultivation and thereby produced the fine crops of the first few years. They were paid 175 piasters per *qinṭār*. As one *faddān* of land produced an average of 5 *qinṭārs*, their income per *faddān* amounted to an average of 875 piasters.[16] It was only in subsequent years that they showed great unwillingness to cultivate cotton. The drain on manpower from conscription was partially responsible, since it made the care of this crop burdensome. Also, the Pasha appears to have cut off his generous advances of the earlier period. Finally, the Pasha reduced the amount of the prices he paid for the crop. Cotton cultivation thereafter became far less attractive to the *fallāḥīn* and not worth the additional trouble it involved. Prices varied then as follows:

1826		100–150 piasters per *qinṭār*;
1827		40[*sic*]–140 piasters per *qinṭār*;
1834	Poorest quality	100–125 piasters per *qinṭār*;
	Medium quality	125–150 piasters per *qinṭār*;
	Best quality	150–200 piasters per *qinṭār*.

As government agents were the sole judges of quality, the *fallāḥīn* were often cheated. As a result, they refused to take any pains to produce a superior quality of cotton for which they usually received only the minimum price. They continued to plant the quantity required of them, but they turned over their worst rather than their best land for this purpose and gave the crop a minimum of attention. They preferred to plant crops which gave two or three harvests, rather than cotton which gave only one. To combat the noticeable lethargy among the *fallāḥīn* towards cotton cultivation, the price was raised during 1834 to 200 piasters for all qualities, but the *fallāḥīn* continued to show a lack of interest. Muḥammad ʿAlī was accordingly forced to send officers and soldiers to cotton plantations to supervise the work. In addition, foreigners were granted land for cotton cultivation on condition that they undertake delivery of their cotton crop to the government *shūnahs* at 10 dollars per *qinṭār*. This decline in the price of cotton in 1837 finally led Muḥammad ʿAlī to fix 1839 cotton payments to the producers at the following rates:

first quality	200 piasters per *qinṭār*;
second quality	150 piasters per *qinṭār*;
third quality	120 piasters per *qinṭār*.

No gradation according to quality was made when the cotton was sold.[17]

Furthermore, the highly centralized form of administration of agriculture was objectionable to the *fallāḥīn*, especially since it gave them very little opportunity for private initiative or private gain. They were helpless against the huge state apparatus and could only combat it by a system of personal sabotage. This was probably not a conscious act of a political nature, but took the form of general lassitude or "laziness," as Muḥammad ʿAlī so often called it. Campbell commented on this phenomenon in 1839: "It is evident from this circumstance that the cultivators do not find any other means of evading the Government Monopoly than by a system of passive resistance which sacrifices his [*sic*] own interests at the same time that it defeats the grasping spirit of the Government. They allow their crops to perish for want of water or neglect to gather them."[18] Government officials also became lax in the performance of their duties and the detailed government regulations concerning cotton cultivation were usually ignored.

Egyptian cotton was placed on the world market by two commercial houses, the British firm of Briggs & Co. and the Swiss firm of Messrs. Violier & Graban, when Muḥammad ʿAlī, in need of money to meet his expenses in the war against the Greek insurgents, asked them to advance him cash on account of the cotton crop.[19] Briggs & Co. received 35,000 bales for sale in England; Messrs. Violier & Graban, 15,000 bales for sale in France and Italy. The head of the British firm went to England, convinced manufacturers there of the value of *al-quṭn al-hindī*, and received favorable conditions from the British government with regard to customs and quarantine expenses.[20] On the other hand, the French firms operating in Egypt lost the business to the British and Swiss, partly because of their lukewarm attitude towards Egyptian cotton, which they had considered to be inferior to American cotton and unable to compete in price. As soon as they realized their mistake, they reversed their opinion and began to claim that Egyptian cotton was equal to American cotton; Drovetti in a report to the French government said that in his opinion conditions in Egypt were so conducive to the cultivation of cotton that the Americans would find it difficult to compete in price or quality.[21] Egyptian cotton was indeed in a favorable position in the competitive world market because of Egypt's proximity to Europe, where the textile industry was expanding rapidly.

Cotton production in Egypt was dependent then both upon the state of the international market and internal factors. Cotton statistics as cited by contemporaries are, however, unreliable, because they were generally based upon Muḥammad ʿAli's inaccurate and exaggerated statements. Every year produced optimistic forecasts of production, but something usually happened to shatter the illusions.[22] It would be profitless to cite all the cases of exaggeration. In 1824, for one example, a report stated that production of long-staple cotton would rise in a four-year period from 400,000 *qinṭārs* to 2,000,000.[23] Since the export figure for 1824, the highest in a fifteen-year period, was only 228,078 *qinṭārs*, it is unlikely either that 400,000 *qinṭārs* were actually produced in 1824 or that the Pasha's expectations of reaching the 2,000,000 mark in the next few years were based on realistic estimates.[24]

The selling price of cotton fluctuated greatly. The first crop was sold at 16 dollars per *qinṭār*. When prices were highest, however, in the boom years of 1835 and 1836, they fluctuated between 25 and 30 dollars per *qinṭār*. But then the international financial crisis of 1836 had its effect on Egyptian trade. The price of cotton dropped to about 10 dollars per *qinṭār* in 1837. There was a moderate increase in 1839; then prices fell once again. The agents in Europe, who held large stocks of Egyptian cotton which had been sitting in the ports of Liverpool, Trieste, and Marseilles since 1839, were forced to allow buyers to choose their purchases. Cotton merchants also had lost confidence in the quality of Egyptian cotton because the finest qualities of cotton were frequently mixed with the *baladī* type, a practice which discredited Egyptian cotton in the European market.[25] Prices decreased steadily. In 1843 the price of Egyptian cotton dropped to 7 dollars and 75 cents. It fluctuated thereafter and by 1848 reached the 7 dollar level.[26]

The area of land utilized for cotton cultivation increased enormously during Muḥammad ʿAlī's reign. In 1824 it was estimated that 50,000 *faddāns* would be devoted to cotton; in 1830 the Pasha claimed that he had planted 400,000 *faddāns* with cotton and expected a yield of 400,000 *qinṭārs* (484,000 cwt.) of clean cotton. The figure of 400,000 *faddāns* was probably exaggerated, since only 213,585 *qinṭārs* of cotton were exported in 1830. In 1836 the amount of land devoted to cotton cultivation was estimated at about 320,000 *faddāns*. In 1844 a total of 224,000 *faddāns* was supposed to be devoted to cotton. A smaller amount was probably sown, as only 153,363 *qinṭārs* of cotton was exported that year. In 1845 there were 344,955 *qinṭārs* of cotton exported and the area of land planted with cotton undoubtedly increased in proportion.[27]

Not only the export figure should be taken into account, however. Part of the cotton crop was used in the Pasha's cotton factories. Figures of amounts of cotton used in the factories are rare and probably inaccurate. In 1828 it was estimated that 25 per cent of the harvest was used locally because of Muḥammad ʿAlī's desire to stimulate industry. The total cotton crop for 1831 was estimated at 160,000 bales, 110,000 of which were for export and 50,000 for use in the native factories, that is to say, about 32 per cent of the total; the figures are exaggerated, but the percentage is probably not too far off.[28] In 1834 60,000 to 70,000 *qinṭārs* were required for Egyptian cotton manufactories. In 1837 it was estimated that the maximum amount of raw cotton which could be consumed if all the cotton factories were in full operation was 80,000 *qinṭārs* for spinning and weaving. The actual figure for those years was about 50,000. Since the highest export figure during Muḥammad ʿAlī's reign was 344,955 *qinṭārs* in 1845 and since the capacity of the factories had not increased from 1837 when the amount of 80,000 *qinṭārs* was the maximum that could have been used in the workshops, then the cotton yield in 1845 would, presumably, have been about 424,995 *qinṭārs*. If one calculates at the minimum figure of 2 *qinṭārs* per *faddān*, the maximum area turned over to cotton cultivation in 1845 would have been around 212,473 *faddāns* or an increase of over 400 per cent in a period of approximately twenty years. Of course, this was the maximum figure. The average probably was closer to a 300 per cent increase.[29]

RICE. Government monopoly of rice began in 1812 as rice constituted a valuable export crop. So much rice was exported, in fact, that it became very expensive in Egypt. As a result, Indian rice was imported for local consumption at a price higher than that of native rice.[30]

Statistical information on rice production is extremely limited. In 1821 the quantity of rice produced was 122,000 *ardabbs* (other figures for that year are 110,000 *ardabbs* and 330,000 hectoliters). In 1836 it was reported that the government *shūnahs* received annually an average of 80,000 *ardabbs* of Damietta rice and 60,000 *ardabbs* of Rosetta rice. Production did not increase in the same proportion as cotton, however, until the 1840's, partly because the limited quantity of land which could be used for *ṣayfī* cultivation was turned over to cotton cultivation. At that time extensive irrigation work and land reclamation and the availability of a greater number of agricultural workers made it possible to expand cultivation of all crops, including rice. The amount of 98,000 *faddāns*, which could produce 490,000 *ardabbs* valued at 44,100,000 piasters, was designated for rice cultivation in 1844. It is not clear whether this figure represents the potential rather than the actual amount cultivated.[31] Rice exports had actually declined in the 1830's because rice at that time, like other foodstuffs, was reserved for internal consumption and for the troops. There had been even less rice available for export than had been exported in the last decade of the eighteenth century.[32] The increase in cultivation in the 1840's, however, led to an increase in exports. The accompanying list shows the varying figures that are available, with figures from other sources in parentheses; all reflect, however, the general movement of rice exports.

1832 46,000 *ardabbs* (50,000 *ardabbs* and 220,000 hectoliters);
1833 26,000 *ardabbs* (25,000 *ardabbs* and 147,200 hectoliters);
1834 25,000 *ardabbs*;
1836 11,192 *ardabbs*;
1843 43,988 *ardabbs* (valued at 10,588,160 piasters);
1844 61,035 *ardabbs* (valued at 17,000,256 piasters).[33]

The pattern of prices paid to the *fallāḥīn* for their rice crop followed that of cotton. Generous payments were made in the early twenties; between 1826 and 1834 there was a decrease, followed by an increase in 1834. Several factors contributed to this trend in prices: Muḥammad 'Alī's involvement in war and various large undertakings reduced his resources considerably; several bad harvests and a serious flood in 1829 contributed to his financial embarrassment; but his situation began to improve after 1834 and the favorable export market made it good policy to stimulate greater productivity by increasing the purchase price.[34]

Rice was transported to Rosetta and Damietta where it was bleached by special machines installed for that purpose. The cost of cleaning one *ardabb* of rice in 1834 was 22½ piasters.[35] Muḥammad 'Alī attempted to improve the system of bleaching rice by importing a modern steam engine for this purpose at a cost of nearly 10,000,000 piasters (£100,000). It operated very well at first, but then suffered several expensive mechanical breakdowns. It was put in order by the English engineers who were then instructed to train Arab apprentices to replace them. As soon as the English engineers were dismissed, the Egyptians in charge allowed the machine to break down through careless treatment. The Pasha's advisers told him he had been cheated by the British contractors who had sent him a defective machine. According to Campbell the contractors laid "the blame on the want of skill in the Egyptian workmen, on the stupidity of the nazirs, or overseers, and on the climate. They say, that the dust or fine sand, the sun, and the humidity, are insurmountable obstacles to the introduction of machines in Egypt."[36] An engineer was brought from England, but he could do nothing to rescue the machine. Later on Muḥammad 'Alī was advised to buy American machines which were supposed to be better. This was done in 1839, but the

American engineer warned Muḥammad ʿAlī that if the machines were left to Egyptians, the same misfortune would occur. In 1841 the Americans left and the machine was placed in the charge of an Italian and two Maltese.[37]

SUGAR. Sugar cane cultivation and refining were known in Egypt and Egyptian cane was in demand in the Mediterranean world long before Muḥammad ʿAlī's reign. It was the practice to send raw sugar to Europe to be refined in two grades, *mukarrar* and *kasīr*. The first was whiter than the second and was used only in the houses of the rich; the second was used by those who were fairly well off. A long-established native industry for refining sugar was located at Cairo and produced a quality of sugar which the native Egyptians favored.[38]

Muḥammad ʿAlī decided in 1818[39] to establish a sugar refinery near the largest of his plantations at Rayramūn[40] in the province of al-Minyā near Mallawī, as a result of which the native industry was stifled and export of raw sugar practically ceased. The Rayramūn refinery was placed under the supervision of Brim, an Englishman who had worked for many years in Trieste. It was later placed under the direction of two Italians. The refinery was not large nor very efficient and could only refine about 30 *qinṭārs* per day at first. It was, however, able to produce sugar more cheaply than the native industry. The quality of the sugar, at first poor, eventually improved. Two other refineries were established at the plantation of ar-Rawḍah and at Sāqiyat Mūsā by Ibrāhīm Pasha, who in 1846 brought several persons from France to direct them.[41] According to two letters in the Egyptian archives dated May 16, 1845, and June 13, 1845, addressed to Mougel, Muḥammad ʿAlī claimed that he installed between 1840 and 1845 five new sugar works. No mention of this fact, however, is made by British Consul Stoddart in his lengthy report on sugar cultivation in Egypt. Muḥammad ʿAlī claimed too in 1827 that 16,000 *faddāns* had been turned over to sugar cultivation. This was probably one of his optimistic exaggerations, as the maximum amount of land devoted to sugar cultivation was 12,100 *faddāns* in 1844, a time when cultivation of all crops was expanding. By 1846 the large estates in Upper Egypt produced 16,500 cwt. to 25,000 cwt. of sugar annually.[42]

Each hectare of land had produced 2,500 kilograms of sugar or around 22 *qinṭārs* per *faddān* in 1827. Approximately ten years later, Bowring estimated that the sugar plantation at ar-Rawḍah of 272 *faddāns* yielded 27½ *qinṭars* per *faddān*. Another plantation of 152 *faddāns* produced

26 *qinṭārs* of sugar per *faddān* and 29 *qinṭārs* of molasses. The increased yield probably resulted from the fact that Ibrāhīm invited two Englishmen, one of whom was named McPherson, from Jamaica to direct the plantations at Rayramūn.[43] They experimented with mixing the West Indies strain with the native type sugar and improved the indigenous type.

Sugar was imported into Egypt from Europe throughout Muḥammad 'Alī's reign, but the amount decreased as native production increased. It was only at the very end of his reign, however, that it seemed likely that Egypt would be able to produce all its sugar needs. By 1845 the quantity of sugar exported exceeded the amount imported. The trend in the 1840's may be seen from the figures in Table 5. Although it has

TABLE 5. Sugar exports and imports (in cwt.)[a]

Year	Export	Import
1843	1,082	9,624
1844	630	6,302
1845	16,020	5,374

[a] Stoddart, May 29, 1846 in F.O. 78/663. Stoddart in his report for 1844 lists the exports of sugar at 705 *qinṭārs* and not 630 as above. The export is valued by him at 112,800 piasters (Stoddart, April 10, 1845 in F.O. 78/624). Campbell says that in 1836 the import of sugar amounted to 2,500,000 piasters (Campbell, July 6, 1840 in F.O. 78/408b).

been maintained that the development of the sugar industry in Egypt suffered from foreign competition,[44] the facts do not warrant such an assumption. Egypt was unable to supply its own needs for a time and was obliged to import sugar. When production increased to take care of local needs, imports dropped.

The price paid to the *fallāḥīn* for sugar in 1826 was between 16 and 36 piasters per *qinṭār* of 37¾ *uqqahs*. The price in 1827 went up to 40½ to 56¼ piasters for a *qinṭār* of 39½ *uqqahs*.[45] Prices paid for raw sugar in the 1830's in Upper Egypt were as shown in Table 6. Sugar refined at Rayramūn was sold at 300 piasters per *qinṭār* for *mukarrar* quality and 150 for *kasīr*. Rum produced at Rayramūn sold at 4 piasters per *uqqah* or 144 piasters per *qinṭār* according to one estimate and 182 according to another. The sugar produced in the Delta on the plantation at ar-Rawḍah was more expensive, however. Here, the *fallāḥīn* received

95 to 100 piasters per *qinṭār* for raw sugar. The finest lump sugar produced at ar-Rawḍah in the refinery there sold at 302 piasters per *qinṭār*.[46] By 1844 it was reported that the price of lump sugar on the Cairo market had dropped to 180 piasters per *qinṭār*, whereas raw sugar sold at 70 piasters. The decrease in the selling price of sugar was due to the reduction in the margin of profit. This fact is borne out by a comparison of profits on sugar in 1837 and 1844. In 1837 the selling price of the product of one *faddān* of land devoted to sugar cultivation was 5,429 piasters, 2 paras, which, less expenses of 2,202 piasters, 20 paras, brought a profit of 3,226 piasters, 22 paras. If the same rate of profit

TABLE 6. Prices (piasters per *qinṭār*) paid for raw sugar and for molasses, Upper Egypt, 1830's

Quality	Raw sugar		Molasses
	According to Bowring[a]	According to Duhamel[b]	
First	60	56	15
Second	58	45	12
Third	34–40	34	10

[a] John Bowring, "Report on Egypt and Candia," A Report addressed to Palmerston and presented to both Houses of Parliament, House of Commons, Sessional Papers 1840, vol. XXI: *Reports from Commissioners*, vol. 6, p. 22.

[b] René Cattaui, *Le règne de Mohamed Ali d'après les archives russes en Egypte*, Société royale de géographie d'Egypte, publications spéciales (Cairo, 1931, Rome, 1933, 1935, 1936), II, Pt. 2, 384.

was earned in 1844, the 12,100 *faddāns* available for sugar cultivation should have produced a profit of 39,046,700 piasters (the selling price of 65,690,900 piasters less expenses of 26,644,200 piasters). However, the gross revenue for 12,100 *faddāns* produced in fact only 12,000,000 piasters. Expenses were not deducted so that the net profit cannot be estimated. At the very most the profit was less than one third that of 1837.[47]

Labor costs at the refineries were kept at a minimum. As one writer put it, Egypt had a class of peasants whom "no revolutions have disturbed from the fields. They toil for bare subsistence. Slaves cannot exist on less. The fellah, besides, is as docile as the negro of Central Africa, whom he greatly excels in strength and in intelligence. Thus his labour is more advantageous."[48] Work was carried on for twenty-four hours a day, the laborers working in shifts. Negro and white child labor was used in addition to men. Wages were as follows:

Adult men	30 paras per day;
Boys and girls (white)	10–15 paras per day;
Negro children	received no pay but could take the upper part of the cane which was used as cattle fodder.

The workers received government bread at 12 paras per *uqqah* instead of the market price of 20 paras. Each worker was entitled to one *uqqah*, its price being deducted from his wages.[49]

INDIGO. Indigo was not a new crop in Egypt. It was used for dyeing the cloth of garments worn particularly by the lower classes and was grown mostly in Upper Egypt and in the Fayyūm. Egyptian indigo before Muḥammad ʻAlī's reign had never been suitable for export because the methods used in preparing it produced a bad quality of dye which had no market in Europe.[50]

The government monopolized indigo as early as 1816. In 1824 forty Armenian families were brought from Bengal to teach the Egyptians their method for preparing it. In addition, the government ordered that indigo should be planted in each village. Indigo works similar to those used in India were built by the government and were directed by *nāẓirs*.[51] During this period the industry was at its most critical stage.

The crop was cut three times at which times the peasants received the following prices:

first cutting	13 piasters 20 paras for 500 *raṭls*;
second cutting	11 piasters 10 paras for 500 *raṭls*;
third cutting	9 piasters for 500 *raṭls*.

After the crop was processed, it was classified and sold as follows:

first quality	75 piasters per *uqqah*	for export to Turkey and Europe;
second quality	55 piasters per *uqqah*	
third quality	36 piasters per *uqqah*	—for local consumption and export to Syria.

The third quality, which was sold to the merchant at 35 piasters, was resold to the Egyptian consumer at a price fixed at 100 piasters per *uqqah*. Merchants would often export all their indigo purchases and then reland the third grade and sell it as contraband to dyers at a price which was profitable to both parties. Muḥammad 'Alī finally recognized the realities of the situation and fixed the price for the native consumer at 40 rather than 100 piasters per *uqqah.*[52]

After the Indian experts left Egypt, the quality of the dye deteriorated. A Frenchman was appointed to direct the factories, but he was unable to correct the situation. As time went on, no discrimination was shown in cutting the crop. Plants which were either insufficiently matured or over-ripe were included with the harvest. They were then loaded on camels and transported to the indigo factories which were usually several hours' journey from the fields. At the works, crops would be thrown under the hot sun and further injured. When the indigo was finally produced, it was greatly inferior to the Indian product and inferior even to that produced by the *fallāḥīn* when employing their primitive methods. Then, in 1835 the Pasha abandoned the operation of the indigo works for his own account because they were expensive to run, and the dye, unsatisfactory for export because of its impurity, often remained unsold in government *shūnahs*. Muḥammad 'Alī decided that it was more profitable to permit the works to be operated by *shaykhs* from neighboring villages on condition that all the indigo manufactured by them be delivered at 30 piasters per *uqqah*, regardless of quality.[53]

Thus, the development of indigo did not fulfill the first flush of optimism. In 1844 indigo formed only an unspecified portion of 27,000 *faddāns* of inundated ground in Middle and Upper Egypt and only part of 3,700 *faddāns* of irrigated ground. In 1845 it did not even appear on the list of exports for the year. In fact, an amount valued at £10,417 was imported from England that year.[54]

TABLE 7. Quantity of sesame produced and exported, 1816–1844[a]

Year	Total production	Amount exported
1816	—	300 *ardabbs*
1833	33,120 hectoliters[b]	—
1843	—	70,285 *ardabbs*
1844	125,000 *ardabbs*	109,495 *ardabbs*

[a] Salt, April 28, 1817 in F.O. 78/89; A. B. Clot, *Aperçu général sur l'Egypte* (Paris, 1840), II, 287; Stoddart, Alexandria, March 23, 1844 in F.O. 78/584.

[b] See Chapter VII, note 21. Because the *ardabb* varies, the original figure has been retained in this table. For purposes of comparison, however, it may be presumed that at that time these 33,120 hectoliters amounted to something in the neighborhood of 17,000 *ardabbs*.

SESAME. Production figures for this item show a phenomenal increase in cultivation (see Table 7).

HENNA. Production figures on henna are as follows:

1821	40,000 *qinṭārs*;
1833	1,555,450 kilograms (about 34,642 *qinṭārs*);
1834	30,000 *qinṭārs*.

It does not appear again as a separate item and was probably not produced in very large amounts.[55]

Shitwī and Nīlī Cultivation[56]

CEREALS AND OTHER FOODSTUFFS. Cereals and other foodstuffs had always been Egypt's principal items of export. During the Napoleonic Wars Muḥammad ʻAlī profited enormously from exports of grain, particularly to the British. Grain exports declined after the wars, but the cultivation of cereals remained an important part of Egyptian agriculture. They not only produced revenue, but also provided the necessary supplies for the Egyptian army, navy, and the local population.

Cereals were produced in varying quantities each year, depending upon the character of the annual flood and the effectiveness of the irrigation system. An insufficient flood produced famine; on the other hand, uncontrolled inundation resulted in devastation, famine, and a decrease in the amount of cereals available for export. The maintenance and extension of the irrigation system was, therefore, essential to cereal cultivation, which consequently benefited from the general measures taken by Muḥammad ʻAlī with regard to irrigation. On the occasions when the dikes were neglected, the excessive flooding of the land resulted in poor crops of cereals and serious losses both to the peasants and to Muḥammad ʻAlī.

Bad floods in two consecutive years, 1824 and 1825, forced Muḥammad ʻAlī to issue an order prohibiting the export of foodstuffs, particularly beans and grain, to assure a sufficient supply in Egypt for local consumption. Wheat had to be imported to meet the deficit at home. The flood of 1826 was the best in several years, however, and eliminated the threat of famine; harvests both in 1826 and 1827 were good. Muḥammad ʻAlī hoped to augment his revenues because of the ukase issued by the Emperor of Russia prohibiting the export of wheat and the closing of the Black Sea during the war between Turkey and Russia in 1828. Demands for wheat did not reach the anticipated amount, though, because of the excellent harvest throughout practically all of southern Europe in 1828.[57] The vegetable harvest, however, failed in Italy so that the price of beans rose considerably. The Pasha sent 40,000 *ardabbs* of beans to his agent at Leghorn, Fernandez, to be sold on his own account, a transaction which annoyed the merchants in Egypt.[58]

In 1828 the flood was good; so orders were issued to devote a considerable part of the sowing to foodstuffs to take advantage of the situation. Muḥammad 'Alī then shrewdly waited to see how events would be shaped before offering his crops for sale. At last he put the crops on sale but at prices which were fixed at an extremely high level. The export price of beans was set at 5 dollars per *ardabb*, although in the spring of 1828 they had sold at between 2.5 to 3 dollars per *ardabb*. Wheat, which had sold at 4.25 dollars per *ardabb* the previous year, rose to 10 dollars. Although these high prices kept prospective buyers away for a time, Muḥammad 'Alī decided not to sell until his demands were met. The merchants eventually capitulated in the hope of benefiting from the fine trading opportunites that the war offered.[59]

Abundant crops caused an overflow in the granaries at Alexandria in the spring of 1829 and were snapped up by the merchants. Because of mismanagement, however, Upper and Lower Egypt were drained of wheat and there was not enough in Cairo to feed the population. One hundred thousand *ardabbs* were ordered back to Cairo from the stores at Alexandria to meet the deficit.[60] The flood of that year, 1829, reversed the export situation. The flood was so high that almost all *nīlī* crops were destroyed and many villages were completely dissolved by the inundation. The whole population of many parts of Egypt worked day and night to repair the dikes, but the water continued to rise. On October 15, 1829, Ibrāhīm Pasha called a meeting of officials to examine official returns of the devastation. The partial or total destruction of ungathered crops amounted to 5,000,000 dollars. About 2,000,000 dollars were also lost on crops which had been harvested, but only partially stored. Other estimates given by foreign consuls were 105,000,000 piasters (210,000 purses) and 15,000,000 to 20,000,000 francs. In addition, the peasants sustained tremendous losses in life and property. Furthermore, the province of Fayyūm remained dry. The river had overflowed its banks, but the water did not enter the irrigation canals and was lost in the desert; famine until the following June seemed certain. Some observers felt that the loss was somewhat exaggerated by Muḥammad 'Alī to support his refusal to help the Sultan meet the first installment of the

Russian indemnity. It was also rumored that some cultivators assisted in the calamity by secretly destroying some of the dikes as a protest against the oppression from which they suffered.[61]

The government's policy in former years of exporting all available foodstuffs had failed to take into account the eventuality of a bad harvest, and the effects of this policy were severely felt during the early part of 1830 when the poor harvest resulting from the disastrous flood of 1829 proved insufficient for the needs of the country. The situation was greatly aggravated by the fact that a large quantity of grain had fallen into the hands of speculators who profited from the suffering of the people to obtain exorbitant prices. Moreover, the wheat which the government supplied to the bakers in the towns had been mixed with beans or barley, a practice which caused a great outcry among the townspeople. Nothing was done to meet the complaints of the native population, but a special concession was made in the case of the Europeans who had complained bitterly about the high price and bad quality of grain. The Pasha commanded that unadulterated wheat should be delivered daily to bakers who supplied the Frank population. Since shipments of grain from Upper Egypt failed to arrive as expected in the spring of 1830, conditions in Egypt grew more critical and it was reported that Egyptians were everywhere dying of hunger. Muḥammad ʿAlī was apparently so affected by the large-scale suffering that he attended public prayers. "Good Muslims," it was said, "are saying that the famine has at least had the merit of converting His Highness." The Pasha was finally forced to import flour to alleviate the famine.[62]

To avoid a similar crisis Muḥammad ʿAlī decided in 1831 to permit the cultivators to sell their grain directly to local consumers. The *fallāḥīn* took advantage of this situation to demand high prices. The government was then forced to compete to bring down prices; on January 1, 1832, it established government markets in Cairo and Alexandria where commodities were sold at fixed prices. At the end of 1832, however, it was reported that the cost of living had gone up from three to five times because of the creation of an artificial scarcity. Wheat bought in Upper Egypt at 25 piasters per *ardabb* was sold in Cairo for as much as 120. Beans were sold in like proportion. Profit on beef, mutton, and fish was about 100 to 150 per cent. One observer commented caustically: "Mehmed Aly can, therefore, never want money, while it is in his power to say to the people of Egypt '*Starve or pay me famine prices for the necessaries of life.*'"[63] By 1837 wheat and barley earned excessively high prices. A shortage of foodstuffs too was felt, largely due to the export of great quantities of cereal to support the armies fighting in al-Ḥijāz. By October 1837 famine conditions actually existed in Egypt. Wheat sold in Cairo at 175 piasters per *ardabb*. Yet large quantities of linseed, grain, and beans which were in the government *shūnahs* at Alexandria were not distributed, as a good flood was anticipated for 1837. The flood, however, proved to be mediocre.[64]

To combat speculation and the prevailing fear of famine Muḥammad ʻAlī issued a decree that the price of wheat should be fixed at 100 piasters per *ardabb* and beans, barley, and lentils at 60 piasters. The prices had risen as high as 160 to 170 piasters for wheat, 78 for beans, 85 for barley, and 105 for lentils. Supplies in Upper Egypt were brought to Cairo to be sold at government prices, but still the situation was not rectified. Egypt, which had been an exporter of grain, was now in the position where imports were urgently required. Merchants were, however, reluctant to import grain because of the prohibition of grain exports. They feared that if they imported grain at high prices, they would find themselves in possession of large quantities of grain which would have to compete with native grain. They knew that, so long as the scarcity existed, there was a fair chance of a gainful return on their investment, but they were apprehensive that a new harvest would glut the market and that they would then suffer great losses. They felt, too, that the exorbitant import taxes which they were forced to pay beyond the legal amount of 3 per cent allowed by the Capitulations had made import of grain into Egypt an unprofitable business venture. To meet the latter objection, Muḥammad ʻAlī now allowed the British merchants to import grain upon payment of 3 per cent duty. He still required the merchants from other countries, however, to pay import duties as high as 19 piasters on an *ardabb* of wheat, although their consuls protested against the discriminatory practices of the Pasha. Then in November 1837 when wheat shipments from Sicily and other ports arrived in Alexandria on consignment to various European merchants and the government insisted upon payment of the higher tariffs by non-British merchants, the latter refused to pay more than was required of the British. After three weeks of negotiations between the foreign representatives and the Pasha, the ships carrying these consignments were permitted to land their cargoes upon a uniform payment of the 3 per cent duty only.[65]

Then, as an experiment, an order was issued on November 26, 1837, which contained the following provisions: first, free import of grain would be permitted as of December 1, 1837, to the end of February 1838; second, the restricted (later modified to read the unrestricted) circulation of grain within Egypt would also be permitted; and third, grain would be subject to government inspection in the markets to insure that standards were maintained and that it was not mixed in any way that was injurious to the health of the population. In consequence of this more liberal policy, grain began to enter the market and by the end of January 1838 the scarcity was relieved. Prices were so high, however, that the *fallāḥīn* could not buy food. Wheat sold at 112 piasters per *ardabb* and was half mixed with barley and lentils; other foodstuffs were equally expensive. Reports came from Upper Egypt of widespread starvation. With the exception of England, Egypt was at the time the most expensive country in the world in which to live. Further corrective measures had to be taken. Not only did the right to free import of grain continue without further publicity into March, but the Pasha also ordered his agents to import more grain. A notice was published in April, asserting that the surplus import duties would not be reinstated upon wheat, barley, beans, rice, and every kind of grain until the next harvest. All internal taxes were also lifted. A drop in the cost of food-stuffs was reported, which in turn promised to reduce the high cost of living. The experience of 1837–38 was not to be repeated in Muḥammad 'Alī's reign; precautions were taken thereafter to have an adequate supply of grain available in the country to obviate the emergency measures which had been necessary.[66]

The floods of 1840 and 1841 brought new setbacks. Just before the 1840 flood, the government warehouses had contained two million *ardabbs* of grain which the Pasha had planned to sell in Europe where foodstuffs were in great demand, due in part to the shortage of Russian wheat, and prices consequently high. The extraordinary flood of 1840 ended the Pasha's hopes of great profit, however, because a large number of government *shūnahs* were destroyed and, also, at least half of the remaining reserves had to be retained in the country for internal consumption. In fact, the Pasha found it necessary to supply the *fallāḥīn* with food and to distribute seed for sowing from government stores. Moreover, the brief blockade of Egypt during the diplomatic crisis of 1840 aggravated the situation further, for prices of all commodities in the country soared as a result of the blockade. The flood of 1841 was far worse, even, than that of 1840, reaching its highest level in living memory. Despite precautions which the government had taken in strengthening and raising the dikes, whole villages were swept away. The crops which were in the ground were completely destroyed. More than eight hundred villages were abandoned along with their animals and agricultural tools. Had the river risen a few inches higher, an immense stock of wheat, about forty feet high, which had been piled at al-ʿAṭf, awaiting shipment to Alexandria, would have been carried away or the greater part of the grain totally spoiled. The island of ar-Rawḍah was completely inundated and suffered considerable damage. The estimated cost of damage was put at 150,000,000 piasters (300,000 purses) for the Pasha and 50,000,000 piasters (100,000 purses) for individuals, making a total of 200,000,000 piasters. A new sowing had to be ordered to provide enough food for local consumption, an amount of 950,000 *ardabbs* of cereals being needed each year so that the native population would have an adequate supply for its sustenance.[67]

A special calamity, which threatened the food supply of the country anew, struck Egypt in 1842. About 150,000 cattle were carried away by a disease reputed to be *cholera morbus.* (One figure quoted 200,000 casualties.) Nearly all the cattle of Lower and Middle Egypt died and the disease extended to sheep as well. The plague spread throughout Egypt as far south as Aṣwān. The mortality was so great in the *chifliks* of the Pasha that he ordered the cavalry horses to work on his farms as well as the artillery horses, which had, since the end of the war with the Sultan, been used for dragging barges on al-Maḥmūdīyah Canal. The lack of animals made it impossible to work the soil or operate the *sāqiyahs.* Muḥammad ʿAlī tried to save the situation by sending to other countries for animals, but they could not be brought quickly enough. The *fallāḥīn* were finally obliged to yoke themselves to the plow to prepare the ground. By November 1842 the disease began to abate. Nevertheless, the Pasha was obliged to issue an order to stop grain sales for export until he could ascertain the effects of the disease on the next harvest. A large stock of wheat was in the granaries, but there was a possibility that only half of the land could be cultivated the following year.[68]

Despite this enormous animal mortality large quantities of foodstuffs were actually harvested in 1843, part of which were available for export. The harvest in 1844 was also satisfactory. Although the harvest of 1845 proved deficient, the export of grain was permitted until prices began to rise locally. Then the Pasha issued an order on October 22, 1845, prohibiting the further export of grain. On February 10, 1846 this prohibition was lifted as a good harvest was expected. The export price of foodstuffs rose in 1846 as a result of European demand. At the time the British government was anxious to import large quantities of food to supply Ireland, and the French, also anxious to procure large quantities of foodstuffs, were willing to pay high prices. It was anticipated that this demand for Egyptian crops would lead to an additional price rise. Prices (in piasters per *ardabb*) quoted in February 1846 were as follows:[69]

Wheat	65	Beans	55
Barley	42	Lentils	55
Maize	45		

Duhamel reported to his government in 1837 that some differences of opinion existed among observers regarding agricultural production in Egypt. Partisans of the government maintained that trade was far more active than in previous years, whereas detractors of the government

TABLE 8. Amount of foodstuffs exported (in *ardabbs*), 1816–1844

Product	1816	1829	1836	1843	1844
Wheat	134,000	150,000	19,426	446,598	287,502
Beans	230,000	160,000	14,724	397,945	430,489
Lentils	26,000	40,000	—	8,645	5,538
Barley	10,000	80,000	24,957	16,988	57,051
Maize	60,000	30,000	—	2,920	—
Dhurah	—	—	—	—	—
Chick peas	20,000	—	—	9,793	8,385
Lupin	12,000	20,000[a]	—	11,221	22,053
Fenugreek	15,000	—	—	—	—
	507,000[b]	480,000[c]	59,107[d]	894,110[e]	811,018[f]

[a] And other grains.
[b] Salt, April 28, 1817 in F.O. 78/89.
[c] René Cattaui, *Le règne de Mohamed Ali d'après les archives russes en Egypte*, Société royale de géographie d'Egypte, publications spéciales (Cairo, 1931, Rome, 1933, 1935, 1936), I, 298, 299.
[d] Cattaui, II, Pt. 2, 409.
[e] Stoddart, March 23, 1844 in F.O. 78/584. Export increases began by 1840. Barnett reports that the total quantity of grain exported in 1840 was 187,500 Imperial Quarters of barley, 375,000 Imperial Quarters of wheat (a quarter approximated an *ardabb*). These shipments were made to replace supplies for Britain drawn from the Mediterranean and Black Sea ports (Barnett, November 15, 1841 in F.O. 78/451).
[f] Stoddart, April 10, 1845 in F.O. 78/624.

claimed it was on the decrease. Duhamel decided to check these statements by an examination of trade figures and came to the following conclusions: first, there was considerable fluctuation in production from year to year, depending upon the extent of the flood; second, cereals, oleaginous grains, and flax had declined in the previous twelve-year period; and third, it was inaccurate to say that cotton cultivation had increased in the same proportion as cereals diminished. He went on to say that though it was clear that production had declined in twelve years, it was none the less true that enormous progress had been made since the Mamlūk rule and the early years of Muḥammad ʻAlī's reign.[70] A study of figures available on cereal exports makes it possible to judge the correctness of Duhamel's analysis. Table 8 gives samples of export figures. These figures demonstrate conclusively that large quantities of cereals and other foodstuffs were produced for export in the period before the development of cotton, that exports dropped moderately in the decade of the twenties, declined enormously in the thirties, and not only rose in the forties, but exceeded by more than 50 per cent the amount exported during the early period when Egyptian produce was

TABLE 9. Total production of foodstuffs, 1821–1844

Product	1821 (*ardabbs*)	1830 (*ardabbs*)	1832 (hecto-liters)	1835 (hecto-liters)	1834 (*ardabbs*)	1844 (*ardabbs*)
Wheat	1,200,000	1,024,565	4,002,000	2,668,000	950,000	2,533,675
Beans	1,200,000	268,368	1,932,000	1,288,000	800,000	2,242,785
Lentils	120,000	6,707	193,200	128,800	70,000	164,000
Barley	600,000	40,428	1,794,000	1,196,000	560,000	3,109,192
Maize	150,000	6,999	441,600	294,400	160,000	—
Dhurah	800,000	—	2,000,000	1,380,000	850,000	4,195,000
Chick peas	80,000	3,335	69,000	46,000	50,000	—
Lupin	40,000	—	55,200	36,800	35,000	—
Fenugreek	130,000	—	165,600	110,400	110,000	—
Total	4,320,000[a]	1,350,402[b]	10,652,600[c]	7,148,400[d]	3,585,000[e]	12,243,652[f]

[a] Felix Mengin, *Histoire de l'Egypte sous le gouvernement du Mohammed-Aly, etc.* (Paris, 1823), II, 372; Georges Douin, *La mission du Baron de Boislecomte. L'Egypte et la Syrie en 1833*, Société royale de géographie d'Egypte, publications spéciales (Cairo, 1927), 86.

[b] John Bowring, "Report on Egypt and Candia," A Report addressed to Palmerston and presented to both Houses of Parliament, House of Commons, Sessional Papers 1840, vol. XXI: *Reports from Commissioners*, vol. 6, p. 17.

[c] Douin, *La mission du Baron de Boislecomte*, 86. A hectoliter is approximately one half an *ardabb.*

[d] A. B. Clot, *Aperçu général sur l'Egypte* (Paris, 1840), II, 287.

[e] Bowring, "Egypt and Candia," 17.

[f] Barnett, December 12, 1844 in F.O. 78/583; Appendix I. This column may represent potential rather than the actual production in 1844. A large figure covering various items not specifically listed has not been included in this column. The figure for lentils also includes onions, kidney beans, lupin, and tobacco.

in great demand in Europe. The figures show also the fluctuation in the demand for individual items.

The available figures on the total production of foodstuffs, however, produce a different picture than is conveyed by the export figures (see Table 9). The crops harvested in 1821 were probably standard for Egypt before the introduction of cotton. Except for some variations because of differences in the flood from year to year, the production of cereals and foodstuffs did not decline radically in the thirties. (In the case of 1830 the figures reflect the results of the excessive flood of 1829.) The great decline in exports in the thirties did not, therefore, reflect a proportional decrease in total production. Egyptian foodstuffs were simply earmarked for destinations other than the foreign export market. This is confirmed by Bowring's analysis of the distribution of the 1830 crop which totaled 1,352,141 *ardabbs* (an additional 1,739 *ardabbs* of peas must be added to the 1,350,402 *ardabbs* listed in Table 9).

Distribution of 1830 crop

To Alexandria	219,756 *ardabbs*
To Damietta	28,244
To al-Manṣūrah	12,732
To Shibīn	27,268
To Rosetta	44,261
Made into biscuits for the garrison of Candia, Sinnār, and al-Ḥijāz	60,000
Cereals used for the army and navy	236,952
Cereals used for the Court and *Ḥarīms* of Muḥammad 'Alī, Ibrāhīm Pasha, and government functionaries	64,148
Sold in Cairo for the consumption of the public	654,280
	1,347,641
Remained in Warehouse	4,500
	1,352,141[71]

An English mechanic once told John Bowring that there had been a decline of one third in the area of cultivation since Muḥammad 'Alī's reign (see Appendix II) and that production had fallen off by two thirds.

His statement was far off the mark.[72] Duhamel came closer to a correct analysis, although he made the essential error of equating exports with production. Both reports were made before the expansion of cultivation in the forties.

In the 1840's the end of the war made possible an expansion of agriculture. Both a good cotton crop and a good crop of cereals and other foodstuffs became available for export as well as for internal consumption. There was, furthermore, no necessity to furnish supplies to troops engaged in war outside Egypt. The expansion of private estates at this juncture and the administration of land by private landholders rather than by a corrupt and inefficient governmental hierarchy may also account in part for the increased production.

CARTHAMUS TINCTORIUS (SAFFLOWER). This plant, cultivated in Egypt even before Muḥammad ʿAlī came to power, was valued because of the oil extracted from its seed, because of its stems which the peasants used for fuel, and especially because of the valuable red vegetable dye, known as safflower, which was derived from the dried petals of the *carthamus* blossom. The quality of Egyptian safflower declined in the early years of Muḥammad ʿAlī's reign because the *fallāḥīn* frequently mixed it with flour made from the chick pea to strengthen its color and to increase its weight. Then in 1816 Muḥammad ʿAlī, wishing to profit from the greater demand for safflower of the expanding European textile industry, added *carthamus tinctorius* to the list of products monopolized by him. From then on, the peasants no longer dared to adulterate this crop in any way.[73]

The statistical information for safflower is very incomplete. In 1821 4,000 *qinṭārs* were produced, all of which were exported to Europe for the Pasha's account. About 3,500 *qinṭārs* were produced annually in the 1830's, although in the fiscal year of 1834–35 only 2,500 *qinṭārs*, valued at 280,000 piasters, were exported. Ten years later, in 1845, the export of safflower amounted to 2,988 *qinṭārs* and was valued at 538,840 piasters.[74] At first, the peasants received a fair price for this crop. In 1826 they received 56 to 112 piasters per *qinṭār* of 39½ *uqqahs* for their safflower. The following year, however, they were paid only 25 to 80 piasters per *qinṭār*.[75] It is impossible, from these few figures, to draw any definite conclusions concerning the trend in production or prices for this crop.

OPIUM. Before Muḥammad ʿAlī's reign opium was scarcely known in Egypt. Its cultivation began around 1824 when a number of Armenians were invited from Smyrna to raise opium in Egypt. In 1831 about 14,500 *uqqahs* were sold at 110 piasters per *uqqah*. The crop of opium in 1832 was 25,000 *uqqahs* which were sold at the following prices: for first quality, 116 piasters per *uqqah*; for second quality, 101 piasters; and for third, 86. In 1833 the annual production was 31,000 kilograms (or about 25,662 *uqqahs*) and was valued at 1,000,000 francs. The annual amount of opium produced in the latter part of the 1830's was estimated at 15,000 to 20,000 *uqqahs* per annum. In 1833 18,450 kilograms (about 14,795 *uqqahs*) were exported. Duhamel claimed that in 1836 Muḥammad ʿAlī exported only 8,642 *uqqahs* and, in turn, received 1,166,693 piasters, although according to Colin the value of the opium export for that year amounted to 884,000 francs (*c.* 2,946,670 piasters). In 1844 the combined area of opium and indigo and other unspecified crops raised in Upper Egypt was 3,700 *faddāns* and was valued at 1,950,000 piasters. The exact percentage of opium is not indicated, but in 1845 the export of opium was merely 1,242 *uqqahs*. This figure clearly indicates that opium as an item of export had declined rather than increased.[76]

TOBACCO. Tobacco was grown in large quantities in Egypt. As it was of inferior quality, it was consumed locally by the lower classes, Syrian tobacco being preferred by the more wealthy people in Egypt. The government did not monopolize tobacco and it was for this reason readily cultivated by the *fallāḥīn* who received the entire profit from the crop for themselves. Bowring put the production figure in 1834 at 100,000 cwt.[77]

HEMP. Although hemp figured as an item of export as early as 1816, no figures are available for the amount produced. In Egypt it was used only as a narcotic known as *hashīsh* until the period of naval expansion during Muḥammad ʿAlī's reign, particularly after 1827, when it was cultivated for use in the manufacture of rope. In 1833 Muḥammad ʿAlī spoke of his desire to increase production of hemp and flax to enable him to replace cotton sails on his ships by cordage sails; since no figures are available, it cannot be known whether he actually increased the production of hemp.[78]

FLAX. Flax was a commodity which had long been cultivated in Egypt; in the days of the Mamlūks between 30,000 and 35,000 *qinṭārs* were produced annually. Although it was claimed in 1801 that Egyptian flax was not of good quality, Boislecomte reported in 1833 that Egyptian flax was the best in the trade. If there was indeed an improvement, it resulted undoubtedly from the fact that flax was included among the crops which were monopolized by Muḥammad 'Alī in 1816 and received special attention in its cultivation.[79]

Flax was produced and exported as shown in the accompanying list. There are many lacunae in these figures, but they point to an increase in production and export.[80]

	Total production of flax	*Export*
1821	45,000 *qinṭārs*	——
1832	——	8,000 *qinṭārs*
1833	800,000 kgms.	——
1834	55,000 cwt.	——
1835	50,000 *qinṭārs*[81]	——
1843	——	59,486 *qinṭārs*
1844	901,445 *qinṭārs*[82]	75,863 *qinṭārs*

LINSEED. Linseed is a by-product of flax. The accompanying figures, showing total production and export, are pertinent.

	Total production of linseed	*Export*
1816	——	30,000 *ardabbs*
1821	50,000 *ardabbs*	——
1833	20,240 *ardabbs* (40,480 hectoliters)	——
1834	60,000 *ardabbs*	——
1836	——	27,217 *ardabbs*
1843	——	60,767 *ardabbs*
1844	614,830 *ardabbs*	29,732 *ardabbs*[83]

As in the case of cereals, it seems there was a steady increase in production, although exports dropped off in the thirties. In the decade of the forties a jump in production and export occurred.[84]

Miscellaneous Crops

DATE TREES. It was estimated in 1833 that there were between five and six million date trees in Egypt. The trees at Damietta gave the following yields: first-class fruit—19–20 kgms. at 9 francs or 45 centimes per kgm.; second-class fruit—10–12 kgms. at 5–6 francs. The date trees in Upper Egypt and Rosetta did not give as good yields. The government bought the foliage of date trees at 9 centimes per tree. The date tree also provided a fiber known as *līf* which was used as cordage and was monopolized by the government. The government price for delivery of *līf* was 22 piasters per *qinṭār*, but the price was so unattractive to the *fallāḥīn* that the government was forced to raise it to 35 piasters per *qinṭār*.[85] The owners earned 6 centimes from branches which fell to the ground.

The date tree was burdened with a tax levied in accordance with the quality of its fruit.[86] The tax bore so heavily on the cultivators of the land that it was not profitable to develop the trees. One man reported that he had asked permission either to uproot the trees or to have its fruit expropriated in lieu of the tax. His request was refused. Many *fallāḥīn* preferred to cut down their trees, whenever they could, rather than pay the tax. The number of date trees diminished in consequence.[87] Export figures on dates are not available except for 1844 when 23,928 *qinṭārs* were exported.[88]

ROSE TREES. This tree was cultivated in the Fayyūm to produce rose water. The government exercised a monopoly over the product and paid such low prices that cultivators were unwilling to develop this branch of agriculture for which the Fayyūm had always been distinguished. The government price was 25 piasters per *qinṭār*. Three qualities of rose water were produced and sold at 3, 5, and 7 piasters per bottle, depending upon the quality.[89]

MADDER. The madder plant was introduced in Egypt in 1825 to provide the dye needed in the *ṭarbūsh* industry newly founded in Egypt. By 1833, 800 *faddāns* were devoted to its cultivation in all Egypt. Alizarin, the red coloring matter of madder, and cochineal were exported in 1832.[90]

VINEYARDS. The Pasha decided in 1828 to raise enough grapes to make brandy and avoid the necessity for importing raisins annually for this purpose. He ordered the *fallāḥīn* who possessed *sāqiyahs* furnished by the government to devote six *faddāns* of their land to grape cultivation.[91] Apparently Ibrāhīm Pasha was particularly interested in this branch of agriculture and made several attempts to extend grape cultivation and to develop the wine industry. No statistics are available, but the number of vineyards reportedly did increase.[92]

MULBERRY TREES AND SILK. The mulberry tree existed in Egypt prior to the reign of Muḥammad 'Alī. Both the black mulberry and the white mulberry were found. The black mulberry dated from ancient times, but the white mulberry was not of ancient origin and had been introduced with the silkworm during the period of the early *khalīfahs*.[93]

During the reign of Muḥammad 'Alī many white mulberry trees were planted. Next to the date tree, it became the most numerous in Egypt, but even so the number planted never sufficed and the failure of the silkworm industry to take permanent hold in Egypt was attributed to this deficiency.[94]

Experiments in the culture of silkworms began as early as 1812 when it was optimistically hoped that Egyptian dependence on imports of raw silk from Syria would cease. The Syrians, brought into Egypt to undertake the culture of silkworms, were unfortunately placed under the supervision of Turk administrators who knew nothing about the industry and were afraid to authorize the necessary outlays. When the silkworms were hatched, an inadequate food supply was available since, particularly at this early date, there were not enough mulberry trees and those in existence were too young to produce sufficiently large leaves. Mallow leaves were substituted to compensate for this shortage, but a great mortality of silkworms resulted nevertheless. Those silkworms which survived produced small and thin cocoons which furnished very little silk of an inferior quality. Muḥammad 'Alī, however, did not allow this early failure to discourage him.[95]

In 1816 Muḥammad 'Alī issued orders for Ra's al-Wādī, which had become a desert during years of neglect, to be reclaimed and for mulberry trees to be planted. The canals which had at one time serviced this area were in a state of ruin. Orders were given by the Pasha for the construction of one thousand *sāqiyahs* to be manufactured at Cairo. They were brought by camel transport to the Wādī and installed. Some time later a canal was dug to bring water to the Wādī from the Nile. Muḥammad 'Alī also appointed an agent in 1816 to go to Syria to purchase silkworm eggs. At the beginning of 1817 Muḥammad 'Alī arranged for specialists in the culture of silkworms to be brought from Syria and Lebanon. He agreed to give them the first harvest of silk and one quarter of the profits of the harvest thereafter. A Syrian colony of five hundred was established.[96] Orders were also issued to the governor of ash-Sharqīyah to bring all the peasants who were not attached to any particular place in the province to work in the Wādī and to learn culture of silkworms. According to al-Jabartī these measures led to the complete reclamation of the Wādī.[97] The area reclaimed amounted to 3,000 *faddāns* and was watered by the new canal that was built. It was drained by 1,000 irrigation ditches that had been dug. Six thousand oxen were brought to aid the irrigation and a total of 1,500,000 mulberry trees were planted. It was soon found, however, that Ra's al-Wādī was not suitable for the mulberry tree. When the tree encountered the secondary strata of the soil, it failed to develop. The trees were eventually uprooted and the land turned over to barley and wheat cultivation.[98]

Muḥammad 'Alī was determined to continue his experiment in establishing the silk industry. He ordered all the provinces, therefore, to plant mulberry trees. The Syrians were brought into the villages to teach the *fallāḥīn* about silkworm culture. Seven thousand additional *faddāns* were planted in ash-Sharqīyah, al-Manṣūrīyah, al-Minūfīyah, al-Gharbīyah, al-Qalyūbīyah, Gīzah, Damietta, and Rosetta. A total of 3,000,000 mulberry trees was planted on the 10,000 *faddāns* of land devoted to this purpose according to Bowring, and 4,000,000 according to Campbell. Muḥammad 'Alī also encouraged experiments in developing another plant suitable for feeding silkworms. According to one estimate the total investment amounted to more than 8,000,000 francs.[99]

The Pasha provided the *fallāḥīn* with the eggs of the silkworm at 1½ piasters per dram. The prices that he paid per *uqqah* in 1833 for raw silk delivered at Cairo were these: for first quality, 125 piasters; for second quality, 95; and for third quality, 85. In 1247/1831–32 the total amount of silk produced in Egypt was 6,748 *uqqahs* and 406 drams (Table 10). Ibrāhīm Pasha also took an interest in the development of the culture of silk. He planted hundreds of *faddāns* of mulberry trees on

TABLE 10. Production of silk, 1247/1831–32

Place produced	*Uqqahs*
Ra's al-Wādī	2,139.200
al-Minūfīyah	1,222.300
al-Manṣūrīyah	1,167.156
al-Gharbīyah	882.050
ash-Sharqīyah	744.050
al-Qalyūbīyah	310.200
Buḥayrah	227.250
Gīzah	56.200
TOTAL	6,748.406

his estates. Egyptian demands for raw silk were not met, however, and the deficiency was supplied by imports from Syria.[100]

Pressure was placed upon Muḥammad ʻAlī in 1835 to end the silk monopoly and to allow the export of raw silk, particularly from Syria. He terminated his monopoly of silk in Egypt by December 18, 1835, and shortly afterwards it was also abolished in Syria. Muḥammad ʻAlī also decided to abandon the silk manufactories which he had established in Egypt and ordered the disposal of all silk remaining in the depot at Cairo. The termination of the monopoly on raw silk made the manufacture of silk textiles in Egypt an unprofitable business, as silk cloth could not be produced at a sufficiently low cost without a cheap source of supply of raw material. Muḥammad ʻAlī explained in a letter to Hamont in 1840 that he had ended the culture of silkworms in Egypt and had abandoned the silk manufactories because his investments of large sums of money had brought inadequate returns and he preferred to employ his money on other projects which would bring greater benefits to Egypt.[101]

Olive trees. When Muḥammad ʻAlī came to power, there were only 2,400 olive trees in Egypt. In 1812 he ordered 30,000 olive trees to be planted in the province of Fayyūm. In 1816 orders were given to plant olive trees in Ra's al-Wādī. Ibrāhīm, however, was responsible for extending olive tree cultivation in Upper Egypt. By 1835, 310,000 trees had been planted in all parts of the country and the average income from each tree was 3 francs. The olive oil produced was used for soap and as an illumination fuel.[102]

The development of gardens and horticultural experimentation. Finally, special attention was given to gardening. Elaborate gardens were laid out in the palaces of members of the royal family as well as in those of members of the upper classes, and plans for al-Azbakīyah Gardens were made. In Cairo the gardens of Ibrāhīm Pasha, who showed a real interest in agriculture and horticulture not only as a source of revenue but for themselves, were particularly distinguished and were open to the public three days a week and to respectable Europeans at all times.[103] Ibrāhīm's gardens were under the supervision of two English gardeners, McCulloch and Trail, the latter, the son of the gardener of the Horticultural Society in London.[104] These men also took charge of Ibrāhīm's estate on the island of ar-Rawḍah which served as an experimental horticultural station.[105] At various times McCulloch was sent to different parts of the world to obtain seeds and plants for experimental purposes. On one occasion he went to India to obtain plants from Bombay, Madras, and Bengal. Lord Auckland, Governor-General of India, used this opportunity to improve Egyptian-Indian relations and gave full support to McCulloch's mission. McCulloch then went to Brazil to obtain plants not available in India, particularly sugar cane plants.[106]

Experimentation with plants which were not indigenous to Egypt was carried on at this time. Several thousand young teak trees were planted at ar-Rawḍah as well as numerous spice and other plants brought from Calcutta. Of these, teak, bamboo, yam, rubber, ginger, arrowroot, and custard apple proved to be cultivable on Egyptian soil, but coffee and tea failed to grow successfully.[107] Experiments on fruit trees were also made, on pineapple, mango, banana, peach, apricot, prune, pear, cherry, and almond trees. The results were not always satisfactory, because of the excessive heat which did not allow the fruit adequate time to mature, and it was consequently often small and tasteless. In other cases, results were good.[108] Tangerines too were introduced from Malta into Egypt by Yūsuf Efendī, one of the students who had been sent to France by Muḥammad ʿAlī and had studied agriculture there. On his voyage back to Egypt, Yūsuf Efendī picked up several tangerine plants at Malta which he later developed in Egypt. Muḥammad ʿAlī was so pleased with the results that he ordered tangerine trees planted at Shubrā. Yūsuf Efendī was placed in charge of these trees and the tangerine became known in Egypt by his name.[109] Also introduced into the country were a number of vegetables and garden fruits, such as artichokes, asparagus, peas, special haricots, and strawberries. Potatoes were also planted, but were smaller and not so good as the European variety.[110]

Agricultural techniques. Despite the experiments which were carried out during Muḥammad ʿAlī's reign Egyptian agricultural practices did not undergo any revolutionary changes. Agricultural techniques, for example, remained traditional, although more attention, particularly in the case of export crops, was paid to standardization of procedures in the preparation of the soil and cultivation. The *Lāʾiḥat zirāʿat al-fallāḥ* contained complete instructions regarding the preparation of land, the amount of seed to be planted per *faddān*, the care of the soil after the crop was planted, and irrigation, harvesting, and transportation of the crop to government *shūnahs*. Scientific methods were used in the case of new crops with varying degrees of success, but the value of scientific farming was not generally comprehended. It was once reported that several students sent by the Egyptian government to Europe on an educational mission had explained to a government official upon their return that they had studied agronomy in Europe. The official had replied in amazement that he was unable to understand why anyone should take as a special field of study that which the most ignorant Egyptian peasant already knew.[111] Indeed, the Egyptian *fallāḥīn* possessed a profound knowledge of the soil which they cultivated; their methods were based on centuries of experience. They venerated their land deeply and always attempted to maintain its fertility. They had practiced crop rotation long before Muḥammad 'Alī's reign, as witnessed by Guillaume Olivier, who traveled in Egypt at the end of the eighteenth century. Olivier noted that the *fallāḥīn* alternated between wheat and barley, rice and clover, and cereals and safflower. The order of rotation, he said, was often determined by the extent of the flood and the prices which various crops could command in the market. If the Nile flood was weak, the farmers sowed barley rather than wheat because barley required less water and was harvested a month sooner. On the other hand, if the flood was strong, they sowed broad beans. Baron de Boislecomte mistakenly considered this practice of crop rotation a revolutionary innovation introduced by Muḥammad 'Alī, and one which, he remarked, France had been attempting to introduce for fifty years with only very limited success because of the ancient prejudices and obstinacy of the French peasants. Actually, Muḥammad 'Alī's "progressive" policy of crop rotation, especially for land devoted to cotton cultivation, was nothing more than the application of an old principle long in use in Egypt, which he quickly observed to be essential because of the exhaustive nature of the cotton crop and the speed at which its quality deteriorated. The order of crop rotation he used was clover followed by wheat, sesame (or other oleaginous plants) followed by clover or barley, and cotton followed by clover or barley. It had also been customary for the *fallāḥīn* to use fertilizers as well as to rotate crops to prevent soil exhaustion. Since animal fertilizer was employed as fuel and not for agricultural purposes, the *fallāḥīn* had used the large supplies of nitrogenous materials to be found in the neighboring ruins. This practice continued unchanged during Muḥammad 'Alī's reign and caused criticism of the government's failure to collect waste material accumulated in villages for use on the land.[112]

Generations of farming experience in Egypt by the *fallāḥīn* had also produced the agricultural instruments most suited to the Egyptian soil. Muḥammad 'Alī recognized this fact and resisted the temptation to introduce European tools, except on the government's model farms that he established. The use of these modern agricultural instruments did not, however, spread beyond these experimental farms. Hamont urged that the *miḥrāth*, or plow, be discarded in favor of the European plow for cotton cultivation, but even he admitted that with all its faults the Egyptian plow worked the land better than the European ones, which made the furrows too wide and deep. Various experiments by the government with European plows demonstrated their unsuitability and no attempt was made to provide *fallāḥīn* with them. As late as 1916 it was confirmed that not a single plow with which experiments had been made had proved superior to the indigenous one, mechancially, agriculturally, and economically, at one and the same time. Although the modern plow gave better results in the preparation of the fields for cotton cultivation, the Egyptian plow still remained, on the whole, most suitable for Egypt. The *fallāḥīn* also continued to use all other traditional agricultural tools. Inundated land was leveled by a tree trunk which was dragged crosswise by oxen. Irrigated land was leveled by the *massāḥah*, a plank about one meter long which was drawn by one or two men. The sickle was used for cutting crops. The ancient methods for threshing the grain were also in use. In the southernmost part of Upper Egypt, cereals were threshed by being spread on the floor and then trampled by oxen. In other parts of Egypt the *nawraj* was used; this was drawn by oxen and is still to be seen in many parts of the Middle East. Irrigating devices also remained unchanged. The *sāqiyah*, *shādūf*, and *tābūt* continued to be used even after the introduction of the deep-water canals. The conversion of canals into *ṣayfī* canals made it possible to retain Nile water for use during the summer, but the water had still to be lifted to the level of the land by means of water-raising devices and during Muḥammad 'Alī's reign the traditional appliances continued to be used almost exclusively.[113]

Although Muḥammad 'Alī's efforts to improve the condition of Egyptian agriculture did not meet with unqualified success and agricultural techniques were not revolutionized, the Pasha's contributions to the development of Egyptian agriculture were nevertheless of paramount importance. Muḥammad 'Alī, first of all, supplied the capital that was needed to transform the Egyptian agricultural economy from a subsistence economy to a cash crop economy and he did this without sacrificing the production of cereals, upon which the Egyptian agricultural economy had always been based. Also, the stress that Muḥammad 'Alī placed upon summer cultivation and the increase in the production of the highly lucrative summer crops made possible by the greater capital outlays provided by the Pasha contributed to this change in the character of Egyptian agriculture. Moreover, the emphasis on summer cultivation stimulated the development of perennial irrigation which, in turn, enabled a further extension of summer cultivation. It is true, of course, that a scientific system of perennial irrigation did not develop until much later, but Muḥammad 'Alī undoubtedly laid the basis for its development. Finally, and extremely important, the extension of summer cultivation and particularly the development of cotton enhanced Egypt's economic importance and provided a crop in great demand in Europe, thus forging a powerful economic link between Egypt and Europe. The extension of summer cultivation and the development of cotton also affected landholding, Egyptian industrial development, the country's administration, and above all furnished a large share of the revenue which made the grandiose projects of the Pasha financially possible. Muḥammad 'Alī's claim, therefore, that he was primarily a cultivator and a merchant was not without some justification.[114]

CHAPTER IX

TRADE AND AGRICULTURE

Commerce follows the variations of the Nile and the politics of the viceroy.

Huder[1]

The revival of Egyptian trade received its first impulse during the period of the Napoleonic Wars when the demand for wheat and other foodstuffs was great. The sale of Egyptian commodities at inflated prices rescued Muḥammad 'Alī's regime from the disaster and collapse which threatened it in 1810 when his economic situation reached a point of crisis. By the end of 1812 the Pasha's financial position was completely transformed; Drovetti was able to assert that Muḥammad 'Alī was not only able to cover the expenses of his army, the cost of administration, the the maintenance of the court, the customary gifts sent to Istanbul, and other extraordinary expenses, but that he was also able to save money to meet future contingencies. He was, in fact, considered the richest pasha in the Ottoman Empire.[2]

By 1810 conditions in Egypt were favorable for the expansion of trade. The life of the country had begun to be stabilized at the end of the civil war and communications between Lower and Upper Egypt were again open. Grain flowed freely from the south and abundant harvests for several consecutive years filled the government granaries with large quantities of grain. Although a shortage of specie in Egypt imposed upon Muḥammad 'Alī the necessity of collecting taxes in kind in lieu of taxes in specie, it was a necessity which he proceeded to turn to his advantage, for he was able to dispose of the crops which he received in payment of taxes in the European market at exceptionally high prices.

Muḥammad 'Alī's trade policy with Europe received its original impetus when the Turkish government, committed to providing Istanbul and the military with grain at government prices fixed at very low rates, found itself in a difficult position in 1810 because of the grain shortage in the capital and in all the cities along the coast of Syria and Asia Minor. The Sultan, therefore, dispatched several firmans prohibiting the export of Egyptian wheat to Turkey at speculative prices. Consequently, Muḥammad 'Alī, unable to obtain his price in the Turkish market and being more concerned with his own difficulties than with those of his sovereign, decided to send very small quantities of wheat to Istanbul and to sell the remainder of his crops to the British and their allies in the Mediterranean (Spain, Portugal, Malta, and the Ionian Islands) at the exorbitant prices they were willing to pay. The Turkish government then countered Muḥammad 'Alī's disobedience to the Sultan's firmans by demanding the observance of one of its long-established regulations prohibiting the export of wheat from the Ottoman Empire. So great, however, was Britain's need—because of the Turkish blockade of the Straits, which prevented the export of Russian wheat—that Stratford Canning issued secret instructions to the British agent in Egypt to arrange with Muḥammad 'Alī for a contraband trade by which the Sultan's order would be circumvented. The British authorities did not undertake to support openly anyone engaged in this trade; those who did so entered it at their own risk. Nevertheless, when the Porte threatened to search ships coming within the range of a line from Candia to Egypt, the British warned that such action would not be tolerated. Muḥammad 'Alī, for his part, ignored the Sultan's commands and continued to export grain. There was little that the Sultan could do to enforce his commands so flagrantly violated by his recalcitrant governor. Muḥammad 'Alī's exclusive dealings with the British soon gave rise to protests by the French also, but this difficulty was overcome in November 1811 when he announced his wish to pursue a policy of nondiscrimination towards the European Powers and promised to sell wheat to France as well as England. His promise availed the French but little, however, since British control of the seas provided them with few opportunities to obtain grain from Egypt.[3]

Having embarked upon a policy of trade with Europe, Muḥammad 'Alī now took several important steps in order to benefit fully from the grain trade. He extended the area of cultivation, reorganized his administration to insure the steady flow of grain into the government warehouses, built a fleet of boats to transport grain from the interior to the ports of embarkation, and levied a high export duty on grain amounting to 10 to 12 Turkish piasters per *ardabb*. Not satisfied with the profits he obtained from the sale of cereals in Egypt and well informed of the great demand for and high price of grain in Malta, Spain, and Portugal, Muḥammad 'Alī also for his own account sent ships to Spain and Malta where he appointed agents to receive and dispose of the cargoes. He commanded the best prices and received payment in specie, manufactured goods, and military supplies. In fact, Egyptian wheat jumped from 22 Turkish piasters per *ardabb* in 1810 to 80 to 100 piasters in 1811 and 1812 and its price to Egyptian consumers rose from 10 to 15 Turkish piasters per *ardabb* in 1810 to approximately 30 Turkish piasters in 1812. Despite the price at which wheat was sold for export and for internal consumption the Egyptian cultivators only received from 15 to 20 piasters per *ardabb*. They were naturally reluctant to sell their crops at the low prices paid by the Pasha and in 1812 were suspected of hiding their grain from government officials. At any rate, the flourishing trade of the previous two years could not be maintained in 1812. Grain surpluses in the government granaries were exhausted and the supply from the current crop was inadequate because the bad flood in 1811 had failed to inundate the land sufficiently. There was barely enough wheat in Egypt to feed the native population and that which existed was sold at exorbitant prices. As the 1812 flood proved a great disappointment also, prospects for the following year were shattered.[4] The seeds of later discord were, in fact, sown during these years. The British resented the high prices that they were obliged to pay for cereals and looked forward to the time when they could buy elsewhere. This resentment was inflamed by numerous complaints concerning Muḥammad 'Alī's discrimination against merchants and his tendency to monopolize every aspect of production and commerce to their disadvantage.[5]

When the Napoleonic Wars ended, Muḥammad 'Alī felt some alarm concerning his position in Egypt because of the rumor that the Treaty of Paris included a program for dismembering the Turkish Empire and for handing Egypt over to the British.[6] Consequently, to strengthen his position with the Porte he contributed large sums of money, as in the following case, described by Frere in a letter to the Foreign Office: "One of the means employed to secure his Sovereign's favour has been a large contribution toward replacing the losses occasioned by the fire that lately consumed the Harem. The Pasha of Egypt has likewise taken this opportunity of making a display of his loyalty and attachment by sending a sum of 1,250,000 piastres, of which he requests that 500,000 may be distributed amongst such of his Ministers as His Highness shall judge most deserving of his favour, and that the rest may be applied to the reparation of the damages caused by the above-mentioned fire."[7] In 1817 Muḥammad 'Alī also undertook to pay an annual sum of 15,000 purses to the Porte, excluding presents which were over and above this amount. Although reinforcing his position with the Sultan by these means, he placed an additional strain on the Egyptian treasury already burdened by the cost of his army, estimated at 40,000 men, of which 20,000 were cavalry.[8]

Muḥammad 'Alī's pressing need for revenue, arising from these demands upon the treasury, posed a problem which he hoped partially to solve through commerce. The exclusive trading privileges which he had enjoyed had been terminated with the end of the wars; nevertheless, he still found enough demand for his produce to maintain a flourishing trade. The threat of famine as a result of the rains in eastern and southern Europe had brought many purchasers to Egypt. In January 1816 one thousand vessels from Alexandria unloaded cereal in Sicily and Naples; moreover, the Egyptian harvest of the spring of 1816 proved to be sufficiently abundant to fulfill the demands of the trade. Muḥammad 'Alī also built ships which plied between Egypt and the Mediterranean ports and in the Red Sea; he appointed representatives in France, England, Malta, Smyrna, Tunis, Naples, Venice, al-Yaman, and India; and he gave large sums of money to trusted servants to bring all kinds of merchandise to Egypt from foreign countries.[9]

Trade was conducted in the manner most profitable to the Pasha. He issued firmans ordering the sale of his commodities to merchants with whom he chose to deal.[10] He also made every effort to keep prices high. If the prices offered were unsatisfactory, he did not hesitate to hold his stocks until he was offered better conditions.[11] Merchants complained bitterly about Muḥammad 'Alī's monopolistic practices and his favoritism. They blamed the Armenians in his entourage for his policies and also blamed Drovetti, the former French consul and an adherent to the Bonapartist economic philosophy favoring monopoly and protectionism, who exercised considerable influence over the Pasha. This commercial system as it finally emerged by 1818 was described at length by the British Consul-General:

> Much of the actual distrust must be attributed to the bad policy of the Pacha in attempting to monopolize the whole produce of the country, as well as to render himself the vendor of all foreign commodities imported into it. Hence it has followed that all commerce among the native traders has ceased and scarcely any means are left by which they can realize an honest livelihood.
>
> It is somewhat difficult to convey any very clear idea of the peculiar system of commerce now carried on in Egypt. More than nine in ten of the

merchants have been originally adventurers, who, in the first instance have no capital of their own. They commence on their arrival by making interest with one of the courtiers to prevail on the Pacha to grant them a firman or order for a certain quantity of grain payable some months after receipt. With this they enter into the market and if they can manage by *jobbing* (which is practised with firmans here as with commissions in England) to realize on this first occasion a profit all goes well—this credit becomes established with the Khasna [*Khazīnah*] or public treasury and as it increases they go on boldly speculating with its funds. I know many not worth a shilling last year now debtors by this line of conduct so far as to the amount of three or four hundred thousand piastres to the Khasna.

When the Pacha is pressed for money, which with all his resources not seldom happens, he levies a contribution on his debtors according to their supposed means and sends a Chaous [*Shāwīsh*] to the parties in question, who waits till the sum required be paid down in effective *dollars* and so urgent is the necessity of keeping a current credit with His Highness, that even Europeans are not only content to bear with this breach of their privileges (the sending a Chaous into their houses being contrary to the capitulation) but are even frequently compelled to dispose of goods at a loss of from twenty-five to thirty per cent to meet the urgency of the demand*—or to borrow of their respective neighbours at an interest of from three to four or even five per cent per month though the ordinary rate of it does not exceed four and twenty per cent per annum.

In favorable years when corn is scarce in Europe everything goes on swimmingly under such a system, the Pacha's coffers being full and the merchants not called upon to settle their accounts—but when grain proves a coming concern as in the present year the merchants become absolutely subjected to the mercy of the Pacha, scarcely one of them being in a state to come to a final settlement.

His Highness, however, with due regard to his own interests, does not seem inclined to press them beyond a certain *point*—except where their inability to pay becomes too apparent or the party loses favor at Court and then he orders their books to be submitted to persons appointed by himself to bring their concern to an issue.[12]

* One of the chief debtors of the Khasna has just failed for eight *millions* which may seem to give some idea of the credit given by the Pacha.

An uncommonly high flood in 1818 caused enormous devastation and loss, but it watered land which had not been inundated for thirty years. Consequently, the 1819 harvest was good, but prices were low and trade stagnant. The cotton crop alone amounted to 32,000 *qinṭārs* for which Muḥammad 'Alī had hoped to obtain no less than 140 francs per *qinṭār*.[13] The decline in cotton and food prices placed merchants indebted to the Pasha in an extremely precarious position and the Pasha's business practices threatened even those merchants still free of debt. Rather than lower his prices, Muḥammad 'Alī at first decided to store his crops. He was finally obliged to reduce his prices to stimulate demand, but he nevertheless monopolized all available trade. No merchant was able to take an independent position against the Pasha's despotism; all feared to displease his agents on whom they depended. The native merchants were forced out of business completely, whereas the foreign merchants, outraged at not obtaining their due share of the trade, finally urged that pressure be placed upon the Porte to control the Egyptian viceroy.[14] The merchants' specific grievances included these:

> The monopoly and exporting on his own account of all such articles as offer any advantage in the foreign markets, of which I may mention, this year, the whole of the Safflower, which the Pasha reserves for himself, and a great part of the lint-seed, which he will only sell for bills on Constantinople—both of which proceedings are, I conceive, in direct contradiction to the spirit of our treaty with the Porte.
>
> A second abuse is the mixing of bad produce with the good, as is too often practiced with the cotton and flax, whence it happens that the article sold to the merchant fetches a less price than that exported on His Highness's account, in the markets of Europe.
>
> A third and very grievous abuse is that of selling largely to the officers engaged in administration at the ports, who thence become naturally interested in thwarting the interests of our merchants. This frequently gives rise to delay in consignment, undue partiality, and unauthorized charges, which though sometimes redressed on application to the Pasha, always occasions delay, and enables his own officers to take the first advantage of the markets.
>
> Another great evil is the uncertain and arbitrary mode of fixing prices that depend entirely on His Highness' caprice, who being surrounded by men of unprincipled character who never hesitate to fill his ears with a thousand falsehoods seldom or ever knows the real state of the market. To these I may add the uncertain value of our specie and its alarming depreciation—the dollar being now worth eleven and a half piastres, Egyptian currency, which is entirely owing to the mal-administration of the Pasha's affairs.[15]

The Pasha decided in 1819 to settle his accounts with the band of merchants who without capital or credit had swarmed to Egypt to make their fortune. After considerable delay and frantic efforts by these merchants to alter the Pasha's decision, Muḥammad 'Alī finally announced in October 1820 that he would agree to make arrangements with his debtors and promised to grant time to those who would pay the entire sum owed to him. In some cases he even reduced the debts by 90 per cent and stated his willingness to accept the balance within five years. Those who could pay nothing or very little were told that their promissory notes would be returned to them, provided they paid what they could and then left Egypt. All foreigners, regardless of national origin, were granted these terms, the regulation being to pay or leave. The foreign consuls attempted to influence Muḥammad ʻAlī to take a less stringent position and pointed out that in some instances debtors did not even have enough passage money to leave Egypt. Bāghūṣ Bey agreed to pay this expense, but stated that no concessions could be made. Although Muḥammad ʻAlī had no right under the terms of the Capitulations to force foreigners to leave, the foreign agents had to agree that his actions were more than generous to those who owed him so much money.[16] There was still, however, a large group of traders who remained in Egypt after Muḥammad ʻAlī expelled the less reputable merchants. Their numbers increased again after the introduction of long-fiber cotton in 1821, and in 1822 there were thirty-five European houses in Alexandria and fifteen in Cairo.[17]

The early monopolistic practices exercised by Muḥammad ʻAlī set the pattern for his commercial policy, which remained in force for the greater part of his reign. All Egyptian produce without exception, as well as produce which came from Sinnār, Kurdufān, and al-Yaman (that is, gums, ostrich feathers, ivory, Mocha coffee, myrrh, incense, and aloes wood) were subjected to monopolies when sold for export. Freedom of trade was nonexistent. Fortunes were made by favorites of the Pasha and privileged trading houses not only profited from monopolistic practices, but sought to perpetuate them. Less favored individuals complained of discrimination to their representatives in shriller and shriller tones as the years passed; they finally accused Muḥammad ʻAlī of contravening the terms of the Treaty of Capitulations. At last in 1825 a group of British merchants, not including Briggs and Company,[18] presented a petition to the British Consul-General asserting that the fifty-third article of the Capitulations ("they may bring and may in like manner buy and export all sorts of merchandise without anyone presuming to prohibit or molest them") entitled them to an exercise of free trade which Muḥammad ʻAlī's commercial practices did not permit. They interpreted this article to imply that nothing should be allowed to interfere with their right to deal directly with the cultivators and that transit trade should not be fettered in any way. Moreover, they recommended that direct treaty relations be established with Muḥammad ʻAlī since the Capitulations no longer had any force in Egypt. Henry Salt explained to the merchants that the exportation of certain articles had always been prohibited in the Ottoman Empire except by the grant of firmans and that the words "prohibited articles" were so vague that it left much latitude to the governors within the Empire for deciding what these words covered, that it had never been the intention of the Porte to permit the right of control over its own internal regulations, and that in his considered opinion a separate treaty could serve no useful purpose. Stratford Canning agreed with Salt's interpretations and could also not recommend that a special treaty between Egypt and Great Britain be signed. The French government at this time took an extremely realistic position and instructed French merchants to conform to the conditions in existence in Egypt without regard for the terms of the Capitulations.

In the years that followed, members of the consular corps would occasionally suggest to Muḥammad ʻAlī modifications of his monopolistic system in Egypt in order to allow greater trading opportunities for European merchants, but the Pasha would invariably point out to them that existing trade was the direct result of his agricultural policy, that when he came to Egypt there were only "three hats" in Alexandria, who were far from prosperous, but that, under his rule, so many European traders had been attracted to the country that Alexandria had the air of a European city. He claimed, in fact, that far from ruining the European merchants, he had been responsible for providing them with commodities of greater value than had formerly existed and had fixed prices at a level which allowed them a small but certain profit. If, on the other hand, he were to modify his system and agree to allow merchants to deal directly with the *fallāḥīn*, they would soon find that all trade would cease for lack of commodities to purchase, as it was only through his system of direct control of agriculture that the proverbial laziness of the *fallāḥīn* could be overcome. Furthermore, the Egyptian peasants would certainly be guilty of bad faith in their dealings with foreign merchants and would cheat them. In 1831 the French Consul-General asserted that it was a great misfortune for the people of Egypt and for the merchant class that the European powers had not prevented the monopolistic trading practices of the Pasha when they had first manifested themselves; in 1838 the British Consul-General said much the same thing, adding that the consular corps had from apathy or a dereliction of duty permitted Muḥammad ʻAlī to contravene the terms of the Capitulations and that with time these infringements had come to be considered a matter of right.[19]

The commercial policies of Muḥammad ʻAlī produced a dramatic change in the role of government in matters of trade from what it had been previously. In the eighteenth century the native merchants had been organized in corporations headed by the *shaykh bandar*, usually the wealthiest of the merchants, while European trade rested in the hands of European and Levantine Christians and Jews who acted as agents for foreign exporters. The government had exercised control over native trade and industry through an official known as the *muḥtasib*, whereas foreign commerce was regulated by the terms of the Treaties of Capitulations.[20] The system remained substantially the same until 1819 when the establishment of a separate *dīwān* to deal with commercial matters appears to have occurred, although the details of its organization are obscure and require investigation in the Egyptian archives.[21] It is probably more than a coincidence that the setting up of a permanent *dīwān* to handle commercial matters occurred in 1819, the year when Muḥammad ʻAlī pushed native and European merchants to the wall by his monopolistic trade policies; it is logical to suppose that he would have attempted to strengthen the control of the government over commerce and to break the old commercial corporations in the same way that he broke, at about the same time, the power of the industrial corporations by his industrial policy (see Chapter X). He was, of course, inhibited in the measures he could take against the foreign merchants because of the Treaties of Capitulations, but, in view of the decline and final elimination of such old trading companies as the Levant Company (May 19, 1825), he needed in this case also an effective government agency that could deal with the individual foreign merchants engaged in Egyptian trade.[22]

Like all other departments of the government, the department dealing with commerce was reorganized periodically. In 1826 it was reported that a new administration had been established in Alexandria for commercial affairs, that the Pasha had appointed Bāghūṣ Bey *nāẓir* in charge of commerce—an appointment which was viewed favorably by European merchants who considered him easier to deal with than a Turk—that he had presented Bāghūṣ with a pelisse, and that Bāghūṣ was to govern the city of Alexandria during the absence of both the Pasha and Muḥarram Bey, governor of Alexandria. Again, when the government was reorganized in 1837, a Ministry of Commerce and Foreign Affairs (*Dīwān at-Tijārah al-Miṣrīyah wa'l-Umūr al-Ifrankīyah*) was formed. Bāghūṣ Bey was appointed minister and remained in this position until his death in 1844. Artīn Bey succeeded him and served as Minister of Commerce and Foreign Affairs until the end of Muḥammad ʿAlī's reign.[23]

Commerce in Egypt functioned in two principal ways, by the system of *appaltos* (farming) and by government monopoly. The former was an arrangement by which exclusive privilege was given to one or several merchants to deal in a particular item of commerce. A contract between the government and the *appaltatore* (contractor, farmer) was entered upon for one or more years and stipulated that the total quantity of the product in question would be delivered to the *appaltatore* at a price fixed in advance. The *appaltos* were put up for auction and the farmer often used his exclusive privilege to compensate himself for the price he had paid.[24]

The items not granted as *appaltos* were disposed of by the government in various ways. At first Muḥammad ʿAlī appointed agents in Mediterranean ports and sent shipments for his own account, but he soon learned by experience that it was more profitable to sell his produce to merchants located in Egypt. When the cotton crop promised to produce large profits, he reverted to his former system in the hope of enriching himself at the expense of the foreign merchants who, he supposed, made enormous profits. Both the French and British consuls felt that this policy would be discontinued as soon as he discovered that profits were less than he thought and risks far greater than he was prepared to accept, but Muḥammad ʿAlī did not relax his trade policy readily and continued either to send shipments to Europe for his own account or to sell his crops to a small group of merchants, mostly Levantines, who were able to obtain his special favor. In 1829 the mounting pressure of complaints led him to announce his decision to end previous practices and to sell Egyptian agricultural products to all merchants in Egypt who would pay his price and could offer adequate guarantees. Some commodities, particularly cereals and indigo, were placed on the market, but Muḥammad ʿAlī was soon accused of selling only part of his crops to the merchants and this at such high prices that they often suffered serious losses.[25]

The pressure for money brought Muḥammad ʿAlī to the practice of selling crops by anticipation. By promising payment in kind at the time of the harvest, he could raise a loan at any time of the year from merchants anxious always to obtain Egyptian produce. This easy method of obtaining money led Muḥammad ʿAlī into the doubtful practice of entering into more agreements with merchants than he could honor.

He often made completely contradictory contracts by which he sold crops in anticipation to one group of merchants and then, when the harvest came, would fail to make delivery and would, instead, sell his crop to another group. Those who had purchased crops in anticipation found their commercial position greatly jeopardized, as they possessed neither their cash nor the crops to which they were entitled. They would seek recourse by demanding that their consuls should place pressure upon Muḥammad 'Alī, but they were frequently obliged to wait for more than a year before the government could honor its commitments and make delivery. The richer firms sought to avoid these difficulties by agreeing to advance cash to the Pasha for half of their purchases, the balance to be paid upon delivery of the first half, but they soon discovered that the government would deliver the first half of the shipment quickly to obtain the balance of the payment and would then delay in shipping the second half.

In 1833 Muḥammad 'Alī finally abandoned the practice of selling by anticipation except as an extraordinary measure, because he could neither keep pace with his commitments nor ever enjoy the full benefits from his current crops. He switched to the system of selling his produce at public sales, either at fixed prices or by auction. Although the merchants had sought this change, they found that prices were driven up by speculators, who were usually the representatives of second-rate business firms operating in Egypt and willing to earn smaller profits. These speculators attended public auctions and bid against the more reputable firms until the prices of Egyptian commodities, particularly cotton, rose to figures which bore no relationship to the prices obtainable in Europe. The larger firms, unwilling to operate on a narrow margin or to take unnecessary risks, soon withdrew from the market. They preferred to make their profit by what they considered much safer means; they assumed the role of bankers and discounted the bills of the smaller firms. When the international financial crisis of 1836 came, the financial instability of the smaller houses in Egypt could not withstand the shock. By April 9, 1837, six bankruptcies had already been reported. The larger houses also found themselves in a serious situation. They had committed large capital amounts to the smaller houses and had thus compromised their own financial position. Auctions were suspended and only rice was sold. The warehouses were glutted with crops, particularly cotton, but no purchasers could be found. Every ship which came from Europe brought more and more discouraging news of the effect of the crisis upon the European market. Business was completely stagnant for several months, for no one would risk any capital. Bankruptcies occurred frequently.[26]

The Pasha was seriously affected by the crisis and his financial position was worse than it had been for a long time. No funds could be raised to pay either the armed forces or government employees; there was even some question whether sufficient funds could be found to pay the annual remittance to the Sultan. The price of cotton dropped to a new low. The merchants, counting upon the Pasha's financial distress, tried to push down prices as far as possible, but Muḥammad 'Alī quickly moved against their tactics by forcing the peasants to pay part of their taxes in advance and by using his reserves, accumulated during the few previous years when cotton had sold at high prices. He let it be known that he had ample resources, even if he could not sell his cotton for two years, and made it clear to the merchants that there was no urgent need for him to submit to their ruthless conditions. When the new crop began to arrive at Alexandria, he refused to place his cotton on the market at the price of 8 dollars per *qinṭār* offered by the merchants, a price which barely covered the cost of cultivation and transportation to Alexandria, and instructed Bāghūṣ Bey to accept nothing below 10 dollars and 75 cents. He then ordered the immediate liquidation of all his debts and by this shrewd move gave the merchants the impression that he was better off than they had believed. By October 1837 they realized they had no alternative but to buy at the Pasha's price. *Al-quṭn al-hindī* went at 11 dollars and 25 cents per *qinṭār*; Sea Island cotton sold at 14 dollars. These prices were about one dollar more per *qinṭār* than had been obtainable three weeks previously.[27] Muḥammad 'Alī showed at this critical moment another aspect of his unusual versatility—he combined real business acumen with the cold-blooded courage which had enabled him to attain his position as ruler of Egypt.[28]

Muḥammad 'Alī's monopolistic policies did not go unchallenged during this era of revolutionary change in the economy of Europe, an era in which the economic philosophy of the Free Trade movement flourished. Increased production in Britain had created a need for greater trading opportunities and had led the British government to examine trading conditions with nations throughout the world with a view to revising existing treaties and obtaining conditions more favorable to British trade. The Treaty of Capitulations by which commercial relations between Great Britain and the Ottoman Empire were regulated was also scrutinized. The Anglo-Turkish Convention of August 16, 1838, signed in the home of Rashīd Pasha at Balta Liman on the Bosporus, grew out of prolonged negotiations begun in 1835 over the revision of the Anglo-Turkish tariff of 1820, which had expired on March 1, 1834, and ended in a commercial convention aimed at the destruction of all monopolistic practices in the Ottoman Empire. Political considerations, particularly Anglo-Russian rivalry and the Turco-Egyptian struggle, also played an important role in negotiations, but these negotiations were essentially economic in character[29] and centered around the problem of the traditional system of monopoly in Turkey by which the right to the exclusive privilege of buying certain articles of produce or of carrying on a particular branch of industry was sold by the government to individuals or a company. According to this system, a person obtained a *tadhkirah* which specified the type of monopoly its holder was entitled to exercise, the price at which he could purchase the article in question, and the amount which he could purchase. He alone was entitled to buy the produce to which monopoly rights had been granted and he was free to dispose of it as he wished. Except for the *appaltos*, which were limited in number and were not of great significance, this monopoly system did not exist in Egypt. Monopolies in Egypt were of another sort and stemmed from Muḥammad 'Alī's control of the land, the direct supervision of agriculture by the government administration, the acquisition by the government of the principal agricultural products, and the active participation in commerce by the Pasha, who possessed the financial means and political power to destroy all competition.[30]

The Anglo-Turkish negotiations proceeded slowly at first, for the Turks were extremely reluctant to end the system that provided their government with an important source of revenue through the sale of monopoly rights. The first important step came when the Sultan consented to instruct Muḥammad 'Alī to rescind his order of July 1834 prohibiting the export of raw silk from Syria. Towards the end of 1835 (Ramaḍān, A.H. 1251), therefore, the Sultan sent a firman to the Pasha directing him to remove all obstacles to British trade in Syria. Although some fear prevailed in Turkey and Europe that Muḥammad 'Alī would refuse to comply with the Sultan's command, thereby causing an international crisis, the Pasha promptly consented to obey the firman concerning British trade in Syria as well as subsequent firmans extending equal privileges to the other nations. It was only in 1838 that the Sultan finally agreed to the policy, urged upon him by the British, of putting an end to all monopolies in the Empire. In giving his consent to the Anglo-Turkish Convention the Sultan was motivated by his animosity towards Muḥammad 'Alī; he became convinced that by destroying one of Muḥammad 'Alī's greatest sources of revenue he would also undermine the Pasha's ability to maintain an army that constituted a permanent threat to the Sultan's sovereignty. He was certainly encouraged in this belief by the British ambassador, Lord Ponsonby, as a means for reaching an agreement,[31] but it must be stressed, as Campbell reported, that the treaty was badly drafted if British intentions in negotiating the Anglo-Turkish Convention of 1838 were primarily directed against Muḥammad 'Alī and his system of government monopolies:

> It appears the treaty contemplated the application of a similar system to the various parts of the Ottoman empire. But as the fiscal regulations of Egypt and Syria—the amount and the manner of collecting and of imposing customs house duties—do not at all resemble those employed in Turkey proper, the application of the terms of the treaty to Egypt and Syria did not only lead to a large increase of the duties paid on imports and exports by British merchants, but placed its merchants in a situation far less favourable than that of the Russians or Greeks or the subjects of powers who have not been parties to the treaty. The general opinion of the merchants of the Levant is, that with oriental governments any system of discriminating duties must be attended with the greatest embarrassments—as trade must naturally flow through the channel which is most favoured.
>
> I would venture humbly to suggest that any commercial arrangements which may hereafter be entered on should take into consideration the necessities of the various localities in as much as the fiscal regulations of various parts of the Empire differ so much from one another. In Egypt the monopolies of which we are entitled to complain are not, like those of Turkey, consequent on the state of exclusive privileges—or on the levying of internal imports. They involve the question of the tenure of the lands. They are complicated by their connection with the miri, or land tax—with the advances made by government to cultivate and with the Mahomedan laws as to the sovereignty exercised by the ruler over the soil.[32]

France, not to be outdone by the British, also negotiated a similar treaty of commerce which was signed in November 1838. Other nations soon followed suit, but Russia, which arranged for a new tariff agreement with the Porte in 1842, only signed a Russo-Turkish commercial treaty on April 30, 1846.[33]

When Muḥammad 'Alī received news of the Anglo-Turkish Convention, he at first told the French Consul-General that he would refuse to submit to its terms, but he informed the French, English, and Austrian Consuls-General on September 15, 1838, that after due reflection he had decided to execute the treaty, for he had found that its terms were advantageous to him. Since his monopolies, he claimed, produced only 50,000 purses (1,250,000 dollars) per year, the additional duties fixed by the treaty would yield him a larger sum. In informing his government of Muḥammad ʿAlī's decision, Campbell explained that the abolition of monopolies as envisaged by the treaty could, in fact, be applied in Egypt only to "some few articles, such as wines, given in appalte (farmed out) by the Pacha—to some articles of produce, as indigo, wool, rice, sugar etc. and to the trade of Soudan and Arabia such as ivory, gold-dust, ostrich feathers, gum, coffee, tea which now can only be exclusively sold to the Pacha." Cotton, on the other hand, Campbell pointed out, was not a monopoly by Muḥammad ʿAlī's definition, but rather the produce of his own land to be sold when and how he liked.[34] It was useless for Palmerston to argue that "a monopoly is not less a monopoly because it extends over a whole country, instead of being confined to part of that country, nor because such monopoly is established by the Governor, and for his exclusive profit, instead of being granted to private individuals; and the monopolies established by Mehemet Ali in Egypt for his own profit are just as much a violation of the Treaty, as if they were granted by him for the profit of other Persons."[35] It was too late to insist that Muḥammad ʿAlī could not be considered the proprietor of the soil which he had not acquired by purchase and which he was only holding as representative of the Sultan. Lord Ponsonby should have seen to it that the treaty which he had so carefully negotiated was more explicit.[36]

As the date approached for the Anglo-Turkish Convention to go into effect (March 13, 1839), Muḥammad ʿAlī appeared reconciled to the need for fulfilling the terms of the treaty. His conciliatory attitude towards the Europeans was undoubtedly prompted by his desire to gain their support in his approaching struggle with Turkey. On March 24, 1839, Campbell wrote that in an interview with the Pasha, Muḥammad ʿAlī informed him that he would "execute the convention between Great Britain and the Porte, faithfully and honestly, as soon as he [should] receive it and the necessary Firman from the Porte." Muḥammad ʿAlī made only one stipulation, that "our Merchants were not to make advances to the Grower for the purchase of the crop before it should be gathered in, but that they could purchase it so soon as the crop should be taken off the Ground, and that the Grower should have free and full liberty to bring his crop to the market and to dispose of it, how and to whom he pleased." The Pasha explained that this stipulation was motivated not only by his desire to save the peasants from the usurious interest that European purchasers would demand when making advances to the peasants, but by a wish to prevent disputes at law between purchasers and cultivators when "the Fellah cultivator in Egypt, having got the money in his possession for his crop, would neglect the cultivation of it."[37] The firman failed to reach Egypt until June 14, 1839, but in the meantime, in April, the Turks had crossed the Euphrates at Bīr and on June 24 Ibrāhīm attacked and vanquished the Turkish forces at Nizzīb in northern Syria.[38]

The crushing defeat inflicted by Ibrāhīm's forces upon the Turks undoubtedly increased Muḥammad 'Alī's confidence in his chances for ultimate victory and accounts for his delay in implementing the terms of the commercial treaty. The former Treaties of Capitulations continued to be respected, but Muḥammad 'Alī said that nothing could be changed until his differences with the Porte were finally settled. He did, however, make limited concessions to the merchants. He allowed them to deal directly with the *fallāḥīn*, but he reserved for himself the right to fix the price of produce. He also reserved the right to purchase produce at the price he fixed, if no one else bought it. There the matter rested until the settlement of the Egyptian Question of 1839–1841. As soon as the struggle was over, Muḥammad 'Alī said that he was ready to carry out the terms of the commercial treaty, and in January 1841 he abandoned his monopoly on cereals and oleaginous seeds to give substance to his statement. Later in the year he told the new British Consul-General, Colonel Barnett, that he was convinced that free trade was a good thing, but stressed that it could only be brought about gradually. Barnett felt certain from his discussion with the Pasha that he would in fact practice every means of evasion and procrastination to prevent the complete exercise of free trade in Egypt; as events turned out, Barnett was fully justified in his belief.[39]

For the next two years the struggle between the foreign consular corps and Muḥammad 'Alī to make the principle of free trade operative in practice as well as in theory grew in intensity. One cause for complaint arose from Muḥammad 'Alī's monopoly of Nile transport. The merchants claimed that even when direct contact with the *fallāḥīn* was established, which occasionally occurred, they were unable to obtain boats to ship their purchases to Alexandria.[40] The Pasha finally issued a public order in October 1841, upon Colonel Barnett's representation, granting permission to Europeans to build boats for their own use which would be free to sail on the Nile and al-Maḥmūdīyah Canal on condition that they were manned by natives and carried the Turkish flag.[41] As soon as the order was issued and before merchants could build boats, they found it difficult to hire any more ships; those who possessed their own boats could find no crews. When the latter group complained to the authorities, they were told that the monopoly on boats had ended, but that the crews were the subjects of Muḥammad 'Alī and could be disposed of as he saw fit.[42]

Although Muḥammad 'Alī continued to circumvent the spirit of the commercial treaty of 1838, the new duties according to the tariff annexed to it went into effect on November 24, 1841, without prior notice to merchants. The old tariff was discontinued; import duties were increased from 3 to 5 per cent; export duties, which under the former tariff had been 3 per cent but had been rarely levied at all or, if so, at an even lower rate, jumped to 12 per cent. The merchants complained bitterly at this change, for the enforcement of the new tariff only burdened them without providing for the compensating advantages guaranteed by the treaty. Free trade, they felt, would remain a dead letter in Egypt until a complete reform of the administration was undertaken. The Russians, who had not yet signed a treaty with Turkey and could continue to operate under the old tariff, were the only ones to profit from this new arrangement.[43] The situation became tense in January 1842 when Barnett informed Artīn Bey that unless all the terms of the Anglo-Turkish Convention were carried out and all articles of export were declared free, including cotton, the British merchants would be instructed to withhold payment of additional duties.[44] A deadline of one month was given. By February most of the merchants had refused to pay the extra duties. Official action by the British and Austrian Consuls-General took place in March when a joint note was presented to the Pasha stating that Austrian and British subjects were no longer bound to pay the additional 2 per cent import duty until all terms guaranteed by the treaty went into effect; the note also claimed the reimbursement of all sums already paid on account of those duties. Muḥammad 'Alī in his reply to the joint note asserted that all articles were in fact free with the exception of cotton, that contravention of his orders by his subordinates was due to their being unaccustomed as yet to the new conditions, that cotton would soon be open to free trade, and that orders had in the meantime been given to customs officials to suspend the collection of the additional 2 per cent duty until further notice.[45] The Pasha also agreed to sell all the produce of his own lands by means of public auction. He announced, furthermore, that the products of as-Sūdān would be free, but vitiated his order to his governor there by instructing him to buy all export products for the Pasha's personal account.[46] In May 1842 Barnett was informed by Bāghūṣ Bey that cotton would be free after the gathering of the next crop, that Muḥammad 'Alī had agreed that, for the period November 23, 1841, to May 26, 1842, the import duty to be collected would be at the old rate of 3 per cent and that the full 5 per cent was to be paid on imports from May 26, 1842. The consuls refused to accept these terms and stated that they would authorize the payment of the additional duty only after the next harvest when, according to Muḥammad 'Alī's promise, cotton would be free. Confronted by a united and uncompromising consular corps, Muḥammad 'Alī finally agreed to sell to the merchants the cotton already in government *shūnahs*. Only then did the consuls order the merchants to pay the additional 2 per cent duty from May 26, 1842.[47]

Trade was now free; at least, theoretically, it was free. The system, however, never really worked. The principal causes for its failure lay in Muḥammad 'Alī's policies of cultivating large estates for his own account and converting, especially after 1838, state lands into private estates which were granted to members of his family or to his favorites (including foreigners) on the condition that certain crops would be raised on a definite proportion of the land granted and would be sold to him at an agreed price. Furthermore, peasants who cultivated land not yet converted into private estates were forced either to remit their taxes in kind or to sell their crops at prices fixed by the government. Thus, most of the country's produce flowed into government *shūnahs*.[48] The merchants too found from experience that it was more convenient and advantageous to purchase crops at government *shūnahs*, for no one dared to undersell the Pasha. In the rare instances where direct contact with producers was made the merchants found that they not only had to pay nearly the same prices as those charged by the government, but could not rely upon the producers for a regular supply.[49]

The concentration of produce in government hands enabled the Pasha to fix his own prices. If merchants refused to meet them, the *shūnahs* closed down and private sales would then be arranged between the government and individuals with influence in high places.[50] "It can by no means be said," wrote Stoddart in 1843, "that there exists an open, fair and settled market, devoid of partiality and undue interference."[51] Barnett in making an evaluation of the Anglo-Turkish Convention remarked caustically on one occasion: "The old Lord of Therapia made a sad mistake when he got up the Convention of 1838. He thought to strike a blow at Mehemet Aly's monopolies, and the Pasha now laughs in his sleeve at the embarrassments we are in. Shall you be able to get us out of them?"[52] The British consul at Cairo, Alfred S. Walne, supported Barnett's view that the Convention of 1838 had placed the British merchants in a less advantageous position. Moreover, Walne contended that a return to the former conditions, although desirable, would no longer be possible since, as he maintained, "by the adoption of the chifflick system and other practical evasions the whole condition of the country [had] been changed."[53] Most of the consuls and foreign merchants, in fact, finally concluded that the inauguration of a uniform system of sales was as much freedom of commerce as could be hoped for in Egypt under existing conditions and urged Muḥammad 'Alī to sell his crops by public auctions held at regular intervals. The Pasha issued an order in November 1843 to this effect and announced that previous notices of sale would be publicized so that every merchant would have an equal opportunity to compete. Nevertheless, despite the Pasha's order about public auctions, he himself still continued to sell his crops by private sales. When the consuls complained about his failure to honor his own promises and attempted to exert pressure upon him, he merely transferred most of his *chifliks* in Upper Egypt to various members of his family to evade the obligation of selling the produce of these lands by public auction.[54]

Until the end of Muḥammad 'Alī's reign the issue of free trade, only partially introduced into Egypt, remained a source of friction between the Pasha and the trading community because of his evasions. An attempt was finally made by the British Board of Trade to face realities with regard to free trade in Egypt and the Ottoman Empire as a whole. When the Turks demanded that the British concede certain rights of monopoly, similar to those granted by the Russians in the commercial treaty signed in 1846, the Board of Trade recommended to the government that concessions be made to allow monopolies and restrictions on trade in the Ottoman Empire. Although Palmerston dogmatically asserted that the

British government, committed to the principle of free trade, could make no concessions of the sort recommended by the Board of Trade, he did agree to a revision of the Anglo-Turkish Tariff of 1839 in order to take into account changes in prices. This tariff, which expired in 1846, actually remained in force until a new tariff, negotiated by Stratford Canning, was signed in October 1850.[55]

CHAPTER X

INDUSTRY AND AGRICULTURE

Muḥammad 'Alī's industrial program,[1] like so many of his other undertakings, did not emerge from a policy clearly conceived and systematically executed. It originated, rather, at a period when the Pasha was searching for ways to increase his revenues and it proceeded along lines determined by time and circumstances. From its inception it followed a double course of development: the exploitation of old established industries for the Pasha's personal profit and the introduction of modern industry.

During approximately the same period that Muḥammad 'Alī introduced his policy of monopolizing agriculture for his own profit, he undertook the monopolization of native industry by closing native workshops which manufactured cotton cloth, abolishing the customary usages of the corporation of weavers, installing looms for weaving cotton cloth in government workshops at Cairo, and ordering the former masters and artisans to enter these workshops as salaried employees. Goods manufactured in government workshops were either retained by the Pasha for his own use or sold to merchants. Drovetti attempted in vain to persuade the Pasha against this policy of monopoly. He argued that state control operated against the true interests of the government, for it annihilated an entire class of workers of long standing and traditions. Not only would it be more equitable, he said, but in the long run more profitable to tax artisans rather than to force them to work for the government.[2] Muḥammad 'Alī did not heed Drovetti, but extended his monopoly to include not only the manufacture of cotton cloth, but of all textiles. He appointed a *dīwān* to supervise the textile industry; agents were sent to villages to purchase for the government's account thread spun by native women; *shaykhs* were appointed in each village to count the village looms and to keep the village weavers steadily employed; and government officials were sent to villages and towns to purchase the finished textile goods at prices fixed by the government. A government stamp was affixed at both ends of each piece so that none could enter the market as contraband and anyone found guilty of dealing in contraband was severely punished by bastinado and a heavy fine. These measures caused hardship to both rich and poor, but particularly to the poor.[3]

The village textile industry was soon confined to the spinning of flax and the manufacture of linen cloth. It was controlled by a government *dīwān* in accordance with the regulations set forth in the *Lā'iḥat zirāʻat al-fallāḥ*. This government ordinance included detailed instructions concerning the duties of the various officials in supervisory positions, the manner in which the work should be carried out, and safeguards for protecting the interests of the workers and the government alike. The spinning of raw flax was carried out by women employed in village *ḥarīms* established for this purpose. In each village these *ḥarīms* were supervised by a commissioner for the women spinners (*wakīl al-ḥarīmāt al-ghazzālāt*) whose duty it was to accompany the women to the yarn store (*shūnat al-ghazl*) to supply them with flax. It was also his responsibility to control the work carried on in the *ḥarīms*, stimulate greater productivity, and inform the *qā'immaqām* (chief of the canton) and the village *shaykhs* of cases of negligence. At the end of each month the *wakīl* assembled the women spinners and together with them brought the linen twist required of the women to the *shūnah*. In order to stimulate greater zeal among the women the *wakīl* also made certain that the manager of the bleaching establishment (*nāẓir al-mabyaḍah*) paid the women spinners the amount due to them (that is, the value of the spun yarn less the value of the raw material). To insure that a proper evaluation was placed on their work, another official, the broker of the spun yarn (*simsār al-ghazl*), checked the deliveries by the women against the amount of raw material that had been issued to them and then made certain that they were paid by the bleaching establishment (*mabyaḍah*) at the current rates.

Each month, after the twist was washed, bleached, dried, and cut at the *mabyaḍah*, the *shaykh* of the weavers (*shaykh al-qazzāzīn*) obtained a supply of the spun yarn from the storekeeper (*makhzanjī*) of the yarn and distributed it to the weavers (*al-qazzāzīn*) according to the capacity of each weaver. Each weaver then took his allotted monthly portion to the weigher of the bleaching establishment (*qabbānī al-mabyaḍah*) to be weighed and registered in his name. This extra precaution was taken in order to enable the weaver to check against any deficiencies and also to determine the wages he could expect on delivery of the finished cloth. The *shaykh* of the weavers was also responsible for the close supervision of the weavers, insuring that none of them worked with yarn other than that supplied through the government stores or wove the pieces of cloth beyond the prescribed length with the intention of keeping the excess for their own clothes or selling it. Should a weaver fall ill and be unable to complete his work, it was then the responsibility of the *shaykh* to distribute the work which he had failed to complete among the other weavers.

The finished pieces of cloth were brought to the bleaching establishment, which was directed by a *nāẓir*, whose responsibilities included the supervision of all the officials in the *mabyaḍah*. These officials included the washer (*ghassāl*) and bleacher (*mubayyiḍ*) who washed and bleached the yarn, the weigher (*qabbānī*) who kept an account of the monthly distribution of raw material to the village *ḥarīms* and the spun yarn delivered to the weavers, the intendant (*mubāshir*) who checked the issues and deliveries to the weavers and then paid them, the assistant (*wakīl*), and the storekeeper (*makhzanjī*). The manager of the *mabyaḍah* checked the cloth which had been brought by the weavers to the storekeeper to determine if it was up to the prescribed standard. Whenever he found that the cloth was not acceptable, he called the matter to the attention of the offending weaver together with the *shaykh* under whose supervision the inferior work had been executed, impressing upon them the necessity of maintaining the standard required by the government. He also supervised the payments due to both the women spinners and the weavers.

The sale of the cloth was under the supervision of another *nāẓir*, assisted by his *mubāshir* who received payments for the merchandise and kept a record of the business transactions. The director of the sale of cloth (*nāẓir mabīʿ al-qumāsh*) was under instructions to sell to *bona fide* merchants only. It was his special responsibility to note which fabrics were in demand and to sell both the unwanted fabrics and those that were wanted in order that there be no loss to the government. Goods that remained unsold were reported to the General Superintendent of Sales (*nāẓir ʿumūm al-mabyūʿāt*) in Cairo for instructions. The director of the sale of cloth also reported cases of bad debts to the *nāẓir al-qism* (director of the department) who, in turn, informed the *maʾmūr* (governor of the province). Action against the debtors, their sureties, or their property was then taken by the *maʾmūr* to prevent a loss to the government. Generally speaking, both the *nāẓir al-qism* and the *maʾmūr* bore ultimate responsibility for the execution of the industrial work carried out in the areas under their jurisdiction, for the deliveries and sale of the finished products, and for the payment of the women spinners and the weavers. The government monopoly of the manufacture of linen cloth so carefully supervised under the provisions of the *Lā'iḥat zirā'at al-fallāḥ* was finally abandoned, however, for in 1834 permission to sell linen cloth in a free market was granted by the government upon payment of a tax on each piece.[4]

The introduction of modern industry into Egypt was urged upon Muḥammad 'Alī as early as 1814, a time when the Pasha was particularly in need of devising ways for increasing his revenues to pursue the war in Arabia and to compensate for the decline in trade.[5] He was greatly influenced by suggestions made by Joseph Bokty, Consul-General of Sweden, and a number of merchants and mercantile consuls. Bokty and his associates argued that by combining the rich supply of raw materials produced in Egypt with the cheap labor force available in the country, industrial goods could be produced at competitive prices in the world market. Their arguments prevailed despite attempts made by Drovetti and members of the Pasha's family to deflect him from a policy which they felt would operate against the true interests of the country.[6] The first step was taken when Muḥammad 'Alī advertised in Malta that he would provide favorable conditions for manufacturers and artisans who would settle in Egypt and engage in their professions and trades. It is unknown whether there was any response to this notice. At any rate, for the next few years Muḥammad 'Alī confined his activities to the monopolization of native industry, but in 1817 reorganization of the textile industry began along European lines. A large factory was built at Khurunfish, followed soon afterwards by the construction of a mill at Būlāq, and both were supplied with the latest machinery for the manufacture of textiles (spinning jennies, carding machines, and looms). A special bleaching establishment, known as *Malta* because of the Maltese who were employed there, was founded at Būlāq to which cotton goods from other factories were sent for bleaching. Two dyeing factories were also established at Būlāq.[7]

Muḥammad 'Alī sent agents to Europe in 1817 to recruit an experienced class of workmen. The British government, however, refused to assist him in his attempts to recruit British workmen and banned all emigration. The French government also tried to prevent the emigration of its workmen,[8] but Egyptian agents managed to convince experienced French workers and managers to emigrate without their government's consent.[9] Recruiting of workmen was more successful in southern Europe where economic conditions were depressed. At the end of 1817 seventeen silk weavers arrived in Egypt from Leghorn; sixty more were expected; and an early report in 1818 stated that male and female workers were on their way from Genoa, Leghorn, and Marseilles to work in the Egyptian silk and cotton factories. Workmen were also recruited in Egypt. At a meeting held in the autumn of 1818 the *shaykhs* of the city quarters in Cairo were instructed to assemble 4,000 youths to work under the orders of the skilled European workmen. Al-Jabartī estimated that the government intended to recruit 10,000 Egyptians for work in the government factories.[10]

Industrial development was accelerated in the early 1820's after the extension of cotton cultivation and the formation of the *Niẓām Jadīd* and Egyptian navy. Muḥammad 'Alī, blinded by his desire for prestige and suffering from illusions, which, as Drovetti put it, sometimes nourish geniuses who are too active and too enterprising, decided that Egypt would have to be able to supply all requirements of his new army and navy. Drovetti, considering the whole venture absurd, pointed out to the Pasha that he would either have to hire foreign workers at such great cost that the final product would be more expensive than foreign imports or he would be forced to use as workers native Egyptians who could not possibly produce merchandise to compete with the products of European factories, factories which had the advantages of advanced technical knowledge and a skilled artisan class and could produce commodities of better quality less expensively than Muḥammad 'Alī could ever hope to do. Drovetti's assessment of Muḥammad 'Alī's industries appeared to be justified when several Egyptian factories stopped operation in 1822. Even Būlāq, which employed three hundred workers, proved an unsuccessful venture. The Pasha went to visit it occasionally, as to a theater, and all the wheels would be set in motion so that the activity and noise of the plant might amuse him. Even great men, wrote Drovetti, have their weaknesses.[11]

The obstinacy of Muḥammad 'Alī's character made it impossible for him to change his mind once a decision had been reached. Although the early results of his industrial program were not impressive, he nevertheless decided upon a fully developed industrial system and proceeded to command its creation. More textile factories were built to manufacture cloth for the uniforms of his new army and navy. Textiles for the local population and for export were also manufactured. A *ṭarbūsh* factory was established to make headgear worn by the soldiers, and native tanneries made their leather accessories. Other branches of industry were also organized to supply the army and navy with military matériel. Finally, an arsenal was built at Alexandria.[12]

According to one estimate the factories cost Muḥammad ʻAlī 200,000 purses, or 5,000,000 dollars, before any return on the investment was realized and of this amount 2,000,000 francs (approximately 380,000 dollars) were spent in France alone over a four-year period to cover the cost of machinery and of bringing French mechanics to Egypt.[13] Exclusive of village spinning wheels, village looms, and the arsenal built somewhat later at Alexandria, Muḥammad ʻAlī's industrial establishments in 1832 were valued at 7,000,000 dollars as follows:

24 manufactories for cotton twist @ 150,000 dollars	3,600,000	dollars
Cloth manufactory at Būlāq, including machinery and wool in store	40,000	
Manufactory for printing calicoes	200,000	
100 manufactories for husking rice @ 1,000 dollars	100,000	
Total manufactories using agricultural goods	3,940,000	
Ṭarbūsh factory	220,000	
Establishment of printing presses and type foundry in Cairo	30,000	
Iron foundries and machinery for making copper plates in Cairo	150,000	
Manufactory at Būlāq for wrought iron for the shipping, containing 50 to 60 forges and stores	300,000	
Two manufactories in Cairo of small arms and cannon producing 500 muskets weekly	1,500,000	
Manufactory of gun powder at ar-Rawḍah with a deposit at the Citadel of 50,000 *qinṭārs*	600,000	
Manufactory of saltpeter at Badrashayn	20,000	
8,000 oxen in the manufactories @ 30 dollars	240,000	
	7,000,000	dollars[14]

Muḥammad ʻAlī in 1837 told Prince Pückler-Muskau that he had spent 10,000,000 Spanish dollars for his factories, that they had already yielded 1,000,000 in clear profit and that more was expected, but Duhamel, on the other hand, asserted that the factories operated at a loss. Campbell confirmed Duhamel's statement. "The manufactories," he wrote, "have cost enormous sums, and it has been necessary to have everything (even to the instructors) brought from Europe, and the receipts are in some cases less than the expenses. I think that Mehemet Ali would gain very much by destroying them, and importing all manufactures from Europe."[15] Moreover, the capital sum invested initially could be considered a dead loss, since everything deteriorated and expensive repairs were always necessary.

The peak of Muḥammad 'Alī's industrial power was actually reached by the middle of the 1830's, but declined steadily thereafter. There were twenty-nine cotton factories in the country in 1837, when the Pasha decided to reduce their number in Upper Egypt. By 1840 only fifteen cotton factories remained. Prince Pückler-Muskau attributed this decline to the fact that war, plague, and cholera had combined to force Muḥammad 'Alī to reduce the number of his factories, but actually the Pasha had discovered that it was more profitable to contract with entrepreneurs to supply him with industrial goods, to allow them to use the government's mule-jennies and looms, and to supply them with raw material at a fixed sum rather than to maintain his factories under the direct administration of the government.[16]

France and Great Britain were both apprehensive at first that Muḥammad 'Alī's industries would compete successfully with them; in fact, in 1829 it was observed with some misgivings that imports of low-quality cloth from England had decreased, while Indian muslin, once in great demand in Egypt, was rarely imported after Egyptian factories had begun to manufacture a similar type of product. Very soon, however, the trend shifted and these fears were dispelled because of the inferior quality of goods manufactured in Egypt. Instead of a diminution of imports from Europe there was a progressive increase. In 1836 European manufactures imported to Egypt amounted to 125,000,000 piasters out of a total import figure of 355,000,000 piasters. By 1844 the import of British cotton goods was particularly heavy; cloth imports amounted to £253,348 and yarns amounted to £14,119. In 1845 cotton goods for £127,541 and yarns for £12,909 were imported from Britain. The average annual imports of cotton manufactures from Great Britain were estimated at between £160,000 to £170,000 (*c.* 16,000,000 to 17,000,000 piasters).[17]

Muḥammad 'Alī's industrial policy failed to achieve its objectives for the following reasons.

1. The *nāẓirs* (managers) were inadequately trained to direct modern factories. They often understood very little about manufacturing or about keeping accounts which they tried to turn to their own private advantage. The *mubāshirs*, the weighers, the storekeepers were all guilty of daily malversation. In the first place, then, failure may be attributed to corruption and mismanagement.[18]

2. Machinery was imported into Egypt without due regard for the country's climatic conditions. Dust, the greatest obstacle, entered the wheels and finer parts of the machines and was particularly injurious to carding and spinning works. Workmen devoted much of their time to cleaning the machinery, but even so mechanical breakdowns could not be avoided. Furthermore, much of the machinery, imported at great expense, was abandoned or neglected upon arrival because of changes in plans or because no one could assemble it. Finally, there were frequently no workmen sufficiently skilled to operate or to maintain the machinery, for the European superintendents were usually dismissed before Egyptians were adequately trained to replace them. Muḥammad ʻAlī's policy of dismissing his European staff before he had trained a class of skilled mechanics contributed greatly to the failure of Egyptian industry.

3. Lack of power was an important deterrent. Muḥammad ʻAlī attempted to overcome this deficiency by employing oxen, but their unequal step and movement, which was either retarded or accelerated, produced a continual jerking movement which shook the machines and caused their breakdown. Several steam engines were introduced into Egypt, but lack of fuel in the country made them expensive to operate. The Egyptians, in whose charge they were placed, were inadequately trained to keep them in order. Consequently only two out of eight steam engines imported into Egypt were still in a good state in 1840.[19]

4. The Egyptian peasants did not wish to be proletarianized. They were conscripted much like soldiers and sent to the factories where they remained until they found the opportunity to escape. So long as factory work protected them from military levies, the adult male workers were not unwilling to work, but they preferred whenever possible to remain in the fields despite the higher wages they received in factories and the food which they could purchase from government warehouses at prices lower than the going market price. Women were forced to enter the cotton factories to work side by side with men, but they often preferred to blind themselves, in the same manner as men mutilated themselves

to escape military service, rather than submit to this violation of the national custom of secluding women. A large percentage of the workers employed in the factories were children, whose mortality rate was very high. Wages, though nominally good, were usually months in arrears and workmen were forced to accept advances on their salaries from the tradespeople at a 15 to 25 per cent discount. Often they received payment in kind rather than in cash. A ration of three loaves of low-quality bread per day was also allowed to all workmen in government factories.[20]

It has been said that the Anglo-Turkish Convention of 1838 was the most significant cause for the failure of Egypt's infant industries, but the evidence does not justify such a conclusion. No European power, above all Great Britain, was greatly concerned by 1838 about the threat of competition from Egyptian industry, for Egyptian industry was doomed before the commercial treaty was negotiated and finally collapsed because of the weaknesses inherent in Muḥammad 'Alī's industrial policy.[21]

There were significant adverse effects of Muḥammad 'Alī's industrial policy on agriculture. In the first place, industry drew from agriculture large capital sums which, if turned back into agriculture, would have furnished greater returns. Also, it kept from agriculture large numbers of needed laborers. The maximum figure of those engaged in the factory system was 40,000 workmen. If to this figure one adds the workers in the village industries, it may be seen that the pressure on Egypt's limited population was considerable. These workmen could have been more profitably engaged in agriculture.[22] Then, too, a large number of oxen were taken from agriculture to provide the power for operating machines in the factories. Finally, the cotton industry did not increase cotton production significantly, as it absorbed 80,000 *qinṭārs* at most. The average amount of raw cotton used in the Egyptian factories amounted to only 50,000 *qinṭārs*. Muḥammad 'Alī's profit would have been greater had he exported the raw cotton.[23] The unanimous opinion of foreign observers (and, incidentally, of Ibrāhīm Pasha) was that Egypt's true source of wealth lay in its agricultural and commercial advantages and that it would have been more profitable to import the necessary manufactured goods and to concentrate on the production of raw materials,[24] a view which, Campbell noted, the Pasha stubbornly refused to accept:

But Mehemet Ali does not willingly surrender his hope he has long cherished, and is fond of exhibiting the effects of his endeavours. The motive is no doubt high and honourable, but the experiment must inevitably prove eventually a failure. The success which has attended most of Mehemet Ali's projects makes him over confident in all. He who has subdued the Bedouins of the Desert (who from time immemorial had prevented all control) and who has established respect for his authority to the tenth degree of north latitude, will not willingly be persuaded that he cannot surmount obstacles mastered by an ordinary European artisan.[25]

CHAPTER XI

MILITARY SERVICE AND AGRICULTURE

Muḥammad 'Alī's agricultural policy was closely linked to his military ambitions, for he relied upon revenues derived from agriculture to pay for his numerous wars. None of the early measures taken by the Pasha to increase revenues had affected the lives of the *fallāḥīn* fundamentally. They had lost some of their former freedom and worked for the benefit of a new master, but otherwise the pattern of existence had remained much as it had been under Mamlūk rule until Muḥammad 'Alī introduced the policy of recruiting troops for his new army and navy from the ranks of the Egyptian peasantry. This new conscription policy, undoubtedly inspired by a similar policy introduced into France at the time of the French Revolution and extended to other parts of Europe during and immediately following the Napoleonic Wars, affected the lives of the Egyptian *fallāḥīn* profoundly and eventually drained the country of its best agricultural workers.

Muḥammad 'Alī did not originally intend to base the *Niẓām Jadīd* upon *fallāḥ* conscription, for the peasants could be used more profitably on the land. Some *fallāḥīn* had been recruited to serve in Arabia in 1815, but it was only when Muḥammad 'Alī failed to form an army with Sudanese conscripts that he began to recruit *fallāḥīn* for his army and navy. The *fallāḥīn* immediately opposed the government's new policy and in May 1823 revolted in al-Minūfīyah Province against conscription and high taxes. Accompanied by palace guards and armed with six cannon, Muḥammad 'Alī hurried to the spot to prevent the insurrection from spreading. The revolt was soon subdued and the rebels were severely punished. In April 1824, however, there occurred another revolt extending from Isnā to Aṣwān which set off the signal for treaty violations by several powerful Bedouin tribes who controlled the Arabian desert from al-Quṣayr to Sawākin (Suakin). The uprising, which for another nation might have become a true revolution,[1] was led by a North African, ash-Shaykh Aḥmad b. Idrīs, who declared that he had been sent by God and His Prophet to end the vexations from which the Egyptian people suffered and to punish Muḥammad ʿAlī for introducing innovations which ran contrary to the dogma of Islām. The revolt gained momentum and the rebels pushed their incursions almost to Girgā. Troops, including several battalions from the newly formed *fallāḥ* army, were ordered to march against the rebels. The *fallāḥ* soldiers remained loyal at first, but within a month many of the new troops deserted and joined the rebels. The insurgents who were successfully dispersed in the early skirmishes soon regrouped themselves and continued the struggle, but the rebellion, after lasting for approximately six weeks, was finally crushed by Turkish troops with the aid of the Bedouin troops who were allies of Muḥammad ʿAlī.[2] The exact number of casualties among the rebels is unknown, but losses by the end of the revolt were sufficiently great to persuade the *fallāḥīn* either to conform to the policy of conscription or to find other means of evading it.[3]

The Egyptian *fallāḥīn* never reconciled themselves to the policy of conscription, however, because of their aversion to military service and their strong attachment to their beloved Nile, their villages, and the soil. For the *fallāḥīn*, whose family ties were very strong, the most odious aspect of the policy was the destruction of family life. A *fallāḥ* was drafted into the army for life. Although families of men stationed in Egypt were permitted to build mud barracks near the camps,[4] when the troops departed from Egypt, wives and children could not accompany them and were left without money or resources of any kind. As a result, marital bonds dissolved automatically and many soldiers' wives soon made other alliances.[5]

The *fallāḥīn* suffered great deprivation in the field. During the war in the Morea, for example, each man received a daily ration of one hundred drams of flour or one hundred drams of biscuits. Occasionally he received, in addition, a handful of beans or lentils. No meat, butter, oil or rice was included in his rations. The soldiers are represented "as having suffered during the winter the utmost extremities of cold and hunger and as having borne and still bearing such privations without a murmur being heard, and to which no other troops could submit."[6] Their officers, who were Turks, bore them no love; when the army was on the move, there were very few higher officers who paid as much attention to the welfare of their troops as their opposite numbers gave to their European forces.[7] Then, too, the army's pay was always in arrears. In August 1825 it was reported that the troops were not receiving their pay; on April 13, 1827, ʿAbdīn Kāshif, governor of an Upper Egyptian province, was killed in Mallawī by soldiers who had mutinied for their pay; in 1828 troops in the Morea were reported to be sixteen months in arrears; in 1832 the army in al-Ḥijāz, unpaid for twenty months, mutinied; during the second Syrian War, the Porte promised to pay arrears outstanding for one year to all those who were captured, a promise which served as an inducement to many of Muḥammad 'Alī's troops to desert his army.[8]

Recruiting was a veritable impressment with extremely brutal methods for conscripting the unwilling peasants. An order would be sent to government officials in the provinces and villages to provide the necessary number of men. Since military assistance was often required to assemble these *fallāḥīn*, a company of soldiers would surround a village and seize as many *fallāḥīn* as necessary. The *fallāḥīn* were then marched off in irons to the chief town in the canton where a European doctor would choose those who were suitable for the army or navy. If demands for conscripts were not fulfilled, officials were either threatened with drastic punishments or were forced to submit lists of inhabitants in the districts under their jurisdiction. These lists were checked to decide whether failure to produce the number of men demanded by the government was justified. Bribery and favoritism provided many opportunities for those who were rich or influential enough to buy their escape from conscription. The peasants, indeed, found it not too difficult to bribe the government functionaries who carried out Muḥammad 'Alī's conscription policy, but they also discovered that they had often to redeem themselves numerous times to evade being conscripted.[9]

Not only *fallāḥīn* were recruited; townsmen also were forced into service. A visiting French naval officer reported that in April 1831 merchants who had come from all parts of Egypt to attend the annual fairs held at Cairo and Alexandria were surrounded by several cavalry regiments; their merchandise was destroyed and they were conscripted into the army. In June 1832 Barker reported that Muḥammad 'Alī intended to raise 60,000 men from the towns of Egypt:

> On the 14th instant the male population of Cairo was suddenly seized by press gangs posted in every quarter at the same appointed time, and, in a few minutes, the streets were deserted by all but troops of females loudly bewailing their captive relatives, and all the shops closed. It is said this violent measure produced 15,000 of all conditions, ages, able-bodied and infirm, out of which 4,000 were retained for the service of the Tyrant.[10]

Copts and Jews, as well as Muslims, were forced into service. "I have now the honour," wrote Barker, "to inform Your Lordship, that today 120 Copts have been brought here, chained two and two to be enrolled in the military service of Mehmed Aly. It is said 5,000 will be raised out of that miserable and degraded race of Egyptian Christians."[11] In January 1833 one hundred Jews were seized in Damietta from a Jewish population of from three to four hundred. At last, during the 1838–1841 crisis Muḥammad ʻAlī's conscription policy and its effects upon the Egyptian population and the country's economy were exposed, although the worst period of conscription had, in fact, already ended by the time these revelations were publicized throughout Europe. The brutality connected with the conscription of the Christian minority, the Copts, was particularly emphasized and, consequently, the Pasha ordered that conscription of Copts should cease in order to avoid the irritation of Christian sensibilities during the crucial years of crisis. At this time, the hostile attitude of the Western Powers towards Muḥammad ʻAlī's military ambitions was undoubtedly the dominant factor determining official response to his policy of conscription rather than any deep feeling of solicitude for the fate of the Egyptian population.[12]

Egyptians, especially the *fallāḥīn*, had their own methods for escaping conscription. Many *fallāḥīn* abandoned their homes rather than submit to the oppressions of Muḥammad ʻAlī. In 1826 General Boyer reported that the Nile Valley was a valley of tears and that large numbers of *fallāḥīn* were emigrating to Syria. Hamont estimated that the number of *fallāḥ* emigrants, accompanied by their wives, children, and flocks, amounted to one or two thousand. ʻAbd-allāh Pasha of ʻAkkah granted land to these Egyptian refugees and exempted them from taxation for a three-year period. Muḥammad ʻAlī demanded the peasants' return, but ʻAbd-allāh replied that the Egyptians were subjects of the Sultan and that he could not, therefore, prevent their settlement in territory under his control. It was this *fallāḥ* emigration, in fact, which was eventually to furnish Muḥammad ʻAlī with a pretext for invading Syria.[13] To escape from the authorities *fallāḥīn* also dug holes in cemeteries or in swamplands near their villages. Often they fled to distant villages or to the desert where they either remained with the Bedouins permanently or returned to their native villages when the danger of conscription had passed. They frequently escaped to the cities, particularly to Alexandria, where they set up "villages" composed of mud huts, three to four feet high, and tried to find work in order to supply their families with the barest necessities. In fact, in July 1831 Muḥammad ʻAlī found that one quarter of the land of Upper Egypt could not be cultivated because of an insufficient number of workers; he consequently issued an order to government officials that all *fallāḥīn* who had fled to Alexandria should be rounded up and led back to their villages under military escort. Those who had no villages or relatives were to be enlisted in the army, navy, or workshops; orphans were to be placed in the workshops of Cairo and its environs. Shortly after this order was issued, troops encircled the "villages" and forced the people to evacuate their mud huts. About six to seven thousand men, women, girls, old people, and children, carrying their few possessions upon their heads, were herded into boats on al-Maḥmūdīyah Canal and returned to their villages. Thereafter, village *shaykhs* came to Cairo and Alexandria each spring and autumn to look for deserters from the villages. The *fallāḥīn* who were captured were placed in government prisons until, chained together and under guard, they could be marched off to their villages.[14]

So unwilling were *fallāḥīn* to enter military service that mothers mutilated their children, blinding or crippling them, so that they would not have to serve. Adult men often cut off the index finger of their right hand, destroyed their right eye, or pulled out their front teeth to avoid conscription. To combat the practice of mutilation Muḥammad 'Alī sent a circular on March 12, 1833, to the heads of districts:

> With respect to the men whom we take for the service of our victorious War Department, some draw their teeth, some blind themselves, and others maim themselves, on their way to us, and for this reason we send back the greater part; and also I see in the Report of the War Department, that there is always a deficiency. Send them, before an hour elapses, all the men wanting, provided they be able-bodied and healthy; and those whom thou dost send, must be in concert with the Sheiks, and when thou dost expedite them, let each know, that he must not maim himself; because I will take from the family of every such offender, men in his place, and he who has maimed himself shall be sent to the galleys all his life; I have already ordered this to the Sheiks in writing, and do thou also take care, in concert with the Sheiks to levy the men demanded, and send them immediately. And the number of the rest of the men who remain in your Department, send me with the least possible delay.—This I demand.[15]

Dr. Gallina, one of Muḥammad 'Alī's doctors who was sent to the provinces to select men for military service, reported in 1834 that conditions were so terrible in the country that Girgā, which had ninety-six villages, could not even furnish seven suitable recruits and that in five other provinces from which the government demanded a levy of four hundred men, he could only find one hundred and seventy men capable of bearing arms. The government ordered those who mutilated themselves to work in its factories, but not only did mutilation continue in an incredible fashion, it was also even introduced in 1838 into districts where it had been unknown for years. The exhaustion of able-bodied men eventually led to the formation of regiments of the blind and of children fourteen or fifteen years of age.[16]

Muḥammad ʿAlī's policies caused much misery and discontent; in fact, when news of the failure of the assault on ʿAkkah on March 9, 1832, reached Egypt, the danger of popular revolt appeared imminent. Muḥammad ʿAlī took punitive action to discourage this discontent from developing into open rebellion: "on the 14th, 21st and 23rd instant the headless trunks of three Turks were exposed in the streets, having on the breast labels, importing, 'This is the fate which awaits those who cannot govern their tongues.' One of these victims of the Tyranny of Mehmed Ali was of the class of the *Ulemas*, and the others of the ancient Turk soldiery; of which it is thought, there are twenty thousand in Egypt ready to act in any popular insurrection."[17] The number of executions for political offenses in 1832 also reflected the unstable political situation in the country.[18] So precarious was Muḥammad ʿAlī's position during the first Syrian War that a decisive victory over the Sultan was deemed essential to prevent a general uprising in Egypt.[19]

The number of men conscripted into the military forces declined for a brief period after the first Syrian War. However, as it became essential to keep the army up to strength to defend the territories under Muḥammad ʿAlī's control, to suppress insurrections such as occurred in Syria in 1834, to deal with the war in al-Yaman, and to send troops to Nubia because of differences which had developed between Abyssinia and the Egyptian government, the policy of conscription was resumed. The supply of able-bodied men of proper age for conscription had been nearly exhausted in Egypt by the first Syrian War, but Muḥammad ʿAlī now had access to new sources of manpower. From 1834 he demanded conscripts not only from Egypt, but also from Syria and Candia.[20]

Widespread dissatisfaction with methods of conscription employed by Muḥammad ʿAlī became too great to be ignored, however, and the need for reform was keenly felt by the Pasha. Muḥammad ʿAlī considered that he did not have sufficient time in which to develop the educational process required for voluntary enlistments, but at the same time he realized he must introduce reforms to overcome the resistance to his policy of conscription. He decided in 1837 to recruit in accordance with military regulations modeled upon the system practiced in France, but nothing was done to implement this decision. Campbell raised the question of reforms with Muḥammad 'Alī in February 1838 and reported his conversation with the Pasha to the British government:

> He said that I could not be ignorant that he (the Pacha) felt how advantageous it was to follow a good system of recruiting—that the inconveniences in that difficult matter proceeded from the ignorance of the people, and the want of tact and knowledge of the officers, and that if I consulted History, I should find that civilized nations, themselves, are not exempt from these inconveniences. He told me that in considering the situation in which he was placed, I would feel that he could not at once carry into execution his benevolent intentions in regard to the conscription—but, he added, that notwithstanding these difficulties he was endeavouring to introduce into his country a good system of recruiting as well as many other ameliorations in which he hoped to succeed, and that Europe would be satisfied with him.[21]

In March 1838 Dr. Bowring tried to influence the Pasha to introduce reforms without delay. Muḥammad 'Alī listened sympathetically, but nothing was done. In April 1838 an uprising in the province of Manfalūṭ in Upper Egypt occurred when the population refused to furnish the contingent claimed from it. The cavalry regiment stationed in the area hesitated to march against the rebels. The Pasha set out personally to supervise repression of the revolt, but because of the low Nile his steamship was unable to get through to Upper Egypt. He, therefore, left the task of repression to Salīm Pasha, inspector-general of Upper Egypt. Some relaxation in the system of conscription did occur in 1839 when it was reported that the current conscription was "unattended by the cruelties and vexations heretofore practised": conscripts were limited to men between fifteen and twenty-five years of age, fathers of families and only sons being exempted.[22] Finally, Muḥammad 'Alī was obliged to abandon recruiting in 1840 when several *mudīrs* and *ma'mūrs* informed him they could recruit no more *fallāḥīn*. He dismissed these officials for their inability to execute his commands, but realized that new expedients had to be found.[23]

In the spring of 1840 Muḥammad 'Alī instituted the National Guard, a new type of military organization modeled upon the French National Guard, which according to Clot was intended to serve as an intermediate step to the army and to prepare the Egyptian peasants for military service. Recruiting for the Guard proceeded with considerable vigor with several leading *shaykhs* even putting on the *Niẓām* costume to stimulate some enthusiasm among *fallāḥīn*:

The recruitment of the National Guard continues everywhere with the utmost activity. At Cairo, Osman Bey Sennari, late Ulema of the Mosque Ashar, has undertaken to raise four regiments, and Mahomet Ali has promised that should he succeed he will make him Pasha of Two Tails. Ibrahim Aref Bey, late a merchant in Cairo, is named Brigadier General and has engaged to raise two regiments. Mohammad Bey, late Ulema, is to assemble other two [*sic*] regiments and to be decorated with the same rank. These eight regiments are to be recruited in the city of Cairo.[24]

Even after nearly twenty years of forced conscription for Muḥammad ʿAlī's regular army the *fallāḥīn* had failed to cultivate a tradition of military service and were extremely dissatisfied with the new wave of conscription under a different guise. Dislike of the new organization, the conscription for which was not confined to peasants alone, was widespread; it was universally believed that an outbreak of numerous fires in Cairo, including the conflagration which entirely consumed al-Azbakīyah Place on May 22, 1840, was attributable to this political discontent. Muḥammad ʿAlī, aware of the dissatisfaction over the Guard and the rumors concerning the causes of the fires, reproved ʿAbbās Pasha, then governor of Cairo, for not taking more stringent measures against the malcontents. He even accused ʿAbbās himself of "tampering in intrigues."

The spirit of the National Guard throughout Egypt was considered highly unsatisfactory; it was reported that Muḥammad ʿAlī eventually became fearful that "a secret understanding amongst the chiefs of the new force extends its ramifications over the whole country."[25] Fuel to the flames of discontent at conditions at home was added when news of the military losses in Syria reached Egypt. It was only when the prospect of settlement of the Egyptian Question became known in January 1841 that the hidden discontent and previous anxiety of the native population partly subsided. Even so, the National Guard remained very unpopular in all parts of the country. In an attempt to pacify the population, Muḥammad ʿAlī went personally to al-Manṣūrīyah Province in the spring of 1841 where he promised tax concessions to the disgruntled peasants to make them amenable to the new military demands which he had imposed upon them; Aḥmad Pasha Miniklī went to Middle Egypt for the same purpose. The National Guard did not long survive, however. By the end of 1841 it was reported that it had been disbanded both in Cairo and Alexandria and this policy of liquidating the Guards was undoubtedly applied universally.[26]

Muḥammad 'Alī by his own estimate had 16,000 troops in 1821 with which to assist the Sultan in his war with the Greek insurgents. By 1829 the army consisted of 62,150 troops, including 15,000 Bedouins. In the summer of 1832 the total number of land forces, stationed in Syria, Candia, al-Ḥijāz, Nubia and Sinnār, and Egypt, amounted to 83,000. In addition to these troops each regiment had artillery men, sappers, pioneers, and a full band of music.[27] Six months later, the full list of government employees was given as 193,932, of which 25,143 were in the marine, 67,998 were part of the civil administration, and approximately 100,000 in the army, three quarters of whom were *fallāḥīn*. It appeared that anyone who could walk was recruited into the forces. In 1838 an attempt was made to raise four regiments but was abandoned because of the manpower shortage. Nevertheless, Muḥammad 'Alī was still able to muster a fighting force of approximately 157,000 men for both his army and navy.[28]

At the end of the second Syrian War Muḥammad 'Alī was confronted with two problems: the reduction of his army to 18,000 men in compliance with the terms of the *khaṭṭ-i-sharīf* of 1841 which accorded him the hereditary government of Egypt, and the reintegration into the agricultural economy of Egypt of the large group of *fallāḥīn* who had been conscripted for life and whose ties with their villages had disappeared. Muḥammad 'Alī evaded the first problem by a subterfuge which could, perhaps, be justified by the difficulties implicit in the second. Instead of demobilizing his troops and returning them to their villages he assigned them to work on agricultural and irrigation projects. The soldiers, however, suffered thereby not only strict military discipline and the burdens of military life, but also the hardships of agricultural labor. These troops, supervised by their officers, repaired dikes which had been neglected for several years, relieving from the *corvée* approximately 25,000 *fallāḥīn* who were permitted to devote their energies entirely to the cultivation of the soil. The newly reformed Third Regiment was ordered to Damanhūr in May 1841 in order to excavate a canal on one of Muḥammad 'Alī's estates; a contingent of soldiers, headed by Sa'īd Pasha, Muḥammad 'Alī's son, and directed by Salīm Pasha, was engaged in repairing canals to reclaim the land lying between Lake Idkū and Lake al-Ma'adīyah; and soldiers and peasants were used in 1842 to work on the excavation of irrigation canals in Upper

Egypt. Naval personnel was used for the same purpose. Out of 14,450 naval recruits, 6,500 were sent in September 1841 to work in the villages. In November 1841 Muḥammad ʿAlī ordered the disarming of five ships of the line, thus relieving 3,000 additional men to work the land. A number of naval vessels were then placed on the Nile as river transports.

Army and naval officers were also affected by the viceroy's new policy. Even Ibrāhīm Pasha turned his swords into plowshares and was busy with the management of his estates. Commanders of Muḥammad ʿAlī's armies, who held the rank of pasha, were appointed to head provincial governments. Aḥmad Pasha Miniklī, however, one of the most distinguished generals in the Syrian army, was offered the governorship of a province, but declined on grounds that he had little aptitude for such an assignment; he was ordered then to withdraw completely from the army. Officers of lesser rank who were accustomed to discipline and to the execution of orders were placed in villages as agents of the government. Those Turkish officers who were discontented with Muḥammad ʿAlī's new policy were authorized, if they so wished, to resign from the Egyptian service.[29]

Thus, when Ibrāhīm Pasha took over from his father the responsibilities of ruling Egypt, in April 1848, the Egyptian army had completely lost its fighting quality because of the nonmilitary character of the work to which it was assigned. At that time Ibrāhīm's position as ruler of Egypt was extremely precarious because of the intrigue taking place in Istanbul to deny him his investiture as the hereditary governor of Egypt in accordance with the terms of the *khaṭṭ-i-sharīf* of 1841. He realized there were many persons, along with the Sultan, who were anxious for the opportunity to pay off old scores.[30] He promptly began then the task of reconstructing and reorganizing the Egyptian army and strengthening the military defenses of the country in order to protect his right to succeed Muḥammad ʿAlī. Orders to conscript men to replenish the ranks of the army were issued and, by July 1848, 19,000 new conscripts were enlisted in the army to fill existing vacancies and to replace the worn-out or infirm soldiers who had been sent back to their villages. This new wave of conscription was also accompanied by the same cruelty and barbarity endured by the Egyptian population during Muḥammad ʿAlī's reign.[31] The regular military force of 52,000 by July 1, 1848, was as follows: infantry, 40,000; cavalry, 6,000; and artillery, 6,000. In addition, 5,000 irregular troops were stationed in the provinces. The naval force amounted to about 11,500 men, half of whom were employed on public works such as the arsenal and Nile Barrages. A total of nearly 70,000 men was to increase to 80,000 men by the end of Ibrāhīm's reign. 'Abbās Pasha, however, reversed his uncle's policies when he succeeded him. He stopped forced conscription, restored town conscripts to their families, and promised to reduce the army to 18,000 in accordance with the terms of the *khaṭṭ-i-sharīf* of 1841. By May 5, 1849, the army was reduced to 22,000, and the old conscripts had been sent home.[32]

An average of 100,000 men or 4 per cent of a population estimated at 2,500,000 had been withdrawn from agriculture to serve in Muḥammad 'Alī's armed forces.[33] In all of Europe only in the Austrian border provinces did there exist an army of comparable size in relation to the total population.[34] In terms of modern warfare and a highly industrialized society an army of 4 per cent would be considered large; in the first half of the nineteenth century, particularly in a country with an agrarian economy, the percentage appeared enormous. Conscription of itself did not produce the picture of desolation in Egypt which foreign observers painted towards the end of the 1830's, but, when conscription was combined with the other burdens imposed upon the peasants, its effects were disastrous. The land was drained of its cultivators by conscription, the *corvée*, and disease;[35] the remaining agricultural population, which had become less competent as a result of voluntary mutilation, could not meet Muḥammad 'Alī's unreasonable demands for more crops and higher taxes. The farmers either abandoned the land to escape the government's heavy exactions or were forced into bankruptcy.[36]

It is not enough to judge Muḥammad 'Alī's conscription policy with reference to its immediate effects upon agricultural developments in Egypt or with sole regard to its effect upon the welfare of the people. Its long-range ramifications are, perhaps, more fundamental considerations which must be taken into account in evaluating the historical consequences of the policy which Muḥammad 'Alī himself justified:

> . . . the Viceroy and his partisans say, that in the East, the principle of force, being paramount and consecrated by religion itself, he was obliged to call into existence and to be surrounded by a very imposing force, in order to repress the excesses of fanaticism, and to oppose those prejudices which would be called up against him, that the adoption of this system has produced two happy results: the first, to establish the unity of power, the security of the country, and a certain homogenous nationality in Egypt; and the second, to initiate the people to an industry far superior to their own.[37]

The *fallāḥīn* themselves, having been conscripted into the Egyptian army, soon acquired habits common to soldiers and looked down upon the peasants, in some cases subjecting the cultivators to the same sort of vexations they had formerly suffered.[38] Gallice remarked in 1841 that the Egyptian soldiers were no longer *fallāḥīn* and were greatly flattered when favorably compared to French soldiers. He felt that conscription of the Egyptian peasants had drawn them out of their state of lethargy and that the soldiers, as a class, inclined towards the European civilization which had influenced the Pasha, civilization which he, in turn, had imposed forcefully upon his contemporaries. Hamont, on the other hand, asserted that no rehabilitation of the peasantry had occurred while they were in service and that as soon as they were released from the army they returned to their former mode of life.[39] Both observers were correct—Hamont in the short run and Gallice in the long run. The soldiers quickly reverted to their former habits, but, at the same time, the awakening of a kind of national self-consciousness among the Egyptians which began during Muḥammad Alī's reign with the formation of an army composed of Egyptian *fallāḥīn* was to bear fruit at a much later date. Nonetheless there remains impressive validity in the contemporary evaluation of Muḥammad 'Alī's policy made by Colonel Campbell, a sympathetic observer, that the arguments in favor of the military program were insufficient to warrant the ill effects of that program upon the economy of the country and the welfare of the people and that Muḥammad 'Alī probably exaggerated the civilizing methods he used, carrying too far the techniques designed to improve the condition of his people.[40]

CHAPTER XII

IRRIGATION

> Use a third of the revenues to increase and maintain canals, dikes, and bridges . . .
>
> 'Amr ibn al-'Āṣ[1]

Muḥammad 'Alī, like all the rulers of Egypt before him, understood that Egypt would be a desert without the Nile and that, without an adequate system of irrigation, the maximum profit from the cultivation of the soil could not be realized. In 1805 the outlines of a highly developed system of irrigation were actually in existence in Egypt, but had been badly neglected.[2] One commentator, in fact, reported that the "present system of irrigation is only the feeble remains of a better state of things. . . ."[3] None of Muḥammad 'Alī's attempts to increase his revenues could succeed then until these conditions were corrected.

The Irrigation System in Lower Egypt

The Nile River from its point of bifurcation formed a network of natural channels including the principal Rosetta and Damietta branches. Through the centuries there had been many shifts in the course of the river as it sought outlets to the sea. Some of the old branches of the river no longer served their function and new branches had formed to replace them. The basin system which had been developed in Egypt in ancient times depended mostly upon these natural branches. In addition, artificial canals had been excavated wherever they were required and dikes had been constructed to complete the system. This system was not altered greatly in Muḥammad 'Alī's time. To be sure, some new canals were excavated, but generally it was only necessary to clean and maintain the old canals. The old watercourses, either natural or man-made, also served as the foundation for the new *ṣayfī* canals. Whenever necessary, they were excavated to a depth ranging from six meters to approximately eight meters fifty centimeters below the level of the soil. In contrast, the *nīlī* canals were four meters in depth at most and could be used only during the period of flood. The accompanying list includes the principal canals in operation in Lower Egypt during the reign of Muḥammad ʻAlī.

West of Rosetta Branch	*Between the Two Branches*	*East of Damietta Branch*
al-Maḥmūdīyah (*ṣayfī*)	Baḥr Shibīn (*ṣayfī*)	Baḥr Muways (*ṣayfī*)
al-Khaṭāṭbah (*ṣayfī*)	Bājūrīyah (*ṣayfī*)	ash-Sharqāwīyah (*ṣayfī*)
Amīn Aghā	Bijayrim (*ṣayfī*)	ash-Sharqāwīyah at Damietta (*ṣayfī*)
Abū Dīb	Ṣarāwah (*ṣayfī*)	Bāsūsīyah (*ṣayfī*)
Damanhūr	al-ʻAṭf (*ṣayfī*)	Ra's al-Wādī (*ṣayfī*)
Buḥayrah	Masjid al-Khiḍr (*ṣayfī*)	Dandīṭīyah (*ṣayfī*)
Canopic branch	al-Jaʻfarīyah	Mīt Yaʻīsh (*ṣayfī*)
	an-Naʻnāʻīyah	Būhīyah (*ṣayfī*)
	Kafr ash-Shaykh	al-Manṣūrīyah (*ṣayfī*)
	Baḥr Qallīn	Baḥr Abū Manājah (*ṣayfī*)
	al-Faraʻūnīyah	Khalīj az-Zaʻfarānī
	Mīt Abū Ghālib	al-Baḥr aṣ-Ṣaghīr
	Baḥr Tīrah	Baḥr Abū 'l-Akhḍar

West of Rosetta Branch—Buḥayrah Province

Even before Muḥammad ʻAlī's time Buḥayrah Province had many canals. In 1802 a British officer reported them to be numerous enough and sufficiently wide and deep to stop the march of an army. Of these the larger canals were natural waterways which were kept clean by the velocity of the water, but the smaller irrigation canals, which required periodic cleaning, had been neglected. Buḥayrah Province itself was plagued by Bedouin raids in the eighteenth and early nineteenth centuries; furthermore, it had been the scene of struggle among the troops of the Mamlūks, the French, the Ottoman Turks, and the British in the period preceding Muḥammad ʻAlī's accession to power. However, the entire province was transformed during Muḥammad ʻAlī's reign because of his public works program and his tribal policy.[4]

The Dike of Abū Qīr. A vital public work which confronted Muḥammad ʻAlī at the beginning of his reign was the repair of the dike of Abū Qīr, a dike of ancient origin considered one of the largest and most solid of the imperial dikes. Governments in the past had always looked to its maintenance, repairing or reconstructing it whenever necessary. The disorders in Egypt at the end of the eighteenth century had resulted in neglect of the dike. As a result, a breach occurred about 1787 which endangered the adjacent land, once part of ancient Lake Maryūṭ. This lake had served as a fresh-water reservoir until the beginning of the eighteenth century and had been fed by canals deriving from the Nile, particularly Canal Buḥayrah. Because of the general neglect of irrigation canals in Buḥayrah Province, water no longer flowed into the lake in great quantity; a large part of the basin consequently became dry and was cultivated by the inhabitants. The breach of 1787 also allowed sea water to inundate numerous villages which lay between Alexandria and Rosetta. It was not until April 1801, when additional breaches at the western extremity of Lake al-Ma'adīyah were made for strategic reasons by the Anglo-Turkish army, that the complete inundation of the basin of Lake Maryūṭ by sea water occurred. By June 1801 the entire basin of Lake Maryūṭ was filled, causing inestimable damage to the cultivable land of this part of Buḥayrah Province. In addition, the salt water penetrated the Canal of Alexandria which supplied the city with its drinking water. Villages and towns were ruined, harvests lost, the routes to Alexandria were cut, and Nile water no longer reached the city. When the Ottoman Turks reoccupied Egypt after the French withdrawal, the Porte sent, according to J. M. Le Père, several Swedish engineers[5] or, according to al-Jabartī, Ṣalāḥ Efendī to repair the dike.[6] After a year and a half the work of reparation was nearly completed when 'Alī Pasha, fearing a Mamlūk attack on Alexandria, decided in 1803 to cut the dike. The dike was once again repaired in 1804 by order of the Ottoman government, but the work was hardly considered satisfactory:

> So incomplete, however, is the work that it is to be feared that it will not be capable of resisting the next winter's gales. No opening having been left between the two lakes, a wall built without mortar cannot long protect the canal against the impulse of the waves when driven by a strong northerly wind.[7]

The matter remained thus until 1811 when Muḥammad 'Alī decided to remedy the situation. Repairs were undertaken that year, but were so badly executed that the waters of Lake al-Ma'adīyah threatened to pass into the interior. In 1816 the Pasha decided to take more effective measures, assembled workers and material, and completed the repair of the dike, which was 1,243 meters in length. The task had been difficult and expensive, for it had been necessary to transport all materials from Alexandria either by sea or on camels.

Some years later Linant attempted to persuade Muḥammad 'Alī to reclaim 220,000 *faddāns* of land ruined by the break in the dike of Abū

Qīr. To reclaim 143,247 *faddāns* of land he proposed building dikes to confine the water of Lake Maryūṭ and to put Canal Buḥayrah into condition. The balance of 76,753 *faddāns* could be reclaimed merely by cleaning out those canals which were already in existence. The total project was estimated at 2,723,075 francs but was not carried through because both money and the necessary manpower to execute the work were lacking.[8]

Al-Maḥmūdīyah Canal (*ṣayfī*). The construction of al-Maḥmūdīyah Canal was the principal public work undertaken and completed by Muḥammad ʿAlī. Its history personifies the history of almost all the major public works which he undertook—a brilliant conception, although not an original one, badly planned, badly executed, and carried on at great cost and suffering to the Egyptian people. It serves, in fact, as a case history of energetic, ambitious, and amateurish despotism.

The old Canal of Alexandria which ran between ar-Raḥmānīyah and Alexandria was described by one early traveler as built solidly enough to last an eternity. Its destruction thus cost Muḥammad ʿAlī much trouble and expense. This canal, which supplied sweet water to the city of Alexandria, also furnished the means for transporting produce and served as an important irrigation canal for the province of Buḥayrah. The bey of Buḥayrah Province was charged with the maintenance of the canal, and his *kāshif*, who was his representative in the province, was to supervise maintenance and repair of the dikes and prevent precipitate cutting of them by the inhabitants bordering the canal. Work on the canal and dikes was to be carried out under his direction by the adjacent villages, numbering about thirty, expenses being borne by the landholders, and was supposed to begin annually on the canal just before the flood at the beginning of June and last thirty or forty days. The *kāshif* was to receive annually a proportion of the customs of Alexandria assigned to him to cover his expenses. In 1797 the amount paid was 18,000 piasters (25,778 francs) and, in 1798, 22,500 piasters (32,223 francs). Payment was to be made to him only upon receipt of a testimonial from the notables of Alexandria confirming that the cisterns of the city had been provided with water; and if an insufficient flood made it impossible for water to come to Alexandria via the canal, he was obliged to convey it by camel transport. Failure to receive the testimonial from the Alexandrians might result in an order of the death penalty by the *Shaykh al-Balad*. After the needs of Alexandria had been satisfied, the *kāshif* was to announce publicly throughout the province that the villagers could open the dikes on their irrigation canals and could fill their cisterns with the water from the Canal of Alexandria. Unfortunately, however, the level of the water was thereby soon lowered in the canal, which usually remained dry for nearly nine months of the year. And, indeed, neglect of public works in the eighteenth century resulted in the gradual silting up of the canal so that it became difficult to navigate and was also inadequate for conducting water to the cisterns of Alexandria. The city therefore relied in large measure upon rain water to fill the cisterns.[9]

The French engineers who accompanied Napoleon considered the Canal of Alexandria of primary importance and placed high on their agenda of public works the re-establishment of this canal. The maintenance of the canal was assigned to two engineers, Moline and Regnault. In 1798 the canal was made navigable by the removal of about eighteen inches of sediment. Small boats were then able to reach ar-Raḥmānīyah for approximately six weeks while the Nile was at its height. An engineer, Bodart, was instructed to survey the canal with an eye to permanent improvement, but he died shortly afterwards. Lancret and de Chabrol replaced him and presented a detailed proposal of the work to be done. The French, however, were unable to take permanent measures for improvement of the canal.[10]

As early as 1811 Muḥammad ʻAlī began to think of restoring the old canal to navigation. No action was taken at the time for military reasons; the opening of the canal would have provided easy access to the interior and thus would have increased the danger of invasion.[11] By 1817 the situation had changed, however. Several factors operated in favor of executing the project rejected in 1811. The increase in commerce had brought many ships to Egypt, which now sailed directly to Rosetta on the Rosetta branch of the river to load the grain. The difficulty of passing the bar or *būghāz* of the Rosetta branch of the river proved a great deterrent to trade, however, as passage could only be made one day in four. At certain times of the year, it was in fact completely impassable and the export of grain which accumulated at Rosetta was thereby delayed.[12] Also, the winter of 1816–17 was a particularly severe one and export of produce from Egypt, therefore, was difficult. Caravans were established to carry the grain from Rosetta to Alexandria, since the failure of the *būghāz* to form for two months in the spring of 1817 had given rise to the fear that no large-scale exports through the Rosetta branch would take place before the flood in August. This situation threatened to ruin those engaged in the trade. The Pasha had sold 545,000 *ardabbs* of various grain by firman that year, but only one fifth could be delivered. The stocks of cotton, hemp, flax, rice, and sugar, which were not included in the figure above, remained almost entirely on hand. Furthermore, the new harvest of the spring of 1817 promised to be an abundant one. Thus, there was a tremendous accumulation of produce which could not be shipped out of the country, a fact which meant that Muḥammad 'Alī was suffering great losses. The first measure which he took to counteract the difficulty was to narrow the mouth of the Nile branch by constructing two piers of stone which were carried out a considerable distance into the sea. It was then decided, possibly upon the urging of Briggs, an English merchant in Alexandria, to open up the Canal of Alexandria to navigation. Briggs himself had suffered greatly that year in his attempt to meet his commitments to ship grain to the government of Malta.[13]

The impression given by various writers is that work was begun on the canal at the end of 1819 and was completed in four months. The facts of the case are quite different. The construction of the canal actually took three years and work was begun in April 1817. The original intention, apparently, was to repair the old Canal of Alexandria; in fact, the first reports concerning the work refer to the course of this canal.[14] The canal was to begin near ar-Raḥmānīyah where the Ashrafīyah Canal started and to end at Pompey's Column in Alexandria where a port was to be dug to accommodate shipping. The canal was to be 10 *qaṣabahs*, a *qaṣabah* equaling 3 meters 64 centimeters, in width and 4 *qaṣabahs* in depth. The *kāshifs* of the provinces in Lower Egypt were ordered to raise a levy of one worker for every ten inhabitants and about 100,000 men participated in the *corvée*. Instructions were also given to the native blacksmiths to make 50,000 picks and shovels. These, along with baskets for carrying the earth, were assembled. Fifteen piasters were paid to each worker to cover his expenses for his trip from the village to the place where other recruits for the *corvée* had assembled. In addition, each worker was to receive 30 paras per day for his work. He was, though, obliged to furnish his own water, as the land through which the canal passed was dry and the well water in the area brackish.

Although the final decision with regard to the canal's course had not yet been made, excavation began as soon as the first workmen were assembled. This procedure produced several very serious consequences for the future canal. The Turkish engineers had not even been informed of Muḥammad 'Alī's decision to build the canal until after the first contingent of workmen had appeared to begin excavation and therefore had not had sufficient time to make the necessary preparations. No leveling was carried out, for the course that the canal was to take had not been decided upon and staked out. Since there was no time to consider where the workers should dig, the excavation was carried on in the general direction of Alexandria at the discretion of the *kāshifs* and *shaykhs al-balad*. It was only after the flood began in June 1817, when the workmen were dispersed, that the engineers were able to draw up the designs for the canal project. The students of the polytechnical school under the supervision of their instructors made a survey in which it was discovered that the distance between ar-Raḥmānīyah and Pompey's Column was 26,000 *qaṣabahs*, whereas the distance between the old canal of Nāṣrīyah, situated at al-'Aṭf near the town of Fuwwah, and Pompey's Column was 5,000 *qaṣabahs* less. It was decided, therefore, to change the course of the canal and to place the head of the new canal at al-'Aṭf. Further justification for placing the head of the canal at al-'Aṭf was found in the fact that the mouth of the canal at ar-Raḥmānīyah was obstructed by an island and that the bank of the river followed a straight line, whereas there was a bend at al-'Aṭf with a great eddy which deepened the river bed and caused the formation of a raised point favorable to the construction of the mouth of the canal. The ill effects of the precipitate beginnings could not, however, be eradicated. Although leveling was undertaken in 1819 after a European engineer was placed in charge, the incline of the canal proved too slight to maintain a steady flow, a difficulty which was never entirely overcome. The tortuous route of the canal that finally emerged was due partially to local conditions, but mostly to the lack of planning and the haphazard digging that made it necessary to join the isolated excavations in the best manner possible.

Work continued in a desultory fashion and figured very little in consular reports until 1819. During this period the port at Pompey's Column was built. Operations on the canal were resumed with increased vigor in January 1819 under the direction of Pascal Coste, a French architect residing in Cairo, and were begun at the mouth of the canal where 60,000 workmen were employed. This number was increased to about 300,000 by March 1819, after orders had been issued to the provincial governors to assemble the number of *fallāḥīn* proportionate to the size of their provinces.[15] The workers, led by their *shaykhs al-balad*, were assembled at the points assigned to them. With their governor at the head, all the contingents of each province arrived accompanied by musicians and carrying banners. Each *fallāḥ* was granted twenty *riyāls* to cover his traveling expenses, ten of which were paid in cash and ten deducted from the taxes he owed. One piaster per day was paid for his labor. Large numbers of carpenters, masons, and blacksmiths were also assembled. Villages which had numerous date trees were ordered to supply baskets and cord, while cities supplied picks and shovels. Pumps were also employed to pump the water which infiltrated at certain points before the excavation had been completed. Work continued until harvest time in 1819, when the *fallāḥīn* were dispersed. It then proceeded at a very slow pace until 100,000 workers were reassembled after the harvest to complete work on the canal. According to al-Jabartī, the governors were obliged to drive them back and were forced to lead the *fallāḥīn* to the *corvée* with cords round their throats.

Because of the continual infiltration of salt water into the canal, Alexandria's drinking water had to be brought from a distance at a great increase in cost to consumers. This situation led Muḥammad ʻAlī to consult two other engineers, Huyot and Lachaise, from Cairo. Huyot executed the construction of a dike, but the work was badly done and had no effect. It was then decided to build a drain to the Nile. It was not well made, though, and only brackish water flowed into the cisterns of Alexandria. Finally, in an attempt to correct the situation and to prevent the infiltration of salt water from Lake Maryūṭ and Lake al-Maʻadīyah two embankments of masonry were built on both sides of the canal, extending from ten to twelve kilometers; but the permanent solution to the problem was to drain Lake Maryūṭ and several drains were excavated for this purpose. The lake, however, was continually replenished by inundation waters. Canal Buḥayrah also continued to bring water to it.

The canal was completed early in 1820 and was called al-Maḥmūdīyah Canal in honor of Sultan Maḥmūd. It was about 72 kilometers long. Its total cost amounted to 35,000 purses (around 7,500,000 francs) which included the cost of labor at 8,795,200 piasters, cost of materials, salaries to the masons and carpenters, the *sāqiyahs* to remove the water that infiltrated, the pelisses that were presented to the *kāshifs*, the gifts made to the *shaykhs al-balad*, and the salaries to those who supervised the work. Also, to this monetary cost must be added the tremendous cost in life. Large numbers of *fallāḥīn* perished because of lack of food and water, fatigue, and exposure. They were badly treated and allowed no respite by the soldiers who acted as overseers and directed the work. They labored from sunrise to sunset; many were obliged to dig with their hands because of the lack of tools and to work in the water which infiltrated as the digging proceeded. Al-Jabartī described how large numbers of *fallāḥīn* collapsed at their work and how earth was thrown over them before it was definitely ascertained that they were dead. Different estimates ranging from 12,000 to 100,000 casualties have been given by various writers for the ten months' period of concentrated work in 1819. So vivid was the recollection of the horrors of those months that when years later the necessity for dredging the canal became vital the government hesitated to call out the *corvée* for that purpose.[16]

Weaknesses in construction became evident after completion of the canal. At first it was necessary to close the mouth of the canal for four months of the year because it was feared that an overflow of water would destroy the dikes designed to prevent infiltration of sea water into the canal. This decision involved transshipment of cargo from boats in the river to boats on the canal and thereby increased transportation costs and caused delays. Al-'Aṭf profited from this necessity, however, and several great fortunes were created in that city. A few years later it was noted that the river did not flow fast enough to move the sediment along with the current because of the insufficient incline of the canal. The yearly deposits of Nile mud on the canal bed also caused increasing shallowness in the channel and made it impossible for larger barges to pass through. Only during flood time was continuous navigation possible. For eight months of the year, therefore, the canal was unserviceable for navigation, particularly near its mouth where deposits concentrated. It was feared that in a few years the new harbor at Alexandria would also be choked with mud. Since dredging boats in operation on the canal were inadequate, in 1830 troops and a *corvée* were called out to clean the canal; only two feet of mud were removed, however, because adequate tools were lacking. The next year it was reported that one hundred *sāqiyahs* were installed at the mouth to cause some movement of water in an attempt to create a slight current where the canal had filled up.[17]

These palliatives did not remedy the situation and much of the traffic was now obliged to go via the Rosetta branch. A permanent corrective was recommended by an English engineer in 1831. He proposed that locks should be built at the canal mouth to render it navigable and that two small irrigation canals should be built on both sides of the canal, but his estimates were so costly that the matter was dropped. In 1833 Coste, who had built the canal, also made proposals for a permanent solution, but no action was taken, as Muḥammad 'Alī's attention was centered entirely on the work which had begun on the Nile Barrages. The canal continued to silt up and by 1834 the canal bed near al-'Aṭf was eighteen inches higher than the river. A new mouth was excavated further upstream, but the same thing occurred. Then a dike was built around the low-lying lands in the vicinity to form a reservoir which could provide water during low Nile. Twenty years after the canal was built, it was so full of mud and debris that boats were in constant danger of being grounded in certain places along the route.[18]

In 1842 or 1843 locks were built at al-'Aṭf to regulate the water and to obviate transshipment. A toll was charged for loaded boats at the rate of 15 paras per *ardabb*; in 1845–46 the amount of 1,684 purses, 39 piasters, was earned. When the locks were closed at low Nile from April to August, the amount of water was increased by water directed through Canal al-Khaṭāṭbah, an irrigation canal only recently built. New complications, however, resulted from this action. The temporary barrages constructed with clods of earth and rice stalks which were built at certain points on this canal to regulate the irrigation of land were carried by the water to al-Maḥmūdīyah Canal upon their removal and thus increased the debris already accumulated. Also, as it was pointed out in 1846, proprietors of land along the Canal of Damanhūr diverted much of the water from Canal al-Khaṭāṭbah so that most of it was lost in Lake Maryūṭ through the lateral canals and not enough water reached al-Maḥmūdīyah to make any real difference.[19] Al-Maḥmūdīyah Canal continued to silt up every year. It was dredged from time to time but without any great effect and hardly warranted the enormous expense and number of workers assembled to perform the necessary labor. After Muḥammad 'Alī's death various devices were attempted to remedy the situation, but in 1887 between 200,000 to 300,000 cubic meters had still to be cleaned out of the canal each year at an expense of approximately £E5,000 each year.[20]

There were, though, some positive achievements: the canal did provide limited possibilities for the transport of goods directly from Cairo to Alexandria; it also served as an irrigation canal. In the first years after the canal was built it irrigated only 4,000 *faddāns* of summer crops, but shortly afterwards this amount increased so much that there was not enough water during low Nile to meet the need. By 1849 there were 11,545 *faddāns* on its banks that depended upon it for irrigation.[21]

Al-Khaṭāṭbah Canal (*ṣayfī*). This canal was an entirely new excavation for most of its course and represented a major irrigation work. It had its head between Banī Salāmah and Abū Nashshābah on the Rosetta branch. Part of it may have been excavated along the course of the old Canal al-ʻAṣṣārah, known also as the Canal of the Pyramids, but it is not clear whether the southern portion of the new canal was built along an old course until aṭ-Ṭarrānah or Ṭayrīyah. At any rate, it ran parallel to the Rosetta branch until Shubrākhīt and then went westward through Damanhūr and joined al-Maḥmūdīyah Canal close to Zāwiyat Ghazāl. According to Clot, al-Khaṭāṭbah was 195,000 meters long, but Linant considered it only 123 kilometers in length; it was 19 meters wide. It watered a large part of Buḥayrah Province at both the time of inundation and low water. Several barrages (Clot mentioned five) were built along its course to regulate the level of the water. The cultivators built smaller barrages of mud and rice stalks to assist the main barrages. It was debris from this canal that aggravated the situation on al-Maḥmūdīyah Canal. Two old canals, Canal Amīn Aghā and Canal Abū Dīb, now derived their source from al-Khaṭāṭbah Canal, but they were used only at flood time and had little water in them at other times of the year.[22]

Damanhūr Canal. This old canal took its waters from the Rosetta branch at ar-Raḥmānīyah and joined al-Khaṭāṭbah Canal at Damanhūr.[23]

Buḥayrah Canal. According to Linant this ancient canal was an extension of Baḥr Yūsuf, which turned westward at Ṭayrīyah, extended along the edge of the desert, and then emptied into Lake Maryūṭ. It was almost 60 miles long (26,000 *qaṣabahs*) and 5 yards wide. After the construction of al-Khaṭāṭbah Canal it branched off from that canal.[24]

Ancient Canopic Branch. The name of this canal cannot be identified, as none of the maps have labeled it other than Canopic Branch. The channel was marked on the early maps as leaving the Rosetta branch at Dayrūṭ and flowing into Lake Idkū. In 1802 it was reported to be full at high Nile and to retain its water for most of the year. It figured in a report during the campaign of 1807, when a British officer stated that the "remains of a deep canal with high banks" were still to be seen. The canal is also marked on Linant's map.[25]

Between the Rosetta Branch and Damietta Branch—Provinces of al-Gharbīyah and al-Minūfīyah

This area contained a number of important canals before the reign of Muḥammad ʻAlī. He did not alter the outlines of the irrigation system in these provinces to any large extent, but he converted a number of the canals into *ṣayfī* canals. Many continued to serve as *nīlī* canals. The water from the canals between the two major branches of the river was carried to the north to the area of the country known as Barrīyah where it was lost in the uncultivated lands bordering the marshlands of Lake Burullus.[26]

Canals deriving their source from the Rosetta branch. The early maps indicate that a series of canals derived their source from the Rosetta branch before Muḥammad ʻAlī's reign. These played a role of minor importance during his time as they were used only as *nīlī* canals. Most of the important ones instead derived their water from the Damietta branch, because the level of water was higher there than in the Rosetta branch. This higher elevation of water was due to the fact that the Damietta branch followed a more sinuous and consequently a longer course and had less of an incline than that of the Rosetta branch. The natural contour of the Delta was also one which permitted a freer flow from the Damietta to the Rosetta branch. For these reasons all the *ṣayfī* canals which supplied these provinces derived their source from the Damietta branch.[27]

Canals deriving their source from the Damietta branch. Before Muḥammad ʻAlī's reign many canals which derived their source from the Damietta branch of the Nile were deprived of water; an appreciable decrease in the flow of water to the sea resulted from the fact that much of the water in the Damietta branch flowed through the lateral canals into the Rosetta branch, which had fewer windings and a greater incline. The consequences were serious to agriculture as the desert encroached upon some of Egypt's most fertile soil east of the river branch, which received an inadequate supply of water to fertilize it. Also, the current became so weak that it could not prevent the water from backing up. As a result, the water of the river branch from Fāraskūr to the sea became salted; further south it was brackish for a considerable distance. Drinking water was therefore scarce and the rice fields which relied upon water from the Damietta branch could not be cultivated.[28]

Al-Fara'ūnīyah Canal. Al-Fara'ūnīyah Canal intersected the Upper Delta obliquely from southeast to northwest; leaving the Damietta branch near the village of Bīr Shams, it traversed the Delta through the city of Minūf and joined the Rosetta branch at Nādir. Originally intended to serve as an irrigation canal only, it had become an important link in the communication system of Egypt between Cairo and the Rosetta branch of the Nile because of the shallowness of that branch upstream of 'Alqām. During the months of low water, boats from Cairo would avoid the upper part of the Rosetta branch by entering al-Fara'ūnīyah Canal from the Damietta branch and by crossing the Delta to the lower part of the Rosetta branch where the water was sufficiently deep for shipping throughout the year. The navigability of al-Fara'ūnīyah Canal proceeded from an increase in the flow of water through two large openings on the Damietta branch near the town of al-Fara'ūnīyah and from the swift current produced by the steep incline of the canal after Kafr al-Fara'ūnīyah. In an effort to regulate the flow of water into this canal, the Mamlūk government had constructed a dike at al-Fara'ūnīyah in the middle of the eighteenth century. Each year when the Nile was low the dike would be cut so water could enter the canal; at flood time the dike would be closed.

The diversion of water from the Damietta branch of the river to al-Fara'ūnīyah Canal had led to a decrease of water in the former, contributing immeasurably to the impoverishment of the provinces lying east of the Damietta branch. Consequently the inhabitants of these provinces deluged the Mamlūk government with their complaints and clamored for the permanent closure of the dike at al-Fara'ūnīyah. The cultivators residing on the banks of al-Fara'ūnīyah Canal as well as the Rosetta branch, beneficiaries of the greater abundance of water in their provinces, insisted, on the contrary, that nothing be altered. The Mamlūk government vacillated between the demands of both groups, generally favoring the one that gave the largest gifts.

Deciding in 1793 to favor the eastern provinces, Murād Bey ordered the construction of two small dikes at al-Fara'ūnīyah in order to close the openings there and commanded that the governor of the province should maintain stringent watch over them so that no breach would occur. After some delay, this work was actually carried out so that by the time the French arrived in Egypt they found the apertures at al-Fara'ūnīyah sealed but the differences between the two parties by no means resolved. Napoleon, confronted by the dilemma of satisfying both groups, ordered an inquest in August 1799, hoping that when a complete survey of the problem had been made, a permanent solution could then be found. Hence reports were prepared, as stipulated by the order, and were presented a year later to Le Père the Elder, the French engineer-in-chief in Egypt.

In the meantime, the residents of Minūf and the nearby villages had persuaded the French officer in command of the area to build a secondary dike at Minūf for the purpose of creating a reservoir between Minūf and the dikes of al-Faraʿūnīyah. This dike of Minūf, built in July 1800, was destroyed soon after during the extraordinarily high flood of September 1800, which also breached the dikes at al-Faraʿūnīyah. The outcome of both disasters was the resumption of navigation between Nādir and the Damietta branch. The French engineers became fearful that unless steps were taken immediately the eastern provinces would again be in trouble. Le Père, therefore, presented recommendations to General Menou for the reconstruction of the dikes at al-Faraʿūnīyah which were to be maintained and carefully guarded until a dam could be built at Minūf. This dam, as conceived by Le Père, would be capable of solving the problem of an equitable distribution of water in the Delta once and for all while at the same time allowing for the navigation of al-Faraʿūnīyah Canal, which, he felt, must eventually play a vital role in the transit through Egypt. The dikes at al-Faraʿūnīyah were accordingly repaired, but the long-term project could not be carried out because of the withdrawal of the French troops from Egypt. Indeed, it remained for Muḥammad ʿAlī many years later to act upon the permanent solution recommended by Le Père.

In the period following the French withdrawal, breaches in the dikes of al-Faraʿūnīyah occurred at different points, undoubtedly from the work of individuals interested in diverting water into al-Faraʿūnīyah Canal. The Turkish administrators made several attempts to blockade these openings, but never completed the task. Thus, when Muḥammad ʿAlī took charge of affairs in Egypt, he found himself confronted by complaints from the inhabitants of the eastern provinces. In 1806 he undertook to stop the flow of water from the Damietta branch into al-Faraʿūnīyah Canal by blocking the breaches in the dikes. The work dragged on for several years until he called upon a European engineer, de Latour Maubourg, to supervise the work. The new director of the project introduced an innovation that speeded up the work; he utilized explosives for excavating the rocks required in the construction of the blockade. Early in 1809 the openings were finally blocked and water flowed uninhibited into the Damietta branch. Al-Fara'ūnīyah Canal now received water from its mouth on the Rosetta branch. As was to be expected, the people of al-Minūfīyah and Buḥayrah provinces now complained to the Pasha. He tried to satisfy these complaints by excavating other canals to compensate for the loss of water from al-Fara'ūnīyah Canal, but the problem of improving the flow of water in the Rosetta branch to facilitate navigation was not undertaken until the Pasha, himself, was severely affected. When Muḥammad 'Alī became interested in monopolizing the trade of Egypt and the transporting of government-owned crops to Alexandria became important, he could no longer afford to ignore the need for correcting the situation. In 1818, therefore, he decided to find some means of increasing the supply of water in the Rosetta branch. He commanded the construction of a dike at Minūf and also closed al-Fara'ūnīyah Canal at Nādir. A large reservoir was formed, fed by numerous canals in the Upper Delta, from which the cultivators could obtain water for irrigation. By these means, he was able to increase the supply of water in the Rosetta branch for the improvement of navigation and at the same time provide for the irrigation of the Delta. A permanent solution to the main problem of equalizing the flow of water in the two river branches still remained, however. The Nile Barrages, reminiscent of Le Père's recommendations, were intended by Muḥammad 'Alī to provide this permanent solution.[29]

Baḥr Shibīn (*ṣayfī*). This canal which followed in part the course of the old Sebennytic branch of the Nile was one of the largest natural channels of the river. It did not, however, appear on the early maps as a continuous arm of the river extending from its head at al-Qarīnayn through Shibīn al-Kūm, Milīj, passing east of al-Maḥallah al-Kubrā, and then flowing north to the Mediterranean. Rather, it was shown as forming part of a network of canals that emptied into Lake Burullus. At the time of the French occupation of Egypt, Baḥr Shibīn had still been navigable throughout the year and its northernmost section (referred to on some of the early maps as the Ashtūm Jamassah Canal) had provided a closer and more navigable route than the Damietta branch between Rosetta and Samannūd and the other principal towns of the interior. After the introduction of summer irrigation by Muḥammad 'Alī the canal became navigable only at flood time because of the settling of silt on the canal bed.

The government attempted to correct this situation by calling out a *corvée* each year to clean the canal. This proved an expensive procedure, however, as approximately 50,000 to 60,000 men had to be called up annually for this purpose. It was then decided that a permanent solution might be found by excavating a new canal mouth at Mīt 'Afīf. After the work at Mīt 'Afīf was completed new difficulties arose. It was soon realized that, unless a new channel was dug annually at the new mouth, water would not enter the canal. The canal mouth at Mīt 'Afīf was finally abandoned in favor of the old one, but to insure the flow of water into the canal at the time of low Nile a barrage was begun in 1839 and completed in 1840 at al-Qarīnayn. The Barrage of al-Qarīnayn was 100 meters long and had 10 arches, each 5 meters wide and included a lock to permit the free passage of boats. When the work was completed, the old channel was closed off by a dike and the water now passed through the new channel. The excavations necessitated by this major project totaled 431,422 cubic meters, the masonry included 50,553 cubic meters, and the cost of the work totaled 1,000,000 francs.[30]

Bājūrīyah Canal (*ṣayfī*). This natural channel took its head upstream of Mīt 'Afīf, passed through the town of Bājūr, and moved northward. It was 62,000 meters long and rarely needed to be cleaned. One of the branches of the Bājūrīyah in the northern part of the Delta was called Baḥr Qallīn and was important as a *nīlī* canal.[31]

Bijayrim Canal (*ṣayfī*). This canal took its head at the village of Bijayrim on the Damietta branch and moved northward. It lay between the Masjid al-Khiḍr Canal and the Damietta branch. It was 62,000 meters in length.[32]

Ṣarāwah Canal (*ṣayfī*). It was 35,000 meters in length, cost 20,000 purses to excavate, and watered only 8,000 *faddāns* even with the help of *sāqiyahs*. This small canal was to be found in the vicinity of Minūf.[33]

Al-'Aṭf Canal (*ṣayfī*). This canal took its head at the town of al-'Aṭf on the Damietta branch (not to be confused with al-'Aṭf on the Rosetta branch where al-Maḥmūdīyah Canal began). This was probably not a new canal.[34]

Masjid al-Khiḍr Canal (*ṣayfī*). It was 62,000 meters in length and took its head at the town of this name on the Damietta branch. It extended northward and ran parallel to the Damietta branch.[35]

Al-Ja'farīyah Canal. The head of this canal was on Baḥr Shibīn at al-Ja'farīyah and passed through Ṭanṭā to join the Canal of Kafr ash-Shaykh. It was 55,000 meters long (or about 30 miles, according to another source), 4 yards wide, and had 4 lockgates to regulate the water.

It appears to have been a new canal, as it does not figure on the older maps, and, presumably, a *nīlī* canal also,[36] as it is not listed by Linant as a *ṣayfī* canal.

An-Na'nā'īyah Canal. This canal, which followed one of the old water courses that had fallen into disuse, took its head on the Damietta branch at an-Na'nā'īyah and was connected to the Rosetta branch near Nādir. It ran almost parallel to the route of al-Fara'ūnīyah Canal. The new canal was 35,000 meters long and was not listed as a *ṣayfī* canal.[37]

Canal of Kafr ash-Shaykh. Canal al-Ja'farīyah flowed into this canal, which was the upper part of an old canal called Baḥr al-Khūr which was described in 1802 as the smallest in the network of canals in this part of the country and as dry by February. Although Linant's map still shows the old canal branching off from Baḥr Shibīn, it appears that its link with the new al-Ja'farīyah Canal made its northern part the most important.[38]

Mīt Abū Ghālib Canal. This old canal which rose on the Damietta branch near Fāraskūr connected the northern part of Baḥr Shibīn (that section often referred to as Ashtūm Jamassah Canal) with the Damietta branch of the river.[39]

Baḥr Tīrah. This was known on the early maps as Canal Tabanīyah. It branched off from the river near Samannūd and emptied into Lake Burullus.[40]

East of the Damietta Branch—Provinces of Daqahlīyah, ash-Sharqīyah, and al-Qalyūbīyah

This part of the country had canals which intersected the provinces lying east of the Damietta branch. Since the early maps did not label many of them, they cannot be identified. The maps and descriptions of the area at the beginning of the nineteenth century show clearly the desolation of the land, particularly in the low lands of the north, once serviced by the Pelusian, Tanitic, and Mendesian branches of the river which because of neglect had become useless by the turn of the century. Only a few miserable villages were to be found on their banks as a reminder of the former fertility of the land. In fact, much of the area was completely inundated for eight or nine months of the year. The only cultivated land near the coast in 1802 was around Lake al-Manzalah from Damietta to Maṭarīyah. Here dams often had to be built to prevent salt water from the lake from backing up into the canals. East of Maṭarīyah the land was uncultivated except in the vicinity of aṣ-Ṣāliḥīyah, which contained about twenty villages surrounded by palm trees. This land was either inundated with salt water from the lake or turned into desert land because of the failure of the government to maintain the canals. By 1845, however, much of the uncultivable land east of the Damietta branch had been reclaimed because of the government's program of draining the land and restoring canals. Many of the older canals were incorporated in the new canals excavated during Muḥammad 'Alī's reign; of these a large number were converted into *ṣayfī* canals, which with the exception of Baḥr Muways had regulating barrages at their heads. The barrage for Baḥr Muways was located at az-Zaqāzīq.[41]

Baḥr Muways (*ṣayfī*). In ancient times this natural waterway was known as the Tanitic branch. It had its head at Kafr Muways on the Damietta branch, passed through az-Zaqāzīq, to Ṣān al-Ḥajar, and emptied into Lake al-Manzalah near Maṭarīyah. The channel was 120 miles long, 150 meters wide, and followed a sinuous course. In 1802 it was reported that the land at the most southern portion of the canal was the richest part of Egypt. In the northern part, about 24 to 27 miles from the lake, the land had become barren and marshy, because the flow of water was insufficient to prevent sea water from backing up for three months of the year and a dam had to be constructed at the northern part of the channel to prevent inundation of the countryside. It was reported to be 12 feet deep at flood time and able to accommodate vessels of the largest tonnage engaged in internal commerce, while during the rest of the year the canal was able to accommodate smaller boats en route to Cairo. After the introduction of summer irrigation, the channel tended to silt and was navigable only at flood time.[42]

Ash-Sharqāwīyah Canal (*ṣayfī*). This canal, which was newly excavated in Muḥammad 'Alī's time, was in the province of al-Qalyūbīyah and took its head downstream of Shubrā. It was 25,000 meters in length. The canal linked up with Baḥr Abū Manājah and both canals watered all of al-Qalyūbīyah. It helped supplement the supply of water to Baḥr Abū Manājah and consequently to Canal Ra's al-Wādī.[43]

Baḥr Abū Manājah (*ṣayfī*). This natural channel began between Shubrā 'l-Khaymah and Bāsūs. It flowed through Shibīn al-Qanāṭar and Bilbays. It then moved north, crossed the canal known as Ra's al-Wādī, continued northward, and ended in the marshlands of Lake al-Manzalah.[44]

Ash-Sharqāwīyah Canal at Damietta (*ṣayfī*). This canal in Daqahlīyah province took its head north of al-Manṣūrah and ran parallel to the

Damietta branch through Fāraskūr close to the city of Damietta. It was 40,000 meters long. Excavation of the canal occurred around 1830; thereafter it served to irrigate the rice fields in the vicinity of al-Manṣūrah to Damietta. There is some question whether this was a new canal as there was at the beginning of the nineteenth century a Canal Fāraskūr which emptied into Lake al-Manzalah whose course corresponded with ash-Sharqāwīyah Canal.[45]

Bāsūsīyah Canal (*ṣayfī*). This canal took its head at the village of Bāsūs upstream of the bifurcation of the river. It was 15,000 meters long. Although not specifically indicated on the earlier maps, there probably was a canal at this point which was put into working order during Muḥammad 'Alī's reign.[46]

Ra's al-Wādī Canal (*ṣayfī*).[47] In former times the flood waters which poured into Valley Ṭumaylāt had remained there so long that it was impossible to sow crops. To rectify this condition attempts had been made to drain the valley through the old Suez Canal to Lake Timsāḥ but these had been unsuccessful. For this reason, the valley became dry through evaporation or infiltration only. When the Nile was low, on the other hand, nothing could be cultivated as there was no water in the valley. Consequently, the whole area had fallen out of cultivation until Muḥammad 'Alī sought to reclaim it in order to grow mulberry trees for his silkworm nurseries.

The canal was built at some time between 1817 and 1821 to furnish water to the valley. Ibrāhīm Pasha was put in charge of the task and Coste was appointed to serve as engineer for the project. A *corvée* was ordered and within eight days 80,000 *fallāḥīn* from ash-Sharqīyah Province were called out. In five days 20,590 cubic meters were dug between the head of the canal on Baḥr Muways, where az-Zaqāzīq now stands, to the dike of al-'Absī situated at the entrance to the valley. Excavations continued along the route of an old canal at al-'Absī, 14,076 cubic meters being cleaned out of the old canal. The total excavation thus amounted to 34,666 cubic meters and the canal was 45 kilometers in length. Dikes were also built to prevent the flow of surplus water into the valley. New drains were cut to carry the water to Lake al-Manzalah. Later, Baḥr Muways ceased to provide an adequate supply of water to this canal, but it was then supplemented by the Bāsūsīyah and ash-Sharqāwīyah canals.[48]

Dandīṭīyah Canal (*ṣayfī*). It had its head at Kafr Kūm an-Nūr and was 50,000 meters long.[49]

Mīt Yaʿīsh (*ṣayfī*). Mīt Yaʿīsh was probably one of the waterways already in existence before Muḥammad ʿAlī's time as Clot does not mention this as a canal which was excavated by Muḥammad ʿAlī.[50]

Būhīyah Canal (*ṣayfī*). With its head north of Mīt Ghamr, this canal was 50,000 meters long and 4 yards wide. It was only partially a new canal, as it appeared to go as far as Ṭanbūl on one early map. During Muḥammad ʿAlī's reign it was extended through Sinbillāwayn and carried almost as far as the marshlands of Lake al-Manzalah.[51]

Al-Manṣūrīyah Canal (*ṣayfī*). The canal, which was 35,000 meters long, took its head north of Būhīyah Canal and emptied into al-Baḥr aṣ-Ṣaghīr. As this canal does not appear on the older maps, it was probably a new canal.[52]

Khalīj az-Zaʿfarānī. This canal was intended to supply Cairo with water and to supplement the water which flowed to Wādī Ṭumaylāt. It was to extend as far as Lake al-Manzalah. For part of its course it was to have followed the ancient Canal of Trajan, known as Canal of Heliopolis. Work on it was begun and several parts were dug to the necessary depth; also several barrages were constructed along its course and at its head. The work was left incomplete, however, and many parts silted up. In 1838 Muḥammad ʿAlī ordered that work should be resumed and commanded Linant to take charge. Over 20,000 troops under the command of the Minister of War were assigned to work on the canal, but the flood that year came before the work was completed. Muḥammad ʿAlī ordered that the Nile waters should not be allowed to enter the canal for fear that it would silt up. Two small canals were therefore dug at the sides of the larger canal to hold the flood waters. The canal was completed, but was not sufficiently deep for the first two kilometers from its head and tended to silt up. Muḥammad ʿAlī had wished this to be a *ṣayfī* canal to be used only during the period of low water, but it proved of no use in the irrigation of the provinces through which it passed. It was incorporated after Muḥammad ʿAlī's reign into the Sweet Water Canal.[53]

Al-Baḥr aṣ-Ṣaghīr. It was a natural watercourse, probably the old Mendesian branch, which originated at al-Manṣūrah, passed through the marshes of Daqahlīyah, and flowed into Lake al-Manzalah near Maṭarīyah.[54]

Baḥr Abū 'l-Akhḍar. This was the ancient Pelusian branch of the river which flowed eastward and fell into Lake al-Manzalah.[55]

Closing the mouth of Lake al-Manzalah at Dibīyah. The purpose of this work was to prevent the too rapid loss of the water which the various canals carried to Lake al-Manzalah. During low Nile the sea water entered the lake in such quantity that it raised the level of the water as much as sixty to eighty centimeters and often caused the destruction of the crops on the border of the lake. The opening was therefore blocked.[56]

The Nile Barrages (al-Qanāṭir al-Khayrīyah)[57]

The introduction of *ṣayfī* canals was no unmixed blessing; the situation grew worse rather than better as the years passed. By 1833 it was noted that a considerable decrease in the flow of water both in volume and velocity in the Damietta branch, from which most of the *ṣayfī* canals took their source, was occurring and that the contrary was the case in the Rosetta branch. The *ṣayfī* canals could only be maintained by annual cleaning, done at a tremendous cost of money and manpower. The latter was perhaps as much a concern as the former because of the steady drain on available manpower after the formation of the *fallāḥ* army. The situation became too serious to ignore and Muḥammad 'Alī sought a solution. No project appeared too great to him; not even the Nile River seemed beyond his personal control. Colonel Barnett, the British Consul-General, reported a discussion with the Pasha about the river. "I once said to the Pasha that when his 'Barrage' was made he might some morning hear that the Nile had escaped through the Lybian Desert, and he replied, 'if that were to happen, do you think Mehemet Aly has not strength enough to bring it back again?'"[58]

Muḥammad 'Alī's first plan at the end of 1833 was to close the Rosetta branch. Linant discouraged the project and pointed out the dangers involved in disturbing the regime of the river in this manner. He argued that the trouble lay not so much in there being less water in the Damietta branch, but in the water not being at a sufficiently high level to feed the *ṣayfī* canals; he maintained, too, that the closing of the Rosetta branch would increase the flow into the Damietta branch at first, but that eventually the water would increase the depth of the canals. Linant then suggested that the scheme envisaged by the engineers of the French occupation forces, that of building regulating barrages on the two branches of the river, would be a better plan to follow.[59] He was ordered to attend immediately a meeting of the Great Council presided over by Ibrāhīm Pasha and to present a list of the materials required to begin the project. Caught unaware, Linant presented a tentative list which bore no relation to real needs. A commission was at once appointed upon his request to study the problem more fully. It proceeded to the place of bifurcation where it remained for a month to study the terrain. Two plans were presented when the commission returned, but Linant's project was finally accepted. Linant then undertook to make a more detailed study and informed Muḥammad ʿAlī that it would be a year before work could begin, but he was no sooner installed on location than workers began to arrive. No preparation had been made to equip them with the necessary tools or provisions. Consequently, Linant was diverted from his major task of studying the problems involved in this gigantic project by the necessity of providing for these workers and of setting them to digging, although he had not yet decided where the digging was to be done. A few days later all the students of the engineering school arrived, also without proper provisions. Again Linant had to make plans for their accommodation and had to decide in which manner to use their services. The same precipitate action continued thereafter and was a curse to the whole project. To aggravate the situation petty intrigues among Linant's assistants developed which created an unpleasant atmosphere. Despite all the initial difficulties, however, the work got under way and within six months some order was introduced. Materials were gathered in the course of the work, workshops were established, a railroad was built to transport materials from the quarries near Cairo, a *corvée* was called out.[60] Linant also received the assistance of a group of Saint-Simonians, headed by Père Enfantin, who set up their quarters on the spot and worked in cooperation with him.[61]

In February 1835 practically all operations, except those in the workshops, ceased because of bubonic plague, which killed a large number of workers employed at the Barrages as well as several Europeans. Linant and his engineers left the site and went into quarantine. During this retirement they studied the project more fully and in July 1835 they presented a detailed plan to Muḥammad ʿAlī which listed the exact work to be carried out, the materials required, and an estimate of costs. To overcome any opposition from the viceroy's advisers Linant suggested that the plan should be submitted to the Council of French Civil Engineers (Conseil des Ponts-et-Chaussées) in Paris for examination, but the viceroy said that he would rely on Linant's judgment. Nevertheless, full-scale operations at the Barrages were not resumed, although the plague had subsided, and only the workshops continued to function.

By May 1836 a shortage of material led Muḥammad 'Alī to suspend all work; it was Colonel Duhamel's opinion that it would never be resumed.[62] Linant was then withdrawn from work on the Barrages and became involved in other projects.

In 1838 the question of the Barrages arose once again and the division of public works was instructed to study the matter to determine the advantages of the Barrages and whether they were commensurate with the cost of construction. A special commission presented its report in July 1838, in which the following points were made.

1. The irrigation of 3,800,000 *faddāns* in Lower Egypt would become possible without the use of water-elevating apparatus.
2. The land between the Barrages and Cairo would be able to be irrigated by use of *tābūts*, which up to that time could only be used in Lower Egypt.
3. The Barrages would make irrigation possible throughout the year, regardless of the nature of the flood.
4. The navigation of the canals would be improved and transportation costs would decrease.
5. Al-Maḥmūdīyah Canal would obtain more water and would thus be improved for navigation.
6. *Ṣayfī* canals would be abandoned in favor of *nīlī* canals which required a depth of only three to four meters. This situation would obviate the great expense of digging the *ṣayfī* canals and maintaining them by annual cleanings.
7. The canal at Cairo would be furnished with adequate quantities of water to supply the population.
8. Water would be supplied to the ancient canal which passed through Ra's al-Wādī to Suez.
9. The use of *sāqiyahs* and *shādūfs* would be suppressed.

The report went on to enumerate in what ways money would be saved by the completion of the Barrages and said that by the annual expenditure of 8,877,773 piasters for a period of five years Muḥammad 'Alī could have his Barrages. It was presented to the Pasha who read it and returned an official reply to the effect that the commission was perfectly right in everything it said, that all its facts had been clearly and justly expounded—but that he no longer wanted the Barrages.

Muḥammad 'Alī's change of mind was variously interpreted. Bowring thought that he might have lost his enthusiasm for the Barrages because he had come to feel distaste after his first experiences, when expenditures had been made so recklessly. Moreover, the development of the steam engine had raised in him doubts as to whether the Barrages were the best irrigation scheme after all. Linant attributed the reversal in Muḥammad 'Alī's position to the fact that members of Muḥammad 'Alī's entourage, envious of his position, had intrigued against the Barrages. It was also his opinion that Muḥammad 'Alī was ruled by a spirit of caprice which could not endure long-term projects but required immediate results. Clot, on the other hand, suggested that war and preoccupation with political matters had absorbed Muḥammad 'Alī's attention at this time and that consequently he could not proceed with so gigantic a public work. Whatever the true reason may have been, the large quantities of materials that had been assembled were transported to other projects and the warehouses and workshops were destroyed so that their wood might be used.[63]

In 1842 the project was revived by Mougel, then engaged in building a graving dock in Alexandria, who suggested to Muḥammad 'Alī that the work on the Barrages could be resumed on a new basis. He was commissioned to present a plan of work. Linant was urged officially to cooperate fully with Mougel and he finally handed him all the plans which had already been prepared. Mougel then drafted his own plan which was presented to the Council of French Civil Engineers in Paris in January 1843, but the Council objected to it on technical grounds and recommended that the matter be studied further. Mougel presented a new plan to the Council in 1845, after receiving Muḥammad 'Alī's promise to commence work on the Barrages as soon as the plan was approved.[64] The Council undoubtedly gave its approval, for work began shortly afterwards under Mougel's supervision.

Muḥammad 'Alī's renewed interest in the Barrages may have stemmed from personal vanity and "his desire to see this great work completed during his lifetime."[65] More probably, it was due to efforts made at this time by the British government, on the one hand, to persuade him to build a railroad across the Isthmus of Suez and by the French and Austrian governments, on the other, to persuade him to build a ship canal. The Pasha, for his part, tried to give the impression that he was too busy with his plans with regard to the Barrages to consider either project and informed both parties that it was his desire to complete them before undertaking any other major public work. In November 1845 large orders for machinery were placed in France and by March 1846 work had already commenced. A report in July 1846 stated that the military was actively engaged in construction work at the Barrages and on April 9, 1847, the foundation stone of the Barrages of the Nile was laid by Muḥammad ʻAlī in a ceremony held in the best oriental tradition. A special gold medal was struck on that occasion and shortly afterwards a brevet (*barā'ah*) was sent by the Sultan commending Muḥammad ʻAlī for his good administration of Egypt and the commencement of the Barrages, which would be of such great advantage to the country. He was also presented the diamond insignia of the decoration of the *Imtiyāz*.[66]

In May 1847 a *corvée* was ordered to begin the excavation of the three canals which formed part of the Barrages irrigation scheme. To insure order and the maintenance of discipline among the workmen, retired army sergeants were appointed as supervisors. The *fallāḥīn* were retained upon the irrigation work for no more than one hundred days so that agriculture would not suffer from lack of manpower.[67] The work, however, though begun precipitately, languished as soon as Muḥammad ʻAlī no longer ruled the country.[68] Mougel informed Murray at the beginning of ʻAbbās Pasha's reign that, if work could be continued steadily, the project could be completed, "but I think he begins to feel that 'Othello's occupation's gone,' and that the 'Barrage,' which was intended to immortalize him [Muḥammad ʻAlī] by doubling the produce of Lower Egypt, is destined to be numbered hereafter among the incomplete monuments of Mahomet Ali's gigantic projects for the extension of his own fame—and the improvement of Egypt."[69]

The story of the Barrages extends beyond the reign of Muḥammad ʻAlī. They were finally completed in 1861 under the supervision of Mazhar Bey, Mougel having been discharged in April 1853. The Barrages, however, never gave satisfactory service and several commissions which examined the work pointed out their many structural weaknesses. The original conception had, to be sure, been a grand one, but the haste with which the work was at the start carried out caused initial failures.[70] Expenses were large,[71] but not unreasonable, provided the Barrages had achieved the ends in view. As it happened, they did not do so. The expenditure on this project represented, then, an additional burden which offered little compensation to justify it. It remained finally for the British engineers after the British occupation of Egypt to carry out effectively Muḥammad ʻAlī's gigantic project.[72]

The Irrigation System in Middle and Upper Egypt

Irrigation works in Middle and Upper Egypt, although not so extensive as those carried out by Muḥammad 'Alī in Lower Egypt, were, nevertheless, extremely important. Since cotton cultivation was limited to the Delta, there was neither the necessity to excavate *ṣayfī* canals in Middle and Upper Egypt nor to alter there the traditional system of basin irrigation. Basin irrigation by its very nature demanded a centralized system of control. The breakdown of any part could mean the collapse of the entire system or at least a decrease in its efficiency. During the period of political confusion in the eighteenth and the beginning of the nineteenth centuries maintenance of the irrigation system had been left in the hands of the village officials who were only concerned with local benefits rather than with the system as a whole. Armed conflicts between inhabitants of various districts of Egypt had resulted, with each group seeking its own advantage. The effects of this political instability on irrigation may be seen from a study of the early maps and the reports of travelers. Napoleon is in fact reputed to have said that twenty more years of an administration like that of the Mamlūks would have meant the loss to Egypt of at least one third of the land under cultivation at the time of the French occupation.[73] Moreover, in 1802 it was reported that thousands of acres of land remained uncultivated in the area between Banī Suwayf and Mallawī through which Baḥr Yūsuf ran—an area which was described as having been in ancient times one of the richest, most populous, and best cultivated parts of the country, but which had become one of the most deserted, the poorest, and the least cultivated.[74]

Irrigation in all of Middle and Upper Egypt was carried out by means of the basin system which had been developed over a period of five thousand years and depended for its efficient operation on the maintenance of dikes constructed both longitudinally and transversely between the Nile and the hills or desert which ran parallel to the river and created the Nile Valley. These formed basins which were inundated annually during the flood. The longitudinal dike which ran parallel to the Nile had to be sufficiently high to protect the basins against direct inundation, while the transverse dikes made possible the regulation of the gradual inundation of all the land extending from Upper Egypt to the Mediterranean Sea. The system also required canals for supplying the waters which entered the basins and drains by which the water could escape to the next basin.

There were two major canals in Middle and Upper Egypt which ran parallel to the Nile on the western bank: Mūsā Sūhājah Canal, which ran from Sūhāj and joined Baḥr Yūsuf near Dayrūṭ (in Upper Egypt), and Baḥr Yūsuf, which took its head in the neighborhood of Dayrūṭ and continued adjacent to the western hills until it approached the Fayyūm, where the channel branched, one branch entering Fayyūm province at 'Ilwān and the other continuing along the desert. It is not known whether Baḥr Yūsuf was a natural or artificial channel, but it had by the nineteenth century taken on all the characteristics of a natural channel. Buḥayrah Canal, which emptied into Lake Maryūṭ, may have been an extension of Baḥr Yūsuf, though it has been claimed instead that Baḥr Yūsuf joined the Rosetta branch either at aṭ-Ṭarrānah or at 'Alqām.[75] In addition to these major canals, there were numerous other canals which completed the system. In the Fayyūm, which was also irrigated by means of the basin system, the irrigation canals derived their water from Baḥr Yūsuf and the small lakes in the province which served as reservoirs.[76]

Numerous works were undertaken during Muḥammad 'Alī's reign in order to strengthen the dikes, construct regulators, and clean out the canals already in existence. Although the work of strengthening or building dikes was neglected for several years in the 1830's, it was resumed after a hiatus when the excessive flood of 1841 destroyed many dikes and demonstrated conclusively that continuous care was essential to avoid similar catastrophes.[77] Clot estimated that during the reign of Muḥammad 'Alī 169,200 meters of canals were excavated in Middle and Upper Egypt and that 183,390 meters of dikes were built, involving earthwork of 30,231,729 cubic meters and 11,788,818 cubic meters respectively, or a total of 42,020,547 cubic meters. He apparently had the mistaken idea that nothing of the former system had remained and that all the irrigation works in Middle and Upper Egypt were developed by Muḥammad 'Alī.[78] Linant was far more conservative: he gave a combined figure of 12,403,812 cubic meters (see Appendix VII) for earthwork on canals and dikes between 1818 and 1842, adding that he could not tell whether work carried out in the most southern part of Egypt before 1831 had been newly executed or merely repaired by Muḥammad 'Alī. The difference of 29,616,735 cubic meters between Clot's and Linant's figures is so great that it suggests that Clot may either have been guilty of gross exaggeration in order to increase the magnitude of Muḥammad 'Alī's accomplishments or may have erred in his statistics. Clot's figures of the masonry work carried out in Middle and Upper Egypt, on the other hand, amounted only to 460,140 cubic meters, as compared to Linant's figure of 787,244 cubic meters for 1818–1842.

In 1833 Linant, in order to improve irrigation in Upper Egypt, proposed the excavation of a large canal which would take its head at Jabal as-Silsilah and would extend to the Fayyūm. The purpose of the canal was to provide water for all the land of Upper Egypt, especially in years when the flood was inadequate. The canal was not intended to interfere with the system of basin irrigation, but to supplement it so that all the basins would receive an adequate supply of water. Another aim was to provide water during low Nile to avoid the necessity of using water-raising machines. The proposal appealed to Muḥammad ʿAlī, who ordered Linant to study the project and work out the course of the canal. Linant prepared a plan which involved a barrage that would enable an area of 601,573 *faddāns* to be used for summer cultivation and presented the project to Muḥammad ʿAlī. No action was taken, however, although in 1834 it was incorrectly reported that work had actually begun. The fulfillment of the proposed scheme took place more than fifty years later when the Aṣwān dam was built.[79]

Works to protect Fayyūm province. In 1819 or 1820 there was a breach in the banks of Baḥr Yūsuf at Hawwārat al-Maqtaʿ near which the head of the natural channel of Baḥr Bilā Māʾ was located. As the dam at ʿIlwān was not adequately closed, the waters entered Baḥr Bilā Māʾ in a torrent and flooded the land. It destroyed the stone dike extending to Ṭāmīyah which had been designed to hold back the water for irrigation purposes. This catastrophe caused so much damage that an effort was made during the flood to close the rupture. It was only six months later, in the period of low water, that it finally was closed by a dike made of stone, supported by a wall and buttresses; it took two years to be completed. The barrage of Ṭāmīyah which was carried away was reconstructed in 1834.[80] The ʿIlwān dam, in existence before Muḥammad ʿAlī's reign, had often been repaired. After the breach at Hawwārat al-Maqtaʿ, it was decided to build a thick barrier at some distance before the dam to serve as a barrage, thereby preventing, if possible, a recurrence of the accident of 1819 or 1820.[81]

The dike of Cocheiche[82] was one of the oldest dikes in Egypt and was essential for regulating the water which flowed into the Fayyūm and Gīzah. During Muḥammad ʿAlī's reign this dike was reinforced by an incasement of masonry. Later it was almost completely covered with stone. It had to be constantly guarded, but even with these precautions, accidents continued to occur.[83]

The administration of the irrigation system

Muḥammad 'Alī's government provided the strong central administration necessary to maintain the irrigation system. The system had previously always functioned on cooperative principles regulated by customary usages, but during Muḥammad 'Alī's reign these usages were incorporated in the *Lā'iḥat zirā'at al-fallāḥ*, in which specific responsibilities were assigned to various members of the government hierarchy. The *qā'immaqām* and *shaykhs al-ḥiṣṣah* in the *nāḥiyah* supervised the irrigation of land, the cleaning of canals during the winter season, the repairing of dams, and the maintenance of irrigation implements in the canton. They also provided workers to perform public works, such as digging canals and repairing dikes in other parts of the *ma'mūrīyah* or province as required. The *qā'immaqām* cut the dikes of the basins in the *nāḥiyah* one by one until the inundation of each basin was completed and all the land in the *nāḥiyah* was watered. Both the *qā'immaqām* and the *shaykhs* were responsible for draining off the water properly. If a dike was found inadequate or damaged in any way, it had to be repaired under the supervision of the *shaykhs*. If an insufficient number of *fallāḥīn* was available to carry out the necessary tasks, the *qā'immaqām* and *shaykhs* informed the officials of the *khuṭṭ* or district who then brought assistance from other *nāḥiyahs*. They also had to inspect the *sāqiyahs* and *shādūfs* and make certain that they were shared by all the *fallāḥīn*. If the number of water-raising machines did not suffice, the *shaykhs al-ḥiṣṣah* had to tell *khuṭṭ* officials to see that help was given for irrigation of the land so that the *fallāḥīn* could not claim they had been unable to meet their quota of crops or taxes because of inadequate irrigating facilities or too little assistance. Whenever the *fallāḥīn* were ordered outside their own *nāḥiyahs* to work in the *ma'mūrīyah*, the *qā'immaqām* was responsible for seeing that they did not escape the *corvée*. He also supervised the people on the job placed in charge of the *fallāḥīn*. The *shaykhs* and the *qā'immaqām* were both responsible for the diligence with which the *fallāḥīn* performed the tasks assigned to them.[84]

Important duties were also assigned to other members of the civil hierarchy. The *ḥākim al-khuṭṭ* and the great *shaykhs* in the district were charged with the task of assembling the officials in the various *nāḥiyahs* within their jurisdiction at the time of the Nile flood. Orders were issued by them regarding the irrigation of each basin.[85] The *nāẓir al-qism* or director of the department was the next person in this chain of authority. His task was to supervise irrigation in a general way and to inspect the dikes. He also recommended to the *ma'mūr* which workers should be transferred to other parts of his *qism* to assist in the cleaning of canals or other works when their sowing was completed.[86] The *ma'mūr* or governor of the *ma'mūrīyah* was in turn in charge of public works in his province. He acted upon information received from the *nāẓirs* in his province or carried out the orders sent from Cairo. It was his duty to make arrangements for an adequate number of water-raising machines. He would also inform the viceroy when he felt a particular canal, dike, or dam was needed in his province which would benefit agriculture. In most cases, these improvements were routine and could be executed by the provincial officials themselves without the assistance of government engineers. Where special engineering skill was required, however, the Pasha, after approving the recommendations of his governor, would instruct his engineers to undertake the task. In the early years these engineers were not formally trained in engineering science but were practical engineers who had learned from experience; as they rarely planned their work adequately, many mistakes resulted.[87]

Centralized control of the irrigation system was further advanced by a reorganization of the public works administration in the 1830's, a reorganization which proceeded through various stages. According to Linant, centralized control actually began in 1830, first in Middle and Upper Egypt where the entire irrigation system was studied by a council of provincial engineers, presided over by Linant himself, chief engineer of Upper Egypt at the time. This council then prepared a report which included a list of works needed to bring the system into good working order. It was submitted to the Great Council in Cairo and on the basis of it firmans were sent by Muḥammad 'Alī to the provinces instructing the governors to carry out specific works. These firmans covered new works as well as routine repairs that had to be done year by year. The same method was then introduced in Lower Egypt. A permanent council (Conseil général permanent des ponts et chaussées) was established in 1834 under the presidency of Linant, who had by then been appointed chief engineer of Egypt and director of the Barrage works. The council discussed the works which were required in the provinces and issued decrees for their execution.

Linant claimed that the Ministry of Public Works and Public Instruction was established in 1835 for the first time[88] and that he was placed at the head of the division of public works.[89] Thereafter, all the engineers-in-chief of the provinces assembled at the department every year after the inundation and discussed the works which had to be carried out in the provinces. The department studied the various projects and then issued orders for their execution.[90] Linant's account is substantially correct. In 1830 the *Dīwān al-Abniyah* was established to direct public works[91] and at the time of the reorganization of the administration in 1837 (see Chapter V) it was stipulated in the *Qānūn as-Siyāsat-nāmah* (Rabī' al-Awwal, A.H. 1253 [June–July 1837]) that the *Majlis Shūrā 'l-Madāris* was to be known henceforth as *Dīwān al-Madāris* and was to be divided into separate bureaus, one of which was to supervise work at the Barrages and include general engineering services. The assignment of engineering services to the *Dīwān al-Madāris*, or Ministry of Public Instruction, was logical, since the Delta Barrages and other engineering services depended for their staff upon students from the School of Engineering (*Polytechnique*). Linant was appointed head of the division of public works in this ministry and took charge of most of the irrigation works in the country. Not all public works fell under the jurisdiction of the *Dīwān al-Madāris*, though, but were kept within the sphere of authority of several of the administrations supervised by the *Dīwān al-Khidīwī*.[92]

The corvée

Labor for public works was provided by means of *corvées*, a system of forced labor employed from the earliest times in Egypt to clear canals, to strengthen dikes during winter and summer, and to guard the banks during the flood when the river threatened to leave its bed. The system had been developed logically from basin irrigation. A basin was, in effect, a large farm; all those who worked part of the land on this farm were personally desirous that canals should supply plenty of water to the basin, that dikes be repaired, and that the banks be adequately protected. So long as the *fallāḥīn* profited directly from the work which they were forced to perform, then, the system seemed justifiable. It became less so when Muḥammad 'Alī introduced the practice of moving *corvées* to any part of Egypt as required and when the *ṣayfī* canals were introduced. Each *fallāḥ* who had benefited from the proper maintenance of the basin system of irrigation did not benefit from a *ṣayfī* canal which was not in his own locality. Often, benefits derived from *ṣayfī* canals, dug and maintained by *fallāḥīn* brought in from other areas of the country, were instead enjoyed exclusively by large landholders who abused their position further by obtaining exemption from the *corvée* for their own *fallāḥīn*, thereby placing all the responsibility for performing the necessary public works on the less fortunate cultivators. Furthermore, the new policy of sending the *corvée* to other parts of the country meant that *fallāḥīn* were unable to care for their own land and livestock and also lost the opportunity that would have been theirs, had they been close to home, to raise an additional crop for their personal profit.[93]

The *corvée* customarily worked during a nine-month period each year. From January 15 to July 15 the work consisted of clearing canals and repairing dikes. From August 1 to November 1 the *corvée* spent its time guarding the dikes of the Nile during the flood. Altogether, approximately 180 days were involved. The average amount of time contributed by each *fallāḥ* was 60 days, not including traveling time. By 1847, however, the average number of working days in which a peasant served in the *corvée* was reduced to about 45 days. It was estimated too that during the course of one year as many as 400,000 men could be called to work in the *corvée*, but dislocation of the rural population could, in fact, double this number, as a *fallāḥ* was often accompanied by his wife, children, and parents. The entire family would establish itself in the open air in the locality to which the peasant had been assigned. If, on the other hand, the family remained in the village, some member was always obliged to bring provisions every few days to the person working in the *corvée*, often traveling a great distance to do so.

The *fallāḥīn* assembled in a particular locality for the *corvée*. Their *shaykh al-balad* put a tent or banner at the place allotted to his men. When the job was completed, the village banner was floated. The job was inspected by the engineers to see if it had been performed to their satisfaction. There was considerable latitude for corruption here, since an engineer might not agree that the work was adequate until he had received some gratuity from the *shaykh*. The *shaykh* himself was not above using the opportunities to make a little extra at the expense of the *fallāḥīn* by agreeing to excuse from the *corvée* those who paid him some bribe.

The peasants received little assistance from the government after being assigned to a *corvée*. Usually, the *fallāḥīn* furnished their own tools, the *fa's*, a kind of hoe, and the *quffah*, a basket made from palm leaves. They also provided lanterns which were placed every fifty meters on both sides of the Nile. In cases where they possessed no tools they scooped up the earth with their hands. In large public works, however, the government sometimes provided tools. The laborers also furnished their own food, which was brought by the women, although sometimes the government provided rations of biscuits or bread, especially when the great canals were being built. Workers were paid approximately one piaster per day on public works like al-Maḥmūdīyah Canal, but it is unclear whether payment was made for all categories of work connected with the irrigation system. The *fallāḥīn* were often quite leisurely about doing their work. One observer even commented that fifty men in England using the proper tools could probably do an equivalent amount of work or even more than five hundred men engaged in digging al-Maḥmūdīyah or any other canal.[94] The natural unwillingness of the *fallāḥīn* to join these *corvées* under these conditions and the brutal methods used to coerce them were described by an English traveler:

> In Egypt, when any public work is to be done, soldiers are sent to surround the villages; the unfortunate peasants are taken prisoners and linked to one another, and marched, sometimes hundreds of miles from their homes and families, to the place of employment. . . . Here the poor naked *fellahs* are to be seen digging the soil with their fingers to excavate a temporary canal, or raising water in baskets to irrigate the soil: how the work is accomplished, Heaven only knows; but the task masters are seen armed with their whips, parading amongst the labourers, lashing right and left the lazy and the weak; and when the work is finished, they get checks on the Sheik or *Kaimacan*, for payment of a piastre a day.[95]

Conclusions

The irrigation system which Muḥammad ʻAlī inherited was of ancient origin and efficient if properly maintained, but it had suffered from neglect. Muḥammad ʻAlī's greatest contribution to Egyptian irrigation was his restoration of the system and his introduction of deep water or *ṣayfī* canals. Actually, his irrigation program fell into two periods. Before 1821 the public works were confined mainly to repairs in the existing system and to the extension of the old system to meet new requirements, whereas after 1821 the expansion of cotton cultivation led to the introduction of *ṣayfī* canals. It must not be supposed, however, that the ancient basins were obliterated and replaced by a completely new system which made perennial irrigation possible for the first time. Actually, basin irrigation remained the only system of irrigation in Middle and Upper Egypt and was used in Lower Egypt for the irrigation of winter crops. It was considered not only efficient, but also salutary for the soil and was far less open to criticism than "the unskilful treatment of the new summer irrigation in Lower Egypt."[96] Basin irrigation was not, however, a faultless system and the following criticisms have been made of it.

(1) Because of the manner in which the system operated, the most valuable deposits of Nile mud remained in the higher basins, whereas the lower basins received water practically devoid of mud.

(2) The system relied entirely on the period and extent of the flood, which was fairly irregular and could cause general disturbance to the agricultural regime.

(3) The system limited the type of crop to those whose cultivation coincided with the Nile floods, such as cereals, whereas crops like cotton, sugar cane, rice, and sesame were sown at the period when the Nile was at its lowest level.[97]

Summer crops, it must be stressed, had always been cultivated in Egypt on the banks of the river or deep canals and water had always been raised by means of the *sāqiyah* and *shādūf* at the period of low Nile, but during Muḥammad 'Alī's reign the area of land made available for summer crops was greatly extended. The Pasha's contribution to summer irrigation, therefore, lay primarily in the fact that the existing deep water canals were cleared of the sediment which had collected and that a number of *nīlī* canals were converted into *ṣayfī* canals. Summer irrigation had its detrimental aspects, though, as well as its positive advantages. Because of the strengthening of the dikes to prevent the flooding of land while the summer crops were still in the ground, the land devoted to summer cultivation no longer received the benefits of periodic washings by the Nile floodwaters and suffered therefrom by an increase of salt efflorescence, an important cause of the decrease in the productivity of this land. Furthermore, the shutting off of the *ṣayfī* canals at flood time to safeguard summer crops, with only the required amount of water being allowed to enter these canals, meant that much of the water carrying the rich Nile mud was lost to the sea. Moreover, the development of large estates led to the subdivision of former inundation basins into smaller basins; this fragmentation of basins also hindered the diffusion of flood waters which in the past had washed the earth and deposited new mud. According to one point of view the final solution to the problem of soil impoverishment lay in a return to the old system of inundation; but the clock could not be turned back and the system of perennial irrigation gradually replaced the use of *ṣayfī* canals as an adjunct to the old basin system, a process completed only after Muḥammad 'Alī's reign.[98]

In addition, a number of problems evolved from the faulty construction of the *ṣayfī* canals. Because the slope of these canals was less than that of the Nile, very little water flowed into the canals when the river was very low and it had to be raised to the soil by means of water-raising machines. This difficulty was overcome by building barrages and locks at regular intervals along the course of the canals to raise the water to the level of the soil so that it could be directed to the land by means of simple trenches.[99] These regulators were also built because even at flood time the *ṣayfī* canals could be used only with great trouble. Under normal circumstances a *nīlī* canal was 6 meters wide and 2.50 meters deep, whereas the *ṣayfī* canals were approximately 6 meters wide and 6 meters deep. Consequently, to insure flush irrigation during the flood the water in the *ṣayfī* canals had to be 6 meters in depth. This necessity for regulators in turn produced several adverse effects. The canals were converted into a series of pools which gathered substantial quantities of silt. Also, the velocity of the river was checked so that mud settled up to a depth of 2 meters. The canals, consequently, required annual cleaning to keep them in working order. The average figure of cubic meters which had to be excavated annually to keep the canals clean amounted to 20,730,118 cubic meters for all the canals of Lower Egypt, of which 13,317,000 cubic meters represent the sum required for cleaning *ṣayfī* canals. Finally, many of the regulators did not possess locks and prevented navigation of the canals, so that the cost of transport increased.[100]

The depth of the *ṣayfī* canals, in turn, necessitated the costly introduction of many more *sāqiyahs*, especially with the extension of summer irrigation. Muḥammad 'Alī told Bowring in 1838 that he had been responsible for the installation of 38,000 *sāqiyahs* in Egypt. An estimated 50,000 *sāqiyahs* and *tābūts* existed in Lower Egypt at that time. The number of *shādūfs* in use was not included in this estimate. Three oxen were required to operate each *sāqiyah* and at least one man was needed to take charge, a total of 150,000 oxen and 50,000 men for these 50,000 water-raising implements. At the rate of 2 piasters per day to feed the oxen and 1½ piasters wages per day for each man, the total cost of operation for 180 days per year amounted to 67,500,000 piasters. To this must be added the cost of maintenance, which was figured at 120 piasters each or 6,000,000 for six months. The total annual expense for 50,000 *sāqiyahs* in 1838, therefore, was calculated at 73,500,000 piasters.[101] The initial cost of installation was 1,200 piasters each or a total of 60,000,000 piasters. As an ox cost 900 piasters each, the total cost of oxen was 135,000,000 piasters or a total capital investment of 195,000,000 piasters for 50,000 *sāqiyahs*. If, as Bowring stated, Muḥammad 'Alī installed 38,000, the capital investment was 136,500,000 piasters. This does not take into account the cost of *shādūfs* for which no precise figures are available. The *shādūf* cost less, however, as animal power was not required; the original capital investment was also less. By 1844 the number of *sāqiyahs* had increased to 52,836 of which 50,836 were found in Lower Egypt. It was this high cost of installation and maintenance of water-raising machines which partially motivated Muḥammad 'Alī to construct the Nile Barrages in the hope that they would no longer be necessary.[102]

A final criticism, and possibly the most significant, may be leveled against the introduction and extension of the *ṣayfī* canals since from them originated the widespread infection of the Egyptian *fallāḥīn* with bilharziasis:

> It is clear that the increase in Bilharziasis had been produced by the substitution of basin irrigation by perennial irrigation. The mollusks, which were unable to withstand conditions created by the system of inundation, have found in the present system an ideal breeding place.[103]

The effects of this debilitating disease upon the health of the vast majority of the Egyptian people is one of the most serious problems confronting modern Egypt.

Care must be exercised in assessing Muḥammad 'Alī's contribution to Egyptian irrigation. Although his program of irrigation works contrasted favorably with the neglect of his immediate predecessors, only 400 leagues (1,200 miles) of great canals existed in Egypt during his reign as compared to 600 leagues (1,800 miles) during the period of the early *khalīfahs*. Of these 1,200 miles, approximately 686 miles (by the most optimistic estimate) were the product of Muḥammad 'Alī's efforts. His judgment was indeed often faulty, his actions hasty, the execution of his commands unsatisfactory. In fact, it even appeared that work had either been confided to people who were blind or had no knowledge of the science of hydraulics and that the division of water was so unequal that it occasioned continual quarrels among the cultivators.[104] In short, the achievements of Muḥammad 'Alī with respect to irrigation seem less impressive when measured against those of greater periods in Egyptian history.

CHAPTER XIII

CONCLUSION

The Ottoman Empire, which had begun to decline in the sixteenth century, was in a state of crisis by the eighteenth. Internal and external enemies alike were undermining the very foundations of the state, and the need for basic reforms of Ottoman institutions was becoming imperative. This need was clearly recognized by Sultan Salīm III; consequently he introduced the *Niẓām Jadīd* in 1792 by means of which he hoped to create a modern army capable of defending the Empire from its enemies. The Sultan, far in advance of Ottoman public opinion, eventually became a martyr to the cause of reforms, for he was murdered by the adherents of the extreme reactionary party which had failed to grasp the significance of his program of reform, viewing it simply as a threat to its own prerogatives.

Salīm was dead but his ideas survived, for before his death he had instilled in his nephew Maḥmūd the conviction that the Empire must change or perish. Therefore, when Maḥmūd became the new Sultan, he ascended the Ottoman throne as an ardent exponent of reform and throughout his reign labored to achieve it and safeguard the integrity of his Empire. Although his objectives were clear from the outset of his reign, Maḥmūd II had to proceed cautiously, for the obstacles which stood in his way appeared almost insurmountable. He was not to be deflected from his course on this account, however. Slowly but steadfastly he moved in the direction of his goal, welcoming in the meantime whatever assistance he could get towards the attainment of the ends for which he was striving.

Muḥammad 'Alī, an obscure Albanian officer who had insinuated himself into the important post of Pasha of Egypt, appeared at first to be a willing tool in the accomplishment of the Sultan's larger objectives. He rid Egypt of the Mamlūks, a rebellious military caste, who had long ignored their obligations towards the central government at Istanbul and whose disregard of the Sultan's authority had added to the centrifugal tendencies which were disrupting the Empire from within while it was being ruthlessly attacked from without. Muḥammad 'Alī also assisted the Sultan in the conquest of the Wahhābīs in Arabia who had challenged the Sultan's position as the guardian of the Holy Cities and, finally, he played a significant role in behalf of his sovereign in the Greek War of Independence. Moreover, Muḥammad 'Alī had drawn the same conclusions from the humiliating defeat of the haughty Mamlūks by Napoleon's army as Sultan Salīm had drawn from the defeat of the Ottoman armies by the Russian troops of Catherine the Great. He recognized, first of all, that the once invincible Ottoman armies were incapable of withstanding the modern armies of Europe which had profited from the technological advances made by the West during the seventeenth and eighteenth centuries while the Ottoman Empire had remained complacent. Second, it was perfectly clear to the Pasha that the ability of the Ottoman Empire to meet the challenge of the West would depend upon Turkey's capacity to absorb new ideas and the speed with which the Ottoman armies were modernized. As a result of these conclusions, Muḥammad 'Alī became an ardent proponent of reform and was, in fact, the first Ottoman official to introduce the *Niẓām Jadīd* into his province with any measure of success.

Indeed, had Muḥammad 'Alī been merely a patriotic Ottoman officer satisfied with playing the role of chief supporter of his sovereign's reform program, the Ottoman Empire might possibly have recovered its former position as a Great Power. Instead, the Egyptian Pasha, consumed by his own ambitions, used Ottoman patriotism as a stratagem for furthering his own private ends and his reform program as the means for achieving his objectives. Instead of safeguarding the Ottoman Empire, Muḥammad 'Alī, in fact, insured its demolition. Perhaps the demise of the Empire was inevitable and the factors making for its dissolution already too firmly entrenched for the trend to have been reversed. Perhaps, also, Muḥammad 'Alī was a prophet of Nationalism who favored bringing to an end the outmoded supranational Ottoman Empire. But if he was such a prophet, his conversion to the ideals of Nationalism was certainly not a conscious one, for Muḥammad 'Alī was no nationalist in the modern sense and above all no Egyptian nationalist. He considered himself a Turk if anything and thought of Egypt simply as a private preserve to be exploited for his own and his family's benefit. His struggle for independence, therefore, was not a struggle for Egyptian independence but rather an attempt to leave to his descendants a secure inheritance. He achieved his goal and thus quite unintentionally launched

Egypt upon the road to national independence; at the same time, he delivered the fatal blow from which the Ottoman Empire never recovered.

Muḥammad ʻAlī's career may be divided into four phases: his struggle for power, his retention of power, the expansion of his power, and the transference of power to his heirs. In each of these stages he required both a strong army and an inexhaustible supply of revenue. Consequently, he formulated a military policy and a fiscal policy which were designed to supply him with both. It is with his fiscal policy that this study has been primarily concerned, for it was intimately connected with agriculture, the source of wealth in Egypt. In fact, insofar as Muḥammad ʻAlī possessed an agricultural policy at all, it was merely as one aspect of his fiscal policy and inseparable from it. At the same time, his military policy has also been taken into account, for it impinged upon Muḥammad ʻAlī's fiscal policy by draining the resources of the country and by exhausting the agricultural manpower of the nation through excessive conscription. Consequently, the assessment of the much narrower problem of Muḥammad ʻAlī's agricultural policy requires an analysis of the broader fiscal policy and a consideration of the effects of the military policy on the economy of the country.

Muḥammad ʻAlī's fiscal policy centered around the problem of increasing his sources of revenue to meet the insatiable demands of the army. To this end he reorganized the system of landholding, consolidated taxes, improved the system of tax collection, and organized a civil administration capable of executing his orders effectively. Furthermore, he introduced an important new crop, long-staple cotton, and attempted to improve all agricultural procedures. He improved irrigation, introduced *ṣayfī* canals, and reclaimed land; he engaged in commerce that was dependent primarily upon agricultural produce; finally, he introduced industry with an eye to utilizing the raw agricultural materials produced in the country and to supplying his army with some of its equipment. The consequences of these measures had both positive and negative results.

On the positive side, Muḥammad ʻAlī provided capital for the cultivation of money crops, transforming Egyptian agriculture from a subsistence economy to a cash crop economy; he introduced *ṣayfī* canals, thereby pointing the way to perennial irrigation upon which the prosperity of modern Egypt is based; he centralized marketing facilities, enabling large quantities of Egyptian agricultural produce to enter the lucrative European market and establishing new horizons for Egyptian trade and a source of great wealth for the country; he attracted large numbers of European merchants who brought with them many Western techniques, Western ideas, and Western customers. These innovations changed the entire pattern of Egyptian trade; henceforth Egyptian commerce was to be linked up closely with Europe. By bringing Egypt within the orbit of European trade Muḥammad ʻAlī brought the country inevitably within the sphere of European civilization, although, unfortunately, on the most superficial level. By opening Egypt to European influences, by stimulating commerce and encouraging the growth of Egyptian cities and towns, by developing an Egyptian bureaucratic class and an Egyptian military class, and by establishing a hereditary dynasty, Muḥammad ʻAlī laid the foundations of the Egyptian national state. These are undeniable achievements which have proved of paramount importance in the development of modern Egypt.

On the other hand, he undermined the Ottoman Empire and opened the way to Western colonial penetration. His Western orientation of Egyptian trade increased the country's dependence upon European markets and made it susceptible to fluctuations in the European economy. The influx of European merchants made Egypt more vulnerable to European interference in the internal affairs of the country on the pretext offered by the European governments that they were entitled to protect their traders and their commercial interests under the terms of the Treaties of Capitulations. Furthermore, by depriving the religious class of its independence, Muḥammad ʻAlī immobilized the only class capable of exercising a restraining influence over the excesses of the ruling class. At the same time, he destroyed the institutions which for centuries had served to protect the people against unlimited oppression. Thus, he weakened the leaders of the people and destroyed the protective institutions without providing simultaneously for the development of new leadership and new institutions upon which a healthy society in Egypt could be based. His policy towards the religious class and the cutting off of revenues from the religious institutions injured Egyptian education, for, restricted as the traditional system of education had been, it had offered some intellectual training to Egyptian children. Muḥammad ʻAlī's government schools and foreign missions could never substitute for an elementary school system and this the Pasha never provided for. In fact, he abandoned his government schools almost completely after 1841. The intellectual dislocation resulting from

Muḥammad ʻAlī's truncated educational policy is impossible to measure, but its effects are unquestionably still being felt in Egypt today.

Muḥammad ʻAlī also destroyed the native merchant class and the native artisan class, inhibiting thereby the development of an Egyptian middle class and Egyptian industrial growth. His own industrial experiments failed miserably; his factories were abandoned, the workers were sent home to their fields, and the development of a skilled industrial proletariat was indefinitely postponed. Moreover, the Pasha created a class of landholders composed of members of his family, his retinue, and his favorites, after European military interference had confined him to Egypt and European diplomatic pressures had forced him to abandon his monopolies. In this way Muḥammad ʻAlī established a pattern of large-scale landholding which prevented the emergence of an independent and responsible class of small farmers. Under Muḥammad ʻAlī's regime the national income rose; yet he failed to improve the conditions of the *fallāḥīn.* It is true that he spoke often of his concern for the welfare of the people over whom he governed, but when this social consciousness was translated into action it invariably took the form of new burdens and crushing exactions. While Muḥammad ʻAlī laid the foundations of the Egyptian national state on the one hand, he thus also laid the foundations on the other for many of the economic and social problems with which Egypt is still grappling.

In short, Muḥammad ʻAlī's contribution to Egypt would undoubtedly have been more impressive had he curbed his private ambitions and had he, instead, devoted his energies to the improvement of the conditions of the people over whom he ruled and to the development of sound institutions to replace those which he so ruthlessly destroyed. He would also have been better advised to have assisted the Ottoman Sultan in the struggle against Western encroachment instead of betraying him and providing the European nations with the opportunity of deciding the fate of the Empire. This was a most dangerous precedent and one which set the pattern for the future. To be sure, the Egyptian Pasha achieved his objective by establishing a hereditary dynasty in the family of Muḥammad ʻAlī, but he also opened the door to European interference before Egypt had evolved institutions that could have aided the Egyptians to meet the challenge of a new age and thus defend their independence against the attacks of predatory European nations.

APPENDIX I

LAND USE IN EGYPT, 1844: ITS DIVISION AMONG LANDHOLDERS, CROPS, AND REVENUES

The tables in this appendix are based on charts prepared by a local official in the office of Colonel Barnett, the British Consul-General in Egypt, from statistical information drawn from Egyptian official documents, apparently made available to the British without restriction. See Barnett, December 12, 1844 in F.O. 78/583.

TABLE 11. Classification of land in Egypt and

Provinces		Taxable land, 1236/1820–21[b]	Village land (*zimām*), 1260 (1844) *Ma'mūr*[c]	*Ab'ādīyah*[d]	Total	*Chifliks*[e]
Lower Egypt						
al-Gharbīyah		225,960	542,475	50,595	593,070	130,000
Buḥayrah[h] (Rosetta)		100,792	257,075	20,067	277,142	60,000
al-Minūfīyah		194,150	292,669	40,344	333,013	10,000
Daqahlīyah (Damietta)		155,860	341,735	32,479	374,214	60,000
ash-Sharqīyah		161,204	313,077	52,145	365,222	90,000
al-Qalyūbīyah		80,000	138,164	24,742	162,906	10,000
Gīzah		85,900	254,284	13,313	267,597	—
TOTAL		1,003,866	2,139,479	233,685	2,373,164	360,000
Middle Egypt						
Banī Suwayf		166,260	168,000	70,000	238,000	—
Fayyūm		70,200	120,000[i]	100,000	220,000	3,000
Upper Egypt						
al-Minyā	148,340	203,340	288,000	170,000	458,000	—
(Aṭfīḥ)	55,000					
Asyūṭ		178,584	588,000	50,000	638,000	—
Qinā (Girgā)		190,400	141,000	40,000	181,000	—
Isnā		143,990	125,000	60,000	185,000	8,000
TOTAL		952,774	1,430,000	490,000	1,920,000	11,000
GRAND TOTAL		1,956,640	3,569,479	723,685	4,293,164	371,000

[a] For the sake of clarity, this table has been reorganized somewhat, and some statistics by Mengin have been added.

[b] According to the Cadastre of A.H. 1236, reproduced by Mengin. Statistics prepared by Felix Mengin have been added to this table to serve as a basis of comparison. See Table 18 for a reproduction of Mengin's table.

[c] According to the original table, *ma'mūr* land was taxed at the rate of between 27 to 90 piasters per *faddān*.

[d] The original table shows that the *ab'ādīyah* lands were lands that had not been cultivated at the time of the survey in 1236/1820–21, but since that time had been granted in limited amounts by Muḥammad 'Alī to individuals who cultivated these lands as private estates on which taxes were demanded only after three to seven years of cultivation.

its division among landholders (in *faddāns*)[a]

Great estates, 1260 (1844)					Peasant lands, 1260 (1844)	Combined totals of great estates and peasant lands, 1260 (1844)	Discrepancy[g]
'Uhdahs[f]				Total			
Muḥammad 'Alī	Ibrāhīm Pasha	Royal family	Favorites				
70,000	50,000	10,000	252,475	512,475	30,000	542,475	—
6,000	10,000	30,000	96,400	202,400	54,675	257,075	—
4,000	8,000	—	24,600	46,600	246,063	292,663	Minus 6
20,000	8,000	20,000	182,910	290,910	50,825	341,735	—
10,000	4,000	15,000	143,480	262,480	50,597	313,077	—
10,000	2,000	—	77,410	99,410	38,754	138,164	—
—	—	—	50,284	50,284	204,000	254,284	—
120,000	82,000	75,000	827,559	1,464,559	674,914	2,139,473	Minus 6
—	—	—	19,000	19,000	149,000	168,000	—
—	—	—	20,000	23,000	100,000	123,000	Plus 3,000
—	—	—	15,000	15,000	273,000	288,000	—
—	10,000	—	20,000	30,000	576,000	606,000	Plus 18,000
—	6,000	—	8,000	14,000	127,000	141,000	—
—	—	—	3,000	11,000	114,000	125,000	—
—	16,000	—	85,000	112,000	1,339,000	1,451,000	Plus 21,000
120,000	98,000	75,000	912,559	1,576,559	2,013,914	3,590,473	Plus 20,994

[e] The original table describes *chifliks* as lands taken over by the Pasha because the villages to which they belonged could not pay their taxes.

[f] *'Uhdahs*, according to the original table, were lands taken over by individuals on the condition that current taxes and arrears were paid by the new landholders.

[g] There are several discrepancies which have not been accounted for in the original table between the combined total for the great estates and the peasant lands on the one hand and the total *ma'mūr* land on the other. See Appendix II for possible explanation.

[h] The original table points out that an amount of 200,000 *faddāns* which were either cultivated by the Bedouins or used by them as pasture land was not included in the survey in the province of Buḥayrah and that the Bedouins did not pay taxes on this land.

[i] The original table shows that there was actually twice this amount of land in the Fayyūm but that only this amount was cultivated each year, the balance being allowed to remain fallow.

TABLE 12. Total area (in *faddāns*) allotted to each crop cultivated by inundation

Provinces	Wheat	Barley	Beans	Flax	Clover	Lentils[a]	Cotton, rice	Indigo and misc. crops	Corrected total	Original total[b]	Discrepancy between original and corrected total
Lower Egypt											
al-Gharbīyah	106,494	162,741	108,494	27,123	20,123	12,544	104,956	—	542,475	542,475	—
Buḥayrah	72,974	58,924	62,468	16,000	15,709	10,142	20,858	—	257,075	257,075	—
al-Minūfīyah	73,165	58,532	58,532	31,268	25,264	14,210	31,698	—	292,669	292,669	—
Daqahlīyah	72,346	77,346	77,346	30,173	20,173	9,921	64,430	—	351,735	341,735	10,000
ash-Sharqīyah	65,614	78,267	58,267	31,307	21,307	18,241	40,074	—	313,077	313,077	—
al-Qalyūbīyah	40,448	25,632	25,632	13,816	15,816	12,121	5,089	—	138,554	138,164	390
Gīzah	84,284	56,856	56,856	29,428	18,142	8,222	1,516	—	255,304	254,284	1,020
TOTAL	515,325	518,298	447,595	179,115	136,534	85,401	268,621	—	2,150,889	2,139,479	11,410
Middle Egypt[c]											
Banī Suwayf	45,000	40,000	42,000	20,000	9,000	10,000	—	2,000	168,000	168,000	—
Fayyūm	40,000	40,000	20,000	8,000	3,000	1,000	—	8,000	120,000	120,000	—
Upper Egypt											
al-Minyā	90,000	60,000	80,000	30,000	11,000	14,000	—	3,000	288,000	288,000	—
Asyūṭ	148,000	140,000	190,000	56,000	19,000	26,000	—	9,000	588,000	588,000	—
Qinā	38,000	34,000	30,000	10,000	8,000	19,000	—	2,000	141,000	141,000	—
Isnā	38,000	40,000	30,000	3,000	—	13,000	—	3,000	127,000	125,000	2,000
TOTAL	399,000	354,000	392,000	127,000	50,000	83,000[d]	—	27,000	1,432,000	1,430,000	2,000

[a] Also onions, haricots, lupin, and tobacco.

[b] The totals on the original table have been retained here, since the copyist may have made an error in the amount of the individual crops rather than in the totals.

[c] The original table for Middle and Upper Egypt specifies that the figures were calculated on the basis of a flood attaining the height of 24 pics. W. Willcocks (*Egyptian Irrigation* [London, 1889], p. 12), put the pic, used for the measurement of the level of the Nile, at 0.54 meters. Another measurement frequently referred to by French authors was the *coudée*, that is, the length of the arm from the elbow to the tip of the middle finger.

[d] The amount 73,000 appears on the original table.

TABLE 13. Total area (in *faddāns*) allotted to each crop cultivated by irrigation or by inundation and irrigation and to *dhurah*

Provinces	Cultivated by irrigation or by inundation and irrigation									Land sown several times annually
	Cultivated by irrigation				Cultivated by inundation and irrigation			Total actual production	Total government requirements[b]	*Dhurah*
	Cotton	Rice	Sesame	Indigo[a]	Sugar	Opium, indigo	Various			
Lower Egypt										
al-Gharbīyah	50,000	40,000	22,000	8,000	—	—	—	120,000	159,000	100,000
Buḥayrah	10,000	9,000	20,800	5,200	—	—	—	45,000	70,000	40,000
al-Minūfīyah	45,000	3,000	30,000	12,000	—	—	—	90,000	100,000	90,000
Daqahlīyah	30,000	38,000	12,000	18,000	—	—	—	98,000[c]	106,666	100,000
ash-Sharqīyah	69,000	8,000	31,000	12,000	—	—	—	120,000	160,000	100,000
al-Qalyūbīyah	20,000	—	10,000	5,000	—	—	—	35,000	40,000	60,000
Gīzah	—	—	—	—	—	—	—	—	—	90,000
TOTAL	224,000	98,000	125,800	60,200	—	—	—	508,000[d]	635,666	580,000[e]
Middle Egypt[f]										
Banī Suwayf	—	—	—	—	300	1,200	300	1,800	1,800	40,000
Fayyūm	—	—	—	—	—	—	2,000	2,000	2,000	30,000
Upper Egypt										
al-Minyā	—	—	—	—	3,000	500	300	3,800	2,800	60,000
Asyūṭ	—	—	—	—	5,900	800	200	6,900	4,900	80,000
Qinā	—	—	—	—	2,500	900	200	3,600	2,000	50,000
Isnā	—	—	—	—	400	300	100	800	800	59,000
TOTAL	—	—	—	—	12,100[g]	3,700[h]	3,100	18,900	14,300	319,000

[a] Also hemp, madder, vegetables, gardening.
[b] The Egyptian government habitually issued orders that all land which could be cultivated by irrigation should be sown, but these commands were frequently not carried out.
[c] Original table reads 88,000.
[d] Original table reads 498,000.
[e] Original table reads 480,000.
[f] See Table 12, note 3.
[g] Original table reads 12,200.
[h] Original table reads 3,900.

TABLE 14. Maximum productivity from inundated and irrigated land, by province

Provinces	Inundated land						Irrigated land			Land sown several times annually
	Wheat (*ardabbs*)	Barley (*ardabbs*)	Beans (*ardabbs*)	Flax (*qinṭārs*)	Linseed (*ardabbs*)	Lentils (*ardabbs*)	Cotton (*qinṭārs*)	Rice (*ardabbs*)	Sesame (*ardabbs*)	*Dhurah* (*ardabbs*)
Lower Egypt										
al-Gharbīyah	319,482	650,964	325,482	81,369	54,246	—	100,000	200,000	22,000	500,000
Buḥayrah	218,922	235,696	187,404	48,000	32,000	—	20,000	45,000	20,800	200,000
al-Minūfīyah	219,495	235,128	175,596	93,804	63,536	—	90,000	15,000	30,000	450,000
Daqahlīyah	217,038	299,384	232,038	90,519	60,346	—	60,000	190,000	12,000	500,000
ash-Sharqīyah	186,842	313,068	174,801	93,921	62,614	—	138,000	40,000	31,000	500,000
al-Qalyūbīyah	121,544	102,528	76,896	41,448	27,632	—	40,000	—	10,000	450,000
Gīzah	252,852	227,424	170,568	88,284	58,856	—	—	—	—	—
Middle Egypt										
Banī Suwayf	112,500	120,000	105,000	51,600	41,600	20,000	—	—	—	200,000
Fayyūm	100,000	120,000	50,000	20,000	16,000	2,000	—	—	—	150,000
Upper Egypt										
al-Minyā	225,000	180,000	120,000	75,000	60,000	28,000	—	—	—	300,000
Asyūṭ	370,000	420,000	475,000	140,000	112,000	52,000	—	—	—	400,000
Qinā	95,000	85,000	75,000	2,500	20,000	36,000	—	—	—	250,000
Isnā	95,000	120,000	75,000	75,000	6,000	25,000	—	—	—	295,000

TABLE 15. Maximum productivity: total yield and total revenue

Produce	Lower Egypt Yield (*ardabbs*)	Lower Egypt Revenue (piasters)	Middle and Upper Egypt Yield (*ardabbs*)	Middle and Upper Egypt Revenue (piasters)
Inundated land				
Wheat	1,536,175[a]	51,532,500	997,500	43,890,000
Barley	2,064,192	51,829,800	1,045,000	38,940,000
Beans	1,342,785	44,759,500	900,000	43,120,000
Flax	537,345[b]	69,646,000 (Flax and Linseed)	364,100[d]	50,800,000 (Flax and Linseed)
Linseed	359,230[c]		255,600	
Lentils	—	—	163,000	8,760,000
Clover	—	13,653,400	—	4,000,000
Various	—	42,700,500	—	13,500,000
Irrigated land				
Cotton	448,000[e]	100,800,000	—	—
Rice	490,000	44,100,000	—	—
Sesame	125,800	18,870,000	—	—
Various	—	24,080,000	—	—
Inundated and Irrigated land				
Sugar	—	—	—	12,000,000
Opium, indigo	—	—	—	1,950,000
Various	—	—	—	1,395,000
Dhurah	2,600,000[f]	48,000,000	1,595,000	31,900,000
TOTAL REVENUE		509,971,700		250,255,000

[a] Original table reads 1,536,176.
[b] Figure is given in *qinṭārs* instead of in *ardabbs*. Original table reads 536,143.
[c] Original table reads 359,228.
[d] Figure is given in *qinṭārs* instead of in *ardabbs*. Original table reads 296,600.
[e] Figure is given in *qinṭārs* instead of in *ardabbs*.
[f] Original table reads 2,900,000.

TABLE 16. Average productivity per *faddān*: net revenue and average yield

Produce	Lower Egypt		Middle and Upper Egypt	
	Net revenue (piasters)	Average yield (*ardabbs*)	Net revenue (piasters)	Average yield (*ardabbs*)
Inundated land				
Wheat	100	3	110	2.5
Barley	100	4	110	3
Beans	100	3	110	2.5
Flax	400	3[a]	400	2[a]
Linseed	—	2	80	2
Lentils	—	—	120	2
Clover	100	—	80	—
Various	500	—	500	—
Irrigated land				
Cotton	450	2[a]	—	—
Rice	450	5	—	—
Sesame	150	1	—	—
Various	400	—	—	—
Irrigated and inundated land				
Sugar	—	—	1,000	—
Indigo, opium	—	—	500	—
Various	—	—	450	—
Dhurah	100	5	100	5

[a] The yields for flax and cotton are given in *qinṭārs* instead of in *ardabbs*.

TABLE 17. Population of Egypt and the division of head and land taxes among the inhabitants of the provinces

Province	Total population	Totals	Laborers who must pay *furdah*	Totals	Land tax revenue (purses)	Totals
al-Gharbīyah	158,800		68,900		60,000	
Buḥayrah	79,900		38,000		16,000	
al-Minūfīyah	188,800		76,400		64,000	
Daqahlīyah	99,000		48,000		40,000	
ash-Sharqīyah	119,080		58,000		48,000	
al-Qalyūbīyah	68,000		28,000		38,000	
Gīzah	89,000	802,580[a]	36,000	353,300[b]	40,000	306,000[c]
Cities						
Alexandria	80,000		—		—	
Cairo	220,000		—		—	
Rosetta	150,000	450,000	—		—	
TOTAL		1,252,580		353,300		306,000
Banī Suwayf	102,000		25,000		12,000	
Fayyūm	63,000		16,000		11,000	
al-Minyā	197,000		48,000		23,000	
Asyūṭ	420,000		100,000		85,000	
Qinā	66,000		16,000		13,000	
Isnā	58,000		16,000		10,000	
TOTAL		906,000		221,000		154,000
GENERAL TOTAL		2,158,580		574,300		460,000

[a] Original table reads 712,580.
[b] Original table reads 355,300.
[c] Original table reads 276,000.

TABLE 18. Cadastre of A.H. 1236, report of Felix Mengin[a]

Province	*Faddāns*	Total for province	Rate of tax per *faddān*		Total revenue		Total for province	
			Piasters	Paras	Piasters	Paras	Piasters	Paras
al-Minūfīyah								
	92,400		38	10	3,534,300			
	54,000		33	30	1,822,500			
	47,750	194,150	29	10	1,396,687	20	6,753,487	20
al-Gharbīyah								
	120,600		38	10	4,612,950			
	55,300		33	30	1,866,375			
	50,060	225,960	29	10	1,464,255		7,943,580	
Buḥayrah								
	50,250		29	10	1,479,812	20		
	30,542		22	20	687,195			
	20,000	100,792	18		360,000		2,527,007	20
ash-Sharqīyah								
	85,800		33	30	2,995,750			
	40,084		27		1,082,268			
	35,320	161,204	22	10	785,850		4,863,868	
al-Manṣūrīyah (Daqahlīyah)								
	80,200		33	30	2,706,750			
	45,000		27		1,215,000			
	30,660	155,860	22	20	689,850		4,611,600	
al-Qalyūbīyah								
	80,000	80,000	38	10			3,080,000	
Gīzah								
	85,900	85,900	38	10			3,275,675	
Fayyūm								
	70,200	70,200	33	30			2,369,250	
Aṭfīḥ								
	55,000	55,000	30	30			1,691,250	
Banī Suwayf								
	85,200		38	30	3,258,900			
	42,660		33	30	1,439,775			
	38,400	166,260	29	10	1,123,200		5,821,875	
al-Minyā								
	75,000		38	10	2,868,750			
	40,840		33	30	1,378,350			
	32,500	148,340	29	10	950,625		5,197,725	
Asyūṭ								
	88,100		38	10	3,369,825			
	48,084		33	30	1,622,835			
	42,400	178,584	29	10	1,240,200		6,232,860	
Girgā								
	96,500		38	30	3,694,950			
	48,000		33	30	1,620,000			
	45,900	190,400	29	10	1,353,550		6,668,500	
Isnā								
	70,100		38	10	2,681,325			
	38,840		33	30	1,310,850			
	35,050	143,990	29	10	1,025,212	20	5,017,387	20
TOTAL		1,956,640					66,054,065	20[b]

[a] Felix Mengin, *Histoire de l'Egypte sous le gouvernement du Mohammed-Aly, etc.* (Paris, 1823), II, 343, 344.
[b] A total of 132,108 purses, 65 piasters, and 10 paras, or 20,000,000 francs (Mengin, II, 344).

APPENDIX II

THE AREA OF CULTIVABLE LAND IN EGYPT

The amount of cultivable land in Egypt during the first half of the nineteenth century cannot be ascertained precisely, for no accurate statistical information is available for this period. It is possible, nevertheless, to arrive at an approximate estimate of the area of cultivable land on the basis of the available statistics, bearing in mind that such an estimate may have to be revised should more convincing statistical information be discovered in future. In this analysis, figures from four periods have been used to serve as a basis of comparison: the French occupation, the Cadastre of 1813–14 (A.H. 1229), the Cadastre of 1820–21 (A.H. 1236), and 1844 (A.H. 1260).[1] Table 19

TABLE 19. Area of cultivable land according to survey figures prepared by Jacotin during the French occupation[a]

Type of land	Large *faddān*[b]	Plus 0.255 per cent	Small *faddān*
Lands cultivated, depending upon extent of flood	3,217,671	820,506.105	4,038,177.105
Uncultivated lands which were cultivable	749,140	191,030.700	940,170.700
Islands in the Nile which were cultivable, depending upon the flood	36,613	9,336.315	45,949.315
	4,003,424	1,020,873.120	5,024,297.120
Lakes and marshes which could be reclaimed	628,540	160,277.700	788,817.700
Land encroached upon by desert which could be reclaimed	113,567	28,959.585	142,526.585
	4,745,531	1,210,110.405	5,955,641.405
Minus:			
Land on which tax was collected by Estève	3,163,618	806,722.590	3,970,340.590
Amount of land formerly cultivated which could be cultivated and taxed	1,581,913	403,387.815	1,985,300.815

[a] Jacotin, *Tableau de la superficie de l'Egypte*, in *Description de l'Egypte, Etat moderne* (Paris, 1822, 1st ed.), I, Pt. 2, 571–578.

[b] Jacotin employed as his unit of measurement a *faddān* of 400 square *qaṣabahs*. The length of the *qaṣabah* used by him was 3 m 85 c; consequently, the size of the *faddān*

contains the results of the survey conducted by Jacotin during the French occupation.

Artin claims that 3,054,710 *faddāns* were cultivated after the Cadastre of 1813–14.[2] Although he does not specify the amount of *ab'ādīyah* (uncultivated) land excluded from the cadastral registers of this period, it is nevertheless possible to ascertain the amount of *ab'ādīyah* land in 1813–14 by using Jacotin's figure of cultivated land as a base.

Cultivated land (Jacotin)	4,038,177.105 *faddāns*
Cultivated land 1813–14 (Artin)	3,054,710.000
Ab'ādīyah land in 1813–14	983,467.105

For the 1820–21 (A.H. 1236) cadastre two figures are available. Mengin lists all the land which was taxed in 1820–21[3] while Barnett reports the amount of land classified as *ab'ādīyah*.[4]

Land taxed 1820–21 (Mengin)	1,956,640 *faddāns*
Ab'ādīyah land 1820–21 (Barnett)	723,685[5]
	2,680,325

A considerable discrepancy exists between these figures for 1820–21 and those of Jacotin and Artin, as may clearly be seen from Tables 20 and 21. This discrepancy of 1,357,852.105 *faddāns* can only be explained by assuming that this quantity of land belonged to a different category than either taxed or *ab'ādīyah* land, possibly being classified either as *waṣīyah* land or land reserved by Muḥammad 'Alī for his own use.

The exclusion of so much land from the cadastral registers of 1820–21 (A.H. 1236), it must be noted, came precisely at the moment when long-staple cotton was introduced and when a special government department was formed to look after the royal estates. These royal estates (*chafālik wa 'uhad*) had formerly been under the control of one of the bureaus of the *dīwān* of the Pasha's lieutenant (*kikhyah*) which had been founded in 1220/1805–06. In 1236/1820–21, however, a new *dīwān*, the *Dīwān 'Umūm al-Chafālik wa'l-'Uhad as-Sanīyah*, was created. Deny in his inventory of Egyptian government records observes that the carton of this new *dīwān* for 1236/1820–21 consisted of "Ifade[6] d'Ibrahim pacha, du 3 Redjeb, relative à la culture

in question equaled 14.8225 m² times 400, or a total of 5,929 m². This *faddān* was considerably larger than the one used during the Cadastre of 1813–14 when both the length of the *qaṣabah* and the area of the *faddān* were reduced, the former to 3 m 64 c and the latter to 333⅓ square *qaṣabahs*. Thus, the *faddān* of the Cadastre of 1813–14 equaled 13.2496 m² times 333⅓, or a total of 4,416.5⅓ m², i.e., approximately 0.255 per cent less than the *faddān* used by Jacotin. So that the statistics of the French survey may be compared with those of the period following the Cadastre of 1813–14 when the smaller *faddān* was adopted by the Egyptian government, the figures reported by Jacotin have been converted to their equivalent in the later period by increasing Jacotin's figures by 0.255 per cent.

TABLE 20. Land excluded from the Cadastre of 1820–21 (A.H. 1236): A comparison of figures for the period of the French occupation (Jacotin) and 1820–21 (Mengin and Barnett)[a]

Type of land	Amount of land (*faddāns*)	
Cultivated land during French occupation	4,038,177.105	
Taxed land 1820–21	1,956,640.000	
Land which, if uncultivated, should have been classified as *ab'ādīyah*	2,081,537.105	
Land actually classified as *ab'ādīyah* in 1820–21	723,685.000	
Land unaccounted for in 1820–21		1,357,852.105

[a] Jacotin, *Tableau de la superficie de l'Egypte*, in *Description de l'Egypte, Etat moderne* (Paris, 1822, 1st ed.), II, Pt. 2, 571–578; Felix Mengin, *Histoire de l'Egypte sous le gouvernement du Mohammed-Aly, etc.* (Paris, 1823), II, 343, 344; Barnett, December 12, 1844 in F.O. 78/583 (see Appendix I).

TABLE 21. Land excluded from the Cadastre of 1820–21 (A.H. 1236): A comparison of figures for 1813–14 (Artin) and 1820–21 (Mengin and Barnett)[a]

Type of land	Amount of land (*faddāns*)	
Cultivated land (1813–14)	3,054,710.000	
Taxed land (1820–21)	1,956,640.000	
		1,098,070.000
Ab'ādīyah land (1813–14)	983,467.105	
Ab'ādīyah land (1820–21)	723,685.000	
		259,782.105
Land unaccounted for in 1820–21		1,357,852.105

[a] Yaqub [J.] Artin, "Essai sur les causes du renchérissement de la vie matérielle au Caire dans le courant du 19me siècle (1800 à 1907)," *Mémoires de l'Institut Egyptien*, V (Cairo, 1908), 67, 68; Felix Mengin, *Histoire de l'Egypte sous le gouvernement du Mohammed-Aly, etc.* (Paris, 1823), II, 343, 344; Barnett, December 12, 1844 in F.O. 78/583 (see Appendix I).

du coton" and included 193 pieces. Deny then lists a second carton for this *dīwān* bearing a date sixteen years later than the first, that is, 1252/1836–37.[7] Since one carton would hardly have sufficed for these sixteen years, it can be assumed that soon after the *dīwān* was created, at the time of the reorganization of the Egyptian administration in the middle twenties (see Chapter V), Muḥammad 'Alī assimilated the land unaccounted for in 1820–21 into the body of taxable village land. A comparison of the statistics of 1820–21 (A.H. 1236) and 1844 (A.H. 1260) bears out this assumption.

Land taxed in 1844[8]	3,569,479 *faddāns*
Land taxed in 1820–21	1,956,640
Area of land subjected to the land tax between 1820–21 and 1844	1,612,839

There can be little doubt that this 1,612,839 *faddāns* includes the amount of land unaccounted for in the Cadastre of 1820–21 (A.H. 1236) (1,357,852.105 *faddāns*) plus an additional amount of 254,986.895 *faddāns*. The latter amount appears to represent an increase in the area of cultivable land and, indeed, corresponds exactly with the increase obtained by comparing the figures of the French occupation with that of Barnett.

Total village land (*zimām*) in 1844	4,293,164.000 *faddāns*
Cultivated land during the French occupation (small *faddān*)	4,038,177.105
	254,986.895

Yet, even this increase may be illusory, if nonexistent, for it is doubtful that the total amount of *zimām* land was actually under cultivation. In fact, the tax data disclose that the total *zimām* land was not cultivated and that instead of an increase in the area of cultivated land during the years between the French occupation and 1844 there was actually a decrease. There follows an analysis of these tax data as proof of this statement.

Total village land (*zimām*) in 1844	4,293,164 *faddāns*
Land taxed (*ma'mūr*) 1844	3,569,479
	723,685[9]

This quantity of untaxed land in 1844 is identical to the amount classified as *ab'ādīyah* land in 1820–21.[10] It may, therefore, be concluded that land classified as *ab'ādīyah* land in 1820–21 continued thereafter to fall within this same category.

Three possibilities exist with regard to this *ab'ādīyah* land. First, all of it may actually have been cultivated, although relieved of tax. Second, the total quantity of 723,685 *faddāns* may have remained uncultivated. Finally, only part of this land may have been cultivated tax free, the balance remaining uncultivated. It is evident from the following calculations that the first two possibilities are implausible, whereas the latter is not only possible, but is surely true.

Land taxed 1844		3,569,479 *faddāns*
Land taxed 1820–21		1,956,640
Land available for distribution to peasants and/or large landholders		1,612,839
Peasant land 1844	2,013,914 *faddāns*	
Land taxed 1820–21	1,956,640	
Increase in land held by peasants	57,274	57,274
Land supposedly available for private estates		1,555,565

The private estates in 1844, however, actually consisted of 1,576,559 *faddāns*, the discrepancy between these two figures (i.e., 1,576,559 minus 1,555,565) being 20,994 *faddāns*. This discrepancy is precisely the one noted in Table 11, Appendix I, and points to the conclusion that this amount of 20,994 *faddāns* granted as private estates was excluded from the column of *ma'mūr* land in the table simply because it represented land drawn from the category of land classified as *ab'ādīyah* land. On the basis of this information alone it is clear that at least 20,994 *faddāns* of the 723,685 *faddāns* of *ab'ādīyah* land were cultivated free of tax. But there still remains the balance of this *ab'ādīyah* land to account for. Part of this balance possibly included the 200,000 *faddāns* of untaxed land in Buḥayrah Province assigned to the Bedouins (see Table 11, note 8).[11] A further 100,000 *faddāns* that may also be included is that land in Fayyūm Province that was allowed to lie fallow each year (see Table 11, note 9). In short, of the 723,685 *faddāns* of land classified as *ab'ādīyah* land in 1820–21, only 320,944 *faddāns* could have been considered cultivated, tax-free land by 1844, the balance of 402,741 *faddāns* (i.e., 723,685 minus 320,944) being classified as uncultivated land.[12]

Therefore, the combined amount of taxed and tax-free land under cultivation in 1844 was only 3,890,423 *faddāns*[13] (i.e., total village land [*zimām*] of 4,293,164 *faddāns* minus 402,741 of uncultivated *ab'ādīyah* land) as compared to the 4,038,177.105 *faddāns* of taxed and tax-free land under cultivation at the time of the French occupation.

Taxed and untaxed cultivable land:	
French occupation	4,038,177.105 *faddāns*
1844	3,890,423.000
Decrease in area of cultivation	147,754.105

There is, of course, the remote possibility that only the land that was taxed by the French was actually cultivated and that no tax-free land existed.[14] Even so, a decrease in the area of cultivation continues to exist.

Taxed cultivated land, French occupation	3,970,340.590 *faddāns*
Taxed and untaxed cultivable land, 1844	3,890,423.000
Decrease in area of cultivation	79,917.590

In other words, the area of cultivated land by 1844 fell short of the level of cultivated land at the time of the French occupation by an amount of about 79,917.590 to 147,754.105 *faddāns*.

It should be stressed, however, that despite Muḥammad ʿAlī's failure to increase the area of cultivable land he nevertheless did increase the cropping area, for by introducing *ṣayfī* canals, he extended summer irrigation, thereby making it possible for a greater proportion of the existing area of cultivable land to produce three and even four crops. In conclusion, Muḥammad ʿAli's improvements were qualitative rather than quantitative and this, in itself, was an important achievement.

APPENDIX III

TRANSLATION OF A NOTICE FROM THE DIVAN ROODAWAY AT ALEXANDRIA*

His Excellency the Chief member of the Heccania (Council of Justice) has addressed me a letter under date 23rd Rabi-Ewel 1260 (10th of April 1844), Sub No. 1 setting forth that Tillage and Agriculture are the foundation of the comfort, happiness and prosperity of the Egyptian population, and in order to obtain the same it is found absolutely necessary that all those who have absented themselves from their primitive homes should return back to their native villages. Former orders have been issued for them to return home and that the punishment of death or the Gallies [*sic*] for life would be awarded to those who harboured them, of which no notice was taken but disregarding this they still continued to keep them in their employ as formerly.

In order therefore to drop the word absconder (Mutasahheb) entirely hereafter, in the month of Moharrem 1260, a meeting of the above named Council was held and a decree was passed that whoever has at present any such absconders from the year 1248 (1832) (to the present time) must give them up to the proper places. If however he does not deliver them up, and even should receive in his service or as a lodger in his house persons newly arrived he will suffer the punishment of the Gallows and death as his reward for doing thus.

Soloman Bedr Iddeen native of Minyat Isserig situated at Shoubra, was requested by the Shieks [*sic*] of that part to give up some absconders he had in his house that they might be seized and sent to their primitive homes, but he denied having them in his house, and caused them to escape and in compliance with instructions the said Soloman was gibbeted in the Public Market of that place, so that if any one harbours, or causes an absconder to escape after proper investigation he will suffer in like manner (as Soloman) according to the decree of the Heccania Council.

Whoever has in his service or in his house any absconder shall neither keep him nor protect him, but consign him to the Diwan of Hoodsaria that he may be returned to his own village and that this decree is given for the purpose of putting in force the said instructions as well as for a lesson to the public, so that every one must take heed and abstain from acting contrary, by observing strictly this notification.

All absconders from the year 1248 (1832) forwards are requested to return to their homes, this is with respect to all places besides Alexandria, but all those who have abandoned or will quit their primitive homes for Alexandria, from the first of the year 1259 (1843) must be delivered up immediately to either the Divan of the *Ferda* (tax) or Mutassahhebeen in obedience to the

* Stoddart, May 24, 1844 in F.O. 78/582. This is an exact copy of the translation contained in the original dispatch.

High Command (of the Pacha) so that they may be forwarded to their own homes. If however any person in future be found keeping (in his house or service) any of the required individuals, he will surely be dealt with in the manner already mentioned. It has been therefore important to circulate widely this notification that it may be known to the public in general. (signed) Ibraheam Zeky. Dated the 29th Rabi-Ewel 1260 (16 April 1844).

APPENDIX IV

TRANSLATION OF A SECRET PRINTED "CIRCULAR" ADDRESSED TO THE CHIEFS OF ALL THE DISTRICTS IN EGYPT, DATED ALEXANDRIA THE END OF RAMADAN (19 FEBRUARY 1833)*

You have already been ordered to send immediately your contribution for last month *Shaban*. Hitherto it has not come to hand—*Ramadan* is over and I am still to expect it. From this it clearly appears, that you are a negligent Blockhead, and affords another proof that you are an Ass. Since you cannot yet comprehend how urgent it is, that the money should be immediately forthcoming, I send you ____ *Cawas*. On his arrival with you, do not detain him one instant, but remit him immediately the contribution due on the expiration of the last month. If you either detain the bearer or delay remitting to him the whole of the money due; as soon as it comes to my knowledge, I will do thee harm; and be assured "*I will tear thee in pieces*" and now act accordingly —This is my will! (sgd.) Mehmed Ali.

* Barker, February 18, 1833 in F.O. 78/231. This is an exact copy of the translation contained in the original dispatch. A copy of the original order was also included.

APPENDIX V

CONSCRIPTION

Several orders to provincial functionaries which were obtained surreptitiously for the British representatives in Egypt have been preserved in the files of the British Public Record Office.[1] They are interesting examples of the tone of administrative instructions during Muḥammad 'Alī's reign and give some insight into the conscription policy of the Egyptian government during the first Syrian War.

Order A[2]

Ordres Imprimés
Au plus honoré parmi ses semblables . . .
Commandant du Département de . . .

Avant cette epoque, on avait envoyé des ordres de notre part, à tous les commandants des Départements, afin qu'ils envoyassent des récrutes militaires au Bureau de la Guerre. Halil-Aga, commandant de la Province d'*Asisié* nous avait répondu qu'il ne pouvait pas nous obéir, attendu qu'il n'y avait pas d'hommes capables de service militaire. En conséquence nous lui avons demandé le Cadastre des Habitants de la Province, afin de pouvoir établir le nombre des absens. C'est alors que nous l'avions nommé au Gouvernement du *Kelioubié* en donnant au commandant de cette dernière Province le commandement de *Asisié*, à peine ce dernier est-il arrivé à *Asisié*, il nous a envoyé les Régistres de la Population, desquels il est résulté que le Rapport de Halil-Aga à ce sujet était faux.

C'est pour le punir d'une telle insolence, et pour qu'il serve d'exemple aux autres, que nous l'avons envoyé à *Aboukir*,* et nous avons cru nécessaire d'envoyer cet ordre circulaire à tous les gouverneurs des Départements maritimes et meridionaux et à vous parmi ceux-ci, afin que vous sachiez, que si vous osez nous contrairier, et transgresser à notre volonté, vous en verriez la conséquence uniforme. Sache-le!

Order B[3]

Ordres litografiés (circulaire) en No. 1300 aux officiers divers des départements de . . .
Au plus honoré de ses égaux le . . .

Avec l'assistance de Dieu tout puissant ayant été publié à tous les habitants de l'Egypte, la Gloire qu'ils ont acquise par leurs troupes de mer et de terre cet honneur qui déjà influe sur la tranquillité de la nation. Et étant en outre bien connu que ces derniers jours, par la grâce de Dieu, nous avons construit

* State Prison.

quatre vaisseaux, fournis de tout le nécessaire, et que nous avons commencé un autre à trois ponts, qui est aussi presque fini; mais il lui manque les hommes nécessaires à la manœuvre. Ce que vous devez donc faire à présent tous, grands, et petits, c'est de concourir à accroître cette gloire à votre Patrie chacun selon son pouvoir. Et comme le présent ordre *doit être*, et que nous désirons cet honneur, nous avons ordonné à tous nos officiers de nous envoyer chacun autant de *Cawas, †Seïs, et Domestiques qu'il pourra et qui seront sous ses ordres; entre autres nous ordonnons à vous . . . de nous faire avoir . . . hommes au plus tôt possible et sans aucun delai. Qu'ils soient sains et sans aucune imperfection. Lesquels arrivant bientôt ici, entreront (jusqu'à ce que de Vaisseau à trois ponts sera prêt) dans l'école de Navigation, afin d'être eux aussi adaptés au service. Et sachez que c'est ce qu'il y a de plus nécessaire. Alexandrie le 3 Rabée el tané 1248

* Janissare. † Palfrenier.

Order C[4]

Au Sheikh de . . .

Avec l'assistance de Dieu tout puissant—ayant été connu à tous les habitants de l'Egypte les grands honneurs et les avantages qui leur sont accrus par la prépondérance de leurs troupes de mer et de terre et que ces honneurs contribuent au bien et au repos du Pays.

Et ces derniers jours nous nous étant determinés à construire 4 Vaisseaux, dont nous avons préparé tout le nécessaire. Et ayant besoin d'hommes pour le service, nous avons déjà ordonné à tous nos commandants et officiers, grands, et petits, de nous envoyer les hommes qui se trouveraient dans leur service, pour le vaisseau dernièrement fini par la Grâce de Dieu. Nous ordonnons à présent à tous les Sheikhs des Villages de ce Royaume de nous envoyer aussi les personnes qui se trouveront dans leur emploi, chacun tant qu'il pourra, pour les Vaisseaux sus-nommés. Et nous vous expédions cet ordre à vous Sheikh . . . pour . . . hommes. Et sur la réception de la présente, vous devez nous les envoyer de suite à Alexandrie. Et il faut qu'ils soient sains et sans aucune imperfection, et celà aussi un moment plus tôt, afin que ceux ci soient prêts quand les vaisseaux seront finis; Et sâchez que c'est ce qu'il y a de plus nécessaire sur toute affaire.
Alexandrie le 5 Rabée el tani 1248.

Order D[5]

Circular addressed to the Governors (Mamours) of several Districts in Egypt.

Last year, we gave orders for the men who ought to have been sent from your department; but they have not yet been all sent. This I have learnt from Mahomed Bey, Minister of War, and he has given me the number of those who have been levied, and those still wanting. And thou ass that thou art! what art thou doing!

Dost thou not know that this affair is of more consequence than any other? Has not thy brain till now been able to comprehend? For want of better men I have placed thee in office and have made thee a governor. And thou! Dost thou neglect thy duty in this way? And delay it so long? What! would'st thou have Mehmed Ali asleep? Mehmed Ali does not sleep, does not sleep. In the instant thou receivest this order, put thy brains in thy head, and send the rest of the men, which thou oughtest to have sent last year, to the Minister of War together with those of this year which the Supreme Council demanded.

Be expeditious—and do not delay—if thou dost not I will make an example of thee to the rest of the Governors of the districts. Open thy eyes and choose between these two alternatives.

Alexandria 2 Ramazan 1248 (22 Jan. 1833)

Order E[6]

Circulars to the Sceiks of Provinces[7]

The present Decree is to be received respected and obeyed by all Sceiks, Nazirs and all of you must know and comprehend that reference has been made to my wisdom, by a note addressed to me, from the Department of War, respecting the number of people not yet sent from the Provinces, and from which I have seen that the number against you is . . .

And of such complaint I give you notice, lest punishment should meet you; you ought to have been already punished in consideration of the unaccountable delay ansuying [*sic*] from your negligence, but for this time I will forgive you, and after you have received this Decree and understood its contents, you will instantly work to its execution, and do everything in your power, and make every exertion towards sending the number of persons required, that is . . .

They are to be as to their height and health without exception, as to be able to serve as soldiers, without being in any way maimed, and this with a view to avoid their being rejected by the Minister of War; and you will consign them to your Nazirs as early as practicable, to be sent to the Council of War; and open your eyes not to be negligent, or retard your duty, because you will bear the consequence, and repent, but too late; and to this end I shall send you this my Decree from my High Court at Alexandria—Learn and execute—

The 13 Zilkadé 1248 (April 1, 1833)

Order F[8]

To the Governor of the District . . . .

With respect to the men whom we take for the service of our victorious War Department, some draw their teeth, some blind themselves, and others maim themselves, on their way to us, and for this reason we send back the greater part; and also I see in the Report of the War Department, that there is always a deficiency. Send them before an hour elapses, all the men wanting, provided they be able-bodied and healthy; and those whom thou dost send, must be in concert with the Sheiks, and when thou dost expedite them, let each know, that he must not maim himself; because I will take from the family of every such offender, men in his place, and he who has maimed himself shall be sent to the galleys all his life; I have already ordered this to the Sheiks in writing, and do thou also take care, in concert with the Sheiks to levy the men demanded, and send them immediately. And the number of the rest of the men who remain in your Department, send me with the least possible delay—This I demand.

Alexandria 21 Shawal 1248 (12th March 1833).

APPENDIX VI

THE POPULATION OF EGYPT DURING THE REIGN OF MUḤAMMAD ʿALĪ

The successful achievement of the various goals set by Muḥammad ʿAlī required a supply of manpower far in excess of the one available to him. His military, administrative, and fiscal policies were unrealistically conceived, having been formulated in the belief that there existed in Egypt a population twice its size. So anxious, in fact, was the Pasha to attain his objectives that he ignored any evidence indicating that fewer resources in manpower were at his disposal than he chose to acknowledge. Admittedly, it was practically impossible to make a correct estimate of population figures because of the deeply rooted prejudice among Muslims to numbering people, the fear that truthfulness in supplying vital statistics would lead to new demands for men and taxes, and the inaccessibility of the *ḥarīms*, which made it impossible to verify statements regarding the number of persons in each household. Furthermore, the police possessed no power to compel the registration of births and deaths. In fact, not until 1846 were registries opened in every city and village for recording of births and deaths by the *shaykhs*, barbers, and *ṣarrāfs*. Even then, only deaths were usually registered in accordance with the law, since permits were required for burials. The registration of births, on the other hand, was frequently omitted because of the failure on the part of midwives, barbers, and doctors to make the necessary declarations.[1]

Since no demographic study of Egypt exists for this period, it is necessary to rely on estimates of eye witnesses, all of whom, while giving different estimates, agree that Muḥammad ʿAlī tended to exaggerate the size of the Egyptian population. Hamont, for example, says that before the Syrian Wars the population had been 2,500,000, declining thereafter to 1,500,000. Baron de Boislecomte, on the other hand, estimates that Egypt contained about 3,000,000 inhabitants with a population density in the settled areas amounting to 500 persons per square mile (1,500 per square league) or twice that of France. Colonel Duhamel dismisses Muḥammad ʿAlī's contention that he had a population of between 3,480,000 to 4,350,000, claiming that the Pasha's estimates were founded on the erroneous assumption that there were 870,000 houses in Egypt, which at the rate of 4 persons per household would equal 3,480,000, and at the rate of 5 persons per household would equal 4,350,000. He feels sure that the government officials falsified the figures and included in the survey abandoned homes, stables, and dovecots (which resembled human habitations). Duhamel finds equally unsound an estimate by Muḥammad ʿAlī based on the amount of cereal consumed in Egypt, stating that the Pasha had made no distinction between cereal consumed by human beings and that consumed by domestic animals. In any case, it is Duhamel's belief that so long as government officials continued to supply the Pasha with false returns, he would never have accurate statistics concerning the amount of cereals grown or consumed in Egypt and, consequently, no accurate population figures so long as they were based on cereal consumption. Bowring also feels that the official estimate in 1840 of 3,200,000 was too high. He points out that the best-informed opinion estimated the population at between 2,000,000 to 2,500,000 at most. Campbell puts the figure at around 2,235,500, of which approximately 800,000 were peasants, while the statistics taken from official records by one of Barnett's employees cite the total Egyptian population at 2,158,580 and the agrarian population at 1,708,580.[2] Contemporary evidence, then, is practically unanimous in placing the Egyptian population below 3,000,000, and most observers put it at less than 2,500,000.

On the other hand, population statistics for Egypt assembled after Muḥammad 'Alī's reign show a rapid growth of population during the Pasha's reign. The figures in Tables 22 and 23 reflect a great increase in population in the period 1821–1846, both in absolute numbers and in rate of increase. Table 23 shows a great decline in the rate of increase in the period immediately following the reign of Muḥammad 'Alī. Both tables are suspect for several reasons. First, the 1846 figures do not conform to the estimates of contemporaries or to the official figure reported by Barnett.[3] Second, although it was certainly Muḥammad 'Alī's policy to force an increase in population by encouraging parents to marry off their children, and under normal conditions such early marriages and the prolificacy of the people would have produced the desired effects, nevertheless the Pasha's conscription policy actually retarded population growth.[4] Furthermore, the sudden decline in the rate of population

TABLE 22. Total population[a]

Period	Population
1798 (French estimates)	2,460,200[b]
1821	2,536,400
1846	4,476,440[c]

[a] Yaqub [J.] Artin, "Essai sur les causes du renchérissement de la vie matérielle au Caire dans le courant du 19me siècle (1800 à 1907)," *Mémoires de l'Institut Egyptien,* V (Cairo, 1908), 83–85.

[b] In his discussion of population de Chabrol cites two figures, 2,442,200 and 2,467,100 inhabitants, without explaining the discrepancy. In neither figure does he include the Bedouins whose number, he claims, could only be roughly estimated and whom he figures at approximately 27,000 fighting men or a total of about 130,000, including men, women, and children (de Chabrol de Volvic, *Essai sur les mœurs des habitans modernes de l'Egypte,* in *Description de l'Egypte, Etat moderne* [Paris, 1822, 1st ed.], II, Pt. 2, 364).

[c] Artin mentions that the French and 1821 estimates included only the area between the Mediterranean Sea and Aṣwān, whereas the later figure included Bedouins and the inhabitants of the Egyptian oases (Artin, "Essai sur les causes," 83).

increase after Muḥammad 'Alī's reign is exceedingly unlikely, since conditions in the years 1846–1882 were no worse than before 1846 and there was not the same drain on the population for military service. The only explanation, therefore, for this sudden decline is that the preceding increase, as shown in both tables, was grossly exaggerated.[5]

TABLE 23. Rate of population increase[a]

Period	Absolute figure	Per cent for entire period	Per cent per year
1800–1821	76,200	3.10	0.15
1821–1846	1,940,039	78.48	3.14
1846–1882	2,105,476	47.03	1.30

[a] A. Boinet, "L'accroissement de la population en Egypte," *Bulletin de l'Institut Egyptien*, 2d Series, VII (Cairo, 1887), 278, 279.

The final conclusion that can be drawn from the evidence is that the population figures were lower than those provided to foreigners by Muḥammad 'Alī and that these foreign observers were fully aware of these inaccuracies and therefore relied on their own sources of information. Muḥammad 'Alī may have genuinely believed that he had at his command a far larger population than actually existed. On the other hand, he may very well have exaggerated the size of the Egyptian population in his effort to justify his military and economic policies.

APPENDIX VII

IRRIGATION WORKS CARRIED OUT BY MUḤAMMAD ʿALĪ

These statistics are based on data contained in Clot (II, 473–476), Linant (*Mémoires* and report of work executed between 1818 and 1842 prepared by Linant for the British Consul-General [Barnett, October 20, 1842 in F.O. 78/502]), and Barnett (December 12, 1844 in F.O. 78/583). Corrections in arithmetic have been made as required and Arabic place names, whenever identifiable, have been changed to conform with the system of transliteration used in this work.

TABLE 24. Earthwork for the principal projects of canalization in Lower Egypt, according to Clot and Linant[a]

Province	Name of work	Clot's figures: Length in meters	Clot's figures: Cubic meters	Linant's figures (cubic meters): 1818–1831	Linant's figures (cubic meters): 1832–1842
Buḥayrah	al-Maḥmūdīyah	80,000	11,520,000		
	al-Khaṭāṭbah	195,000	15,120,000		
		(275,000)	(26,640,000)	26,640,000	357,700
al-Gharbīyah	Masjid al-Khiḍr	62,000	3,720,000		
	Bijayrim	62,000	2,970,000		
	al-Jaʿfarīyah	55,000	2,750,000		
		(179,000)	(9,440,000)	10,190,000	48,650
al-Minūfīyah	an-Naʿnāʿīyah	35,000	3,150,000		
	Ṣarāwah	35,000	4,950,000		
	Bājūrīyah	62,000	7,440,000		
		(132,000)	(15,540,000)	12,358,000	276,500
Daqahlīyah	Dandīṭīyah	50,000	4,500,000		
	Būhīyah	50,000	4,500,000		
	al-Manṣūrīyah	35,000	2,600,000		
	ash-Sharqāwīyah (Damietta)	40,000	2,000,000		
		(175,000)	(13,600,000)	13,600,000 }	
ash-Sharqīyah	Ra's al-Wādī	45,000	2,200,000		
	Maṣrif Bilbays[b]	35,000	1,400,000	}	216,300
		(80,000)	(3,600,000)	2,000,000 }	
al-Qalyūbīyah	Zaʿfarānī	56,283	5,820,300		
	ash-Sharqāwīyah	25,000	4,375,000		
	Bāsūsīyah	15,000	1,500,000		
		(96,283)	(11,695,300)	5,875,000	254,100
Gīzah		—	—	—	63,140
TOTALS		937,283[c]	80,515,300	70,663,000	1,216,390
Less Maṣrif Bilbays			1,400,000		
			79,115,300	71,879,390[d]	

[a] A. B. Clot, *Aperçu général sur l'Egypte* (Paris, 1840), II, 474, and Linant's dispatch to Barnett, October 20, 1842 in F.O. 78/502.

[b] Maṣrif Bilbays was a drain rather than a canal and should not have been included by Clot in his list of canals.

[c] Approximately 581 miles.

[d] In his book, on the other hand, Linant claims that excavations of the principal *ṣayfī* canals totaled 110,000,000 cubic meters and cost £3,300,000 (*Mémoires sur les principaux travaux d'utilité publique executés en Egypte, etc.* [Paris, 1872, 1873], 30). See W. Willcocks, *Egyptian Irrigation* (London, 1889), p. 90.

TABLE 25. The annual excavation required for the maintenance of canals in Lower Egypt

Province	Name of canal	*Ṣayfī* canals only[a] (cubic meters)	Average total all canals[b] (cubic meters)
Buḥayrah	al-Maḥmūdīyah	2,500,000	
	al-Khaṭāṭbah	1,800,000	
		(4,300,000)	2,634,624
al-Gharbīyah	Ṣarāwah	120,000	3,824,673
	Bājūrīyah	114,000	
and	Baḥr Shibīn	7,000,000	
	Masjid al-Khiḍr	360,000	
al-Minūfīyah	Bijayrim	125,000	2,524,678
		(7,719,000)	
Daqahlīyah	ash-Sharqāwīyah (Damietta)	200,000	3,201,436
and	Mīt Ya'īsh	150,000	
	Dandīṭīyah	150,000	
	Būhīyah	150,000	
ash-Sharqīyah	al-Manṣūrīyah	288,000	3,943,678
al-Qalyūbīyah	ash-Sharqāwīyah	260,000	2,200,789
	Bāsūsīyah	100,000	
		(1,298,000)	
Gīzah		—	2,400,240
TOTALS		13,317,000	20,730,118[c]

[a] M. A. Linant de Bellefonds, *Mémoires sur les principaux travaux d'utilité publique executés en Egypte etc.* (Paris, 1872, 1873), 30.

[b] A. B. Clot, *Aperçu général sur l'Egypte* (Paris, 1840), II, 474.

[c] It can probably be assumed that the additional 7,413,118 cubic meters in this column covers the amount excavated annually from *nīlī* canals.

TABLE 26. Cubic meters of masonry for barrages, locks, and dikes, Lower Egypt

Province	Clot[a]: Specific works mentioned	Clot[a]: Cubic meters	Linant (including dikes)[b]: 1818–1831	Linant (including dikes)[b]: 1832–1842
Buḥayrah	Barrage/lock at:			
	Shubrākhīt[c]	15,000		
	Locks/dikes for al-Maḥmūdīyah	132,000		
		(147,000)	608,600	51,440
al-Gharbīyah	Barrage/lock at:			
	Rahbayn	21,000		
	Damīrah	21,000		
	Biyalah	15,000		
	Nashart	15,000		
	Sirrī	15,000		
	Soutta [*sic*]	21,000		
		(108,000)	228,000 (al-Gharbīyah and al-Minūfīyah)	24,000
al-Minūfīyah	Barrage/lock at:			
	an-Naʿnāʿīyah	9,000		
	Ṣarāwah	9,000		
	Bājūrīyah	21,000		
	Mīt ʿAfīf	21,000		
		(60,000)		103,000
al-Qalyūbīyah	Barrage/lock on:			
	ash-Sharqāwīyah	15,000		
	Abū Manājah	9,000		
	8 Locks on Zaʿfarānī	71,000		
		(95,000)	76,000	12,000
ash-Sharqīyah	Barrage/lock at:		48,000	
	az-Zaqāzīq	45,000		
and	Sufrah	15,000		66,000 (ash-Sharqīyah and Daqahlīyah)
	Būhīyah	9,000		
Daqahlīyah	al-Manṣūrīyah	9,000	27,000	
		(78,000)		
Gīzah	Lock/weir on Dike of Raqqah	15,000	19,000	13,500
			1,006,600	269,940
TOTALS		503,000	1,276,540	

[a] A. B. Clot, *Aperçu général sur l'Egypte* (Paris, 1840), II, 475, 476.
[b] Barnett, October 20, 1842 in F.O. 78/502.
[c] Shubrākhīt is probably correct, although Clot lists it as Burergotte.

TABLE 27. Volume of earthwork (in cubic meters) for the principal projects of canalization and dike construction in Middle and Upper Egypt, according to Linant [a]

Province	1818–1831	1832–1842
Middle Egypt		
Banī Suwayf	1,830,000	162,060
Fayyūm	—	
al-Fashn	903,903	213,692
Bibā	—	
Banī Nuṣayr (Naṣīr)	618,555	203,364
al-Minyā	692,196	150,832
Upper Egypt		
Mallawī	1,376,000	26,460
Asyūṭ	3,240,120	291,179
Manfalūṭ	1,081,638	
Ṭahṭā	64,000	152,785
Sūhāj	—	
Girgā	—	342,944
Farshūṭ	—	269,206
Qinā	—	461,653
Isnā	—	323,225
TOTALS	9,806,412	2,597,400
	12,403,812	

[a] Barnett, October 20, 1842 in F.O. 78/502.

[b] Linant says that he is unable to determine whether the work done in Sūhāj, Girgā, Farshūṭ, Qinā, and Isnā in the period 1818–1831 was executed by Muḥammad 'Alī or merely repaired by him.

TABLE 28. Earthwork for the principal projects of canalization in Middle and Upper Egypt, according to Clot[a]

Province	Name of canal	Length (meters)	Volume (cubic metres)
Middle Egypt			
Banī Suwayf	al-Barānqah	14,500	705,438
al-Fashn	al-Fashn	15,750	430,000
Upper Egypt			
Asyūṭ	Kawm	10,500	435,375
Sūhāj	Islāmīyah	12,250	507,916
Girgā	Sabaykah	7,700	1,960,000
Farshūṭ	al-Marāshdah	21,000	1,806,000
Qinā	Shallāl	14,000	860,000
	Najiḥ	14,000	860,000
	Sanhūr	5,250	774,000
	al-Bayāḍīyah	28,000	20,000,000
Isnā	Ramādi	12,250	603,000
	Aqlīt	14,000	1,290,000
		169,200[b]	30,231,729

[a] A. B. Clot, *Aperçu général sur l'Egypte* (Paris, 1840), II, 473, 474.
[b] Approximately 105 miles.

TABLE 29. Earthwork for the principal projects of dike construction in Middle and Upper Egypt, according to Clot[a]

Province	Name of dike	Length (meters)	Volume (cubic meters)
Middle Egypt			
Banī Suwayf	Raqqah	12,250	564,375
al-Fashn	al-Barānqah	10,850	473,903
Banī Nuṣayr	al-Qays to Banī ʻAdī	9,590	618,555
al-Minyā	Ṭahnashāwī	23,450	592,196
Upper Egypt			
Mallawī	Kudyah	14,000	1,376,000
Asyūṭ	Donhea [*sic*]	8,750	175,000
Manfalūṭ	Banī Kalb, Maharriq	17,500	551,638
Sūhāj	Mishtā	17,000	2,150,000
	ash-Shabāsāt	5,250	465,776
	Wādīyah	5,250	516,000
Girgā	Manshīyah	15,750	1,935,000
Farshūṭ	(1) Farshūṭ	17,500	903,000
	(2) Farshūṭ	17,500	903,000
Qinā	Abū Dīb	8,750	564,375
		183,390	11,788,818

[a] A. B. Clot, *Aperçu général sur l'Egypte* (Paris, 1840), II, 473, 474.

TABLE 30. The annual excavation required for the maintenance of canals in Middle and Upper Egypt, according to Clot[a]

Locality	Cubic meters	Totals
Middle Egypt		
Banī Suwayf	1,491,805	
Fayyūm	1,350,997	
al-Fashn	1,685,241	
Banī Nuṣayr	1,630,709	
al-Minyā	1,978,324	8,137,076
Upper Egypt		
Mallawī	1,842,314	
Asyūṭ	1,746,523	
Manfalūṭ	1,967,942	
Sūhāj	1,003,804	
Girgā	1,045,996	
Farshūṭ	1,091,368	
Qinā	1,572,288	
Isnā	1,238,400	11,508,635
Middle and Upper Egypt		19,645,711
Lower Egypt		20,730,118
Total for Egypt		40,375,829[b]

[a] A. B. Clot, *Aperçu général sur l'Egypte* (Paris, 1840), II, 474.

[b] Linant confirms this figure, stating that an average of 40,000,000 cubic meters was dug each year in Egypt (Barnett, October 20, 1842 in F.O. 78/502; Linant, *Mémoires*, p. 379).

Footnotes to Table 31 on page 287

[a] A. B. Clot, *Aperçu général sur l'Egypte* (Paris, 1840), II, 475, 476.

[b] Barnett, October 20, 1842 in F.O. 78/502

[c] Linant could not be sure that new works were carried out in Sūhāj, Girgā, Farshūṭ, Qinā, and Isnā before 1831 and therefore gave no figures for these areas.

[d] An average of 2,799,140 francs was spent annually for building locks, weirs, barrages, and dikes (Barnett, October 20, 1842 in F.O. 78/502; Linant, *Mémoires*, p. 380).

TABLE 31. Cubic meters of masonry for barrages, locks, and dikes, Middle and Upper Egypt*

	Clot[a]		Linant, including dikes[b]	
Province	Specific works mentioned	Cubic meters	1818–1831	1832–1842
Middle Egypt				
Banī Suwayf	Locks on Dike			29,500
	Shūshah	82,500		
Fayyūm	Reservoir at:		236,400	94,436
	Ṭāmīyah	59,200		
	Sannūris	35,232		
al-Fashn	Weir/locks:		—	
	Dike Chinestad [*sic*]	12,000		
	Dike Arjanūs	6,000		33,000
	Dike Bimbal [*sic*]	12,000		
Bibā	—	—	—	
Banī Nuṣayr	—	—	44,100	30,000
al-Minyā	Weir/locks:		—	51,000
	Dike Ṭahnashāwī	24,000		
	Dike Ṭaḥāwī	18,000		
Upper Egypt				
Mallawī	Weir/locks:		—	9,000
	Dike Khaṭā Abū 'Afrīt	9,000		
Asyūṭ	Aqueduct 'Alī Bey near Bānūb Zahr al-Jamal	9,000	21,200	85,000
	Barrage/locks:			
	Baṣrah	12,000		
	Entrance to Asyūṭ	12,000		
	Dike Asyūṭ	12,000		
	Dike Qalaye [*sic*]	19,000		
	Banī Samī'a	30,000		
Manfalūṭ	Weir/locks:		—	14,608
	Dike al-'Atāmnah	14,608		
Ṭahṭā	—	—	10,000	—
Sūhāj[c]	Lock of Sūhāj	24,600	—	15,000
	Weir/locks: Dike ash-Shabāsāt	21,000		
Girgā	Weir/locks:		—	21,000
	Dike Samhūd	9,000		
	Dike al-Maṣālḥah	12,000		
Farshūṭ	Barrage/locks on Canal Marāqīdī	27,000	—	27,000
Qinā	—	—	—	15,000
Isnā	—	—	—	51,000
TOTALS		460,140	311,700	475,544
			787,244[d]	

* For footnotes see page 286.

TABLE 32. Number of *sāqiyahs*[a]

Provinces	Number in province	Total	Number of *faddāns* per *sāqiyah*
Lower Egypt			
al-Gharbīyah	7,500		26
Buḥayrah	7,000		16
al-Minūfīyah	11,110		9
Daqahlīyah	5,926		24
ash-Sharqīyah	12,000		12
al-Qalyūbīyah	6,600		6
Gīzah	700		6
TOTAL		50,836	99
Middle and Upper Egypt			
Banī Suwayf	150		
Fayyūm	150		
al-Minyā	400		
Asyūṭ	800		
Qinā	300		
Isnā	200		
TOTAL		2,000	
GRAND TOTAL		52,836	

[a] Barnett, December 12, 1844 in F.O. 78/583. See Appendix I for other statistics contained in this dispatch.

BIBLIOGRAPHY

NOTES

GLOSSARY

COMPARATIVE TABLE OF DATES

INDEX

BIBLIOGRAPHY

Unpublished Manuscripts

France, *Les archives du ministère des affaires étrangères*, Paris.

Documents in the Ministry's Alexandria and Cairo files were examined. As the diplomatic and consular reports for the years preceding 1841 have been published by the Société royale de géographie d'Egypte, only the files covering the years 1841–1849 were consulted at the Quai d'Orsay. They contain useful information, some of which is highly critical of the Egyptian government during the closing years of Muḥammad 'Alī's reign.

Great Britain, British Museum, London, MSS division, the Hekekyan Papers.

A collection of private papers left by Yūsuf Hekekyān, an Armenian who studied engineering in England while on an Egyptian educational mission and later became director of the School of Engineering in Egypt.

Great Britain, Public Record Office, London.

The Foreign Office records in the following series were extensively used: F.O. 24, F.O. 78, F.O. 95, F.O. 97, F.O. 141, F.O. 142, F.O. 195, F.O. 196. In addition, the following records were consulted: Board of Trade (B.T.), Levant Company (S.P. 105), War Office (W.O.), and the Stratford Canning papers. Many of the unpublished reports in these files are of inestimable value. Several of the Foreign Office series are especially useful, i.e., *Turkey* (F.O. 78), *Egypt* (F.O. 24), *Egypt* (F.O. 141), and *Egypt* (F.O. 142). The last, consisting of copies of correspondence sent by the British Consul-General in Egypt, should be checked against the F.O. 78 series, which includes all the originals and enclosures received in London from British representatives in the Ottoman Empire. The F.O. 142 series also contains interesting letters sent locally to persons in Egypt or to British officials other than the ambassador at Istanbul or to the Foreign Office in London.

In the War Office series, the most useful of the files dealing with Egypt are W.O.1/345, W.O.1/346, W.O.1/347, W.O.1/348, and W.O.1/349. These War Office files contain not only military reports but also political and economic reports for the years 1801–1816. The State Papers (S.P. 105 [Levant Company]) supply some useful data on trade in Egypt. The Board of Trade (B.T.) files, however, are disappointing. Statistical material on trade essential to the subject and forwarded by the British consuls in Egypt to the Board of Trade has recently been destroyed and copies do not exist. The Stratford Canning papers add little to Canning's official dispatches regarding Egypt contained in the Foreign Office files.

The United States, National Archives, Washington, D.C.

The Department of State records for Turkey, Vols. I–VIII, and Cyprus, Alexandria, Stancho, Vol. I, cover the period of this work. The separate Egypt series dates from 1849 only.

Materials here are not so rich as those in London and Paris, because American interests in the Levant were extremely limited and American representation almost nonexistent. In the early years of the nineteenth century American trade with the Ottoman Empire was chiefly under English protection and subject to the tariff and consular fees of the Levant Company, which had a monopoly on British trade in the Levant until its dissolution in 1825. Independent representation then became necessary and a Treaty of Commerce and Navigation between the United States and Turkey was consequently ratified in 1831. In 1832 John Gliddon, a British merchant in Alexandria, was appointed consular agent for the United States Government, and his son, George Gliddon, was appointed the same for Cairo. These and other consuls did not have direct access to Muḥammad ʻAlī during his reign, as only diplomatic representatives with the rank of consul-general could demand an audience with him. Throughout the reign of Muḥammad ʻAlī the Americans had to rely on foreign consuls-general to present their views to the Pasha. Direct diplomatic relations between the United States and Egypt only began in 1849 during the reign of ʻAbbās Pasha, when the United States Government appointed D. Smith McCauley to serve as America's first Consul-General to Egypt.

Published Works

Abū Yūsuf (Yaʻkūb b. Ibrāhīm) [Abou Yousof Yaʻkoub], *Le livre de l'impôt foncier (Kitāb el-Kharādj)*, trans. by E. Fagnan, Paris, 1921.
Basic theoretical study of land tenure in Islamic countries by early Ḥanafī jurist.

Aghnides, Nicolas, *An Introduction to Mohammedan Law and a Bibliography*, New York, 1916.

d'Allemagne, Henri René, *Les saint-simoniens, 1827–1837*, Paris, 1930.
An analysis of the theories of Count Claude Henri de Saint-Simon and a detailed account of the activities of his followers.

Altundag, Şinası, *Kavalalı Mehmet Ali Paşa isyanı: Mısır meselsi, 1831–1841*, Ankara, 1945.
Study of the Egyptian Question by a Turkish historian. His sources include material from the Turkish archives.

Arminjon, Pierre, *La situation économique et financière de l'Egypte, le Soudan égyptien*, Paris, 1911.
Historical section of little value for period covering the reign of Muḥammad ʻAlī. Draws upon conventional sources.

Artin, Yaqub [J.], "Essai sur les causes du renchérissement de la vie matérielle au Caire dans le courant du 19me siècle (1800 à 1907)," *Mémoires de l'Institut Egyptien*, V (Cairo, 1908), 57–116.
Contains some information about Egyptian agriculture and useful statistical information.

——— *The Right of Landed Property in Egypt*, trans. E. A. van Dyck, London, 1885.
Important nineteenth-century monograph dealing with the problems of land tenure in Egypt. The author describes the changes which occurred during the reign of Muḥammad 'Alī but fails to use his sources critically. This work has, in the past, influenced numerous Egyptian and European historians and economists. It is now out of date.

Audebeau, Charles and Victor Mosséri, "Le labourage en Egypte," *Bulletin de l'Institut Egyptien*, 5th Series, X (Cairo, March 1917).
Deals specifically with the problems of plowing in Egypt and the advantages of the traditional Egyptian plow.

Bainville, Jacques, "L'expédition française en Egypte (1798–1801)," in *Précis de l'histoire d'Egypte*, ed. Mohamed Zaky el-Ibrachy, Vol. III, Cairo, 1933.
Short historical summary of the French expedition to Egypt. Exaggerates the influence on Egypt of the French occupation.

Baldwin, George, *Political Recollections Relative to Egypt*, London, 1801.
The author was the British representative in Egypt at the close of the eighteenth century. He was finally recalled by the British Government owing to the decline in British trade in Egypt. He tells of the political anarchy existing in Egypt under Mamlūk domination.

Barker, John B. B., *Syria and Egypt under the Last Five Sultans of Turkey; being Experiences during Fifty Years of Mr. Consul-General Barker*, 2 vols., London, 1876.
A laudatory account of Consul-General John Barker by his son. Consul-General Barker represented the British Government in Egypt briefly during Muḥammad 'Alī's reign. The author exaggerates Barker's importance and supplies little information of interest. Barker's own dispatches to the Foreign Office at the time of the first Syrian War are of far greater value.

Barois, J., *Irrigation in Egypt*, trans. Major A. M. Miller, U.S. Congress, House of Representatives, 50th Cong., 2d Sess., Mis. Doc. No. 134, Washington, D.C., 1889.
A technical study of Egyptian irrigation written in the nineteenth century by an authority on irrigation problems. Not particularly useful for the period of Muḥammad 'Alī's reign but furnishes the historian with helpful information about Egyptian irrigation before the introduction of a well-developed system of perennial irrigation.

Becker, C. H., "Egypt," *The Encyclopedia of Islām*, ed. M. Th. Houtsma *et al.*, II (1927), 4–23.

——— *Islamstudien*, 2 vols., Leipzig, 1924.

Belin, Alphonse, *Etude sur la propriété foncière en pays musulman et spécialement en Turquie (rite hanéfite)*, Paris, 1862.
An important work for a study of the theory and practice of landholding in Turkey after the promulgation of the Ottoman Land Law of 1858. Throws considerable light on prevailing concepts regarding landholding in Islamic countries, especially Egypt.

Bendetti, Comte, "Mehemet Ali durant ses dernières années," *Revue des deux mondes*, 129 (June 1, 1895), 509–532.
A general account of the author's experiences in Egypt from 1840 until Muḥammad 'Alī's death. Of particular interest is his report of the financial embarrassments of the Egyptian Government, the events leading up to the Crisis of 1844 when signs of mental decay in Muḥammad 'Alī were first observed, and the final loss of the Pasha's mental faculties at the end of his career.

Benis, Adam Georges, *Une mission militaire polonaise en Egypte*, 2 vols., Société royale de géographie d'Egypte, publications spéciales, Cairo, 1938.
Contains Polish diplomatic and consular documents.

Bertrand, Henri-Gratien, *Napoleon at St. Helena*, trans. Frances Hume, New York, 1952.

——— *Campagne d'Egypte et de Syrie (1798–1799), mémoires pour servir à l'histoire de Napoléon, dictés par lui et publiés par le général Bertrand*, 2 vols., Paris, 1847.
Napoleon's own views on his work in Egypt seen in retrospect. Bonaparte's memory tends to fail him on occasion and he glosses over events which are distasteful to him. Nevertheless the work is an important account of the French Expedition by the man who was responsible for its successes and failures.

Boaz, T., *Egypt*, London, n.d.
An early nineteenth-century work which deals very generally with Egypt during the Muḥammad 'Alī regime. Has some useful appendices of weights, measures, and coins.

Boinet, A., "L'accroissement de la population en Egypte," *Bulletin de l'Institut Egyptien*, 2d Series, VII (Cairo, 1887), 272–295.

——— *Dictionnaire géographique de l'Egypte*, Cairo, 1899.
Useful reference work for Arabic spelling of Egyptian place-names.

Boutros Ghali, "Rapport de S.E. Boutros Pacha Ghali, membre de la commission d'enquête de l'impôt foncier, présenté à cette commission le 18 février 1880," *Répertoire de la législation et de l'administration égyptiennes*, ed. Philippe Gelat, Supplément, Alexandria, 1890.
On the subject of land taxes and legislation pertaining to them.

Bowring, John, *Autobiographical Recollections of Sir John Bowring*, London, 1877.
Contains very little about Egypt.

——— "Report on Egypt and Candia," A Report addressed to the Right Hon. Lord Viscount Palmerston and presented to both Houses of Parliament, House of Commons, Sessional Papers 1840, vol. XXI: *Reports from Commissioners*, vol. 6, London, 1840.
Published text of the MS in the Public Record Office (F.O. 78/381). An exhaustive study of the economic conditions of Egypt, based largely on statistics provided by the British Consul-General Patrick Campbell and by officials in the Egyptian Government. Although long considered an authoritative source, the report should be used with care, as it was believed by persons in Egypt and in the British Foreign Office that Bowring was in the pay of Muḥammad ʻAlī.

Bréhier, Louis, *L'Egypte de 1798 à 1900*, Paris, 1901.
A survey of Egyptian history in the nineteenth century. Is somewhat critical of Muḥammad ʻAlī.

Brown, Robert Hanbury, *History of the Barrage at the Head of the Delta of Egypt*, Cairo, 1896.
A brief historical account of the Barrage with special emphasis on the period following the British occupation. The early history of the project is inadequately dealt with.

Bulwer, Sir Henry Lytton, *The Life of Henry John Temple, Viscount Palmerston*, 3 vols., London, 1870–1874.

Burckhardt, John Lewis, *Arabic Proverbs; or the Manners and Customs of the Modern Egyptians, Illustrated from their Proverbial Sayings Current at Cairo*, 2d ed., London, 1875.
In addition to the proverbs, Burckhardt has included a description of cooperative farming in Egypt in the early years of Muḥammad ʻAlī's reign and gives statistical information of the revenues earned by the peasants participating in the cooperative venture. Also includes incidental information concerning Egyptian agriculture.

de Cadalvène, Ed. and J. de Breuvery, *L'Egypte et la Nubie*, 2 vols., Paris, 1841.
Traveler's account. Of limited usefulness.

Cameron, D. A., *Egypt in the 19th Century; or Mehemet Ali and His Successors until the British Occupation in 1882*, London, 1898.

Carré, Jean Marie, *Voyageurs et écrivains français en Egypte* (1517–1869), 2 vols., Cairo, 1932.
Many works were published by Europeans who visited Egypt briefly and then returned to their homes to write accounts of their travels. These writers, for the most part, never understood the country, the administration, or the people. Nevertheless their accounts are interesting because they sometimes convey bits of information which confirm other

sources, and they recreate something of the atmosphere of the early nineteenth century in Egypt as well as the prejudices of Europe in its relationship to Egypt. Carré's work is an important guide to the writings of French travelers to Egypt. Includes a short biography of each author and a critical evaluation of his work.

Cattaui, René, *Le règne de Mohamed Ali d'après les archives russes en Egypte*, Vol. I: *Correspondance des consuls de Russie en Egypte, 1819–1833*, Société royale de géographie d'Egypte, publications spéciales, Cairo, 1931; Vol. II, *La mission du Colonel Duhamel, 1834–1837*, Société royale de géographie d'Egypte, publications spéciales, Part 1, Rome, 1933, Part 2, Rome, 1935; Vol. III, *La mission du Comte Médem, 1837–1841, et la mission de M. Krehmer, 1841–1844*, Société royale de géographie d'Egypte, publications spéciales, Rome, 1936.
Contains extremely important Russian diplomatic and consular documents sent to the home government. Russian representatives were less impressed with the achievements of Muḥammad 'Alī than were their French counterparts and maintained a degree of objectivity.

Cattaui, René and Georges, *Mohamed-Aly et l'Europe*, Paris, 1950.

de Chabrol de Volvic, *Essai sur les mœurs des habitans modernes de l'Egypte*, in *Description de l'Egypte, Etat moderne*, 1st ed., Vol. II, Pt. 2, Paris, 1822.
Prepared by a French scholar accompanying Napoleon. Good description of Egyptian society before traditional relationships began to disintegrate in the conflict with Western ideas.

Charles-Roux, François, *Autour d'une route. L'Angleterre, l'Isthme de Suez et l'Egypte au XVIIIème siècle*, Paris, 1922.

——— *Bonaparte: Governor of Egypt*, trans. E. W. Dickes, London, 1937.
Defense of Napoleon's administration of Egypt by a French historian. Relies almost entirely on French sources.

——— *L'Egypte de 1801 à 1882*, in *Histoire de la nation égyptienne*, ed. Gabriel Hanotaux, Vol. VI, Paris, 1936.
A standard account. Deals favorably with the Muḥammad 'Alī dynasty.

——— *La production du coton en Egypte*, Paris, 1908.
Uncritical reliance on French sources resulting in numerous inaccuracies. Nevertheless the work stands as a useful monograph on the subject of Egyptian cotton cultivation in the nineteenth century.

——— *Thiers et Méhémet Ali*, Paris, 1951.

Clerget, Marcel, *Le Caire: Etude de géographie urbaine et d'histoire économique*, 2 vols., Paris, 1934.

Clot, A. B., *Aperçu général sur l'Egypte*, 2 vols., Paris, 1840.
A panegyric upon the Muḥammad 'Alī regime by a French doctor long in the employ of the Egyptian Pasha. If critically used, this work can serve as an indispensable source of useful information about life in Egypt during this period.

Colin, Auguste, "Lettres sur l'Egypte," Part 1, "Budget et administration," *Revue des deux mondes*, XIII (January 1, 1838), 101–114. Part 2, "Rétablissement de l'ancienne route de l'Inde," *Revue des deux mondes*, XIII (March 1, 1838), 236–248; Part 3, "Commerce," *Revue des deux mondes*, XVII (January 1, 1839), 63–81.
Contains some statistical information for governmental revenues and expenditures and for Egyptian trade.

Colucci, "Note de M. Colucci-Bey sur les mesures prises par S. A. Mehemet-Ali, relativement aux haras et à l'élevage des bestiaux," Séance of October 3, 1863, *Bulletin de l'Institut Egyptien*, IX (Alexandria, 1866).

Combe, Etienne, "L'Egypte ottomane de la conquête par Selim (1517) à l'arrivée de Bonaparte (1798)," in *Précis de l'histoire d'Egypte*, ed. Mohamed Zaky el-Ibrachy, Vol. III, Cairo, 1933.
Short but competent historical survey of Egypt under Ottoman rule.

Combes, Edmond, *Voyage en Egypte, en Nubie, dans les déserts de Beyouda, des Bicharys, et sur les côtes de la mer Rouge*, Paris, 1846.
Traveler's account.

Copies of Original Letters from the Army of General Bonaparte in Egypt Intercepted by the Fleet under the Command of Admiral Lord Nelson, 3 parts, London, 1798, 1799, 1800.
A fascinating collection of intercepted letters written by members of the French Expeditionary Force in Egypt. Many of the letters are highly critical of Egypt, Napoleon, and the French occupation. A salutary antidote to the customary eulogies upon the expedition.

Creasy, E. S., *History of the Ottoman Turks: from the beginning of their empire to the present time*, 2 vols., London, 1856.
Traditional approach to Ottoman history. Contains very little about Egypt.

Crouchley, A. E., *The Economic Development of Modern Egypt*, London, 1938.
An excellent historical account of economic developments in Egypt but needs to be revised to include the findings of recent research in European and Egyptian archives.

"De la culture du ver à soie en Egypte," Lecture given by the Secretary on a Mémoire of M. Grégoire at the Séance of November 4, 1859, *Bulletin de l'Institut Egyptien* (Marseilles, 1860).

Dennett, Daniel C., Jr., *Conversion and the Poll Tax in Early Islam*, Cambridge, Mass., 1950.
Important contribution to our knowledge about *jizyah* and *kharāj.*

Denon, Vivant, *Travels in Upper and Lower Egypt, during the Campaigns of General Bonaparte*, trans. E. A. Kendal, 2 vols., London, 1802.
First-hand account of the French Expedition by an artist who accompanied Napoleon. A splendid description of Egypt and Egyptian monuments by a keen observer.

Deny, Jean, *Sommaire des archives turques du Caire*, Société royale de géographie d'Egypte, publications spéciales, Cairo, 1930.
Indispensable for a study of the Egyptian administration. Not only does the author provide an inventory of the Turkish archives in Cairo, but he also describes the functions of government officials and government departments.

Description de l'Egypte; ou recueil des observations et des recherches qui ont été faites en Egypte pendant l'expédition de l'armée française. Etat moderne, 2 vols. in 3 parts, 1st ed., Paris, 1809, 1813, 1822.
A monumental work by the French *savants* who accompanied Napoleon to Egypt. Contains many articles dealing with all aspects of contemporary Egyptian life and institutions. An invaluable source.

——— *Planches*, Vol. I, 1st ed., Paris, 1809; *Planches de grand format*.
Maps of Egypt and illustrations of Egyptian scenes prepared by artists and draughtsmen who accompanied the French Expeditionary Forces to Egypt.

Digeon, J. M., *Nouveaux contes turcs et arabes*, 2 vols., Paris, 1779, 1781.
Vol. II contains French translation of the *Qānūn-nāmah* promulgated by Sulaymān the Magnificent after the Ottoman conquest of Egypt.

el-Djabarti. See al-Jabartī.

Dodwell, Henry, *The Founder of Modern Egypt: A Study of Muhammad Ali*, Cambridge, England, 1931.
A survey of Muḥammad 'Alī's career by an English historian who manipulates his material in order to reveal the Egyptian Pasha in the most favorable possible light.

Douin, Georges, *L'Angleterre et l'Egypte*, Vol. II: *La politique mameluke (1803–1807)*, Société royale de géographie d'Egypte, publications spéciales, Cairo, 1930.
A collection of official British and French dispatches and reports sent by representatives to their home governments.

——— *L'Egypte de 1802 à 1804*, Société royale de géographie d'Egypte, publications spéciales, Cairo, 1925.
A collection of official French dispatches and reports sent by representatives to the home government.

——— *L'Egypte de 1828 à 1830*, Société royale de géographie d'Egypte, publications spéciales, Rome, 1935.
A collection of official French dispatches and reports sent by representatives to the home government.

——— *La mission du Baron de Boislecomte. L'Egypte et la Syrie en 1833*, Société royale de géographie d'Egypte, publications spéciales, Cairo, 1927.
A collection of official French dispatches and reports sent by representatives to the home government.

——— *Une mission militaire française auprès de Mohamed Aly* (*Correspondance des Généraux Belliard et Boyer*), Société royale de géographie d'Egypte, publications spéciales, Cairo, 1923.
A collection of official French dispatches and reports sent by representatives to the home government.

——— *Mohamed Aly et l'expédition d'Alger* (*1829–1840*), Société royale de géographie d'Egypte, publications spéciales, Cairo, 1930.
A collection of official French dispatches and reports sent by representatives to the home government.

——— *Mohamed Aly, Pacha du Caire* (*1805–1807*), Société royale de géographie d'Egypte, publications spéciales, Cairo, 1926.
A collection of official French dispatches and reports sent by representatives to the home government.

——— *La première guerre de Syrie*, Vol. I: *La conquête de la Syrie* (*1831–1832*), Société royale de géographie d'Egypte, publications spéciales, Cairo, 1931; Vol. II: *La paix de Kutahia* (*1833*), Société royale de géographie d'Egypte, publications spéciales, Cairo, 1931.
A collection of official French dispatches and reports sent by representatives to the home government.

Douin, Georges and E. C. Fawtier-Jones, *L'Angleterre et l'Egypte*, Vol. I: *La politique mameluke* (*1801–1803*), Société royale de géographie d'Egypte, publications spéciales, Cairo, 1929.
A collection of official British and French dispatches and reports sent by representatives to their home governments.

——— *L'Angleterre et l'Egypte* (*La campagne de 1807*), Société royale de géographie d'Egypte, publications spéciales, Cairo, 1928.
A collection of official British and French dispatches and reports sent by representatives to their home governments.

Driault, Edouard, *L'Egypte et l'Europe. La crise de 1839–1841*, Vol. I: *Nezib—Le destin de l'empire ottoman* (*avril-octobre 1839*), Société royale de géographie d'Egypte, publications spéciales, Cairo, 1930; Vol. II: *L'intervention de l'Europe* (*novembre 1839–juin 1840*), Société royale de géographie d'Egypte, publications spéciales, Cairo, 1931; Vol. III: *L'Egypte et la France contre l'Europe* (*juillet-octobre 1840*), Société royale de géographie d'Egypte, publications spéciales, Cairo, 1931; Vol. IV: *Les négociations de la paix* (*novembre 1840-mars 1841*), Société royale de géographie d'Egypte, publications spéciales, Rome, 1933; Vol. V: *Les solutions—l'Egypte héréditaire dans la famille de Mohamed-Aly* (*mars-décembre 1841*), Société royale de géographie d'Egypte, publications spéciales, Rome, 1934.
A collection of official French dispatches and reports sent by representatives to the home government.

——— *L'expédition du Crète et de Morée* (*1823–1828*), Société royale de géographie d'Egypte, publications spéciales, Cairo, 1930.

A collection of official French dispatches and reports sent by representatives to the home government.

——— *La formation de l'empire de Mohamed Aly de l'Arabie au Soudan (1814–1823)*, Société royale de géographie d'Egypte, publications spéciales, Cairo, 1927.
A collection of official French dispatches and reports sent by representatives to the home government.

——— "Mohamed-Aly et Ibrahim," in *Précis de l'histoire d'Egypte*, ed. Mohamed Zaky el-Ibrachy, Vol. III, Cairo, 1933.
An uncritical work. Not to be relied upon.

——— *Mohamed Aly et Napoléon (1807–1814)*, Société royale de géographie d'Egypte, publications spéciales, Cairo, 1925.
A collection of official French dispatches and reports sent by representatives to the home government.

Dubois-Aymé, *Mémoire sur les tribus arabes des déserts de l'Egypte*, in *Description de l'Egypte, Etat moderne*, 1st ed., Vol. I, Paris, 1809.

Dubois-Aymé and Jollois, *Voyage dans l'intérieur du Delta, contenant des recherches géographiques sur quelques villes anciennes, et des observations sur les mœurs et les usages des Egyptiens modernes*, in *Description de l'Egypte, Etat moderne*, 1st ed., Vol. II, Paris, 1813.

Elgood, P. G., *Bonaparte's Adventure in Egypt*, Oxford Bookshelf Ed., London, 1936.
A frank appraisal of Napoleon's experiences in Egypt. Uses published British and French sources and relies upon al-Jabartī for his Egyptian source. Concludes that the French occupation was too short and its program too ambitious to have any lasting effects on Egypt.

Estève, Comte, *Mémoire sur les finances de l'Egypte depuis sa conquête par le sultan Selym Ier, jusqu'à celle du général en chef Bonaparte*, in *Description de l'Egypte, Etat moderne*, 1st ed., Vol. I, Paris, 1809.
Basic source for the study of Egyptian finances prepared by one of the experts who had accompanied Napoleon to Egypt and who was later appointed Director-General of the Egyptian Department of Finance by General Menou.

Fahmy, Moustafa, *La révolution de l'industrie en Egypte et ses conséquences sociales au 19e siècle (1800–1850)*, Leiden, 1954.
An uncritical study of Muḥammad 'Alī's industrial program. The author has somewhat exaggerated views concerning the social consequence of this industrial program and insists that Egyptian industrial development atrophied after the signing of the Anglo-Turkish Commercial Treaty of 1838.

al-Gabartī. See al-Jabartī.

Gatteschi, D., "Mémoire sur le droit de propriété foncière dans l'empire ottoman et en Egypte," *Bulletin de l'Institut Egyptien*, X (Alexandria, 1869), 42–49, 51–60.

Discusses historical and legal background of property rights in Egypt.

——— *Real Property, Mortgage and Wakf according to Ottoman Law*, trans. Edward A. van Dyck, London, 1884.

A nineteenth-century study of Ottoman law as it applied to problems of land tenure.

Gelat, Philippe, ed., *Répertoire de la législation et de l'administration égyptiennes*, Alexandria, 1887–1897.

The French edition of an encyclopedia of legislative and administrative acts and also explanatory articles concerning these acts. Constitutes an important collection of Egyptian legal documents in translation.

Ghorbal, Shafik, *The Beginnings of the Egyptian Question and the Rise of Mehemet Ali*, London, 1928.

A first-rate account of the years between the expulsion of the French from Egypt and the seizure of power by Muḥammad 'Alī. Draws heavily upon material in the British archives.

——— "Miṣr 'inda mafriq aṭ-ṭuruq 1798–1801," *Majallat Kullīyat al-Âdāb, Bulletin of the Faculty of Arts*, IV, Pt. 1 (Cairo, 1938).

Reproduction of a memorandum by Ḥusayn Efendī, an official in the *Rūznāmah* during the French occupation.

——— *Muḥammad 'Alī al-Kabīr*, Cairo, 1944.

A popular account of the Pasha's career.

Gibb, H. A. R. and Harold Bowen, *Islamic Society and the West*, Vol. I: *Islamic Society in the Eighteenth Century*, 2 parts, London, 1950, 1957.

A splendid study of Islamic society and Islamic institutions by two distinguished British Orientalists. The work is based on the most intensive research in European and Oriental sources and reflects the authors' profound understanding of the Islamic world.

Girard, P. S., *Mémoire sur l'agriculture, l'industrie et le commerce de l'Egypte*, in *Description de l'Egypte, Etat moderne*, 1st ed., Vol. II, Paris, 1813.

Study of economic institutions in Egypt at the end of the eighteenth century. This important source is based on the author's personal observations and data collected while he was in Egypt.

Gliddon, George R., *A Memoir on the Cotton of Egypt*, London, 1841.

Served as United States consul at Cairo. Describes cotton cultivation during Muḥammad 'Alī's reign and criticizes the Pasha's monopolistic practices.

Gouin, Edouard, *L'Egypte au XIX siècle*, Paris, 1847.

Gouvernement égyptien, Ministère des Finances, *La législation en matière immobilière en Egypte; recueil des lois, règlements et instructions administratives relatifs à la propriété immobilière*, 2d ed., Cairo, 1901.

Deals with real property, land taxation, and irrigation laws.

Grégoire, "De la culture du coton en Egypte," *Mémoires de l'Institut Egyptien*, I (Paris, 1862), 437–478.
Historical survey of cotton cultivation in Egypt.

Guémard, Gabriel Alphonse, *Les réformes en Egypte* (*d'Ali-Bey el Kébir à Mehemet-Ali*) (*1760–1848*), Cairo, 1936.
Emphasizes military reforms.

Hamilton, William Richard, *Remarks on Several Parts of Turkey*, Part I: *Aegyptiaca, or, Some Account of the Antient and Modern State of Egypt, as Obtained in the Years 1801, 1802*, London, 1809.

Hammer-Purgstall, Joseph, *Des Osmanischen Reichs Staatsverfassung und Staatsverwaltung dargestellt aus den Quellen seiner Grundgesetze*, Vienna, 1815.
Pioneer study of the Ottoman government based on Turkish sources. Now out of date, but still an important source.

Hamont, Pierre Nicolas, *L'Egypte sous Méhémet-Ali*, 2 vols., Paris, 1843.
A bitter indictment of Muḥammad 'Alī's government. Contains much valuable material on government, economics, and society during this period but should be used cautiously.

Ḥanayn, Jirjis [Girgis], *Al-aṭyān wa'ḍ-ḍarā'ib fī 'l-quṭr al-miṣrī*, Cairo, 1904.
Deals with problems of land tenure and taxes in Egypt.

Hanotaux, Gabriel, ed., *Histoire de la nation égyptienne*, 7 vols., Paris, 1931–1940.
An uneven but valuable collection of works on all periods of Egyptian history prepared by a distinguished group of historians.

Hasenclever, Adolf, *Geschichte Egyptens in 19 jahrhundert 1798–1914*, Halle, 1917.
Still one of the best general surveys of nineteenth-century Egyptian history.

Henniker, Sir Frederick, *Notes during a Visit to Egypt, Nubia, the Oasis, Mount Sinai, and Jerusalem*, London, 1823.
A traveler's account. Of little use but reflects amusing prejudices.

Heyworth-Dunne, J. [Gamal-Eddine], *An Introduction to the History of Education in Modern Egypt*, London, n.d. [1938].
A balanced re-evaluation of Egyptian educational policies in the nineteenth century. Commendable for its critical use of the sources.

——— *Land Tenure in Islam 630 A.D.–1951 A.D.*, in *The Muslim World Series*, No. 3, Cairo, 1952.
Brief historical survey of traditional Muslim concepts regarding land tenure and a translation of a *fatwā* on private property dated April 18, 1948.

al-Ḥitta, Aḥmad Aḥmad, "Marāji' ta'rīkh az-zirā'ah al-miṣrīyah fī 'ahd Muḥammad 'Alī," *al-Majallah at-Ta'rīkhīyah al-Miṣrīyah*, Société royale d'études historiques, I, Nos. 1–2 (1948), 239–254.

Good bibliographical article which lists the sources for the study of the history of Egyptian agriculture at the time of Muḥammad ʻAlī.

——— *Ta'rīkh az-zirāʻah al-miṣrīyah fī ʻahd Muḥammad ʻAlī al-Kabīr*, Cairo, A. H. 1369 (1950).
Draws too heavily on European and Egyptian secondary sources rather than on Egyptian archives.

Hurst, H. E., *The Nile*, London, 1952.
Survey of the history of the river, irrigation problems, and life along its banks.

el-Ibrachy, Mohamed Zeky, ed., *Précis de l'histoire d'Egypte*, 4 vols., Cairo, Rome, 1932, 1933, 1934.
Surveys briefly all of Egyptian history. The separate studies made by different contributors vary greatly in value. Sections dealing with the Muḥammad ʻAlī dynasty reflect an understandable though regrettable lack of critical analysis.

Issawi, Charles, *Egypt at Mid-Century*, London, 1954.
A good economic survey of Egypt.

al-Jabartī, ʻAbd ar-Raḥmān, *Merveilles biographiques et historiques ou chroniques du Abd-el-Rahman el Djabarti*, trans. Chefik Mansour Bey, Abdulaziz Kahil Bey, Gabriel Nicolas Kahil Bey, and Iskender Ammoun Effendi, 9 vols., Cairo, 1888–1896 (in Arabic, *ʻAjā'ib al-âthār fī 't-tarājim wa'l-akhbār*, 4 vols., Cairo, 1322/1904–05).
Invaluable as source for the early period of Muḥammad ʻAlī's reign. Probably the principal Egyptian source for 1805–1820, because the fire in the Citadel in 1820 destroyed important documents. Translation is faulty and calls for scholar's use of the original Arabic text in conjunction with it. Each reference to the French edition is accompanied by the corresponding reference in the Arabic text.

Jacotin, *Mémoire sur la construction de la carte d'Egypte*, in *Description de l'Egypte, Etat moderne*, 1st ed., Vol. II, Pt. 2, Paris, 1822.
A description of procedures used in drawing the map of Egypt included in this publication.

——— *Tableau de la superficie de l'Egypte*, in *Description de l'Egypte, Etat moderne*, 1st ed., Vol. II, Pt. 2, Paris, 1822.

Jallād, Filib. See Philippe Gelat.

Jaubert, Amédée, *Nomenclature des tribus d'arabes qui campent entre l'Egypte et la Palestine depuis khân Younes et Ghazzah jusqu'à l'Oronte, et dans la partie septentrionale du désert qui sépare la Mecque de la Syrie*, in *Description de l'Egypte, Etat moderne*, 1st ed., Vol. II, Paris, 1813.

Jomard, Edme. François, *Coup d'œil impartial sur l'état présent de l'Egypte, comparé à sa situation antérieure*, Paris, 1836.
A slight book in which author fails to be impartial. Rather, he is uncritical in his praise of Muḥammad ʻAlī's accomplishments.

——— *Observations sur les arabes de l'Egypte moyenne*, in *Description de l'Egypte, Etat moderne*, 1st ed., Vol. I, Paris, 1809.

de la Jonquière, A., *L'expédition d'Egypte*, 5 vols., Paris, 1900.
A detailed study of the French expedition to Egypt.

——— *Histoire de l'empire ottoman depuis les origines jusqu'au traité de Berlin*, Paris, 1881.
Brief survey of Ottoman history.

Jorga, N., *Geschichte des Osmanischen Reiches*, 5 vols., Gotha, 1913.

Juchereau de Saint-Denys, Antoine de, *Histoire de l'empire ottoman depuis 1792 jusqu'en 1844*, Paris, 1844.

Lā'iḥat zirā'at al-fallāḥ watadbīr aḥkām as-siyāsah biqaṣd an-najāḥ, 2d ed., Būlāq, Dhū'l-Ḥijjah 1, A.H. 1258 (January 3, 1843).
Administrative code issued by Muḥammad 'Alī; deals specifically with the duties and obligations of the *fallāḥīn* and government officials regarding agricultural production, with village industries, and with punishments set for infringement of the rules in the *qānūn*.

Lambton, Ann Katherine Swynford, *Landlord and Peasant in Persia. A Study of Land Tenure and Land Revenue Administration*, London, 1953.
A masterful work based on intensive study in the sources and on personal observation in Persia. Attention has been given to both the theory and practice of land tenure and land revenue administration from the time of the Arab conquest to the present.

Lancret, Michel-Ange, *Mémoire sur le système d'imposition territoriale et sur l'administration des provinces de l'Egypte, dans les dernières années du gouvernement des Mamlouks*, in *Description de l'Egypte, Etat moderne*, 1st ed., Vol. I, Paris, 1809.
An important source for study of government and taxation in Egypt at the end of the eighteenth century. Prepared by one of the *savants* who accompanied Napoleon to Egypt.

Lancret, Michel-Ange and de Chabrol, *Mémoire sur le canal d'Alexandrie*, in *Description de l'Egypte, Etat moderne*, 1st ed., Vol. II, Paris, 1813.
A description of the old Canal of Alexandria which was later destroyed by Muḥammad 'Alī and replaced by Canal al-Maḥmūdīyah.

Lane, Edward William, *The Manners and Customs of the Modern Egyptians*, Everyman Ed., London, 1944.
Invaluable source for information about people of Egypt in Muḥammad 'Alī's reign, less useful regarding political institutions and administration.

Lane-Poole, Stanley, *The Life of the Rt. Honourable Stratford Canning Viscount Stratford de Redcliffe*, 2 vols., London, 1888.
Based on official documents and the private papers of Stratford Canning. Has been corrected although not superceded by a more recent biography.

Leake, Lieutenant-Colonel W. M., *Map of Egypt*, London, January 2, 1818.

Leiper, Dr. R. T., "La production expérimentale des bilharzioses égyptiennes," *Bulletin de l'Institut Egyptien*, 5th series, X (Cairo, March 1917).

Le Père Ainé, *Mémoire sur la vallée du Nil et le nilomètre de l'île de Roudah*, in *Description de l'Egypte, Etat moderne*, 1st ed., Vol. II, Pt. 2, Paris, 1822.

Le Père, Gratien, *Extrait d'un mémoire sur les lacs et les déserts de la basse Egypte*, in *Description de l'Egypte, Etat moderne*, 1st ed., Vol. II, Paris, 1813.

Le Père, J. M., *Mémoire sur la communication de la mer des Indes à la Méditerranée par la mer Rouge et l'isthme de Soueys*, in *Description de l'Egypte, Etat moderne*, 1st ed., Vol. I, Paris, 1809.

Lewis, Bernard, "The Islamic Guilds," *The Economic History Review*, VIII, No. 1 (November 1937), 20–37.

——— "The Ottoman Archives as a Source for the History of the Arab Lands," *Journal Royal Asiatic Society*, Parts 3, 4 (1951).

Linant de Bellefonds, M. A., *Carte hydrographique de la Basse Egypte et d'une partie de l'Isthme de Suez où sont indiqués les travaux exécutés ou à exécuter d'après les ordres de son altesse Méhémet-Ali vice-roi d'Egypte. Avec le projet de la communication directe des deux mers au travers de l'Isthme*, Paris, 1855.

——— *Carte hydrographique de la Moyenne Egypte etc.*, Paris, 1854.

——— *Carte hydrographique de la Haute Egypte etc.*, Paris, 1855.

——— *Mémoires sur les principaux travaux d'utilité publique executés en Egypte depuis la plus haute antiquité jusqu'à nos jours*, Paris, 1872, 1873.
Linant was a French engineer who served Muḥammad 'Alī in that capacity for many years. This work serves as an important source of information regarding the irrigation works.

Lokke, Carl Ludwig, "The French Agricultural Mission to Egypt in 1801," *Agricultural History*, X, No. 3 (July 1936), 111–117.

Løkkegaard, Frede, *Islamic Taxation in the Classic Period*, Copenhagen, 1950.
Traces the evolution of Islamic theory of taxation. This work contributes greatly to an understanding of the problem of land tenure in Islamic countries, especially in Iraq.

Lorin, Henri, *Bibliographie géographique de l'Egypte*, Société royale de géographie de l'Egypte, 2 vols., Cairo, 1928, 1929.

Lybyer, Albert Howe, *The Government of the Ottoman Empire in the Time of Suleiman the Magnificent*, Cambridge, Mass., 1913.
A good study of Ottoman institutions. Should be used in conjunction with Gibb and Bowen's *Islamic Society and the West*, Vol. I: *Islamic Society in the Eighteenth Century*.

MacBrair, Robert Maxwell, *Sketches of a Missionary's Travels in Egypt, Syria, Western Africa, etc.*, London, 1839.
A traveler's account.

Madden, R. R., *Egypt and Mohamed Ali*, London, 1841.
Critical of the Pasha's government.

——— *Travels in Turkey, Egypt, Nubia, and Palestine in 1824, 1825, 1826, and 1827*, 2 vols., London, 1829.
Describes the oppressive aspects of the Muḥammad 'Alī regime.

Makrizi, Taki-eddin-Ahmed, "Description topographique et historique de l'Egypte," Parts 1 and 2, trans. U. Bouriant, *Mission archéologique au Caire, Mémoires*, XVII (1895); Part 3, trans. Paul Casanova, *Institut Français d'Archéologie Orientale du Caire, Mémoire*, III (1906).

——— "Histoire d'Egypte de Makrizi," trans. Edg. Blochet, *Revue de l'Orient Latin*, VI (1898), 435–489; VIII (1900–1901), 165–212, 501–553; IX (1902), 6–163, 466–530; X, (1903–1904), 248–371; XI (1905–1908), 192–260.

——— *Histoire des sultans mamlouks de l'Egypte*, trans., Etienne Marc Quatremère, 2 vols., Paris, 1837.

Malcolm-Smith, E. F., *The Life of Stratford Canning, Lord Stratford de Redcliffe*, London, 1933.
A more objective biography of Stratford Canning than Lane-Poole's.

Marcel, J., *Egypte depuis la conquête des arabes jusqu'à la domination française*, in *L'univers. Histoire et description de tous les peuples. Egypte*, Paris, 1877.
A brief survey of Egyptian history dealing with the Arab, Mamlūk, and Ottoman periods.

Marin, Scipion, *La vérité sur les affaires d'orient, après des études faites sur lieux de l'Egypte et de la Turquie*, Paris, 1841.
A political tract by a journalist who had come to Egypt to work in his profession but had left in disgust. One of the few Frenchmen to write unfavorably about the Muḥammad 'Alī regime.

Martin, P. D., *Description hydrographique des provinces de Beny-Soueyf et du Fayoum*, in *Description de l'Egypte, Etat moderne*, 1st ed., Vol. II, Paris, 1813.

Masson, Paul, *Histoire du commerce français dans le Levant au XVIIIe siècle*, Paris, 1911.

Maunier, René, *Bibliographie économique, juridique et sociale de l'Egypte moderne (1798–1916)*, in *Travaux spéciaux de la société sultanieh d'économie politique, de statistique et de législation*, No. 1, Cairo, 1918.

Mazuel, Jean, *L'œuvre géographique de Linant de Bellefonds*, Société royale de géographie d'Egypte, publications spéciales, Cairo, 1937.
Adds nothing to Linant's book.

——— *Le sucre en Egypte*, Cairo, 1937.
Deals briefly with the development of the sugar industry by Muḥammad 'Alī and then goes on to describe the expansion which took place later on in the nineteenth and twentieth centuries.

Memoirs relative to Egypt, written in that Country during the Campaigns of General Bonaparte in the Years 1798 and 1799 by the Learned and Scientific Men who accompanied the French Expedition, trans. from the French, London, 1800.
Learned articles on various subjects by some of the experts who came to Egypt with Napoleon.

Mengin, Felix, *Histoire de l'Egypte sous le gouvernement du Mohammed-Aly; ou récit des événemens politiques et militaires qui ont eu lieu depuis le départ des français jusqu'en 1823*, 2 vols., Paris, 1823.
A study of Muḥammad 'Alī's regime in its early years by a sympathetic observer. Should be used with extreme caution.

——— *Histoire sommaire de l'Egypte sous le gouvernement de Mohamed Ali (1823–1838)*, Paris, 1839.
Brings Mengin's earlier work up to date.

Merruau, Paul, *L'Egypte contemporaine, 1840–1857, de Méhémet-Ali à Said Pacha*, Paris, 1858.
Propaganda for the Egyptian ruling house. Not to be relied upon.

Michaud, J., "Lettre sur l'Egypte," *Revue des deux mondes*, III (September 1834), 671–685.
Traveler's impressions of Egypt.

Michaud, J. and Baptistin Poujoulat, *Correspondance d'orient par M. Michaud et M. Poujoulat*, Vols. V, VI, VII, Paris, 1834, 1835.

Mouriez, Paul, *Histoire de Méhémet-Ali, vice-roi d'Egypte*, 4 vols., Paris, 1855–1858.
Biased in favor of the Pasha. Should be used cautiously.

——— *Notes et documents historiques*, Paris, 1857.

Nahas, Joseph F., *Situation économique et sociale du fellah égyptien*, Paris, 1901.
A slight work. Sees Muḥammad 'Alī's economic policies as socialistic in character.

Nahum, Hayyīm, *Recueil de firmans impériaux ottomans adressés aux valis et aux khédives d'Egypte, 1006 H–1322 H (1597 J.C.–1904 J.C.)*, Cairo, 1934.
A useful collection of Ottoman imperial firmans translated from Turkish into French.

Nakoula el-Turk, *Histoire de l'expédition des français en Egypte*, trans., Alix Desgranges ainé, Paris, 1839.
An eye-witness account of the French occupation of Egypt by a Syrian Christian. Is particularly interesting when contrasted with the observations of his Muslim contemporary, al-Jabartī.

Norden, Frederick Lewis, *Travels in Egypt and Nubia*, trans., Dr. Peter Templeman, London, 1758.
A description of a trip to Egypt in 1737 and 1738 by an officer in the Danish navy.

Olin, Stephen, *Travels in Egypt, Arabia, Petraea, and the Holy Land*, 2 vols., New York, 1843.
A traveler's account.

Olivier, Guillaume Antoine, *Voyage dans l'empire othoman, l'Egypte, et la Perse*, 3 vols., Paris, 1801–1807.
A traveler's account. Describes conditions in Egypt at the end of the eighteenth century.

P. and H., *Egypte sous la domination de Méhémet Aly*, in *L'univers. Histoire et description de tous les peuples. Egypte*, Paris, 1877.
A bitter indictment of the Muḥammad 'Alī regime. This work is especially interesting because it repeats some of the gossip which circulated in Egypt during this period.

Paton, A. A., *A History of the Egyptian Revolution*, 2d ed., 2 vols., London, 1870.
The historical sections of this work are out of date, but the author's personal observations of life and society in Egypt in the last years of Muḥammad 'Alī's reign remain a valuable contemporary source.

Poliak, A. N., *Feudalism in Egypt, Syria, Palestine, and the Lebanon, 1250–1900*, London, 1939.
Interesting but not dependable. Attempts unsuccessfully to fit Middle Eastern institutions into the mold of European feudal institutions.

Polites, Athanasios G., *L'hellénisme et l'Egypte moderne*, Vol. I: *Histoire de l'hellénisme égyptien de 1798 à 1927*, Paris, 1929; Vol. II: *Contribution de l'hellénisme au développement de l'Egypte moderne*, Paris, 1930.
History of the Greek community in Egypt and an analysis of the specific contributions made by the Greeks in the development of modern Egypt.

Politis, Athanese G. [Athanasios G. Polites], *Le conflit turco-égyptien de 1838–1841 et les dernières années du règne de Mohamed Aly, d'après les documents diplomatiques grecs*, Société royale de géographie d'Egypte, publications spéciales, Cairo, 1931.
Collection of Greek diplomatic documents.

——— *Les rapports de la Grèce et de l'Egypte pendant le règne de Mohamed Aly (1833–1849)*, Rome, 1935.
Collection of Greek diplomatic documents.

Poujoulat, Baptistin, *Voyage à Constantinople dans l'Asie Mineure, en Mésopotamie, à Palmyre, en Syrie, en Palestine, et en Egypte*, 2 vols., Paris, 1840, 1841.
Traveler's account.

Prokesch-Osten, Anton, *Mehemed-Ali vize-König von Aegypten. Aus meinem Tagebuch, 1826–1841*, Vienna, 1877.
A description of Egypt and its ruler by the diplomatic representative from Austria.

Pückler-Muskau, Hermann, prince von, *Egypt and Mehemet Ali*, trans. H. Evans Lloyd, London, 1845.
The prince was enormously impressed by his host, Muḥammad ʻAlī, and presents the Pasha's views. He seems to have made no attempt to examine conditions for himself or to reach an independent judgment of the true situation.

Puryear, Vernon John, *International Economics and Diplomacy in the Near East*, Stanford, 1935.
A good general survey.

Qānūn al-Chafālik, Būlāq, Ṣafar, A. H. 1259 (March 1843).
Deals with the administration of the *chifliks* or the private domains of the royal family and favorites who received concessions of land from Muḥammad ʻAlī.

Qānūn as-Siyāsat-nāmah. See Zaghlūl, Aḥmad Fatḥī.

ar-Rafi'ī, ʻAbd ar-Raḥmān, *Ta'rīkh al-ḥarakah al-qawmīyah*, 3 vols., Cairo, 1929–1930.
A history of Egypt's development by an Egyptian historian. The Muḥammad ʻAlī period is treated in Vol. 3.

de Regny, E., "Notice sur l'introduction de la culture du coton en Egypte et sur Jumel," *Bulletin de l'Institut Egyptien* (Cairo, 1876), 78–84.

Rifaat, Mohammed, *The Awakening of Modern Egypt*, London, 1947. The section on Muḥammad ʻAlī is weak.

Rigault, Georges, *Le Général Abdallah Menou et la dernière phase de l'expédition d'Egypte (1799–1801)*, Paris, 1911.
An excellent objective study of the last stage of the French occupation of Egypt. The author draws upon sources sometimes overlooked by other writers.

Rodkey, Frederick S., "The Attempts of Briggs and Company to Guide British Policy in the Levant in the Interest of Mehemet Ali Pasha, 1821–1841," *Journal of Modern History*, V (1933), 324–351.

Rustum, Asad [Assad] Jibrail, *Materials for a Corpus of Arabic Documents relating to the History of Syria under Mehemet Ali Pasha*, 5 vols., Beirut, 1930–34.
A collection of Arabic documents.

——— ed., *Les campagnes d'Ibrahim Pacha en Syrie et en Asie Mineure 1831–1840*, Heliopolis, Egypt, n.d.
A collection of Arabic documents.

Ryme, Amédée, *Egypte sous la domination française*, in *L'univers. Histoire et description de tous les peuples, Egypte*, Paris, 1877.
A brief survey of the French occupation. Traditional French view of the benefits derived from French rule.

Sabry, Mohammed, *L'empire égyptien sous Mohamed-Ali et la question d'Orient, 1811–1849*, Paris, 1930.
A diplomatic history of the Eastern Question based on research in the French, British, and Austrian archives. Deals sympathetically with the Muḥammad 'Alī regime in Egypt and in the conquered countries.

Saint-Marc Giradin, "Mehemet Ali," *Revue des deux mondes*, XXIII (September 1840).
Uses comments on Clot's book which he is reviewing in this article as starting point for his own analysis of the Egyptian ruler.

Sāmī, Amīn, *Taqwīm an-Nīl*, 6 vols., Cairo, A. H. 1334–1355 (1916–1935).

Sammarco, Angelo, *Histoire de l'Egypte moderne, 1801–1882*, Cairo, 1937.
A general survey of the period. Favorable to the Muḥammad 'Alī dynasty.

——— *Il regno di Mohammed Ali nei documenti diplomatici italiani inediti*, Vol. VIII: *Genesi e primo svolgimento della crisi egiziano-orientale del 1831–1833 (gennaio 1831-gennaio 1832)*, Société royale de géographie d'Egypte, publications spéciales, Rome, 1931; Vol. IX: *La presa di San Giovanni d'Acri (febbraio-guigno, 1832)*, Société royale de géographie d'Egypte, publications spéciales, Rome, 1932; Vol. X: *La conquisto egiziana della Siria (luglio-ottobre, 1832)*, Société royale de géographie d'Egypte, publications spéciales, Rome, 1932.
Collection of Italian diplomatic documents.

Samuel-Bernard, *Mémoire sur les monnoies d'Egypte*, in *Descripton de l'Egypte, Etat moderne*, 1st ed., Vol. II, Paris, 1813.
Indispensable source for a study of currency in Egypt at the end of the eighteenth century.

Savary, C. E., *Lettres sur l'Egypte*, 2d ed., 3 vols., Paris, 1786.
Collection of letters by an observant eighteenth-century traveler.

Schoelcher, Victor, *L'Egypte en 1845*, Paris, 1846.
Traveler's account.

Schweinfurth, "Sur la flore des anciens jardins arabes d'Egypte," *Bulletin de l'Institut Egyptien*, 2d Series, VIII (Cairo, 1888), 294–337.

Scott, C. Rochfort, *Rambles in Egypt and Candia, with details of the military power and resources of those countries, and observations on the government, policy, and commercial system of Mohammed Ali*, London, 1837.
A traveler's account.

Sékaly, A., "Le problème des wakfs en Egypte," *Revue des études islamiques*, Cahier I, II, III, IV (1929), 75–126, 277–338, 395–454, 601–659.
The question of family *waqfs* in modern Egypt is of special interest in view of Muḥammad 'Alī's policy with regard to *waqfs* and *rizqahs*.

Shaw, Stanford J., "The Financial and Administrative Organization and Development of Ottoman Egypt, (1517–1798)," unpublished dissertation presented to the Faculty of Princeton University in candidacy for the degree of Doctor of Philosophy, June 1958.
An important study. His sources include new material from the Turkish and Egyptian archives.

Silvestre de Sacy, "Sur la nature et les révolutions du droit de propriété territoriale en Egypte, depuis la conquête de ce pays par les musulmans jusqu'à l'expédition de François," Part 1, *Mémoires de l'Institut Royal de France, classe d'histoire et de littérature ancienne*, I (Paris, 1815), 1–165; Part 2, *Mémoires de l'Institut Royal de France, académie des inscriptions et belles-lettres*, V (Paris, 1821), 1–75; Part 3, *Mémoires de l'Institut Royal de France, académie des inscriptions et belles-lettres*, VII (Paris, 1824), 55–124.
A significant work based on Arabic sources. One of the earliest attempts by a European Orientalist to explain the evolution of landholding in Egypt. Has been superseded by the work of other scholars but continues to be useful.

Sonnini de Manoncourt, Charles Nicolas Sigisbert, *Voyage dans la haute et basse Egypte, fait par ordre de l'ancien gouvernement, et contenant des observations de tous genres*, Paris, 1799.
A traveler's account.

St. John, James Augustus, *Egypt and Mohammed Ali, or Travels in the Valley of the Nile*, 2 vols., London, 1834.
A traveler's account.

——— *Egypt and Nubia; their scenery and their people*, London, 1845.

Temperley, Harold, *The Crimea—England and the Near East*, London, 1936.
A diplomatic history based on a thorough study of British documents. The best work on the subject.

Tewfik, Mohamed M., *L'abolition du système de l'Iltizam sous le règne de Mohamed Ali*, trans. from the Arabic by Ibrahim El Mouelhy, in *Etude documentaire sur l'histoire de l'Egypte moderne*, Cairo, 1941.
A brief and not very profound study of the subject.

Thédénat-Duvent, P. P., *L'Egypte sous Méhémed-Ali, ou aperçu rapide de l'administration civile et militaire de ce Pacha*, Paris, 1822.
A slight work of little importance.

Toussoun, Omar, *Le cadastre de Mohammed Ali*, in *Mémoires de la société royale d'archéologie d'Alexandrie*, Vol. VIII, Cairo, 1936.
Not reliable.

——— *Mémoire sur les finances de l'Egypte depuis les pharaons jusqu'à nos jours*, in *Mémoires présentés à la société archéologique d'Alexandrie*, Vol. II, Cairo, 1924.
Bases his work on European authors. Has introduced no new material from his own research in the Egyptian archives.

——— *Mémoire sur l'histoire du Nil*, in *Mémoires présentés à l'Institut d'Egypte*, Vols. VIII, IX, X, Cairo, 1925.
A general study of the subject.

'Umar Ṭūsūn. See Toussoun, Omar.

de Vaulabelle, A., *Histoire moderne de l'Egypte (1801–1834)*, in *Histoire scientifique et militaire de l'expédition française en Egypte*, Vols. IX, X, Paris, 1830–1836.
Adds little new material but is a useful summary.

Viesse de Marmont, Auguste Frédéric Louis, duc de Raguse, *The Present State of the Turkish Empire*, trans. Col. Sir Frederic Smith, 2d ed., London, 1854.
A traveler's account.

Volney, C. F. C., *Travels through Syria and Egypt in the Years 1783, 1784, and 1785*, trans. from the French, 2 vols., Dublin, 1793.
The author was one of the keener observers among the eighteenth-century travelers. His report on conditions in the latter part of the eighteenth century serve as valuable background material.

al-Waqā'i' al-Miṣrīyah
Government gazette containing official reports, commands, and decisions of the government, in both Arabic and Turkish. As an official publication, it did not reflect the opinions of the Egyptian people.

War Office, *Lower Egypt in 4 Sheets compiled at the Intelligence Branch War Office, from the original French Survey in 1818 by M. Jacotin, from the Manuscript of Mahmud Bey and from the most recent Information*, lithographed at the Intelligence Department, War Office, June, 1882.
Map is not based on a new survey but brings the earlier French survey up to date.

Warburton, Eliot, *The Crescent and the Cross; or, Romance and Realities of Eastern Travel*, 2 vols., New York, 1845.
A traveler's account.

Webster, Sir Charles, *The Foreign Policy of Palmerston 1830–1841. Britain, the Liberal Movement and the Eastern Question*, 2 vols., London, 1951.
The causes for Palmerston's opposition to Muḥammad 'Alī are thoroughly explored. The author bases his study on the public and private papers of Lord Palmerston.

Wiet, Gaston, ed. and tr., *Nicolas Turc. Chronique d'Egypte 1798–1804*, Cairo, 1950.
A recent translation of this interesting Arabic source. See Nakoula el-Turk.

Wilkinson, Sir Gardner, *Modern Egypt and Thebes; being a Description of Egypt; including the Information Required for Travellers in that Country*, 2 vols., London, 1843.
A traveler's account. Contains useful information on weights and measures and local currency.

Willcocks, W., *Egyptian Irrigation*, London, 1889.
An analysis of the problems of Egyptian irrigation by a British irrigation engineer who served as an inspector in the Egyptian Irrigation Department.

Wilson, Sir Robert Thomas, *History of the British Expedition to Egypt*, 2d ed., London, 1803.

Wood, Alfred C., *A History of the Levant Company*, London, 1935.
The best work on the subject.

Worms, Dr., "Recherches sur la constitution de la propriété territoriale dans les pays musulmans," *Journal asiatique*, I (1843), 126–178.
An analysis of the nature of landholding in Muslim lands.

Yates, William Holt, *The Modern History and Conditions of Egypt, Its Climate, Diseases, and Capabilities; Exhibited in a Personal Narrative of Travels in that Country; with an Account of the Proceedings of Mohammed Ali Pasha from 1801 to 1843; Interspersed with Illustrations of Scripture History, the Fulfilment of Prophecy and the Progress of Civilization in the East*, 2 vols., London, 1843.
A traveler's account.

Zaghlūl, Aḥmad Fatḥī, *al-Muḥāmāh*, Cairo, 1900. Contains a reproduction of the *Qānūn as-Siyāsat-nāmah*, Būlaq, Rabī'al-Awwal, A.H. 1253 (June, 1837), official regulation reorganizing the Egyptian administration.

Zinkeisen, Johann Wilhelm, *Geschichte der europäischen Staaten, Geschichte des osmanischen Reiches in Europa*, Vol. VII, Gotha, 1863.

NOTES

Chapter I. Introduction

1. Salīm had appointed Khayr Bey, a Circassian chief who had supported him, as the first *Beylerbeyi* or Pasha of Egypt. The principal limitations on Khayr Bey's authority included the obligation to remit a fixed sum annually to Istanbul and to accept control by the military establishment of 12,000 Turkish soldiers left by Salīm to protect his interests in Egypt. The Ottoman troops, stationed in Cairo and at key points in the country, were organized into six corps or *ūjāqs* under the control of a military chief who resided in the Citadel at Cairo and were assigned the task of defending Egypt, policing the country, and collecting taxes. The chiefs and officers of the *ūjāqs* met as a *dīwān*, presided over by the pasha. The pasha had to obtain the *dīwān's* consent to all measures and its members could refuse to execute his orders until confirmation was received from the sultan that they should do so. They could also recommend to the sultan that the pasha should be deposed whenever they felt he was betraying the interests of the sovereign.

2. There follows a more detailed description of the Ottoman administrative system established by Sulaymān; for description of administration under Muḥammad 'Alī see Chapter V.

The Great *Dīwān* consisted of the three principal officers from each *ūjāq*—the *aghā* (commanding officer), *daftardār* (secretary), and *rūznāmjī* (controller and archivist); a representative from each *ūjāq* other than these listed above; the *amīr al-ḥajj* (leader of the annual pilgrimage to the holy cities of Makkah and al-Madīnah); the chief *qāḍī* (judge) of Cairo, appointed by the *Shaykh al-Islām* at Istanbul; the principal *shaykhs* and *sharīfs*; the *muftī* of each of the four schools of law; the heads of the four orthodox rites; and the *'ulamā'*. It met only occasionally and was not presided over by the pasha who could only listen to the discussions from behind a curtain. Orders from the Sublime Porte were addressed officially to the Great *Dīwān*, but were received by the pasha, who alone had the right to convoke this assembly. His *kikhyah* or lieutenant (from the Persian *katkhudā* meaning "Lord of the House"; in Egypt the term was written *katkhudā* but pronounced *kikhyah*) and the *daftardār* or chancellor were charged with the task of submitting his orders to both the Great and Small *Dīwāns* for their deliberation and to inform him of their decisions. His task was to sanction resolutions and to issue orders for their execution. The Small *Dīwān* met daily in the pasha's palace, but the pasha was excluded from its meetings also, his intermediaries being the *kikhyah* and *daftardār*. The Small *Dīwān* was composed of the *kikhyah* of the pasha, the *daftardār*, the *rūznāmjī*, one representative from each *ūjāq*, the *aghā* and principal officers of the corps of the *Mutafarriqah* and the *Shāwīshīyah*.

Seven corps of *ūjāqlīs* were stationed in Egypt: (1) *Mutafarriqah*, which had been formed from the elite of Salīm's guards and were known as his "Noble Guard"; (2) *Shāwīshīyah*, formed originally from the noncommissioned officers of Salīm's army whose special task was to enforce the collection of taxes; (3) *Jamulyan* or cavaliers (pronunciation in colloquial Arabic of the Turkish term *gönüllü*, meaning *volunteer*, caused the misconception that this was a Camel Corps when it was, in fact, a Cavalry Corps—see H. A. R. Gibb and Harold Bowen, *Islamic Society and the West*, Vol. I: *Islamic Society in the Eighteenth Century* [London, 1950, 1957], Pt. 1, 181 n. 4, 192; Jean Deny, *Sommaire des archives turques du Caire*, Société royale de géographie d'Egypte, publications spéciales [Cairo, 1930], 26, 27; A. N. Poliak, *Feudalism in Egypt, Syria, Palestine, and the Lebanon, 1250–1900* [London, 1939], 53); (4) *Tufankjīyah* or artillerymen; (5) *Sharākisah* (Circassians), a new corps added by

Sulaymān from the ranks of the Mamlūks of the previous reign who had escaped annihilation by the Turks at the time of the conquest and had begged the Sultan for the privilege of serving in his armies; (6) *Inkishārīyah* (Janissaries) or *Mustaḥfiẓan* (guardians), called thus because they were in charge of policing the cities, who, though not first in the military hierarchy, were greatest in number and power, their chief being recognized not only as the head of the corps but as General-in-Chief of the entire military establishment; and (7) *'Azab* (bachelors) who were armorers of the military force and responsible for the manufacture and repair of arms and the manufacture of munitions for the infantry. Each corps was commanded by its own commanding officer (*aghā*) under whom there was a lieutenant-colonel (*kikhyah*), a secretary (*daftardār*), treasurer (*khazīnah-dār*), and controller and archivist (*rūznāmjī*). The military establishment was fixed by Sulaymān at 20,000 men, but it rarely reached that number. Each corps was assigned a definite revenue and received salaries from the *efendīs*, officials connected with the financial administration. Its business was dealt with in a special *dīwān* composed of the officers and representatives of the noncommissioned officers; this assembly received accounts of the *efendīs*, made appointments in the lower ranks, and submitted the names of higher officers to the pasha for his confirmation. The members of the *ūjāqs* soon formed the dominant caste in Egypt and transmitted their privileges and military obligations to their descendants.

Salīm had divided Egypt into twelve *sanjaqs* or provinces, each of which was controlled by a *sanjaq beyi*. The number of provinces did not remain fixed at twelve, however, but varied instead, whereas the rank held by provincial governors might be either that of *sanjaq beyi* or *kāshif*. In Sulaymān's reign an additional twelve beys were appointed, making a total of twenty-four, of which four were the direct appointees of the sultan. The remaining twenty beys were elected for life by the *dīwān* from among the members of the *ūjāq* of the *Mutafarriqah*. The pasha then submitted their names to the sultan for confirmation, and as soon as the beys received their appointments, they were dropped from the rolls of the *ūjāq* of the *Mutafarriqah*. The principal government posts were alternated on an annual basis among these twenty beys; those with no office in any particular year carried out special jobs or were held in reserve for an emergency. The twelve principal beys were: (1) the *kikhyah bey*, lieutenant of the pasha; (2–4) the *qapūdān beys*, direct appointees of the sultan in charge of the seaports at Suez, Damietta (Dimyāṭ), and Alexandria (al-Iskandarīyah), who were in no way controlled by the pasha or the Cairo *dīwāns* and only recognized orders received from the Imperial *Dīwān* at Istanbul; (5) the *daftardār*, originally appointed annually by the sultan but by the eighteenth century usually one of the Egyptian beys whose appointment had to be confirmed by the sultan for a period of tenure, the duration of which cannot be stated as the sources are not clear; (6) the *amīr al-ḥajj*, who led the annual pilgrimage to the holy cities and took with him the *Maḥmal*, the litter containing the Holy Tapestry, and the gifts sent annually from Egypt in the name of the sultan; (7) the *amīr al-khaznah* (treasurer) who brought the annual remittance from Egypt to Istanbul; (8–12) governors of the provinces of Girgā, Buḥayrah, al-Minūfīyah, al-Gharbīyah, and ash-Sharqīyah. The provinces of al-Qalyūbīyah, al-Manṣūrīyah, Gīzah, and Fayyūm were governed by *kāshifs* rather than beys. The authority of the provincial beys and *kāshifs* was limited by provincial *dīwāns* composed of the officers or *chūrbājīs* of the *ūjāq* units (*ūrṭahs*) which were stationed in all the provinces. Only three of the beys had access to the governmental *dīwāns*: the *kikhyah bey*, the *daftardār bey*, and the *amīr al-ḥajj*.

3. Gibb and Bowen, I, Pt. 1, 208–216.

4. Or *'Alamdār* (standard bearer). See Gibb and Bowen, I, Pt. 1, 319 n. 7.

5. Louis Bréhier, *L'Egypte de 1798 à 1900* (Paris, 1901), 22, 23; "On the 'Consilium Aegyptiacum' or 'Egypt Project,' an unpublished memoir by Leibnitz," attached to a letter of T. L. Stoddart to Lord Palmerston dated London, February 23, 1850 in F.O. 78/842.

6. Jacques Bainville, "L'expédition française en Egypte (1798–1801)," in *Précis de l'histoire d'Egypte*, ed. Mohamed Zaky el-Ibrachy (Cairo, 1933), III, 133.

7. Bréhier, 30; Bainville, III, 131.
8. Bainville, III, 135, quoting the academician Arnault in *Souvenirs d'un sexagénaire.*
9. *Copies of Original Letters from the Army of General Bonaparte in Egypt Intercepted by the Fleet under the Command of Admiral Lord Nelson* (London, 1798–1800), Pt. 2, 121, 128–137, 147–152, 181–186, 216–221.
10. Bréhier, 52.
11. *Copies of Original Letters*, Pt. 3, 38–52.
12. *Copies of Original Letters*, Pt. 3, 122–151, 136, 142.
13. ʻAbd ar-Raḥmān al-Jabartī, *Merveilles biographiques et historiques ou chroniques du Abd-el-Rahman el Djabarti*, trans. Chefik Mansour Bey, Abdulaziz Kahil Bey, Gabriel Nicolas Kahil Bey, and Iskender Ammoun Effendi (Cairo, 1888–1896), VI, 168 (in Arabic, *ʻAjā'ib al-âthār fī 't-tarājim wa'l-akhbār* [Cairo, A. H. 1322/1904–05], III, 88).
14. Bréhier, 57.
15. The Arabic spelling of Muḥammad ʻAlī's name in this work has been determined by the present practice of identifying him with the founding of modern Egypt, which is Arabic rather than Turkish in its allegiance, but it must be emphasized that in Muḥammad ʻAlī's day he was considered a Turk and his name was spelled accordingly.
16. The Turkish term *delī* (Ar. *dalī*) was applied to irregular troops.
17. Al-Jabartī, VII, 375, 376 (III, 331, 332).
18. Al-Jabartī, VII, 373 (III, 330).

Chapter II. Landholding in Egypt before the French Occupation

1. See Silvestre de Sacy, "Sur la nature et les révolutions du droit de propriété territoriale en Egypte, depuis la conquête de ce pays par les musulmans jusqu'à l'expédition de François," *Mémoires de l'Institut Royal de France*, I (Paris, 1815), 1–165, V (Paris, 1821), 1–75, VII (Paris, 1824), 55–124; Poliak.
2. Land in the Ottoman Empire was classified as (1) *mulk*, land held in full ownership; (2) *mīrī*, land whose revenues accrued to the state; (3) *waqf*, land whose revenues accrued to pious foundations; (4) *mawāt*, barren or uncultivated land; and (5) *maṭrūq*, pasture land or meadows used in common by the entire community. See Alphonse Belin, *Etude sur la propriété foncière en pays musulman et spécialement en Turquie* (*rite hanéfite*) (Paris, 1862), 180–186; D. Gatteschi, *Real Property, Mortgage and Wakf according to Ottoman Law*, trans. Edward A. van Dyck (London, 1884), 7–20; D. Gatteschi, "Mémoire sur le droit de propriété foncière dans l'empire ottoman et en Egypte," *Bulletin de l'Institut Egyptien*, X (Alexandria, 1869), 44–48.
3. The *mīrī* was the tax on state land, the proceeds of which were for the State Treasury. See Gibb and Bowen, I, Pt. 1, 128 n. 5, 133 n. 4; Pt. 2, 9–12, 40, 40 n. 2.
4. Etienne Combe, "L'Egypte ottomane de la conquête par Selim (1517) à l'arrivée de Bonaparte (1798)," in *Précis de l'histoire d'Egypte*, ed. Mohamed Zaky el-Ibrachy (Cairo, 1933), III, 68, 69; Poliak, 36, 40, 46; Gibb and Bowen, I, Pt. 2, 172, 173; de Sacy, I, 51–89.
5. Al-Jabartī, VIII, 206 (IV, 93).
6. J. M. Digeon, *Nouveaux contes turcs et arabes* (Paris, 1779, 1781), II, 196–198, 204–208, 210–213, 254, 255; de Sacy, I, 90–128; Gibb and Bowen, I, Pt. 2, 38, 39.
7. De Chabrol de Volvic, *Essai sur les mœurs des habitans modernes de l'Egypte*, in *Description de l'Egypte, Etat moderne* (Paris, 1822), 1st ed.), II, Pt. 2, 481; A. B. Clot, *Aperçu général sur l'Egypte* (Paris, 1840), II, 193; Campbell, July 6, 1840 in F.O. 78/408b.
8. The spelling *fā'iẓ* rather than *fā'iḍ* has been used to conform with the spelling used by al-Jabartī and other nineteenth-century authors.
9. Yaqub [J.] Artin, *The Right of Landed Property in Egypt*, trans. E. A. van Dyck (London, 1885), 48, 49.

10. Artin, *Landed Property*, 49, 50; de Chabrol, II, Pt. 2, 480; Michel-Ange Lancret, *Mémoire sur le système d'imposition territoriale et sur l'administration des provinces de l'Egypte, dans les dernières années du gouvernement des Mamlouks*, in *Description de l'Egypte, Etat moderne* (Paris, 1809, 1st ed.), I, 236, 257; Gibb and Bowen, I, Pt. 1, 260.

11. Artin, *Landed Property*, 48; de Chabrol, II, Pt. 2, 480; Lancret, I, 240, 241, 257; Gibb and Bowen, I, Pt. 1, 260, 261.

12. De Chabrol, II, Pt. 2, 479, 480; Lancret, I, 236, 246; Artin, *Landed Property*, 59 n.

13. *Kharouqah*, according to Lancret, I, 236.

14. Lancret, I, 235, 236, 246, 257, 258; de Chabrol, II, Pt. 2, 479.

15. Lancret, I, 244.

16. Lancret, I, 245; al-Jabartī, VIII, 132 (IV, 61).

17. Amédée Jaubert, *Nomenclature des tribus d'arabes qui campent entre l'Egypte et la Palestine depuis Khân Younes et Ghazzah jusqu'à l'Oronte, et dans la partie septentrionale du désert qui sépare la Mecque de la Syrie*, in *Description de l'Egypte, Etat moderne* (Paris, 1813, 1st ed.), II, 249–276; E. Jomard, *Observations sur les arabes de l'Egypte moyenne*, in *Description de l'Egypte, Etat moderne* (Paris, 1809, 1st ed.), I, 545–576; Dubois-Aymé, *Mémoire sur les tribus arabes des déserts de l'Egypte*, in *Description de l'Egypte, Etat moderne* (Paris, 1809, 1st ed.), I, 577–606; P. S. Girard, *Mémoire sur l'agriculture, l'industrie et le commerce de l'Egypte*, in *Description de l'Egypte, Etat moderne* (Paris, 1813, 1st ed.), II, 510–514, 585, 586; Lancret, I, 238, 245–248; Poliak, 60; al-Jabartī, III, 71–88 (I, 343–349), VII, 63 (III, 199); Digeon, II, 204–210; Combe, III, 77–79; Georges Rigault, *Le Général Abdallah Menou et la dernière phase de l'expédition d'Egypte (1799–1801)* (Paris, 1911), 74, 75, 163–165.

18. For comparison with functions of government officials during the reign of Muḥammad 'Alī see the latter half of Chapter V.

19. Comte Estève, *Mémoire sur les finances de l'Egypte depuis sa conquête par le sultan Selym Ier, jusqu'à celle du général en chef Bonaparte*, in *Description de l'Egypte, Etat moderne* (Paris, 1809, 1st ed.), I, 310; Lancret, I, 249.

20. Lancret, I, 241, 242.

21. Lancret, I, 241, 244; Estève, I, 311; Gibb and Bowen, I, Pt. 1, 263.

22. Lancret, I, 242; Estève, I, 311, 318, 319.

23. Both Lancret and Estève err when they refer to the *mishadd* as the *mechhed* (Lancret, I, 241, 244; Estève, I, 311). This mistake was apparently due to the use of an incorrect transcription of the Arabic term by Lancret. Silvestre de Sacy calls attention to this fact and says that the correct term should be *mishadd*, meaning *inspector* or *controller* (de Sacy, 121 n. 165). De Sacy's view is borne out by two Arabic sources, one contemporary with Lancret and Estève and one a generation later (*Lā'iḥat zirā'at al-fallāḥ watadbīr aḥkām as-siyāsah biqaṣd an-najāḥ* [Būlāq, Dhū'l-Ḥijjah 1, A.H. 1258 (January 3, 1843), 2d ed.], 46; Shafiq Ghorbal, "Miṣr 'inda mafriq aṭ-ṭuruq 1798–1801," *Majallat Kullīyat al-Âdāb, Bulletin of the Faculty of Arts*, IV, Pt. 1 [Cairo, 1938], 41).

24. Ghorbal, "Miṣr 'inda mafriq aṭ-ṭuruq," 41.

25. Estève, I, 311.

26. Lancret, I, 243–245; Estève, I, 311, 312; Girard, II, 587–589.

27. Lancret, I, 246, 247; Estève, I, 321–323; Girard, II, 586. According to Estève, the *ṣarrāf* in Upper Egypt was known as *'āmil* and frequently delegated part of his responsibilities to officials known as *qābiḍs*. Lancret, on the other hand, says that the *ṣarrāf* collected the *māl*, the tax in specie, whereas the Copt who collected the *kharjah*, the tax in kind, was sometimes known as *wakīl* and sometimes as *'āmil*.

28. Lancret, I, 248, 249; Gibb and Bowen, I, Pt. 2, 42 n. 1.

29. So listed by Estève, although Ḥusayn Efendī who supplied him with information makes no mention of it in his report. See note 30.

30. Combe, III, 68, 69; de Sacy, I, 73–77; Estève, I, 304, 331, 332; Ghorbal, "Miṣr 'inda mafriq aṭ-ṭuruq," 45, 47, 58, 61; al-Jabartī, VII, 113 (III, 222); Gibb and Bowen, I, Pt. 2, 166, 167, 171, 172, and 172 n.3.

31. Gibb and Bowen, I, Pt. 2, 173.
32. Gibb and Bowen, I, Pt. 2, 167–169.
33. Estève, I, 332.
34. Lancret, I, 239.
35. De Sacy, I, 67–73, 161–163; Estève, I, 304, 305, 332; Lancret, I, 238, 239; al-Jabartī, VIII, 206, 207 (IV, 93, 94), IX, 93 (IV, 209); Poliak, 32–40; Belin, 98–102, 124; Gibb and Bowen, I, Pt. 2, 172, 173.
36. Al-Jabartī, VIII, 206–208 (IV, 93–95); Estève, I, 336, 337; Lancret, I, 240; Ghorbal, "Miṣr 'inda mafriq aṭ-ṭuruq," 31; Gibb and Bowen, I, Pt. 2, 173, 175.
37. One of these officials was usually the descendant of the donor, but it is not at all clear which it was. Only a study of the registers of *waqfs* and *rizqahs* would solve this problem. See Gibb and Bowen, I, Pt. 2, 170, but Sir Hamilton Gibb in a conversation with the author suggested that the matter needs further investigation.
38. Lancret, I, 240, 243; Gatteschi, *Real Property, Mortgage and Wakf*, 85, 86, 88, 93, 94; al-Jabartī, VIII, 207 (IV, 93, 94); Gibb and Bowen, I, Pt. 2, 169, 170.
39. Lancret, I, 239.
40. Al-Jabartī, VII, 60, 61 (III, 198), VII, 95, 96 (III, 211, 212), VIII, 206 (IV, 93), IX, 93–95 (IV, 209–210); Belin, 181–186; Rigault, 257; J. [Gamal-Eddine] Heyworth-Dunne, *Land Tenure in Islam 630 A.D.–1951 A.D.*, in *The Muslim World Series*, No. 3 (Cairo, 1952), 16–20; A. Sékaly, "Le problème des wakfs en Egypte," *Revue des études islamiques* (1929); Charles Issawi, *Egypt at Mid-Century* (London, 1954), 131, 132; Gibb and Bowen, I, Pt. 2, 174, 175, 177, 178. The Ottoman Land Laws of 1858 distinguished between *waqf ṣaḥīḥ* and *waqf ghayr ṣaḥīḥ* (sound and unsound *waqfs*) and questioned the immutability of *waqfs* constituted from *mīrī* land. It was decreed that henceforth unsound *waqfs* were to be regulated, like *mīrī* land, by *qānūn* law, enforcing, thereby, the idea that the rights of the state were no longer to be disregarded. On the other hand, the land laws recognized as sound and therefore legal all *waqfs*, either *waqf khayrī* or *waqf ahlī*, that had been constituted from property held in *mulk* and acknowledged that such *waqfs* were to remain subject to the *Sharī'ah* (Belin, 183–186).

Chapter III. Changes in Egyptian Land Tenure: 1798–1815

1. The reforms which Salīm sought to introduce envisaged the eventual substitution of a modern European-type military system for the old Turkish system. Some of these reforms seem to be of a nonmilitary character, but actually they were introduced by the Sultan in order to facilitate the reform of the existing military establishment. During Muḥammad 'Alī's reign, the *Niẓām Jadīd* was extended to Egypt but there the term frequently referred to the military organization on the European (French) model. The term eventually became synonymous with the new Egyptian army created by Muḥammad 'Alī (see Chapter XI).
2. These are military fiefs to support the knights (*sipāhī*). The *tīmārs* and *zi'āmats* differed in the amount of their revenue. The former yielded revenue from 2,000 or 3,000 to 19,999 aspers (120=1 piaster), while the latter yielded 19,999 to 99,999 aspers. See Gibb and Bowen, I, Pt. 1, 47, 47 n.5, 48, 48 n.5; I, Pt. 2, 49, 49 n.2.
3. E. S. Creasy, *History of the Ottoman Turks: from the beginning of their empire to the present time* (London, 1856), II, 331, 332, 446–451; Johann Wilhelm Zinkeisen, *Geschichte der europäischen Staaten, Geschichte des osmanischen Reiches in Europa* (Gotha, 1863), VII, 324, 325.
4. Al-Jabartī, VII, 43 (III, 192).
5. Al-Jabartī, VII, 38, 39 (III, 190), VII, 48, 49 (III, 193, 194), VII, 52 (III, 195), VII, 57 (III, 196), VII, 60, 61 (III, 198), VII, 95, 96 (III, 211, 212).
6. Salīm to George III, Rajab 13, A.H. 1216 (November 20 [19], 1801) in F.O. 95/496; Georges Douin and E. C. Fawtier-Jones, *L'Angleterre et l'Egypte. Vol. I: La politique mameluke (1801–1803)*, Société royale de géographie d'Egypte, publications spéciales (Cairo, 1929), 131, 151; al-Jabartī, VII, 67–75 (III, 200–203).

7. Caven, May 5, 1802, Anstruthen, May 8, 1802 in W.O. 1/346; Georges Douin, *L'Egypte de 1802 à 1804*, Société royale de géographie d'Egypte, publications spéciales (Cairo, 1925), 32, 33; al-Jabartī, VII, 86 (III, 208), VII, 115–117 (III, 223, 224), VII, 128, 129 (III, 228), VII, 231 (III, 267).

8. F. Charles-Roux, *Bonaparte: Governor of Egypt*, trans. E. W. Dickes (London, 1937), 46–49, 55–58, 60, 181; al-Jabartī, VI, 36 (III, 16); *Copies of Original Letters*, Pt. 3, 100–121.

9. So complex is the currency situation in Egypt for the entire period under review that no attempt at conversion into a single currency has been made. All currency references have been given as they appear in the sources and can merely serve, therefore, as a measure of magnitude in a specific instance rather than as a basis of comparison. See al-Jabartī, Vols. VII-IX (III, IV); Samuel-Bernard, *Mémoire sur les monnoies d'Egypte*, in *Description de l'Egypte, Etat moderne* (Paris, 1813, 1st ed.), II; Gibb and Bowen, I, Pt. 2, 49–59; Sir Gardner Wilkinson, *Modern Egypt and Thebes; being a Description of Egypt; including the Information Required for Travellers in that Country* (London, 1843), I, 102, 103, 104; William Holt Yates, *The Modern History and Conditions of Egypt, Its Climate, Diseases, and Capabilities etc.* (London, 1843), I, 352, 459.

10. Henri-Gratien Bertrand, *Campagne d'Egypte et de Syrie (1798–1799), mémoires pour servir à l'histoire de Napoléon, dictés par lui et publiés par le général Bertrand* (Paris, 1847), I, 239–243; Charles-Roux, *Bonaparte*, 109–111, 175–181, 184–187; al-Jabartī, VI, 42–44 (III, 19, 20), VI, 52–55 (III, 23–25), VI, 63 (III, 29), VI, 86 (III, 41), VI, 114 (III, 56).

11. Rigault, 240–260; Carl Ludwig Lokke, "The French Agricultural Mission to Egypt in 1801," *Agricultural History*, X, No. 3 (July 1936), 111–117.

12. Muḥammad 'Alī suffered the same kind of financial pressure from his mercenary troops that he had himself imposed upon his predecessors before he became Pasha of Egypt (Missett, April 28, 1805 in W.O. 1/347). The constant demands by these mercenary troops bore heavily not only upon him but also upon the people of Egypt, for the usual method by which these demands were met was by permitting the troops to range the countryside and exact whatever they could from the peasantry. The peasants often resisted these depredations and pitched battles occurred (al-Jabartī, VII, 371, 372 [III, 329]). The situation for the peasants at this time was, in fact, extremely bad, for they not only had to meet the demands of the mercenaries but also those of the Mamlūks in the areas under their control (Georges Douin, *Mohamed Aly, Pacha du Caire (1805–1807)*, Société royale de géographie d'Egypte, publications spéciales [Cairo, 1926], 32, 100).

13. Muḥammad 'Alī, by one account, paid 4,000 pounds for the original confirmation of his appointment. He then paid large sums to retain his post and gave rich presents to visiting dignitaries (A. de Vaulabelle, *Histoire moderne de l'Egypte (1801–1834)*, in *Histoire scientifique et militaire de l'expédition française en Egypte* [Paris, 1830–1836], IX, 397, 398). In 1806 he paid 2,500 purses to bribe the Turkish admiral (Missett, October 1, 1806 in F.O. 24/2).

14. Al-Jabartī, VIII, 22 (IV, 10), VIII, 129 (IV, 60), VIII, 132 (IV, 61), VIII, 174–178 (IV, 80, 81); de Vaulabelle, IX, 407–410.

15. Al-Jabartī, VIII, 206 (IV, 93). The date 1808 is usually the one that appears in European sources, but if al-Jabartī's chronology is correct 1809 is the correct date.

16. Al-Jabartī, VIII, 206 (IV, 93), VIII, 209–211 (IV, 95); Creasy, II, 372–377; Clot, II, 195; Pierre Nicolas Hamont, *L'Egypte sous Méhémet-Ali* (Paris, 1843), II, 631.

17. See Gibb and Bowen, I, Pt. 2, 93, 94, 100, 101.

18. The purse (*kīs*) in this period equaled 500 piasters. See Wilkinson, I, 102; Yates, I, 352, 459; Gibb and Bowen, I, Pt. 2, 58 n.2.

19. See Gibb and Bowen, I, Pt. 2, 101.

20. See Gibb and Bowen, I, Pt. 2, 133–138.

21. Al-Jabartī, VIII, 212–223 (IV, 96–101), VIII, 321 (IV, 142); de Vaulabelle, IX, 410–417.

22. Edouard Driault, *Mohamed Aly et Napoléon (1807–1814)*, Société royale de géographie d'Egypte, publications spéciales (Cairo, 1925), 71.

23. Driault, *Mohamed Aly et Napoléon*, 11, 34, 82, 97; al-Jabartī, VIII, 202, 203 (IV, 91, 92), VIII, 224, 225 (IV, 101), VIII, 314, 315 (IV, 138, 139).

24. Al-Jabartī, VIII, 242, 243 (IV, 108, 109).

25. Al-Jabartī, VIII, 243–245 (IV, 109, 110).

26. Al-Jabartī, VIII, 277–279 (IV, 123, 124); Driault, *Mohamed Aly et Napoléon*, 106; Georges Douin, *La mission du Baron de Boislecomte. L'Egypte et la Syrie en 1833*, Société royale de géographie d'Egypte, publications spéciales (Cairo, 1927), 79.

27. Shafik Ghorbal, *The Beginnings of the Egyptian Question and the Rise of Mehemet Ali* (London, 1928), 280 n.2; Edouard Driault, "Mohamed-Aly et Ibrahim," in *Précis de l'histoire d'Egypte*, ed. Mohamed Zaky el-Ibrachy (Cairo, 1933), III, 221, 222; Driault, *Mohamed Aly et Napoléon*, 123, 184, 199.

28. Al-Jabartī, VIII, 321 (IV, 141, 142), VIII, 347, 348 (IV, 153, 154), IX, 22 (IV, 177), IX, 34–38 (IV, 183–185); Driault, *Mohamed Aly et Napoléon*, 138.

29. Hamont, II, 434, 500.

30. Driault, *Mohamed Aly et Napoléon*, 231.

31. De Vaulabelle says that the announcement was made Ṣafar 24, A.H. 1229 (X, 70, 71); according to al-Jabartī, it was made on Rabī' al-Awwal 1, A.H. 1229 (IX, 79 [IV, 203]), that is, February 15 or 21, 1814.

32. Al-Jabartī, IX, 79, 80 (IV, 203, 204), IX, 87 (IV, 207); Missett, March 22, 1814 in F.O. 24/5; Driault, *Mohamed Aly et Napoléon*, 241, 242; Artin, *Landed Property*, 54, 55.

33. Al-Jabartī, IX, 88 (IV, 207).

34. Artin says that each family in all parts of Egypt received an allocation of from 3 to 5 *faddāns* (Artin, *Landed Property*, 52). Boutros Ghali, however, who prepared a detailed report in 1880 on land tax, included no information about the allocation of land to the peasants, nor is there anything in al-Jabartī's work to indicate that a distribution of land such as Artin recorded did take place. Al-Jabartī does, though, mention that the *fallāḥīn* were allowed to retain the land in their possession upon payment of the additional taxes imposed by the government (IX, 87 [IV, 207]).

35. Al-Jabartī, IX, 91, 92 (IV, 208, 209), IX, 316 (IV, 311); Artin, *Landed Property*, 51, 169; Douin, *La mission du Baron de Boislecomte*, 82; Driault, *Mohamed Aly et Napoléon*, 241, 242; Athanasios G. Polites, *L'hellénisme et l'Egypte moderne* (Paris, 1929, 1930), II, 94; Boutros Ghali, "Rapport de S. E. Boutros Pacha Ghali, membre de la commission d'enquête de l'impôt foncier, présenté à cette commission le 18 février 1880," *Répertoire de la législation et de l'administration égyptiennes*, ed. Philippe Gelat, Supplément (Alexandria, 1890), 116; Aḥmad Aḥmad al-Ḥitta, *Ta'rīkh az-zirā'ah al-miṣrīyah fī 'ahd Muḥammad 'Alī al-Kabīr* (Cairo, 1950), 48.

36. Al-Jabartī, IX, 91 (IV, 208, 209).

37. Al-Jabartī, IX, 91–93 (IV, 209), IX, 97, 98 (IV, 211).

38. Al-Jabartī, IX, 121–123 (IV, 221, 222).

39. Al-Jabartī, IX, 123–138 (IV, 222–229), IX, 170, 171 (IV, 244), IX, 195 (IV, 256), IX, 263 (IV, 287), IX, 294 (IV, 301); Missett, August 5, 1814 in F.O. 24/5; Artin, *Landed Property*, 53–55; Boutros Ghali, 116; J. Michaud, "Lettre sur l'Egypte," *Revue des deux mondes*, III (September 1834), 675.

40. Douin, *La mission du Baron de Boislecomte*, 79, 80, 131, 132; Auguste Colin, "Lettres sur l'Egypte," Pt. 1, "Budget et administration," *Revue des deux mondes*, XIII (January 1, 1838), 104; Campbell, July 6, 1840 in F.O. 78/408b; René Cattaui, *Le règne de Mohamed Ali d'après les archives russes en Egypte*, Société royale de géographie d'Egypte, publications spéciales (Cairo, 1931, Rome, 1933, 1935, 1936), II, Pt. 2, 374, 413, 414; Murray, May 28, 1847 in F.O. 78/707.

41. Douin, *La mission du Baron de Boislecomte*, 80.

Chapter IV. Muḥammad 'Alī and Landholding Reform after 1815

1. Douin, *La mission du Baron de Boislecomte,* 111.
2. Hamont, I, 119–123; Gatteschi, *Real Property, Mortgage and Wakf,* 30; Artin, *Landed Property,* 56, 57, 153, 170–172, 174–176, 224–227; al-Ḥitta, *Tarīkh az-zirā'ah al-miṣrīyah,* 52, 54, 55; Barnett, December 12, 1844 in F.O. 78/583 (see Appendix I); Belin, 104–120, 186, 230–232; Boutros Ghali, 123, 124; John Bowring, "Report on Egypt and Candia," A Report addressed to The Right Hon. Lord Viscount Palmerston and presented to both Houses of Parliament, House of Commons, Sessional Papers 1840, vol. XXI: *Reports from Commissioners,* vol. 6 (London, 1840), pp. 9, 10, 16. See Appendix I, Table 11, note 8 and Appendix II.
3. Polites, *L'hellénisme et l'Egypte moderne,* II, 95, 96, 98–100; Hodges, August 17, 1840 in F.O. 78/408A.
4. Gatteschi, *Real Property, Mortgage and Wakf,* 38–40; Bowring, "Egypt and Candia," 124; Campbell, July 6, 1840 in F.O. 78/408b.
5. Hamont, I, 126.
6. Hamont, I, 89, 121–127; Artin, *Landed Property,* 174–176.
7. Artin, *Landed Property,* 160.
8. Edouard Driault, *L'Egypte et l'Europe. La crise de 1839–1841,* Société royale de géographie d'Egypte, publications spéciales (Cairo, Rome, 1930–1934), V, 371, 372.
9. Bowring, "Egypt and Candia," 45; Gatteschi, *Real Property, Mortgage and Wakf,* 30.
10. Al-Ḥitta, *Tarīkh az-zirā'ah al-miṣrīyah,* 51 n.3 and n.4.
11. Artin, *Landed Property,* 79–81; Campbell, February 26, 1838 in F.O. 142/9.
12. Barnett, December 12, 1844 in F.O. 78/583; Hamont, II, 520–523.
13. Artin, *Landed Property,* 81, 82; Campbell, July 6, 1840 in F.O. 78/408b; Deny, 130, 498–500, 502, 504, 505, 507, 508, 512; Stephen Olin, *Travels in Egypt, Arabia, Petraea, and the Holy Land* (New York, 1843), I, 40–44.
14. Driault, *L'Egypte et l'Europe,* V, 564; Hamont, I, 328; Barnett, January 3, 1842 in F.O. 195/209.
15. Hamont, I, 188–193; Olin, I, 40; Polites, *L'hellénisme et l'Egypte moderne,* I, 184; Murray, December 4, 1849 in F.O. 78/804.
16. Belin, 245, 246. Gliddon's definition of *chiflik* is inaccurate: "The Turkish appellation 'Chiflik' belongs exclusively, in Mohammedan law, to farms owned by, and cultivated for the Sultan and his royal blood alone, which, as crown lands, are exempt from all imposts. In applying, therefore, the name 'Chiflik' to the territories he has appropriated to himself, Mohammed Ali arrogates to his own person attributes belonging exclusively to the Supreme Ruler of the Faithful; in the same manner as he has usurped the government itself" (George R. Gliddon, *A Memoir on the Cotton of Egypt* [London, 1841], 25).
17. Al-Jabartī, VIII, 184 (IV, 84), VIII, 352 (IV, 156).
18. Boutros Ghali, 124; Bowring, "Egypt and Candia," 124; Hamont, I, 82, II, 520–523; Barnett, December 12, 1844 in F.O. 78/583 (see Appendix I); al-Ḥitta, *Tarīkh az-zirā'ah al-miṣrīyah,* 56. See Appendix I, Table 11, note 3.
19. Deny believes this should read Baḥr al-Gharb, p. 508.
20. Al-Ḥitta, *Tarīkh az-zirā'ah al-miṣrīyah,* 56 n.3 and n.4; Deny, 501–503, 506–513; Gatteschi, "Mémoire sur le droit de propriété foncière," 57; Grégoire, "De la culture du coton en Egypte," *Mémoires de l'Institut Egyptien,* I (Paris, 1862), 442.
21. Barnett refers to *mudīrs* of *chifliks* instead of *nāẓirs* (Barnett, March 16, 1845 in F.O. 142/13), but the *qānūn* clearly refers to the head of a *chiflik* as the *nāẓir* (*Qānūn al-Chafālik* [Būlāq, Ṣafar, A.H. 1259 (March 1843)], 25–31).
22. *Qānūn al-Chafālik;* Deny, 107, 108, 126–129, 150–153, 502, 507, 510, 511; Barnett, May 15, 1842 in F.O. 78/502. See Chapter V for further discussion of these officials.
23. Gliddon, 25–27; Bowring, "Egypt and Candia," 119; Adam Georges Benis,

Une mission militaire polonaise en Egypte, Société royale de géographie d'Egypte, publications spéciales (Cairo, 1938), II, 48; Barnett, March 19, 1844 in F.O. 142/13.

24. Barnett, March 16, 1845 in F.O. 78/623.
25. Hamont, I, 64–86, 126, 132, 133, 136.
26. See p. 85.
27. Stoddart, August 6, 1844 in F.O. 78/582.
28. Stoddart, July 27, 1844 in F.O. 78/582; Lyons, July 27, 1844 in F.O. 78/585.
29. Stoddart, July 27, 1844 and August 6, 1844 in F.O. 78/582.
30. Stoddart, July 27, 1844, August 7, 16, 1844 in F.O. 78/582; Lyons, July 27, 1844 in F.O. 78/585; A. A. Paton, *A History of the Egyptian Revolution* (London, 1870, 2d ed.), II, 234–236.
31. Barnett, April 16, 1845 in F.O. 78/623.
32. See Appendix I for statistics and Appendix II for a discussion regarding the problem of the extent of cultivated land in Egypt during Muḥammad 'Alī's reign. The evidence contained in Appendix II reveals that Muḥammad 'Alī did not increase the area of cultivation as a whole and that the increase in peasant holdings was minute. He did, however, increase the cropping area by introducing summer canals, thus facilitating the development of summer cultivation. Landholders in areas of improved irrigation benefited enormously, since they could raise as many as four crops on the same amount of land. The peasant holdings, now concentrated in Upper Egypt where summer irrigation did not exist, were consequently at a definite disadvantage.
33. Artin, *Landed Property*, 186, 187; Boutros Ghali, 117.
34. "Tous les règlements administratifs faits ou à faire par ma Sublime Porte, seront également appliqués à la dite province, suivant les exigences de la localité et les principes de la justice" (Hayyīm Nahum, *Recueil de firmans impériaux ottomans adressés aux valis et aux khédives d'Egypte, 1006H–1322H* [*1597 J.C.–1904 J.C.*] [Cairo, 1934], 234).

Chapter V. Administration of Egypt under Muḥammad 'Alī

1. Lancret, I, 235; Digeon, II, 189–194 (see de Sacy, Vol. I, for an analysis and criticism of and additions to Digeon's translation); Gibb and Bowen, I, Pt. 2, 38–42.
2. Gibb and Bowen, I, Pt. 2, 17, 17 n.3, 41, 41 n.7.
3. Al-Jabartī, VII, 302, 303 (III, 294), VII, 312–314 (III, 298, 299), VII, 371, 372 (III, 329), VII, 397, 398 (III, 343, 344); Missett, October 10, 1804 in W.O. 1/347. The period is treated fully in Shafik Ghorbal, *The Beginnings of the Egyptian Question.*
4. Digeon, II, 246, 247; Deny, 33, 34, 104–111; Campbell, May 25, 1837 in F.O. 78/319 and February 26, 1838 in F.O. 142/9.
5. Deny, 126–129, 150–153; Cattaui, II, Pt. 2, 370; Campbell, January 25, 1838 in F.O. 78/342.
6. Reproduced in Aḥmad Fatḥī Zaghlūl, *al-Muḥāmāh* (Cairo, 1900), Appendix II, 4–26.
7. Deny, 104–108; Campbell, May 25, 1837 in F.O. 78/319; Cattaui, II, Pt. 2, 313, 314; Bowring, "Egypt and Candia," 121. The terms *minister* and *ministry* frequently employed by foreigners in Egypt are retained here for the sake of convenience, but must be qualified in accordance with Hamont's observations: "There has never existed, properly speaking, ministries or ministers in Egypt. The Europeans alone have given this name to various administrations and to the directors of them. Muḥammad 'Alī is the unique master, supreme in the country; he receives advice, opinions, propositions; he orders, he accepts or refuses. . . . What one calls ministers in the realm of the Pasha are only secretaries, delegates of the viceroy, representing his authority or executing his orders. None of them can take the initiative" (Hamont, II, 52, 53).
8. Deny, 115; Zaghlūl, Appendix II, 4, 5; Campbell, July 6, 1840 in F.O. 78/408b.
9. Gibb and Bowen, I, Pt. 1, 129f, 148; Digeon, II, 198.
10. Al-Jabartī, VII, 415 (III, 350), VIII, 136 (IV, 63), VIII, 161 (IV, 74), IX, 22 (IV, 177), IX, 25 (IV, 179).

11. Lancret, I, 252–255; Gibb and Bowen, I, Pt. 2, 46, 47; al-Jabartī, VIII, 313 (IV, 138), IX, 14 (IV, 174), IX, 91 (IV, 208, 209), IX, 184 (IV, 251).

12. Al-Jabartī, VIII, 242 (IV, 108, 109); Poliak, 48 n.3.

13. Al-Jabartī, VIII, 240 (IV, 107, 108), VIII, 242 (IV, 108, 109), VIII, 247–249 (IV, 111, 112), VIII, 275, 276 (IV, 122, 123), IX, 6–9 (IV, 170, 171), IX, 13, 14 (IV, 173, 174), IX, 16, 17 (IV, 174, 175), IX, 166, 167 (IV, 242, 243), IX, 227, 228 (IV, 271), IX, 263 (IV, 287).

14. Deny, 131–138.

15. Deny, 116–120; Zaghlūl, Appendix II, 5; Cattaui, II, Pt. 2, 321, 322, 326.

16. Campbell, January 22, 1838 in F.O. 78/342, Part 1; Cattaui, II, Pt. 2, 327.

17. Campbell, February 26, 1838 in F.O. 142/9.

18. Deny, 118.

19. Campbell, May 25, 1837 in F.O. 78/319 and July 6, 1840 in F.O. 78/408b; Zaghlūl, Appendix II, 5.

20. Campbell, July 6, 1840 in F.O. 78/408b; Zaghlūl, Appendix II, 5.

21. Campbell, July 6, 1840 in F.O. 78/408b; Zaghlūl, Appendix II, 6.

22. Campbell, July 6, 1840 in F.O. 78/408b; Zaghlūl, Appendix II, 6.

23. Zaghlūl, Appendix II, 6.

24. Cattaui, II, Pt. 2, 314; Edme. François Jomard, *Coup d'œil impartial sur l'état présent de l'Egypte, comparé à sa situation antérieure* (Paris, 1836), 23.

25. Deny, 108, 121, 122.

26. Deny, 90–95; Cattaui, II, Pt. 2, 313; Campbell, February 26, 1838 in F.O. 142/9; Bowring, "Egypt and Candia," 121; Hamont, I, 99–103; Zaghlūl, Appendix II, 7, 8.

27.

Egyptian provinces at the time of French Occupation	*Egyptian provinces at the time of the Cadastre of 1236/1820–21*
1. Buḥayrah	1. Buḥayrah
2. Rashīd	2. al-Gharbīyah
3. al-Gharbīyah	3. al-Minūfīyah
4. al-Minūfīyah	4. al-Manṣūrīyah
5. Dimyāṭ	5. ash-Sharqīyah
6. al-Manṣūrīyah	6. al-Qalyūbīyah
7. ash-Sharqīyah	7. Gīzah
8. al-Qalyūbīyah	8. Fayyūm
9. Gīzah	9. Aṭfīḥ
10. Fayyūm	10. Banī Suwayf
11. Aṭfīḥ	11. al-Minyā
12. Banī Suwayf	12. Asyūṭ
13. al-Minyā	13. Girgā
14. Asyūṭ	14. Isnā
15. Girgā	
16. Thebes	

(Felix Mengin, *Histoire de l'Egypte sous le gouvernement du Mohammed-Aly; ou récit des événemens politiques et militaires qui ont eu lieu depuis le départ des français jusqu'en 1823* [Paris, 1823], II, 343, 344; C. H. Becker, "Egypt," *The Encyclopaedia of Islām*, ed. M. Th. Houtsma *et al.*, II [1927], 12.)

28. Mengin, *Histoire de l'Egypte*, II, 340, 341; al-Jabartī, IX, 185 (IV, 251), IX, 228 (IV, 271), IX, 231, 232 (IV, 273).

29. Edouard Driault, *L'expédition du Crète et de Morée (1823–1828)*, Société royale de géographie d'Egypte, publications spéciales (Cairo, 1930), 33.

30. Asyūṭ and Girgā were known as *Mudīrīyah* of the First Half of Upper Egypt and Qinā and Isnā as *Mudīrīyah* of the Second Half of Upper Egypt. Their *mudīrs*, Ḥusayn Aghā and Muḥarram Aghā, were appointed in 1250/1834–35 (Deny, 130). Reorganization of *mudīrīyahs*, as well as of the other administrative units, often occurred, a fact which probably accounts for the differences among the various sources shown in Table 33. In 1836 Jomard said that there were 7 *mudīrīyahs*, 14 provinces, and 64

departments subdivided into cantons. In 1840 Clot listed 64 departments (*qisms*) and 3,500 villages, while Campbell counted 6 *mudīrīyahs*, 60 departments divided into districts (*khuṭṭs*), subdivided into cantons and finally into villages (Jomard, *Coup d'œil*, 23; Clot, I, 186; Campbell, July 6, 1840 in F.O. 78/408b).

TABLE 33. The *mudīrīyahs* of Egypt during Muḥammad 'Alī's reign as given by four different sources

Clot		Duhamel	Murray	Deny
Mudīrīyahs	Composed of *ma'mūrīyahs*	*Mudīrīyahs*	*Mudīrīyahs*	*Mudīrīyahs*
I	Buḥayrah Gīzah al-Qalyūbīyah	I Buḥayrah II Gīzah III al-Qalyūbī-yah	I Buḥayrah II Gīzah III al-Qalyūbī-yah	I Buḥayrah II Gīzah
II	al-Minūfīyah	IV al-Minūfīyah	IV al-Minūfīyah	III al-Minūfī-yah
	al-Gharbīyah	V al-Gharbīyah	V al-Gharbīyah	IV al-Gharbī-yah
III	al-Manṣūrīyah	VI al-Manṣūrī-yah	VI Daqahlīyah (al-Manṣūrīyah)	
IV	ash-Sharqīyah	VII ash-Sharqīyah	VII ash-Sharqīyah	V ash-Shar-qīyah
V	Banī Suwayf and Fayyūm	VIII Banī Suwayf and Fayyūm	VIII Banī Suwayf	VI Banī Suwayf and al-Minyā
VI	Name not given	IX Asyūṭ	IX Asyūṭ	VII Asyūṭ and Girgā
VII	Name not given	X Qinā and Isnā		VIII Qinā and Isnā

Source: Clot, I, 186, 187; Cattaui, II, Pt. 2, 376; Murray, May 28, 1847 in F.O. 78/707; Deny, 130.

31. Murray claims that the number of blows of the *kurbāj* depended upon no law, but the caprice of the judge. If, for example, a laborer stole a sheep from the Pasha or governor of a province, he might get 300 blows and be crippled for months. The severity of a punishment, however, Murray contends, is not to be measured alone by the number of blows awarded by a judge but, rather, by the degree of brutality with which the sentence is carried out (Murray, March 18, 1848 in F.O. 142/16). The *lā'iḥah* certainly attempted to prevent this sort of abuse, but as it remained to a great extent a theoretical rather than a working instrument, it failed to do so. Even members of Muḥammad 'Alī's family were guilty of contravening his regulations. In 1845 Sa'īd Pasha killed a *fallāḥ* with his own hands at Damanhūr, because he was dissatisfied with the severity of the beating which he had ordered for an offending *fallāḥ*. He took the *kurbāj* himself and finished off the unfortunate *fallāḥ* (Barnett, March 26, 1845 in F.O. 142/13).

32. Deny, 130.

33. This responsibility was finally assumed by the department in charge of public works (see section in Chapter XII on the administration of the irrigation system) and the *mudīr* and other provincial administrators were required only to supply men and materials as requested by public works officials.

34. Zaghlūl, Appendix II, 8; Clot, II, 186; Paul Merruau, *L'Egypte contemporaine, 1840–1857, de Méhémet-Ali à Said Pacha* (Paris, 1858), I, 13, 14; Campbell, July 6,

1840 in F.O. 78/408b. Failure of the *Lā'iḥat zirāʿat al-fallāḥ* to mention the *mudīr* indicates that this officer was not yet active on a national scale.

35. *Lā'iḥat zirāʿat al-fallāḥ*, 32.

36. Orders were communicated to the provincial officers either by courier or by the telegraph system established between Alexandria and Cairo (Campbell, July 6, 1840 in F.O. 78/408b).

37. *Lā'iḥat zirāʿat al-fallāḥ*, 55–58. See the first pages of Chapter X.

38. It is difficult to distinguish between legal and illegal cheating of *fallāḥīn*. The British representative in Egypt obtained copies of budgets for two consecutive years which listed as a source of revenue an item referred to as "overplus of measurement," amounting to 6,282 purses and 103 piasters for the Coptic year 1845–46 and 8,779 purses and 479 piasters for the Coptic year 1846–47 (Murray, January 1, 1847 in F.O. 78/707 and March 17, 1848 in F.O. 78/757). The Pasha resorted to an old trick of the Copts by using two measures, one when he purchased commodities from the *fallāḥīn* and a smaller one when he sold the commodities (Cattaui, I, 357). Murray justified the government's action on the grounds that the *fallāḥīn* or the boatmen cheated the government by mixing dust, sand, and water with the grain to increase its bulk and weight. The government simply retaliated by cheating the *fallāḥīn* in return (Murray, March 17, 1848 in F.O. 78/757).

39. *Lā'iḥat zirāʿat al-fallāḥ*, 53–55.

40. *Lā'iḥat zirāʿat al-fallāḥ*, 52, 53.

41. Cattaui, I, 376.

42. *Lā'iḥat zirāʿat al-fallāḥ*, 40–43.

43. *Lā'iḥat zirāʿat al-fallāḥ*, 34–43; Zaghlūl, Appendix II, 9; Clot, II, 185; Merruau, I, 14–16; Campbell, July 6, 1840 in F.O. 78/408b; Bowring, "Egypt and Candia," 121.

44. See paragraph on *khawlī*.

45. *Lā'iḥat zirāʿat al-fallāḥ*, 43–45; Zaghlūl, Appendix II, 9.

46. *Lā'iḥat zirāʿat al-fallāḥ*, 45, 46.

47. *Lā'iḥat zirāʿat al-fallāḥ*, 46.

48. Auguste Colin, "Lettres sur l'Egypte," Pt. 3, "Commerce," *Revue des deux mondes*, XVII (January 1, 1839), 66, 67, 70–72.

49. *Lā'iḥat zirāʿat al-fallāḥ*, 50–52.

50. *Lā'iḥat zirāʿat al-fallāḥ*, 58.

51. Campbell, January 22, 1838 in F.O. 78/342, Part 1; Cattaui, II, Pt. 2, 376.

52. According to Malivoire, the dismissal of Maḥmūd Bey was the result of his venality and his open opposition to all the progressive measures of the Pasha; Sharīf Bey, on the other hand, had been an excellent provincial governor in al-Manṣūrīyah and was willing to cooperate with Muḥammad ʿAlī in his plans for the general improvement of the country (Driault, *L'expédition du Crète et de Morée*, 104). Salt believes exactly the reverse. He says that Sharīf had nothing to recommend him, that Maḥmūd had attended very closely to business and was highly experienced. His single shortcoming, according to Salt, was his unwillingness to decide upon any question without the Pasha's concurrence; consequently, public business was always several months in arrears. However, Maḥmūd had displeased Muḥammad ʿAlī by calling a meeting to discuss certain matters which the Pasha felt should not have been discussed. Furthermore, he displeased the French party because of the difficulties he placed in their way in the formation of the new army (Salt, April 4, 1826 in F.O. 78/147). Partisan reporting of this kind is typical and complicates the historian's task. In this instance, however, it is not very important to decide which is correct, as Ibrāhīm Pasha became *kikhyah* in 1827 after his return from the war in Greece.

53. Georges Douin, *Une mission militaire française auprès de Mohamed Aly* (*Correspondance des Généraux Belliard et Boyer*), Société royale de géographie d'Egypte, publications spéciales (Cairo, 1923), 108; Driault, *L'expédition du Crète et de Morée*, 138–140; Salt, April 4 and August 12, 1826 in F.O. 78/147.

54. Salt, April 4, 1826 in F.O. 78/147.

55. Barker, September 22, 1829 in F.O. 78/184.

56. Campbell, October 26, 1833 in F.O. 78/228, September 15, 1835 in F.O. 78/258, and July 6, 1840 in F.O. 78/408b; Bowring, "Egypt and Candia," 121; Clot, II, 183; Deny, 108–111.

57. Campbell, October 8, 1834 in F.O. 78/247, October 28, 1834 in F.O. 142/7, December 11, 1833 and March 24, 1835 in F.O. 142/6, January 24, 1836 in F.O. 78/282, February 6, 1837 in F.O. 142/9, March 30, 1837 in F.O. 78/319, July 6, 1840 in F.O. 78/408b; Cattaui, II, Pt. 1, 190, 249, 266, II, Pt. 2, 442.

Chapter VI. The Failure of the Egyptian Administrative System: Civil Service and Government Regulation of the Agricultural Population

1. Al-Jabartī, IX, 225, 226 (IV, 270).
2. Cattaui, II, Pt. 2, 267, 268.
3. Driault, *L'Egypte et l'Europe*, V, 284, 285.
4. Campbell, November 30, 1838 in F.O. 142/6.
5. Cattaui, II, Pt. 2, 415, 416.
6. Hamont, II, 635.
7. Hamont, II, 634, 635, I, 90–94, 137–139.
8. Yaqub [J.] Artin, "Essai sur les causes du renchérissement de la vie matérielle au Caire dans le courant du 19me siècle (1800 à 1907)," *Mémoires de l'Institut Egyptien*, V (Cairo, 1908), 89, 90.
9. Georges Douin, *L'Egypte de 1828 à 1830*, Société royale de géographie d'Egypte, publications spéciales (Rome, 1935), 455; Barker, April 10, 1832 in F.O. 78/213 and January 25, 1833 in F.O. 78/231; Barnett, September 18, 1841 in F.O. 78/451; Cattaui, II, Pt. 1, 307, II, Pt. 2, 6, 442, 443; Driault, *L'Egypte et l'Europe*, I, 9, 10, III, 93.
10. Hamont, I, 32.
11. Douin, *La mission du Baron de Boislecomte*, 111; Hamont, I, 228. Lists of salaries paid to the pashas of Egypt were included in British dispatches in 1847. These salaries, as shown in Table 34, were supplemented by other sources of income, often irregularly acquired.

TABLE 34. Salaries of Egyptian pashas

Name	Place of origin	Salaries in purses	Rations in piasters
Ibrāhīm (son)	Cavalla	6,000	not given
Sa'īd (son)	Egypt	300*	not given
'Abbās (grandson)	Egypt	300*	not given
Aḥmad (nephew)	Cavalla	4,000	not given
Ibrāhīm (nephew)	Cavalla	600	not given
Kāmil (son-in-law)	Turkey	300*	not given
Sharīf	Cavalla	2,400	not given
Salīm	Abaza	300**	17,856
Salīm	Abaza	300	17,856
Khūrshīd	Georgia	300	17,856
Aḥmad Miniklī	Turkey	300	17,856
Aḥmad Daramallī	Turkey	300	17,856
Sulaymān	France	300	17,856
Ḥusayn	Georgia	300	17,856
Samī	Morea	4,300	17,856
Khālid	Turkey	300	17,856
Aḥmad Ṭāhir	Turkey	dismissed	

* Reduced from 600 to 300 purses.
** Reduced from 2,000 to 300 purses.
Source: Murray, January 1 and January 18, 1847 in F.O. 78/707.

12. Douin, *Une mission militaire française*, 120; Salt, August 12, 1826 in F.O. 78/147. It was reported in 1826 that Muḥammad 'Alī had scarcely enough funds to pay for ships which he had ordered from France. No one was being paid, not even the Europeans in his service (Douin, *Une mission militaire française*, 108).

13. Artin, *Landed Property*, 80, 81; Campbell, February 26, 1838 in F.O. 142/9; Barnett, April 16, 1845 in F.O. 78/623.

14. Barnett, October 16, 1843 in F.O. 142/13.

15. Douin, *La mission du Baron de Boislecomte*, 145.

16. Salt, April 4, 1826 in F.O. 78/147. The proposal made by Drovetti included also the dismissal of all Turkish officers and soldiers who refused to join the new Egyptian army (the *Niẓām Jadīd*). It was not until 1829, however, that Muḥammad 'Alī accepted the idea in principle and began to act upon it by dismissing a group of Turks from the army and navy (Salt, April 4, 1826 in F.O. 78/174; Barker, August 1, 1829 in F.O. 78/184).

17. Campbell, June 13, 1833 in F.O. 78/227 and October 8, 1834 in F.O. 78/247; Bowring, "Egypt and Candia," 6–9; Clot, I, 261, 262; Hamont, I, 290.

18. Hamont, I, 287.

19. Douin, *La mission du Baron de Boislecomte*, 140.

20. Edward William Lane, *The Manners and Customs of the Modern Egyptians* (London, 1944), 293.

21. Hamont, I, 291.

22. Hamont, I, 397; Clot, II, 186; Cattaui, II, Pt. 2, 372; Driault, *L'Egypte et l'Europe*, IV, 395, V, 368, 369.

23. Lane, 293.

24. Hamont, I, 294, 295.

25. Hamont, I, 288.

26. Bowring, "Egypt and Candia," 197.

27. Polites, *L'hellénisme et l'Egypte*, I, 174.

28. Larking, January 24, 1840 in F.O. 78/414 and January 21, 1841 in F.O. 78/452; Barnett, November 12, 1841 and December 1, 1841 in F.O. 142/13; Driault, *L'Egypte et l'Europe*, IV, 235, 236; Bowring, "Egypt and Candia," 9; Prince Hermann von Pückler-Muskau, *Egypt and Mehemet Ali*, trans. H. Evans Lloyd (London, 1845), I, 60, 61.

29. See Chapter VII, note 20.

30. Al-Jabartī, VIII, 322, 323 (IV, 142), VIII, 344 (IV, 152), VIII, 346 (IV, 153), VIII, 348 (IV, 154), IX, 185 (IV, 251, 252); de Vaulabelle, IX, 400; Driault *Mohamed Aly et Napoléon*, 195.

31. Al-Jabartī, IX, 190–194 (IV, 254–256).

32. Al-Jabartī, IX, 185 (IV, 251, 252), IX, 230 (IV, 272), IX, 232 (IV, 273); Edouard Driault, *La formation de l'empire de Mohamed Aly de l'Arabie au Soudan (1814–1823)*, Société royale de géographie d'Egypte, publications spéciales (Cairo, 1927), 106; Douin, *La mission du Baron de Boislecomte*, 87; Bowring, "Egypt and Candia," 196, 197.

33. Campbell, April 25, 1834 in F.O. 142/7.

34. Douin, *La mission du Baron de Boislecomte*, 87–89; Cattaui, II, Pt. 1, 61, 67, 68; Colin, Pt. 3, 70–71; Bowring, "Egypt and Candia," 11, 14, 46; Hamont, I, 26–30; Clot, II, 198; Campbell, January 22, 1838 in F.O. 78/342, Part 1, and July 6, 1840 in F.O. 78/408b.

35. Campbell writes concerning price fixing: "If the government gave the fellahs the price at which the produce would be sold to the merchants, after deducting a fair remuneration (say 8 or 10 per cent) for commission and expenses, the system would be a just one, and in its general outline well calculated for Egypt. But in order not only to avoid all risk of loss but even to gain, the government always takes care to levy a difference of from 60 to 80 per cent and sometimes more between the price given to the fellah, and the probable price to be paid for the produce by the merchants at Alexandria. The charges for transportation and warehousing do not exceed 7 to 8 per

cent, so that an immense sum goes to the Pasha on raw produce" (Campbell, July 6, 1840 in F.O. 78/408b).

36. Cattaui, II, Pt. 1, 261, II, Pt. 2, 115; Campbell, July 6, 1840 in F.O. 78/408b; Merruau, 52–54; R. R. Madden, *Travels in Turkey, Egypt, Nubia, and Palestine in 1824, 1825, 1826, and 1827* (London, 1829), I, 293; Yates, II, 56–67.

37. Hamont, I, 48–62, 198; Madden, *Travels*, I, 246–248; Wilkinson, I, 468–470; Merruau, 58–60; Cattaui, I, 95, 124; Barnett, March 16, 1845 in F.O. 142/13.

38. Hamont, I, 107, 108.

39. Both Duhamel and the British Consul in Alexandria confirmed this, although other writers did not. See Clot, II, 206; Merruau, 56, 57; Douin, *La mission du Baron de Boislecomte*, 129; Cattaui, II, Pt. 2, 137, 375, 376; Sloane, May 12, 1836 in F.O. 78/285; Campbell, September 15, 1835 in F.O. 78/258 and July 6, 1840 in F.O. 78/408b; Baptistin Poujoulat, *Voyage à Constantinople dans l'Asie Mineure, en Mésopotamie, à Palmyre, en Syrie, en Palestine, et en Egypte* (Paris, 1840, 1841), II, 540, 541; C. Rochfort Scott, *Rambles in Egypt and Candia, etc.* (London, 1837), II, 162–165; Joseph F. Nahas, *Situation économique et sociale du fellah égyptien* (Paris, 1901), 44. See Chapter VII for further commentary on the breakdown of the administrative system.

Chapter VII. The Failure of the Egyptian Administrative System: Finances

1. John Lewis Burckhardt, *Arabic Proverbs, etc.* (London, 1875, 2d ed.), 279.

2. See Appendix VI.

3. For the amount of revenue sent to Istanbul in the eighteenth century see Gibb and Bowen, I, Pt. 2, 40–42. In 1829 the amount remitted to Istanbul by Muḥammad ʿAlī was as follows: fixed tribute—2,000,000 francs at 35 centimes per piaster (*c.* 6,400,000 piasters); gifts—110,000 francs at 35 centimes per piaster (*c.* 352,000 piasters) (Douin, *La mission du Baron de Boislecomte*, 128). After the first Syrian War the amount remitted to Istanbul totaled 8,750,000 piasters (17,500 purses) broken down as follows: 6,000,000 piasters (12,000 purses) for Egypt; 2,750,000 piasters (5,500 purses) for Syria, i.e., 750,000 piasters (1,500 purses) for Damascus, 750,000 piasters (1,500 purses) for Aleppo, 750,000 piasters (1,500 purses) for Acre, Tripoli, Sidon, 500,000 piasters (1,000 purses) for Adana (Colin, Pt. 1, 106; Campbell, September 13, 1833 in F.O. 78/228, February 7, 1835 in F.O. 142/6, July 6, 1840 in F.O. 78/408b). After the second Syrian War the annual remittance to the Sultan was 30,000,000 piasters (60,000 purses), which amounted to £300,000 or 7,500,000 francs (at 25 centimes per piaster) (Murray, January 1, 1847 and May 28, 1847 in F.O. 78/707). In other words, the remittance between the years just preceding the first Syrian War and those immediately following the second Syrian War had tripled in value when cited in francs and had increased about five times when cited in piasters, the difference simply reflecting the decrease in the value of the piaster in the intervening years.

4. Barker, November 28, 1827 in F.O. 78/160.

5. Barker, January 15, 1831 in F.O. 78/202; Cattaui, II, Pt. 1, 17, 18, 370, II, Pt. 2, 47; Campbell, August 22, 1833, February 28, 1834, and February 7, 1835 in F.O. 142/6, September 13 and October 25, 1833 in F.O. 78/228.

6. Campbell, May 21, 1833 in F.O. 142/7. The exaggeration of Egyptian revenues was not confined to Muḥammad ʿAlī alone. The Administrator-General of Egyptian Finances for the French army of occupation, E. Poussielgue, pointed out in his report of September 22, 1799 (1 Vendémiaire, an VIII), that the prevailing estimate of 49,000,000 to as high as 60,000,000 francs for the ordinary revenues of the country, including customs, did not, in fact, reflect the real situation. Instead, he claimed, the figures were closer to 19,000,000 in peacetime and, at most, 20,000,000 if commerce was well managed and well protected and 12,000.000 to 13,000,000 francs in wartime (*Copies of Original Letters*, Pt. 2, 123).

7. Douin, *La mission du Baron de Boislecomte*, 125. The following are figures submitted by other observers. Barker estimated in 1827 that Muḥammad ʿAlī's revenues

amounted to less than £4,000,000 in the best years (Barker, November 28, 1827 in F.O. 78/160). Mimaut sent his government a semi-official budget which he obtained in 1829 which placed the Pasha's total revenue at 30,290,000 dollars, but he mentioned that the *Journal du Commerce* of July 20, 1829, put it at only 20,580,000 dollars. In his opinion, the two estimates were exaggerated in opposite directions and he would himself put the amount at 25,000,000 dollars or 131,250,000 francs (Douin, *L'Egypte de 1828 à 1830*, 380, 381). Even this compromise figure far exceeded the amount in Boislecomte's budget for 1829 which listed Muḥammad 'Alī's revenues as follows.

In his capacity of sovereign	45,293,000 francs
In his capacity of landowner, manufacturer, and merchant	44,170,000 francs
	89,463,000 francs

Boislecomte claimed that the revenue of Egypt was about equal to that of France and five times that of Russia (Douin, *La mission du Baron de Boislecomte*, 125–127). Muḥammad 'Alī and Bāghūṣ Bey, according to Barker, claimed in 1832 that the annual revenue of Egypt amounted to 40,000,000 dollars, but Barker felt that the maximum could be no more than 35,000,000 (£ 7,000,000) (Barker, June 22, 1830 in F.O. 142/3 and April 10, 1832 in F.O. 78/213). Colin said that the total revenue for 1250/1834–35 amounted to 311,400,000 piasters (622,820 purses) (Colin, Pt. 1, 105). Campbell's figure for this year approximated Colin's. Campbell also mentioned that Muḥammad 'Alī had claimed that his annual income amounted to 1,200,000 purses, or 30,000,000 dollars, which Campbell felt was an exaggeration, as the revenue of Egypt was usually 18,000,000 to 23,000,000 dollars and only once exceeded 25,000,000 (Campbell, July 6, 1840 in F.O. 78/408b). In 1836 Duhamel said that the total revenue at Muḥammad 'Alī's disposal was 612,860 purses (306,430,000 piasters) of which 137,128 purses (68,564,000 piasters) were derived from trade. He claimed that when commerce was in a flourishing state Egyptian revenues could come to 15,321,500 dollars; the estimated 20,000,000 to 22,000,000 dollars, given by some as the amount which could be attained, he felt to be based on faulty research (Cattaui, II, Pt. 2, 409, 410). Count Medem said in 1838 that the Pasha's annual revenues were estimated at an average of 18,000,000 dollars or 360,000,000 piasters (720,000 purses) (Cattaui, III, 255).

8. This figure, taken from the Egyptian budget for the Coptic year ending September 28, 1847, shows the amount of the Egyptian revenue at the end of Muḥammad 'Alī's reign. The figure is 600,403 purses, 229 piasters (300,201,729 piasters). At approximately this period one purse equaled 125 centimes or 0.25 centimes per piaster. Thus the 1846–47 revenue amounted to 75,050,432 francs (Murray, May 28, 1847 in F.O. 78/707 and March 17, 1848 in F.O. 78/757).

9. Baron de Boislecomte does not make clear whether the amount given for 1825 and 1826 is for each year or for the two years, but in view of conditions in the country at that time (see below, Chapter VII), his figure probably covers the two-year period.

10. See Gibb and Bowen, I, Pt. 2, 49–59; Samuel-Bernard, II; al-Jabartī, VII–IX (III, IV).

11. Douin, *La mission du Baron de Boislecomte*, 130.

12. In 1838 Muḥammad 'Alī prohibited the circulation of Turkish piasters and the merchants, refusing to take a loss, exported them. The Pasha then began to mint his own coins, bearing the mark of the Sultan on one side and "coined in Cairo" on the reverse, this measure being taken to avoid any accusation of impinging upon the Sultan's prerogative to mint coins for the Empire. The intrinsic value of the new money was made equal to its nominal one, the imperial dollar of Austria valued at 20 piasters serving as the base and other foreign money being fixed at proportional values. Although the new specie became standard currency and circulated freely in the country along with European money, these monetary changes did not overcome the shortage of specie. Consequently, there was an inadequate supply of specie in circulation to serve the commercial needs of the country (Campbell, October 1, 1838

in F.O. 142/9; Cattaui, III, 88,89). Another currency change occurred in 1842. The Pasha regulated the prices at which all foreign coins could pass in Egypt, declaring that infringements of his tariff (see Yates, I, 351, 352, II, 459; Wilkinson, I, 102–104) would invoke severe penalties. Nevertheless, the decrease in the value of Turkish coins, reintroduced after the second Syrian War, as well as that of some Egyptian coins, caused great confusion (Barnett, January 13, 1842 in F.O. 142/13). Much of the specie of the Turkish mint, exported from Egypt to Istanbul at this time, was not replaced so that once again there was an insufficient supply of specie in circulation (Stoddart, January 21, 1842 in F.O. 78/504).

13. Stoddart, January 21, 1842 in F.O. 78/504.

14. Douin, *La mission du Baron de Boislecomte*, 125.

15. The sources differ as to whether payments were made in cash or in kind. Payments were, undoubtedly, demanded in both categories as was customary in Egypt (Douin, *Une mission militaire française*, 10; see also note 16 below).

16. Salt, August 12, 1826 in F.O. 78/147.

17. Cattaui, I, 113; Barker, March 10, 1828 in F.O. 78/170 and January 25, 1833 in F.O. 78/231; Barnett, June 10, 1843 in F.O. 78/541; Stoddart, March 23, 1844 in F.O. 78/584.

18. The figures in Table 35, like all statistics for this period, are tentative; nevertheless, they provide some basis by which to compare the value of the land tax with the total revenue. They also reveal the rate of increase in land taxes.

TABLE 35. Value of the land tax, period of the French occupation until 1846–47

Period (and source)	Land tax		
	In Egyptian currency (piasters)	Conversion rate (centimes per piaster)	In francs
French occupation (Estève)	6,855,700 and 29 paras	—	9,672,946 and 24 centimes
1236/1820–21 (Mengin)	66,054,065 and 20 paras	—	20,000,000
1829 (Boislecomte)	*c.* 55,390,000	0.35	19,400,000
1250/1834–35 (Colin and Campbell)	140,500,000	.30	*c.* 42,575,757
1835 (Bowring)	112,500,000	.30	*c.* 33,787,878
1835–36 (Duhamel)	160,000,000	.30	*c.* 48,484,848
1844 (Barnett)	230,000,000	.25	*c.* 57,500,000
1262/1845–46 (Murray)	219,000,000	.25	54,750,000
1846–47 (Murray)	152,545,149	0.25	38,136,287 and 25 centimes

Source: Estève, I, 309; Mengin, *Histoire de l'Egypte*, II, 343, 344; Douin, *La mission du Baron de Boislecomte*, 126; Colin, Pt. 1, 102; Campbell, July 6, 1840 in F.O. 78/408b; Bowring, "Egypt and Candia," 16, 17; Cattaui, II, Pt. 2, 406; Barnett, December 12, 1844 in F.O. 78/583 (see Appendix I); Murray, May 28, 1847 in F.O. 78/707 and March 17, 1848 in F.O. 78/757.

19. Lancret, I, 236–252; Gibb and Bowen, I, Pt. 2, 40–42.

20. The German *reichsthaler* or *thalari* was commonly used in commerce as a medium of exchange and was known in Egypt as *abū ṭāqah*. (The Spanish pillared

dollar was called *abū midfa'* [Gibb and Bowen, I, Pt. 2, 50 n.6].) The term *abū ṭāqah* became corrupted into the French *pataque* which then passed into colloquial Arabic. Taxes were calculated in paper currency known as *pataques* which were fixed at 90 paras, although the coin, known also as *pataque*, fluctuated in value and was worth considerably more (Samuel-Bernard, II, 322 and 322 n.5, 342–344). Forty paras (or *medins*) = 1 piaster (see Gibb and Bowen, I, Pt. 2, 39 n.8, 57, 57 n.3).

21. A dry measure which, at the present time, is 5.447 U.S. bushels. At the time of Muḥammad 'Alī it varied in different parts of Egypt; its capacity was generally five English bushels, but could be as much as eight (Yates, I, 462; Wilkinson, I, 105; Clot, II, 560).

22. Girard, II, 586–589; al-Jabartī, VIII, 244 (IV, 109), VIII, 323 (IV, 142).

23. Al-Jabartī, VIII, 111 (IV, 52).

24. Five *riyāls* amounted to 450 paras when the *riyāl* (dollar) was valued at 90 paras, but the official rate of the *riyāl* (see Gibb and Bowen, I, Pt. 2, 50, 50 n.4) was fixed at 220 paras in Ramaḍān, A.H. 1223 (November 1808), and by Rabī' al-Awwal, A.H. 1224 (April–May 1809), it was being exchanged at a higher rate. Consequently, the five *riyāls* levied on land at the end of the month of Ramaḍān, A.H. 1224 (November 1809), amounted to 1,100 paras minimum and possibly as much as 1,250 paras (al-Jabartī, VIII, 180 [IV, 82], VIII, 203 [IV, 92]).

25. Lancret, I, 249, 250; al-Jabartī, VIII, 22 (IV, 10), VIII, 129 (IV, 60), VIII, 134, 135 (IV, 62), VIII, 150–153 (IV, 69, 70), VIII, 162 (IV, 74), VIII, 200, 201 (IV, 91), VIII, 224, 225 (IV, 101); Petrucci, n.d. in W.O. 1/638 and February 6, 1808 in F.O. 24/3; Douin, *Mohamed Aly, Pacha du Caire*, 207, 208.

26. Gibb and Bowen, I, Pt. 2, 40, 40 n.2; Artin, *Landed Property*, 75, 76, 209, 210; Jacotin, *Tableau de la superficie de l'Egypte*, in *Description de l'Egypte, Etat moderne* (Paris, 1822, 1st ed.), II, Pt. 2, 573; de Vaulabelle, IX, 402, 403; Mengin, *Histoire de l'Egypte*, II, 338.

27. Al-Jabartī, IX, 22 (IV, 177); IX, 77, 78 (IV, 203); IX, 91 (IV, 208). Artin says that classification of lands was placed in the hands of *shaykhs* chosen by the government from each district and that the *shaykhs* of Lower Egypt classified the lands of Upper Egypt and vice versa (Artin, *Landed Property*, 76, 77). There is nothing in al-Jabartī's journal to confirm Artin's statement for the 1813–14 cadastre, but it does report the foundation in 1231/1815–16 of a school for the training of engineers and surveyors. Students were chosen from among Egyptians and Muḥammad 'Alī's personal Mamlūks and the school was placed under the direction of Ḥasan Efendī. A Turk, Rūḥ ad-Dīn Efendī, and several Europeans instructed the students in mathematics and the use of survey instruments brought especially for this purpose from England (al-Jabartī, IX, 192, 193 [IV, 255]). Boutros Pasha Ghali claims that the procedure described by Artin took place during the survey of 1236/1820–21 (Boutros Ghali, 116). Al-Jabartī mentions, however, that Ibrāhīm brought 60 surveyors from Upper Egypt to carry out the 1236/1820–21 cadastre, that European engineers and surveyors, assisted by Copt surveyors, made the survey, and that the more exact methods of the Europeans were employed despite resistance on the part of the Copt chief, al-Mu'allim Ghālī (IX, 329, 330 [IV, 318]). Mengin writes that the Cadastre of 1236/1820–21 was directed by Masi, a Florentine engineer, with the assistance of several young men instructed by him (Mengin, *Histoire de l'Egypte*, II, 342).

28. De Vaulabelle, IX, 403; Burckhardt, 158–160; Wilkinson, I, 105. The size of the Egyptian *faddān* has since been reduced. It now equals 4,200.786 m^2 (1.038 acres) as compared to 4,416.5⅓ m^2 in 1813–14.

29. Al-Jabartī, IX, 87 (IV, 207).

30. Al-Jabartī, IX, 91 (IV, 208); Boutros Ghali, 116. Burckhardt claims that the decrease in the size of the *faddān* produced an increase in the government's revenues estimated by him at between £ 20,000 to £ 30,000 per annum ((Burckhardt, 160).

31. Artin, *Landed Property*, 76, 77, 127.

32. Clot, II, 204; Mengin, *Histoire de l'Egypte*, II, 340; al-Jabartī, IX, 91 (IV, 208). See Chapter VI.

33. Copts were removed from the *dīwān* of Ibrāhīm ad-Daftardār in 1812 on the grounds that they were disloyal to the interests of the Pasha. Al-Jabartī, however, remarks that the true reason for their removal was that Muḥammad 'Alī wished to have all the profits from the country, whatever their importance, and to prevent every-one else from making any profit (VIII, 313, 314 [IV, 138]).

34. Mengin, *Histoire de l'Egypte*, II, 340, 341.

35. Mengin, *Histoire de l'Egypte*, II, 341; al-Jabartī, IX, 185 (IV, 251, 252), IX, 228, 229 (IV, 271, 272).

36. Bowring, November 23, 1837 in F.O. 78/323: Muḥammad 'Alī said that "notwithstanding the wars in which I have been engaged, I have not augmented the amount of taxes. Other princes always do this."

37. Al-Jabartī, 276 (IV, 292, 293).

38. Al-Jabartī, IX, 310 (IV, 308, 309), IX, 316 (IV, 311).

39. Driault, *La formation de l'empire de Mohamed Aly*, 275; Boutros Ghali, 116, 117; Mengin, *Histoire de l'Egypte*, II, 342–344.

40. A weight which is equivalent to 99.049 lbs. or 44.927 kgms. In Muḥammad 'Alī's day, it was generally thought of as equal to a British cwt., although weighing about 98¾ lbs. avoirdupois. The *qinṭār* varied, however, from 100 *raṭls* (a *raṭl* equaling *c.* 15¾ oz. avoirdupois, frequently referred to as 1 lb.) to 150, according to the commodity (Yates, I, 460, 461; Wilkinson, I, 105; Bowring, "Egypt and Candia," 195).

41. Salt, April 4, 1826 in F.O. 78/147; Artin, "Essai sur les causes," 135. A decline in European cotton prices in 1825 led Muḥammad 'Alī to suspend the sale of his cotton rather than lower prices. This may account, in part, for the decreased cotton exports in 1825 (Driault, *L'expédition du Crète et de Morée*, 112).

42. Driault, *L'expédition du Crète et de Morée*, 191; Salt, August 12, 1826 in F.O. 78/147; Barker, November 5, 1827 in F.O. 142/2; Cattaui, I, 101, 109, 110.

43. Several other examples of remission of taxes may be cited: a decree dated Rabī' al-Awwal 16, A.H. 1238 (December 16, 1822), exempted from tax the lands whose harvest had been accidentally burned; the decree dated Jumādā 'l-Ūlā 20, A.H. 1238 (February 2, 1823), gave a remission of taxes retroactive from A.H. 1237 (1821) for the total tax of land whose harvest had been destroyed by severity of weather such as frost and dry wind or by parasitical plants (Gouvernement égyptien, Ministère des Finances, *La législation en matière immobilière en Egypte, etc.* [Cairo, 1901, 2d ed.], xiii; Boutros Ghali, 117; Artin, *Landed Property*, 166, 167).

44. Douin, *La mission du Baron de Boislecomte*, 129. The distribution of taxes in 1826 on inundated lands was as follows: class I, good quality, 674,000 hectares, 21 francs; class II, medium quality, 264,000 hectares, 13 francs; class III, poor quality, 221,000 hectares, 11 francs.

45. The dispatch in which this figure appears (Salt, March 3, 1827 in F.O. 78/160) is somewhat vague as to the precise amount of the indebtedness.

46. Salt, March 3, 24, April 4 and August 27, 1827 in F.O. 78/160; Cattaui, I, 91.

47. The foreign representatives felt certain that Muḥammad 'Alī's sudden personal preoccupation with administrative affairs was due to his desire to appear indifferent to diplomatic events after his defeats in Greece; Consul-General Barker suggested that Muḥammad 'Alī feared a blockade of Alexandria and had decided to remain in the Delta, for "a blockading squadron sailing to and fro before his palace windows is a view, that it is thought, he is anxious to avoid" (Barker, May 17, 1828 in F.O. 142/2; Cattaui, I, 215, 220).

48. Barker, February 29, 1828 in F.O. 142/2; Douin, *L'Egypte de 1828 à 1830*, 336.

49. Barker, April 10, 1832 in F.O. 78/213.

50. Douin, *La mission du Baron de Boislecomte*, 128; Benis, II, 47. Other writers give varying tax rates (see Boutros Ghali, 117; Clot, II, 204; Bowring, "Egypt and Candia," 45; Cattaui, II, Pt. 2, 405).

51. Campbell, April 25, 1834 in F.O. 78/245 and October 8, 1834 in F.O. 78/247; Cattaui, II, Pt. 1, 76.

52. Campbell, June 25, 1835 in F.O. 78/257 and September 15, 1835 in F.O. 78/258; Sloan, May 12, 1836 in F.O. 78/285; Cattaui, II, Pt. 1, 351; Pückler-Muskau, I, 59.

53. Cattaui, II, Pt. 2, 137, 138; Campbell, March 30, 1837 in F.O. 142/9 and May 25, 1837 in F.O. 78/319.

54. Cattaui, II, Pt. 2, 294, 314, 315, 442, 443.

55. Campbell, January 25, 1838 in F.O. 78/342.

56. Muḥammad 'Alī appeared less concerned with affairs in Upper Egypt, primarily because Salīm Pasha, *mufattish* of Upper Egypt, enjoyed the Pasha's complete confidence. Furthermore, the documents on Upper Egypt had not been completed for presentation at the meetings.

57. 'Abd ar-Raḥmān was a renegade Copt who had by measures of extreme cruelty extracted 60,000 purses from the provinces in 1837 on account of the arrears amounting to 190,000 purses. He had also managed to force the *fallāḥīn* of ash-Sharqīyah province to pay 150,000 purses, a province from which, he claimed, only 18 had previously been paid. In the course of this latter feat of tax collection he caused the death of 36 *fallāḥīn* under bastinado (Campbell, May 25, 1837 in F.O. 78/319; Poujoulat, II, 547–551). Cruelty of this kind was said to be of daily occurrence (Barnett, March 26, 1845 in F.O. 142/13).

58. Cattaui, II, Pt. 1, 17, 18, 261, 266; Benis, II, 106.

59. It was precisely this situation which led to Muḥammad 'Alī's policy of conceding tax farms, *'uhdahs*, to wealthy individuals, native and foreign. In other words, the principal cause for creating *'uhdahs* stemmed from the peasants' inability to meet the burden of taxation and Muḥammad 'Alī's desire to protect his income from heavy losses which would result from the bankruptcy of an increasing number of villages.

60. Campbell, February 26, 1838 in F.O. 142/9; Cattaui, III, 45.

61. Driault, *L'Egypte et l'Europe*, III, 398, 399. Previously, Muḥammad 'Alī had received offers of large loans which he had refused because of the ruinous conditions attached to them. He usually tapped resources available in Egypt, such as merchants who often made advances. On several occasions he contracted loans, but these were always kept to a minimum. The request for a large foreign loan at the time of the second Syrian War was therefore an unusual occurrence (Campbell, September 17, 1833 and September 23, 1834 in F.O. 142/7, October 12 and 24, 1833 in F.O. 78/228, November 12, 1833 in F.O. 142/6; Sloan, June 3, 1836 in F.O. 78/285; Cattaui, II, Pt. 2, 53).

62. Campbell, March 21, 1838 in F.O. 78/342, Part 1, September 8 and 10, 1838 in F.O. 78/343, Part 2, July 6, 1840 in F.O. 78/408b; Hodges, February 21, March 20, and June 6, 1840 in F.O. 78/404; Driault, *L'Egypte et l'Europe*, I, 9, 10, II, 61, 62, 294, III, 93; Cattaui, II, Pt. 2, 314, 315, III, 188, 199, 216, 254–256.

63. Larking, January 21, 1841 in F.O. 78/452.

64. The *kharāj* (in this context, the poll tax, *jizyah*) continued to be levied on non-Muslims. The budget for 1250/1834–35 listed the amount of *kharāj* at 400,000 piasters (800 purses) collected from Jews and Christians at the rate of 9, 18, and 36 piasters per person (Colin, Pt. 1, 102). The amount of *kharāj* collected for the year 1835–36 was 900 purses; approximately ten years later it amounted to 480 purses or 60,000 francs (Cattaui, II, Pt. 2, 405, 406; Murray, May 28, 1847 in F.O. 78/707 and March 17, 1848 in F.O. 78/757). But see Boislecomte's figures which do not tally with any of these amounts (Douin, *La mission du Baron de Boislecomte*, 128).

65. Clot set the figure at 15 to 500 piasters and said that the tax was levied on individuals and cities and on houses in villages (Clot, II, 204).

66. Barker, December 4, 1832 in F.O. 78/214; Cattaui, I, 43, II, Pt. 2, 405. The *furdah* produced the following revenues: in 1829, on 780,000 families at 8 dollars, 6,240,000 dollars, or, according to another estimate, 12,250,000 francs; in 1250/1834–35, 37,500,000 piasters; 1835–36, 30,000,000 piasters; 1262/1845–46, 40,000,000 piasters (10,000,000 francs); 1846–47, 52,718,895 piasters (Douin, *La mission du Baron de Boislecomte*, 126; Douin, *L'Egypte de 1828 à 1830*, 381; Colin, Pt. 1, 102; Campbell, July 6, 1840 in F.O. 78/408b; Cattaui, II, Pt. 2, 406; Murray, May 28, 1847 in F.O. 78/707 and March 17, 1848 in F.O. 78/757).

67. A report in 1848 mentioned that the *furdah* deduction was made from the salaries of public servants to serve as a retirement fund from which pensions and allowances were drawn (Murray, March 17, 1848 in F.O. 78/757).

68. Hamont noted that failure to pay the tax resulted in imprisonment for the head of the family until it was paid (Hamont, I, 110).

69. A Turkish word derived from the Persian, meaning annual tax (Gibb and Bowen, I, Pt. 1, 148 n.1).

70. Salt, May 10, 1822 in F.O. 78/112; Barker, December 4, 1832 in F.O. 78/214.

71. Lancret, I, 242, 243; Artin, *Landed Property*, 118, 119; al-Jabartī, IX, 317 (IV, 311); Salt, May 10, 1822 in F.O. 78/112; Douin, *La mission du Baron de Boislecomte*, 85, 130; Bowring, "Egypt and Candia," 24; Cattaui, II, Pt. 2, 406; Clot, II, 205.

72. Clot, II, 205. A government monopoly had previously existed in cattle. They had been sold at fixed prices to the government which sold them to those to whom it had farmed out the right to kill and sell meat. The monopoly ended in 1834 and was replaced by this tax (Campbell, April 25, 1834 in F.O. 78/245).

73. Boutros Ghali, 117; Cattaui, II, Pt. 2, 406; Bowring, "Egypt and Candia," 47.

74. Pückler-Muskau, on the other hand, points out that, although the *fallāḥīn* suffered great hardships and arbitrary oppressions, they were "still in a position, which many of our proletarian population would envy . . ." (I, 50).

75. Hamont, I, 200, 201; Driault, *L'Egypte et l'Europe*, IV, 399, 400, V, 288, 289; Cattaui, II, Pt. 2, 470; Campbell, January 22, 1838 in F.O. 78/342, Part 1; Paton, II, 319, 320; Scipion Marin, *La vérité sur les affaires d'orient, etc.* (Paris, 1841), 4–22.

76. The much vaunted improvement in housing conditions had little or no effect in Egypt. It was carried out on too limited a scale to make any difference. An item (listed as an irregular expense) in the budget of 1846–47 covered the building of three new villages in the European style and amounted to 282 purses, 35 piasters. This amount must be compared with an expense for the same year which covered maintenance of private gardens amounting to 225 purses, 136 piasters, or with the item in the 1845–46 budget covering the wedding expenses of Muḥammad 'Alī's daughter, including a pair of diamond earrings, which totaled 25,162 purses, 61 piasters (Hamont, II, 359, 360; Driault, *L'Egypte et l'Europe*, V, 18, 19; Murray, January 1, 1847 in F.O. 78/707 and March 17, 1848 in F.O. 78/757).

77. Barker, May 20, 1829 in F.O. 78/184.

78. Hamont, I, 31–33, 329, II, 290; Clot, I, 285, 286; Bowring, "Egypt and Candia," 14, 15, 26, 64; Douin, *La mission du Baron de Boislecomte*, 98, 99; Campbell, December 20, 1836 in F.O. 142/9 and January 22, 1838 in F.O. 78/342, Part 1.

79. Michaud, 676, 677.

80. Hamont, I, 36; Clot, II, 104; Bowring, "Egypt and Candia," 19, 123.

81. By 1847 Muḥammad 'Alī was not attending to public business as he had done a decade before. In fact, after the conclusion of the second Syrian War in 1841, the strain, shock, and disappointment which he had suffered from the conflict and from the diplomacy of the Great Powers had begun to affect his nervous system. He was already in his seventies (he was born in Cavalla in A.H. 1182 [1769]) and though apparently physically fit, he already showed signs of senility and mental deterioration. He had become morbidly suspicious and subject to hysterical outbursts, as demonstrated by his behavior at the time of the crisis of July 1844. Generally, he allowed things to slide with little sustained personal supervision. Both he and his son, Ibrāhīm Pasha, old and sick, indulged themselves in a last vacation from the affairs of state: Ibrāhīm traveled to Europe and Muḥammad 'Alī visited Istanbul and Cavalla in 1846. Thus, his exhortation to his officers was rather incongruous. By April 1848 his mind had given way completely and the government then passed into the hands of Ibrāhīm Pasha. (Barnett, October 18, 1841 in F.O. 78/451 and August 29, 1846 in F.O. 142/14; Stoddart, August 23, 1846 in F.O. 78/661B; Murray, June 9, 1847 in F.O. 78/707 and April 9, 1848 in F.O. 78/757).

82. Murray, December 24, 1847 in F.O. 78/708.

83. Georges Douin, *La première guerre de Syrie*, Société royale de géographie d'Egypte, publications spéciales (Cairo, 1931), I, 25, 26, II, 288; Douin, *La mission du Baron de Boislecomte*, 144, 145; Douin, *L'Egypte de 1828 à 1830*, 171, 172; Georges Douin, *Mohamed Aly et l'expédition d'Alger (1829–1830)*, Société royale de géographie d'Egypte, publications spéciales (Cairo, 1930), 221–230; Salt, March 3, 1827 in F.O. 78/160; Bowring, "Egypt and Candia," 145, 146, 150–152.

84. Barker, December 4, 1832 in F.O. 78/214; Douin, *La première guerre de Syrie*, I, 445, 446.

Chapter VIII. Agricultural Practices under Muḥammad ʿAlī

1. Girard points out that agriculture could produce either an absolute profit or a relative profit, depending on the amount of land and capital that was available. In countries possessing an abundance of land but a scarcity of money, it was customary for farmers to cultivate crops requiring a minimum of investment but from which they received only a relative profit. On the other hand, in countries where land was scant or expensive and money plentiful, it was customary to plant crops that could produce the maximum or absolute profit. In Egypt, where capital was deficient and land abundant, crops producing a relative profit would have been the most economical had it not been for the shortage of a third essential in agricultural economics, namely, labor. This shortage of labor made the cultivation of cereals uneconomic, but the Egyptian peasant could not turn to the cultivation of other more profitable crops until he had the capital to invest (Girard, II, 521–525).

2. The greatest absolute profits were earned by crops like sugar, rice, and indigo. There were a few instances when groups of *fallāḥīn* formed associations to raise indigo and process it for commercial purposes, but usually the more prosperous *multazims* cultivated this crop. Sugar was also grown by a few wealthy Mamlūks in Girgā who supplied the raw sugar to the sugar refineries and shared the profits with the manufacturers (Girard, II, 521–525, 545–548, 581–586; Gibb and Bowen, I, Pt. 1, 272, 273).

3. The agricultural seasons, corresponding to the regime of the Nile River, were the following.

1. Flood	summer	*ṣayfī*	planted around April 1 and harvested at the end of July.
2. Recession of flood	autumn	*nīlī*	planted around end of July.
3. Period prior to the flood	spring		planted around March.
4. Low water	winter	*shitwī*	In Upper Egypt, planted around October and harvested in March. In Lower Egypt, planted about November and harvested in April.

(Girard, II, 499, 500; Clot, II, 275, 276, 281, 282; Hamont, I, 154; Mengin, *Histoire de l'Egypte*, II, 345–370; J. Barois, *Irrigation in Egypt*, trans. Major A. M. Miller, U.S. Congress, House of Representatives, 50th Cong., 2d Sess., Mis. Doc. No. 134 [Washington, D.C., 1889], IX, 26, 27.)

4. Hamont, I, 173; Girard, II, 542–544; Driault, *Mohamed Aly et Napoléon*, 147, 148; François Charles-Roux, *La production du coton en Egypte* (Paris, 1908), 151, 152; Gabriel Alphonse Guémard, *Les réformes en Egypte* (*d'Ali-Bey el Kébir à Mehemet-Ali*) (*1760–1848*) (Cairo, 1936), 341, 342.

5. The term *al-quṭn al-hindī* is the one by which long-staple cotton was known in Egypt (see *Lāʾiḥat zirāʿat al-fallāḥ*, 10), while in Europe it was known either as Maho or Jumel cotton. This discrepancy may be traced to the differing versions which exist regarding the introduction of long-staple cotton into Egypt. The conflicting versions appear in these works: Charles-Roux, *La production du coton en Egypte*, 21, 22; Guémard, 343; Polites, *L'hellénisme et l'Egypte moderne*, II, 122, 123; Grégoire, 438,

439; E. de Regny, "Notice sur l'introduction de la culture du coton en Egypte et sur Jumel," *Bulletin de l'Institut Egyptien* (Cairo, 1876), 78–84; Clot, II, 278; Bowring, "Egypt and Candia," 19, 65; Mengin, *Histoire de l'Egypte*, II, 363. The French, wishing to take credit for the introduction of this valuable crop into Egypt, tend to call it Jumel cotton after the Frenchman Jumel who brought Muḥammad 'Alī's attention to the plant. The British, on the other hand, call it Maho cotton after Maho, the Turkish official in whose garden Jumel was said to have first seen the plant. The British term appears to have been used earlier than the French one by Frenchmen themselves, for at the time of the introduction of long-staple cotton, Drovetti, the French representative in Egypt, calls it Maho cotton rather than Jumel cotton (Driault, *L'expédition du Crète et de Morée*, 26–29). The fact that the Russian representative also referred to long-staple cotton as Maho cotton is further evidence that in the early period, at least, the term Maho was more commonly used among Europeans (Cattaui, I, 66, 256).

6. Charles-Roux, *La production du coton en Egypte*, 156; Grégoire, 439, 440; Driault, *L'expédition du Crète et de Morée*, 28.

7. Water-raising devices such as the *sāqiyah, shādūf*, and *tābūt* (Archimedean screw) had long been in use in Egypt. The *shādūf*, which could be built at different levels, was usually used to irrigate summer crops in Upper Egypt where the level of the river was often 8 to 10 meters below the soil (Barois, 26).

8. *Lā'iḥat zirā'at al-fallāḥ*, 10–12, 18, 19; Grégoire, 449; Charles-Roux, *La production du coton en Egypte*, 159, 160. Clot and Bowring also describe cotton cultivation minutely (Clot, II, 278–281; Bowring, "Egypt and Candia," 20).

9. In his article on cotton Grégoire (pp. 444, 448) distinguishes between two grades of cotton, *zavnati* (*sic*), produced on the large estates, and *barrani* (*sic*), usually cotton raised by peasants. *Baladī* was undoubtedly intended for *barrani*, whereas *zavnati* should have been transcribed as *dhawāt*, a word used in Egypt to mean aristocracy. This term, to designate a grade of cotton, probably came into existence after Muḥammad 'Alī's reign (Grégoire published his article in 1862). The American Consul-General, Mr. Thayer, used the term correctly: "It may be observed here that the cotton gathered on the estates of members of the ruling family, being raised under European superintendance with special care, is quoted under the name of 'Zawatt' or Princes' cotton, and ordinarily bears the highest price in the market" (Thayer, March 5, 1863, in Department of State, *Egypt*, Vol. III).

10. Charles-Roux, *La production du coton en Egypte*, 157; Polites, *L'hellénisme et l'Egypte moderne*, II, 123–124; Cattaui, I, 66, II, Pt. 2, 47.

11. Charles-Roux, *La production du coton en Egypte*, 156–160; Polites, *L'hellénisme et l'Egypte moderne*, II, 122–128; Cattaui, I, 256, 299.

12. Stoddart, March 21, 1843 in F.O. 78/542. Grégoire, writing in 1862, noted that when the older *fallāḥīn* spoke of the attention lavished upon the first cotton crops, the younger generation of *fallāḥīn* was astonished and scarcely able to believe its elders (Grégoire, 449).

13. *Lā'iḥat zirā'at al-fallāḥ*, 11, 12, 45, 46; Bowring, "Egypt and Candia," 20; Mengin, *Histoire de l'Egypte*, II, 362; Douin, *Une mission militaire française*, 92, 93; Campbell, March 2, 1837 in F.O. 142/9.

14. Clot, II, 281. A bale weighed 100 kgms. and measured 1 meter high and 1½ meters in diameter (Bowring, "Egypt and Candia," 20).

15. *Nīlī* crops consisting of *dhurah* and kitchen crops like onions provided the Egyptian population with its principal supplies of food and were consequently of great importance to the peasants. Since there was an overlapping of the period of cultivation of *ṣayfī* crops with the harvest of the spring *nīlī* crop, the sowing of the autumn *nīlī* crop, and sometimes the sowing of *shitwī*, *ṣayfī* crops had never been sown in the inundation basins before the reign of Muḥammad 'Alī, but only on the high land rarely reached by the floodwaters. In this way, the peasants' food supply had been safeguarded. Muḥammad 'Alī, on the other hand, gave precedence to the *ṣayfī* crops at the expense of the *nīlī* crops, thereby jeopardizing the food supply of the native population (Bowring, "Egypt and Candia," 19, 26).

16. Bowring claims that one *faddān* of land could produce as little as 2 *qinṭārs* and as much as 7 or 8, but that the average was 5 ("Egypt and Candia," 19). Compared to the profit that could be made upon one *faddān* of wheat, this was very good. Bowring estimates that a profit of 26 piasters and 20 paras could be earned on one *faddān* of wheat land which sold at 50 piasters per *ardabb* (p. 18).

17. Barker, July 10 and December 31, 1827 in F.O. 142/2; Campbell, July 6, 1840 in F.O. 78/408b; Driault, *L'expédition du Crète et de Morée*, 28; Cattaui, II, Pt. 1, 187, 190, 191, II, Pt. 2, 21, 137, 138; Charles-Roux, *La production du coton en Egypte*, 40, 43–45, 69; Bowring, "Egypt and Candia," 19–21; Grégoire, 441; Gliddon, 22–27; Poujoulat, II, 529.

18. Campbell, February 14, 1839 in F.O. 142/9.

19. The Egyptian grain trade had declined after the Napoleonic Wars, inflicting a serious loss of revenue upon Muḥammad ʿAlī. By the cultivation of long-fiber cotton in demand in the export market Egyptian trade received a new stimulus. Stoddart confirms this point. "The previous consignments of linseed, and sometimes beans, had been an insufficient aliment to useful traffic, but the new export struck root at once in our markets and became the origin of a very important commerce. In 1824 the cargoes of cotton to Liverpool were 44, in 1825 they had augmented to 65" (Stoddart, August 4, 1846 in F.O. 78/663).

20. Muḥammad ʿAlī was quick to recognize the political advantages of cotton cultivation. He offered Great Britain his entire cotton crop in the event of a war between Great Britain and the United States, hoping in this way to obtain certain concessions from Great Britain for furthering his own political aims (Barker, March 8, 1830 in F.O. 78/192).

21. Driault, *L'expédition du Crète et de Morée*, 26, 27, 29.

22. Douin, *L'Egypte de 1828 à 1830*, 436.

23. Douin, *Une mission militaire française*, 10; Driault, *L'expédition du Crète et de Morée*, 28.

24. The figures in Table 36, obtained from the Société Khédiviale d'Agriculture, do not always correspond with other sources, but on the whole they seem fairly reliable. The first figure of 99 *qinṭārs* for 1821 apparently applies to *al-quṭn al-hindī* only, as Mengin, undoubtedly referring to *baladī* or short-staple cotton, mentions that 60,000 *qinṭārs* were raised in the provinces of ash-Sharqīyah and al-Manṣūrīyah in 1821. The figures are in *qinṭārs* (44.927 kgms. or 99.049 lbs.).

TABLE 36. Cotton exports, 1821–1849, in *qinṭārs*

Year	Cotton	Year	Cotton	Year	Cotton
1821	99	1831	186,675	1841	193,507
1822	35,108	1832	136,127	1842	211,030
1823	159,426	1833	56,067	1843	261,064
1824	228,078	1834	143,892	1844	153,363
1825	218,312	1835	213,604	1845	344,955
1826	216,181	1836	243,230	1846	202,040
1827	159,642	1837	315,470	1847	257,492
1828	59,225	1838	238,833	1848	119,965
1829	104,920	1839	134,097	1849	257,510
1830	213,585	1840	159,301		

Source: Artin, "Essai sur les causes," 135.

25. Cattaui, III, 547.

26. Polites, *L'hellénisme et l'Egypte moderne*, II, 125–127; Driault, *L'expédition du Crète et de Morée*, 31, 128, 218; Cattaui, I, 260, II, Pt. 1, 299, II, Pt. 2, 272, 431, 432, 440, III, 58; Douin, *L'Egypte de 1828 à 1830*, 364, 365, 429, 430; Benis, I, 242; de Regny, 81; Campbell, January 24, 1836 in F.O. 78/282; Stoddart, March 23, 1844 in F.O. 78/584; Murray, August 10, 1847 in F.O. 142/15.

27. Driault, *L'expédition du Crète et de Morée*, 28; Barker, March 8, 1830 in F.O. 78/192 and July 6, 1830 in F.O. 142/3; Cattaui, II, Pt. 2, 47, 96; Appendix I.

28. Cattaui, I, 299; Douin, *La mission du Baron de Boislecomte*, 83, 84.

29. Campbell, August 7, 1834 in F.O. 78/246; Cattaui, II, Pt. 2, 381–383.

30. Hamont, I, 179.

31. Mengin, *Histoire de l'Egypte*, II, 357–359, 372; Appendix I.

32. Rice exports from Damietta were given by Girard as follows: 1791, 38,853 *ardabbs*; 1792, 31,039; 1793, 26,256; 1794, 19,242; 1795, 24,275; 1796, 22,315; 1797, 29,544; 1798, 36,863, making a total of 228,387 *ardabbs* (*Memoirs relative to Egypt, written in that Country during the Campaigns of General Bonaparte in the Years 1798 and 1799 etc.*, trans. from the French [London, 1800], 416).

33. Bowring, "Egypt and Candia," 19; Cattaui, II, Pt. 1, 42, II, Pt. 2, 409; Benis, II, 49; Douin, *La mission du Baron de Boislecomte*, 86; Clot, II, 287; Colin, Pt. 3, 70, 71; Stoddart, March 23, 1844 in F.O. 78/584 and April 10, 1845 in F.O. 78/624.

34. At the beginning of the 1820's the price for rice was 122½ *pataques* (about 275½ piasters) for one Damietta *ḍarībah* and 87½ *pataques* (about 197 piasters) for one Rosetta *ḍarībah*. (The Damietta *ḍarībah*, a measurement used in connection with rice and equivalent to about 2 *ardabbs*, was larger than the Rosetta *ḍarībah*. A Damietta *ardabb* weighed 225 *uqqahs*; the Rosetta *ardabb* weighed 155 *uqqahs* [Mengin, *Histoire de l'Egypte*, II, 359].) In 1826 the *fallāḥīn* received from 50 to 60 piasters for a Rosetta *ardabb*. The price was increased slightly in 1827 to 113½ piasters for 208 *uqqahs*. In 1834 the *fallāḥīn* were paid 80 *pataques* (180 piasters) per Damietta *ḍarībah*, although the price at which Muḥammad 'Alī had fixed rice was 109 *pataques* (about 245 piasters) per *ḍarībah*. This is borne out by another set of figures which give, for a Damietta *ardabb*, the price paid to the *fallāḥīn* for each of three different qualities of rice and the price at which each was sold for export: *manzalāwī* rice, bought for 90 piasters, sold for 270 piasters; *kafrāwī* rice, bought for 90 piasters, sold for 270; and *baladī*, bought for 90 piasters, sold for 247½. The Rosetta *ardabb* sold at 200 piasters in 1833, which approximates the 1834 price (Barker, July 10 and December 31, 1827 in F.O. 142/2; Cattaui, II, Pt. 1, 187; Benis, II, 48, 49).

35. Benis, II, 48.

36. Campbell, July 6, 1840 in F.O. 78/408b.

37. Hamont, I, 179–183.

38. Mengin, *Histoire de l'Egypte*, II, 359; Girard, II, 547, 548, 610, 611.

39. Stoddart claims that the refinery was established in 1816 (May 29, 1846 in F.O. 78/663).

40. Referred to by various writers as Reyremoun, Karamoun, Radamoun, Rhadamone, Radamon, and Eraramon.

41. In 1821 a total of 24,000 *qinṭārs* of sugar was produced in Egypt. The refinery at Rayramūn produced 11,000 *qinṭārs* of sugar in 1831 and also molasses from which Egyptian rum was distilled. In 1833 the sugar refined in Egypt was 21,395 *qinṭārs* plus molasses and rum, broken down as follows: 12,995 *qinṭārs* of raw sugar processed at Rayramūn; 30 *qinṭārs*, *mukarrar* quality; 5,198 *qinṭārs*, *kasīr* quality; 20 *qinṭārs*, second quality; 10 *qinṭārs*, third quality; 5 *qinṭārs*, fourth quality; 5 *qinṭārs* crystallized sugar; 9½ *raṭls* brown sugar which was sold to foreigners; 4,800 *qinṭārs* of molasses, 48,000 *uqqahs* of rum of 28 per cent alcohol; at Sāqiyat Mūsā 5,200 *qinṭārs* of raw sugar were refined, producing 2,080 *qinṭārs* of *kasīr* quality; ar-Rawḍah processed 3,200 *qinṭārs* of raw sugar. The total quantity of sugar produced in 1834 amounted to 32,000 *qinṭārs* (Mengin, *Histoire de l'Egypte*, II, 372, Jean Mazuel, *Le sucre en Egypte* [Cairo, 1937], 31; Colin, Pt. 3, 70; Bowring, "Egypt and Candia," 17, 21–23; Clot, II, 293, 294).

42. Mazuel, *Le sucre en Egypte*, 30, 31; Colin, Pt. 3, 71; Stoddart, May 29, 1846 in F.O. 78/663; Mengin, *Histoire de l'Egypte*, II, 361; Hamont, I, 177, 178; Cattaui, II, Pt. 2, 384; Douin, *La mission du Baron de Boislecomte*, 84, 85; Appendix I.

43. Campbell mentions that 'Umar Efendī, an Egyptian who had been trained in England, had been sent to Jamaica to recruit these men (December 25, 1838 in F.O.

78/343, Part 3). He had also been sent there to examine the manufacture of rum in order to introduce into Egypt the best methods for its production (Bowring, "Egypt and Candia," 23). Furthermore, Ibrāhīm Pasha assigned his second gardener, Mr. McCallogh, an Englishman, to go to Rio de Janeiro to study sugar cultivation there and to bring back the best varieties of sugar cane (Campbell, December 25, 1838 in F.O. 78/343, Part 3).

44. Mazuel, *Le sucre en Egypte*, 31.

45. Barker, July 10 and December 31, 1827 in F.O. 142/2. An *uqqah* equals 2.73 lbs. avoirdupois and consists of 400 drams (drachms [Ar. *dirham*]). One *uqqah* equals 2¾ *raṭls*. It should, however, be noted that the number of *uqqahs* per *qinṭār* varied in accordance with the commodity or the part of the country (Yates, I, 460, 461; Wilkinson, I, 105; W. Willcocks, *Egyptian Irrigation* [London, 1889], 347).

46. Bowring, "Egypt and Candia," 22; Campbell, July 6, 1840 in F.O. 78/408b; Cattaui, II, Pt. 2, 384. Campbell claims that sugar imported from France was cheaper than Egyptian sugar. Duhamel, on the other hand, says that European sugar was more expensive, but of a finer quality.

47. Stoddart, May 29, 1846 in F.O. 78/663; Bowring, "Egypt and Candia," 22; Appendix I.

48. Stoddart, May 29, 1846 in F.O. 78/663. This statement was made in connection with an official inquiry by the British government, as part of the movement to ban all goods produced by slave labor, whether or not slave labor was employed in Egypt for sugar production.

49. Bowring, "Egypt and Candia," 21, 22.

50. Girard, II, 545–547; Cattaui, II, Pt. 2, 385.

51. Douin, *Une mission militaire française*, 10; Cattaui, II, Pt. 2, 385, 386; Clot, II, 294; Bowring, "Egypt and Candia," 23; Campbell, July 6, 1840 in F.O. 78/408b. There is some disagreement about the number of indigo works established. Clot put the number at 17; Duhamel, 12; Bowring, 9; and Campbell, only 7.

52. Cattaui, II, Pt. 2, 385; Campbell, January 22, 1838 in F.O. 78/342, Part 1, and January 25, 1838 in F.O. 142/9.

53. Colin, Pt. 3, 71, 72; Douin, *La mission du Baron de Boislecomte*, 84; M.A. Linant de Bellefonds, *Mémoires sur les principaux travaux d'utilité publique executés en Egypte depuis la plus haute antiquité jusqu'à nos jours* (Paris, 1872, 1873), 364, 365.

54. Stoddart, April 10, 1845 in F.O. 78/624 and May 29, 1846 in F.O. 78/663; Appendix I.

55. Mengin, *Histoire de l'Egypte*, II, 372; Clot, II, 287; Bowring, "Egypt and Candia," 17.

56. Winter (*shitwī*) crops consisted of wheat, beans, barley, flax, clover, fenugreek, safflower (*carthamus tinctorius*), lentils, chick peas, lupin, tobacco, and opium. *Nīlī* crops were divided into two classes: *damīrah* and *nabarī*. The former was planted on low land, whereas the latter was planted on high land and required artificial irrigation. Since the period in spring and autumn was short, only those crops which matured quickly could be accommodated (Girard, II, 499, 500).

57. Driault, *L'expédition du Crète et de Morée*, 35, 36, 128, 140, 217, 218; Douin, *Une mission militaire française*, 59; Cattaui, I, 256, 299, 300; Salt, October 28, 1824 in S.P. 105/142, April 4 and August 12, 1826 in F.O. 78/147.

58. Cattaui, I, 290. Abraham Abro, the cousin of Bāghūṣ Bey, was ceded 10,000 *ardabbs* of beans at 3 dollars per *ardabb* for bringing the news of the rise in price to Muḥammad 'Alī. It was estimated that Abro would make a profit of at least 1½ dollars per *ardabb* on the transaction.

59. Cattaui, I, 292, 300, 326; Barker, May 30, 1827 in F.O. 78/160 and March 10, 1828 in F.O. 78/170. Artin gives the average price of foodstuffs per *ardabb* between 1825 and 1836 as wheat, 10 dollars; beans, 9 dollars; lentils, 130 piasters; barley, 9 dollars; maize and *dhurah*, 10 dollars; peas, 70 piasters; lupin, 30 piasters; fenugreek, 19 piasters (Artin, "Essai sur les causes," 101).

60. Barker, March 10, 1829 in F.O. 78/184; Cattaui, I, 345.

61. Barker, October 2, 9, and 20, 1829 in F.O. 78/184; Douin, *L'Egypte de 1828 à 1830*, 382; Cattaui, I, 365, 366. Excessive flood was not the only scourge from which agriculture suffered in Egypt. Locusts were not infrequent, although rarely mentioned by consular representatives. Muḥammad 'Alī took active measures to combat an invasion of locusts by offering a government award for every pound of dead locusts brought in by the *fallāḥīn* (Murray, March 20, 1849 in F.O. 78/804; Paton, II, 226).

62. Douin, *L'Egypte de 1828 à 1830*, 213–215; Hamont, I, 111; Georges Douin, *La première guerre de Syrie*, I, 483, 484, 528. Pezzoni claims that Muḥammad 'Alī managed to profit from the misery of the people by adulterating the flour. He earned 10,000 purses in this manner (Cattaui, I, 376).

63. Barker, September 14, 1832 in F.O. 142/3, December 4, 1832 in F.O. 78/214, and January 4, 1833 in F.O. 142/4.

64. Cattaui, II, Pt. 2, 322, 432, 440, 442, 464, 488; Campbell, October 8, 1837 in F.O. 78/320; Bowring, "Egypt and Candia," 14.

65. Cattaui, II, Pt. 2, 496; John Bowring, *Autobiographical Recollections of Sir John Bowring* (London, 1877), 181–183; Campbell, November 7, 1837 in F.O. 78/321; Thurburn, December 1, 1837 in F.O. 78/322.

66. Cattaui, III, 2, 7, 8, 15, 16, 27, 45, 55, 69, 91, 92, 95, 96; Campbell, January 22 and January 25, 1838 in F.O. 78/342, Part 1, and April 24, 1838 in F.O. 78/342, Part 2; Thurburn, December 1, 1837 in F.O. 78/322; Driault, *L'Egypte et l'Europe*, III, 167; Athanase G. Politis [Polites], *Le conflit turco-égyptien de 1838–1841 et les dernières années du règne de Mohamed Aly, d'après les documents diplomatiques grecs*, Société royale de géographie d'Egypte, publications spéciales (Cairo, 1931), 15.

67. Driault, *L'Egypte et l'Europe*, III, 120, 167, 398, 399, IV, 131, 132; Cattaui, III, 560, 561, 566; Barnett, October 17, 1841 in F.O. 78/451.

68. Barnett, October 16 and November 13, 1842 in F.O. 142/13, October 18, November 16, December 10, 1842 in F.O. 78/502, and October 25, 1842 in F.O. 142/14; Stoddart, October 21, 1842 in F.O. 78/504; Politis [Polites], *Le conflit turco-égyptien*, 142; Paton, II, 224–226.

69. Barnett, October 25, 1845 in F.O. 78/624 and February 16, 1846 in F.O. 78/663; Stoddart, March 23, 1844 in F.O. 78/584, April 10, 1845 in F.O. 78/624, and February 17, 1846 in F.O. 78/663; Murray, October 22, 1846 in F.O. 142/15.

70. Cattaui, II, Pt. 2, 388–391. Campbell says of the situation during Mamlūk times with regard to foodstuffs: "In regard to the extraordinary augmentation in the price of the generality of produce, it must be understood that all the ground which was cultivated in the time of the Mamlouks was, in great part, employed for the production of objects of nourishment—viz.—wheat, barley, beans, Indian corn, garden stuffs, etc., etc., the produce of which was immense, and the people were also enabled to rear fowls, sheep, goats, etc., and consequently the prices, in comparison with those of the present time, were but a sixth or eighth part, and in some cases a tenth part" (Campbell, January 22, 1838 in F.O. 78/342, Part 1).

71. Bowring, "Egypt and Candia," 17. Campbell also mentions that the Pasha took foodstuff to supply the army and navy. Furthermore, the Pasha provided rations for the people employed in the manufactories (Campbell, January 22, 1838 in F.O. 78/342, Part 1). Medem also reports that the governors of Lower Egypt were ordered in 1838 to collect 450,000 *ardabbs* of *dhurah* for the army (Cattaui, III, 45).

72. Bowring, "Egypt and Candia," 200. The report made by this English mechanic is typical of similar statements made by other people. The literature produced at that time was almost entirely polemical. One could only be an advocate of Muḥammad 'Alī or an enemy. Estimates reflected exaggerations in one direction or the other. With very few exceptions no one seems to have taken the trouble to make an objective study which would have presented to the European reading public or even the foreign ministries of various nations a clear picture of Egypt's true situation.

73. Girard, II, 538, 539; Clot, II, 277, 278; Mengin, *Histoire de l'Egypte*, II, 368, 369; Douin, *La mission du Baron de Boislecomte*, 84; al-Jabartī, IX, 185 (IV, 251).

74. Mengin, *Histoire de l'Egypte*, II, 374; Colin, Pt. 2, 104, Pt. 3, 70. Exports to Great Britain of safflower amounted to 40 caskets valued at 10,325 piasters in 1824 and 19 caskets valued at 19,658 piastres in 1825 (Salt, April 25, 1825 in F.O. 78/135). Clot notes, too, that in 1833 2,760 hectoliters of *carthamus* seeds were produced in Egypt (II, 287). Export figures for these seeds are not available.

75. Barker, July 10 and December 31, 1827 in F.O. 142/2.

76. Driault, *L'expédition du Crète et de Morée*, 33; Bowring, "Egypt and Candia," 17, 23, 24; Campbell, July 6, 1840 in F.O. 78/408b; Angelo Sammarco, *Il regno di Mohammed Ali nei documenti diplomatici italiani inediti*, Société royale de géographie d'Egypte, publications spéciales (Rome, 1931, 1932), X, 234; Douin, *La mission du Baron de Boislecomte*, 84; Clot, II, 287; Colin, Pt. 3, 70, 71; Cattaui, II, Pt. 2, 409; Stoddart, April 10, 1845 in F.O. 78/624; Appendix I.

77. Bowring, "Egypt and Candia," 17, 19; Cattaui, II, Pt. 2, 361, 362; Colin, Pt. 3, 70, 71.

78. Girard, II, 542; Salt, April 28, 1817 in F.O. 78/89; Campbell, August 4, 1833 in F.O. 78/228; Wilkinson, I, 459; Guémard, 347; Dubois-Aymé and Jollois, *Voyage dans l'intérieur du Delta, etc.*, in *Description de l'Egypte. Etat moderne* (Paris, 1813, 1st ed.), II, 96, 97; *Lā'iḥat zirā'at al-fallāḥ*, 16, 17 (the term for hemp used in the *lā'iḥah* is the Turkish word *kendir*).

79. Girard, II, 539–542; Hutchinson, August 16, 1801 in W.O. 1/345; al-Jabartī, IX, 185 (IV, 251), IX, 190 (IV, 254); *Lā'iḥat zirā'at al-fallāḥ*, 5, 6; Douin, *La mission du Baron de Boislecomte*, 85; Campbell, January 22, 1838 in F.O. 78/342, Part 1.

80. Mengin, *Histoire de l'Egypte*, II, 372; Sammarco, *Il regno di Mohammed Ali*, X, 234; Clot, II, 287; Bowring, "Egypt and Candia," 17; Stoddart, March 23, 1844 in F.O. 78/584 and April 10, 1845 in F.O. 78/624; Barnett, December 12, 1844 in F.O. 78/583; Appendix I; Colin, Pt. 3, 70, 71.

81. This figure is an estimate of the average annual production.

82. This may be the potential rather than actual production figure.

83. Salt, April 28, 1817 in F.O. 78/89; Mengin, *Histoire de l'Egypte*, II, 372; Clot, II, 287; Bowring, "Egypt and Candia," 17; Colin, Pt. 3, 70, 71; Cattaui, II, Pt. 2, 409; Stoddart, March 23, 1844 in F.O. 78/584 and April 10, 1845 in F.O. 78/624; Barnett, December 12, 1844 in F.O. 78/583; Appendix I.

84. Cotton seed and lettuce seed were two oleaginous grains which were exported. Cotton seed figured for the first time as an export item in 1844 when a quantity of 4,233 *ardabbs* was exported (Stoddart, April 10, 1845 in F.O. 78/624). Cotton seed not used for planting was employed as animal fodder or fuel (*Lā'ihat zirā'at al-fallāḥ*, 12). Clot mentions that 14,720 hectoliters of lettuce seed were produced in 1833 (II, 287).

85. Bowring, "Egypt and Candia," 24, 26.

86. Douin, *La mission du Baron de Boislecomte*, 85. The following figures represent the amount of revenue obtained from the date trees: in 1829, at 20–60 paras on 6,000,000 trees, 400,000 dollars, or, according to another estimate, 1,960,000 francs; in 1250/1834–35, 10,700,000 piasters; in 1835–36, 3,000,000 piasters; in 1262/1845–46, 1,800,000 piasters; in 1846–47, 4,094,607 piasters (Douin, *La mission du Baron de Boislecomte*, 127; Douin, *L'Egypte de 1828 à 1830*, 381; Colin, Pt. 1, 102; Campbell, July 6, 1840 in F.O. 78/408b; Cattaui, II, Pt. 2, 406; Murray, May 28, 1847 in F.O. 78/707 and March 17, 1848 in F.O. 78/757).

87. Hamont, I, 176; Barker, December 4, 1832 in F.O. 78/214.

88. Stoddart, April 10, 1845 in F.O. 78/624. One source states that dates sold at two dollars per *qinṭār* in 1828. No export figure is given (Barker, March 10, 1828 in F.O. 78/170).

89. Bowring, "Egypt and Candia," 24, 25.

90. Bowring, "Egypt and Candia," 25; Cattaui, I, 514, 552.

91. Cattaui, I, 214, 215.

92. Bowring, "Egypt and Candia," 25; Douin, *La mission du Baron de Boislecomte*, 85; Hamont, I, 185.

93. There seems to be a difference of opinion on this point. A statement was made at a meeting of the Institut Egyptien in 1859 that the use of mulberry leaves to feed silkworms was unknown in Egypt until the period of Muḥammad 'Alī ("De la culture du ver à soie en Egypte," *Bulletin de l'Institut Egyptien* [Marseilles, 1860], 50).

94. Schweinfurth, "Sur la flore des anciens jardins arabes d'Egypte," *Bulletin de l'Institut Egyptien*, 2d Series, VIII (Cairo, 1888), 307.

95. Hamont, I, 38; Driault, *Mohamed Aly et Napoléon*, 177, 178.

96. Hamont claims that the Syrians did not know much more about this business than the native Egyptians (II, 310). Artin says that Maronite Christians and Syrian Bedouins were settled in Egypt for this purpose. The Syrian Bedouins received land by tribes and were exempted from taxes and conscription. This writer is the only one to speak of Bedouin settlement in Ra's al-Wādī (Artin, "Essai sur les causes," 71).

97. Al-Jabartī, IX, 194 (IV, 256), IX, 196 (IV, 257), IX, 233, 234 (IV, 274).

98. Douin, *La mission du Baron de Boislecomte*, 84; Linant, *Mémoires*, 24, 25.

99. Bowring, "Egypt and Candia," 20; Campbell, July 6, 1840 in F.O. 78/408b; Clot, II, 285; Douin, *La mission du Baron de Boislecomte*, 84.

100. Bowring, "Egypt and Candia," 20, 21; Clot, II, 285, 286. There is not much agreement among writers concerning the quantity of silk produced in Egypt. Amounts produced in Egypt were often confused with those imported from Syria (Clot, II, 286; Bowring, "Egypt and Candia," 21; Douin, *La mission du Baron de Boislecomte*, 84). The 65,000 *uqqahs* reported to have entered the government *shūnahs* in 1834 represented the total quantity of silk available to the government, whether locally produced or imported (Bowring, "Egypt and Candia," 17; Colin, Pt. 3, 70, 71). When the monopoly on silk ceased, only 20,000 *uqqahs* entered the government *shūnahs* (Campbell, July 6, 1840 in F.O. 78/408b).

101. Cattaui, II, Pt. 1, 420, II, Pt. 2, 129, 130; Campbell, December 23, 1835 in F.O. 142/6; Hamont, II, 313–315.

102. Al-Jabartī, IX, 194 (IV, 256); Driault, *Mohamed Aly et Napoléon*, 177; Douin, *La mission du Baron de Boislecomte*, 85; Bowring, "Egypt and Candia," 24.

103. Schweinfurth, 333; Linant, *Mémoires*, 596–602; Campbell, July 6, 1840 in F.O. 78/408b.

104. Ibrāhīm's plantations were under the management of a Frenchman, Bonfort, who employed 10,000 *fallāḥīn* for all of Ibrāhīm's plantations in Upper and Lower Egypt. They were reputed to be the best-run estates in Egypt. Their workers were also better paid than other workers; they received 1½ to 3 piasters a day and were paid regularly on Fridays (Pückler-Muskau, I, 164).

105. Hamont claims that his own efforts to start a botanical garden at the school at Abū Za'bal were unsympathetically viewed by members of the Ministry of Education. The project was abandoned. Ibrāhīm was distinctive in Egypt for his advanced notions concerning the value of experimentation (Hamont, II, 307, 308).

106. Campbell, March 30, 1837 in F.O. 78/319, June 28 and December 25, 1838 in F.O. 78/343, and July 6, 1840 in F.O. 78/408b. Schweinfurth (p. 333) mentions that it was Mr. Trail who was sent to India. Campbell does not refer to this fact.

107. Campbell, December 25, 1838 in F.O. 78/343, Part 3; Bowring, "Egypt and Candia," 26.

108. Douin, *La mission du Baron de Boislecomte*, 85; Hamont, I, 174, 175.

109. Schweinfurth, 311, 335, 336.

110. Hamont, I, 185, 186.

111. Hamont, II, 193; J. Heyworth-Dunne, *An Introduction to the History of Education in Modern Egypt* (London, n.d.), 168.

112. Guillaume Antoine Olivier, *Voyage dans l'empire othoman, l'Egypte, et la Perse* (Paris, 1801–1807), II, 163, 165; Charles-Roux, *La production du coton en Egypte*, 157; Douin, *La mission du Baron de Boislecomte*, 89, 90; Hamont, I, 168–172, II, 291, 292.

113. Hamont, I, 155–167, II, 278–295, 304, 305; Heyworth-Dunne, *History of Education in Modern Egypt*, 151, 152; Clot, II, 271–274; Bowring, "Egypt and Candia," 27; Grégoire, 450, 451; Charles Audebeau and Victor Mosséri, "Le labourage en Egypte," *Bulletin de l'Institut Egyptien*, 5th Series, X (Cairo, March 1917), 125, 127.

114. Barker, March 8, 1830 in F.O. 78/192.

Chapter IX. Trade and Agriculture

1. Douin, *Mohamed Aly et l'expédition d'Alger*, 230.

2. Driault, *Mohamed Aly et Napoléon*, 203; Paul Masson, *Histoire du commerce français dans le Levant au XVIIIe siècle* (Paris, 1911); Alfred C. Wood, *A History of the Levant Company* (London, 1935), ch. X; Henry Dodwell, *The Founder of Modern Egypt: A Study of Muhammad Ali* (Cambridge, England, 1931), 29–31; Ghorbal, *The Beginnings of the Egyptian Question*, 281, 282.

3. Nahum, 35, 42, 48, 49, 54, 55; de Vaulabelle, IX, 443–445; Artin, *Landed Property*, 144, 145; Douin, *L'Egypte de 1802 à 1804*, 93; Driault, *Mohamed Aly et Napoléon*, 65, 82; Stratford Canning, September 17, December 10, 1810 in F.O. 78/70, November 11, 1810 in F.O. 196/1, January 21, 1811 in F.O. 196/2; Cotton, November 26, 1810 in F.O. 78/75; Morier, April 15, July 7, 1810, Briggs, June 27, 1810, Schutz, July 7, 1810, Maltass, December 17, 1810 in S.P. 105/132; Maltass, July 15, 1811 in S.P. 105/133; Waldgrave, January 24, 1811 in F.O. 24/4; Missett, July 14, 1811 in W.O. 1/349, August 4, November 6 and 23, December 2 and 8, 1811 in F.O. 142/1.

4. Driault, *Mohamed Aly et Napoléon*, 77, 78, 87, 88, 97, 104, 133, 136, 139, 148, 165, 173, 177, 183, 186, 187, 196, 197; Missett, July 4, 1811 and December 3, 1812 in F.O. 24/4, September 11, 1811 in F.O. 78/76, December 2, 1811 in F.O. 142/1 and November 30, 1812 in W.O. 1/349; Maltass, June 22, 1811 in S.P. 105/133; al-Jabartī, VIII, 317, 318 (IV, 140), VIII, 344 (IV, 152), VIII, 346 (IV, 153).

5. Missett, September 11, 1811 in F.O. 78/76; Stratford Canning, December 8, 1811 in F.O. 196/3; Driault, *Mohamed Aly et Napoléon*, 170.

6. "A strong suspicion has certainly prevailed amongst some persons of high authority, founded perhaps upon imperfect knowledge which they may have previously possessed of this Treaty, that the European Powers have concerted a plan for the dismemberment of the Turkish Dominions; and my last letters from Egypt mention that Colonel Missett has had great difficulty in satisfying the Pasha that Great Britain could not be concerned in such a project and had not stipulated for the acquisition of Egypt as her share of the plunder. But though His Majesty's Government, not having part in the Treaty in question, is probably exempted from the jealousy that it has produced in the minds of the Ottoman ministers, they are confidently persuaded, as they themselves assert, from good information, that several secret articles were agreed on at Paris to which Great Britain was a party and of the tendency of which, as they are entirely ignorant of it, they are naturally suspicious" (Frere, February 24, 1816 in F.O. 78/86).

7. Frere, November 11, 1816 in F.O. 78/86.

8. Driault, *La formation de l'empire de Mohamed Aly*, 37, 38, 89. This figure was reduced by 1821 (see p. 209) because of Muḥammad 'Alī's dissatisfaction with these troops who had resisted the introduction of the *Niẓām Jadīd* (see p. 57). Some were therefore discharged from the Pasha's army. Others died in the Arabian and Sudanese campaigns.

9. De Vaulabelle, X, 120, 121; Salt, January 23, 1816 in F.O. 24/6 and May 14, 1816 in S.P. 105/135; al-Jabartī, IX, 196 (IV, 256, 257). In 1816 Muḥammad 'Alī and Messrs. Briggs and Company formed a trading company for commerce with India with a capital fund of 5,000,000 piasters (Driault, *La formation de l'empire de Mohamed Aly*, 31).

10. Henry Salt (April 12, 1817 in F.O. 78/89) lists the grain which Muḥammad 'Alī sold in 1816 by firman. The lists come from the books of the *khazīnah* and are probably reliable.

Commodity	*Ardabbs*
Wheat	134,000
Beans	230,000
Lupin	12,000
Lentils	26,000
Linseed	30,000
Indian Corn	60,000
Barley	10,000
Fenugreek (*ḥulbah*)	15,000
Sesame	300
Chick peas	20,000
Pea (*julubbān*)	8,000
	545,300

11. Driault, *La formation de l'empire de Mohamed Aly*, 59, 66, 85, 86, 101.

12. Salt, June 6, 1818 in F.O. 78/91.

13. Driault, *La formation de l'empire de Mohamed Aly*, 180. The figure 32,000 probably refers only to the amount available for export. The cotton crop of 1818 was 70,000 *qinṭārs* and that of 1821, 60,000 *qinṭārs* (Driault, *La formation de l'empire de Mohamed Aly*, 150, 151; Mengin, *Histoire de l'Egypte*, II, 372).

14. Al-Jabartī, IX, 275, 276 (IV, 292); Driault, *La formation de l'empire de Mohamed Aly*, 106, 122, 166, 167, 177, 188, 189, 202, 203, 205; Salt, September 27, 1818 in S.P. 105/136 and October 10, 1818 in F.O. 78/91; Cattaui, I, 21.

15. Salt, June 30, 1820 in F.O. 78/96.

16. The French foreign minister noted on the margin of the dispatch containing the news of the plight of French merchants in Egypt that it was true that the Pasha could not expel French nationals under the terms of the Capitulations, but that it would be considered that anyone who decided to leave Egypt in order to extinguish his debts would be doing so voluntarily and that no contravention of the Capitulations would therefore be involved (Driault, *La formation de l'empire de Mohamed Aly*, 204).

17. Driault, *La formation de l'empire de Mohamed Aly*, 204, 273.

18. Briggs and Company acted as the viceroy's agents for goods sold in Britain. They benefited greatly from their position of favor which they owed to their long existence in Egypt and possibly to close family ties with leading Egyptians. Officials at the Foreign Office noted when Consul Larking was dismissed from his post that he belonged to the "clique" of Thurburn and other supporters of Muḥammad 'Alī, that he was the brother-in-law of Briggs, that he was married to the stepdaughter of Thurburn, and that there was a family connection between the Thurburns, Briggs, and Bāghūṣ Bey (Internal Minute, August 14, 1841 in F.O. 78/452).

19. Cattaui, II, Pt. 1, 67, 68; Douin, *L'Egypte de 1828 à 1830*, 347, 364, 365; Douin, *La première guerre de Syrie*, I, 533, 534; Douin, *La mission du Baron de Boislecomte*, 98, 99; Driault, *L'expédition du Crète et de Morée*, 221; Salt, May 20, 1825 and encl. and June 15, 1825 and encl. in F.O. 78/135; Barker, August 24, 1827 and encl. in F.O. 142/2, March 10, 1825 in F.O. 78/170; London *Times*, May 11, 1829 in F.O. 78/184; Campbell, May 15, 1833 in F.O. 142/4, July 24, 1833 in F.O. 142/6, September 5, 1835 in F.O. 78/258, January 22, 1838 in F.O. 78/342, Part 1, and March 24, 1839 in F.O. 78/373.

20. Gibb and Bowen, I, Pt. 1, 299–313.

21. As early as 1816 Bāghūṣ Bey was referred to as Minister of Foreign Affairs, but this was a misnomer. He was Muḥammad 'Alī's chief interpreter and in this capacity often dealt with his commercial and diplomatic affairs (Driault, *La formation de l'empire de Mohamed Aly*, 31).

22. Deny says that a permanent *dīwān*, the *Dīwān at-Tijārah wa'l-Mabyū'ah*, was established in 1234/1818–19, whereas Dodwell refers to an order to the *kikhyah bey* dated Sha'bān 12, A.H. 1235 (May 25, 1820), which Dodwell incorrectly cited as being in 1819, authorizing the establishment of a *dīwān* of seven persons to deal with commercial transactions between the Treasury and European merchants. Without reference to the archives it is difficult to know whether these two writers are discussing the same *dīwān* or two separate ones (Deny, 125, 461; Dodwell, 205). In any event, the *Qānūn as-Siyāsat-nāmah* of A.H. 1253 (June/July 1837) listed the *Majlis at-Tujjār* and the *Majlis Tujjār Awruba* as two of the nineteen administrations for which the *Dīwān al-Khidīwī* was responsible. It is unclear what the relation was between these two bodies and the Ministry of Commerce and Foreign Affairs established at this time (Zaghlūl, Appendix II, p. 5; Deny, 115).

23. Salt, April 4, 1826 in F.O. 78/147; Driault, *L'expédition du Crète et de Morée*, 112; Zaghlūl, Appendix II, p. 6; Barnett, January 15 and January 17, 1844 in F.O. 78/582; Paton, II, 231.

24. Cattaui, II, Pt. 1, 68; Campbell, December 12, 1838 in F.O. 78/373, Part 3. The list of *appaltos* included the following, with the price paid for each to the government, in piasters.

Customs of Alexandria	3,000,000
Customs of Būlāq and Damietta	3,676,700
Customs of Old Cairo	525,000
Appalto for the sale of hides	2,497,950
Appalto on jugglers and prostitutes	2,250,000
Appalto on *khurdah* which included 72 kinds of taxes	2,225,000
Appalto on the sale of salt	1,283,000
Appalto on the sale of wines and spirits	1,385,880
Appalto for hunting and fishing at Lake al-Manzalah	1,007,500
Appalto for the sale at the bazaar of Rūmīlyah	280,000
Appalto for the boats on the Nile	184,500
Appalto for the trade of senna	130,500
Appalto for the octrois of Fayyūm and fishing in Lake Qārūn and Baḥr Yūsuf	50,000
	18,496,030

(Ed. de Cadalvène and J. de Breuvery, *L'Egypte et la Nubie* [Paris, 1841], I, 382; Gibb and Bowen, I, Pt. 1, 277, n. 1.) There were undoubtedly many more *appaltos* than those listed here. A report in 1838 said that the Pasha suppressed in Cairo alone 33 *appaltos*, which had netted the treasury 104,445 piasters (Cattaui, III, 27).

25. Salt, June 15, 1825 & encl. in F.O. 78/135; Barker, August, 27, 1827 & encl. in F.O. 142/2; Driault, *L'expédition du Crète et de Morée*, 221; Cattaui, II, Pt. 2, 389; Douin, *L'Egypte de 1828 à 1830*, 157, 364, 365, 390, 391, 404, 405, 415.

26. Douin, *L'Egypte de 1828 à 1830*, 435, 436, 439, 456–459; Cattaui, I, 459; II, Pt. 1, 66, 67, 425, II, Pt. 2, 282, 294, 473; Sammarco, *Il regno di Mohammed Ali*, IX, 70, 71; Barker, March 13, 1833 in F.O. 142/4; Bowring, "Egypt and Candia," 48; Colin, Pt. 3, 71–73.

27. Cattaui, II, Pt. 2, 96, 115, 325, 431, 432, 442, 443; Campbell, January 24, 1836 in F.O. 78/282, May 25, July 13, August 7, and September 24, 1837 in F.O. 78/319, October 8, 1837 in F.O. 78/320.

28. According to Bowring, Muḥammad 'Alī did not rely entirely upon his native business ability, but tried to learn something about economic theory. Bowring claims that Muḥammad 'Alī ordered the translation into Turkish of several articles on the trade of Egypt from MacCulloch's dictionary as well as the translation of an elementary work on political economy. In discussions with Bowring he showed keen interest in economic problems and attempted to draw from him as much information as he could

regarding the economy of various nations, particularly that of the United States. He also inquired into the causes of the commercial crisis and other economic matters (Bowring, November 23, 1837 in F.O. 78/323).

29. Sir Charles Webster, *The Foreign Policy of Palmerston 1830–1841. Britain, the Liberal Movement and the Eastern Question* (London, 1951), II, 548–557.

30. Campbell, September 28, 1838 in F.O. 142/9.

31. Webster, II, 548–557.

32. Campbell, July 6, 1840 in F.O. 78/408b.

33. Campbell, April 15, 1835 in F.O. 78/257, January 23, 1836 in F.O. 142/6, May 25, 1837 in F.O. 78/319, June 12, 1837 in F.O. 142/9; Cattaui, II, Pt. 2, 114, 115; Nahum, 191, 192, 194–197; Vernon John Puryear, *International Economics and Diplomacy in the Near East* (Stanford, 1935), 38–45, 107–130, 197–199; Webster, II, 556; Hamont, II, 517; René and Georges Cattaui, *Mohamed-Aly et l'Europe* (Paris, 1950), 135, 136.

34. Campbell, September 28, 1838 in F.O. 142/9.

35. Palmerston, October 12, 1839 in F.O. 78/372.

36. *Abstract of Correspondence respecting Mehemet Ali's intended Declaration of Independence*, 69–73, unpubl. MS. in F.O. 78/482.

37. Campbell, March 24, 1839 in F.O. 78/373, December 12, 1838 in F.O. 142/9, February 14, 1839 in F.O. 78/373, March 18, 1839 in F.O. 142/11. Clot feels that if the merchants were allowed to deal directly with the *fallāḥīn*, they would be oppressed by them (II, 202). Hamont, on the other hand, claims that the Egyptian *fallāḥīn* were very shrewd and that if anyone was to be cheated, it was certain not to be the *fallāḥīn* (I, 28).

38. Dodwell, 169–175.

39. Campbell, July 12, 1839 in F.O. 142/11; Hodges, March 31, 1840 in F.O. 78/404, May 22, 1840 in F.O. 142/11; Larking, January 21, 1841 in F.O. 78/452; Foreign Office, August 26, 1841 in F.O. 78/451; Barnett, August 18, 1841 in F.O. 78/451, November 6, November 26, December 17, and December 31, 1841 in F.O. 142/14, December 1, 1841 in F.O. 142/13, January 3, 1842 in F.O. 195/209, January 20, 1843 in F.O. 142/14; Driault, *L'Egypte et l'Europe*, II, 33, V, 109, 110, 342, 366; Hamont, II, 517–522; Dodwell, 221, 222.

40. Barnett, October 20, 1841 in F.O. 97/408, November 30, 1841 in F.O. 142/14; Hamont, I, 236, 237. Campbell had foreseen this difficulty in 1837 before the negotiations of the Anglo-Turkish Convention had been completed and had urged the British government to include in the terms of the treaty a clause guaranteeing freedom of transport and the right to hire laborers. His recommendations were not acted upon (Campbell, December 28, 1837 in F.O. 78/321, January 22, 1838 in F.O. 78/342, Part 1).

41. The Austrians protested the order on the grounds that requiring European vessels to fly the Turkish flag was an infringement of existing treaties between Austria and the Porte. Upon the examination of the treaties in question dating from February 24, 1784, Barnett said that in his opinion the Austrian view could not be upheld. The treaties covered the navigation of rivers which could be entered from the sea by foreign merchant vessels. Such was not the case with the Nile whose mouths were passable only for small craft. Navigation of the Nile was to be considered inland navigation and the hoisting of national colors could not, therefore, be justified. Barnett was supported by the French and Russian Consuls-General in his interpretation (Barnett, November 12, 1841 in F.O. 142/13).

42. Barnett, October 18 and October 23, 1841, December 1, 1841 in F.O. 142/13, December 18, 1841 in F.O. 78/451; Hamont, II, 518–520.

43. Stoddart, December 23, 1841 in F.O. 78/452; Barnett, December 1, 1841 in F.O. 142/13, November 30, 1841 in F.O. 142/14, November 30, 1841 in F.O. 78/451; Driault, *L'Egypte et l'Europe*, V, 352–363. High export taxes amounting to 10 to 12 Turkish piasters had, in fact, been levied previously in the Pasha's reign. See discussion of the Pasha's early commercial policies.

44. Not only did Muḥammad 'Alī collect a higher import as stipulated in the treaty, but also higher export duties which were contrary to the terms of the treaty. In May 1842 export duties were for cotton about 22 per cent, for wool 20 to 25 per cent, for safflower 50 per cent, for Mocha coffee 14 per cent, for buffalo and oxen horns 22 per cent, for opium 15 per cent, for cereals much above 12 per cent (Barnett, May 20, 1842 in F.O. 78/502).

45. Barnett, January 10, 17, 18 and March 19, 1842 in F.O. 78/502, January 14, March 3 and March 16, 1842 in F.O. 142/13, March 14, 1842 in F.O. 142/14; Foreign Office, April 4, 1842 in F.O. 78/502; Cattaui, III, 626, 627, 631, 632.

46. Stoddart, April 21, 1842 in F.O. 78/504; Barnett, March 20, May 15, 1842 in F.O. 78/502, April 6, May 16, 1842, and February 12, 1844 in F.O. 142/13; Murray, September 9, 1847 in F.O. 78/708, July 30, 1848 in F.O. 78/757; Foreign Office, November 9, 1847 in F.O. 78/706.

47. Boghos [Bāghūṣ], May 11, 1842 in F.O. 78/502; Barnett, May 13 and May 31, 1842 in F.O. 142/14, May 16 and May 26, 1842 in F.O. 142/13, May 15 and June 10, 1842 in F.O. 78/502; Cattaui, III, 641, 644; Politis [Polites], *Le conflit turco-égyptien*, 138–140.

48. The commodities listed in Table 37, constituting the largest proportion of Egyptian exports, entered the government *shūnah* at Alexandria. All the amounts except those for cotton and flax are in *ardabbs*.

TABLE 37. Export commodities entering the government warehouse at Alexandria, in *ardabbs*, 1840–1843[a]

Commodity	1840	1841	1842	1843
Wheat	454,897	590,698	409,512	484,977
Beans	482,900	362,131	266,306	572,644
Barley	363,600	117,794	12,681	80,648
Chick peas	13,066	6,987	3,771	1,284
Lupin	3,069	9,676	13,016	9,430
Lentils	60,769	19,526	22,813	13,975
Maize	6,083	1,802	—	—
Linseed	1,145	4,473	10,275	18,930
Sesame	—	16,496	9,468	17,005
Green peas	—	—	—	2,458
Rice of Damietta	—	—	—	8,952
Rice of Rosetta	—	—	—	5,390
TOTAL	1,385,529	1,129,583	747,842	1,195,693
Cotton	205,836	228,189	228,036	272,160
Flax	—	—	—	79,024

Source: Stoddart, March 23, 1844 in F.O. 78/584.
[a] The figures for cotton and for flax are in *qinṭārs* instead of in *ardabbs*.

49. Larking, January 21, 1841 in F.O. 78/452; Barnett, December 1, 1841 in F.O. 142/13, January 3, 1842 in F.O. 195/209, March 20 and August 19, 1843 in F.O. 78/541; Driault, *L'Egypte et l'Europe*, V, 364–369.

50. It was announced early in 1843 that the Pasha had signed a contract with two merchants to form a bank. The other merchants protested loudly to their consuls that the formation of such a bank would lead to the concentration of economic wealth in the hands of these two individuals and to the inevitable ruin of the rest of the trading community. This outcry made Muḥammad 'Alī less anxious to encourage the venture. He did not break the contract, however, but he never contributed his share of the capital fund which he was to have invested in the bank (Barnett, February 10, March 20, and June 10, 1843 in F.O. 78/541; Stoddart, March 21, 1843 in F.O. 78/542).

51. Stoddart, March 21, 1843 in F.O. 78/542.

52. Barnett, June 6, 1843 in F.O. 78/542.

53. Barnett, July 6, 1843 and encl. in F.O. 78/542.

54. Foreign Office, July 25, 1843 in F.O. 78/541; Barnett, June 10 and August 19, 1843 in F.O. 78/541, August 19, 1843 in F.O. 142/14, January 15, 1844 (dispatches nos. 2 and 3) in F.O. 78/542.

55. Board of Trade [B.T.] 1/463, No. 1823; Puryear, 212–215.

Chapter X. Industry and Agriculture

1. See Moustafa Fahmy, *La révolution de l'industrie en Egypte et ses conséquences sociales au 19e siècle (1800–1850)* (Leiden, 1954). It is not the object of the present chapter to duplicate Dr. Fahmy's work but rather to evaluate the effect of Muḥammad 'Alī's industrial policy on his agricultural policy.

2. Al-Jabartī, IX, 196 (IV, 257); Driault, *La formation de l'empire de Mohamed Aly*, 275; Girard, II, 594–605.

3. Cotton cloth increased in price from 100 paras per piece to 300 in 1817. Canvas went from 200 to 600 paras. Clothing increased in price as a result of the government's monopoly of both textile manufacturing and indigo, the dye most frequently used by native Egyptians for their clothes. Some years after Muḥammad 'Alī established his monopolies, MacBrair was impressed by the fact that the poor people seemed more ragged than ever. He attributed this to their no longer being free to make their own cloth for domestic use (al-Jabartī, IX, 192 [IV, 255], IX, 252, 253 [IV, 282, 283]; Robert Maxwell MacBrair, *Sketches of a Missionary's Travels in Egypt, Syria, Western Africa, etc.* [London, 1839], 67).

4. *Lā'iḥat zirā'at al-fallāḥ*, 47–50, 54, 55, 57; Fahmy, 32, 34; Campbell, April 25, 1834 in F.O. 78/245. The monopoly for the manufacture of mats was also abandoned at the same time.

5. Other explanations have been given for Muḥammad 'Alī's decision. Drovetti claims that he wished to become self-sufficient; Clot says that he wished to establish industry in Egypt to free himself from the yoke of foreigners; finally, Campbell maintains that he was motivated by his desire to acquire acclaim in Europe as a progressive ruler and wanted "to give a certain impulse to the Arab nation by giving it a new sort of education" (Driault, *Mohamed Aly et Napoléon*, 242, 243; Clot, II, 298; Campbell, July 6, 1840 in F.O. 78/408b). These opinions probably reflect Muḥammad 'Alī's efforts to justify his policy after its introduction rather than his original motives for launching it.

6. Driault, *La formation de l'empire de Mohamed Aly*, 275. Drovetti's position was consistent with that taken at the time of the French occupation when General Menou was dissuaded from his plan to instruct Egyptians in modern industrial methods on the grounds that it could eventually injure French industry (Rigault, 169–173). Bokty and the other mercantile consuls who urged Muḥammad 'Alī to establish a modern industry were probably anxious to obtain cheap industrial goods with which to undersell their colleagues representing industrial nations.

7. Full details about the cotton factories in Egypt are to be found in Bowring, "Egypt and Candia," 29–39, Cattaui, II, Pt. 2, 381–383, and Campbell, July 6, 1840 in F.O. 78/408b.

8. Roussel, the French Consul-General in Egypt, called attention to the fact that the establishment of a textile industry along European lines might eventually prove competitive (Driault, *La formation de l'empire de Mohamed Aly*, 64).

9. Soon after arriving in Egypt, a number of French workmen, becoming dissatisfied with the situation, nevertheless demanded repatriation (Driault, *La formation de l'empire de Mohamed Aly*, 207, 208).

10. Al-Jabartī, IX, 273, 274 (IV, 292); Driault, *La formation de l'empire de Mohamed Aly*, 63, 64, 89, 99; Fahmy, 14, 15.

11. Driault, *La formation de l'empire de Mohamed Aly*, 274.

12. Campbell, July 6, 1840 in F.O. 78/408b; Cattaui, I, 552, II, Pt. 1, 68–70. Campbell asserts that Muḥammad 'Alī's industry which was geared to serve his military needs also incited him to war.

13. Campbell, January 22, 1838 in F.O. 78/342, Part 1; Driault, *La formation de l'empire de Mohamed Aly*, 274.

14. Barker, April 10, 1832 in F.O. 78/213.

15. Campbell, July 6, 1840 in F.O. 78/408b.

16. Campbell, March 30, 1837 in F.O. 78/319, January 22, 1838 in F.O. 78/342, Part 1, July 6, 1840 in F.O. 78/408b; Cattaui, II, Pt. 1, 69, II, Pt. 2, 381–383; Pückler-Muskau, I, 142.

17. Bowring, "Egypt and Candia," 35; Campbell, July 6, 1840 in F.O. 78/408b; Stoddart, May 29, 1846 in F.O. 78/663; Douin, *Une mission militaire française*, 109.

18. Campbell, January 22, 1838 in F.O. 78/342, Part 1.

19. Douin, *Mohamed Aly et l'expédition d'Alger*, 221, 222; Bowring, November 23, 1837 in F.O. 78/323; Campbell, January 22, 1838 in F.O. 78/342, Part 1, July 6, 1840 in F.O. 78/408b.

20. Douin, *La mission du Baron de Boislecomte*, 91; Campbell, January 22, 1838 in F.O. 78/342, Part 1; Bowring, "Egypt and Candia," 37; Hamont, II, 365, 366; Fahmy, 85–95. Dr. Fahmy has greatly exaggerated Muḥammad 'Alī's "humanitarian" labor policies.

21. Fahmy, 104–107; Puryear, 114.

22. Campbell, January 22, 1838 in F.O. 78/342, Part 1; Bowring, "Egypt and Candia," 35, 37, 39; Campbell, July 6, 1840 in F.O. 78/408b; Linant, *Mémoires*, 364. Dr. Fahmy's figures (pp. 84, 85) are misleading and his conclusion debatable. It seems erroneous in a discussion of the formation of a new social class in Egypt to lump together the workers in the village industries with those in the modern factories established by Muḥammad 'Alī.

23. Campbell, July 6, 1840 in F.O. 78/408b; Cattaui, II, Pt. 2, 382, 383; Barker, April 10, 1832 in F.O. 78/213.

24. Douin, *La mission du Baron de Boislecomte*, 93, 94; Driault, *L'Egypte et l'Europe*, V, 285; Hamont, II, 365, 366; Bowring, December 17, 1837 in F.O. 78/342, Part 1.

25. Campbell, July 6, 1840 in F.O. 78/408b.

Chapter XI. Military Service and Agriculture

1. Clot, II, 107.

2. By 1829 fifteen thousand Bedouins were in Muḥammad 'Alī's pay. "These are principally employed in scouring the country, for the purpose of preventing the escape of deserters, *as well of the villages as of the army*, a service they willingly perform, from their rooted and hereditary hatred of the Arab Peasantry. His Highness depends upon these Bedoweens in case of the revolt of any of his Regiments, or the rising of a Province, for though the desert Arabs have been from the remotest antiquity, remarkable for their love of independence, they would become ready and powerful instruments, in suppressing any effort that the miserable inhabitants of Egypt might make to throw off the yoke of the Viceroy" (Barker, July 7, 1829 in F.O. 78/184).

3. Guémard, 120–123; Artin, *Landed Property*, 194, 195; Driault, *La formation de l'empire de Mohamed Aly*, 37, 38, 285; Driault, *L'expédition du Crète et de Morée*, 13, 14, 16; Cattaui, I, 45; Clot, II, 217; Hamont, II, 11, 12.

4. Bowring claims that the state provided the families with supplies and assistance ("Egypt and Candia," 52). Hamont, on the other hand, claims that the government provided nothing for the wives and children of conscripts who were obliged to share their own moderate rations of bread, beans, and lentils with their families (I, 199).

5. Hamont, I, 42, 43; Salt, February 8, 1824 in F.O. 78/126; Douin, *La mission du Baron de Boislecomte*, 116, 117; Douin, *La première guerre de Syrie*, I, 7.

6. Barker, April 26, 1828 in F.O. 142/2.

7. Hamont, II, 28; Barker, June 23, 1829 in F.O. 78/184. Several writers express

the opinion that the lot of the *fallāḥīn,* once in the army, improved materially as compared with their lives before conscription or with the lot of those who had remained behind. They found that they were better fed and clothed in the army than ever before and gradually became accustomed to their new life. Desertions were fewer than might have been expected; in fact, after the first Syrian War Muḥammad 'Alī felt absolute confidence in the loyalty of his Egyptian troops. Hamont, on the other hand, disagrees with these views. He believes that the *fallāḥīn* were better off in their villages than in the army where they suffered a far greater rate of mortality. Whichever view is the correct one, one thing is certain: the *fallāḥīn* never accepted conscription willingly (Clot, II, 218; Bowring, "Egypt and Candia," 52; Douin, *La première guerre de Syrie*, I, 7; Campbell, July 30 and August 12, 1834 in F.O. 142/6; Hamont, II, 36).

8. Salt, August 12, 1826 in F.O. 78/147 and April 25, 1827 in F.O. 78/160; Barker, April 26, 1828 in F.O. 142/2 and April 10, 1832 in F.O. 78/213; Campbell, October 8, 1834 in F.O. 78/247, May 25 and August 7, 1837 in F.O. 78/319; Barnett, September 18, 1841 in F.O. 78/451, May 15, 1842 in F.O. 78/502, and June 10, 1843 in F.O. 78/541; Driault, *L'Egypte et l'Europe*, IV, 131; Cattaui, II, Pt. 2, 442, 443, 473; Guémard, 198–200.

9. Campbell, February 26, 1838 in F.O. 142/9; Barker, July 8, 1829 in F.O. 78/184 and August 23, 1832 in F.O. 142/3; Campbell, February 7, 1838 in F.O. 142/9; Driault, *L'Egypte et l'Europe*, II, 213; Benis, II, 39; Clot, II, 255-260; Hamont, II, 11, 12; Appendix V.

10. Barker, June 21, 1832 in F.O. 142/3.

11. Barker, August 27, 1832 in F.O. 142/3.

12. Barker, June 4, 1832 in F.O. 142/3 and January 25, 1833 in F.O. 78/231; Campbell, June 23, 1834 in F.O. 142/6, January 6 and January 25, 1838 in F.O. 142/9; Douin, *La première guerre de Syrie*, I, 25.

13. Douin, *Une mission militaire française*, 120; Hamont, II, 381, 382; Guémard, 170, 171; Cattaui, I, 376; Auguste Frédéric Louis Viesse de Marmont, duc de Raguse, *The Present State of the Turkish Empire*, trans. Col. Sir Frederic Smith (London, 1854, 2d ed.), 244; Asad Jibrail Rustum, *Materials for a Corpus of Arabic Documents relating to the History of Syria under Mehemet Ali Pasha* (Beirut, 1930–1934), 5 vols.; *Les campagnes d'Ibrahim Pacha en Syrie et en Asie Mineure 1831–1840*, ed. Assad J. Rustum (Heliopolis, Egypt, n.d.).

14. Hamont, I, 43, II, 12; Douin, *La première guerre de Syrie*, I, 25, 543, 544; Guémard, 121, 122; Cattaui, I, 429, II, Pt. 2, 49, 89; Bowring, "Egypt and Candia," 197.

15. Barker, March 16, 1833 in F.O. 78/231. In a report dated March 30, 1835, Colonel Duhamel says that Muḥammad 'Alī had at first condemned to forced labor all those who had mutilated themselves, but that the situation had become so serious by 1835 that he would have been obliged to send three quarters of the Egyptian population to the galleys because of voluntary mutilation (Cattaui, II, Pt. 1, 267).

16. Benis, II, 39; Hamont, II, 41; Campbell, February 25, 1838 in F.O. 142/9.

17. Barker, March 29, 1832 in F.O. 78/213.

18. Sixty executions took place in 1832, half of which were for political reasons (Douin, *La mission du Baron de Boislecomte*, 144, 145).

19. Douin, *L'Egypte de 1828 à 1830*, 130; Barker, October 13, 1832 in F.O. 142/3.

20. Barker, March 15, 1833 in F.O. 142/4; Campbell, April 1, 1833 in F.O. 78/227, April 7, 1833 in F.O. 142/7, July 30 and August 12, 1834, July 24, 1835 in F.O. 142/6, September 5, 1835 in F.O. 78/258, November 7, 1837 in F.O. 78/321, December 21, 1837, March 20 and March 21, 1838 in F.O. 142/9.

21. Campbell, February 7, 1838 in F.O. 142/9.

22. Campbell, April 1, 1839 in F.O. 78/373.

23. Campbell, May 25, 1837 in F.O. 78/319, January 6 and May 20, 1838 in F.O. 142/9; Hodges, January 24 and February 21, 1840 in F.O. 142/11; Bowring, "Egypt and Candia," 152, 153; Cattaui, III, 70, 71.

24. Hodges, April 20, 1840 in F.O. 142/11.

25. Hodges, March 19 and June 6, 1840 in F.O. 142/11.

26. Larking, January 22, 1841 in F.O. 78/452; Clot, II, 261; Guémard, 196, 201; Hodges, April 18, 1840 in F.O. 78/404, May 26, 1840 in F.O. 142/11; Barnett, December 1, 1841 in F.O. 142/13; Driault, *L'Egypte et l'Europe*, IV, 404, 405.

27. Barker reports that one regiment had "a complete band of forty musicians, all Arab lads, who play European airs from written music in the best Italian style" (Barker, June 23, 1829 in F.O. 78/184).

28. Guémard, 178, 188; Salt, October 10, 1821 in F.O. 78/103; Barker, July 7, 1829 in F.O. 78/184, July 21, 1832 in F.O. 142/3, and February 18, 1833 in F.O. 78/231; Campbell, May 14, 1838 in F.O. 142/9; Sammarco, *Il regno di Mohammed Ali*, X, 16. Guémard's figure for 1840 amounted to almost 300,000 men in all of Muḥammad 'Alī's armies, of which between 68,000 to 82,560 were Egyptian (pp. 195, 201). The National Guard, according to Guémard, was formed because of Muḥammad 'Alī's wish to increase his military forces to 400,000. He commanded that recruiting for the National Guard should be carried out both in Egypt and Syria (p. 196).

29. Chasseaud, May 15, 1841 in F.O. 195/169; Barnett, September 18, 1841 in F.O. 78/451, November 12 and December 1, 1841 in F.O. 142/13; Stoddart, September 23, 1846 in F.O. 78/661B; Driault, *L'Egypte et l'Europe*, IV, 235, 236, V, 108, 109, 133, 134, 249, 286, 371, 372; Cattaui, III, 620, 621; Hamont, II, 510; Paton, II, 222.

30. British Consul-General Murray felt that Ibrāhīm's fears were groundless and that "even if the Porte had any such intentions as those above referred to, the Great Powers would, in spite of the revolutions that have convulsed Europe, coincide and cooperate in securing to Ibrahim tranquil succession to his father's government" (Murray, April 9, 1848 in F.O. 142/16).

31. "The Mudirs, or Governors of Provinces, having been made to send in returns of the population in their respective administrations, orders are then issued to them by the Central Government to make a conscription amounting to a certain percentage on that population. These orders are then forwarded by the mudir to the Scheikh, or Chief of each village, enjoining him to secure three, four, or five conscripts, according to their population. These Scheikhs are if possible more cruel and brutal in their tyranny than the Mudirs themselves, and no sooner do they get the order than they proceed to seize upon and lock up 50 or 60 of the laborers, in short, ten times more than the number required. Most of these are, of course, fathers of families, and they look with such dread and horror upon being dragged from their homes to serve in the Egyptian army, that they are prepared to buy their exemption at any price, even although [*sic*] it should involve their being reduced to absolute penury. In this manner the Scheikh is able to 'squeeze' his prisoners of every farthing they possess; he then dismisses them, retaining only the number required from among those who are most unable or unwilling to satisfy his rapacity. These poor wretches are then chained together two and two like felons, and having been first collected in the chief provincial town, are thence driven, like flocks of sheep, under a guard to the capital or to the camp.

"This being the system, Your Lordship may easily imagine that no sooner is it known or rumoured in the villages that a conscription is on foot, than the labourers leave their homes and families and fly in every direction, some hiding themselves in barns or thickets, and the greater part taking refuge in the desert. On this last occasion the time selected for the conscription was just as the harvest was ripe so that thousands, I might say millions, of acres of good crops have been lost, or spoilt, for want of hands to cut and carry them.

"To the preceding account I must add a necessary corollary, namely, that bodies of soldiers are, of course, sent out in every direction to catch and bring back the fugitive labourers. These *enlightened* Turks cannot be made to understand that, apart from the misery, disaffection, and ruin thus caused among the Arab peasantry, a bounty for enlistment, large enough to ensure an ample supply of volunteers, would not amount to one fourth of the cost and loss thus indirectly inflicted on the resources of the country. And, after all, what dependence can be placed on a half disciplined army thus constituted? There is no doubt that they are, each and all, only waiting for the first favorable opportunity to break away and return to their own homes" (Murray, June 1, 1848 in F.O. 78/757).

32. Murray, May 5, July 1 and December 5, 1848 in F.O. 78/757, April 20, 1848 in F.O. 142/16, May 5, 1849 in F.O. 78/804.

33. See Appendix VI.

34. Douin, *La mission du Baron de Boislecomte*, 113. Ibrāhīm Pasha, reported the British Consul-General, had once asserted that "he thought every Government had the right to one-third of the male adults of a proper age for the army. Mr. Thurburn . . . endeavoured to combat this opinion by pointing out to him the excessive drain which it would be on any country, particularly on one so thinly populated as Syria, but Ibrahim said that he deemed it a fair proportion, as one-third would still remain for agriculture and the other third for trades and professions" (Campbell, June 19, 1834 in F.O. 142/6).

35. Egypt was often visited by epidemics and plagues. The cholera epidemic of 1831 was very serious, but the estimate of 150,000 deaths was considered somewhat exaggerated (Douin, *La première guerre de Syrie*, I, 585). The plague of 1835 was one of the worst in many years. It was estimated that about 150,000 people in all Egypt died, of which 75,000 were in Cairo and 18,000 in Alexandria (Campbell, May 18, 1835 in F.O. 78/260, June 25, 1835 in F.O. 78/257, June 30, 1835 in F.O. 142/7; Cattaui, II, Pt. 1, 350).

36. Cattaui, I, 456, 457, II, Pt. 1, 350, III, 254–256; Sammarco, *Il regno di Mohammed Ali*, IX, 352, 353; Benis, II, 39; Barker, July 17, 1832 in F.O. 142/3, April 15, 1835 in F.O. 142/6; Campbell, January 24, 1836 in F.O. 78/282, March 30, 1837 in F.O. 78/319.

37. Campbell, July 6, 1840 in F.O. 78/408b.

38. Clot, II, 260; Douin, *La mission du Baron de Boislecomte*, 117. Contrary to the opinion of others, Bowring felt that the *fallāḥ* soldiers protected the class from which they originated ("Egypt and Candia," 49).

39. Driault, *L'Egypte et l'Europe*, V, 287, 288; Hamont, II, 29.

40. Campbell, July 6, 1840 in F.O. 78/408b.

Chapter XII. Irrigation

1. Quoted by P. and H., *Egypte sous la domination de Méhémet Aly*, in *L'univers. Histoire et description de tous les peuples. Egypte* (Paris, 1877), 71.

2. Indispensable descriptions of the irrigation system as it existed prior to Muḥammad 'Alī's reign may be found in articles contained in the *Description de l'Egypte*. Four maps have been used here for purposes of comparison: (1) the frontispiece and plate VI in *Description de l'Egypte, Etat moderne. Planches* (Paris, 1809, 1st ed.), I, and Plate X in *Description de l'Egypte, Etat moderne. Planches de grand format* (cf. Jacotin, *Mémoire sur la construction de la carte d'Egypte* in *Description de l'Egypte, Etat moderne* [Paris, 1822, 1st ed.], II, Pt. 2, 1–118); (2) *Map of Egypt* prepared by Lieutenant-Colonel W. M. Leake and published in London, January 2, 1818; (3) M. A. Linant de Bellefonds, *Carte hydrographique de la Basse Egypte et d'une partie de l'Isthme de Suez où sont indiqués les travaux exécutés ou à exécuter d'après les ordres de son altesse Méhémet-Ali vice-roi d'Egypte. Avec le projet de la communication directe des deux mers au travers de l'Isthme* (Paris, 1855); *Carte hydrographique de la Moyenne Egypte etc.* (Paris, 1854); *Carte hydrographique de la Haute Egypte etc.* (Paris, 1855). These maps not only show the canals discussed in this chapter but also many others which were either less important or did not play an important part in the public works program of Muḥammad 'Alī; and (4) *Lower Egypt in 4 sheets compiled at the Intelligence Branch, War Office, from the original French Survey in 1818 by M. Jacotin, from the Manuscript of Mahmud Bey and from the most recent Information*, lithographed at the Intelligence Department, War Office, June 1882.

3. Le Père Ainé, *Mémoire sur la vallée du Nil et le nilomètre de l'île de Roudah*, in *Description de l'Egypte, Etat moderne* (Paris, 1822, 1st ed.), II, Pt. 2, 539.

4. Douin and Fawtier-Jones, *L'Angleterre et l'Egypte. La politique mameluke*, I, 412; Bryce, July 2, 1802 in W.O. 55/1553 (5).

5. J. M. Le Père, *Mémoire sur la communication de la mer des Indes à la Méditerranée par la mer Rouge et l'isthme de Soueys*, in *Description de l'Egypte, Etat moderne* (Paris, 1809, 1st ed.), I, 124 n.3., 125.

6. Al-Jabartī, VII, 217–219 (III, 262).

7. Missett, August 23, 1804 in W.O. 1/347.

8. Bryce, July 2, 1802 in W.O. 55/1553 (5); Michel-Ange Lancret and de Chabrol, *Mémoire sur le canal d'Alexandrie*, in *Description de l'Egypte, Etat moderne* (Paris, 1813, 1st ed.), II, 192; Gratien Le Père, *Extrait d'un mémoire sur les lacs et les déserts de la basse Egypte*, in *Description de l'Egypte, Etat moderne* (Paris, 1813, 1st ed.), II, 470; al-Jabartī, IX, 198, 199 (IV, 258); Driault, *Mohamed Aly et Napoléon*, 104, 150, 151; Ghorbal, *The Beginnings of the Egyptian Question*, 212, 213.

9. Olivier, II, 35, 36; Lancret and de Chabrol, II, 188; J. M. Le Père, I, 133, 134; Bryce, July 2, 1802 in W.O. 55/1553 (5); Linant, *Mémoires*, 349.

10. Lancret and de Chabrol, II, 192–194; J. M. Le Père, I, 129, 130; Charles-Roux, *Bonaparte: Governor of Egypt*, 286, 287.

11. Driault, *Mohamed Aly et Napoléon*, 104; Driault, *La formation de l'empire de Mohamed Aly*, 53, 54.

12. Barker, October 20, 1828 in F.O. 78/170; Bryce, July 2, 1802 in W.O. 55/1553 (5); Bowring, "Egypt and Candia," 65.

13. Salt, April 28, 1817 in F.O. 78/89; al-Jabartī, IX, 241 (IV, 277); Madden, *Travels*, I, 292; Driault, *La formation de l'empire de Mohamed Aly*, 64. Military reasons may also have entered into Muḥammad 'Ali's decision. Roussel suggests that Muḥammad 'Alī's secret motive was to divert the Nile waters in such a way as to render the mouth of the Rosetta branch even more impassable in order to close it to the fleet of the Turkish admiral which he feared in 1816. The canal would also serve as a means for defending Alexandria from invasion from the land side (Driault, *La formation de l'empire de Mohamed Aly*, 154).

14. The old canal had its head near ar-Raḥmānīyah. It passed through a section called the Ashrafīyah Canal which linked up with the Damanhūr Canal which also had its head at ar-Raḥmānīyah. It moved north to the town of Zāwiyat Ghazāl and then struck out westward to Alexandria. Writers on the subject often referred to the new project as the Ashrafīyah, the Damanhūr, or ar-Raḥmānīyah Canal. It is clear that there was a very indistinct idea of the route which the canal was to take (Mengin, *Histoire de l'Egypte*, II, 332; al-Jabartī, IX, 237 [IV, 276]).

15. Linant (*Mémoires*, 351) says that up to 360,000 workers were employed on the construction of the canal (see Table 38, however).

TABLE 38. The *corvée* of 1819 employed in the excavation of al-Maḥmūdīyah Canal

Governor	Rank	Province	Number of *fallāḥīn*	Number of *qaṣabahs*	Number of meters
Ismā'īl	pasha, director	——	——	——	——
Muḥammad	*kāshif*	al-Gharbīyah	109,000	7,694	28,083
'Alī	*kāshif*	ash-Sharqīyah	30,000	2,092	7,635
Muḥammad	*kāshif*	al-Manṣūrīyah	42,000	2,915	10,639
Tamir	*kāshif*	al-Qalyūbīyah	17,000	1,196	4,365
Ibrāhīm	*kāshif*	Gīzah	12,000	899	3,281
'Umar	bey	al-Minūfīyah	65,000	4,510	16,461
Ḥasan	bey	Buḥayrah	38,000	2,682	9,789
TOTAL			313,000	21,988	80,253

Source: Mengin, *Histoire de l'Egypte*, II, 335.

16. Salt, May 6, 1819 in F.O. 78/93; al-Jabartī, IX, 237 (IV, 276), IX, 239–241 (IV, 277), IX, 293–296 (IV, 301, 302), IX, 299, 300 (IV, 304), IX, 316 (IV, 311); Driault, *La formation de l'empire de Mohamed Aly*, 104, 148, 149, 152, 153, 154, 170 178, 180, 188; Mengin, *Histoire de l'Egypte*, II, 331–336; Linant, *Mémoires*, 350, 351; Madden, *Travels*, I, 293.

17. Linant, *Mémoires*, 351; Mengin, *Histoire de l'Egypte*, II, 333; Madden, *Travels*, I, 302–304; Douin, *L'Egypte de 1828 à 1830*, 435; Douin, *La première guerre de Syrie*, I, 486.

18. Campbell, June 2, 1834 in F.O. 142/6; Cattaui, I, 429, 430, 439; Hamont, I, 210; Merruau, 119; Jean Mazuel, *L'œuvre géographique de Linant de Bellefonds*, Société royale de géographie d'Egypte, publication spéciales (Cairo, 1937), 395; Willcocks, 101.

19. Linant, *Mémoires*, 351, 352; Mazuel, *L'œuvre géographique de Linant de Bellefonds*, 396; Stoddart, March 23, 1844 in F.O. 78/584; Barnett, June 2, 1846 in F.O. 142/14; Murray, January 1, 1847 in F.O. 78/707.

20. Linant, *Mémoires*, 353; Mazuel, *L'œuvre géographique de Linant de Bellefonds*, 396.

21. Linant, *Mémoires*, 353.

22. Clot, II, 471, 474; Linant, *Mémoires*, 20, 21. Maps by Leake and Linant and in *Description de l'Egypte*.

23. Charles-Roux, *La production du coton en Egypte*, 216. Maps by Linant and in *Description de l'Egypte*.

24. Bowring, "Egypt and Candia," 14. Maps by Leake and Linant and in *Description de l'Egypte*.

25. Bryce, July 2, 1802 in W.O. 55/1553 (5); Stewart, April 25, 1807 in W.O. 1/303.

26. Linant, *Mémoires*, 23. Only the most important canals will be mentioned in the following analysis.

27. Linant, *Mémoires*, 21.

28. Bryce, July 2, 1802 in W.O. 55/1553 (5).

29. Linant, *Mémoires*, 342–345; al-Jabartī, V, 180, 181 (II, 240), VIII, 20, 21 (IV, 9), VIII, 184 (IV, 84), VIII, 194, 195 (IV, 88, 89), VIII, 202 (IV, 91); Bryce, July 2, 1802 in W.O. 55/1553 (5); Douin, *Mohamed Aly, Pacha du Caire*, 15; Driault, *Mohamed Aly et Napoléon*, 32, 35, 41; Driault, *La formation de l'empire de Mohamed Aly*, 115, 116; Dubois-Aymé and Jollois, II, 93–95; J. M. Le Père, I, 114–118. Maps by Leake and Linant and in *Description de l'Egypte*.

30. Linant, *Mémoires*, 22, 23, 376–380; Clot, II, 469; Bryce, July 2, 1802 in W.O. 55/1553 (5). Maps by Linant, Leake, War Office, and in *Description de l'Egypte*. Baḥr Shibīn was known in its entirety or in certain of its parts by various names, each name being spelled according to the preference of the particular source.

31. Linant, *Mémoires*, 22, 34; Clot, II, 474. Also called Bagourieh, Bayourie. Map by Linant.

32. Linant, *Mémoires*, 22; Clot, II, 474. Also called Bekerem, Bequidi. Map by Linant.

33. Bowring, "Egypt and Candia," 14; Linant, *Mémoires*, 22; Clot, II, 474. Also called Sersawe, Sersaoue, Serdawi. Map by Linant.

34. Linant, *Mémoires*, 22. Map by Linant.

35. Linant, *Mémoires*, 22; Clot, II, 474. Also called Messid-el-Khradr, Messid-el-Radrah. Map by Linant.

36. Bowring, "Egypt and Candia," 14; Clot, II, 470, 474. Also called Canal of Tanta, Safargeh, Giafferie. Maps by Leake and Linant.

37. Linant, *Mémoires*, 431; Clot, II, 474. Also called Nanayeh. Map by Linant.

38. Bryce, July 2, 1802 in W.O. 55/1553 (5). Maps by Leake and Linant.

39. Maps by Leake and Linant.

40. Charles-Roux, *La production du coton en Egypte*, 215. Maps by Leake, Linant, War Office, and in *Description de l'Egypte*.

41. Bryce, July 2, 1802 in W.O. 55/1553 (5); Douin and Fawtier-Jones, *L'Angleterre*

et l'Egypte. La politique mameluke, I, 412; Linant, *Mémoires*, 26; Mazuel, *L'œuvre géographique de Linant de Bellefonds*, 117.

42. Bryce, July 2, 1802 in W.O. 55/1553 (5); Clot, II, 469; Linant, *Mémoires*, 23, 25. Called also Bahr Moeze. Maps by Leake and Linant and in *Description de l'Egypte*.

43. Linant, *Mémoires*, 23, 24. Called also Charawe, Chercaoue. Map by Linant.

44. Charles-Roux, *La production du coton en Egypte*, 216; Linant, *Mémoires*, 24. Maps by Leake, Linant, and War Office, and in *Description de l'Egypte*.

45. Bryce, July 2, 1802 in W.O. 55/1553 (5); Charles-Roux, *La production du coton en Egypte*, 216; Clot, II, 474; Linant, *Mémoires*, 26; Mazuel, *L'œuvre géographique de Linant de Bellefonds*, 117. Also called Chercawe, Chercaoue. Map by War Office.

46. Linant, *Mémoires*, 25; Clot, II, 474. Called also Bessoussieh, Bessous.

47. Mengin refers to this as the Scander Canal, named after the newborn son of the viceroy. As this name appears in no other work, it seems clear that the name Ra's al-Wādī was the name by which it was actually known (*Histoire de l'Egypte*, II, 336).

48. Linant, *Mémoires*, 24, 25; Clot, II, 474.

49. Linant, *Mémoires*, 25; Clot, II, 474. Also called Donded, Doudeh.

50. Linant, *Mémoires*, 25. Also called Mityaheche.

51. Linant, *Mémoires*, 25; Clot, II, 470, 471, 474; Bowring, "Egypt and Candia," 14. Called also Boukieh, Bouhie, Bouhyeh, Bouseyeh. Maps by Linant and Leake.

52. Linant, *Mémoires*, 25, 26; Clot, II, 474. Also called Mansourieh, Mansourie.

53. Linant, *Mémoires*, 427–429; Charles-Roux, *La production du coton en Egypte*, 216. Maps by Leake and Linant and in *Description de l'Egypte*.

54. Also known as Canal of Ashmun, Bahr Serayer. Maps by Leake and Linant and in *Description de l'Egypte*.

55. Linant, *Mémoires*, 23, 34; Bryce, July 2, 1802 in W.O. 55/1553 (5). Maps by Leake, Linant, and War Office.

56. Linant, *Mémoires*, 345.

57. Linant, *Mémoires*, 431–477 (see Planche VI of the Atlas published with this work for the plans prepared by Linant; also Linant's map of Lower Egypt sketches it in and indicates how it differed from Mougel's plan); Mazuel, *L'œuvre géographique de Linant de Bellefonds*, 134–189; Robert Hanbury Brown, *History of the Barrage at the Head of the Delta of Egypt* (Cairo, 1896).

58. Barnett, October 20, 1842 in F.O. 78/502.

59. Bowring, "Egypt and Candia," 60; Clot, II, 478, 479; Hamont, I, 213.

60. Muḥammad 'Alī ordered the Pyramids to be dismantled and the stone used for the construction of the Barrages. Linant successfully dissuaded him from this action (Linant, *Mémoires*, 420–424; Willcocks, 148).

61. Cattaui, II, Pt. 1, 158; Bowring, "Egypt and Candia," 60; Henri René d'Allemagne, *Les saint-simoniens, 1827–1837* (Paris, 1930). There was, nevertheless, feeling that the engineers in charge were not equipped to handle a task of such magnitude. Both Campbell and Marmont recommended that Muḥammad 'Alī should send to England or France for more expert advice. The Pasha promised to act upon this advice, but there is no record that he ever did (Campbell, November 1, 1834 in F.O. 78/247; Hamont, I, 214, 215).

62. Cattaui, II, Pt. 2, 46, 345; Bowring, "Egypt and Candia," 195, 196.

63. Bowring, "Egypt and Candia," 60; Clot, II, 482; Linant, *Mémoires*, 448–455.

64. Linant makes no reference in his book to this second attempt to obtain the Council's approval for the Barrage plan, but Colonel Barnett's dispatch of April 12, 1845, clearly says that such approval was sought (Barnett, April 12, 1845 in F.O. 142/13).

65. Barnett, October 20, 1842 in F.O. 78/502.

66. Barnett, November 1, 1845 in F.O. 78/623 and March 7, 1846 in F.O. 78/661B; Stoddart, July 29, 1846 in F.O. 142/15 and September 23, 1846 in F.O. 78/661B; Linant, *Mémoires*, 457; *Transit through Egypt: Navigation of the Nile 1841–1848*, unpubl. ms. in F.O. 97/408; *Suez Canal 1843–1851*, unpubl. ms. in F.O. 97/411; Murray, June 9, 1847 in F.O. 78/707; Politis [Polites], *Le conflit turco-égyptien*, 164, 165; Nahum, 244.

67. Murray, May 13, 1847 in F.O. 78/707.
68. Brown, 14, 18.
69. Murray, April 19, 1849 in F.O. 78/804.
70. Brown, 63.
71. It is not clear whether the figure given in the budget for the year 1846–47 included the cost of the Barrages from its inception in the thirties or merely from the commencement date of the second attempt. The figures for 1846–47 were as follows:

	Purses	*Piastres*
Expenses of the Barrage and its Canals (not placed in Account):		
All the expenses for the Barrage from the commencement to the end of the Coptic Year 1263 [1846–47]	30,837	292
Calculation of probable expenses for the year 1264 [1847–48] —purses 41,258 and 127 piastres; from which has been already spent to last month	18,258	52
Expenses for the opening of the three canals near the barrage (last year)	9,610	480
Calculation of the probable expenses of the same for the year 1263 [1846–47]—purses 18,000.		

The total was 58,706 purses and 324 piasters or 29,353,324 piasters by September 28, 1847 (the end of the Coptic year). The additional anticipated expense was 41,000 purses and 75 piasters or 20,500,075 piasters, making a total of 49,853,399 piasters (*c.* £ 488,535) by the end of Muḥammad ʻAlī's reign (Murray, March 17, 1848 in F.O. 78/757).

Brown says that the Barrages eventually cost £ 1,880,000, excluding the cost of the *corvée*, adding that Willcocks had placed the total cost of the Barrages, fortifications, canal heads, etc., at £ 4,000,000 (Brown, 17). Linant, who says that his plan would have cost only 21,000,000 francs (*c.* £ 840,000), all expenses included, points out that in 1853 when Mougel left the project, the expenses had already reached the amount of 47,000,000 francs (*c.* £ 1,880,000), not including the wages of the workers of the *corvée*. At that time, the works were far from completed (Linant, *Mémoires*, 464).

72. The British engineers decided not to abandon Muḥammad ʻAlī's Barrages entirely, although doing so had perhaps been considered a cheaper and more efficient procedure, but determined instead to restore them and to correct the structural flaws. Experiments began in 1884 under Willcock's supervision and work began in 1887. The underwater work was completed by June 16, 1890. The total cost of restoration was £E 465,000 and the total masonry was 113,397 cubic meters (Brown, 37, 41–52).

73. Clot, I, 172; Polites, *L'hellénisme et l'Egypte moderne*, II, 53.

74. Douin and Fawtier-Jones, I, 410, 411; Charles-Roux, *La production du coton en Egypte*, 210–215; Linant, *Mémoires*, 1, 2; Clot, II, 467, 468.

75. Clot, II, 468; Mazuel, *L'œuvre géographique de Linant de Bellefonds*, 215. Maps by Leake and Linant and in *Description de l'Egypte*.

76. Mazuel, *L'œuvre géographique de Linant de Bellefonds*, 234, 235; Olivier, II, 165; Willcocks, 36–38, 46, 47; Barois, 22–25; Linant, *Memoires*, 13–19.

77. Driault, *L'Egypte et l'Europe*, V, 296.

78. Clot says that a dike was built by order of Muḥammad ʻAlī which extended along the entire length of the Nile on both sides of the river from Jabal as-Silsilah to the sea and around the Delta, the dike being on the average 6 meters in width and 2 meters high. The total length, according to Clot, was 2,320,000 meters, involving earth work of 27,840,000 cubic meters (II, 472; Willcocks, 90).

79. Campbell, January 1, 1834 in F.O. 142/6; Linant, *Mémoires*, 397–406; Mazuel *L'œuvre géographique de Linant de Bellefonds*, 195–197, 200, 201.

80. Linant, *Mémoires*, 346, 347.

81. Linant, *Mémoires*, 347, 348.

82. The author has been unable to trace its Arabic name.

83. Linant, *Mémoires*, 345, 346.
84. *Lā'iḥat zirā'at al-fallāḥ*, 33, 35, 37, 46.
85. *Lā'iḥat zirā'at al-fallāḥ*, 41, 42.
86. *Lā'iḥat zirā'at al-fallāḥ*, 53.
87. *Lā'iḥat zirā'at al-fallāḥ*, 56; Linant, *Mémoires*, 38.
88. Linant must be in error, as it was only on Ramaḍān 19, A.H. 1251 (January 8, 1836) that Muḥammad 'Alī ordered that a general council be formed to investigate educational problems (Heyworth-Dunne, *History of Education in Modern Egypt*, 190–191). Mukhtār Bey was appointed president, or *nāẓir*, of the council which was called *Majlis Shūrā 'l-Madāris*. A number of professional schools were set up under its jurisdiction, including a polytechnical school which was to train students (Heyworth-Dunne, *History of Education in Modern Egypt*, 198).
89. Elsewhere in his book Linant mentions that in 1837 he was appointed head of the division of public works in the Ministry of Public Works and Public Instruction (*Mémoires*, 445). Mazuel gives the date as March 1838 (*L'œuvre géographique de Linant de Bellefonds*, 173).
90. Linant, *Mémoires*, 38, 39; Barois, 100.
91. Heyworth-Dunne's date for the creation of this *dīwān* is 1829 (*History of Education in Modern Egypt*, 209). It is interesting to note that the *dīwān*'s records include a bundle of 216 documents bearing the date Rajab, A.H. 1242 (January/February 1827). There is then a gap in the records until 1245/1829–30 and thereafter the records run consecutively (with some lacunae) (Deny, 459).
92. Heyworth-Dunne, *History of Education in Modern Egypt*, 142–145, 208, 209; Deny, 115, 122, 125; Zaghlūl, Appendix II, 5, 6.
93. Linant, *Mémoires*, 37, 38; Willcocks, 272–274; Barois, 63–65; Madden, *Travels*, I, 224, 225; Nahas, 154–159.
94. Madden, *Travels*, I, 224; Hamont, I, 227–230.
95. Madden, *Travels*, I, 293.
96. Willcocks, 47; Barois, 25, 26.
97. Omar Toussoun, *Mémoire sur l'histoire du Nil*, in *Mémoires présentés à l'Institut d'Egypte* (Cairo, 1925), IX, 451; Mazuel, *L'œuvre géographique de Linant de Bellefonds*, 131, 234.
98. Willcocks, 89, 90, 96, 131, 300, 301; Barois, 107; Linant, *Mémoires*, 36. The construction or strengthening of dikes to protect summer crops against the annual flood could even be considered detrimental to the Nile River itself, as Colonel Barnett reported:

> But a serious question arises—whether those Dikes which the Pasha has made to prevent the overflow of the Nile, although works of apparent utility, may not hereafter be productive of very injurious consequences. The waters of the Nile being no longer allowed as formerly to spread over the adjacent country, but being now confined within a comparatively narrow channel the whole of the alluvial soil brought down by the flood will be deposited in the bed of the river which will of course be raised every year, while the level of the land under its banks will remain the same. This level is already in many places as much as twenty feet below the level of the water at high Nile. The earth of which the Dikes are formed is mostly of a light sandy nature, and not such as to offer for a length of time an effectual resistance to the great pressure of water which will every year rise in proportion to the increased deposit in the bed of the river. It has been ascertained, as I am informed by Mr. Linant, that a lesser body of water comes down from the Upper Country although the rise in Lower Egypt was greater as I have already stated than during the last season. The consequences of the Dikes giving way in any part, an accident always to be apprehended through the negligence of those whose duty it is to keep them in repair would be most disastrous, but the Pasha does not appear to be aware of the danger of interfering with the course of a river as the Nile.

(Barnett, November 17, 1842 in F.O. 142/13; Mazuel, *L'œuvre géographique de Linant de Bellefonds*, 128, 129.)

99. Linant, *Mémoires*, 20.

100. Willcocks, 95, 96; Linant, *Mémoires*, 36; cf. Appendix VII.

101. Linant, *Mémoires*, 452; Clot, II, 268, 269. Hamont puts the total number of *sāqiyahs* in Lower Egypt at 40,000, but says that they were probably not all in operation (I, 164, II, 305, 306). MacBrair mentions that he had seen many *sāqiyahs* during his travels, but that many had been allowed to fall into a state of decay. He also says that those in use were so badly constructed that half the power was lost (MacBrair, 83, 84).

102. Bowring, "Egypt and Candia," 12, 13. Duhamel puts the cost of the initial investment at a higher figure. He claims that it cost 5,000 piasters for each *sāqiyah* and that the maintenance cost was 1,500 piasters (Cattaui, II, Pt. 2, 355, 356; Clot, II, 270, 271; Appendix VII).

103. R. T. Leiper, "La production expérimentale des bilharzioses égyptiennes," *Bulletin de l'Institut Egyptien*, année 1916, 5th series, X (Cairo, March 1917), 225, 226.

104. Campbell, July 6, 1840 in F.O. 78/408b; Hamont, I, 209, 210.

Appendix II. The Area of Cultivable Land in Egypt

1. Numerous references to the area of cultivated land are to be found scattered throughout the works of contemporary observers of the Egyptian scene. Some confirm the figures here employed, others do not. The latter have been rejected as being unreliable, being based either on optimistic statements made by Muḥammad 'Alī in his attempt to impress foreigners with his achievements or on prejudiced opinions of persons unfavorable to his administration.

2. Artin, "Essai sur les causes," 67, 68. See Omar Toussoun, *Le cadastre de Mohammad Ali*, in *Mémoires de la société royale d'archéologie d'Alexandrie* (Cairo, 1936), VIII, 508. Figures given by Prince Omar are incomplete and have probably been inflated.

3. Mengin, *Histoire de l'Egypte*, II, 343, 344 (see Appendix I). With the exception of Barnett's figure for *ab'ādīyah* land in A.H. 1236, all future references to the Cadastre of 1820–21 (A.H. 1236) are drawn from Mengin's report.

4. Barnett, December 12, 1844 in F.O. 78/583 (see Appendix I).

5. The decrease in the amount of *ab'ādīyah* land after 1813–14 probably means that land which had been considered *ab'ādīyah* land in 1813–14 was later placed in a different category. It may, of course, reflect a certain amount of land reclamation in the period after 1813–14, but it is more likely that this land was *waṣīyah* land, *rizqah* land, or the private estates of the Pasha and his officers.

6. *Ifādah* (plu. *ifādāt*), according to Deny, were letters which emanated from the administrative bureaus of the viceroy's cabinet. These letters could be addressed to a bureau, to individuals, or to the viceroy (Deny, 150).

7. Deny, 116, 130, 497.

8. Barnett, December 12, 1844 in F.O. 78/583 (see Appendix I). All future references to the statistics of 1844 are drawn from Barnett's report.

9. It should be noted that at the time of the French occupation the difference between the cultivated land and taxed land was as follows.

Cultivated land	4,038,177.105 *faddāns*
Taxed land	3,970,340.590
	67,836.515

Since the French did not tax all the cultivable land such as *rizqah* land, for example, all or part of this 67,836.515 *faddāns* represents the amount of land on which taxes were not levied.

10. By an interesting coincidence the difference between the *zimām* land and the land taxed during the French occupation plus the difference between the land taxed during the French occupation and the land taxed in 1844 also equals 723,685 *faddāns*.

Total village land (*zimām*) in 1844	4,293,164.000 *faddāns*	
Land taxed during French occupation	3,970,340.590	322,823.410 *faddāns*
Land taxed during French occupation	3,970,340.590	
Land taxed (*ma'mūr*) 1844	3,569,479.000	400,861.590
		723,685.000

It should also be noted that the area of land taxed by Muḥammad 'Alī decreased by 400,861.590 *faddāns*, although the area of cultivable land had supposedly increased by 254,986.895 *faddāns*. These figures appear to substantiate the statement that no increase had actually occurred.

11. The tribes of Buḥayrah province had for generations held land in the province but had been dispossessed by the French because of the latter's anti-Bedouin policy. These lands were, however, restored to them by an imperial decree after the French withdrawal (al-Jabartī, VII, 78–80 [III, 204–206]). Muḥammad 'Alī, anxious to retain these Bedouins as allies, allowed them to keep their land. Eventually, the Bedouins became dissatisfied with Muḥammad 'Alī's land policies, for in a report by Colonel Barnett there appears an account of a nocturnal visit to Ciani, the British agent at al-'Aṭf, from a Bedouin chief of Buḥayrah province who appeared at Ciani's home in disguise. Barnett mentions that he had always been under the impression that the Bedouins were better off than either the peasants or the town residents, enjoying more liberty and being less oppressed. "I am ignorant," he wrote, "of the nature of the grievances of which they so loudly complain, and I did not think it prudent, by further enquiring into their complaints to encourage in them a hope that I might have it in my power to obtain redress for them . . ." (Barnett, October 6, 1844 in F.O. 78/582).

12. It is interesting that the figures of 320,944 and 402,741 approximate those of 322,823.410 and 400,861.590 as shown above in note 10. It can, therefore, be assumed that with the allowance for a narrow margin of error the figures arrived at here are substantially correct.

13. This figure is roughly equal to the one given by Clot who claimed that Egypt consisted of a total area of 7,014,000 *faddāns* of which 3,856,226 (Lower Egypt, 2,249,000, Middle Egypt, 856,826, Upper Egypt, 750,400) were under cultivation and 3,157,774 uncultivated (II, 265).

14. See note 9 above.

Appendix V. Conscription

1. Consul-General Barker, describing how one of these orders came into his possession, writes: "It was hardly out of the press, when Mr. George Adib, my first Drogoman through his intimate connexions with the principal officers of the Government was enabled *clandestinely* to obtain it" (Barker, January 22, 1833 in F.O. 78/231). Translations of these orders were prepared in Egypt by an employee in the Consulate-General and forwarded together with the original to England.

2. Sent in August 1832 to 500 Egyptian villages "for the purpose of compelling each head of a village to furnish a certain number of men under diverse punishment to those who may endeavor to evade that injunction" (Barker, August 27, 1832 in F.O. 78/214).

3. Addressed to 1,300 employees of every grade (Barker, September 3, 1832 in F.O. 78/214).

4. Addressed to 3,500 *shaykhs al-balad* (Barker, September 3, 1832 in F.O. 78/214).

5. Barker thought this order was dictated by Muḥammad 'Alī personally (Barker, January 22, 1833 in F.O. 78/231).

6. Campbell, April 1, 1833 in F.O. 78/227.

7. Addressed also to *nāẓirs al-qism*.

8. Barker, March 16, 1833 in F.O. 78/231.

Appendix VI. The Population of Egypt during the Reign of Muḥammad 'Alī

1. Bowring, "Egypt and Candia," 4, 5; A. Boinet, "L'accroissement de la population en Egypte," *Bulletin de l'Institut Egyptien*, 2d Series, VII (Cairo, 1887), 277.

2. Hamont, II, 640; Douin, *Mohamed Aly et l'expédition d'Alger*, 230; Douin, *La mission du Baron de Boislecomte*, 109, 110; Cattaui, II, Pt. 2, 350, 351; Bowring, "Egypt and Candia," 4; Campbell, July 6, 1840 in F.O. 78/408b; Barnett, December 12, 1844 in F.O. 78/583 (see Appendix I); Clot, I, 166, 167.

3. See Appendix I.

4. Cattaui, I, 215; Bowring, "Egypt and Candia," 5.

5. Artin's statement that Bedouins and inhabitants of the oases were included in the 1846 figure (see Table 22, note 3) does not explain the huge increase; for so large a Bedouin or oasis population in 1846 is inconceivable. In any event, there still remains to be explained the sudden drop in the rate of population increase after 1846.

GLOSSARY

ab'ādīyah: The uncultivated and uncultivable land excluded from the land survey at the time of the Cadastre of 1813–14. Term applied to estates granted from this land.

abū midfa': Term by which Spanish pillared dollar was called in Egypt.

abū ṭāqah: Egyptian term for the German reichsthaler or thalari. *Pataque* is the French corruption of the Arabic. Its value was fixed at 90 paras for purposes of tax collection.

'ādat awrāq shitwī waṣayfī: A gift which, according to custom, had to be paid to the messengers who brought letters to the villagers informing them that someone would soon be coming to collect taxes.

aghā: A Turkish officer.

aḥbās (sing. *ḥubus*)*:* Mortmain.

aḥbāsīyah: See *ar-rizaq al-aḥbāsīyah.*

ahlī: Family. See *waqf ahlī.*

ajr: Small annual rent. Remuneration.

'āmil: Agent selected from among rich individuals who could pay the government for the privilege of acting as its agent. Forerunner of the *multazim.* In the eighteenth century certain tax collectors in Upper Egypt were called by this term.

amīr: Commander.

amīr al-ḥajj: Commander of the pilgrimage; leader of the annual pilgrimage to the holy cities of Makkah and al-Madīnah.

amīr al-khaznah: Commander of the treasure; the officer charged with the responsibility for bringing the annual remittance from Egypt to Istanbul.

appalto: Farming. Exclusive privilege given by the government to one or several merchants to deal in a particular item of commerce.

appaltatore: Contractor, farmer.

ardabb: An Egyptian dry measure. At present equal to 5.447 U.S. bushels. In Muḥammad 'Alī's time it varied in different parts of Egypt. It was generally equal to 5 English bushels but could be as much as 8.

arḍ al-fallāḥ: Portion of the *iltizām* assigned to the peasant.

arḍ al-waṣīyah: Portion of the *iltizām* assigned to the *multazim* for his exclusive enjoyment.

'aṣāyah: Cane, stick.

aṣḥāb al-amlāk: Owners of *mulk* property.

assignation: Paper currency constituting a promissory note on the Egyptian treasury or *khazīnah.*

athar (plu. *âthār*)*:* Fixed area of *arḍ al-fallāḥ* (peasant land) cultivated by individual families and handed down from father to son.

atharīyah: See *athar.*

awqāf al-Ḥaramayn: A group of *waqfs* (*awqāf*) from whose revenues the holy cities of Makkah and al-Madīnah were provided with annual payments in money and kind.

al-awqāf as-sulṭānīyah: Royal *waqfs* (*awqāf*) established by the sultans, the revenues of which were allotted to Makkah and al-Madīnah and to charitable works.

balad: Village.

baladī: Indigenous.

barā'ah: Brevet, diploma.

barrānī: A tax originally imposed upon the peasants by the *multazims* as an extraordinary tax, but in time collected regularly along with the prescribed taxes.

baṣāṣīn: Secret police, spies.

bayt al-māl: The state treasury.

bey: Title of rank. There were 24 beys in Egypt before Muḥammad 'Alī became Pasha of Egypt.

beylerbeyi: Bey of beys, title given to viceroys or governors of Ottoman provinces. See *wālī*.

bi'l-masāḥah: (Land) by the measure.

būghāz: Channel, strait, bar.

bushārat al-furdah (*firdah*)*:* Announcement tax paid to agent sent by tax collector to announce to villagers that the tax collector was about to come to the village to gather the taxes.

chafālik wa 'uhad: Royal estates and tax farms.

chiflik (plu. *chafālik*)*:* Farm. Royal estate.

chūrbājī: Colonel of a regiment of Janissaries. This officer headed the *dīwān* of the provincial *ūjāqs*.

daftar: Register.

daftardār: Chancellor. Official appointed annually by the sultan. By the eighteenth century, however, the sultan merely confirmed the appointment of one of the Mamlūk beys. The same situation continued under Muḥammad 'Alī, with the sultan simply confirming the Pasha's appointee. The term *daftardār* is used also for the secretary of a military corps.

dalī (*delī*)*:* Irregular soldier.

dalāt: Irregular soldiers.

damīrah: Term used for *nīlī* crops planted on low land.

ḍarībah: A measurement used in connection with rice. A Damietta *ḍarībah* equaled approximately two *ardabbs* of 225 *uqqahs* each; a Rosetta *ḍarībah* equaled two *ardabbs* of 155 *uqqahs* each.

dhawāt: Aristocracy. A term used to designate a high grade of cotton.

dhurah: Maize, Indian corn, millet.

dīwān: Council, ministry.

dirham: An Arabian measure of weight; a small silver coin.

efendī: Muslim official employed in the government finance office (*Rūznāmah*).

faddān: A surface measure which varied in size before 1813–14 but was fixed at 4,416.5⅓ square meters during the reign of Muḥammad 'Alī. Now equal to 4,200.8 square meters (1.038 acres).

fā'iẓ: Profit, revenue. The *fā'iẓ* represented the portion of the land tax that the *multazim* was entitled to retain for his own profit.

fallāḥ (plu. *fallāḥīn*)*:* Peasant.

faramān: An imperial order, rescript; a royal decree. A firman.

fa's: Hoe.

fatwā: Legal decision or opinion given by a *muftī*.

furdah (*firdah*)*:* See *furdat ar-ru'ūs*.

furdat ar-ru'ūs: Head or capitation tax. Levied on Muslims as well as non-Muslims.

ghafīr: Village policeman.

gharūqah: A form of mortgage by which a peasant could lease his land to another peasant. As soon as he returned the loan, he was entitled to reclaim his land.

ghassāl: Washer.

ḥākim: Governor.

ḥākim al-khuṭṭ: Official in charge of the administrative unit known as a *khuṭṭ* (district).

ḥaqq aṭ-ṭarīq: A tax paid to officials who came to villages on government business.

ḥarīm: Harem. Women's apartment. Workshop in which women were employed by the government to spin flax.

hashīsh: Dried hemp smoked for its intoxicating effects.

ḥiṣṣah: A portion of a village.

ḥubus (plu. *aḥbās*)*:* Mortmain.

ḥujjah: Title deed.

ḥukkām al-aqālīm: Governors of provinces.

ḥulbah: Fenugreek.

ḥulwān: A tax which the heir of a deceased *multazim* paid to the Pasha in order to obtain the privilege of inheriting the deceased's *iltizām*. Constituted a kind of repurchase of the land.

ifādah (plu. *ifādāt*)*:* Letters emanating from the administrative bureaus of the viceroy's cabinet.

al-ifrāj: Title deed employed for *rizqahs*.

iltizām: Tax farm on state land granted by the government to a tax farmer (*multazim*).

imām: Leader of prayer in the mosque. Head of the Islamic Community.

iqlīm: Province.

jizyah: Poll tax, capitation tax paid by non-Muslims. Sometimes called *kharāj*. Differs from *furdah*, which was paid by Muslims and non-Muslims alike.

julubbān (*gilbān*)*:* Pea, vetch.

jurnāl (plu. *jurnālāt*)*:* Inspection report.

jurnāljī: A provincial official who prepared inspection reports.

kafrāwī: Grade of rice.

kallāf: Official in charge of animals on estates. Served as village veterinarian.

kāshif: Governor of a district or province.

kasīr: Grade of sugar.

kātib: Clerk, scribe, secretary.

kātib 'arabī: A scribe employed in a *chiflik*.

kātib adh-dhimmah: Supervisor appointed to control the activities of the employees in the *Rūznāmah*.

kātib ar-rizaq: An official (*efendī*) attached to the *Dīwān ar-Rizaq al-Aḥbāsīyah* where records concerning *rizqahs* were maintained.

katkhudā: See *kikhyah*.

kayyāl: Grain measurer.

khalīfah: Caliph.

kharāj: Land tax, but sometimes refers to capitation tax (i.e., *jizyah*).

kharjah: Tax in kind paid in Upper Egypt.

khaṭṭ-i-sharīf: Imperial edict.

khawlī: An official who supervised cultivation and frequently made land surveys after the Nile flood.

khayrī: Good. See *waqf khayrī.*

khazīnah: Treasury.

khazīnah-dār (*khaznadār, khāzindār, khizindār*)*:* Treasurer.

khidmah: Service tax to cover fees or salaries of officials.

khidmat (*māl*) *al-kushūfīyah:* Tax to cover the administrative expenses of the district governed by a *kāshif.*

khurdah: Term including 72 special taxes.

khuṭbah: Sermon.

khuṭṭ: District (subdivision of a province).

kikhyah: Steward. The *kikhyah* (*katkhudā*) bey was the official who acted as lieutenant to the pasha and ruled Egypt in his absence.

kīs: Purse. 500 piasters.

kundur (*kendir*)*:* Hemp.

kurbāj: Whip of the hide of a hippopotamus.

lā'iḥah: Ordinance, regulation.

līf: Fiber from date trees used as cordage.

mabyaḍah: Bleaching establishment.

maḥkamah: Tribunal, court.

Maḥmal: Litter in which the Holy Carpet or Tapestry was brought to Makkah at the time of the annual pilgrimage.

majlis (plu. *majālis*)*:* Deliberative council.

makhzanjī: Storekeeper.

māl: Tax.

māl al-ḥimāyah: Tax of protection.

al-māl al-ḥurr: Tax consisting of the *mīrī* and the *fā'iẓ* collected by the *multazim* in the *iltizām.*

māl al-kushūfīyah: See *khidmat al-kushūfīyah.*

ma'mūr: Cultivated (land).

ma'mūr: Governor of a province (*ma'mūrīyah*).

ma'mūrīyah: Province.

manzalāwī: Grade of rice.

mashāyikh al-'arab: Bedouin *shaykhs.*

masmūḥ al-maṣāṭib: Land grants to village notables who undertook the responsibility of feeding the poor and travelers.

masmūḥ al-mashāyikh: Lands granted to the *shaykhs al-balad* in payment for services rendered the government and to cover the cost of entertaining officials passing through or stopping in the villages.

masmūḥ ash-shaykh: See *masmūḥ al-mashāyikh.* In Mamlūk days it referred to village land granted by *multazims* to pay for various administrative duties performed by the *shaykh al-balad* as well as his expense in providing for hospitality to travelers.

massāḥ: Surveyor.

massāḥah: Plane for leveling ground.

maṭrūq: Pasture land or meadows used in common by the entire community.

mawāt: Barren or uncultivated land.

medin: Another term for para.

micht: 90 paras.

miḥrāth: Plow.

mīrī: Tax destined for State Treasury. *Mīrī* land refers to the category of land whose revenues accrue to the state.
mishadd: An official in the village who carried out the instructions of the *dīwān* in connection with law enforcement. Inspector, controller.
mu'adhdhin: Caller to prayer.
mubāshir: Steward, intendant, bailiff.
mubayyiḍ: Bleacher.
muḍāf: An extraordinary tax levied by the *multazim*. See *barrānī*.
al-muddah aṭ-ṭawīlah: A type of loan on land granting to the lender a temporary cession of the right to the use of the land.
mudīr: Director, manager, governor of a *mudīrīyah*.
mudīr ad-dīwān: Director of a ministry.
mudīrīyah: Several provinces (*ma'mūrīyahs*) grouped together to form a larger administrative unit, the *mudīrīyah*, headed by a *mudīr*.
mufattish: Inspector.
muftī: Member of the religious classes who issues *fatwās*, legal decisions or opinions; expounder of the law of the Qur'ān.
muḥāsib: Accountant.
muḥtasib: Official who controlled native trade and industry on behalf of the government.
mukarrar: Fine grade of sugar.
mulāhiz: Police officer on a *chiflik*.
mulāzim: Clerk.
mulk (*milk*)*:* Land held in full ownership.
multazim: Tax farmer, i.e., holder of an *iltizām*.
muta'ahhid: Concessionaire of an *'uhdah*.
mutaṣarrif: Beneficiary of a *rizqah*.
mutawallī: Administrator of a *rizqah*. Superintendent.
nabarī: *Nīlī* crop planted on high land and requiring artificial irrigation.
nabbūt: Club, cudgel.
nāḥiyah: Canton (subdistrict of a province).
namīqah: Letter addressed to notables and inhabitants of an *iltizām* instructing the villagers to obey the *multazim* and to pay him the amount of taxes authorized by the terms of the title deed of the *iltizām*.
Naqīb al-Ashrāf: Chief of those claiming descent from the house of the Prophet.
nawraj: Threshing machine.
nāẓir: Director, superintendent, supervisor, inspector, administrator.
nāẓir mabī' al-qumāsh: Overseer of the sale of linen cloth.
nāẓir al-mabyaḍah: Manager of the bleaching establishment.
nāẓir al-qism: Director of the *qism* (department).
nāẓir 'umūm: General director.
nāẓir 'umūm al-mabyū'āt: General superintendent of sales.
nīlī: Refers to period in regimen of Nile River prior to the flood (spring) and at the time of the recession of the flood (autumn).
Niẓām Jadīd: New system, regulation; the name given to the reforms introduced in the Ottoman Empire in 1792 by Sultan Salīm III.
pārah (para)*:* 40 paras = 1 piaster.
pāshā (*bāshā*)*:* High-ranking Ottoman official. The Ottoman governor of Egypt was a pasha of three tails.
pāshāliq (*bāshāliq*)*:* An Ottoman province governed by a pasha.

pataque: 90 paras.
qabbānī: Weigher.
qabbānī al-mabyaḍah: Weigher of the bleaching establishment.
qābiḍ: Tax collector's assistant (Upper Egypt).
qāḍī: Muslim judge.
qā'immaqām: Lieutenant-colonel. Governor of Cairo. An official who protected the interests of the *multazim* in the *iltizām* and in Muḥammad 'Alī's time was administrator of the *nāḥiyah* (canton).
qānūn: Administrative law.
qapūdān: Captain of a ship. Skipper. The *qapūdān* pasha was the admiral of the Ottoman fleet.
qaṣabah: Unit of measurement. Before 1813–14, it varied in length from between 3 m 75 c to 3 m 99 c. After 1813–14 it was fixed at 3 m 64 c.
qaṣṣāb: An official who assisted the surveyor (*massāḥ*).
qazzāzīn: Weavers.
qinṭār: A unit of weight, 99.049 lbs. It varied, however, in Muḥammad 'Alī's day, depending on the commodity being weighed.
qīrāṭ: The one-twenty-fourth part of anything.
qism: Department (subdivision of a province).
quffah: A basket made from palm leaves.
al-quṭn al-hindī: A variety of long-staple cotton.
ra'īs: Chief, foreman.
raqabah: Substance of the land as distinguished from *taṣarruf*, use of the land only.
raṭl: A unit of weight, 0.981 lb.
Rayah: Non-Muslim. Protected person.
riyāl: A dollar; 90 paras.
ar-rizaq al-aḥbāsīyah: Pensions held by religious beneficiaries in land, money, or payment in kind. By the eighteenth century the term referred to lands converted into *aḥbās*, rather than pensions from such lands.
ar-rizaq al-jayshīyah: Pensions held by soldiers in land, money, or payment in kind.
rizqah (plu. *rizaq*)*:* Estate, farm. See *ar-rizaq al-aḥbāsīyah.*
rizqah bilā māl: *Rizqah* land free from tax.
Rūznāmah: One of the bureaus of the central financial administration.
rūznāmjī: Head of the *Rūznāmah*; controller and archivist of an *ūjāq* (army corps).
sālyān: Income tax. Tax on houses.
sanad: Deed, title, document.
sanjaq: A minor province.
sāqiyah: Water-raising device.
ṣarrāf: Tax collector, money changer.
ṣayfī: Summer.
shādūf: Water-raising device.
shāhid: Witness, village representative.
sharāqī: Land remaining uninundated at the time of the Nile flood.
Sharī'ah: Muslim law.
sharīf: Descendant of Muḥammad the Prophet.
shaykh (plu. *mashāyikh*)*:* Elder. Chief of an Arab tribe, leader of a religious order, guild, village.

shaykh al-balad: Head of a village or part of a village.
Shaykh al-Balad: Title given in the eighteenth century to the chief Mamlūk bey who served as governor of Cairo and who was *de facto* ruler of Egypt.
shaykh bandar: Head of the corporation of native merchants.
shaykh al-ḥiṣṣah: An official in charge of a subdivision of the village (*ḥiṣṣah*).
Shaykh al-Islām: Muftī of Istanbul; head of the religious hierarchy of the Ottoman Empire.
shaykh al-mashāyikh: Chief *shaykh* in a village.
shaykh al-qazzāzīn: Shaykh of the weavers.
shitwī: Winter.
shūnah: Warehouse.
shūnat al-ghazl: Yarn stores.
shūrā khāṣṣah: Special council, privy council.
simsār (plu. *samāsir*)*:* Broker, agent.
simsār al-ghazl: Broker of the spun yarn.
ṣūfī: A member of a Muslim religious fraternity.
sulṭān: Sultan.
tābūt: Water-raising device. Archimedean screw.
tadhkirah: Note, identity card.
taqsīṭ: Title deed.
ṭarbūsh: Head gear.
taṣarruf: Right to the use of the land. See *raqabah.*
tīmār: Ottoman fief yielding revenue amounting to from 2,000 to 19,999 *akçes* a year.
ṭurrah: Monogram, signet.
'uhdah (plu. *'uhad*)*:* A concession of land made by the state to an individual undertaking the collection of land taxes.
ūjāq: Ottoman army corps.
ūjāqlī: Member of an *ūjāq.*
'ulamā' (sing. *'alīm*)*:* The learned scholars. In Egypt refers usually to those who have graduated from al-Azhar.
uqqah: A unit of weight equal to 2.73 lbs. avoirdupois and consisting of 400 drams (*dirhams*). It is equal to 2¾ *raṭls.*
ūrṭah: Ūjāq unit stationed in the provinces.
'ushr: Tithe.
'Uthmānlī: Ottoman.
wādī: Valley.
wakīl: Steward, assistant.
wakīl al-ḥarīmāt al-ghazzālāt: Commissioner for the women spinners.
wālī: Governor of an Ottoman province (*beylerbeyi*).
waqf (plu. *awqāf*)*:* Pious foundation in favor of a religious or charitable institution.
waqf ahlī: Pious foundation whose revenues went to the descendants of the donor until extinction of his line when these revenues reverted to the religious or charitable institution for whom endowment was made.
waqf ghayr ṣaḥīḥ: Unsound *waqf*, that is, one involving the donation of *mīrī* land.
waqf khayrī: Pious foundation whose revenues went to the religious or charitable institution as soon as the donation was made.
waqf ṣaḥīḥ: Sound or true *waqf*, that is, one involving the donation of *mulk* land.
warshah: Workshop. A subdivision of a *dīwān* (ministry).

waṣīyah: See *arḍ al-waṣīyah.*

wazīr: Minister.

zi'āmat: Ottoman fief yielding revenue amounting to from 19,999 to 99,999 *akçes* a year.

zimām: Limit, boundary. Refers specifically to all the land falling within the boundaries of a village.

COMPARATIVE TABLE OF ISLAMIC AND CHRISTIAN DATES

A.H. 1164—1267
A.D. 1750—1850

Islamic year	*Christian date*	*Islamic year*	*Christian date*
1164*	30 November 1750	1201	24 October 1786
1165	20 November 1751	1202*	13 October 1787
1166*	8 November 1752†	1203	2 October 1788†
1167	29 October 1753	1204	21 September 1789
1168	18 October 1754	1205*	10 September 1790
1169*	7 October 1755	1206	31 August 1791
1170	26 September 1756†	1207*	19 August 1792†
1171	15 September 1757	1208	9 August 1793
1172*	4 September 1758	1209	29 July 1794
1173	25 August 1759	1210*	18 July 1795
1174	13 August 1760†	1211	7 July 1796†
1175*	2 August 1761	1212	26 June 1797
1176	23 July 1762	1213*	15 June 1798
1177*	12 July 1763	1214	5 June 1799
1178	1 July 1764†	1215	25 May 1800
1179	20 June 1765	1216*	14 May 1801
1180*	9 June 1766	1217	4 May 1802
1181	30 May 1767	1218*	23 April 1803
1182	18 May 1768†	1219	12 April 1804†
1183*	7 May 1769	1220	1 April, 1805
1184	27 April 1770	1221*	21 March 1806
1185	16 April 1771	1222	11 March 1807
1186*	4 April 1772†	1223	28 February 1808†
1187	25 March 1773	1224*	16 February 1809
1188*	14 March 1774	1225	6 February 1810
1189	4 March 1775	1226*	26 January 1811
1190	21 February 1776†	1227	16 January 1812†
1191*	19 February 1777	1228	4 January 1813
1192	30 January 1778	1229*	24 December 1813
1193	19 January 1779	1230	14 December 1814
1194*	8 January 1780†	1231	3 December 1815
1195	28 December 1780†	1232*	21 November 1816†
1196*	17 December 1781	1233	11 November 1817
1197	7 December 1782	1234	31 October 1818
1198	26 November 1783	1235*	20 October 1819
1199*	14 November 1784†	1236	9 October 1820†
1200	4 November 1785	1237*	28 September 1821

* Leap year, in which Dhū'l–Ḥijjah has 30 days.
† Leap year, in which February has 29 days.

Islamic year	*Christian date*	*Islamic year*	*Christian date*
1238	18 September 1822	1253	7 April 1837
1239	7 September 1823	1254*	27 March 1838
1240*	26 August 1824†	1255	17 March 1839
1241	16 August 1825	1256*	5 March 1840†
1242	5 August 1826	1257	23 February 1841
1243*	25 July 1827	1258	12 February 1842
1244	14 July 1828†	1259*	1 February 1843
1245	3 July 1829	1260	22 January 1844†
1246*	22 June 1830	1261	10 January 1845
1247	12 June 1831	1262*	30 December 1845
1248*	31 May 1832†	1263	20 December 1846
1249	21 May 1833	1264	9 December 1847
1250	10 May 1834	1265*	27 November 1848†
1251*	29 April 1835	1266	17 November 1849
1252	18 April 1836†	1267*	6 November 1850

* Leap year, in which Dhū'l–Ḥijjah has 30 days.
† Leap year, in which February has 29 days.

The Islamic era dates from July 16, A.D. 622, the start of the year in which the *hijrah* or migration of the Prophet Muḥammad from Makkah to al-Madīnah took place. The calendar adopted by the Muslims is based on the lunar rather than the solar year; there are 354 days in the year except when the last month adds an extra day and has 30 instead of 29 days. The twelve lunar months are al-Muḥarram, Ṣafar, Rabīʿ al-Awwal, Rabīʿ ath-Thānī, Jumādā 'l-Ūlā, Jumādā 'l-Âkhirah, Rajab, Shaʿbān, Ramaḍān, Shawwāl, Dhū'l-Qaʿdah, Dhū'l-Ḥijjah. Since these months do not always fall in the same season, it was customary in Egypt to use the Coptic year, a solar year beginning on September 10, for fiscal and other practical purposes. The starting date of the Coptic era is A.D. 284; the twelve Coptic months are Tūt, Bābah, Hātūr, Kīhak, Ṭūbah, Amshīr, Barmahāt, Barmūdah, Bashans, Ba'ūnah, Abbīb, Misrā.

In the absence of a conversion table it is possible to derive the Muslim date for the Gregorian year by using the formula: $H = G - 622 + \frac{G - 622}{32}$.

INDEX